NetWare Training Guide: Networking Technologies

3rd Edition

D1514839

Debra Niedermiller-Chaffins

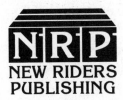

NEW RIDERS PUBLISHING

New Riders Publishing, Indianapolis, Indiana

NetWare Training Guide: Networking Technologies, 3rd Edition

By Debra Niedermiller-Chaffins

Published by:
New Riders Publishing
201 West 103rd Street
Indianapolis, IN 46290 USA

Printed in the United States of America   5 6 7 8 9 0

```
Niedermiller-Chaffins, Debra R., 1963-
NetWare training guide : networking technologies / Debra Niedermiller-
Chaffins. — 3rd ed.
            p.        cm.
2nd ed. entered under NetWare training guide.
Includes index.
ISBN 1-56205-363-9
1. NetWare (Computer file) 2. Local area networks (Computer networks)
I. Title.
TK105.7.N545  1994
004.68—dc20                        94-33319
                                   CIP
```

Warning and Disclaimer

This book is designed to provide information about the NetWare computer program. Every effort has been made to make this book as complete and as accurate as possible, but no warranty or fitness is implied.

The information is provided on an "as is" basis. The author and New Riders Publishing shall have neither liability nor responsibility to any person or entity with respect to any loss or damages arising from the information contained in this book or from the use of the disks or programs that may accompany it.

Publisher	LLOYD J. SHORT
Associate Publisher	TIM HUDDLESTON
Product Development Manager	ROB TIDROW
Marketing Manager	RAY ROBINSON
Director of Special Projects	CHERI ROBINSON
Managing Editor	MATTHEW MORRILL

About the Author

Debra R. Niedermiller-Chaffins is Education Director for Computer Data, Inc. in Madison Heights, Michigan. Ms. Niedermiller-Chaffins started the education department at Computer Data, Inc. in 1988 to help organizations develop autonomy and self-sufficiency in training future Certified NetWare Engineer (CNE) operations. She is a Certified NetWare Instructor (CNI) and a CNE. Ms. Niedermiller-Chaffins also supports a small client base, which provides her with a background of real-world networking scenarios. She is the author of *Inside Novell NetWare, Special Edition*, *Inside NetWare Lite,* and *NetWare Training Guide: Managing NetWare Systems*, also published by New Riders Publishing.

Trademark Acknowledgments

All terms mentioned in this book that are known to be trademarks or service marks have been appropriately capitalized. New Riders Publishing cannot attest to the accuracy of this information. Use of a term in this book should not be regarded as affecting the validity of any trademark or service mark. NetWare is a registered trademark of Novell, Inc.

PRODUCT DIRECTOR
DREW HEYWOOD

PRODUCTION EDITOR
STEVE WEISS

EDITORS
MELINDA TAYLOR
LILLIAN YATES

ACQUISITIONS EDITOR
JIM LEVALLEY

TECHNICAL EDITORS
KIM GREEN
ART MELLOR
KURT SCHERNEKAU

ACQUISITIONS COORDINATOR
STACEY BEHELER

EDITORIAL ASSISTANT
KAREN OPAL

PUBLISHER'S ASSISTANT
MELISSA LYNCH

COVER DESIGNER
JEAN BISESI

BOOK DESIGNERS
FRED BOWER
ROGER S. MORGAN

GRAPHICS IMAGE SPECIALISTS
CLINT LAHNEN
DENNIS SHEEHAN

PRODUCTION IMPRINT MANAGER
JULI COOK

PRODUCTION IMPRINT TEAM LEADER
KATY BODENMILLER

PRODUCTION ANALYSTS
DENNIS CLAY HAGER
MARY BETH WAKEFIELD

PRODUCTION TEAM
MICHAEL BRUMITT, ELAINE BRUSH
MARY ANN COSBY, JUDY EVERLY
DONNA HARBIN, ALEATA HOWARD
BETH LEWIS, SHAWN MACDONALD
STEPHANIE MCCOMB, TIM TAYLOR
JACKIE THOMPSON, SCOTT TULLIS
HOLLY WITTENBERG

INDEXERS
JEANNE CLARK

Acknowledgments

It is at this point, after having relaxed for the first time in months, I can thankfully acknowledge all the wonderful people who have helped make this book possible.

First, I would like to thank Computer Data, Inc. for graciously giving me the support and encouragement to complete this project. Without all of you, I would lack the wonderful analogies you've helped me develop. Thank you, Jim Weyand, for giving me the opportunity to learn and create.

Thanks to all my instructors, Gary Dall, Bill Myers, Tom Weyand, Mary Jane Heleski, Al Balash, Paulette Bemis, Bob Hopkins, and assistant Teresa Hassell, for their assistance and saintly patience. I hope I can give back to you all you've given to me.

Thanks to NRP, Cheryl Wilhite, Dorothy Cady, Steve Weiss (who I immensely enjoyed working with), and the technical editors for their time and fortitude. And thanks to Rob Tidrow, for understanding most of the time.

A special thanks to the remarkable Drew Heywood for his empathetic shoulders, patience, and desire to help make this book as good as it could possibly be. Without you, well, I can't even imagine what it would have been without you.

Raging gratitude to my parents for their excitement and their concern. I especially appreciate that you still find me worth bragging about.

Thanks also to my friends and family for finally realizing that it's better NOT to ask how the book is going!

To my readers, I want to say thank you for picking this book out of all the others. I hope that it provides what you are looking for.

To all the trees that gave their lives so this book could be possible, thank you. I will now tend my garden in your honor.

Appreciation to Novell, Inc., lest I forget, for their tremendous products and programs.

Finally, thanks to my husband and best friend, Brian. Without you, not only would this book truly not be possible, but the royalties would not be nearly as much fun!

Contents at a Glance

Table of Contents

Introduction

Welcome to the third edition of New Riders Publishing's *NetWare Training Guide: Networking Technologies*. The first two editions of this book have assisted thousands of NetWare users in reaching their goal of becoming Certified NetWare Engineers. This third edition has been updated to reflect the evolution of network technology, to prepare you for the newly revised Service and Support test, and to introduce you to TCP/IP.

The need for well-trained, competent individuals in today's computer industry is greater than ever. Novell, Inc. has seen the need to educate users who support NetWare products and has created the following certifications to meet the industry's needs:

- **Certified NetWare Administrators (CNAs)** are tested to ensure basic competence with managing a specific NetWare operating system. CNA certifications can be obtained for NetWare versions 2.2, 3.1*x*, and 4.01.

- **Certified NetWare Engineers (CNEs)** are tested for their knowledge of a wide variety of NetWare server products, as well as for their understanding of LAN hardware, software, and communication technologies. This certification is in high demand by systems engineers, consultants, and administrators of NetWare products.

- **Enterprise CNEs** are additionally certified for their competence with a variety of NetWare products, which may include network management and diagnostic tools, UNIX or Macintosh support products, or communication and gateway products.

Candidates for these certifications must pass one or more tests. A variety of methods of preparation are available, including classroom instruction from Novell Authorized Education Centers (NAECs) and self-study kits available from Novell. The test objectives for each test are public, and candidates can choose to study by using their own materials. Novell, Inc. also provides assessment disks with sample test questions to help users prepare for taking the necessary tests. These disks can be acquired through most NAECs, as well as through the NetWire forum on CompuServe.

Most candidates use a variety of these training methods, and many may feel the need for additional training help. New Riders' *NetWare Training Guide* series is intended to provide supplemental study information to help you pass the tests required to achieve Novell certification.

Who Should Read This Book?

NetWare Training Guide: Networking Technologies, 3rd Edition, is written for individuals who need to learn more about Novell NetWare because of a job responsibility, and for those who need to know more about system administration and the operating system. The following chapters guide you through the various revisions of the NetWare product in an effort to acquaint you with the variety of security and functionality that NetWare offers.

What Is Covered in This Book?

NetWare Training Guide: Networking Technologies, 3rd Edition, was written to help you pass the certification curriculum, which includes the following tests:

- Networking Technologies
- Service and Support

- TCP/IP Transport
- Installation and Configuration

This book is intended to be an aid in studying for the CNE, ECNE, and CNI certification programs. Two additional methods are available for studying for these programs. The first method is to obtain actual hands-on experience with the products. Second, Novell instructor-led courses provide hands-on experience as well as instructor expertise and additional study materials. These excellent courses are taught around the world.

Conventions Used in the Book

A few basic conventions will appear throughout this book to help make studying easier.

Objectives help set your study goals, introducing you to material that will be focused upon in the tests.

The Study Notes help you review for your test. They enable you to skim through chapters you have already studied, reviewing major points.

Notes are sidebars of information related to, but not directly involved in, the discussion at hand.

Practical Tips are helpful things to know when working with NetWare and networking technologies, but don't necessarily cover material on the Novell tests.

 Warnings basically speak for themselves; read them, heed them, and remember them. It could save you a headache later on.

The Details of This Book

This book is divided into four parts. Each chapter is introduced, and then the topics are covered in depth. At the end of each chapter are review questions.

These review questions are designed to simulate the Drake testing format for the actual Novell tests. Most of the questions are multiple choice with either one, or more than one, correct answer. Single correct answers are indicated with a small circle (○) next to the answers; multiple correct answer questions show a small square (□) next to the answers. Additonal questions are True/False and fill-in-the-blank. Answers are provided at the end of each chapter. The following sections outline the topics covered in each chapter.

Part 1 Technologies Used in Local Area Networks

This section teaches you about the Networking Technologies test.

Chapter 1, "Learning Network Technology Terminology," helps you learn about the following subjects:

 ◆ Analog versus digital

 ◆ ASCII versus EBCIDIC

- Signal transmissions
- Multiplexing
- Asynchronous versus synchronous
- Switching techniques

Chapter 2, "Topologies," helps you explore the following:

- Architectures
- Access methods

Chapter 3, "Building the Blueprint," explains the following topics:

- The OSI model
- Definitions of the layers

Chapter 4, "Exploring the Lower Layers," teaches you about the following:

- Physical Layer specifications
- Data-Link Layer specifications
- IEEE 802 workgroups
- ARCnet
- LocalTalk
- FDDI
- Format comparisons

Chapter 5, "Exploring Protocol Suites," defines the following protocols:

- OSI
- SNA
- DEC
- TCP/IP
- NetWare
- AppleTalk

Part 2 Installing, Upgrading, and Troubleshooting Local Area Networks

Part 2 helps you study for the Service and Support test.

Chapter 6, "Working with Network Interface Card Configurations," explains how to configure the following:

- ARCnet
- Ethernet
- Hard drives
- Disk coprocessor boards

Chapter 7, "Using Novell DOS," covers the fundamentals of using the following:

- Novell's DR DOS version 6.0
- Novell's DOS version 7.0

Chapter 8, "Addressing Your Network," defines the methods used for the following:

- Addressing your network workstations
- Addressing your network servers

Chapter 9, "Installing the Client," covers the various methods of configuring workstations, now called clients, to access the network. You will learn about the following:

- Configuring the NetWare Shell
- Configuring ODI drivers
- Using the new DOS Requester

Chapter 10, "Working with Storage Devices on a Network," introduces you to the range of technologies that can be used for storing files on NetWare servers. You will learn about the following:

- Hard drives, CD-ROMs, and magneto-optical disks
- How to mirror and duplex hard drives to improve system reliability

Chapter 11, "Printing with NetWare," explores printing with NetWare. The topics you will study include the following:

- Understanding the basics of printing with NetWare
- Setting up network printing using PCONSOLE, PSERVER.NLM, PSERVER.EXE, and RPRINTER.EXE
- Connecting to network printing through Windows
- Troubleshooting network printing problems

Chapter 12, "Troubleshooting Concepts and Tools," examines the following topics:

- The troubleshooting process
- Troubleshooting tools
- Problem prevention

Chapter 13, "Optimizing the Network," covers a variety of techniques that can improve the performance of your network, including the following:

- Viewing file server performance with MONITOR
- Tuning the server with SET commands
- Basics of using LANalyzer for Windows
- Using PATCHMAN for loading NetWare enhancements
- Understanding Packet Burst
- The basic functions of bridges and routers
- Creating a disaster recovery plan

Part 3 Installation and Configuration for NetWare

Chapters 14, 15, and 16 consist of installation and configuration workshops on NetWare versions 3.11 and 3.12.

Chapter 17, "Upgrading," examines the tools and procedures required for upgrading to NetWare 3.11, 3.12, and 4.01.

Part 4 NetWare TCP/IP

Part 4 contains six chapters dealing with NetWare and TCP/IP.

Chapter 18, "Learning the History of TCP/IP and the Internet," examines the following subjects:

- The history of the ARPANET
- The Internet
- Why TCP/IP became so popular
- The basic goals of TCP/IP
- Who were the principal players in developing the TCP/IP protocol suite

Chapter 19, "Investigating the TCP/IP Protocol Suite," enables you to learn the following:

- List the layers of the DoD model
- Identify the protocols used at each layer
- Create a hosts file
- Evaluate an IP Address
- Determine how subnet masks are used

Chapter 20, "Combining NetWare and TCP/IP," explores the following subject areas:

- The products Novell produces that rely upon the TCP/IP Protocol Suite
- The supported interfaces, their frame types, and what is needed to use them on a NetWare server
- The database file used by NetWare
- The NLMs that NetWare servers use
- The syntax for loading and binding the TCP/IP protocols

Chapter 21, "Managing TCP/IP," consists of these topics:

- Simple Network Management Protocol (SNMP)

- SNMP Managers and SNMP Agents

- Community names

- The console menu utility for monitoring and managing SNMP File Server Agents—TCPCON

- Simple TCP/IP troubleshooting

Chapter 22, "Routing IP Over NetWare," examines the following:

- Internetworking terms and devices

- Setting up your NetWare server to allow IP Packets to cross the router

- Creating an IPTUNNEL network

Chapter 23, "Using Simple UNIX Commands," covers two general areas of interest:

- The most common FTP commands and how to use them

- The most common TELNET commands and their syntax

Following Part 4 are four appendixes.

Appendix A is a glossary of NetWare and networking terms.

Appendix B is an extensive list of acronyms used in this book.

Appendix C helps you toward studying for the NetWare 4.*x* Installation and Configuration test.

Appendix D is an introduction to the networking tools NSEPro and MicroHouse Technical Library (MTL) (MTL is included on the *Networking Technologies, 3rd Edition* CD-ROM discs). Mastering these tools is a CNE testing requirement, and this appendix gives you test scenario questions, hints and strategies for finding solutions, and the correct answers.

Learning More about NetWare

NetWorking Technologies covers three tests that are required to qualify as a Certified NetWare Engineer:

- ◆ DOS/Microcomputer Concepts

- ◆ Networking Technologies

- ◆ Service and Support

In addition to those three tests, you need to be certified on NetWare 3.11, 3.12, or 4.01. Other books in NRP's *NetWare Training Guide* series can assist you with these tests.

NetWare Training Guide: Managing NetWare Systems assists CNEs who choose to be certified on a NetWare 3.*x* track. Additionally, those who wish to be Certified NetWare Administrators for NetWare 2.2 or 3.*x* will find the training they require in this volume. The tests covered by Managing NetWare Systems include the following:

- ◆ DOS/Microcomputer Concepts

- ◆ Certified NetWare Administrator, versions 2.2, 3.1*x*, and 3.12

- ◆ NetWare 3.1*x* Administration (v3.12 and v3.11)

- ◆ NetWare 3.11 Administration

- ◆ NetWare 3.1*x* Advanced Administration

- ◆ NetWare 3.11 Advanced Administration

If you are among the increasing numbers of CNEs who want to be certified with NetWare version 4.01, NRP has two training guides that will interest you.

NetWare Training Guide: NetWare 4 Administration assists NetWare administrators to pass the NetWare 4.01 Administration and Advanced Administration tests. Choose this volume if you are new to NetWare or if you want the most thorough NetWare 4.01 coverage available.

NetWare Training Guide: NetWare 4 Update is intended to help experienced NetWare 3.1*x* administrators become certified for NetWare 4.01. Choose this volume if you are comfortable with NetWare 3.1*x* and want to be certified on NetWare 4.01 as efficiently as possible by studying only the new features.

Both of these guides, as well as *NetWare: The Professional Reference*, also by New Riders Publishing, contain extensive coverage of NDS (NetWare Directory Services), as mentioned in Appendix C, "Installing NetWare 4.01" of this book.

Earning a Novell certification is an expensive and time-consuming process. *New Riders' Guide to NetWare Certification* shows you how to achieve your certification goals efficiently, reliably, and economically. The author, an experienced CNE and CNI, shows you how to best become a CNA, CNE, CNI, or ECNE.

New Riders Publishing

The staff of New Riders Publishing is committed to bringing you the very best in computer reference material. Each New Riders book is the result of months of work by authors and staff who research and refine the information contained within its covers.

As part of this commitment to you, the NRP reader, New Riders invites your input. Please let us know if you enjoy this book, if you have trouble with the information and examples presented, or if you have a suggestion for the next edition.

Please note, though: New Riders staff cannot serve as a technical resource for Novell NetWare or for questions about software- or hardware-related problems. Please refer to the documentation that accompanies your version of Novell NetWare or to the appropriate electronic Help systems.

If you have a question or comment about any New Riders book, there are several ways to contact New Riders Publishing. We will respond to as many readers as we can. Your name, address, or phone number will never become part of a mailing list or be used for any purpose other than to help us continue to bring you the best books possible. You can write us at the following address:

New Riders Publishing
Attn: Associate Publisher
201 W. 103rd Street
Indianapolis, IN 46290

If you prefer, you can fax New Riders Publishing at (317) 581-4670.

You can send electronic mail to New Riders from a variety of sources. NRP maintains several mailboxes organized by topic area. Mail in these mailboxes will be forwarded to the staff member who is best able to address your concerns. Substitute the appropriate mailbox name from the list below when addressing your e-mail. The mailboxes are as follows:

ADMIN	Comments and complaints for NRP's Publisher
APPS	Word, Excel, WordPerfect, other office applications
ACQ	Book proposal inquiries by potential authors
CAD	AutoCAD, 3D Studio, AutoSketch, and CAD products
DATABASE	Access, dBASE, Paradox and other database products
GRAPHICS	CorelDRAW!, Photoshop, and other graphics products
INTERNET	Internet
NETWORK	NetWare, LANtastic, and other network-related topics
OS	MS-DOS, OS/2, all OS except Unix and Windows

UNIX	Unix
WINDOWS	Microsoft Windows (all versions)
OTHER	Anything that doesn't fit the above categories

If you use an MHS e-mail system that routes through CompuServe, send your messages to:

mailbox @ NEWRIDER

To send NRP mail from CompuServe, use the following address:

MHS: *mailbox* @ NEWRIDER

To send mail from the Internet, use the following address format:

mailbox@newrider.mhs.compuserve.com

NRP is an imprint of Macmillan Computer Publishing. To obtain a catalog or information, or to purchase any Macmillan Computer Publishing book, call (800) 428-5331.

Thank you for selecting *NetWare Training Guide: Networking Technologies, 3rd Edition*!

PART 1

Technologies Used in Local Area Networks

Learning Network Technology Terminology

As you read this book, you will be challenged to learn large amounts of terminology. Networking and data communication, like all technical fields, have developed a technical vocabulary. You need to ground yourself in this vocabulary and in the underlying technologies if you want to become a networking expert.

The first set of terms in this chapter focuses on the distinction between analog and digital data. Data communication is frequently involved in converting data between analog and digital forms, and a wide variety of devices have been developed for this purpose. These devices become the focus of later sections in this chapter, and you learn about modems, codecs, and other communication devices.

You then examine media and techniques for transmitting analog and digital data. After considering the characteristics of various media types, you are introduced to asynchronous and synchronous communication. Then you are introduced to techniques for switching signals through complex networks. Finally, this chapter examines the public telephone network as a medium for data communication.

Describe computer network development.

The first business computers came into use in the 1950s and were huge machines, large enough to require their own rooms. These first computers were terribly expensive and were normally found only in the larger corporations. These computers, much like those we use today, were made up of a central processing unit (CPU), random access memory (RAM), and secondary storage devices.

As the need for the processing power of the computers increased, the need to distribute the resources of the computer system became evident. The original *islands of automation*, where one vendor supplied a workgroup's computing needs and other workgroups had to fend for themselves, became a cumbersome element. The need for these islands of automation to communicate with each other was the key element to the early stages of network development.

Identify the major standards organizations and their responsibilities.

To aid in the development of standards, which all computer network designers needed to be able to connect such computer diversity as existed, several standards organizations were created. The following is a list of several popular standards organizations that have helped to define the networking industry:

EIA—Electronic Industries Association

Definition:

The EIA is a standards organization made up of U.S. electronics manufacturers.

Contribution:

The EIA developed the RS-232 standard interface.

ISO—International Standards Organization

Definition:

ISO is a voluntary, nontreaty organization that issues standards on a vast number of topics.

Contribution:

The ISO developed the OSI blueprint and protocol suite discussed in Chapter 3.

ANSI—American National Standards Institute

Definition:

ANSI is the U.S. representative in the ISO. ANSI is a private, nonprofit, nongovernmental organization made up of manufacturers, common carriers, and other interested parties.

Contribution:

ANSI is responsible for creating the American Standard Code for Information Interchange (ASCII).

IEEE—Institute of Electronic and Electrical Engineers

Definition:

IEEE is a standards organization dealing with electronics.

Contribution:

IEEE governs the 802 workgroups for networking topology standards described in Chapter 4.

CCITT—Consultative Committee for International Telegraphy and Telephony

Definition:

CCITT is an international standards committee, making technical recommendations about telephone, telegraph, and data communication interfaces.

Contribution:

CCITT has contributed the X series standards and the V series standards described in Chapter 4.

Now that you are familiar with the necessity of interconnecting computer systems, the rest of this chapter helps develop the methods used to accomplish this task.

Understanding Analog and Digital Data

 Differentiate between analog and digital data.

You are probably most familiar with analog and digital data as they appear on watch dials. The hands on an analog watch move continuously. You can estimate half minutes by watching the minute hand move between two marks on the dial.

A digital watch, however, represents time in the form of a number that has a specific value at any given time. The dial does not move gradually between 8:05 and 8:06; the time changes all at once. Digital data cannot represent in-between values that are more precise than the limits designed into the measurement device.

Defining Data

It is useful to have a working definition of data, which simply put is information. Data is organized. Peas rattling in a can do not carry much information. Peas dropped in rhythmic patterns into the can can be made to carry information; Morse code is an obvious possibility.

 Data stands in sharp contrast to noise, which is random information with no informational content. The static on a phone line does not convey any information to the listener. In fact, the static noise tends to obscure the data on the line, the voice that the listener is attempting to hear.

Noise is a serious concern in communication, because noise can insinuate itself into any message. Noise places limits on the distances that data can be transmitted and on the environments in which some media can be employed. In addition, the presence of noise makes it necessary for a communication system to check for errors in transmissions.

Data is the thing that computers (and humans) manipulate. Data can take two forms. One form can be observed in nature: sounds, vibrations, textures, and so on. This form of data is continuously changing. Vibrations in the air become sound data when they are organized in such a way that a person can listen and extract information. This data is known as *analog* data. Music and speech are two examples.

Another form of data was invented by humans. This is symbolic information. Stop signs are examples of symbols that can carry two messages. A corner with a stop sign conveys one message. A street corner without a stop sign conveys another message. Stoplights are similar, but they can provide three distinct messages. This sort of symbolic information is closely related to the digital data that is the life's blood of computers and data communication. Digital data consists of numbers that function as symbols. In a symbolic coding scheme, numbers can represent a shade of red, middle C on a piano, or customer satisfaction with a mouthwash brand, to select a few diverse examples.

Differentiate between analog and digital signals and how they are measured.

Defining Analog Data

Most, if not all, data you encounter in nature is analog. In fact, the concept of digital data was principally a mathematical concept until computers made their way into common experience.

Analog data varies along a scale: from dark to light, low to high, short to long, or cold to hot, for example. Examples of analog data surround us. When a number is assigned to measure an analog value, it is understood that the number represents a value on a continuous scale of measurement and that the value can slide along any point on that scale. Look at a ruler for a common example; each space between marks on the ruler can be divided and divided again.

Most analog values change continuously, and many analog phenomena are conveniently represented by waves much like waves in a pool of water. Sound is perhaps the best known example of wave-like analog data. You have probably seen sound represented by a wave similar to that depicted in figure 1.1. This wave falls into a special category known as *sine waves* because they take the form of a curve related to the mathematical sine function. The most obvious characteristics of sine waves are that they vary smoothly along a range of values, and that they alternate their motion, first moving in a positive direction, then reversing to move in a negative direction. All these characteristics can be viewed directly in water waves.

Figure 1.1

An example of an analog sine waveform.

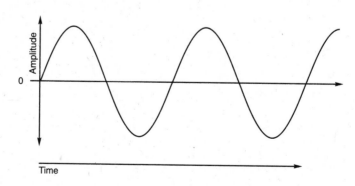

Analog signals have three important characteristics: amplitude, frequency, and phase. The first two characteristics can be easily illustrated by examining our own experiences with sound.

Amplitude is the measure of the strength of the signal, and is usually determined by the heights of the peaks of the waveform. Figure 1.2 shows two examples of analog waves that are identical except for their amplitudes. In sound, the amplitude is related to loudness.

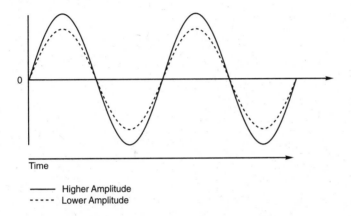

Time

——— Higher Amplitude
- - - - - Lower Amplitude

Figure 1.2

Two analog waveforms differing in amplitude.

Frequency is the measure of the rapidity with which the analog waveform repeats itself. Examine the analog waveforms in the figures and take note of the following characteristics:

◆ The wave's characteristics are considered in reference to a zero (0) reference point. Above the zero point, the wave is said to have a positive value; below the zero point, the wave is said to have a negative value.

◆ The amplitude value of the wave changes with time, which is usually represented going from left to right.

◆ The waveform has two peak values, one on the plus side of the zero point; one on the minus side.

◆ The waveform periodically crosses the zero point.

◆ The waveform repeats itself.

To determine the frequency of a waveform, identify a point on the wave and see how much time elapses until the waveform returns to a similar point. The peaks of the wave are frequently used reference points, as shown in figure 1.3.

Figure 1.3

Two analog wave forms differing in frequency.

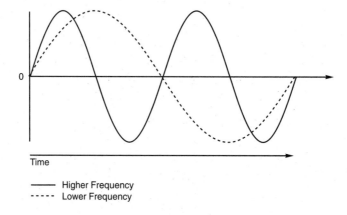

A complete wave is usually called a *cycle*. Frequency is usually specified in the number of cycles that repeat in a second. The measure of cycles-per-second is the *Hertz*. 1,000 Hertz (abbreviated as Hz) is equivalent to 1,000 cycles-per-second. Frequencies can be referred to as high (high Hz values) or low.

With sound, frequency is related to pitch. The high-pitched sounds of a flute have a high frequency. The notes produced by a tuba have a low frequency.

Electrical signals also can be analog in nature. The sound carried by a telephone system is transferred from your phone to the telephone central office via analog, electrical signals.

The amplitude of an electrical wave is measured in volts. Most electronic devices operate with voltages somewhere between a 1.5 -volt flashlight battery and 110- volt house current.

Phase is harder to understand; you cannot usually hear the difference between two sounds that differ in phase. (Stereo buffs will, however, be well acquainted with the phenomenon of "out of phase" speakers.) Phase, however, is a characteristic of analog data often relied on in data communication.

Phase also has to do with the timing of the waveform. Whereas frequency has to do with the duration of a cycle, phase has to do with when the cycle begins. Two waves of the same frequency differ in phase when they do not begin their cycles at the same time.

Figure 1.4 illustrates two waves that are identical except for phase. Note that one wave begins a quarter of a cycle before the other. Such waves are said to be "out of phase." Phase is commonly measured along a scale from 0 to 360 degrees. The waves shown are out of phase by one-quarter cycle or 90 degrees. Figure 1.5 shows various phase relationships measured in degrees.

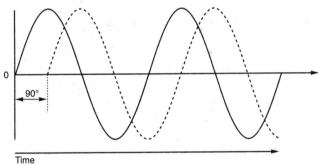

Figure 1.4

Two analog waveforms differing in phase by 90 degrees.

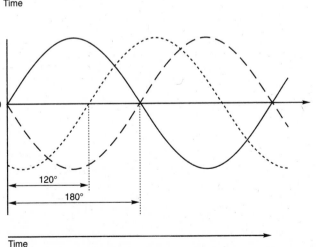

Figure 1.5

Analog waveforms differing in phase by various values.

Defining Digital Data

Digital data takes on specific values as on the digital watch discussed earlier. Digital is the natural form of computer data because computers are, at their hearts, machines made of on/off switches. With very few exceptions, electronic computers are digital computers. Therefore, all data coming out of a computer is digital, and all data going in must be given a digital form.

Data that can have only two values—on/off, yes/no, true/false—is *binary*. Because computers rely on on/off switches, they are binary devices, and you encounter data in binary form frequently as you work with digital communication. These on/off values are usually represented by the digits 1 and 0, although no universal rule determines whether 1 represents true or false, on or off.

Figure 1.6 shows an electrical signal used to represent digital data. The digital electronic signal can have only two voltage values, one representing a one value and another representing a zero value. If any other voltages appear, they are noise and can be ignored.

Figure 1.6

Representing digital data with an electrical signal.

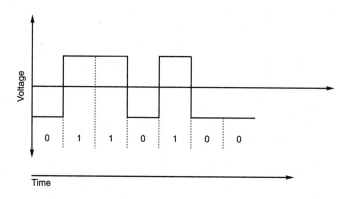

The voltages of the digital signal are measured in comparison to a reference voltage, which is assigned the value of zero volts. In figure 1.7 a signal of +5 volts represents a value of one, whereas a signal of -5 volts represents a zero.

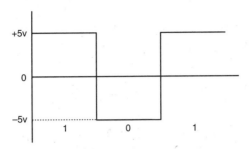

Figure 1.7

Voltages associated
with a digital signal.

Voltage is the measure of the difference between the electrical potentials of two points in an electrical circuit. Most often, a reference point is assigned for the entire circuit, and that reference point is assigned an arbitrary voltage value of zero. Other points have voltages that are either more positive or more negative than the reference.

The zero volt reference is often referred to as signal ground. The term *ground* refers to the technique of actually attaching the equipment's signal ground to a metal stake driven into the earth. The ground circuits on electronic devices are frequently attached to earth ground through the ground conductor of their power cords. Regardless of whether the device is grounded to the earth, however, the ground voltage serves as a reference for the measurement of other voltages.

An analog signal can vary quite freely within broadly defined limits. That is one reason digital communication is regarded as more reliable than analog communication. If outside interference changes the waveform of an analog signal (adds noise to the signal), the receiver has no way of distinguishing the original signal from the noise. You hear noise frequently as you listen to an AM radio: motors, lightning, and other nearby phenomena can add electrical interference to the signal.

Digital signals can take on only specific, well-defined values. Therefore, when noise is added to a digital signal, it is usually obvious. The signal does not take on one of the allowable values, and the receiver can readily spot the problem.

 For the purposes of CNE certification, consider analog data to be data that changes with time or that represents a range of values. Here are some examples of analog data from the perspective of the CNE exams:

- The time represented by the second hand on a watch

- The sound of an ambulance siren

- The rate of rainfall during a storm

The CNE exams consider digital data to be data that is not changing or that represents a discrete measurement. Some examples are:

- The capacity of a container

- The current time

- The brightness in lumens of an electric light

Digital signals are characterized by amplitude and data rate. Figure 1.8 illustrates both characteristics. Amplitude is simply the difference in voltage between the lowest and highest signal values. Notice that the peak voltages do not change, however. The information in a digital signal is not reflected in changes in amplitude. The signal shown in figure 1.8 is digital because it has a limited number of states.

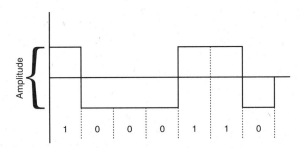

Figure 1.8

The characteristics of a digital signal.

Information is coded into digital signals by changing the signal between the positive and negative states. The timing of the changes is also a factor. You soon will learn several techniques that can be used to "encode" digital information on an electric signal. Data rate is related to the number of bits that the signal can represent in a given time.

In figure 1.8, notice the signal representing three adjacent zero bits. The signal does not change between bits. This presents a problem: how is the receiver to know how many bits are represented by this portion of the signal?

To resolve this problem, devices communicating via digital signals must be careful to synchronize themselves. The receiver must know the rate at which bits are being transmitted. Figure 1.9 shows a transmitted message along with two receivers. Receiver A is synchronized with the transmitter and perceives the data bits correctly. Receiver B expects the bits to be arriving more slowly and interprets the data incorrectly.

The technique for synchronizing sender and receiver is known as *clocking*. The communicating devices agree on a clock tick mechanism that enables them to agree when a bit occurs. The rate of the clock mechanism is sometimes specified in *baud*, the number of times per second that the signal value is set or read. (Jean Baudot was an early pioneer in data communication. The baud unit is named in his honor.) Later in this chapter, you encounter some of the mechanisms used to add clocking to digital signals.

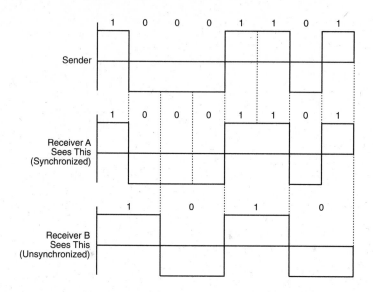

Data rate for digital signals is usually specified in terms of bits per second, abbreviated bps. LANs typically transmit digital data at rates ranging from one million to 16 million bits per second (1-16 Mbps), although much higher rates are available.

  Identify the major coding techniques and their key characteristics for analog and digital signals.

Transmitting Analog and Digital Data

Both analog and digital data can be transmitted either by analog or digital signals. This is fortunate because many devices do not converse using digital signals, and computers do not naturally converse in analog. Here are the possibilities:

◆ Analog signals can carry analog data. Radios, telephones, shouting across the street: all these are examples of using an analog signal to carry analog data.

◆ Analog signals can carry digital data. To carry digital data over a voice phone line, a modem represents ones with signals of one frequency and zeros with signals of another frequency.

◆ Digital signals can carry digital data. When computer devices exchange data, they use digital signals. That is how a computer sends text to a printer, for example.

◆ Digital signals can carry analog data. If you have ever heard sound from a computer arcade game, you have heard digital sound. Each of many numeric values in the game's computer memory is translated into a short sound. When enough digital values are converted to analog and reproduced through a speaker, the result can be music, voice, or sound effects.

From the preceding examples, you should easily reach the conclusion that digital and analog data conversion is performed frequently. Next, you will examine the technologies involved.

Using Analog Signals To Encode Digital Data

The technique that enables an analog signal to carry digital data is *modulation*. You are familiar with the names of two types of modulation employed in radio broadcasting: *amplitude modulation* (AM) and *frequency modulation* (FM).

Modulation requires two things: data to be transmitted and an analog carrier. The carrier is simply an analog wave, which can be electrical signals on a wire, radio signals in the air, or light waves in a glass fiber, to give a few examples. Modulation means that the data is used to modify the amplitude, frequency, or phase of the analog wave, so that the wave represents the ones and zeros of the digital data.

Amplitude-Shift Keying

Amplitude modulation, when used with digital data, is called *amplitude-shift keying* (ASK). With this technique, the amplitude of a signal varies between two distinct values. One example is to represent zeros with a signal amplitude of one volt, and ones with an amplitude of five volts. ASK is shown in figure 1.10.

Figure 1.10

Methods of encoding digital data on analog waveforms.

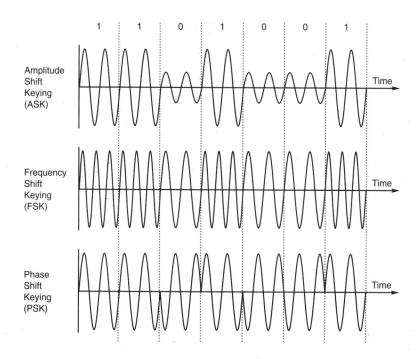

Like AM radio broadcasts, ASK can be susceptible to noise. A noise pulse might raise the one volt used to represent a zero to five or more volts, in which case the signal at that point might be received as a one.

Frequency-Shift Keying

Frequency-shift keying (FSK) is employed by some slower types of modems, and you can often hear the data-modulated carrier when the modem's speaker is turned on. One of the frequencies you hear represents a one, and another frequency represents a zero. Figure 1.10 contrasts FSK with ASK.

Frequency-shift keying shares with FM radio the virtue of being less sensitive to interference. Most noise affects the amplitude of the signal, not the frequency, but changes to the amplitude are ignored by the receiver of the signal. The data rates that can be used with FSK are limited, however. Modems generally employ FSK only for data rates of 1,200 bps and below.

Phase-Shift Keying

Phase-shift keying (PSK) varies the phase of the signal. The signal used to represent a zero might be 180 degrees out of phase with the signal used to represent a one. (Figure 1.10 contrasts PSK and the other modulation techniques.)

PSK is highly resistant to noise and can often be used at higher data rates than FSK. Modems operating at 2,400 bps employ PSK encoding. Higher speeds can be attained by combining PSK with ASK.

Using Digital Signals To Encode Digital Data

The majority of LANs, including Ethernet and Token-Ring, transmit digital data via digital signals. A variety of techniques are employed for encoding digital data, and several are examined here.

The following three characteristics must be examined for each encoding scheme:

◆ The voltages used to represent one and zero values. Recall that voltages are measured in relation to a signal ground, which is assigned a reference value of zero volts.

◆ The portion of the signal sampled to determine the bit value.

33

◆   How the sender and receiver perform clocking to synchronize themselves.

This section describes eight methods of encoding digital data on
digital signals. While reading this discussion, refer to figure 1.11
for pictorial examples. The figure also summarizes the characteristics of the encoding methods.

Figure 1.11

Examples of digital
encoding.

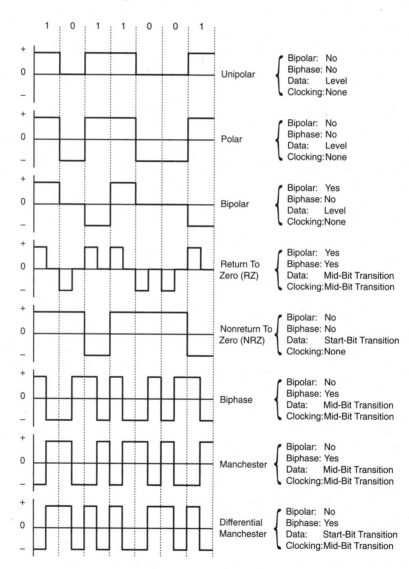

Unipolar Encoding

In *unipolar encoding*, only one voltage, which can be positive or negative, is used in addition to the zero reference. In figure 1.11, a positive voltage represents a one and zero volts represents zero. Teletypes (TTY devices) were examples of devices that used unipolar encoding.

If you examine the figure and recall the discussion about clocking earlier in this chapter, you will recognize a problem with unipolar encoding: it is necessary to devise a separate clocking mechanism to synchronize the sending and receiving devices. This can be accomplished by providing a clocking signal on an additional wire in the data communication circuit.

Polar Encoding

Polar encoding resembles unipolar encoding except that both a positive and a negative signal are used. This reduces susceptibility to noise by increasing the voltage range. The need remains, however, to provide a separate clocking mechanism.

Bipolar Encoding

Bipolar encoding is characterized by the use of three distinct voltages, typically plus, minus, and zero.

The example in figure 1.11 uses a system called alternate mark inversion (AMI). A zero is represented by a zero voltage. Ones are represented by alternately driving the voltage high and low. With AMI, noise-induced errors can be easily recognized; however, the need for a separate clocking mechanism remains.

Return to Zero Encoding

Return to zero (RZ) encoding is another example of bipolar technique. With RZ encoding, the signal voltage is zero for a portion of each bit. This is the first scheme you have seen that guarantees a voltage transition for each bit. This is an advantage because the signal encodes both clocking information and data. RZ is, therefore, self-clocking.

 Return to zero is also the first scheme in which a voltage transition is used to designate a bit rather than simply a voltage level. Although voltage levels can be distorted by noise or by the electrical characteristics of the transmission medium, voltage transitions are less easily masked. Transition-based encoding schemes are less susceptible to noise and are, therefore, employed in most high-performance networks.

In figure 1.11, the transition in mid-bit is used to encode the data. If the signal transitions from positive to zero, it encodes a one. A mid-bit transition from negative to zero encodes a zero value.

Non-Return to Zero

The *non-return to zero (NRZ) encoding* technique also uses transitions to represent data. If the transition occurs at the start of the bit, a one is represented. The lack of a transition indicates a zero. Because NRZ does not guarantee a signal transition for each bit, it is not self-clocking.

NRZ is simple to implement and is frequently used for terminal-to-host and terminal-to-modem communication. Because of the absence of self-clocking, however, NRZ is infrequently used in LANs. A desirable characteristic of NRZ is its efficient use of channel bandwidth, and an ingenious system was used to enable high-performance FDDI networks to use NRZ encoding. You read about FDDI in Chapter 4.

Biphase Encoding

Biphase encoding requires at least one voltage transition per bit. Biphase encoding techniques, therefore, are self-clocking. They also are more noise-resistant than other systems because the lack of a transition is a ready indicator of a network error.

Manchester and Differential Manchester encoding are examples of biphase codes.

Manchester Encoding

Manchester encoding utilizes a mid-bit transition to encode data. For example, a negative-to-positive transition can indicate a one, whereas a positive-to-negative transition can indicate a zero. Because each bit is characterized by a voltage transition, Manchester encoding is an example of a biphase code and is self-clocking. The mid-bit transition provides both clocking and data encoding.

Ethernet LANs employ Manchester Encoding.

Differential Manchester Encoding

Differential Manchester encoding uses the mid-bit transition to provide clocking. However, data is encoded in a voltage transition at the beginning of the bit. The presence of a transition at the start of the bit encodes a one; the absence of a transition encodes a zero.

Differential Manchester encoding is an example of a biphase code and is self-clocking.

Differential Manchester encoding is employed in 802.5 Token-Ring LANs.

Exploring Codes for Representing Data

Identify common message codes and reasons for using codes for message transmission.

Until now, the discussion in this chapter has focused on how bits are encoded for transmission through analog and digital signal-carrying media. Because a bit can have only two values, very little information can be encoded unless bits are combined into groups. A common example of a group of bits is the unit called a *byte*, which consists of eight bits. A byte can represent numbers corresponding from decimal values of 0 through 255. That is enough to assign a number to each letter, number, and punctuation mark and leave some numbers available for other purposes.

This is the essential principle underlying the ASCII and EBCDIC character sets discussed in this section. These are the most commonly used character sets employed in data communication. They are used by the computers internally, to represent characters in memory, and they are also used externally when computers need to exchange character information.

Circumstances exist that require characters to be translated between character sets. If, for example, a microcomputer is emulating a terminal connected to an IBM mainframe, the characters sent to the mainframe must use EBCDIC coding, the coding that IBM computers understand. Because the microcomputer uses ASCII in its own memory, a translation process must take place whenever sending or receiving characters.

ASCII

The *American Standard Code for Information Interchange* (ASCII) is the character code most commonly employed in computers.

Virtually all micro- and minicomputers utilize ASCII, as do most mainframes not based on IBM mainframe architectures. ASCII is a formal United States government standard, designated as ANSI standard X3.4. In addition to having almost universal acceptance in the United States, ASCII is a broadly accepted *de facto* standard in many other nations.

The ASCII code uses seven bits, representing 128 values (ranging from 0 through 127), to define codes for 33 control codes and 95 printable characters. Figure 1.12 summarizes the ASCII character set. (It also shows an extended ASCII character set, discussed later.) The left-hand columns describe bits 1 through 4, while three rows along the the top describe bits 5 through 7. Do not forget that these bits are written from right to left: bit 1 is the rightmost bit, and bit 7 is the leftmost bit.

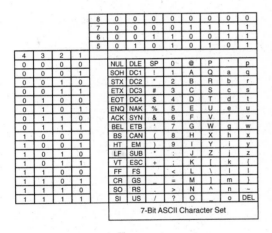

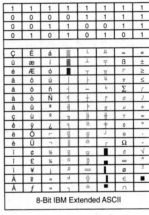

Figure 1.12

The ASCII and IBM Extended ASCII character sets.

7-Bit ASCII Character Set

8	7	6	5		4	3	2	1								
0	0	0	0		0	0	0	0	NUL	DLE	SP	0	@	P	`	p
0	0	0	1		0	0	0	1	SOH	DC1	!	1	A	Q	a	q
0	0	1	0		0	0	1	0	STX	DC2	"	2	B	R	b	r
0	0	1	1		0	0	1	1	ETX	DC3	#	3	C	S	c	s
0	1	0	0		0	1	0	0	EOT	DC4	$	4	D	T	d	t
0	1	0	1		0	1	0	1	ENQ	NAK	%	5	E	U	e	u
					0	1	1	0	ACK	SYN	&	6	F	V	f	v
					0	1	1	1	BEL	ETB	'	7	G	W	g	w
					1	0	0	0	BS	CAN	(	8	H	X	h	x
					1	0	0	1	HT	EM	)	9	I	Y	i	y
					1	0	1	0	LF	SUB	*	:	J	Z	j	z
					1	0	1	1	VT	ESC	+	;	K	[	k	{
					1	1	0	0	FF	FS	,	<	L	\	l	|
					1	1	0	1	CR	GS	-	=	M	]	m	}
					1	1	1	0	SO	RS	.	>	N	^	n	~
					1	1	1	1	SI	US	/	?	O	_	o	DEL

8-Bit IBM Extended ASCII

It is worthwhile to consider the following examples from the ASCII character set:

- ◆ Bit pattern 1000001 represents the decimal value 65 and the character A. Most of the ASCII codes represent printable characters, starting with the ASCII 32, the space character, and ending with ASCII 126, the ~ character.

- ◆ Bit pattern 0001010 represents the decimal value 10 and the character LF. "LF" stands for "line feed" and is an example of a control character. ASCII values from 0 through 31 are used to represent communication control functions. LF informs the receiver that a new line of data is about to start. ASCII value 127 is assigned the DEL or delete function. Other control codes are encountered later in this book.

 Take some time to examine figure 1.12 closely. Notice that the table can be divided into four major groups: control codes, punctuation, uppercase, and lowercase. In particular, notice that upper and lowercase letters differ only in bits 5 through 7. Bits 1 through 4 are identical for any given pair of letters. The ASCII code is quite organized, and it is easy and useful to commit key values to memory.

The ASCII code uses only seven bits, whereas computers usually group bits into eight-bit bytes. That eighth bit can be put to two distinct uses: parity and character set extension.

Parity

Parity is a technique for detecting errors. When a character is transmitted, the eighth bit can be designated as a parity bit. The sender sets the value of the parity bit to represent the number of one bits that appear in the character. The receiver examines the parity bit and determines whether it still correctly reflects the number of one data bits, enabling the receiver to detect many types of communication errors.

Two types of parity are commonly employed: even and odd. In each case, the parity bit is set so that the byte transmitted has an even or an odd number of ones.

◆ With even parity, the sender counts the ones in the character and sets the parity bit so that the total number of ones is even. If the character contains three ones, the parity bit is set to the value of one. If the character contains six ones, the parity bit is set to zero.

◆ With odd parity, the sender counts the ones in the character and sets the parity bit so that the number of ones is odd. If the character contains three ones, the parity bit is set to the value of zero. If the character set contains six ones, the parity bit is set to one.

Note When even parity is employed, every byte transmitted contains an even number of ones.

When odd parity is employed, every byte transmitted contains an odd number of ones.

Parity techniques are commonly used in modem communication.

Character Set Extension

Examination of the ASCII character set reveals that it is extremely limited. The ASCII character set has an English bias, and many characters in non-English alphabets are unavailable. ASCII has no graphics characters, so you cannot draw boxes, for example, and many common mathematical symbols are absent.

Because computers can easily work with groups of eight characters, a variety of extended character sets have been developed. Most retain the ASCII character set for values 0 through 127. However, an eighth bit adds the possible values of 128 through 255.

A common extended character set was created by IBM for the IBM personal computers. The extended characters appear alongside the seven-bit ASCII characters in figure 1.12. Although the IBM character set has been widely implemented by other vendors, it is not an official standard, and many other character sets are possible.

EBCDIC

IBM defined the EBCDIC character code for use in IBM mainframe computers. The Extended Binary Coded Decimal Interchange

Code uses eight bits to represent 256 characters. The EBCDIC character set is summarized in figure 1.13.

Figure 1.13

The EBCDIC character code.

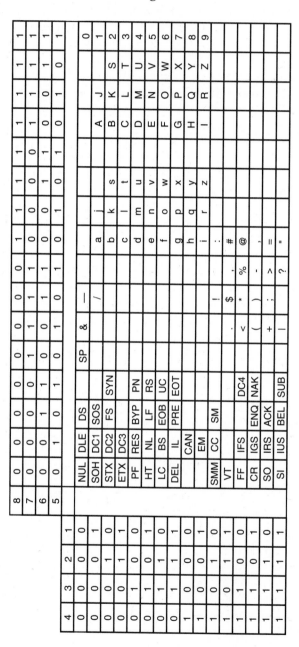

Because EBCDIC uses all eight bits, parity cannot be used for error detection. When data is transmitted, another system, known as a *checksum*, is employed. Checksum is discussed along with other error detection techniques later in this book.

Understanding Modems and Codecs

From an earlier discussion, you may gather that it is extremely common to convert data between analog and digital forms. Two types of devices are involved in these conversions: modems and codecs.

Modems

 Define modem and identify reasons for using a modem.

Modem is derived from the phrase "modulator/demodulator." Earlier in this chapter, you examined how *modulation* can be used to encode a digital signal onto an analog carrier. *Demodulation* is the process of recovering the original digital signal.

Figure 1.14 depicts the modulation/demodulation process. Notice that the modem is capable of carrying the process in either direction depending on whether it is receiving data destined for the digital device or transmitting data to a remote device.

Figure 1.14

Modulation and
demodulation.

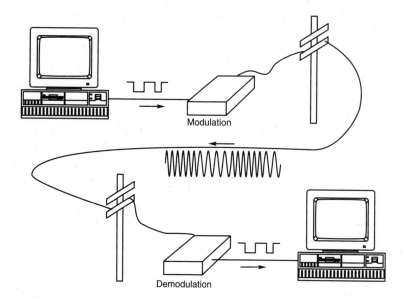

 Note Two terms you encounter often in data communication are *DCE* and *DTE*. Both have their origins far back in the history of data telecommunications, when the most common application of data communication was to connect remote terminals to mainframes via modems.

Terminals and computers are classified as Data Terminal Equipment (DTE), whereas modems are examples of Data Circuit-Terminating Equipment (DCE). Figure 1.15 illustrates a typical telecommunication circuit consisting of DTEs, DCEs, and a telephone-type medium. You encounter the terms DTE and DCE frequently in telecommunications, particularly with regard to the RS-232 interface standard, which is the most frequent standard for interfacing terminals and other devices with modems.

You may also encounter the use of DCE to mean Data Communication Equipment.

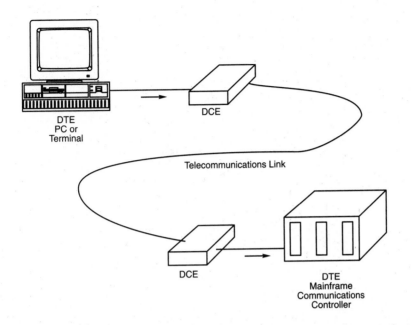

Figure 1.15

DTE and DCE devices used in telecommunications.

A modem is a type of DCE that interfaces a DTE (which is digital in nature) with an analog transmission medium. A modem accepts the signal from its attached DTE and modulates it with an analog carrier. The modulated carrier is an audio frequency that can be transmitted through the transmission medium. At the receiving end, a modem demodulates the signal to extract the original digital information from the carrier.

Modems have evolved from simple, slow devices to highly sophisticated signal processors. The old Bell-103 modem, which operated at 300 bps, has largely been superceded by higher performing standards. Some standards define means of achieving higher data rates, and others define error detection and data compression protocols. Many of these standards originated as vendor standards, but have since been codified into various standards, for example the CCITT V-series of standards, discussed in Chapter 4.

Most frequently, modems are employed to take advantage of public or private telephone facilities for long-distance communication. Such uses can range from light-duty, dial-up systems to use

45

of high-data rate leased lines. A dedicated leased line can be an effective way of internetworking distant hosts or LANs.

Modems, however, also can be employed locally. It may occasionally be desirable to use two short-range modems to interconnect two devices in the same building but located beyond the 50-foot range of a simple serial connection. When devices are located within 50 feet of each other, the modems can be eliminated by connecting the devices with a *null-modem*. A null-modem is simply a connector or a cable that crosses the wires between two computer devices so that the send circuits of each device are connected to the receive circuits of the other.

 Most frequently, modems (DCEs) are connected to computers (DTEs) through serial ports. In Chapter 4, the discussion of the RS-232 standard describes the most commonly employed standard used for designing serial ports.

Codecs

 Define codec and identify reasons for using a codec.

In some respects, *codecs* function as mirror images of modems. Whereas a modem converts digital data so that it can be transmitted on an analog communication medium, a COder/DECoder converts analog data for transmission on a digital medium.

Figure 1.16 illustrates a codec transmitting voice data via a digital medium. This might be done for several purposes. Digital encoding enables your LAN or wide-area digital network to transmit voice data or data from analog instruments. Voice mail might be tied to electronic mail by using a codec to encode the voice messages digitally. Because data is transmitted digitally, it is possible to take advantage of the greater reliability inherent in digital data transmission.

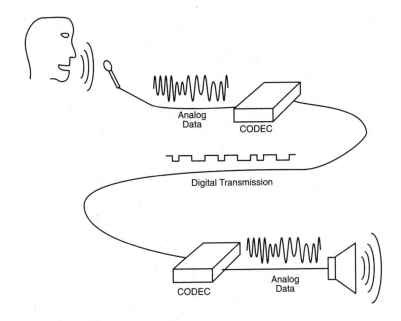

Figure 1.16
The operation of a codec.

Exploring Data Transmission Media

Identify a variety of media types and their key characteristics, including cost, ease of installation, speed/capacity, and resistance to interference.

Data transmission is the process of conveying data between two points by way of a communication medium. A wide variety of media are available, but they fall into two classes: bounded and unbounded.

Bounded media confine the data to specific physical pathways. Common examples of bounded media are wire and optical fiber cables. Cable TV uses bounded media.

Unbounded media transmit the data-carrying signal through space, independent of a cable. Broadcast radio and television are examples of unbounded media.

Identify transmission modes and their advantages and disadvantages.

Bounded Media

By far the most common media employed for data transmission are defined as bounded—the data signal is confined in a specific transmission pathway. When practical, cable represents a low-cost and reliable means of transmitting data between computing devices.

Practicality is a relative thing. Certainly cables are likely to be the logical choice within a building or even a building complex. It may not be possible, however, to run a cable between two buildings on different sides of a public road, and it is certainly not practical when the buildings are located on different continents. Such conditions may call for use of unbounded media.

You should be alert to several characteristics when examining cables:

1. Resistance to electrical magnetic interference (EMI). See the following note for more information.

2. Bandwidth, the range of frequencies that the cable can accommodate. LANs generally carry data rates of 1 to 16 megabits per second and require moderately high bandwidth.

3. Attenuation characteristics. *Attenuation* describes how cables reduce the strength of a signal with distance. Resistance is one factor that contributes to signal attenuation.

4. Cost.

Electrical magnetic interference, or EMI, can be a major headache for LAN technicians. Many electrical devices generate magnetic fields that produce unwanted electrical currents in data cables. The noise that results from these currents can degrade data signals, sometimes stopping communication altogether due to excessive error rates. Electrical motors and fluorescent lights are common sources of EMI, and it can be a genuine challenge to cable a network in environments such as factories that contain many electrical devices.

Cable Types

Cables fall into two broad categories—electrical conductors and fiber optic—with various types of cables available in each category. Prior to an examination of fiber-optic cables, this section examines two types of electrical cables: *coaxial* and *twisted pair*.

Electrical cable types are frequently referred to as "copper" because that metal is the most frequently used conductor. You may hear fiber-optic cables called simply "fiber" or "glass."

Coaxial Cable

As you can see in figure 1.17, this cable is called coaxial (or coax for short) because two conductors share a COmmon AXIS. A typical coaxial cable has the following components:

Figure 1.17

The structure of a coaxial cable.

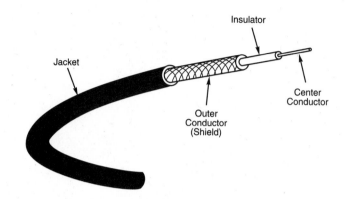

- **Center conductor.** This conductor usually consists of a fairly heavy, solid yet flexible wire; stranded wires can also be used. Solid conductors are preferred for permanent wiring, but stranded conductors make the cable more flexible and easier to connect to equipment.

- **Insulation layer.** Also called a *dielectric layer*, this layer provides electrical insulation and keeps the inner and outer conductors in precise coaxial relationship.

- **Outer conductor or shield.** This layer shields the inner conductor from outside electrical interference. The shield can consist of braided wires, metal foil, or a combination of both. Because of this shield, coax is highly resistant to electrical magnetic interference (EMI).

- **Jacket.** A durable plastic or Teflon jacket coats the cable to prevent damage.

Coax has many desirable characteristics. It is highly resistant to EMI and can support high bandwidths. Some types of coax have heavy shields and center conductors to enhance these characteristics and to extend the distances that signals can be transmitted reliably.

A wide variety of coax cable is available. You must use cable that exactly matches the requirements of a particular type of network. Coax cables vary in a measurement known as the *impedance* (measured in a unit called the *ohm*), which is an indication of the cable's resistance to current flow. The specifications of a given cabling standard indicate the required impedence of the cable. Here are some common examples of coaxial cables used in LANs, along with their impedances and the LAN standards with which they are associated:

◆ RG-8 and RG-11 are 50-ohm cables required for thickwire Ethernet. (See the discussion of the 10BASE5 standard in Chapter 4.)

◆ RG-58 is a smaller 50-ohm cable required for use with thinwire Ethernet. (See the discussion of the 10BASE2 standard in Chapter 4.)

◆ RG-59 is a 75-ohm cable most familiar when used to wire cable TV. RG-59 is also used to cable broadband Ethernet, also discussed under the 802.3 standards in Chapter 4.

◆ RG-62 is a 93-ohm cable used for ARCnet. It is also commonly employed to wire terminals in an IBM SNA network.

Some advantages of coaxial cable are as follows:

◆ Highly insensitive to EMI.

◆ Supports high bandwidths.

◆ Heavier types of coax are sturdy and can withstand harsh environments.

◆ Represents a mature technology that is well understood and consistently applied among vendors.

Coax also has some disadvantages, including the following:

◆ Although fairly insensitive to EMI, coax remains vulnerable to EMI in harsh conditions such as factories.

◆ Coax can be bulky.

◆ Coax is among the most expensive types of wire cables.

Twisted–Pair

Figure 1.18 shows how two wires are twisted together to form the wire type known as twisted pair (TP). Cables can be constructed of multiple pairs of cables contained by a common jacket.

Figure 1.18

Twisted-pair wire.

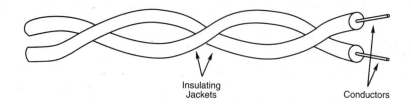

Insulating
Jackets

Conductors

The twists in the wire pairs are an important part of the electrical characteristics of TP cable. Twists reduce the cable's sensitivity to outside EMI and the degree to which the cables radiate radio frequency signals. Remember that the frequencies at which LANs operate fall into the range of radio signals. If TP cable is insufficiently twisted, it can function as an antenna and radiate significant amounts of radio signals that can interfere with local broadcast reception equipment.

Until recently, twisted-pair cable used in networks was most frequently surrounded by a braided shield that served to reduce both EMI sensitivity and radio emissions. An example of STP cable is the IBM Type 1 cable shown in figure 1.19. Shielded twisted pair cable (STP) was required for all high-performance networks such as IBM Token-Ring until a few years ago. STP cable, however, is expensive and bulky, and manufacturers of network equipment have devoted extensive research to enabling high-speed networks to work with unshielded twisted-pair (UTP).

Figure 1.19

IBM Type 1 cable is an example of shielded twisted-pair.

Jacket

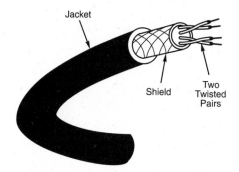

Shield

Two
Twisted
Pairs

UTP is the cost leader among network cables. The 10BASE-T standard defines an Ethernet configuration that utilizes UTP. Recent work by IBM and other vendors also has developed network equipment that can use UTP even for high-speed 16-megabit per second Token-Ring. In most cases, UTP cable is implemented using modular telephone-type connectors such as the RJ-11 (two pair) and RJ-45 (four pair) connectors, shown in figure 1.20. Telephone modular connectors are inexpensive and easy to install, serving to further reduce the cost of UTP cabling systems.

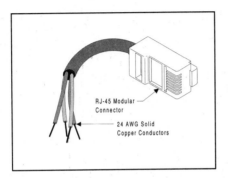

Figure 1.20

UTP cable with an RJ-45 modular connector.

 UTP looks much like the wire used to wire voice telephones. In newer telephone installations, it may indeed be possible to use wiring installed for the voice telephone system as cable in a network. UTP cable comes in a variety of grades, ranging from level 1 (lowest quality) to level 5 (highest quality). When investigating the use of UTP cabling, be sure to determine the wire quality required for your network.

When utilizing UTP cable, it is necessary to ensure that all components in the data network are data grade. Voice grade components used in voice telephone systems are not of sufficiently high quality.

Shielded twisted-pair cable is the standard cable specified for IBM Token-Ring networks and for Apple's LocalTalk.

Unshielded twisted-pair cables can be utilized for some configurations of Token-Ring, Ethernet, and ARCnet networks.

Here are some advantages of twisted-pair wiring:

◆ Telephone cable standards are mature and well established. Materials are plentiful, and a wide variety of cable installers are familiar with the installation requirements.

◆ It may be possible to use in-place telephone wiring if it is of sufficiently high quality.

◆ UTP represents the lowest cost cabling. The cost for STP is higher and is comparable to the cost of coaxial cable.

Some disadvantages of twisted-pair are as follows:

◆ STP can be expensive and difficult to work with.

◆ Compared to fiber optic cable, all TP cable is more sensitive to EMI. UTP especially may be unsuitable for use in high-EMI environments.

◆ TP cables are regarded as being less suitable for high-speed transmissions than coax or fiber optic. Technology advances, however, are pushing upward the data rates possible with TP. Cable segment lengths are also more limited with TP.

◆ Some uses for TP have not been sanctioned by international standards. For example, a variety of vendors produce equipment that enables UTP to be used with a 16-megabit per second Token-Ring, although a standard is currently only in the early stages of the IEEE approval process.

Fiber Optic

Fiber optic cables utilize light waves to transmit data through a thin glass or plastic fiber. The structure of a typical fiber optic cable is shown in figure 1.21. The parts of the cable are as follows:

◆ The light conductor is a very fine fiber core. Glass is the most common material, allowing signals to be transmitted for several kilometers without being refreshed. Plastic is used in some circumstances, but plastic cables enable only short cable runs.

◆ The cladding is a glass layer that surrounds the optical fiber core. The optical characteristics of the cladding reflect light back to the core, ensuring that little of the light signal is lost.

◆ A sheath or jacket protects the cable from damage. A single sheath can be used to bundle multiple core/cladding fibers into a multi-fiber cable.

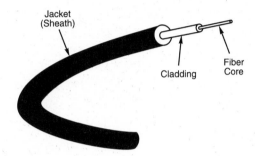

Jacket
(Sheath)

Cladding

Fiber
Core

Figure 1.21

The structure of a fiber optic cable.

The light signals on fiber optic cables are generated either by *light emitting diodes* (LEDs) or by *injection laser diodes* (ILDs), which are similar to LEDs but produce laser light. The purity of laser light is desirable, increasing both data rates and transmission distance. Signals are received by *photodiodes*, solid state devices that detect variations in light intensity.

The interface devices required to operate with fiber optic cable are more expensive than those required for copper cable. The higher cost is the result of several factors, including cost of the components and tighter design characteristics because fiber optic cables generally are operated at high data rates. The cost of fiber optic cable installation, however, is trending downward.

Fiber optic cables have many desirable characteristics. Because the fibers are small in diameter, a cable of a given size can contain more fibers than copper wire pairs. Because fiber optic cables use light pulses instead of electrical signals, they offer very high bandwidth. Bandwiths of 100 million bits per second are commonplace, and bandwidths in the gigabit (billion bit) per second range are available.

Because the signal in a fiber optic cable consists of light pulses, the signal cannot be affected by electromagnetic interference. Nor can the cables radiate radio frequency noise. Optical fibers are, therefore, suitable for use in the noisiest and most sensitive environments. Because these cables radiate no electromagnetic energy, it is impossible to intercept the data signal with electronic eavesdropping equipment. Fiber optic transmissions are extremely secure.

Installation of fiber optic cable requires greater skill than is necessary to install most copper cables. Cables must not be bent too sharply, and connectors must be installed by skilled technicians using special tools. However, new connector technologies have simplified installation and reduced cost.

Here are some advantages of fiber optic cable:

◆ Very high bandwidth.

◆ Immunity to EMI; fiber optic cables can be used in environments that make wire cables unusable.

◆ No radio frequency emissions; signals on fiber optic cables cannot interfere with nearby electronic devices and cannot be detected by conventional electronic eavesdropping techniques.

Summary of Cable Characteristics

Table 1.1 summarizes the characteristics of the cables discussed in this section.

Table 1.1
Comparison of Cable Characteristics

Cable Type	Cable Cost	Installation Cost	EMI Sensitivity	Bandwidth
UTP	Lowest	Lowest (may already be in place)	Highest	Lowest
STP	Medium	Moderate	Low	Moderate

Cable Type	Cable Cost	Installation Cost	EMI Sensitivity	Bandwidth
Coax	Medium	Moderate	Low	High
Fiber-optic	Highest	Highest	None	Very High

Unbounded Media

Unbounded media do not confine data signals to conductors. Rather, they broadcast data signals through space. Signals can be directed in narrow beams to specific receivers or in broad beams to multiple receivers. Examples of unbounded media are microwaves, laser light, and infrared light.

Unbounded media are desirable under a number of circumstances. If equipment will be relocated frequently, movement is simplified because new cables need not be run. Compare the flexibility of broadcast versus cable television. You can relocate a TV much easier if it relies on broadcast signals received through its antenna.

This comparison also illuminates a potential disadvantage of unbounded media. Cable TV is popular in part because reception quality is often superior. The effects of atmospheric interference and many other factors are reduced when the signal is transmitted through a reliable cable.

Unbounded media also can have cost advantages. Radio transmission via satellite has evolved into a cost-effective way of transmitting data between any locations in the world. It would be prohibitively expensive to run a cable for each required connection on an earthly scale. Unbounded media may even be the best way to bridge a short gap. If you need to connect two buildings located on opposite sides of a public road, you probably will be prohibited from stretching a wire over the roadway. A private microwave link, however, may prove less expensive than leasing a high-speed line from a commercial provider.

This section considers four examples of unbounded media: microwaves, radio, laser light, and infrared light.

Microwaves

Microwaves are electromagnetic waves that fall between radio waves and light. Microwaves have frequencies that extend into the gigahertz (billion hertz) range.

Unlike radio waves, microwaves transmit by "line-of-sight" and cannot transmit around the curvature of the earth. If microwaves are to be transmitted more than a few miles, it is necessary to make use of terrestrial relay stations or to relay the signal through a communication satellite. These possibilities are illustrated in figure 1.22.

Figure 1.22

The options for microwave communication.

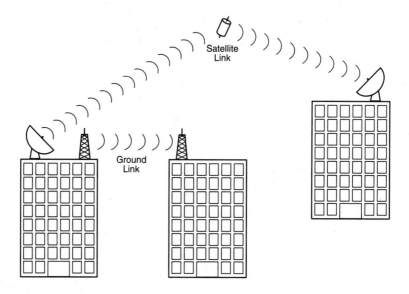

The high frequencies of microwave signals have high bandwidth, and very high data rates are possible. Telephone transmissions usually *multiplex* (see the discussion later in this chapter) several signals onto a single microwave transmission.

The high frequencies of microwaves carry two liabilities. One, as mentioned, is that the signals are transmitted only by line-of-sight.

The other is that microwave signals can be attenuated or interfered with by atmospheric phenomena such as rain.

Although an FCC license is required, microwave communication may be the best method of establishing a communication link. Leases on high-speed lines can be quite expensive, whereas a private microwave link represents a fairly fixed cost investment. Equipment for higher frequency microwaves is generally reasonable in cost.

Satellite microwave communication makes use of satellites in geosynchronous orbit, meaning that they orbit above the same point on earth at all times. This orbit places the satellites approximately 23,000 miles above the surface of the earth. Because the minimum transmission distance of a microwave signal is, therefore, 46,000 miles, a small time delay is introduced, known as *propagation delay*. This time delay can seriously affect the efficiency of some high-speed, two-way communication. However, the time delay is about the same regardless of the distance between the two earth-bound endpoints of the communication link. Whether communicating between Ohio and Indiana or between California and England, the delay encountered is about the same because the majority of distance traveled is encompassed in the satellite up and down links.

The signal transmitted by a satellite can be narrowly focused on a single receiver, or can be broad enough to cover a large area. Satellites carrying commercial television transmit a broad-beam signal so that they can reach receivers in many states with a single transmission.

A recent variation on microwave transmission uses technology similar to that employed in cellular phones. Microwave LANs use very low-power microwave signals to link workstations with central communication hubs. The office is divided into small "cells" within which a group of workstations can communicate. This technology makes it possible to greatly reduce the amount of physical cable required to wire an office and eliminates the need to rewire when a workstation is relocated. The cost-per-workstation for initial installation is higher than for a wired LAN. Given the mobility require-ments of modern industry, however, this use of unbounded media may prove to be a significant direction for the future of office-based LANs.

Some advantages of microwave communication are as follows:

♦ High bandwidth.

♦ Possible significant cost savings.

Some disadvantages include the following:

♦ Requires license and approved equipment.

♦ Potential for atmospheric interference.

♦ Susceptibility to electronic eavesdropping.

Satellite links have their own advantages and disadvantages. Here are some of the advantages:

♦ No relay stations are required.

♦ High bandwidths are available.

♦ Satellite signals can have narrow or broad beams.

♦ Both fixed and mobile earth stations are supported.

♦ Propagation delay is independent of the distance between the earth-bound communication stations.

The disadvantages of satellite communication are as follows:

♦ High cost of earth-bound and satellite equipment.

♦ Need for an FCC license.

♦ Propagation delay may reduce efficiency of two-way com-munication.

♦ Possibility of electronic eavesdropping.

♦ Sensitivity to atmospheric interference.

Radio

Radio consists of electromagnetic waves lower in frequency than microwaves (although the dividing line is fuzzy). Radio frequencies extend from the kilohertz range (for example, AM radio broadcasts), through the megahertz range (commercial FM radio, television, and many other services), and into the low gigahertz range.

Especially with lower frequencies, radio frequencies can extend beyond line-of-sight communication. You have certainly listened to AM radio transmissions that originated hundreds of miles away. These lower frequencies are also less sensitive to atmospheric attenuation than are microwaves.

Radio signals are usually transmitted on a wide beam. Radio is an effective way to transmit to a large number of receivers.

Equipment for transmitting and receiving radio is relatively inexpensive. However, FCC licenses are required to transmit on all but a very few frequencies. The FCC allocates all radio frequencies for specific types of use. Despite the apparent immensity of the available frequencies, most were allocated long ago, and few of the frequencies classified as radio are currently available for commercial data transmission. In actual practice, radio frequencies are used only infrequently for data communication.

The advantages of radio are as follows:

◆ Low cost

◆ Exceeds line-of-sight communcation in many instances, so relay facilities are less frequently required

◆ Both mobile and stationary stations are supported

◆ Equipment costs are moderate

The disadvantages of radio are as follows:

◆ Few frequencies are available

◆ Signals are often affected by noise and interference

◆ Susceptible to eavesdropping

◆ Bandwidths are limited

Laser

Laser light has two properties that make it ideal for data communication. A given laser beam consists entirely of light of a single frequency. Also, all the individual light waves are oriented in parallel; this property is referred to as *coherency*. Because laser light is coherent, it does not diverge in a cone like light from a flashlight. Beams of laser light remain in tight focus, and can be made to diverge only a few miles, even in the distance between the earth and the moon. The coherency and purity of laser light also make it possible to create powerful beams of light.

Laser light does not occur in nature, but is produced by a variety of sophisticated man-made devices. The first laser was constructed of a rod of pure, artificial ruby. Modern lasers use solid materials, gases (helium and neon are a common combination, referred to as HeNe lasers), or solid-state devices. Laser diodes were mentioned in the preceding discussion about fiber optic cables.

Most laser light used in data communication falls in the range of infrared light and is, therefore, invisible. Light has a higher frequency than microwaves, and laser signals can have even higher bandwidth. Laser beams are much tighter than microwave transmissions. Tight laser beams are difficult to intercept with electronic eavesdropping equipment; however, great care is required to properly align the transmitting and receiving equipment.

Laser light can be transmitted over moderate distances (up to a few miles) through the atmosphere. Being light, these signals are, of course, susceptible to all sorts of atmospheric interference. An example of a laser communication link is shown in figure 1.23.

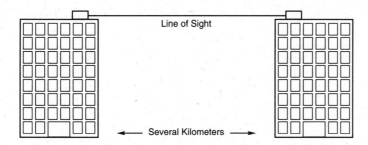

Line of Sight

Several Kilometers

Figure 1.23
An example of a laser
communication link.

Equipment for laser communication is available "off the shelf," and no license is required. Care is required, however, because the laser beams are powerful enough to damage eyesight.

Laser has the following advantages for data communication:

◆ No FCC license is required

◆ Equipment is moderate in cost

◆ Undetected eavesdropping is difficult

Laser has the following disadvantages:

◆ Strictly line-of-sight transmission

◆ Sensitivity to attenuation from atmospheric phenomena

◆ Need for careful alignment of transmitter and receiver

Infrared Transmission

You use a form of infrared data transmission every time you change the channel on a television by pushing a button on the remote control. The remote transmits a series of digital pulses using an infrared LED (ILD); the infrared light is received at the television and decoded to determine the intended command.

This technology can be used to create wireless LANs. One method is to transmit tight-beam signals from station to station. Another is to bounce broad-beam signals off walls or special reflective surfaces. These methods are illustrated in figure 1.24.

Figure 1.24

The options for
infrared data
communication.

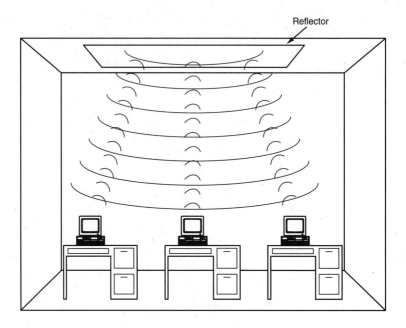

The advantages of infrared media are as follows:

◆ Light beams can have high bandwidth

◆ Reduced cost of relocating equipment

Infrared media have the following disadvantages:

◆ Short distances, usually within a room

◆ Sensitivity to interference, especially when tight-beam
transmissions are used

Summary of Unbounded Media

Table 1.2 summarizes some of the characteristics of the unbounded media discussed.

Table 1.2
Characteristics of Unbounded Media

Media	Coverage	EMI Sensitivity
Terrestrial Microwave	Narrow beam	Moderate

Media	Coverage	EMI Sensitivity
Satellite Microwave	Narrow or broad beam	Moderate
Radio	Broad beam	High
Laser	Very narrow	None
Infrared	Narrow or broad beam	None

Understanding Simplex and Duplex Communication

You will encounter the terms *simplex* and *duplex* many times in regard to modems and data communication. These terms simply refer to whether communication is taking place in one direction or two directions. Simplex and duplex communication are illustrated in figure 1.25.

With simplex communication, the sender only sends and the receiver only receives. In other words, communication flows in one direction only. A fire alarm is a simplex device; it sends an alarm signal to the fire station, but is incapable of receiving any signals.

When all communicating devices can both send and receive, communication is considered to be duplex in nature. Duplex communication has the following two modes:

◆ In half-duplex mode, only one device can transmit at a given time and the devices must take turns. Half-duplex communication requires small amounts of bandwidth, but has a low data rate.

◆ In full-duplex mode, all devices can transmit simultaneously. In other words, multiple messages may be present in the communication channel at a given time. In the next section, you discover methods of transmitting multiple, simultaneous messages through a communication channel.

Figure 1.25

Simplex and duplex
communication
modes.

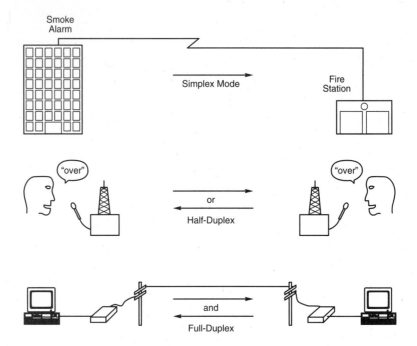

Understanding Multiplexing

 Define multiplexing and identify reasons for
multiplexing.

You have been introduced to the concept of *bandwidth*, a measure
of the range of frequencies or data rates that can be accommo-
dated by a transmission medium. The media discussed in this
chapter range from the low bandwidth of voice telephone communications to very high bandwidths of microwave and laser media.

The full capacity of a high bandwidth channel is frequently
underutilized by a single data stream. This makes possible a
variety of techniques for combining messages to share the bandwidth. Thus, many messages can be transmitted through the same
communication channel. The technique of combining multiple
data messages for transmission on a single, high-bandwidth
channel is called *multiplexing*.

Before discussing the techniques used to multiplex data, it is necessary to clarify the terms *baseband* and *broadband*.

Baseband and Broadband

Identify the key characteristics of baseband and broadband transmissions.

All the bandwidth of a baseband channel is designated for use by a single analog or digital message. The telephone wire that services your phone is a baseband channel capable of supporting a single voice signal. LAN cabling systems such as Token-Ring and Ethernet are generally configured to enable only one message at a time.

Broadband channels, on the other hand, have the capacity to support more than one simultaneous message. Cable TV is a common example of a broadband channel. The video signal for each channel is modulated by an analog carrier signal of a distinctive frequency. This enables a single run of coaxial cable to carry over a hundred individual video signals into your home. Your television's tuner selects one of the available frequencies and can recover the video signal used to modulate that frequency. Broadband data systems are closely related to the technologies used to implement cable TV (CATV), and data and CATV systems share much of the same equipment.

Although the original signals can be analog or digital, the carriers in a broadband system are always analog. Digital baseband and broadband transmission are contrasted in figure 1.26. This figure illustrates how baseband signals utilize the full available bandwidth for a single signal, whereas a broadband transmission allocates portions of the total bandwidth to each of several signals.

Figure 1.26

A comparison of digital baseband and broadband signals.

Digital baseband signals are subject to attenuation and distortion, and cannot be transmitted beyond a kilometer or two without becoming unusable. For longer distances, repeaters are placed at intervals to amplify and clean up the digital signal.

Analog broadband signals are less affected by distance and can often be transmitted several kilometers without the need for intermediate amplification and processing.

Broadband circuits can have two configurations, as shown in figure 1.27. In a dual-cable system, the stations transmit on the same frequency, but avoid conflict by using separate cables. A passive headend at each device processes the two signals. Because it is unnecessary to separate the two signals, a passive headend is a relatively simple device. The term "passive" in an electronic circuit indicates that the circuit does not contain any amplifying circuits, which makes such circuits low in cost.

Figure 1.27

Dual-cable and "split" configuration broadband circuits.

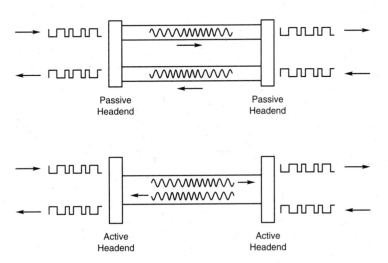

In a "split" configuration, the devices use the same cable, but each device transmits with a different carrier frequency. An active headend is required to recover the two original signals from the same broadband cable. Active headends are more complicated devices than passive headends, and rely on amplifying and other active circuits to separate the signals by frequency. Active headends are more expensive than passive headends.

Most LANs, including Ethernet and Token Ring, are baseband systems. However, a broadband configuration of Ethernet was established by the IEEE committee that developed the 802.3 Ethernet standards. See Chapter 4 for a discussion of baseband and broadband 802.3 networks.

Multiplexing

Identify key characteristics of frequency-division and time-division multiplexing.

Multiplexing is the general term for enabling a single high-bandwidth transmission medium to carry multiple low-bandwidth signals. You have already seen this process in use with broadband transmission systems.

Figure 1.28 illustrates the general process. A multiplexer at the transmission end combines several signals. At the receiving end, a demultiplexer separates out the individual signals. In most cases, multiplexing and demultiplexing capabilities are built into the same device. A multiplexer device frequently is referred to as a "mux."

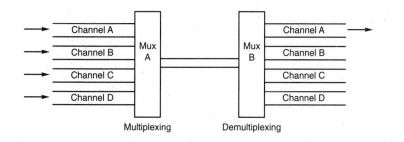

Figure 1.28

The process of multiplexing.

Multiplexing is an effective technique for using transmission channels efficiently. Many voice telephone signals can be muxed for transmission on a high-bandwidth microwave link. A high-bandwidth network backbone can be used to carry the signals of several slower local networks in a multi-building "campus."

It is also possible to use the multiplexing process in reverse, separating a high-bandwidth signal into multiple signals that can be sent through lower-bandwidth channels. The various component signals can be recombined into the original high-bandwidth signal at the receiving end.

It is important to emphasize that multiplexing is an invisible process from the perspective of the communicating devices, which function as though they are connected by a dedicated channel.

Multiplexing makes use of two techniques: frequency-division and time-division, each of which is discussed in the following sections.

Frequency-Division Multiplexing (FDM)

Frequency-division multiplexing is the technique discussed in the earlier description of broadband transmission. The bandwidth of a broadband transmission medium is divided into *sub-bands* or channels, each of which is associated with a carrier frequency. The transmitter can modulate each carrier with an individual signal. The receiver uses a mechanism identical in principle to a television tuner to recover each of the original signals. This technique is illustrated in figure 1.29.

Figure 1.29

Frequency-division multiplexing.

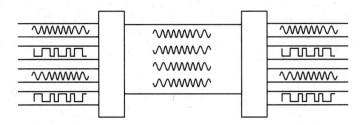

Frequency-division multiplexing is extremely versatile. Digital signals can be modulated using any modulation technique (ASK, FSK, PSK, or a combination) and can share the broadband medium with analog signals such as video or audio. It is possible to allocate the available bandwidth in any combination, and a single broadband network can service a wide variety of information networking requirements.

Time-Division Multiplexing (TDM)

TDM is a technique for subdividing the signal bandwidth of a high-speed digital channel. As figure 1.30 illustrates, TDM functions by dividing transmission time into time slots. Each of the incoming signals is allocated a time slot. The receiving mux sorts out the various signals and reassembles them.

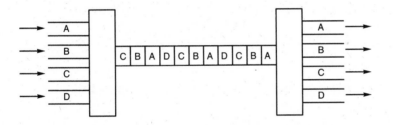

Figure 1.30

Time-division multiplexing.

Because each signal has access to the full bandwidth of the channel at any given time, TDM is essentially a baseband technique.

The simplest form of TDM uses fixed-length time allocations for each subchannel. Different time allocations can be assigned to each channel, but the times remain fixed when configured. This approach is simple but wastes a portion of the total bandwidth if any subchannels are utilized below their configured capacities. TDM systems of this type are sometimes described as *synchronous TDMs* because the transmitter and receiver synchronize themselves based on the subchannel time allocations.

Statistical TDM systems dynamically adjust the time allocations depending on the demands of the individual subchannels. The data for each slot is identified by a control field so that the individual subchannels can be recovered. "Stat muxes" make more efficient use of the channel bandwidth, but are more expensive because of their higher degree of sophistication.

Understanding Asynchronous Communication

Identify asynchronous and synchronous communication, their key characteristics, and their advantages and disadvantages.

Asynchronous communication is quick and dirty. The technology is simple, and the equipment required is inexpensive. This low cost is desirable when communication requirements call for relatively light traffic loads. Asynchronous communication is also well suited to terminal communication, because terminals transmit individual characters at random intervals depending on user input.

The term *asynchronous* is applied because no clocking mechanism is employed. Recall that a clock is a mechanism that ensures that the sending and receiving devices are in lockstep agreement about the timing of bits being communicated. The general asynchronous technique is to synchronize sender and receiver, and then to transmit a small amount of data—generally only a 7- or 8- bit character—before they can drift out of synchronization.

Format of an Asynchronous Character

Asynchronous communication transmits a character at a time. Each character is accompanied by information that ensures that communication will be reliable. The format of a character, along with its control information, is shown in figure 1.31. The parts of the character are discussed in the following sections.

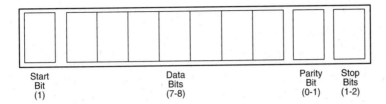

Start Bit (1) Data Bits (7-8) Parity Bit (0-1) Stop Bits (1-2)

Figure 1.31

The format of a character for asynchronous communication.

Start and Stop Bits

Because the sending and receiving devices are not synchronized by a clocking mechanism, each character is "framed" by start and stop bits.

One *start bit* warns the receiver that a character is coming. This enables the receiver to synchronize itself with the transmitter. Only eight to 11 bits follow the start bits, so the receiver needs to remain "in sync" for a relatively short time. After the receiver synchronizes with the incoming character, it ignores the start bit.

Note One bit time is not much time for the receiver to adjust its clock. Therefore, asynchronous communication devices are always preconfigured so that they have a general understanding of the speed at which they will operate. Whenever you configure communication software, you probably need to define a bits-per-second rate. After the software is configured, the sender and receiver operate at nearly the same rate, and the receiver needs to make only a small adjustment to synchronize with the incoming signal. (This is a bit of an oversimplification because BPS configuration also sets the communication standards that the modems utilize.)

Most modern modems are capable of "negotiating" a bit rate when they establish a connection. If you listen to the sounds produced by two high-speed modems when they first connect, you can hear them try a variety of data rates until they determine the highest rate that matches their design capabilities and the conditions of the communications medium.

73

Stop bits (consisting of binary ones) are added following the character data to signal the end of the character and prepare the receiver for the next character. Stop bits can be 1, 1.5, or 2 bit times in length. (You do not see 1.5 stop bits very often. This option is a legacy of long obsolete mechanical teletypes.)

Data

The data is usually an ASCII or Extended ASCII code. It can, therefore, consist of 7 or 8 bits.

Parity

If parity is used, a parity bit follows the data. Even and odd parity was explained in the discussion about the ASCII character set. Parity is generally used only with 7-bit data.

Parity is infrequently used with 8-bit data. You probably will encounter communication devices configured for "no parity."

Configuring Asynchronous Communication Options

This section summarizes the options available for asynchronous communication:

- **Data**—7 or 8 bits
- **Parity**—1 bit (even or odd) or none
- **Stop Bits**—1, 1.5, or 2

Because options are available in each case, the sending and receiving devices must be configured to agree on the options they will use. In addition to configuring the bps rate, a technician usually needs to configure the devices or the controlling software for data, parity, and stop bits.

Configurations are usually abbreviated. For example, 8-N-1 designates eight data bits, no parity, and one stop bit. This is, incidentally, the default configuration for most bulletin boards. Eight data bits are chosen so that the IBM extended graphics set can be used to draw boxes and, of course, happy faces.

Flow Control

Asynchronous communication works smoothly when data is transmitted in small, irregular clumps. Asynchronous techniques are commonly employed to transmit the characters a user types on a terminal, for example. In many such circumstances, the speed capability of the communication and receiving devices exceeds the demand placed on them by the sending computer. The sender simply transmits as it desires with the implicit understanding that the data transmitted will be communicated, and that the receiver will attentively receive all data.

When large blocks of data are transmitted, however, it is possible that the data might overwhelm the communication link or the receiving device. Most receiving devices are equipped with a buffer to temporarily store characters that have been received but not processed. If the buffer fills up, the receiving device must be able to signal the sender to cease transmitting. Otherwise, the sender may continue to send data that the receiver does not have the capacity to receive.

Flow control is frequently referred to as *handshaking*.

Two methods of flow control are employed: hardware and software.

Hardware Flow Control

Hardware flow control requires a direct cable connection between devices, which are frequently configured using the RS-232 serial communication interface. In addition to the wires that allow data to be transmitted, the RS-232 standard specifies additional wires that allow the devices to indicate their readiness to send and receive.

In Chapter 4, you examine the RS-232 standard in detail, and the lines commonly employed to interface devices. Various combinations of signals on the available lines can be used to halt or resume communication.

Hardware flow control is used between a DTE and a local DCE, such as a PC and a modem.

Software Flow Control

When devices are not connected via an interface such as RS-232, they can employ software flow control. One signal from the receiver indicates that it is ready to receive. Another signal indicates that it is unable to receive.

The most common means of software flow control is called XON/XOFF (transmit on/transmit off) after the two ASCII characters used to signal handshaking conditions. When the receiver's buffer is nearly full, it transmits an XOFF character (ASCII character 19, Control+S) to indicate that transmission should cease. When the receiver again has available buffer space, it sends an XON character (ASCII 17, Control+Q) to notify the sender that it can again transmit.

Ctrl+S and Ctrl+Q are commonly used to control asynchronous communication. If you are communicating with a bulletin board system and if characters are scrolling too fast for you to read, you can frequently halt transmission by pressing Ctrl+S. Typing Ctrl+Q notifies the BBS that it can resume transmission.

Software flow control is used between a DCE and a remote DCE, such as two modems connected through a telephone line.

Advantages and Disadvantages

Asynchronous communication technology is relatively simple. Because the need for a clocking mechanism is eliminated, the hardware can be manufactured at low cost. High demand for asynchronous modems has driven the prices to extremely low levels.

Asynchronous communication, however, has several significant limitations, including the following:

◆ Each character is framed by start, stop, and parity bits. These framing bits add two or more bits of overhead to each character transmitted. With large messages, this 20- to 30-percent overhead can be a serious liability.

◆ Parity is a limited way of detecting errors and may not even be implemented. If two bits in a character are damaged, parity may not detect the error.

◆ The general level of performance is low and can be unacceptable for high-volume traffic.

Uses

Asynchronous communication is frequently used to connect devices within a building. A printer might be connected through a serial communication line to a server on another floor. Short-haul modems are an inexpensive way of making this connection.

Asynchronous communication also is frequently employed for dial-up communications that have moderate data transfer requirements. A common example is the use of terminal emulation software to dial into a bulletin board.

Asynchronous communication, however, also can be a useful method of interconnecting LANs. A good example is a mail system that stores messages and periodically establishes a dial-up connection with a remote LAN to send the stored messages and receive waiting messages. If it is not essential that messages be transferred as soon as they are stored in the mail system, a dial-up connection is a low-cost method of linking remote LANs. Novell makes a mail system called MHS (Message Handling System) that can operate in store-and-forward mode.

Understanding Synchronous Communication

 Identify asynchronous and synchronous communication, their key characteristics, and their advantages and disadvantages.

When large amounts of data must be communicated without error, technicians usually resort to synchronous communication techniques. *Synchronous communication* improves efficiency and reliability by eliminating the need for framing bits on each character and employing more sophisticated error-detection techniques.

Structure

Synchronous communication transmits data in blocks. The data for many characters can be strung together into a block inside the same framing mechanism. A clocking mechanism keeps sender and receiver synchronized throughout lengthy messages, and a single error check verifies an entire block of data. The features of a synchronous message block are shown in figure 1.32. These features are then discussed individually.

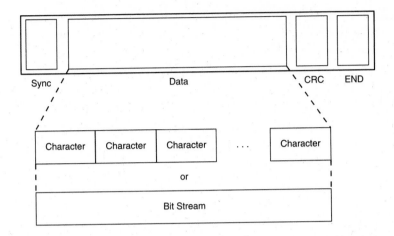

Figure 1.32

The features of a synchronous transmission block.

Sync

A series of bits is transmitted to synchronize the receiver with the transmitter. Following synchronization, the receiver's clock must remain in step with the sender for the duration of the block, which can be hundreds or thousands of bits long. This is accomplished through a clocking mechanism.

Clocking can be provided in two ways as follows:

◆ A separate clocking signal can be transmitted, perhaps over a separate conductor.

◆ Clocking can be made a part of the data encoding method by using techniques such as those discussed earlier in this chapter.

Data

The data can be organized in characters or simply as a long series of bits. *Binary synchronous communication* (BSC) is an IBM standard protocol that treats data as characters.

Character or byte-oriented protocols are less efficient than bit-oriented protocols. *High Level Data-Link Control* (HDLC) and *Synchronous Data-Link Control* (SDLC) are common bit-oriented protocols. Each is discussed in Chapter 4.

79

Error Detection

Synchronous communication requires a sophisticated error-detection mechanism if errors in long bit streams are to be detected. A commonly used method is the *Cyclic Redundancy Check* (CRC).

The CRC mechanism applies a formula (algorithm) to the data and computes a CRC value that is appended to the data frame in the CRC field. This CRC value "summarizes" all the bits of the data field. The receiver repeats the CRC calculation on the received data and compares its calculation to the CRC value that was sent. If the two CRC values agree, the transmission is assumed to be error free. The CRC algorithm is carefully chosen to make it unlikely that errors go undetected.

Advantages and Disadvantages

Several advantages can be cited for synchronous communication, including the following:

◆ High efficiency because framing information services entire blocks, rather than single characters.

◆ Sophisticated error detection.

◆ High speed. Because error detection is improved, synchronous modems can be driven to higher speeds without fear of undetected data corruption.

Uses

Synchronous communication is used primarily when large amounts of data must be transferred. Synchronous modems operating at 56 Kbps (thousand bps) over dedicated, data-quality telephone lines have long been a mainstay of mainframe computer communication. Above that speed, most communication is accomplished through digital media.

Synchronous communication also can be used to link LANs through dedicated telephone lines. The speed limitations of standard leased lines, however, do not enable them to be used at LAN speeds. This is a mechanism for transferring moderate levels of data, such as file transfers and electronic mail.

Exploring Switching Techniques

 Identify the characteristics of circuit switching, message switching, and packet switching.

Until now, this chapter makes the assumption that data communication takes place between two devices connected directly by a transmission medium. Data communication networks, however, are seldom this simple. Instead of resembling the hookup of a printer to a PC's printer port, data networks more frequently resemble the public telephone system, with many devices conversing with many other devices in different combinations.

It is not possible to string a wire for each possible pair of devices. Imagine the expense of a telephone system that requires millions of wires to terminate at each telephone! Instead, networks implement some type of switching mechanism to route messages through a network consisting of a large but manageable collection of wires and other media channels. In this section, you learn about three techniques for switching messages through complex networks: circuit, message, and packet switching.

Figure 1.33 shows a network consisting of two computers, A and B. Connecting them is a complex of wires (or other media channels) and switches. You will discover that the differences among the three types of switching largely consist of how much intelligence is built into the switches.

Figure 1.33

A representative
switching network.

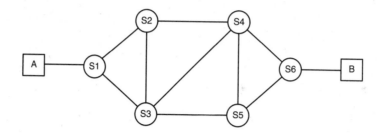

Circuit Switching

When *circuit switching* is used to connect two devices, a continuous, physical link is established to carry transmissions between
the end points. Figure 1.34 illustrates how circuit switching establishes a connection in this hypothetical network.

Figure 1.34

Circuit switching.

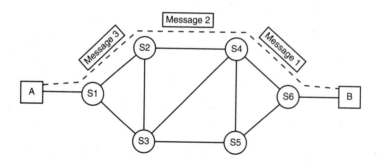

The switching devices consist essentially of multi-position
switches that set themselves at the beginning of the communication session and remain set until the session is over. Each time the
computers request a connection, the switches probably configure a
different path through the network. Once established, however,
the path does not change until the computers end communication
and release their network connection.

Circuit switching establishes a transmission path and reserves that
path for the exclusive use of the communicating devices. This path
is a physical circuit. When a physical circuit is established, it
functions as though it consisted of a single, continuous wire.

If you have ever seen a film or television drama where technicians are "tracing" a phone call, you have a picture of circuit switching. It is literally possible to trace a pathway through the maze of wires and switches dedicated for the sole use of the communicating devices.

Because the data circuit is completely dedicated to servicing a single connection, multiple data transmissions need not compete for bandwidth. The end devices experience little or no delay in the channel.

This approach, however, is decidedly inefficient. If the devices are momentarily idle, the entire channel is idle. This makes it necessary to build considerable excess capacity into the system. If no circuit is available when two devices want to communicate, they must wait until a circuit is released.

Message Switching

Two things are added to a *message switching* network. Each communicating device is assigned a unique identification, usually a numeric identifier, called an *address*. This address is added to each message.

The switching devices are more than dumb, mechanical switches. They have the capacity to store entire messages, examine the address for the message, and forward the message along an appropriate route. Other devices can forward the message to other parts of the network until the message reaches its destination. Because of this process, these networks are sometimes referred to as *store-and-forward networks*.

Examine figure 1.35 to see how this works. Notice that the two messages in this figure follow different routes. This might result because different parts of the network are available at different times. The switching devices are intelligent enough to select a new route.

Figure 1.35

Message switching.

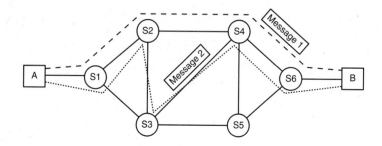

The switches can now be referred to as network *nodes* because they are intelligent, special-purpose computers. Because entire messages must be received and stored at each node, the node must have a significant amount of memory. Because the entire message is stored before any of it is retransmitted, a significant time delay may be introduced. Message switching, therefore, is poorly suited to real-time communication, and is a weak approach for monitoring processes where rapid response is a requirement.

With message switching, a given network segment is monopolized only for the duration of an individual message. The segment is then released to service another message. Traffic congestion can be controlled, and bandwidth can be fully utilized. The intelligent devices at the nodes can even establish message priorities, forwarding high-priority messages before less urgent ones. The addressing system can also be designed to enable a single message to be sent to multiple destinations.

Store-and-forward switching is a useful approach when timeliness is less important than low cost. Mail systems frequently utilize store-and-forward delivery. A mail node might accumulate several messages before establishing a connection with the next mail node in the network. This enables the system to utilize low-performance but low-cost transmission systems.

Message switching has the following advantages:

◆ Makes efficient use of bandwidth. Messages can be stored until a channel is available.

◆ Priority mechanisms are available.

◆ Messages can be directed to multiple destinations.

Disadvantages of message switching are as follows:

◆ Messages may be delayed because the entire message is stored prior to forwarding.

◆ The delays inherent in message switching make it poorly suited to real-time applications.

◆ Message switching is poorly suited to video, audio, and other high-data rate or highly interactive communication.

Packet Switching

Packet switching resembles message switching but avoids the problem imposed by large message sizes by breaking messages into small packets. The message is disassembled into packets at the transmitting device, and the packets are reassembled in proper order at the receiver. You can see how this works in figure 1.36.

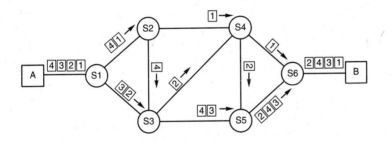

Figure 1.36

Packet switching.

When the message is disassembled into packets, each packet is labeled with the address of the source device, the address of the destination, and a sequence number indicating the packet's position in the message. Each packet contains a data field that has a maximum allowable size. The overall size of the packet is kept fairly small to reduce storage requirements in the switching nodes and improve efficiency.

Notice in figure 1.36 that the packets can be routed through the network by different paths. Each switching node receives the packet, examines the destination address, and retransmits the packet on an appropriate network segment. Although the switch nodes can be specifically programmed with route information, many modern devices learn the network and route packets along what appears to be the most efficient route.

The key difference between packet switching and message switching is that packets are kept small and each message can be stored entirely in the switch's high-speed memory. This enables the switch to receive, process, and forward the message at high speeds. Message switches must be capable of forwarding messages of arbitrary length and can be quite long. Message switches, therefore, generally rely on disk storage, which is considerably slower than memory.

Virtually all local-and wide-area networks are based on some form of packet switching. You encounter the mechanisms in various standards used to manage packets in Chapter 4. In that chapter, you are exposed to two major types of packet switching services: *datagram* and *virtual circuit*. These switching approaches are examined in the next sections.

Datagram Services

Datagram services treat each packet as an independent message. Each packet is routed individually through the network, with each node deciding what segment should be used for the next step in the packet's transmission. If a particular segment is busy when a node is required to forward a packet, the node selects a different segment. This is the approach shown in figure 1.36. Notice that the packets can arrive in an order that differs from the original order. The tasks of creating the packets from a long message and of reassembling the packets in the correct order at the receiving node are handled by a *Packet Assembly and Disassembly* (PAD) device.

Datagram services are fairly informal. Packets are sent into the network on the good faith expectation that they will be delivered safely. It is up to the network to accomplish the delivery, and the sending and receiving devices do not much concern themselves with how delivery is accomplished. This simplicity makes datagram services lean and efficient and a common choice on LANs, which generally are regarded as reliable delivery mechanisms.

Virtual Circuits

A more formal approach than datagrams is for the communicating devices to establish a logical connection. When devices want to communicate they go through a formal process of establishing a connection, agreeing on how they will communicate (message sizes, protocols, and so on) and on the route that messages will take through the network. Because the devices have agreed to communicate in a formal mode, mechanisms can be put in place to verify that packets are delivered and to request retransmission if a packet is lost or damaged. When the devices are through communicating, a formal procedure for breaking or "tearing down" the connection is performed.

Even though the devices may agree on a route for their shared messages, they do not monopolize that route as was the case with circuit switching. Any given segment can be used to carry packets in transit between any two devices. From the viewpoint of the end devices, the network appears as though a circuit has been established for their exclusive use. The reality, however, is a far more efficient, if more complicated, approach.

All these procedures are established for the sake of reliability. Some performance is lost due to the overhead of establishing, maintaining, and breaking the connection. However, the overhead is justified if there is a reasonable expectation that packets will be lost or damaged. This is frequently the case in wide-area networks, which can be less reliable due to the longer distances and greater complexity of the network components.

The word "virtual" is used because the end devices view the network as though a dedicated circuit has been established for them. Computer terminology frequently employs the word virtual when something is being simulated. In this case, the network is simulating a simple, circuit switched network.

Advantages and Disadvantages

Some advantages of packet switching are the following:

◆ Packet switching makes efficient use of the network.

◆ Small packets require little node storage and can be quickly routed through the network.

◆ Packet routes can be selected to avoid busy, slow, or bad segments.

◆ No network resource is monopolized for any given message. Available network bandwidth is shared by the entire network.

The disadvantages of packet switching are as follows:

◆ Complexity translates into high implementation cost. The protocols and devices employed for packet switching can be quite complex.

◆ With complexity comes lower reliability. Packet switching networks can lose or damage packets, and reliability mechanisms must be put into place.

Exploring the Public Switched Telephone Network

 Identify the components of the public switched telephone network and how they impact data communications.

Until now discussion has skirted around the *public switched telephone network* (PSTN) without explicitly mentioning it. The PSTN is essentially a huge circuit switching network that can accommodate both analog and digital signals. In fact, the PSTN can be considered to be the first network; it remains perhaps the largest.

Because it can be used to interconnect virtually any two points in the United States and far beyond, the PSTN is a powerful tool for data communication.

This section examines the components of the PSTN. It also covers the *Integrated Services Digital Network* (ISDN), which is a set of standards that holds the promise of evolving the PSTN into a worldwide, digital network.

Structure of the PSTN

The PSTN is a complex organization of many different components. These components are classified into four groups, based upon the party responsible for the component:

- ◆ The subscriber is responsible for equipment and wiring within his or her premises.

- ◆ The local phone company maintains the central office and the local loop—the wire that connects the subscriber to the central office co.

- ◆ The local phone company also maintains local trunk lines that interconnect various central offices.

- ◆ Long-distance carriers maintain services that interconnect various local telephone services.

Each of these component areas are examined in the following sections.

Subscriber Equipment

A *demarcation point* (demarc) on the subscriber's premises marks the dividing line between equipment, which is the rsponsibility of the subscriber, and the local loop, which is the responsibility of the local phone company. The relationship of the subscriber equipment to the local loop is shown in figure 1.37.

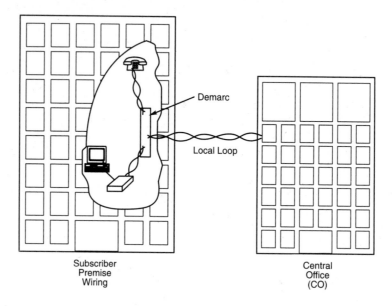

The subscriber is responsible for wiring, telephones, and all other equipment on the subscriber's side of the demarc. Most of the wiring is telephone twisted-pair, which may or may not be suitable for data. RJ-11 and RJ-14 connectors are commonly used for three-pair wiring. RJ-45 connectors are the standard for four-pair wiring.

The Local Loop

The local loop consists of twisted-pair wiring that begins at the demarc and generally extends to the central office (CO). With the commonly employed centrex system of wiring, all local loops terminate at a CO.

A single pair wire is sufficient for each telephone being serviced. Within the local loop, cables containing many pairs of wires can be employed. Within the subscriber's premises, however, the wires extending to each telephone jack are generally red and green and are assigned to the center pair of conductors on the RJ-11 or RJ-14 connectors.

These wires are referred to as the *tip* and *ring*. If you could examine the plugs on the wires of an old-fashioned telephone switchboard, you would see that one conductor is at the tip of the plug, and the other is a ring around the circumference of the plug's barrel.

Telephone terminology is rich in its historic roots. The phrase "off hook" describes a telephone actively connected to the telephone network. The phrase derives from old phones where the listening device was literally hung on a hook to disconnect the phone.

Central Offices

Operated by the local telephone provider, the CO provides power and switching facilities for the subscribers in its service area. Each CO is identified by a combination of the area code and the first three digits of the local phone number. Within a given CO, communications are carried out using full-duplex, baseband audio signals.

When an area supports many subscribers, multiple COs are distributed through the service area. These COs are interconnected through high-bandwidth trunk lines. The trunk lines utilize frequency-division multiplexing to support large numbers of connections.

The bandwidth of each voice channel is limited to 3,000 Hz. This bandwidth is adequate to support understandable voice communication, but imposes limits on the data rates that can be achieved with modem communication. A telephone voice circuit can reliably support up to 2,400 data signal changes per second. Therefore, when only one modulation technique is employed, modem communication is limited to 2,400 bps. As mentioned in the discussions about modulation techniques, faster modems combine phase-shift and amplitude-shift keying to achieve data rates as high as 9,600 bps by encoding four bits into each signal change.

Digital services are available when the limitations of voice telephone circuits are unacceptable. You will encounter the digital T1 and T3 services in Chapter 4.

Long-Distance Providers

When the telephone system was reorganized in 1984, the United States was divided into *local access and transport areas* (LATAs). Calls within a LATA are intra-LATA calls and are handled as local CO-to-CO connections. Such calls may be tariffed as local or as local long-distance.

Calls that cross LATA boundaries are classified as inter-LATA long-distance. For such calls, a subscriber is serviced by a long-distance provider such as AT&T, MCI, or US Sprint.

Summary of the PSTN Organization

In 1984, the United States telephone system, formerly owned almost entirely by AT&T, was broken into seven *regional Bell holding companies* (RBHCs). Each RBHC in turn maintains *Bell operating companies* (BOCs) that service local areas. BOCs are responsible for all intra-LATA services.

One requirement of the reorganization was that all long-distance service providers be granted equal access to COs. This is accomplished by granting the long-distance provider a *point of presence* (POP) in the CO through which subscribers can gain access to that provider's services. These providers supply inter-LATA services as described in the preceding section.

Integrated Services Digital Network (ISDN)

 Identify the standard networking services provided by ISDN.

As extensive as it is, the PSTN is limited in its capability to cope with many modern communication needs. ISDN consists of a set of standards promoted by the CCITT (see Chapter 4 for information about this standards organization), with the goal of enhancing the worldwide telephone network to support audio, video, and a wide variety of digital services.

ISDN uses multiplexing techniques to provide multiple data channels in high-bandwidth circuits. The channels are frequently referred to as bit pipes. These channels are classified in terms of their bandwidth and service as follows:

- A channels provide 4 kHz voice analog telephone.

- B channels provide 64 kbps digital data.

- C channels provide 8 or 16 kbps digital data for out-of-band signaling.

- D channels provide 16 or 64 kbps service, also for out-of-band signaling. This channel supports subchannels for signaling, telemetry (data from meters, and so on), and low-bandwidth packet data. Currently, this is one of the most popular configurations.

- E channels provide 64 kbps signaling for internal ISDN signaling.

- H channels provide a 384, 1,536, or 1,920 kbps digital channel.

These channels usually are provided in the following standard combinations:

- Basic rate includes two B channels and one D channel.

- Primary rate includes one D channel and 23 B channels (for the U.S. and Japan) or 30 B channels (for Europe). These different allocations are based on the different standard data rates in these areas. The U.S. and Japan are standardized on the T1 rate of 1.544 Mbps. The European standard has a data rate of 2.048 Mbps.

- Hybrid provides one A channel and one C channel and can provide standard telephone service.

There is little question that the existing analog telephone system is insufficient for the needs of today's information-intensive communication systems. ISDN is one of the new technologies that will adapt the PSTN to the future of data communication.

Review Questions

1. Which is not an example of analog data?
   - ○ a. The amount of gasoline in your car while traveling.
   - ○ b. The temperature at 4:30 this afternoon.
   - ○ c. The time of day shown on a watch with a second hand.
   - ○ d. The speed of the wind measured at an airport.

2. Which is not an example of digital data?
   - ○ a. The amount of gasoline it takes to fill an approved container from empty.
   - ○ b. The temperature during the daylight hours.
   - ○ c. The time of day currently shown on a watch without a second hand.
   - ○ d. The decibel level of a jet as it gets ready for takeoff.

3. Which term is not used to describe analog data?

   ○   a. Amplitude

   ○   b. Frequency

   ○   c. Mode

   ○   d. Phase

4. Which statement about signals is false?

   ○   a. Electrical signals are digital.

   ○   b. Phase refers to when the cycle of a signal begins.

   ○   c. Digital data goes from a binary one to a binary zero instantaneously because no state exists between one and zero.

   ○   d. Information is coded into digital signals by changing the signal between positive and negative.

5. The technique for synchronizing sender and receiver is known as:

   ○   a. Synching

   ○   b. Clocking

   ○   c. Timing

   ○   d. Ticking

6. Which is not a characteristic of digital encoding?

   ○   a. Voltage is used to represent one and zero values.

   ○   b. The portion of the signal that is sampled to determine bit value.

   ○   c. How the sender and receiver perform clocking to synchronize themselves.

   ○   d. Positive voltage signifies a binary one and negative voltage signifies a binary zero.

7. AMI is considered an example of:

   ○   a. Bipolar encoding

   ○   b. Biphase encoding

   ○   c. NRZ

   ○   d. Manchester

8. Ethernet LANs use:

   ○   a. Polar encoding

   ○   b. Differential Manchester encoding

   ○   c. Manchester encoding

   ○   d. NRZ

9. Which statement about code sets is true?

   ○   a. ASCII is a seven-bit code with the eighth bit used for error checking.

   ○   b. EBCDIC uses the eighth bit for error checking.

   ○   c. EBCDIC is as popular as ASCII.

   ○   d. ASCII uses CRC error checking.

10. Which is not correct?

   ○   a. MODEMs code digital data onto an analog carrier, whereas CODECs code analog data onto a digital carrier.

   ○   b. DTEs are usually computers, whereas DCEs are usually modems.

   ○   c. Whereas a modem is always connected to a DTE, a CODEC does not require a DTE.

   ○   d. DCE is known as both Data Communication Equipment and Data Circuit-Terminating Equipment.

11. Which is the least significant characteristic of bounded media?

   ○ a. Resistance to EMI

   ○ b. Attenuation

   ○ c. Bandwidth

   ○ d. Mobility

12. Which type of unbounded media has the characteristics of very narrow coverage and no sensitivity to EMI?

   ○ a. Infrared

   ○ b. Laser

   ○ c. Radio

   ○ d. Microwave

13. Which type of multiplexing dynamically adjusts slot allocation?

   ○ a. TDM

   ○ b. Stat Mux

   ○ c. FDM

   ○ d. Synchronous TDM

14. Which statement about synchronous communication is false?

   ○ a. Synchronous communication is good when large amounts of data must be communicated without error.

   ○ b. Synchronous communication uses clocking.

   ○ c. Synchronous communication is frequently used to connect devices within a building.

   ○ d. Synchronous communication improves efficiency over asynchronous communication.

15. Which statement about circuit switching is true?

   ○ a. Circuit switching establishes a transmission path for the exclusive use of the communicating devices.

   ○ b. Message switching functions without the need of an individual address.

   ○ c. With message switching, a given network is monopolized for the entire conversation.

   ○ d. Packet switching packets are usually large and must be stored on disk.

16. Which ISDN channel is most popular in emerging technology?

   ○ a. A

   ○ b. B

   ○ c. C

   ○ d. D

17. Which statement about coaxial cable technology is true?

   ○ a. It is mature and stable

   ○ b. It is expensive

   ○ c. It guards adequately against interference and tapping

   ○ d. It does not support high bandwidths

18. Which statement about analog data is true?

   ○ a. Analog data represents specific, well-defined values

   ○ b. Analog data has an unlimited number of values

   ○ c. Analog data is used between a computer and a printer

   ○ d. Analog data cannot be carried by digital signals

19. Which type of network represents a LAN rich with diverse computer architecture?

   O   a. Wide area

   O   b. Enterprise

   O   c. Heterogeneous

   O   d. Homogeneous

20. Which device enables a single high-bandwidth transmission medium to carry multiple low-bandwidth signals?

   O   a. CODEC

   O   b. MUX

   O   c. MODEM

   O   d. HUB

21. Which communication systems use half-duplex transmission mode? Pick all that apply.

   ☐   a. Television

   ☐   b. Walkie-Talkie

   ☐   c. Telephone

   ☐   d. Ship-to-shore radio

   ☐   e. Intercom System

   ☐   f. Home Stereo

22. Flow control is also referred to as _____.

23. A network that uses a _____ channel can support more than one simultaneous message. An example is CATV systems.

24. Standard ASCII uses ____ bits per character.

25. What are synchronous communications often used for? Pick all that apply.

   ☐ a. Transmission of multimedia

   ☐ b. Transmission of characters

   ☐ c. Transferring large blocks of data

   ☐ d. High-speed transmissions

26. TDM is used for:

   ○ a. Variable length time allocations for each subchannel

   ○ b. Dividing transmission time into time slots

   ○ c. Dividing bandwidth

   ○ d. Asynchronous transmissions

27. A _____ circuit simulates a pathway that is established for the exclusive use of two devices during the length of the communication, then are torn down.

28. Which switching technique creates a continuous physical circuit that is dedicated to servicing a single connection?

   ○ a. Circuit Switching

   ○ b. Message Switching

   ○ c. Packet Switching

   ○ d. Virtual Switching

29. The PSTN is made up of which of the following components? Pick all that apply.

   ☐ a. Subscribers responsible for equipment and wiring on the premises

   ☐ b. Local phone company maintaining a Central Office, local loop, and local trunk lines.

   ☐ c. Integrated Service Digital Network

   ☐ d. Long-distance carriers

30. The _____ is the standards committee that promotes ISDN.

Answers

1. B

2. D

3. C

4. A

5. B

6. D

7. A

8. C

9. A

10. C

11. D

12. B

13. B

14. C

15. A

16. D

17. A

18. B

19. C

20. B

21. B,D,E

22. Handshaking

23. Broadband

24. 7
25. A,C,D
26. B
27. Virtual
28. A
29. A,B,D
30. CCITT

Topologies

2
CHAPTER

Identify common network topologies, their key characteristics, and when each might be used.

The word *topology* is commonly used to discuss the properties of various types of networks. Topology is the branch of mathematics that examines the characteristics of geometric shapes. Networks have shapes, and the shape a network takes has much to do with the way it functions.

Two different definitions of topology are as follows: physical and logical. You encounter the distinction between physical and logical frequently in networking. The distinction is necessary because the way something looks can be quite different from the way it functions.

A motion picture may look like a natural moving scene, but it actually consists of many snapshots flashed on the screen so quickly that your eye interprets the individual pictures as moving. The logical, moving picture is much different from the physical reality.

So it is with computer networks. Your eye may tell you one thing as you examine the cabling, but the network may operate very differently at the invisible level of electrical signals in the wire.

The following rule of thumb distinguishes physical from logical:

◆ If you can see it and touch it, it is physical.

◆ If you cannot see it or touch it, it is logical.

The physical topology of a network is the layout or actual appearance of the cabling scheme used on a network.

The logical topology of a network describes how the data flows through the physical topology. You soon discover that similar-looking networks can have quite different logical topologies.

A network's logical topology is closely related to the mechanism used to manage the way stations access the network. Because a given cable in a baseband network services only one station at a time, it is necessary to have procedures in place that manage network access so that all stations have access without conflicting with each other. These procedures are called *access control methods* (discussed at the end of this chapter).

Exploring Physical and Logical Topologies

All physical topologies are variations of two fundamental methods of connecting devices: *point-to-point* and *multipoint*. After examining these two fundamental topologies, several variations are examined.

Methods of Connecting Devices

This section discusses point-to-point and multipoint connection methods, which are the building blocks for all network topologies.

Point-to-Point Topology

Point-to-point (PTP) topology connects two nodes directly together. The following examples are pure point-to-point links:

- Two computers communicating via modems
- A mainframe terminal communicating with a front-end processor
- A workstation communicating along a parallel cable to a printer

In a PTP link, two devices monopolize a communication medium. Because the medium need not be shared, a mechanism is not needed to identify the computers. Therefore, a simple two-device PTP network has no need for addressing.

PTP links can be simplex, half-duplex, or full-duplex. When devices must engage in bidirectional communication on a half-duplex link, some turnaround mechanisms must be in place to switch the roles of the sending and receiving devices.

Figure 2.1 shows examples of point-to-point topologies.

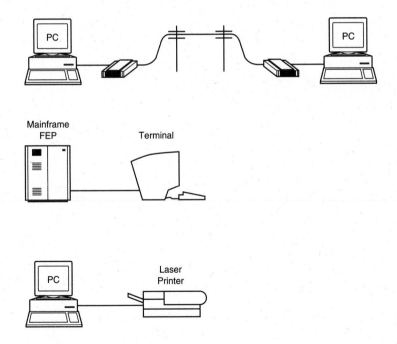

Figure 2.1

Point-to-Point topologies.

Multipoint Topology

Multipoint topologies link three or more devices together through a single communication medium. Multipoint topologies work much like a party-line telephone service where several subscribers are connected to the same telephone line.

Because multipoint topologies share a common channel, each device needs a way to identify itself and the device to which it wants to send information. The method used to identify senders and receivers is called *addressing*.

Figure 2.2 shows some examples of multipoint topologies.

Figure 2.2

Multipoint topologies.

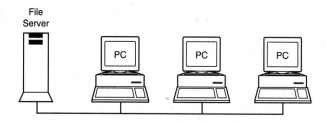

Examples of Point-to-Point and Multipoint Topologies

The following five types of physical topologies are frequently used in computer networking:

- ◆ Mesh
- ◆ Star
- ◆ Ring
- ◆ Bus
- ◆ Hybrid

Note Most of the preceding topologies are discussed in greater detail in later chapters.

Mesh

It may appear that the simplest method of interconnecting more than two computer devices is to establish a point-to-point link between each pair of devices, similar to the networks shown in figure 2.3.

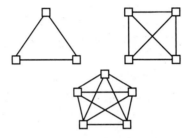

Figure 2.3

Examples of mesh topology.

Large mesh networks are not very practical, however. The difficulty with this approach is that the number of PTP links increases to impossible levels when just a few nodes are being connected. Each device must be equipped with a network interface for every other device in the network. True mesh networks, therefore, are seldom used to connect large numbers of devices.

Partial mesh networks are more common and are frequently employed in networks that span several distant sites. A company might establish a partial mesh network like the one in figure 2.4 to interconnect its various networks across the United States. An advantage of a partial mesh is that redundant paths can be built in. Notice that New York can still communicate with Los Angeles if the link to Chicago is temporarily disabled.

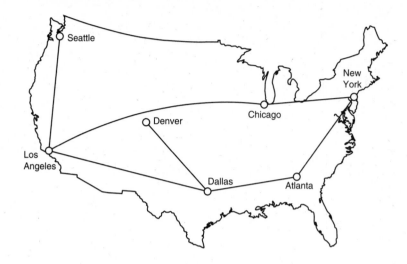

Figure 2.4

An example of a
partial mesh topology.

Benefits of Mesh Topology

The benefits of mesh topology are as follows:

◆ Multiple links exist.

◆ If the nodes are capable of routing signals, a path is always available in the event of a cable or route failure.

◆ Multiple routes can be used for multiplexing. An original message can be broken into multiple message packets that can be routed through multiple routes simultaneously, thus taking advantage of the bandwidth available in several channels.

Disadvantages of Mesh

Mesh topology has the following disadvantages:

◆ Devices require multiple interface cards.

◆ Requires the most cable of all the topologies.

Examples of Mesh

Mesh networks are seldom used in local environments. A possible exception might be to interconnect several mainframe computers or minicomputers. In most cases, however, local area networks employ one of the other topologies discussed in the following sections.

Mesh networks are commonly employed in wide-area networking. You can see examples of mesh network technologies in the discussion about switching technologies in Chapter 1.

Star Topology

The star topology is a popular method of connecting the cabling in a computer network. In a star, each device connects to a central point via a point-to-point link. Depending on the logical architecture used, several names are used for the central point including the following:

- ◆ Hub

- ◆ Multipoint Repeater

- ◆ Concentrator

The central hubs also can be classified in the following manner:

- ◆ **Passive.** A passive hub is a simple signal splitter. Its main function is to connect the arms of the star while maintaining the proper electrical characteristics.

  A passive hub routes all traffic to all nodes. This means that a tremendous load can be created when much communication takes place between computers. Every computer has the additional burden of reading the address of each piece of information it receives to determine if the information is intended for that computer. Information containing other addresses is discarded.

Figure 2.5 illustrates a star topology using a passive hub.

Figure 2.5

Star topology using a passive hub.

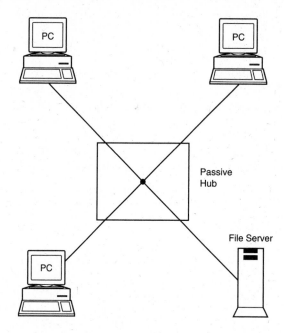

◆ **Active.** An active hub performs the same function as a passive hub, but contains electronic circuits that regenerate and retransmit the information. Thus, active hubs can be used to extend the size of a network.

◆ **Intelligent.** Intelligent hubs perform the same functions as passive and active hubs; however, they can make informed path selections and perform some network management. Intelligent hubs route traffic only to the branch of the star on which the receiving node is located. If redundant paths exist, an intelligent hub can route information around normally used paths when cable problems occur.

Routers and bridges are examples of hub devices that can route transmissions intelligently. They are discussed in Chapter 3.

Intelligent hubs can also incorporate diagnostic features that make it easier to troubleshoot network problems.

Benefits of Stars

Most modern cabling systems are designed in a star physical topology. The benefits of the star topology are many, including the following:

◆ Each device is isolated on its own cable. This makes it easy to isolate individual devices from the network by disconnecting them from the wiring hub.

◆ All data goes through the central point, which can be equipped with diagnostic devices that make it easy to troubleshoot and manage the network.

◆ Hierarchical organization allows isolation of traffic on the channel. This is beneficial when several, but not all, computers place a heavy load on the network. Traffic from those heavily used computers can be separated from the rest or dispersed throughout for a more even flow of traffic.

Disadvantages of Star

Star topology has the following disadvantages:

◆ Because point-to-point wiring is utilized for each node, more cable is required.

◆ Hub failures can disable large segments of the network.

Examples of Star

The following types of networks are examples of star topologies:

◆ ARCnet

◆ 10BASE-T

◆ StarLAN

Token Ring is also wired in a physical star; however, as you learn later in this chapter, the physical wiring and the logical characteristics of Token Ring are quite different.

Ring

The ring topology is a physical, closed loop consisting of point-to-point links. In figure 2.6, you can see how each node on the ring acts as a repeater. It receives a transmission from the previous node and amplifies it before passing it on.

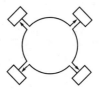

Benefits of Ring

Ring topology has the following advantage:

◆ Each repeater duplicates the data signals so that very little signal degradation occurs.

Disadvantages of Ring

Ring topology has the following disadvantages:

◆ A break in the ring can disable the entire network. Many ring designs incorporate extra cabling that can be switched in if a primary cable fails.

◆ Because each node must have the capability of functioning as a repeater, the networking devices tend to be more expensive.

Examples of Ring

The following is an example of a ring topology:

◆ Fiber Distributed Data Interface (FDDI)

Bus

In a bus topology, all devices attach to the same transmission medium. The medium has a physical beginning and end. All buses are implemented using electrical cable, usually coaxial, and the ends of the cable must be terminated with a terminating resistor that matches the impedance of the cable. The terminating resistor prevents data reflections from coming across as data corruption. The bus is considered a multipoint system because all devices tap into the same backbone cable.

An important characteristic to remember in bus topologies is that all data signals are broadcast throughout the bus structure. In figure 2.7, if node B sends a signal to node C, the signal propagates for the length of the cable and is seen by nodes A, D, and E. It is necessary to have an addressing mechanism so that each node understands which messages it is to receive and which to ignore.

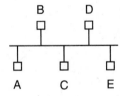

Figure 2.7
Bus topology.

Benefits of Bus

Bus topology has the following advantage:

◆ Cabling costs are minimized because of the common trunk.

Disadvantages of Bus

Disadvantages of bus topology are as follows:

◆ Difficult to troubleshoot because no central distribution points exist.

◆ Cable breaks can disable the entire segment because they remove the required termination from each of the two cable fragments.

Examples of Bus

The following networks are examples of bus topology:

◆ Token bus

◆ Ethernet

Hybrid

The hybrid topology scheme combines multiple topologies into one large topology. The hybrid network is common in large wide-area networks. Because each topology has its own strengths and weaknesses, several different types can be combined for maximum effectiveness.

Figure 2.8 is an example of hybrid topology.

Figure 2.8

Hybrid topology using ring, bus, and star topologies.

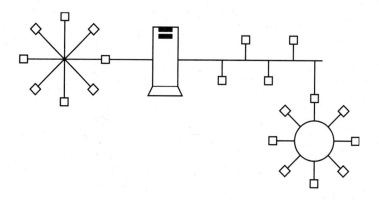

Benefits of Hybrid

Hybrid topology has the following advantages:

◆ One company can combine the benefits of several different types of topologies.

◆ Workgroup efficiency and traffic can be customized.

Disadvantages of Hybrid

The disadvantages of hybrid topology include the following:

◆ Devices on one topology cannot be placed into another topology without some hardware changes.

Examples of Hybrid

An example of a hybrid topology is as follows:

◆ A company can place its accounting database users on a ring for better throughput and its secretarial staff on a bus for ease of cabling.

 Throughput is the amount of data transferred per unit of time. It is viewed in terms of bits, bytes, or packets per second.

Exploring Logical Topologies

You have just examined five types of physical topologies. Now you examine two types of logical topologies. Logical topologies have the same names as physical topologies, but keep in mind that the physical topology describes the network you can see, whereas the logical topology describes the network from the viewpoint of the data travelling on the network. Networks can have different physical and logical topologies.

Types of Logical Topologies

The following two logical topologies are discussed in the following sections:

- Ring
- Bus

Ring Logical Topologies

Ring topologies function by passing data transmissions from one node to the next. This operation is clearest when the physical topology is also a ring. Review figure 2.8 to see how a ring topology works.

Any time data is passed from node to node, the network has a ring logical topology.

Another way to identify a ring is to determine whether each node has separate receive and transmit circuits. If that is the case, the node is functioning as a repeater and is probably connected in a logical ring network.

Bus Logical Topologies

In a bus topology, each data transmission passes by each node on the network. Essentially, each transmission is broadcast throughout the network, and the nodes use addresses to determine whether they should pay attention.

Any time all transmissions are available to all nodes on the network, the network has a bus logical topology.

If the nodes on a network use the same circuits to transmit and receive, the logical network is a bus.

Examining Logical and Physical Topologies of Common Networks

As mentioned earlier, a network can have a logical topology different from its physical topology. In this book, you work with the following four common types of networks:

◆ Ethernet

◆ Token Ring

◆ ARCnet

◆ FDDI

The following sections examine the topologies of each network.

Ethernet

The most common wiring system for Ethernet uses coaxial cable in a linear bus topology. In the most common type of Ethernet, each node connects to the coax through a T-connector that taps into the signals on the coaxial cable. The nodes both transmit and receive through the same connector. Therefore, Ethernet is a logical as well as a physical bus.

A newer variation of Ethernet, 10BASE-T, is cabled using wiring hubs, as shown in figure 2.9. Each station is connected to the hub via an individual twisted pair cable. Within the hub, however, the individual signals are combined into a bus. 10BASE-T is a physical star but a logical bus.

Figure 2.9

Topology of a
10BASE-T network.

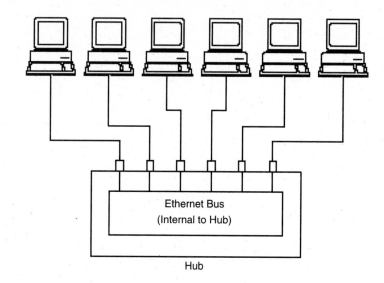

Figure 2.9

Topology of a
10BASE-T network.

Token Ring

If you examine the wiring of a Token Ring, it meets all the specifications of a star. Token Ring uses central wiring hubs, and each node is wired to the hub with an individual run of cable.

If you look inside the hubs and wires, however, you can see why this is called a ring network. Figure 2.10 shows the path that a transmission follows through the network. Starting at the hub, the signal travels through a pair of wires to the receiving circuit on the node's network interface. The receiving circuit passes the signal to the transmit circuit, which repeats the signal on a separate pair of wires and sends the signal back to the hub.

If you follow the signal around the entire network, you can see that it completes a circuitous path, proving that Token Ring has a ring logical topology.

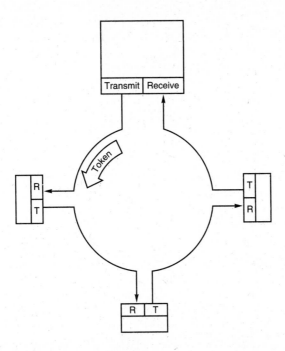

Figure 2.10

The path a token
follows around a ring.

Token Ring is wired in a physical star to obtain the advantages of
a central wiring hub. All stations can be connected and disconnected at a central point, and the wiring hub can be equipped with
hub management and diagnostic systems.

ARCnet

ARCnet is wired in a star using coaxial cable. Figure 2.11 shows
an extremely simple ARCnet using a single, passive hub.

Recall from the earlier discussion about passive hubs, that they
simply split the signal and pass it on to all the nodes connected to
the hub. This is an indication that ARCnet is a logical bus: all
nodes see all signals on the network.

Figure 2.11

A simple ARCnet.

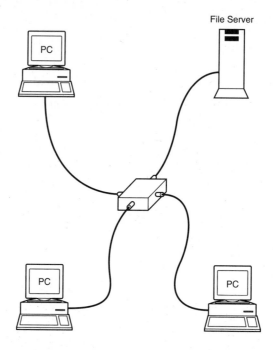

That ARCnet is a logical bus can also be determined by examining the network cards. They both receive and transmit through the same coaxial connector.

ARCnet is wired as a physical star and has some of the advantages of a star network. However, ARCnet functions as a logical bus.

FDDI

Fiber Distributed Data Interface (FDDI) can be configured as both a physical and a logical ring. FDDI is commonly used to connect widely dispersed areas with a high-speed fiber network. When doing so, a physical ring is the most cost-effective cabling plan. Figure 2.12 shows an FDDI network covering a large metropolitan area. FDDI uses the same mechanism as Token Ring; each node repeats the incoming signal and transmits it to the next node in the ring.

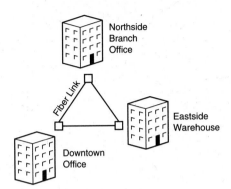

Figure 2.12

Example of an FDDI ring network.

Exploring Channel Access Methods

Identify common network topologies, their key characteristics, and when each might be used.

Channel access methods are theoretically independent of the topologies you just learned about. In reality, however, only a few combinations of physical and logical topologies work well together.

When several entities share the same communications medium, some mechanism must be in place to control access fairly. It is unproductive to have everyone in a meeting speak at once, so rules of order were defined long ago for managing meetings. Similar rules, or access methods, are applied to networks.

In this section, you learn about the three most common channel access methods and the topologies with which they are associated. These access methods are as follows:

- Polling
- Token passing
- Contention

121

The channel access methods discussed in the following sections include general rules that govern the devices as they access and transmit across the channel. Access methods use a certain amount of the channel's bandwidth for access control. The usable portion of the channel's bandwidth is limited by the access method being used. Each method has a different effect on network traffic.

Polling

Polling resembles a well-ordered meeting in which the chairman must recognize an attendee before that person is allowed to speak. The chairman's responsibility is to maintain order in the meeting and ensure that each person who wants to speak has an opportunity to do so.

Polling is most closely associated with mainframe computer networks. By using polling, one device such as a mainframe's front-end processor is designated as the primary device. Primaries are also known as the *channel access administrators, controllers,* or *masters.* All access to the network is controlled by the primary.

The primary queries (polls) each of the secondary devices, also known as *slaves.* As each secondary is polled, the primary inquires if the secondary has information to be transmitted. Only when it is polled does the secondary have access to the communication channel. Each system has rules pertaining to how long each secondary can transmit data.

The process of polling is much like a committee chairman who asks each member in turn to vote on an issue.

As shown in figure 2.13, polling can be utilized in virtually any network topology.

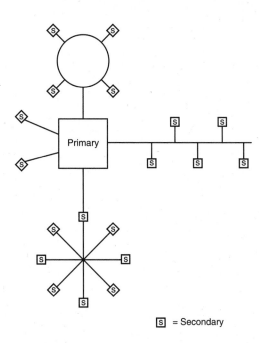

Figure 2.13

Secondaries connected to primaries in different network configurations.

⬓ = Secondary

Advantages of Polling

The advantages of polling are as follows:

♦ Many characteristics of polling can be determined centrally, including the polling order and node priorities.

♦ Polling ensures that channel access is predictable and fixed. Because the time delays between the primary and secondary devices can be calculated, this access method is called *deterministic*. Deterministic access methods are suitable for controlling some automated equipment because each piece of equipment is guaranteed access to the network at predetermined intervals.

♦ Polled channels cannot be over saturated with traffic. As demand increases, traffic increases up to a maximum level. The polling mechanism ensures that maximum traffic level cannot be exceeded. Nor can excess traffic reduce the performance of the network.

Disadvantages of Polling

Polling has the following disadvantages:

- ◆ Some applications cannot function with the time delays required for polling other devices.

- ◆ The process of polling involves large numbers of messages that take up available bandwidth. Traffic is required to poll each node, even nodes that are idle.

- ◆ Some polled networks use half-duplex transmission lines. This means that the primary and secondary devices must "turn around" the line, requiring some bandwidth.

- ◆ Polling requires a sophisticated central control mechanism that requires extensive configuration.

Contention

Contention on a network resembles conversation in a meeting. Every attendee can attempt to speak at any time. When two speakers interfere, however, the conversation is garbled and the speakers must begin again. Any speaker can speak at any time, and the speakers must contend for openings in the conversation in which to state their messages.

Similarly, on a contention network, any device can transmit whenever it needs to send information. To avoid data collisions, specific contention protocols were developed requiring the device to listen to the cable before transmitting information.

Contention is also known as *random access* because, unlike polling and token passing, there is no fixed order in which the nodes can transmit.

 The act of "listening" to the channel to see if any traffic exists is called *carrier sensing*, and contention-based networks are called *Carrier Sense Multiple Access* (CSMA) networks.

Even though each station listens for network traffic before it attempts to transmit, it remains possible for two transmissions to overlap on the network. This overlap is called a *collision*. As figure 2.14 shows, collisions occur because it takes time for signals to propagate through the network. Both stations A and D have found the network clear and transmit a message. A few microseconds are required for the signal from A to reach D. During that period, D is free to transmit, and a collision can occur.

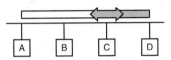

Figure 2.14

Collisions on a CSMA network.

With pure CSMA, recovering from a collision is the responsibility of layers above the Data-Link Layer. When the Data-Link Layer fails to get a response, it then starts a retransmission. This requires the transmitting device to wait for responses. The overhead from depending on upper layers is substantial.

As a result of collisions, access to a CSMA network is somewhat unpredictable, and CSMA networks can be referred to as *random* or *statistical access networks*.

Collisions are part of the normal operation of a CSMA network. Two specialized methods of collision management have been developed to improve performance: *Collision Detection* (CD) and *Collision Avoidance* (CA).

Collision Detection

The collision detection approach listens to the network traffic as the card is transmitting. By analyzing network traffic, it is possible to detect collisions and initiate retransmissions with mechanisms that operate entirely below the Data-Link Layer. Carrier Sense Multiple Access with Collision Detection (CSMA/CD) is the access method utilized in Ethernet and IEEE 802.3.

Collision Avoidance

Collision avoidance uses *time slices* to make network access smarter and avoid collisions. Carrier Sense Multiple Access with collision avoidance is the access mechanism used in Apple's LocalTalk network, which is described in Chapter 4.

Benefits of Contention

Contention offers the following benefits:

◆ Contention is a very simple access method that has low administrative overhead requirements. No network traffic is necessary to manage the access scheme.

◆ Actual user data throughput is rather high at low-traffic levels in comparison to the total amount of utilized network bandwidth.

Disadvantages of Contention

The disadvantages of contention are as follows:

◆ At high traffic levels, data collisions and the resulting retransmission diminish performance dramatically. It is theoretically possible that collisions can be so frequent at higher traffic levels that no station has a clear chance to transmit.

◆ Channel access is probabilistic rather than deterministic. Because of retransmissions and the time it takes to sense collisions, automated equipment that cannot tolerate delays cannot use this type of access. Contention offers no means of establishing the frequency of a station's opportunities to transmit.

Examples of Contention

Examples of networks that use contention are as follows:

◆ Ethernet

- IEEE 802.3
- LocalTalk

Token Passing

Token passing resembles a children's story-telling game in which the players pass a ball around a circle. When a player receives the ball, he or she is expected to tell part of a story. Players can talk only when the ball is in their possession.

Token passing uses a special authorizing packet of information to inform devices that they can transmit data. These packets are called *tokens* and are passed around the network in an orderly fashion from one device to the next. Devices can transmit only if they have control of the token. This method distributes the access control among all the devices.

Two approaches to token passing are available. Token Ring uses a ring topology. Each station passes the token to the next station in the ring. ARCnet also uses token passing; however, with ARCnet, each station passes the token to the station with the next higher address, regardless of its physical location on the network.

Figure 2.15 shows examples of token passing in Token Ring and ARCnet networks.

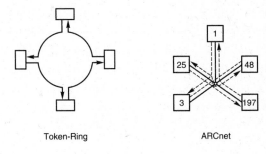

Token-Ring   ARCnet

Figure 2.15

Token passing in Token Ring and ARCnet networks.

127

Advantages of Token Passing

Token passing provides the following advantages:

◆ Token passing offers the highest data throughput possible under high-traffic conditions. Only one transmission can occur at a time, and collisions cannot occur. Therefore, token passing experiences less performance degradation at higher traffic levels than contention.

◆ Token passing is deterministic. Each station is guaranteed an opportunity to transmit each time the token travels around the ring.

◆ Some token-passing systems enable you to set priorities for devices that need controlled access to the token.

◆ As the traffic increases, data throughput also increases to a certain level, and then stabilizes.

Disadvantages of Token Passing

The disadvantages of token passing are as follows:

◆ Token passing involves complicated protocols for managing the network and recovering from errors. The traffic associated with these protocols has a higher bandwidth overhead than is required for CSMA.

◆ All devices require complicated software that needs to be modified whenever a station is added or removed.

◆ Some systems require an additional central controller that adds to the overhead and reduces throughput. Cabling and network hardware can be more expensive for token-passing networks than for CSMA networks.

Examples of Token Passing

Examples of token-passing networks include the following:

◆ IEEE 802.4, also known as token bus. A token bus uses token-passing access control and a bus topology.

◆ IEEE 802.5, also known as Token Ring. Token Ring uses token-passing access control and a ring topology.

◆ ARCnet uses token passing based on node addresses, using a star-wired network with a logical bus topology.

◆ TokenTalk is Apple's standard for networking Macintosh computers on Token Ring networks.

Performance Comparisons

Token access and CSMA, the most common access methods used in LANs, have different performance characteristics (see fig. 2.16). The "Load" axis represents the demand being placed on the network. The "Throughput" axis represents the data actually being transmitted.

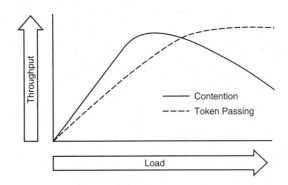

Figure 2.16

Throughput characteristics of token passing and CSMA networks.

Notice that the throughput of a CSMA network rises smoothly with increased traffic levels up to a point. At that point, collisions begin to occur with greater frequency, resulting in a gradual reduction in network throughput. At some point, network throughput reaches unacceptably low levels.

Token-passing exhibits reduced performance at lower traffic levels than CSMA. This is a result of the many administrative mechanisms required for token access. Throughput rises smoothly until the network is fully utilized. At that point, throughput stabilizes. Throughput does not degrade because no collisions can

129

occur. However, beyond the plateau, all workstations are sharing a strictly limited bandwidth. Although total throughput remains stable, the bandwidth available to a given station diminishes as demand increases.

The user's perception is that the network's performance is diminishing as the load demand increases. Figure 2.17 illustrates how throughput decreases as a percentage of demand. Basically, as demand increases, a smaller percentage of the demand can be satisfied. With contention-based networks, the fall-off after a certain point is fairly rapid until the number of collisions interferes with virtually all traffic on the network and few, if any, packets are actually delivered.

Figure 2.17

User's perceived throughput as a percentage of load.

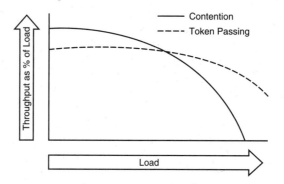

Perceived performance of a token-passing network also declines, but never reaches zero. Each user is guaranteed a fair share of the network's bandwidth, although this share may, at some point, be considered inadequate for the user's needs.

Combining Architectures and Access Methods

Table 2.1 summarizes common types of networks in terms of their topologies and access methods.

Table 2.1
Summary of Networks, Topologies, and Access Controls

Network	Physical Topology	Logical Topology	Access Control
Coax Ethernet	Bus	Bus	CSMA/CD
10BASE-T	Star	Bus	CSMA/CD
LocalTalk	Bus	Bus	CSMA/CA
Token Ring	Star	Ring	Token passing
FDDI	Ring/Star	Ring	Token passing
ARCnet	Star	Bus	Token passing

Notice that CSMA technologies are only applicable in networks that are logical buses. This is the case because each station must be able to sense all network traffic to determine if the network is busy. On a ring network, a node can detect only the data transmissions that happen to pass it and cannot determine whether traffic exists elsewhere on the network. CSMA is, therefore, not applicable to rings.

On the other hand, the only access method that works with rings is token passing.

Review Questions

1. Which topology connects to a central point via point-to-point?

  ○ a. Star

  ○ b. Bus

  ○ c. Mesh

  ○ d. Ring

2. Which is not an example of a star topology?

○ a. ARCnet

○ b. 10BASE-T

○ c. StarLAN

○ d. Ethernet

3. Which topology incorporates a physical, closed loop?

○ a. Star

○ b. Bus

○ c. Mesh

○ d. Ring

4. Which is not a disadvantage to the mesh topology?

○ a. Each device requires multiple interface cards

○ b. Excessive bandwidth

○ c. Redundant links

○ d. Excessive cable

5. Which is not an example of an access method?

○ a. Polling

○ b. Token transition

○ c. Token passing

○ d. Contention

6. Which topology defines the use of secondaries?

○ a. Polling

○ b. Contention

○ c. Token passing

○ d. Token bus

7. Which is not an advantage of polling?

○ a. Centralized administration

○ b. Predictable channel

○ c. Polling uses half-duplex communications

○ d. Priority assignment

8. Which is not an advantage of contention?

○ a. Low overhead

○ b. High user throughput at low traffic levels

○ c. Simple access method

○ d. Probabilistic

9. Which is not an example of Contention?

○ a. Ethernet

○ b. 10BASE-T

○ c. LocalTalk

○ d. TokenTalk

10. FDDI is considered:

○ a. Token passing on bus

○ b. Contention on star

○ c. Token passing on ring

○ d. Contention on bus

11. CSMA/CA is considered:

○ a. Token passing on bus

○ b. Contention on star

○ c. Token passing on ring

○ d. Contention on bus

12. Token Ring is considered:

    ○ a. Token passing on bus

    ○ b. Contention on star

    ○ c. Token passing on ring

    ○ d. Contention on bus

13. In a _____ topology, you can actually see and touch the cabling scheme.

14. Which physical topology connects all possible nodes to each other?

    ○ a. Star

    ○ b. Bus

    ○ c. True Mesh

    ○ d. Partial Mesh

15. "Each repeater duplicates the data signals so that very little signal degradation occurs" is a benefit of which topology?

    ○ a. Star

    ○ b. Ring

    ○ c. Bus

    ○ d. Mesh

16. "Hub failures can disable large segments of the network" is a disadvantage of which topology?

    ○ a. Star

    ○ b. Ring

    ○ c. Bus

    ○ d. Mesh

17. 10BASE-T uses a _____ Physical Topology, a _____ Logical Topology and _____ Access Control.

○ a. Star, Bus, Token Passing

○ b. Star, Bus, CSMA/CD

○ c. Bus, Bus, CSMA/CA

○ d. Star, Ring, CSMA/CD

18. A large WAN would most likely use a _____ topology.

○ a. Star

○ b. Ring

○ c. Bus

○ d. Hybrid

Answers

1. A

2. D

3. D

4. C

5. B

6. A

7. C

8. D

9. D

10. C

11. D

12. C

13. Physical
14. C
15. B
16. A
17. B
18. D

Building the Blueprint

Network communication can be complicated, and it is useful to have some models that organize the various concepts involved. A commonly used model is the *Open Systems Interconnection* (OSI) Reference Model, which is the major topic of this chapter. After you examine the OSI Reference Model, you will see how the model organizes discussion of various internetworking devices, including repeaters, bridges, routers, and gateways.

Exploring the Open Systems Interconnection Reference Model

The OSI model was developed in the late 1970s by the *International Organization for Standardization* (ISO), an international standards organization of industry representatives and government organizations. The United States' representative is the *American National Standards Institute* (ANSI).

The ISO organized a subcommittee of computer professionals to help establish standards to encourage interoperability among computer and data communication vendors in the industry.

When the ISO group was first established, some vendors were reluctant to comply. These vendors felt they could maintain their "sales" channels with all the proprietary equipment they had already entrenched.

Gradually, however, vendors recognized the need to support connectivity for all types of equipment to maintain their customer base. Because there are more variables in providing components that can establish interoperability, greater understanding of the "big picture" and the tasks that put the project together is essential.

 Identify the seven layers of the OSI Reference Model and the key responsibilities of each layer.

The OSI Reference Model organizes network communication into the following seven layers:

- Application—Layer 7

- Presentation—Layer 6

- Session—Layer 5

- Transport—Layer 4

- Network—Layer 3

- Data-Link—Layer 2

- Physical—Layer 1

 The following phrase can help you to remember the names and order of the OSI layers:

All People Seem To Need Data Processing

In Chapter 5, you discover that the OSI also has established a suite of protocols that corresponds to the layers of the OSI Reference Model. However, the model is discussed in this chapter not as a standard but as a basis for understanding many diverse protocol suites. Although protocol suites such as SNA, DECnet, and TCP/IP are different in design and implementation, they must provide similar services and can be examined using a layered approach. The OSI Reference Model facilitates the comparison of these various protocol suites.

Purpose of the OSI Model

 Recognize the interrelationship of the OSI model, protocols, and standards.

The purpose of establishing the OSI Reference Model is not to create physical communications, but to provide a plan for functionality among the layers. The functionality among layers is specified by the protocol blueprints developed by standards organizations and vendors. Each layer has a job to perform. Theoretically, OSI-compliant products can be substituted for other compliant products at any layer.

When two devices communicate, each level in one device communicates with the comparable level in the other. These communicating levels are called *peers*.

Peers can communicate with each other by attaching a *header* to the packet. Any layer can add its own header to the message before passing it on to the next lower layer. The headers are removed in reverse order when the destination computer receives the *information unit* (headers and data). The following sections discuss how each layer communicates with each other to allow information to flow back and forth.

Concepts of Layered Protocols

Figure 3.1 shows an example of a layered protocol in an everyday setting. As you read the following discussion, take note of these points:

- ◆ Each person at each layer has a specific, clearly defined responsibility.

- ◆ Each person has clearly defined interfaces with the layers above and below them.

- ◆ As items go down through the layers, each layer adds something to the item to facilitate processing.

- ◆ As items go up through the layers, each layer removes the items added at the corresponding sending layer. These items are used to facilitate processing at that layer.

Figure 3.1

A layered communication situation.

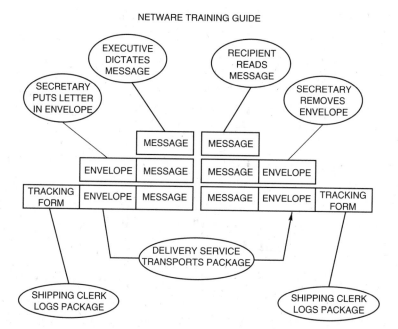

An example of a layered approach for delivering a registered message is as follows:

1. An executive dictates a message to his secretary.

2. The secretary types a letter and places it in a registered shipping envelope.

3. The mailroom attaches a shipping form to the envelope, makes a record of the package and its ship date, and hands the package over to a delivery service.

4. The delivery service transmits the package to the customer's receiving department.

5. After receiving the package, the receiving department removes the packing list, logs the package in, and transmits the package and packing list to the appropriate secretary.

6. The secretary removes the letter from the shipping envelope and delivers it to the recipient.

7. The recipient reads the message.

The seven layers of the OSI model work similarly. As figure 3.2 shows, each layer transfers data between the layers above and below it. At any transmitting layer, a header can be added to the data. This header can be removed at the corresponding receiving layer to facilitate processing of the data.

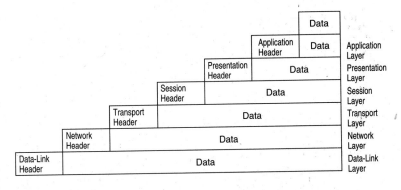

Figure 3.2

Headers and OSI-layered communication.

 The header and data from a given layer taken together constitute the data transmitted by the lower layer. As each lower layer adds its own header, the complete message becomes larger. The overall growth in the message is the overhead required to ensure that the original data is delivered safely and efficiently.

141

The Layers of the OSI Reference Model

In the following sections, you examine the functions of each of the seven layers of the OSI model.

Physical—Layer 1

The Physical Layer transmits bits to and receives bits from the communication medium.

The information unit at the Physical Layer is the bit. The Physical Layer does not regard the bits as being grouped into meaningful patterns. This layer is concerned only with transmitting bits to and receiving bits from the transmission medium.

This layer describes the mechanical characteristics of the network as well as the rules by which bits are transmitted. As such, the Physical Layer is concerned with the connectors employed, particularly the pin configurations, the signals that appear at the pins, the voltage characteristics of the signals, and so forth.

You can compare this layer to a telegraph sending dots and dashes. On the wire, each dot and dash is an independent unit. They are not organized into letters until they are interpreted by the telegraph operator, who corresponds to higher-level OSI protocols.

A familiar Physical Layer protocol is RS-232C. This protocol describes the connectors used to interface devices as well as the signal protocols employed. RS-232C is described in Chapter 4.

Other common Physical Layer protocols are RS-449, and many CCITT's X and V-series protocols. In part, the IEEE 802.5 (Token Ring) and 802.3 (Ethernet) standards also describe Physical Layer characteristics.

Data-Link—Layer 2

The Data-Link Layer receives the zeros and ones (bits) from the Physical Layer and organizes them into logical groups called *frames*. The Data-Link Layer includes the rules that control the network access protocols—when a station can transmit, what to do when a node fails, and how to check for errors.

The Data-Link Layer is comparable to a telegraph operator who translates incoming dots and dashes into groups that represent letters and sentences.

The Data-Link Layer adds a header to its data component that frequently contains address information about the sender and the intended receiver. Both Token Ring and Ethernet protocols add address information to the frame. This address information is used to route the frame to the appropriate destination and ensure that the destination computer is aware of the frame's origin.

At this level, the address is regarded as a physical address because it usually is derived from hardware settings. Both Ethernet and Token Ring rely on addresses "burned" into the hardware ROMs at the factory. A standards organization assigns each manufacturer a range of addresses, and the manufacturer assigns a unique address from that range to each card. Such physical addresses are guaranteed to be unique across all cards produced by all manufacturers. No two Ethernet cards anywhere in the world have the same physical addresses.

Other standards, such as ARCnet rely on addresses configured using switches on the cards. Physical address duplication with such cards is a common cause of LAN problems.

Network—Layer 3

The Network Layer routes messages through complex networks. The information unit at the Network Layer is the *packet*.

In simple networks, physical source and destination addresses are enough to move messages efficiently between computers. When networks span large areas and have many network segments, it is useful to have more information. Such complex networks are called *internetworks* or *internets*. An example is shown in figure 3.3.

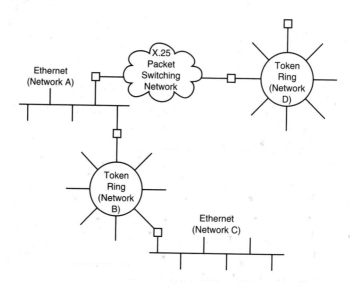

Figure 3.3

Example of an
internetwork.

In an internet, each network segment is assigned a logical network
identification. This assignment is managed at the Network Layer.
In this diagram, the networks are identified as LANs A through D.
NetWare identifies individual network segments with eight-digit
hexadecimal numbers.

The network information in a packet is used at the Network Layer
to route the packet efficiently through the internetwork in a way
completely transparent to the upper-layer protocols. The Transport Layer and higher layers are unaware of the configuration of
the network and of the way routers forward messages between
their sources and destinations.

If a telegraph message is to be transmitted across the country, it is
necessary to relay it in several hops. Each operator consults the
address for the message and sends it on to the next appropriate
telegraph station. The sender and receiver of the telegram are
completely unaware of the route taken by the message.

A common example of a Network Layer protocol is X.25.

Transport—Layer 4

This layer ensures "reliable" data delivery between processes running on the source and destination computers. Notice that now communication is between processes, not devices with network addresses. The information unit of this layer is called a *segment.*

The Transport Layer is responsible for ensuring that data units are transmitted without error, in sequence, and without loss or duplication. "Reliable" does not mean that data cannot be lost or damaged, only that all such loss or damage can be detected. Either the error must be corrected by the Transport Layer or higher layer protocols must be informed of the error.

The Transport Layer is responsible for taking message strings and breaking them into smaller units that can be handled by the Network Layer. The Transport Layer then controls the flow of the data, provides for error recovery, reorders the message units, and provides acknowledgment between communicating devices.

Telegraph operators are alert for errors in transmission. If letters are garbled, for example, or if a message is received without an appropriate end-of-message signal, the receiver might ask the sending operator to retransmit.

Session—Layer 5

This layer manages dialog between two computers by establishing, synchronizing, and terminating communications.

If two parties want to converse, they will establish rules of conversation. For example, they might agree to converse in French using appropriate rules of courtesy to ensure that messages are communicated in an orderly manner. At the end of the conversation, the parties engage in a polite exchange to establish that no further messages are expected.

Telegraph operators obey well-established rules of communication to signal the beginnings and ends of messages and sentences.

The period when the two parties expect communication between themselves is similar to a session between two computers. When establishing a session, the computers negotiate the protocols to be used, communication modes, error checking and recovery, and other communication issues. When the computers no longer need to communicate, a procedure is used to discontinue the session in an orderly manner.

Dialogs can be performed in full-duplex or half-duplex modes. When operating in full-duplex, the Session Layer is responsible for synchronizing the dialogs. For example, it may be the task of the Session Layer to ensure that multiple related actions all take place or that complex, multipart messages are delivered in their entirety.

Remote procedure calls (RPCs) are frequently regarded as services of the Session Layer. RPCs are protocols that enable computers to transmit data or to request services of other computers. RPCs are used extensively in NetWare and other network environments such as TCP/IP.

Telegraph operators have rules whereby they agree to transmit messages and then turn over the circuit so that a response can be received. Finally, an end-of-message dialog terminates the communication session.

Presentation—Layer 6   NOInf Unit

The Presentation Layer is concerned with the syntax—the grammar rules—utilized when communicating between two computers.

This layer provides a variety of data translation services. Presentation Layer protocols also are responsible for translating data into a uniform syntax understood by diverse computers and applications.

The Presentation Layer can be compared to the function of a human language translator, who is responsible for interpreting one language into another.

Among the services that can be performed by the Presentation Layer are *data encryption* and *data compression*. It is important, however, to realize that both of these services can be performed at other layers as well.

The name Presentation Layer is extremely misleading. It does not mean that this layer presents data to the user as is frequently construed.

The Presentation Layer ensures that data is presented to the Application Layer in a form consistent with the needs of the particular host.

Application—Layer 7

The Application Layer is closest to the user; however, this layer does not consist of applications such as word processors, spreadsheets, or such.

In part, this layer provides a uniform interface between end-user applications and the network. Your word processor does not comprehend network protocols and cannot directly interface with network software. The Application Layer, however, can make the network look like a standard DOS file system, for example. For all the application knows, the network is DOS, and the many network functions are hidden.

Users do interface directly with some utilities that reside at the Application Layer. File transfer programs such as NFS (see Chapter 5) are examples. A user can employ a file transfer program to access the files on another networked computer.

The information units at the Application Layer are messages. — Info Unit

Understanding OSI Internetwork Implementation

 Identify the functions and capabilities of repeaters, bridges, routers, and gateways, and of the OSI model layers each involves.

The OSI Reference Model is especially useful for conceptually organizing the devices used in internetworking. Four types of devices are commonly used to extend networks in size and complexity:

◆ Repeaters

◆ Bridges

◆ Routers

◆ Gateways

 Evaluate the advantages and disadvantages of repeaters, bridges, routers, and gateways.

These devices can be distinguished easily by examining the OSI layers at which they function.

Repeaters

The specifications for a network describe a maximum size for a segment of the network. Beyond that size, signal strength and quality deteriorate to the point that reliable communication is not possible. The input and output of a repeater are shown in figure 3.4.

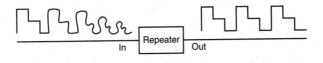

Figure 3.4

A repeater amplifies and reshapes a signal.

Repeaters can be used to combine several segments into a large network. Figure 3.5 illustrates an Ethernet consisting of two network segments and a repeater.

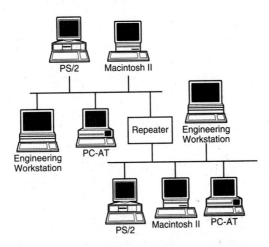

Figure 3.5

An Ethernet network incorporating a repeater.

Repeaters operate at the Physical Layer. Figure 3.6 illustrates how a repeater functions in relation to the OSI model. Notice that the signal is examined only at the Physical Layer. A repeater can amplify a signal or reshape it to extend the range of the network. Because they are Physical Layer devices, repeaters only comprehend bits. They cannot segment large internetworks into smaller network segments. To segment a network, a device must have access to the device or network information available at the Data-Link or Network Layers.

Figure 3.6

Repeaters function at
the Physical Layer.

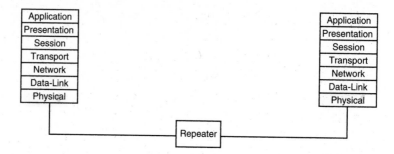

Because repeaters function at the Physical Layer, they are tied to a specific Physical Layer standard. Repeaters cannot be used to interconnect Ethernet and Token Ring segments, for example, because the Physical Layer signalling conventions and the message formats at higher layers are different.

Bridges

A *bridge* is an intelligent device that provides connectivity for two separate networks that can include different protocols and/or different medium types.

Because they operate at the Data-Link Layer (see fig. 3.7), bridges have access to the physical addresses of the source and destination nodes. As shown in figure 3.8, the bridge can then route traffic in the following way:

1. The bridge examines all data frames on LAN A and retrieves the destination address.

2. If the destination address is for a device on LAN A, the bridge ignores the frame.

3. If the destination address is for a device on LAN B (or for LAN C, which is accessible through LAN B), the frame is forwarded to LAN B.

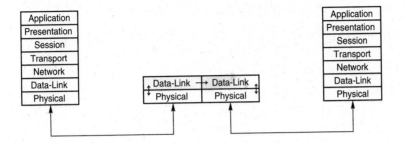

Figure 3.7

Bridges function at
the Data-Link Layer.

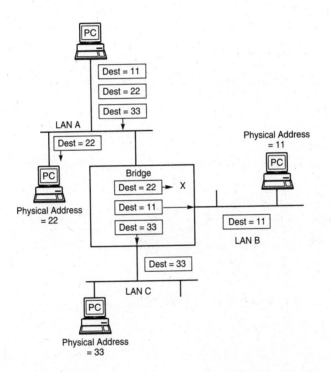

Figure 3.8

How a bridge routes
packets.

In figure 3.8, three frames are shown with physical destination
addresses (DEST=) of 11, 22, and 33. The bridge determines that
the PC with physical address 11 is on LAN segment B and for-
wards the frame with DEST=11 to that LAN. Similarly, the frame
with DEST=33 is forwarded to LAN C. However, the PC with
physical address 22 is on LAN A, which was the segment that
delivered the DEST=22 frame to the router. The router does not
forward the frame to its originating LAN segment and simply
drops it.

In this way, a bridge can be used to divide network traffic and isolate the traffic onto the segment where it belongs. When a network is extended by repeaters, all messages travel throughout the network. When bridges extend a network, they segment the network and confine traffic to the appropriate segments.

Bridges can be of two physically located types: local or remote. A *remote bridge* can control traffic for networks located at different sites by forwarding packets across a serial connection such as a T1 link (see fig. 3.9).

Figure 3.9

Local and remote bridges.

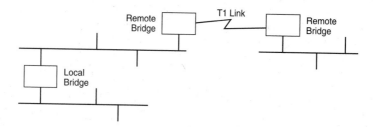

A local bridge is located in the same physical site as the network segments to which it is connected. This bridge configuration is also shown in figure 3.9.

Bridges can be of two types: *source-routing* or *transparent*. Source-routing bridges are found primarily in IBM Token Ring networks. Transparent bridges are found in many types of networks and are also known as *learning* or *spanning tree bridges*.

Source-routing relies on the communicating devices to determine the best route. When one computer needs to open communication with another, it has the capability of discovering the most efficient route. The routing information is included in the header for each frame. The router's job is simply to examine the routing information in the data frame and forward the frame as specified. Source-routing bridges are simpler than transparent bridges. However, each device on the network must be equipped with the mechanism for discovering routes.

A transparent bridge can "learn" and "remember" the location of the devices on the network. Transparent bridges build routing tables of destination device addresses, and route packets to the segment where the destination device of the addressed packet exists. This is the type of bridge depicted in figure 3.8.

Routers

Whereas bridges operate based on the physical addresses of the sending and receiving devices, routers route information based on logical addresses set by the LAN administrator. Routing algorithms are used to determine the most efficient path through the internetwork. Because a router has access to the Network Layer of the OSI model (see fig. 3.10), it can determine the logical address associated with a frame.

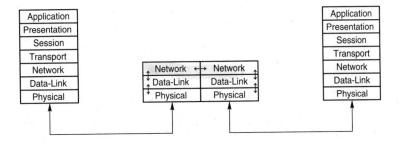

Figure 3.10

A router functions at the Network Layer.

Bridges work with only a single route through the internetwork for a given pair of devices. Source-routing establishes this route when the devices first begin to communicate. Once determined, this routing information remains fixed as long as the devices remain in communication. Transparent bridges learn a route through the network and work with that route until it fails, at which time another route is determined.

The operation of a router is shown in figure 3.11. The packet shown has a destination network address of C. The routers forward the packet to the appropriate network. Notice that the packet is routed between two Token Rings by way of an Ethernet. This is quite acceptable when routers are employed.

153

Figure 3.11

Operation of a router.

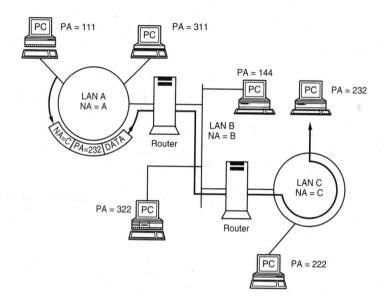

Unlike bridges, routers can manage multiple routing paths through a network. As network traffic patterns change, routers can dynamically adjust their routing tables to reoptimize the chosen paths. Routers employ complex algorithms to estimate the costs of transmitting frames by different routes. As conditions change, routers recalculate the "cost" of transmitting by the various routes and select the least expensive path.

Several different algorithms can be used to estimate the cost of a path. One is to count the number of *hops*—the number of router devices a message must cross. Other algorithms take transit time into account. In many cases, the LAN administrator can adjust the parameters used by routers. The selection and tuning of router algorithms is an important task in optimizing the performance of a network.

The task of a router is more complicated than that of a bridge. Routers must translate data up to the Network Layer, which requires more processing than translation to the Data-Link Layer. Also, routers use more complex algorithms for determining internetwork paths—paths continuously adjusted for optimum performance. Traditionally, therefore, routers are regarded as having lower performance and higher cost than bridges. However, the additional sophistication of a router can outweigh its lower packet-per-second data throughput.

Routers function above the Data-Link Layer. One consequence of this is that routers can easily internetwork data among different types of networks. If data traffic must internet from an Ethernet to a Token Ring, a router is the most efficient device for making the interconnection.

A number of new devices combine bridging and routing functionality. *Brouters* ("bridging routers") use bridging or routing as appropriate—bridging when possible to enhance performance, and routing when a given packet cannot be bridged. Routing bridges incorporate some routing intelligence, but still function with physical addresses at the Data-Link Layer.

 If you have ever installed a NetWare server, you have been required to assign a network address to each LAN segment that attaches to the server. This network address is managed at the Network Layer and is the logical address used by NetWare routers. Every NetWare server has the built-in capability to route messages among several LAN segments. In addition, you can configure separate NetWare routers using ROUTEGEN. For more about addresses see Chapter 7. For information about NetWare routers see Chapter 12.

Gateways

Gateways are devices that connect two ~~completely~~ Radically different network formats. A common example is an SNA gateway, a device that enables PCs on a LAN to operate as terminals that access IBM mainframe computers. The LAN and IBM terminal environments are so different that much more than forwarding and simple translation is required to link them. For example, IBM networks use polling to control network access, whereas LANs generally use contention or token-passing. Translating between these access control methods is a sophisticated job and calls for a gateway.

The term gateway describes any device that interconnects computer environments at a higher level than the OSI Network Layer, as depicted in figure 3.12. The gateway performs a variety of data translation and protocol conversion services, and operates at several OSI layers.

Figure 3.12

Gateways function above the Network Layer.

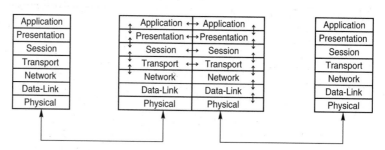

Gateways are often, but not always, stand-alone devices as depicted in figure 3.13. A common example of a gateway in the NetWare environment is NetWare for SAA (IBM's System Application Architecture). This gateway can be run in a dedicated workstation on the LAN that provides only gateway services, or it can operate as a communication service on a NetWare 3.11 server.

Figure 3.13

An SNA gateway on a LAN.

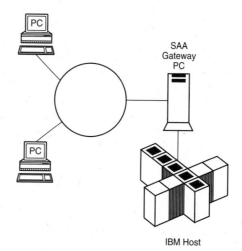

Gateways can also be used in other environments, such as forwarding electronic mail between dissimilar systems.

Summary of the OSI Reference Model

In summary, the OSI model is an integral part of the networking environment. It is important to use this as a reference for establishing a format for interconnectivity. The internetworking devices can help provide the physical connections to expand communications. To further develop networking, all computer professionals must be able to think and verbally translate the functionality of the OSI Reference Model.

The following table summarizes the information in this chapter. It also adds some information about protocols related to the various OSI layers.

Table 3.1
Summary of the OSI Reference Model

Layer	Information Units	Examples	Functions	Hardware
Application	Messages	Telnet X.400, NFS NCOPY	Application interfaces	Gateways
Presentation		OSI Pres. protocol Sun's XDR NetWare password encryption	Language translator	Gateways
Session		Sun's RPC OSI Sess. protocol Novell's TTS	Dialog management	Gateways

continues

157

Table 3.1, Continued
Summary of the OSI Reference Model

Layer	Information Units	Examples	Functions	Hardware
Transport	Segments	TCP, SPX OSI's TP4	Reliable data delivery	Gateways multi-plexors
Network	Packets	IP, IPX	Routing over segments, message fragmentation and reassembly	Routers
Data-Link	Frames	Ethernet Token Ring ARCnet	Package and unpackage data	Bridges
Physical	Bits	RS232, V.28	Move bits across medium	Repeaters

Review Questions

1. The OSI is:
   - ○ a. An organization for networking standards
   - ○ b. A blueprint for building network operating systems
   - ○ c. A subcommittee for networking standards
   - ○ d. An end-user support group for networking models

2. Layer 4 is:
   - ○ a. Session
   - ○ b. Network
   - ○ c. Transport
   - ○ d. Data-Link

3. The OSI model defines __ layers?
   - ○ a. 7
   - ○ b. 6
   - ○ c. 5
   - ○ d. 4

4. Which is not a feature of Layer 1?
   - ○ a. Transmits bits and bytes
   - ○ b. Defines mechanical characteristics
   - ○ c. Concerned with connectors and pin configurations
   - ○ d. Groups bits into a logical pattern

5. Which responsibility does not belong to the Data-Link Layer?
   - ○ a. When a station can transmit
   - ○ b. What should be done when a node fails
   - ○ c. How to check for errors
   - ○ d. Ensuring reliability

159

6. Layer 5 does not:

   ○ a. Establish communications

   ○ b. Synchronize communications

   ○ c. Condense communications

   ○ d. Terminate communications

7. The Transport Layer:

   ○ a. Is responsible for reliable data delivery

   ○ b. Guarantees a connection

   ○ c. Calls the information unit a packet

   ○ d. a and c

8. The Network Layer does not:

   ○ a. Route messages

   ○ b. Ensure reliability

   ○ c. Deal with packets

   ○ d. Concern itself with efficient routing

9. The Application Layer:

   ○ a. Includes word processing and spread sheet applications

   ○ b. Makes the network look like a standard DOS file system

   ○ c. Helps translate data

   ○ d. Sets the language module

10. Layer 6:

    ○ a. Provides RPC services

    ○ b. Presents data to the user

    ○ c. Is concerned primarily with syntax and grammar rules

    ○ d. b and c

11. Which layer is not needed for routing?

- ○ a. Transport
- ○ b. Network
- ○ c. Data-Link
- ○ d. Physical

12. Gateways can function all the way up to the _____ Layer.

- ○ a. Transport
- ○ b. Session
- ○ c. Presentation
- ○ d. Application

Answers

1. B
2. C
3. A
4. D
5. D
6. C
7. A
8. B
9. B
10. C
11. A
12. D

Exploring the Lower Layers

4

CHAPTER

This chapter discusses the lower layers of the OSI model: Physical and Data-Link.

While exploring the Physical Layer specifications, you learn about the following topics:

◆ RS-232 and RS-449

◆ CCITT V Series and X Series

◆ Digital transmission

The discussion of Data-Link Layer specifications helps you learn the following important popular protocols:

◆ SDLC

◆ ADCCP

◆ HDLC

◆ LAPB

In this chapter, you also learn about the following specific implementations of the lower-layer protocols:

◆ IEEE specifications

◆ FDDI

◆ ARCnet

◆ LocalTalk

Learning About Physical Layer Protocols

Identify the interface standardized by the RS-232 standard.

In this section, you learn about the RS-232 standard interface. You also learn the handshaking signals used with RS-232. Finally, other important communication protocols are defined, including RS-449, CCITT specifications, and T-1 technology.

One of the most common connections between Data Terminal Equipment (DTE) and Data Circuit Terminating Equipment (DCE) is the RS-232 connector.

RS-232 Connector

The original RS-232 connector was designed to specify the point at which the PC and modem interact. The Electronic Industries Association (EIA) developed the RS-232 specification. This specification helped relieve the problems of signal connection incompatibilities that arose because no prior standard existed. Each of the pins that comprise the RS-232 standard communicates the status information from the modem to the serial port on the computer.

The RS-232 standard, also referred to as RS-232-C, was renamed in 1987 to EIA-232-D. EIA-232-D was redesigned slightly to be more compatible with several internal specifications: ISO 2110, V.24, and V.28.

The specification breaks down into the four areas discussed in the following sections.

Mechanical: Wires and Connections

RS-232 recommends that the maximum cable length be limited to 50 feet. Another part of the mechanical specification is the 25-pin connector, called the DB25, and the specific pin arrangement.

Table 4.1 is a list of the pins and their assignments as defined by the EIA.

Table 4.1
RS-232 Connector Pin Assignments

Pin Number	Assignment
1	Protective Ground
2	Transmitted Data
3	Received Data
4	Request to Send
5	Clear to Send
6	Data Set Ready
7	Signal Ground
8	Data Carrier Detect
9	Reserved
10	Reserved
11	Unassigned
12	Secondary Data Carrier Detect
13	Secondary Clear to Send
14	Secondary Transmitted Data
15	Transmit Clock
16	Secondary Received Data
17	Receiver Clock
18	Unassigned

continues

Table 4.1, Continued
RS-232 Connector Pin Assignments

Pin Number	Assignment
19	Secondary Request to Send
20	Data Terminal Ready
21	Signal Quality Detector
22	Ring Indicator
23	Data Rate Select
24	External Clock
25	Unassigned

The DB25 connector is laid out in two rows of pins. One row consists of pins 1 through 13. The second row contains pins 14 through 25. Other connectors are also used in place of the DB25. The DB9 is one popular alternative. This connector uses the nine pins required for computer-to-modem communications. Table 4.2 shows pin assignments, the pin numbers for the DB25 and DB9 connectors, and the general order in which they are called.

Table 4.2
RS-232 Connector Pin Assignments for DB-25 and DB-9 Connectors

Pin Assignment	Standard Abbreviation	DB25 Pin number	DB9 Pin number
Ground	(GND)	7	5
Data Terminal Ready	(DTR)	20	4
Data Set Ready	(DSR)	6	6
Request to Send	(RTS)	4	7
Clear to Send	(CTS)	5	8
Ring Indicator	(RI)	22	9

Pin Assignment	Standard Abbreviation	DB25 Pin number	DB9 Pin number
Data Carrier Detect	(DCD)	8	1
Transmit Data	(TD)	2	3
Receive Data	(RD)	3	2

Draw, label, or sequence the flow of the RS-232 handshaking signals.

The following example shows the communication between two DTE-DCEs:

When a modem is connected to the computer, the serial port determines that a modem is ready and waiting. When this happens, the DTR and RTS are high. The term *high* means that a standard voltage has been applied to the pin, and the pin indicates an active status.

After a command is given by the communication software to the modem to dial, the modem "hears" a dial tone. At this point, the DSR goes high. The number is then dialed. If you listen to a modem, you hear the number being dialed followed by ringing or a busy signal.

If the remote system is not busy, the call is answered. At this point, DCD goes high and handshaking occurs. *Handshaking* is the protocol two modems use to decide on communication. The two types of handshaking are: Hardware—CTS/RTS and Software—Xon/Xoff. CTS/RTS uses these two pins on the RS-232 interface and is faster than software handshaking. Xon/Xoff uses a software command with which one system tells the other when to start and when to stop communication.

On the receiving side of the original call, the modem's RI goes high, indicating that a call is coming in. If the receiving modem's DTR is active, its DSR also goes high.

At this point, the originating modem's CTS goes high, and the modem sends out a mark condition to the receiving modem. The tone is the same frequency used to indicate a binary one. When the receiving modem receives the mark condition, its DCD goes high.

The original modem then starts transmitting data over the RD pin.

Electrical: Voltage Levels (Signals) across the Interface

RS-232 recommends that the electrical specifications for each pin be as follows:

◆ -3V (negative 3 volts) is a binary one

◆ +3V (positive 3 volts) is a binary zero

◆ Maximum signal rate less than 20 Kbps (20,000 bits per second)

Function: Each Signal's Purpose

The RS-232 standard supports one data circuit in each direction, which makes full-duplex transmission possible. The four areas of functions are as follows:

1. Data
   - Transmitted Data (Pin 2)
   - Received Data (Pin 3)
   - Secondary Transmitted Data (Pin 14)
   - Secondary Received Data (Pin 16)

2. Ground
   - Protected Ground (Pin 1)
   - Signal Ground (Pin 7)

3. Timing
   - Transmit Clock (Pin 15)
   - Receiving Clock (Pin 17)
   - External Clock (Pin 24)

4. Control
   - Request to Send (Pin 4)
   - Clear to Send (Pin 5)
   - Data Set Ready (Pin 6)
   - Data Carrier Detect (Pin 8)
   - Secondary Data Carrier Detect (Pin 12)
   - Secondary Clear to Send (Pin 13)
   - Secondary Request to Send (Pin 19)
   - Data Terminal Ready (Pin 20)
   - Signal Quality Detector (Pin 21)
   - Ring Indicator (Pin 22)
   - Data Rate Select (Pin 23)

Procedures

This section discusses how each function covers the sequencing of signals and actions taken by the computer and modem. The signals are matched in pairs for their action and the intended response. Some examples of pairs include the following:

- ◆ Transmitted Data—Received Data
- ◆ Request to Send—Clear to Send
- ◆ Data Set Ready—Data Terminal Ready
- ◆ Transmit Clock—Receiver Clock

RS-232 has become very popular and is now used in many situations, such as connecting computers to other computers and to serial printers. The method used to connect computers using RS-232 involves using a *null modem cable*. A null modem cable does not have a DCE, so a problem arises in the standard interface. The null modem cable "tricks" the serial ports into believing they are connected to a modem. These devices are not standardized, do not provide synchronization, and only operate with asynchronous equipment. Null modems use combinations of cross connections—usually RD and TD; RTS and CTS; and DSR, CD, and DTR. Check equipment specifications to determine the proper combination of cross connections.

Other Standard Interfaces

Identify and discuss other important Physical Layer interfaces.

Among the other widely used interface standards are the RS-449, CCITT V-Series and CCITT X-Series, and AT&T's T-1. The EIA developed RS-232 and RS-449 while the Consultative Committee for Telegraphy and Telephony (CCITT) created the V series and X series.

RS-449

EIA sponsored RS-449 to overcome the distance and speed limitations of RS-232. RS-449 relies on the RS-422 (balanced transmission, two wires, no common ground) and RS-423 (unbalanced, common ground shared by all circuits) standards to specify electrical characteristics of the pins. More signal lines are in RS-449, which allows several lines to be dedicated for return signals.

To satisfy several international requirements, RS-449 requires two connectors, which makes it an expensive alternative to RS-232. The main channel connector is a 37-pin connector. The secondary channel connector is a 9-pin connector. The EIA released EIA530, which is electrically compatible to RS-449, but uses a DB25 connector.

V Series

The CCITT V Series Recommendations are the most widely used international specifications for defining the transmission of data between computers via the telephone network. Almost every modem and multiplexor in use today conforms to V Series protocols. Among the areas defined in the V Series Recommendations are the following:

- Physical Layer interfaces such as V.24, which is similar to RS-232
- Voice-band and wide-band modems *Voice & Data Modems*
- Error control for modems
- Diagnostic procedures
- Internetworking (including Integrated Services Digital Network [ISDN], discussed in Chapter 1)

X Series

The CCITT's X Series applies to Public Data Networks (PDN). Every day, communications networks send billions of bytes of

171

data around the world. The X Series is designed to ensure the system's compatibility, which is essential for this tremendous data exchange. Among the areas defined in the X Series Recommendations are the following:

◆ Services and facilities

◆ Interfaces (including X.25 data packets, X.29 PAD, X.31 internetworking, and X.32 dial-and-answer)

◆ Transmission and signaling

◆ The OSI Model's X.200 standard

◆ ISDN, telephone, packet, and satellite networks through X.300

◆ Message-handling system, X.400

◆ Directory applications, X.500

AT&T's T-1

T-1 is a digital, full-duplex, time-division multiplexed transmission technology introduced by AT&T in the early 1960s. Its main focus is digitizing the telephone system. T-1 uses time-division multiplexing to allow transmission along 24 different eight-bit-wide voice channels. Combined bandwidth using the American and Japanese implementations is 1.544 Mbps (1,544,000 bits per second). This is attained by the transmission of 193 bit frames at a rate of 8,000 frames per second. A synchronization bit is added every 193 bits. European implementations can offer single-channel access at speeds up to 2.048 Mbps.

To comply with the T-1 physical signal specifications, the DCEs used are CSU/DSUs (Channel Service Units/Data Service Units). CSUs address the output pulse requirements. DSUs provide unipolar-to-bipolar signal conversion.

T-1 lines offer high-speed, high-capacity transfer of digitized voice or data. In addition to T-1 there are T-2, T-3, T-4, and SONET technologies. T-1 and T-3 are currently the two most widely implemented forms of the T-Carrier technology. T-2 has a data transfer rate of 6.312 Mbps. T-3 offers data transfer rates up to 44.54 Mbps, which are more frequently used to multiplex 28 T-1 voice lines. The T-3 technology can be leased from telephone companies. T-4 has a data transfer rate of 274.76 Mbps. The SONET (Synchronous Optical Network) was developed around fiber-optic technology and can offer data rates from 51.85 Mbps to 2.5 Gbps.

Learning About Data-Link Protocols

Identify the principal organizations that promulgate or champion SDLC (Synchronous Data Link Control), HDLC (High-level Data Link Control), and LAPB (Link Access Procedure Balanced) protocols and the target environment of each protocol.

When the Physical Layer finishes receiving data, a stream of bits is passed to the Data-Link Layer. This section discusses several bit-oriented Data-Link protocols introduced after the mid-1970s: SDLC, HDLC, ADCCP, and LAPB.

◆ **Synchronous Data-Link Control (SDLC_1975),** an IBM product, is the major bit-oriented, full-duplex, synchronous protocol in use today. Although IBM developed SDLC, many other vendors use SDLC in conjunction with SNA-based products.

◆ **Advanced Data Communication Control Procedure (ADCCP_ 1979)** is an ANSI specification for a bit-oriented, full-duplex, synchronous protocol.

◆ **High-level Data-Link Control (HDLC_1979)** is the International Standards Organization (ISO) specification for a bit-oriented, full-duplex, synchronous protocol.

173

◆ **Link Access Procedure Balanced (LAPB_1984)** is the CCITT's specification for a bit-oriented, full-duplex, synchronous protocol. LAPB is an earlier subset of HDLC. LAPB is the Data-Link Layer protocol for the X.25 network. Besides LAPB are Link Access Procedure for D-Channel (LAPD) and Link Access Procedure for Modems (LAPM). The CCITT V.42bis protocol uses LAPM.

SDLC, ADCCP, and HDLC grew out of the work started within ANSI. SDLC arrived on the market first as an IBM product. ADCCP was expanded by the ISO into HDLC, which is rapidly becoming the standard Data-Link Control protocol throughout the world.

Whereas LAP is based on a primary-to-secondary communication scheme, LAPB allows communications between combined stations. A *combined station* is one that can act alternately as either a primary or secondary. This allows the computer to initiate and respond to communications.

Identify the key characteristics of SDLC, HDLC, and LAPB.

Identify the major services provided by SDLC, HDLC, and LAPB.

SDLC

The SDLC protocol was developed by IBM to allow high performance data communication between two computers with large amounts of data to be transferred.

SDLC uses a frame as the basic unit of communication. The frame consists of a beginning group bit of a specific bit pattern, 01111110, used for synchronization. The second field is an eight-bit address field. The third field is an eight-bit special control field.

The fourth field is the user data of any length because SDLC does not restrict this field length. The fifth field is a 16-bit error checking field. The sixth and last field is an ending group bit with the pattern 01111110, which is the same as the beginning group.

 Identify/label the fields of an SDLC frame and their functions.

Figure 4.1 shows the fields of an SDLC frame.

1	2	3	4	5	6
Flag	Address	Control	User Data	Error Checking	End
01111110	8 Bit	8 Bit	Variable	16 Bits	01111110

Figure 4.1
SDLC frame fields.

Field 1: Flag Field

The first field in an SDLC frame is made up of eight bits in a predetermined pattern of 01111110.

 The pattern 01111110 is only allowed to occur as a beginning or ending flag. Elsewhere, SDLC inserts a zero into the bitstream after every occurrence of five adjacent ones. This procedure is called *bit stuffing*.

Field 2: Address Field

Every secondary in an SDLC system identifies itself in each frame using this field.

Secondaries also can have multiple addresses, one each for unicast, multicast, and broadcast address to primaries.

Primaries use this field to place the address of the secondary to which it is communicating.

175

Because the primaries are always involved in communications, it is assumed that every secondary knows the address of the primary, so the primary's address is not required in the frame.

Field 3: Control Field

The three types of Control fields are as follows: information format, supervisory format, and unnumbered format.

Information Format

The information format is made up of eight bits, as shown in figure 4.2:

Figure 4.2

Information control format.

```
Bits
┌─────┬─────┬───┬─────┬───────────┬─────┬───┬───┐
│  1  │  2  │ 3 │  4  │     5     │  6  │ 7 │ 8 │
├─────┼─────┴───┴─────┼───────────┼─────┴───┴───┤
│  0  │ Send Sequence │ Poll/Final│ Receive Sequence │
└─────┴───────────────┴───────────┴──────────────┘
```

- ◆ Bit one is a zero, which indicates that the frame is an information frame.

- ◆ Bits two through four make up the send sequence.

- ◆ Bit five is a poll/final bit.

- ◆ Bits six, seven, and eight make up the receive sequence.

By using the send sequence, poll/final bit, and receive sequence, the sender and receiver can communicate with each other at a rate upon which they both agree.

The send-and-receive sequence contributes to the flow control and error control in the SDLC frame.

The poll/final bit allows the primaries and secondaries to state whether another frame will be sent or acknowledged.

Each frame is numbered when sent. The send sequence is the number of the next frame the sender is expected to send. The receive sequence is the next frame number the receiver expects to get from the sender. Sender and receiver monitor these numbers. If a frame is out of sequence, an error is detected and the receiver does not accept frames after the frame with an error. After the sender detects that the frames are not being received, it retransmits beginning with the frame where the error was detected.

SDLC integrates a facility to allow multiple frames to be sent with acknowledgment upon request. The poll/final bit allows the sender or receiver to communicate subsequent frame acknowledgment. When the sender sets this bit to one, an acknowledgment of all frames sent since the last acknowledgment is requested. The receiver sets this bit to one when the frame it is sending is the final response frame.

 The send and receive sequence together allow the sender to get several frames ahead. A one-byte control field allows the sender to get up to seven frames ahead. A two-byte control field allows the sender to get up to 127 frames ahead of an acknowledgment.

If the Control field uses the Information format, it is followed by the Information field.

Supervisory Format

Figure 4.3 shows the bit designation for the supervisory format of the Control field.

Bits

1	2	3	4	5	6	7	8
1	0	Function		Poll/Final	Receive Sequence		

Figure 4.3

Supervisory control format.

- The Supervisory format starts with bit one as a one and bit two as a zero.
- Bits three and four are for the function.
- Bit five is for the poll/final bit.
- Bits six, seven, and eight make up the receive sequence.

The function bits are used for positive and negative acknowledgments, specifying Receiver Ready (RR), Receiver Not Ready (RNR), and Frame Reject (REJ).

Supervisory formats do not include the Information field and are followed by the checksum.

The final three bits designate the receive sequence number.

Unnumbered Format

Figure 4.4 shows the Unnumbered Format of the Control field.

Figure 4.4

Unnumbered control format.

Bits

1	2	3	4	5	6	7	8
1	1	Function		Poll/Final	Function		

This format is used to start or disable the link between the primary and secondary. They are also used to select a one- or two-byte control field.

Most unnumbered frames are not followed by an Information field. The exceptions are Unnumbered Information (UI) and Frame Reject (FRMR).

Field 4: User Data Field

This is the Information field that follows the Information Format Control Frame field. Select Unnumbered Format Control Frame.

Field 5: Error Checking Field

This field is for the checksum bits. This field is 16 bits and the process is *Cyclic Redundancy Check Remainder*. This check is performed on the following fields:

- ◆ Address
- ◆ Control
- ◆ Information

Field 6: End Field

This field is a string of bits in the pattern 01111110, the same as the first field.

HDLC

The following characteristics describe HDLC:

- ◆ Synchronous
- ◆ Full-duplex
- ◆ Very similar to SDLC

HDLC and SDLC share the same frame format. HDLC adds some features and provides many of the same functions as SDLC.

HDLC differs from SDLC in the following ways:

- ◆ HDLC can have a 32-bit checksum.
- ◆ When an error is detected, SDLC must retransmit the entire string, whereas HDLC can resend the specified frame.
- ◆ HDLC includes three different transfer modes: NRM, ARM, ABM.

179

♦ HDLC does not include group or broadcast addresses.

♦ HDLC does not communicate using support loop or hub go-ahead as SDLC does.

HDLC has three different modes of transferring data, as shown in table 4.3.

Table 4.3
HDLC Data Transfer Modes

Mode	Station Types	Who Starts Communication
Normal Response Mode (NRM)	Primary, Secondary	Primary
Asynchronous Response Mode (ARM)	Primary, Secondary	Either
Asynchronous Balanced Mode (ABM)	Combined	Either

Normal Response Mode (NRM)

NRM is used by SDLC and involves both primary and secondary stations, where the secondaries are not allowed to initiate communication.

Asynchronous Response Mode (ARM)

ARM is the least common of the three transfer modes. This mode has primaries and secondaries, and either can start communication.

Asynchronous Balanced Mode (ABM)

ABM is used with stations that can alternately be primaries and secondaries, called *combined stations*. Any combined station can initiate communication. This is very useful in local area networking.

LAPB

LAPB uses the same frame format as SDLC and HDLC. The LAPB protocol, defined by CCITT as part of the X.25 protocol, uses the ABM transfer mode, which works well because LAPB does not allow information to be transmitted in the response frames. LAPB uses the poll/final bit in a slightly different manner than SDLC.

Learning About the Institute of Electrical and Electronic Engineers (IEEE)

Identify key characteristics of the IEEE 802 series standards.

Because standards are so important to achieving connectivity among computers, the IEEE was assigned the task of defining LAN standards in 1980. The original plan was to have one standard provide the promised interoperability at a reasonably low cost. It was not long before they realized that this was not feasible. The needs of the marketplace were too diverse. This meant that they would have to devise several different standards.

By 1985, four standards were announced as the IEEE Project 802. These standards are known as 802.2 through 802.5. The American National Standards Institute (ANSI) and the OSI adopted these standards.

181

The IEEE Project 802 is concerned with the lower two OSI layers, Physical and Data-Link. The Data-Link Layer is further subdivided into two sublayers: Media Access Control (MAC) and Logical Link Control (LLC).

The MAC sublayer is defined by: CSMA/CD (802.3), Token Bus (802.4), and Token Ring (802.5).

The LLC is defined by 802.2 and is responsible for providing an error-free, transparent transmission path to the Network Layer.

The following sections define 10 of the 802 standards, with special emphasis on the most popular standards: 802.2 LLC, 802.3 Ethernet, and 802.5 Token Ring.

Identify and briefly describe some of the lesser-known IEEE 802 specifications.

802.1

Title: Overview, Systems Management, and Internetworking

802.1 introduces the rest of the standards. It addresses how the rest of the standards interrelate and discusses the problems of internetworking.

Although the 802.1 standard is not yet finished, it is responsible for the popular spanning-tree algorithm for transparent bridges. The spanning-tree algorithm operates in the following manner. One bridge is chosen to be the root, which is usually the station with the lowest physical address. All bridges determine the shortest path and count the number of hops from the segments to which they are connected to the root bridge.

If two or more bridges connect to the same segment with the same number of hops, the bridge with the higher physical address is blocked. Blocking a bridge allows it to continue to receive packets but requires that all packets to be routed be discarded. The spanning-tree algorithm functions dynamically, with each bridge periodically informing all other bridges of its location and status.

802.2

Identify key characteristics of the 802.2 standard and its relationship to the remaining 802 series standards.

Title: Logical Link Control

LLC is modeled after the HDLC protocol, with modifications to the functions of the frame formats.

802.2 works in conjunction with the 802.3 through 802.6 MAC layer protocols. FDDI, although it is an ANSI standard, also uses 802.2 at the LLC sublayer.

The LLC is responsible for offering services to the Network Layer. This is done through passageways called *Service Access Points* (SAPs). The LLC uses the SAPs to identify the Network Layer process. The Network Layer uses the SAPs to leave messages for the LLC about what services are required.

Figure 4.5 shows an LLC frame format.

Field 1	Field 2	Field 3	Field 4	Field 5	Field 6
	1 Byte	1 Byte	1 or 2 Bytes		
Mac Header	DSAP	SSAP	Control	Information	MAC CRC

Figure 4.5
LLC frame format.

The LLC frame is made up of four fields—DSAP, SSAP, Control, and Information—and is bordered by a MAC layer header and CRC.

LLC frames are also called PDUs, or *Protocol Data Units.*

183

DSAP

Length: 1 byte

This is the destination SAP, which is the address of the Network Layer to receive the PDU.

Seven of the eight bits are used for the address. The eighth bit is used for control, specifying whether the destination is a group or individual address.

SSAP

Length: 1 byte

This is the source SAP, which is the address of the Network Layer to send the PDU.

Seven of the eight bits are used for the address. The eighth bit is used for control, specifying whether the PDU is a request or response.

Control

Length: 1 or 2 bytes

The length of this field depends on the service being requested or supplied. Upper layers define the contents of this field.

Information

Length: Variable

This field is present only when the service requires upper-layer information to be included.

The error control provided by LLC is provided by accounting for end-to-end link guarantees. The MAC layer is responsible for CRC testing. The LLC is responsible for reporting whether the link is established or not established because of some network anomaly, such as authentication of failure or an unreachable destination.

The LLC also can reset a connection should the link fail because of noise.

Flow control at the LLC layer is done through one of two methods: Stop and Wait or Sliding Window.

Stop and Wait

In the Stop and Wait method, the sender must wait for a positive acknowledgment before continuing to send PDUs. This is not the most efficient method, because the sender must wait for the acknowledgment after each PDU.

Sliding Window

In the Sliding Window method, the receiver sets the size of the window. The sender can get that specified number of PDUs ahead. If the window size is eight, then the sender can send eight PDUs before having to wait for an acknowledgment. Sliding window protocols are full-duplex.

LLC supports both connection-oriented and connectionless services. Connection-oriented services use a logical connection that must be established before data can be transferred and is considered to be reliable. Connectionless services do not rely on a preset path, so data transfer is faster. It also is considered to be unreliable because no acknowledgments are required. Three types of services for sending and receiving data are provided by LLC.

Type 1: Unacknowledged, Connectionless Service

Type 1 is the fastest and most unreliable transfer method because it does not require an acknowledgment.

The reason that Type 1 is so popular is because most protocols use a reliable transport at other layers. Redundancy at the Data-Link Layer is not required.

Type 2: Connection-Oriented Service

Type 2 provides more control and reliability, including facilities to recover the link if it is lost. A logical connection is established between the sender and receiver for the length of the conversation. Either party can terminate the session when finished. All communication is acknowledged using the sliding window method for flow control.

Type 3: Acknowledged, Connectionless Service

Type 3, although connectionless, does require acknowledgments. This is done using the stop and wait flow control mechanism. This is effective for automated equipment with limited storage capabilities. The lack of a logical link also cuts down on overhead.

Because each station can perform combinations of these three services, the LLC also defines four LLC classes that combine the services the station can provide. Table 4.4 shows the possible combinations.

Table 4.4
802.2 LLC Service Classes

	Type 1	Type 2	Type 3
Class I	Yes		
Class II	Yes	Yes	
Class III	Yes		Yes
Class IV	Yes	Yes	Yes

802.3

 Identify the characteristics of and major services provided by IEEE 802.3.

Characteristics: 802.3 defines Ethernet-like protocol and Carrier Sense Multiple Access/Collision Detection (CSMA/CD) access scheme.

Media Access Method: CSMA/CD

Media: Table 4.5 compares different 802.3 and Ethernet standards for cabling.

Topology: Bus and Star

Table 4.5
Ethernet and 802.3 Specification

Rate	Topology	Media	Segment Length in Meters	Data Mbps
Ethernet	BUS	50 ohm thick coax	500	10
10BASE5	BUS	50 ohm thick coax	500	10
10BASE2	BUS	50 ohm thin coax	185	10
10BASET	STAR	Unshielded twisted pair	100 (3 23 Ft)	10
10Broad36	BUS	75 ohm coax	1800	10
1BASE5	STAR	Unshielded twisted pair	250	1

In most cases, the first number stands for the speed, the middle word is the media, and the last number is the maximum segment length in 100 meter lengths. The T of 10BASET stands for twisted pair, the 36 in 10Broad36 is derived from the requirement that 10Broad36 needs two segments, the maximum length being 1,800 for each. Finally, the 2 in 10BASE2 is derived by rounding 185 up to 200.

Although the term Ethernet, invented by Digital, Intel, and Xerox, is often used in conjunction with the 802.3 workgroup, the frame types are significantly different, and one frame type cannot be arbitrarily substituted for the other.

802.3 standards were released approximately three years after the invention of the Ethernet packet. Both Ethernet and 802.3 use the CSMA/CD channel access method.

CSMA/CD works in the following way:

1. When a station wants to transmit data, it listens to the cable to see if it can detect existing traffic. If the cable is idle _not being used to send data_ the station can send its data. If the channel is in use, the station monitors the channel until it detects the idle state.

2. After the sending station detects an idle state, it can begin to send data, and then check for collisions.

A collision happens when a station tries to transmit data at the same time as another station.

If a collision is detected, the detecting station stops transmitting the data and starts transmitting a "jamming" pattern. The jamming pattern can be from 32 to 48 bits of any pattern with the exception of the 32-bit CRC value of the frame being transmitted when the collision was detected. The jamming pattern is sent for a period of time to ensure that all stations receive the pattern.

The station needs to send the transmission again and needs to determine slot times for the retransmission. Because multiple stations may need to retransmit, an algorithm must be enforced to guarantee cable availability. A *slot time* is 512 bit times, which is slightly longer than the time it takes for a packet to make a round trip on an 802.3 network. The slot time ensures that the collision signals are no longer on the cable when the next station attempts to transmit.

Slot times are determined as follows:

The station selects a slot time from a set of numbers recalculated for each retry. The number set is defined as {0,..,2m - 1}. "m" is defined as the minimum (n,10). The "n" is the number of previous unsuccessful attempts at transmission, not to exceed 10 in the calculation. This means that the largest possible set is {0,..,1023}. The maximum transmissions before a failure is reported is 16.

On the first attempt at retransmission, the number set is {0, 2^1-1} or {0,1}. The station has two slot time choices. If the attempt fails, then the next attempt allows the station to choose from the number set of {0,..2^2-1} or {0,1,2,3}. This continues until either the retransmission takes place or 16 attempts are made. At that time an upper layer is responsible for reporting the problem.

A significant difference between 802.3 and Ethernet is the frame types. Figure 4.6 shows both frame types.

Identify the frame format and field functions of IEEE 802.3.

Identify major differences between IEEE 802.3 and Ethernet.

Ethernet

8 Bytes		6 Bytes	6 Bytes	2 Bytes	46-1500 Bytes	4 Bytes
Preamble		Dest. Address	Source Address	Type	Data	CRC

802.3

7 Bytes	1 Byte	6 Bytes	6 Bytes	2 Bytes	46-1500 Bytes	4 Bytes
Preamble	Start of Frame	Dest. Address	Source Address	Length	802.2 Header and Data	CRC

Figure 4.6

IEEE 802.3 and Ethernet frame types.

Preamble and Start of Frame Delimiters

Significant differences occur in two places. The first is the Preamble and the Start of Frame Delimiter. The Ethernet frame has an 8-byte preamble that consists of alternating ones and zeros. The 802.3 frame has seven bytes of alternating ones and zeros, but the eighth byte ends in two ones, which signifies the start of the frame.

Destination Address

The destination address is usually a 6-byte address, which is the hardware address of the network board, but it can be a 2-byte address. This is the address of who gets the frame. The destination address also can include unicast (single host), multicast (multiple selected hosts), or broadcast addresses (all hosts).

Source Address

Source address is a 6-byte address, which is the hardware address of the sender. The first three bytes of this 6-byte hardware address are assigned by the IEEE. The vendor is responsible for the second set of three bytes.

Length versus Type

802.3 uses Length, whereas Ethernet uses Type. *Length* signifies the number of bytes in the frame from the data field and is used to delineate the LLC packet. *Type* is the type of frame being sent.

Data and Padding

In the 802.3 packet, this field contains the frame's data. The number in the length field describes the portion of this field that is the LLC packet. The pad includes any other bytes up to the Frame Check Sequence.

The padding is necessary to increase the length of the packet so that defective frames and collisions can be detected through the use of slot times. Packets shorter than 64 bytes are discarded *(Runts)* because they are not sufficient to complete a round trip and be detected.

Frame Check Sequence

The frame check sequence is the CRC value assigned to the packet.

Another feature of both Ethernet 2.0 and IEEE 802.3 is the *Signal Quality Error* (SQE), or heartbeat. SQE determines whether the transceiver or *Medium Attachment Units* (MAUs), which are the connection point between the network board and the cable, can be trusted to be working. Because collision detection is integral to CSMA/CD, these devices must be operational. The heartbeat tests these units.

Mixing the older Ethernet 1.0 with 802.3 or Ethernet 2.0 is not recommended, because the heartbeat is viewed as a jamming signal.

802.4

Characteristics: 802.4 defines a token passing MAC sublayer and bus and tree topologies. 802.4 is deterministic but complex.

Media:

- ◆ Single channel
- ◆ Broadband
- ◆ 75 ohm CATV
- ◆ Fiber optic

Media Access Method: Token Bus

Topology: Bus and Tree

Token Bus was created to focus on the needs of automation, which makes it very attractive to General Motor's Manufacturing Automation Protocol (MAP). GM adopted Token Bus to fill the needs of MAP. However, GM exhibited limited follow-up of Token Bus, so it has not achieved the popularity initially forecast.

Token Bus offers exceptional performance under heavy loads and is useful for situations that require low delay, such as process control.

802.5

 Identify the characteristics of and major services provided by IEEE 802.5.

Characteristics: 802.5 is a token passing ring network in which each station functions as a unidirectional repeater. Each station reads, stores into memory, and then passes the transmitted bits to the next station. Most token passing ring networks include wire centers to which all stations are attached. These are called *MultiStation Access Units* (MAUs or MSAUs). MAUs include the capability to bypass stations having problems or that are not connected to the ring. Multiple MAUs can be connected to form a large ring; however, the cables connecting the MAUs cannot be bypassed in the event of a cable failure.

Media: Mostly unstated as part of the standard of 802.5, the choice of media usually conforms to the IBM Token Ring specifications. Table 4.6 describes the cable specifications for both IBM Token Ring and 802.5.

Table 4.6
IBM Token Ring and 802.5 Specification

	IBM Token Ring	*IEEE 802.5*
Media	Twisted pair	No specification
Data rates	4 or 16 Mbps	1 or 4 Mbps
Stations per segment	72 unshielded TP 260 shielded TP	250
Topology	Star	No specification

Both Token Ring and 802.5 use Differential Manchester encoding and baseband signaling.

Media Access Method: Token Passing

Topology: Ring or Star

Token passing, as the name implies, involves a special frame called a *token*. A station can communicate only when it has control of a token. At any moment, only one token can exist on the ring. The token frame is passed from station to station around the ring until it reaches a station that has data to be transmitted.

When a station receives a token, it is converted into a frame and passed to the next station. The frame continues to travel the ring, passing through each station until it reaches its destination and then on to the original sending node. If the packet reaches its destination, the packet is marked to let the sending node know that it was received without error. The destination node passes the frame to the next station in line, and the frame continues until it reaches the sending node. The sending node looks at the frame to see if it was received by the destination. If all is well, the frame is converted back into a token and passed back onto the ring.

When a station needs to transmit, it must wait until it receives the token. After the token frame is received, it is converted into a data frame that includes address information and the data to be transmitted. This data frame is passed to the next station. The data frame continues to travel the ring, passing through each station until it reaches its destination station. The destination station marks the frame as received and then allows the frame to continue around the ring until it reaches the original sending node. The sending node looks at the frame to see if it was received by the destination. If all is well, the frame is converted back into a token and passed back onto the ring.

Some rings support early token release, which allows for a new token to be created immediately after the sending station finishes transmitting the frame. By allowing more than one token to exist on the ring, the available bandwidth on the ring is used more efficiently.

One of the stations on the ring performs a function called an *active monitor*. The active monitor provides the following services:

◆ Places 24 or more bit delays onto the ring so that each station can finish sending the token before it starts receiving the token back. It is possible for the sending node to receive the frame it is sending back before it finishes transmitting. The bit delays hold the token so that the node can finish transmitting the entire frame.

◆ Removes frames that cannot find their destination.

◆ Performs various maintenance functions.

Any station can act as an active monitor, although the active monitor usually is the first node to attach to the ring. When no active monitor is present, the ring starts a procedure to force a station to become the active monitor.

One maintenance function that can be performed by an 802.5-compliant system is called *beaconing*. Beaconing occurs when a fault is detected in the ring. The node that senses the failure starts to send beacon frames until it can find its nearest upstream neighbor, which is the node farthest along the normal path of the ring before returning to the beaconing node. The link between the beaconing node and its nearest upstream neighbor is called the *failure domain*. When the failure domain is found, this process also starts an autoreconfiguration in an attempt to route around the failure.

Nine potential fields comprise the three frames that occur on an 802.5 ring. These fields and frames are described in figure 4.7.

 Identify IEEE 802.5 frame fields and discuss their functions.

```
Command Frame Format (MAC frames carrying maintenance information)
Data Frame Format (LLC frames carrying upper-layer information)

Fields:             1  2  3  4  5   6    7   8  9
Length in Bytes:    1  1  1  6  6   >0   4   1  1
Field Name:         SD AC FC DA SA  INFO FCS ED FS

Abort Frame Format (sent for early termination of transmission)

Fields:             1  2
Length in Bytes:    1  1
Field Name:         SD ED

Token Format (used for media access order only)

Fields:             1  2  3
Length in Bytes:    1  1  1
Field Name:         SD AC ED
```

Figure 4.7

802.5 fields and frames.

SD—Start Delimiter

This field alerts the receiver that a frame should be expected. The alert is generated by violating the Differential Manchester code used on the ring.

AC—Access Control

The AC byte is for priorities and token reservation.

The first three bits are for priority, the fourth bit is a token bit, the fifth bit is a monitor bit, and the last three bits are for reservation, as shown in figure 4.8.

```
Bits      1   2   3    4     5      6    7    8
          |  Priority  |Token|Monitor|  Reservation  |
```

Figure 4.8

AC bit designation.

The reservation and priority bits work in the following way. A station can convert a token to data or command frame only when their priority is the same or higher than the priority set in the token. When a station receives a token, it looks at the priority bit.

If the priority of the station needs to transmit data, but has a priority lower than the token's priority, the station can set the reservation bit to its assigned priority.

The token is then passed to the next station until a station with a priority that is the same or higher than the token is reached. When that station regenerates the next token, it sets the priority to the reservation number. This way, another station can use the token. Each station using the token is responsible for resetting the priority so that everyone has a chance to transmit.

When the token bit is set to zero, the frame is known to be a token. When the bit is set to one, it is considered to be a command or data frame.

The monitor bit is used by the active monitor. When a frame is passed to the active monitor, it sets this bit to one. If the active monitor receives a frame with this bit set to one, it assumes that it has seen this frame before and removes it from the ring.

FC—Frame Control

This byte specifies data or control information. This field is used to do the following:

- Attempt to become the active monitor
- Declare that it has become the active monitor
- Initialize the ring

DA—Destination Address

This field is used to specify the unicast, multicast, or broadcast address of the designation receiver.

SA—Source Address

This is the sending station's hardware address.

INFO—Information

This field holds the data targeted for the upper layers.

FCS—Frame Check Sequence

This is a CRC remainder, calculated from the FC, DA, SA, and INFO fields. This remainder is checked by the receiving station for errors.

ED—End Delimiter

The ED field signals the end of the frame by again violating the Differential Manchester encoding scheme.

FS—Frame Status

This byte specifies the source of the frame and its condition. The byte is divided into two address resolution bits and two frame copied bits. The sending station sets both sets of bits to zero. When the sender receives the frame back, these bits should be set to one.

- If the bits are still zeros, the destination is considered un-reachable.

- If the frame was not acceptable to the receiver because of errors or no buffer space, the address resolution bits are set to one, and the frame copied bits are left at zero.

- If the frame is acceptable to the receiver, both sets of bits are set to one.

802.6

Title: Metropolitan Area Networks (MAN)

Characteristics: 802.6 uses Distributed Queue Dual Bus (DQDB) and is considered to be a city-wide network. MAN supports synchronous or asynchronous transfer, and data, voice, and video data.

Media: Fiber

Topology: Dual Bus

The MAN was developed to solve a particular problem, unlike the rest of the standards, which standardize existing technology. Many wide-area networking solutions are too expensive (leased lines) or too slow (PDNs). The MAN attempts to solve this by using DQDB.

DQDB was proposed by the University of Western Australia. DQDB utilizes unidirectional buses, each functioning in a different direction. Because of the capability to transport voice, video, and data, MAN technology can be viable in the home entertainment arena as well as for commercial endeavors.

802.7

Title: Broadband Technology

Characteristics: Although still under development, the 802.7 workgroup's goal is to incorporate standards for broadband technology for use in existing networks.

The main focus for 802.7 is installation and maintenance of broadband networks.

802.8

Title: Fiber Optic Technology

Characteristics: 802.8 is still in development stages. IEEE's objective is to look into fiber optic options for the 802.3, 802.4, and 802.5 workgroups.

Another objective is to set up standards for installation of fiber optics and training documentation.

802.9

Title: Integrated Voice and Data

Characteristics: 802.9 is responsible for integrating voice and data standards for the desktop. Its purpose is to make the standard ISDN compatible.

802.9 will use 802.2 Logical Link Control.

Media: Unshielded twisted pair

802.10

Title: LAN Security

Characteristics: 802.10 will work out standards for the following:

- Encryption schemes
- Managing networks
- Security of data for transfer
- OSI compliance for security

Learning About Fiber Distributed Data Interface (FDDI)

 Identify the principal organizations that promulgate and/or champion FDDI protocols and their target environment.

 Identify the major services provided by FDDI.

FDDI is the ANSI standard for high-speed, fiber optic networks, designed to overcome the 10 Mbps Ethernet and 4 Mbps Token Ring limitations. FDDI was introduced in 1986 by the X3T9.5 committee. It is most useful for network backbones, computer room networks where mainframes and minis need connections, and LANs that require high data rate throughput.

FDDI assumes that 802.2 will be used along with a MAC sublayer. FDDI also includes a station management (SMT) specification, still under development.

FDDI is most similar to IEEE 802.5. Table 4.7 compares the two protocols.

Table 4.7
FDDI and IEEE 802.5 Comparison

	FDDI	*802.5*
Media	Fiber optic	Twisted pair fiber optic
Data rate	100 Mbps	1 or 4 Mbps
Encoding	NRZI 4B/5B	Differential Manchester

Similarities between FDDI and 802.5 include the following:

- Ring and star topologies
- Token passing access method
- Baseband signaling
- 16- and 48-bit addressing

 Identify the characteristics of FDDI.

An important characteristic of FDDI is the use of two counter-rotating rings. Traffic normally flows on the primary ring. If a break occurs in the primary ring, the secondary ring can be used to bridge the break and continue an unbroken physical ring. This is important to know when planning the ring and making it possible for the secondary ring to patch breaks. The maximum number of nodes is 1,000, and the total cable length cannot be longer than 200 kilometers.

If the secondary ring is used to patch a failure, every station will be counted twice because they exist on the primary cable as well as the secondary ring. The length of the cable also will be doubled. Because of this peculiarity, FDDI states that <u>500 workstations and 100 kilometers</u> of cable are practical limitations. Figure 4.9 demonstrates the reconfiguration of the secondary ring.

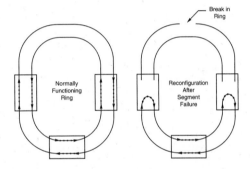

Figure 4.9
Reconfiguration of the secondary ring.

Fiber specifications are fairly stringent to ensure a reliable system. Repeaters are required every two kilometers. FDDI star configuration defines two classes of stations. <u>Class A</u> stations are <u>connected</u> to <u>both rings,</u> while Class B stations are only connected to the primary ring. If the primary ring has a fault, only Class A stations can participate in the reconfiguration.

FDDI uses a token passing scheme in which a token is generated at the end of each transmission. Any station needing to send data can absorb the token and generate a frame. In FDDI, multiple frames can be on the ring.

FDDI uses an encoding scheme significantly different from Manchester and Differential Manchester. Because those encoding schemes require two bit transitions per bit time, the signal must be twice the speed of transfer. This results in 50 percent efficiency.

FDDI uses a method called 4 bit of 5 bit (4B/5B) encoding. In this scheme, each group of four data bits is encoded into a five-bit code group called a *symbol*. This encoding method yields 80 percent efficiency because it take five bits to convey four bits of information. Symbols are defined for the hexadecimal numbers 0 through F and for several communication functions. 4B/5B is a self-clocking serial data transmission scheme.

The symbols were chosen so as to guarantee a line transition at least every three bit times. The actual transmission is accomplished through the non-return to zero inverted (NRZI) transmission scheme. NRZI uses the presence of a one to cause a change in the level of the signal; a zero produces no change. The 4B/5B symbol list has no symbol with more than three consecutive zeros. This ensures the transmission of a one, and therefore a line transition at least every three bit times.

FDDI also specifies the following:

◆ 100 Mbps total bandwidth

◆ Synchronous or asynchronous transmissions

◆ Extended asynch dialogs that provide uninterrupted node-to-node transmission using restricted tokens

◆ Eight levels of priority assignments with asynchronous transmissions

Ten fields define two frame formats in FDDI. Figure 4.10 shows the fields and frames for FDDI.

 Identify/label the fields of an FDDI frame and their functions.

Figure 4.10

FDDI field and frame formats.

Data or Command Frame

A	B	C	D	E	F	G	H	I
16+	2	2	4 or 12	4 or 12	0+	8	1	3+

# of symbols

Token Frame

A	B	C	H
16+	2	2	2

The fields are as follows:

- Field A: Preamble
- Field B: Start Delimiter
- Field C: Frame Control
- Field D: Destination Address
- Field E: Source Address
- Field F: Information
- Field G: Frame Check Sequence
- Field H: End Delimiter
- Field I: Frame Status

Field A: Preamble

Length: 16 or more symbols

Whenever a station is not transmitting frames, it transmits an IDLE symbol, which is all ones. At least 16 of these symbols must be between frames.

Field B: Start Delimiter

Length: Two symbols

Two start delimiter symbols signal the receiver that the frame will begin.

Field C: Frame Control

Length: Two symbols

This frame indicates synchronous/asynchronous, 16/48-bit address, data/command, and type of command.

Field D: Destination Address

Length: 4 or 12 symbols

This is the address of the destination station.

Field E: Source Address

Length: 4 or 12 symbols

This is the address of the original sending station.

Field F: Information

Length: Zero or more symbols

This is information intended for upper layers.

Field G: Frame Check Sequence

Length: Eight symbols

A CRC is performed on the Control, Address, and Information fields.

Field H: End Delimiter

Length: One symbol for data/command frames; two symbols for tokens

This field contains one T (01101) symbol if the frame is a data or command frame, and two T symbols if the frame is a token.

Field I: Frame Status

Length: Three or more symbols

The three symbols in the Frame Status field can be manipulated to indicate if the frame is acceptable and copied into memory or unacceptable, or if the destination is unreachable.

The maximum length of a packet from field B to field I cannot be larger than 4,500 bytes.

Learning About LocalTalk

 Identify the principal organization that champions LocalTalk.

LocalTalk is Apple Computer's proprietary physical and Data-Link Layer implementation for small workgroup networks. LocalTalk is also called LocalTalk Link Access Protocol, or LLAP. Apple's Macintosh computer is popular because of the inclusion of a network board in each computer and other built-in network capabilities.

 Identify the characteristics of and major services provided by LocalTalk.

Characteristics: AppleTalk was designed to provide a seamless integration from a stand-alone workstation into a networked computer. LocalTalk uses baseband signaling and a biphase encoding scheme referred to as FM-0 or *biphase space*. FM-0 includes a transition at the beginning of each bit for clocking.

Media: Shielded twisted pair spanning up to 300 meters

Physical Layer specifications: EIA RS-422

Topology: Bus, with a maximum of 32 devices

In keeping with Apple's image of user-friendly computing devices, LocalTalk's method of addressing each node is performed by the network. As each node is turned on, it checks in its long-term memory for the address it had last on the network. If this is the first time the node is attaching to the network, it chooses a number at random.

After a number is chosen either from memory or at random, it is broadcast across the cable. In essence, each node says "I'd like to be number 98. Is anyone else using this number?" If another node answers that its address is set to the requested address, the requesting node chooses again. Workstation addresses are in the range of 1 to 127, while server addresses are in the range of 128 to 254.

Access Method: CSMA/CA, Carrier Sense, Multiple Access/ Collision Avoidance; LocalTalk attempts to avoid collisions by using Request To Send (RTS) and Clear To Send (CTS) packets.

The transmission is controlled through dialogs in which multiple frames begin a logical conversation. The directed transmission dialog is done between one sending and one receiving node. A broadcast transmission dialog is done between the sender and all other receivers. A minimum gap of 400 microseconds is required between dialogs. This is called an *interdialog gap* (IDG). Frames within a dialog must be separated by a minimum gap of 200 microseconds, which is called an *interframe gap* (IFG).

The following scenario depicts a directed transmission dialog. The sequence of events in a directed transmission is illustrated in figure 4.11. The sending node senses the cable for traffic. This sensing must last at least 400 microseconds. An IFG must pass, and then an RTS is sent, alerting all nodes that a data transmission is about to begin. Again an IFG passes, and then the CTS is sent by the receiving node to say that it is ready for transmission, also giving the network enough time to sense a collision. Once more an IFG passes, and then the data is sent. When sending is complete, an IDG must pass before another dialog can begin.

Should a collision be detected, the sending node is deferred. The amount of time that it is deferred depends on the deferral history plus a random element. If either 32 collisions or 32 deferrals take place during one transmission, a network failure is reported to the upper layers.

Figure 4.11

Sequence of events in a LocalTalk directed transmission.

LocalTalk's frame format consists of nine fields and two frame types. The frame types are Control and Data. Valid frame size is from 5 to 603 bytes from the Destination Node ID to the Data field. Field 1 is the packet preamble, whereas fields 7, 8, and 9 are the frame trailer. Figure 4.12 depicts a LocalTalk frame format.

Identify the frame format and field functions of a LocalTalk frame.

	1	2	3	4	5	6	7	8	9
Size in Bytes	2+	1	1	1	10 Bits	0-600	2	1	12-18 Bits

Figure 4.12

LocalTalk frame format.

The LocalTalk fields are as follows:

◆ Field 1: Preamble Flags

◆ Field 2: Destination Node Identification

◆ Field 3: Source Node Identification

◆ Field 4: Type

◆ Field 5: Data Length

◆ Field 6: Data

◆ Field 7: Frame Check Sequence

◆ Field 8: Trailer Flag

◆ Field 9: Abort Sequence

Field 1: Preamble Flags

Length: Two or more bytes

Contains two or more bytes that have the value of 7E, hexadecimal. This pattern is not allowed anywhere else in the packet.

Field 2: Destination Node Identification

Length: One byte

This contains the address of the destination node.

Field 3: Source Node Identification

Length: One byte

This contains the address of the sending node.

Field 4: Type

Length: One byte

If the value is from 1 to 127, this field is a data frame. Values of 128 to 255 are control frames. Control frames do not include a data field.

The four types of control frames are discussed in the following four sections.

RTS

This is a request-to-send frame specifying that data is ready to be sent.

CTS

This is a clear-to-send frame used to respond to the RTS, which indicates that the receiver is ready for transmission.

ENQ

This is an enquiry used to determine node address availability.

ACK

This is an acknowledgment frame sent to respond to the ENQ frame.

Field 5: Data Length

Length: Ten bits

This is the length of the entire data field.

Field 6: Data

Length: 0 to 600 bytes

This field contains the upper-layer protocol information.

Field 7: Frame Check Sequence

Length: Two bytes

A CRC is calculated on all fields except the flags, FCS, and abort sequence fields.

Field 8: Trailer Flag

Length: One byte

The Trailer flag is similar to the Preamble flag but is only one byte of the pattern 7E.

Field 9: Abort Sequence

Length: 12 to 18 bits

This is a series of 12 to 18 ones that force all nodes to lose synchronization, thereby indicating that the transmission is complete.

Learning About ARCnet

Identify the principal organizations that promulgate or champion ARCNET.

Attached Resource Computer Network (ARCnet) was created by Data Point Corporation in 1977. ARCnet was licensed to Standard Microsystems Corporation (SMC), which developed an ARCnet chipset. It is the simplest and most inexpensive of the protocols you have learned about. An ARCnet Trade Association (ATA) maintains the standards for ARCnet.

Identify the key characteristics of and major services provided by ARCNET.

Media: RG-62/U Coax, fiber optic, and unshielded twisted pair (UTP)

Access Method: Token passing

Topology: Bus and Star

Addressing an ARCnet system is done by setting DIP switches on the network boards. Each station knows its own address, which is known as the Source Identifier (SID). Tokens are passed to the next highest numbered node, whose address is called the Next ID (NID). During certain network faults, or when a node enters or leaves the network, an autoreconfiguration (recon) is performed. Recon disrupts the token passing scheme, causing all nodes to set both the IDs to the source ID. The node with the highest SID tries to find the next highest node by incrementing the address by one until the next node is reached. This continues until all nodes are rediscovered.

ARCnet defines five frame types. Figure 4.13 shows the ARCnet frame types and the fields.

 Identify the frame format and field functions of an ARCNET frame.

Invitation to Transmit (ITT) this is an ARCnet Token Frame

	6 Bits	1 Byte	1 Byte	1 Byte
Length				
Name	Alert	EOT	DID	DID

Free Buffer Enquiry (FBE) sent to the receiver by the sender

	6 Bits	1 Byte	1 Byte	1 Byte
Length				
Name	Alert	ENQ	DID	DID

Acknowledgment (ACK) sent by the receiver in answer to the FBE or PAC

	6 Bits	1 Byte
Length		
Name	Alert	ACK

Negative Acknowledgment (NAK) sent by the receiver in answer to the FBE or PAC

	6 Bits	1 Byte
Length		
Name	Alert	NAK

Data Packet (PAC) - the data frame sent after receiving an ACK

	6 Bits	1 Byte	1 Byte	1 Byte	1 Byte	1-2 Bytes	1-508 Bytes	2 Bytes
Length								
Name	Alert	SOH	SID	DID	DID	Count	Data	CRC

Figure 4.13

ARCnet frames and field formats.

Alert

This field alerts the receiver of the impending frame.

EOT—End of Transmission

This field is sent in the ITT frame only.

DID—Destination Identifier

This field is the address of the destination; this field is set to the NID.

SID—Source Identifier

This is the address of the sending node.

ENQ—Enquiry

This is an ASCII enquiry. This field signifies that an ACK or NAK response is required.

ACK—Acknowledgment

This field signifies a positive acknowledgment.

NAK—Negative Acknowledgment

This field signifies a negative acknowledgment.

SOH—Start of Header

SOH designates the beginning of the information portion of the frame.

Count

This field indicates the number of bytes in the INFO field.

Data

This is the upper-layer information.

CRC

CRC is done on SOH to data fields.

Review Questions

1. Which statement is not part of the EIA's RS-232 specification?

   ○ a. The connector defined is a DB29.

   ○ b. The maximum cable length is 50 feet.

   ○ c. It uses a 25-pin connector.

   ○ d. It supports full-duplex transmission.

2. Which statement regarding HDLC and SDLC is false?

   ○ a. SDLC includes Group and Broadcast addresses.

   ○ b. HDLC supports NRM, ARM and ABM.

   ○ c. SDLC supports Loop and Hub Go-Ahead.

   ○ d. HDLC retransmits entire strings upon error detection.

3. Which pin assignment of the EIA's RS-232 specification is not part of the timing mechanism?

   ○ a. 15

   ○ b. 17

   ○ c. 20

   ○ d. 24

4. Which IEEE workgroup is responsible for integrating voice and data?

   ○ a. 802.7

   ○ b. 802.8

   ○ c. 802.9

   ○ d. 802.10

5. Which IEEE workgroup is most like Token Ring?

   ○ a. 802.2

   ○ b. 802.3

   ○ c. 802.4

   ○ d. 802.5

6. Which IEEE workgroup defined CSMA/CD?

   ○ a. 802.2

   ○ b. 802.3

   ○ c. 802.4

   ○ d. 802.5

7. Which 802.3 definition uses a bus topology, thinnet cable, provides 10 Mbps data rate, and specifies a maximum cable segment not to exceed 185 meters?

   ○ a. 10BASE2

   ○ b. 10BASET

   ○ c. 1BASE5

   ○ d. 10BASE5

8. Which statement about 802.5 and the Active Monitor is not true?

   ○ a. One station on the ring must become the active monitor.

   ○ b. The active monitor removes frames that are not able to reach their destination.

   ○ c. When no active monitor is present, the system looks for who logged in first, then assigns that station to become the active monitor.

   ○ d. The active monitor is responsible for introducing bit delays to the ring.

9. FDDI is most similar to:

   ○ a. 802.4

   ○ b. 802.5

   ○ c. 802.6

   ○ d. 802.7

10. The committee that introduced FDDI is:

   ○ a. IEEE 802 workgroup

   ○ b. CCITT

   ○ c. X3T9.5

   ○ d. EIA

11. LocalTalk uses the _____ access method.

   ○ a. Contention

   ○ b. Polling

   ○ c. CSMA/CD

   ○ d. CSMA/CA

12. Which is not part of the ARCnet specification?

   ○ a. ARCnet uses coax, fiber optic, and UTP cabling.

   ○ b. ARCnet supports bus and star topologies.

   ○ c. ARCnet uses the token passing access method.

   ○ d. ARCnet has three different frame types.

13. On an RS-232 connector, the signal goes _____ when a standard voltage has been applied to the pin indicating an active status.

14. _____ occurs when two modems decide on a protocol, usually CTS/RTS or Xon/Xoff.

15. Which pin is assigned the same on both the DB25 and DB9 connectors?

    ○ a. 7

    ○ b. 6

    ○ c. 3

    ○ d. 2

16. Which of the following pins are used for timing on a DB25 connector? Pick all that apply.

    ☐ a. 15

    ☐ b. 17

    ☐ c. 20

    ☐ d. 24

17. Which item below is not a normal pairing?

    ○ a. Transmitted Data - Received Data

    ○ b. Request to Send - Clear to Send

    ○ c. Data Rate Select - Data Set Ready

    ○ d. Transmit Clock - Receiver Clock

18. Which standards group and supported interface is not a valid combination?

    ○ a. IEEE - 802 Workgroups

    ○ b. EIA - RS-449

    ○ c. CCITT - X Series

    ○ d. AT&T - PDN

19. Which protocol is the ISO specification for a bit-oriented, full-duplex, synchronous protocol.

  ○ a. SDLC

  ○ b. ADCCP

  ○ c. HDLC

  ○ d. LAPB

20. The _____ protocol is the CCITT's specification for a bit-oriented, full-duplex, synchronous protocol.

21. Who starts the communication in Asynchronous Balanced Mode?

  ○ a. Primary

  ○ b. Secondary

  ○ c. Either

  ○ d. Neither

22. Which of the following MAC layer protocols use 802.2? Pick all that apply.

  ☐ a. 802.3

  ☐ b. 802.4

  ☐ c. 802.5

  ☐ d. 802.6

  ☐ e. 802.7

  ☐ f. 802.8

  ☐ g. FDDI

Answers

1. A

2. D

3. C

4. C

5. D

6. B

7. A

8. C

9. B

10. C

11. D

12. D

13. High

14. Handshaking

15. B

16. A,B,D

17. C

18. D

19. C

20. LAPB

21. C

22. A,B,C,D,G

ISO also has defined a suite of protocols to conform to the reference model. This suite of protocols is intended to provide a versatile and robust basis for international networking. In many cases, protocols were borrowed from other sets of standards, particularly in the Physical and Data-Link Layers. Higher level protocols often were developed from scratch specifically for the OSI protocol suite.

Because of the international character of the ISO, the process of developing and finalizing a standard is involved and lengthy. Standards at some layers have been established, whereas other standards remain under development. Consequently, the OSI protocol suite is more a promise of future international cooperation than a statement of current reality.

Due to its committee origins, the OSI protocols tend to pack more options than needed for a given set of requirements. Some of the protocols are full-featured rather than lean and fast. In many cases, organizations have established subsets—called *profiles*—of the OSI protocol suite better tuned to their specific requirements. GOSIP, discussed shortly, is such a profile.

In the United States, acceptance of OSI has been lethargic. In part, this is a result of the Internet, which already provides multi-platform connectivity in a nationwide network. The Internet protocols, such as TCP/IP, are robust and supported on mature, affordable hardware. By contrast, OSI is in its infancy as far as the United States is concerned.

Widespread acceptance of OSI most likely will be fueled by an increasing emphasis in United States government agencies on GOSIP (Government Open System Interconnection Profile), a subset of the full OSI protocol suite selected to support the needs of government. The Defense Department, which originated the Internet as a project of DARPA (the Defense Advanced Research Project Agency), has announced that all defense systems will move toward GOSIP. The move to GOSIP is also policy for all other U.S. government organizations. These changes almost certainly will result in increased interest in the OSI protocols in industry and in lowered costs of implementation as equipment and expertise become more readily available.

Identify the major services provided by OSI.

Figure 5.1 diagrams the OSI protocols with respect to the layers of the OSI Reference Model. Under this model, each layer provides services to the next higher layer. Each layer has a service interface, consisting of *service access points* (SAPs) whereby a higher layer can request services of a lower layer.

Figure 5.1

OSI protocols in regard to the OSI Reference Model.

| APPLICATION | MHS CMIP/CMIS DS |
| | VT FTAM |

 Identify the characteristics of OSI.

At most layers, OSI provides for protocols that are either connectionless or connection-oriented. A connection-oriented protocol establishes a virtual circuit between the communicating end systems. A connectionless protocol does not establish a virtual connection. Although connectionless and connection-oriented services are available at several layers, they are most commonly associated with the Transport and Network Layers, and are discussed in those contexts.

OSI separates devices into two broad categories. An *end system* (ES) is a device at an end point of a communication link. End systems must implement all seven layers of the OSI protocol model. An *intermediate system* (IS; also called an intermediate working unit or an IWU) is a device that routes traffic between end systems, such as a router. An intermediate system typically implements only the lower three layers of the OSI model.

The following sections discuss the protocols selected for the OSI protocol suite, starting at the Physical Layer.

Physical Layer OSI Protocols

The ISO has selected recognizable standards at this layer. Many of them are discussed elsewhere in this book, including X.21, V.35, ISDN, RS-232, and RS-449. Local area network standards include the Physical Layer components of the IEEE 802.3, 802.4, and 802.5 standards.

Data-Link Layer OSI Protocols

HDLC and LAPB have been accepted by the ISO for the Data-Link Layer. Also included are the MAC sublayers of the IEEE 802.3, 802.4, and 802.5 standards. The IEEE 802.2 standard is included as a specification for logical link control.

Network Layer OSI Protocols

Two major classes of service are provided at the Network Layer:

◆ Connection-Oriented Network Service (CONS), implemented using the CCITT X.25 Packet-Level Protocol (PLP)

◆ Connectionless Network Service (CLNS), implemented using OSI's own Connectionless Network Protocol (CLNP)

The relationships of these services and layers to the OSI model are illustrated in figure 5.2.

Figure 5.2

OSI Network Layer services and protocols.

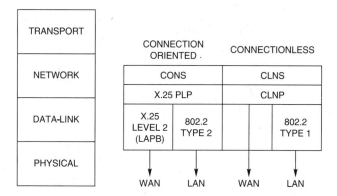

When connection-oriented services are required on LANs, X.25 PLP can be run over IEEE 802.2 Type 2. WAN connection-oriented services are provided by implementing the full X.25 protocol, including LAPB (X.25 Level 2) at the Data-Link Layer.

CLNP can provide connectionless services over wide area networks. To provide similar service on LANs, CLNP is run over IEEE 802.2 Type 1, which provides unacknowledged connectionless service.

The Network Layer is the layer with which network routing is associated. As mentioned earlier, OSI distinguishes between two types of systems: end systems and intermediate systems. This distinction establishes the two types of OSI routing protocols, depicted in figure 5.3:

◆ The ES-IS protocol is concerned only with traffic on the immediate network, and the ES needs to make only relatively simple routing decisions. If the destination ES is on the local network, the ES can transmit its information to the destination. Otherwise, the ES needs simply to select an available IS that can provide the next hop toward the destination ES.

♦ The IS-IS protocol is implemented in ISs, the OSI equivalent of routers. IS-IS is considerably more complicated than ES-IS because it can involve routing traffic through complex internetworks. ISs must be capable of determining which routes are available and promise the greatest efficiency. Because network conditions are dynamic, the algorithms required can be quite involved.

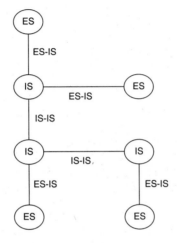

Figure 5.3
OSI routing protocols.

ES = END SYSTEM
IS = INTERMEDIATE SYSTEM

Transport Layer OSI Protocols

The Transport Layer offers a wide variety of types and levels of service. In this section, you examine the five OSI connection-oriented transport protocols, named TP0, TP1, TP2, TP3, and TP4.

Generally, TP0 offers the most rudimentary capabilities, whereas the higher numbered protocols add additional capabilities. Table 5.1 summarizes these capabilities along with the protocols with which they are associated.

Table 5.1
Capabilities of OSI Transport Protocols

	TP0	TP1	TP2	TP3	TP4
Fragmentation and Reassembly	✓	✓	✓	✓	✓
Error recovery		✓		✓	✓
Connection, multiplexing, and demultiplexing			✓	✓	✓
Flow control				✓	✓
Reliable service					✓

The information unit at the OSI Transport Level is the Transport Protocol Data Unit (TPDU).

All OSI transport protocols are capable of performing TPDU fragmentation and reassembly. When a TPDU is larger than can be accepted by an underlying service, the transport layer divides the TPDU into manageable fragments. Fragments are reassembled into the original TPDU at the Transport Layer of the receiving end system.

TP0 performs only packet fragmentation and reassembly, and is most suitable when error detection and recovery are performed at lower protocol layers. When error recovery must be performed at the Transport Layer, TP1, TP3, or TP4 is used. When error recovery is performed, each transmitted TPDU is numbered and receipt is acknowledged by the destination end system. Non-acknowledged TPDUs are retransmitted.

TP2, TP3, and TP4 can perform circuit multiplexing and demultiplexing. This capability manages multiple data streams on the same virtual circuit. This can result in more efficient use of circuit bandwidth and can reduce telecommunication charges by enabling multiple data streams to coexist on the same connection.

Notice that TP3 includes the services of TP1 and TP2, combining error correction with multiplexing/demultiplexing.

TP4 combines the services of the lower-numbered protocols with reliable service. TP4 is a full-duplex, connection-oriented, reliable protocol. When the OSI Transport Layer is running over a connectionless network, TP4 reliable service can deal with many problems that can occur and ensure a more robust communication environment. TP4 is comparable to TCP in the Internet protocol suite.

Session Layer OSI Protocols

The Session Layer is the first layer not concerned with simply delivering information between end systems. The OSI Session Layer protocol is concerned with maintaining well-managed dialogs between end systems. Although such dialogs can be full-duplex, with each system communicating freely with the other, in most cases dialogs are half-duplex with each end system speaking in turn.

Dialogs are managed using a token-passing technique, which has an effect similar to the token-passing access control method introduced in Chapter 2. Token passing ensures that dialogs take place in an orderly manner.

In part, the Session Layer is concerned with executing transactions. A *transaction* is a set of related activities, all of which must be completed to complete the transaction. The OSI Session Layer dialog controls are designed to ensure that all the activities associated with a transaction are completed. If the transaction fails irretrievably, the Session Layer returns the system to its pre-transaction state and signals an error to upper layers. (NetWare's Transaction Tracking System provides similar services to those discussed here.)

Accounting provides the most common example of a transaction. When a check is cashed, two activities must take place without fail: (1) the check amount must be deducted from the payer's checking account, and (2) the exact same amount must be credited to the account in which the check is deposited. If only one of these two related activities takes place, the bank's books are out of balance.

One technique for managing such dialogs is *checkpointing*. Prior to initiation of an activity, the Session Layer takes a checkpoint, a record of conditions prior to the activity. Then, if one of the activities is not reported as being completed, the transaction can be rolled back to the checkpoint and reinitiated. Complex transactions involve multiple checkpoints.

If the two activities in the example are executed on different computers interconnected with a network, it is conceivable that network or system failure can prevent one of the activities from being completed. If the Transport Layer notifies the Session Layer that network errors are excessive, the Session Layer notifies upper layers that the transaction cannot be completed.

Presentation Layer OSI Protocols

Although the OSI Presentation Layer protocol is capable of establishing connections and managing dialogs, this layer typically is implemented as a simple pass-through layer between the Application and Session Layers.

Besides the OSI Presentation Layer protocol, the ASN.1 protocol is frequently implemented at the Presentation and Application Layers. Abstract Syntax Notation One is derived from the CCITT X.409 specification. The purpose of ASN.1 is to establish machine-independent data structures that permit dissimilar computers to communicate.

ASN.1 consists of extensible syntax rules for establishing data types and structures. These rules are described in the Basic Encoding Rules (BER) portion of the ASN.1 standard. Data types encoded in accordance with BER have the following three fields:

◆ The *tag field* identifies the data type (real, character string, Boolean, integer, and so on), a concept that will be familiar to all programmers.

◆ The *length field* specifies the size of the value field in bytes.

◆ The *value field* contains the actual data value.

Figure 5.4 shows how these fields are used to encode a character string value. The values shown will actually be encoded in binary form into the tag, length, and value fields. They are presented in decimal form here for clarity.

TAG	LENGTH	VALUE

TAG = 19 (PRINTABLE STRING)

LENGTH = 4

VALUE = 74 79 72 78 = "JOHN"

Figure 5.4

Example of BER encoding of ASN.1 data types.

The function of the Presentation Layer is to provide a standard data interface between applications and the network. Abstract Syntax Notation One (ASN.1) provides such an interface using the Basic Encoding Rules.

Application Layer OSI Protocols

The Application Layer is home to *Application Service Elements* (ASEs), which provide a communication interface between applications and the lower layer protocols. Prior to discussing several important OSI applications, you will examine three of these ASEs.

Association Control Service Element (ACSE)

This service element enables OSI applications to communicate with one another. Incorporated in each application is an ACSE that establishes a title whereby the application is identified. At the Transport Layer, this application title is associated with a reference number applied to every protocol data unit for that association.

229

Reliable Transfer Service Element (RTSE)

This service element provides an easy-to-use interface between applications and the reliability services provided by the Session Layer. Through RTSE, applications are informed of the success or failure of a transfer.

Remote Operations Service Element (ROSE)

This service element is similar to Remote Procedure Calls. ROSE provides a means of requesting remote operations of a host and enables either end system to function as a performer, which provides remote services.

OSI Applications

Recall that users seldom interact directly with applications in the OSI Application Layer. Rather, these applications provide an interface between user applications and the network services. In this section, you learn about five prominent OSI applications.

Message Handling Systems (MHS)

MHS provides a store-and-forward mechanism for delivering electronic mail and other messages, and is derived from the CCITT recommendation X.400. The ISO set of MHS standards is described as Message Oriented Text Interchange Systems (MOTIS).

As shown in figure 5.5, users and programs request MHS services through a *user agent* (UA) that communicates with a *message transfer system* (MTS). An MTS consists of one or more *message transfer agents* (MTAs) responsible for routing the message to its destination.

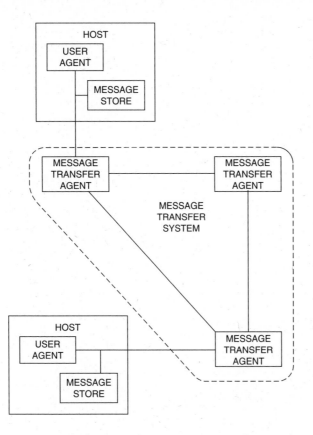

Figure 5.5

Organization of MHS services.

File Transfer, Access, and Management (FTAM)

FTAM is an OSI standard that describes a wide variety of services for accessing files across OSI systems. FTAM *responders* (servers) provide the following services to *initiators* (clients):

◆ **File transfer**—movement of entire files or portions of files between systems

◆ **File access**—reading, writing, erasure, or partial replacement of files

◆ **File management**—creation and deletion of files; management of file attributes

The OSI defined a virtual filestore mechanism. Each real system is responsible for mapping its physical filestore into this virtual model. The virtual filestore serves as a common reference point, enabling systems to exchange files without any knowledge of each other's physical data storage structures. In the virtual filestore are provisions for defining such file characteristics as the file name, owner, attributes, and modification/access dates. The virtual filestore also supports access controls, for example whether files are shareable.

FTAM does not utilize the remote operation services provided by ROSE. Rather, FTAM establishes an association between systems using ACSE. All file operations, such as opening, access, movement, and closing, are performed with reference to this application association.

FTAM is an extremely elaborate file service. Due to this complexity, FTAM generally provides lower performance compared to NFS or FTP (discussed later). Consequently, FTAM is currently implemented less widely than NFS or FTP. However, FTAM is a component of the GOSIP protocol suite defined by the United States government and is expected to grow in popularity. FTAM support is available as an option on NetWare file servers.

Directory Services (DS)

A *directory service* provides a database that contains descriptions for all entities on a network. In addition, a DS provides a variety of security functions ranging from passwords to data encryption. The OSI DS is derived from the CCITT X.500 standards (as is the directory service of the new NetWare 4.0 product).

A wide variety of network entities can be described in the directory services *Directory Information Base* (DIB). Examples are users, hosts, and files. Entities in the DIB are referred to as *objects*, and their characteristics are called *attributes*. The information in the DIB can be accessed by applications such as electronic mail, network management, or end-user applications.

As figure 5.6 illustrates, DIBs can be distributed through a large directory system. *Directory Service Agents* (DSAs) are responsible for accessing and maintaining the information in the DIBs. Users access the DIBs via *Directory User Agents* (DUAs).

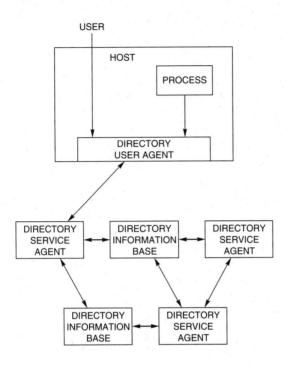

Figure 5.6

Organization of OSI directory services.

 Note Novell has implemented a similar directory service, called *NetWare Directory Service* (NDS) in NetWare 4.*x*.

Virtual Terminal (VT)

Virtual Terminal provides terminal emulation services in mixed-vendor environments. By now, you have seen the term "virtual" used frequently to describe a common model interposed between computer systems. FTAM utilizes a virtual filestore that provides a common point of reference between two different file systems, for example.

A *virtual terminal* is a conceptual representation of a terminal display. Both the host and the terminal emulating device maintain a copy of this model in a data structure called a *conceptual communication area*. The terminal-emulating device and the host maintain their respective virtual terminal images, and the Virtual Terminal

233

protocol ensures that the images are synchronized. This process is illustrated in figure 5.7.

Figure 5.7

Operation of the Virtual Terminal protocol.

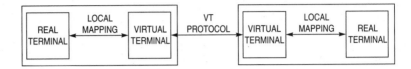

The conceptual communication area consists of the following components:

♦ The *conceptual data store* maintains screen display information and stores information about characters and their positions by column and line (and page on terminals capable of managing multiple screen displays).

♦ The *device object* controls the input/output devices by converting between the virtual terminal representation and the hardware representation required for the terminal.

♦ The *control object* controls other hardware functions, such as the bell.

♦ The *token object* manages the token control mechanism when synchronous communication is employed.

♦ The *parameters object* maintains any parameters that define the communication session, such as character sets and mode (synchronous/asynchronous).

When the terminal and host are communicating via synchronous communication, a single terminal image is maintained as in figure 5.7. A token control updates to this single image to ensure that it is maintained in an orderly manner.

When asynchronous communication is employed, it is necessary to maintain separate input and output structures at each end of the link, as shown in figure 5.8. The terminal-emulating device updates its output image, which in turn updates the input image of the host. The host can read its input image, perform any required actions, and update its output image, which in turn updates the input image of the terminal-emulating device. This mechanism does not require that the input and output images be synchronized, and no token mechanism is required.

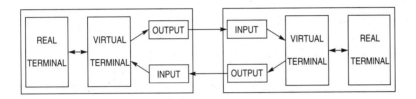

Figure 5.8

Virtual Terminal asynchronous communication.

Common Management Information Protocol (CMIP)

CMIP is the OSI network management application and provides for management in the following areas:

- **Accounting.** Reports on resource usage

- **Performance.** Analyzes and controls network performance characteristics

- **Security.** Controls access to resources

- **Fault management.** Analyzes and corrects network faults

- **Configuration management.** Maintains information about the system configuration

As shown in figure 5.9, each managed device on the network has a CMIP agent that communicates with a manager, which can be located on a host computer or in a specialized network management workstation. Agents can transmit data on a regular basis or in response to commands from the manager. This data is connected in a *Management Information Base* (MIB). Users (network technicians) can interact with the CMIP manager to assess the status of the network. For example, the user can instruct the manager to "get" network utilization information from the MIB or to "set" an alarm threshold level when network utilization exceeds 40 percent.

Figure 5.9

The CMIP network management model.

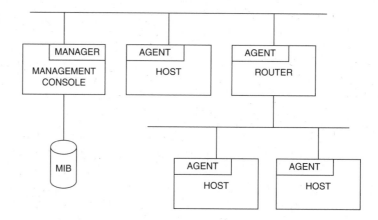

Exploring System Network Architecture (SNA)

 Characterize the major services SNA provides.

For almost 20 years, System Network Architecture has defined IBM's evolving network strategies. SNA is more than a family of protocols, also describing the hardware and Physical Layer components of an IBM network. Although SNA was originally a self-contained set of standards that embraced little that was not IBM, the market has pressured IBM to open SNA to other standards and protocols. Although SNA retains a distinctly IBM flavor, it is now possible to internetwork SNA with most other network environments.

The Organization of SNA

 Discuss the basics of SNA hierarchical terminal-to-host connectivity, which includes Network Addressable Units (SSCP, PU, and LU), mainframe-based networking, sessions, and network management.

 Contrast SNA hierarchical networking with SNA peer-to-peer networking.

SNA networks are organized hierarchically. Figure 5.10 illustrates the general organization of an SNA network. An SNA network consists of *Network Addressable Units* (NAUs). An NAU is a device capable of working in an SNA networking environment. The following are three types of NAUs:

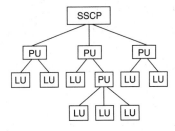

Figure 5.10

The hierarchical organization of SNA networks.

◆ Systems Services Control Point (SSCP)

◆ Physical Units (PUs)

◆ Logical Units (LUs)

A given SNA network can consist of several domains that provide access to different computers and resources. Each domain in a network is organized in a hierarchy that originates from a location called a *Systems Services Control Point*, or SSCP, which controls all connection requests and network flow. Each SNA network is organized around an SSCP.

Every device on an SNA network incorporates a PU, which provides physical connectivity between the devices. Generally speaking, PUs are managed by the SSCP (or by other PUs), and are not directly addressed by programs.

Logical Units are the end points of most SNA communication. LUs can be terminal-type devices, such as 3270 display terminals or printers. However, programs also can communicate with other programs via SNA mechanisms, and such programs also are defined as LUs. LUs, therefore, are not always physical devices, and the name "logical" can be understood in that context. LUs do not network directly, but are dependent on PUs to provide physical connectivity.

LUs are the devices most commonly associated with sessions. A *session* is a formally established communication between two NAUs. The protocols for establishing, maintaining, and tearing down a session are discussed later. Sessions between LUs are called LU-to-LU sessions. A typical terminal session is between a terminal LU and a program LU running on the host.

Mainframe networks are fundamentally different from networks managed by LAN network servers in that there is a hardware division of labor.

Mainframes evolved when terminals were little more than character input/output devices. When you issue a program command from a mainframe terminal (or from a PC running in terminal emulation mode), that request is transmitted to the mainframe's CPU and executed there. When a terminal opens a session on a mainframe, any processing it requests places demands on the mainframe's CPU. In addition to all the tasks performed by a NetWare server (file access, security, network management, and so on), a mainframe CPU must execute all user programs.

Because a mainframe CPU such as an IBM 3090 is quite expensive, it is desirable to offload as much of its responsibility as possible. It is wasteful to have the CPU perform such a repetitious task as polling each LU to determine if it requires attention. This is particularly the case in wide area networks where polling requires an appreciable amount of time. The CPU is required to run the operating system and user's programs, but such things as managing I/O from terminals are tasks that can be performed by less expensive devices. This division of labor is quite common in mainframe networks and is the rule with SNA. It is the responsibility of communication and cluster controllers to make sure that the mainframe communicates with the network as efficiently as possible.

Figure 5.11 illustrates a prototypical IBM SNA network. At the center of the network is a mainframe CPU, in this case one of the 3090 models. Like a NetWare server, the host operates under control of an operating system, which may be MVS (Multiple Virtual Storage), VM (Virtual Machine), or VSE (Virtual Storage Extended).

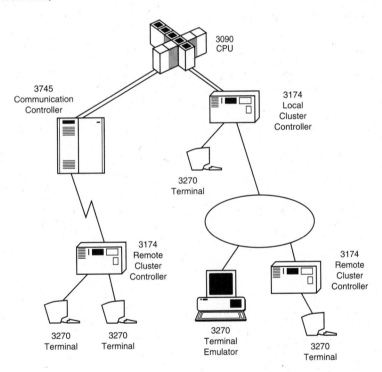

Figure 5.11

Example of an SNA network.

The OS is the heart of the mainframe and manages all other resources. Unlike a LAN operating system such as NetWare, however, a mainframe OS directly performs only the core tasks on the host. Additional programs are required to support user programs, provide security, or manage the network. Before the mainframe can support terminals, a terminal-access support program must be installed on the host. Typically, this is a program called *virtual terminal access method* (VTAM).

As explained earlier, at the heart of an SNA network domain is the Systems Service Control Point (SSCP) that manages access to all services on the network. VTAM is the program most commonly used to implement the SSCP on an IBM mainframe. VTAM runs under the mainframe OS (MVS, VM, or VSE), and is configured with information about the terminals on the network and the resources each terminal can access.

Responsibility for managing the physical connectivity of network devices is assigned to several types of PUs called *communication controllers*. The network in figure 5.11 incorporates three types of communication controllers. In the figure, you see two types of 3174 cluster controllers, which directly support terminals. You also see a 3745 front-end processor that supports wide-area networks.

LUs such as terminals do not connect directly to the mainframe. Rather, they connect to cluster controllers such as the 3174. The cluster controller functions as the primary and the terminals as secondaries in a polled environment. The mainframe is thus relieved of the responsibility of polling the terminals. Two types of cluster controllers exist: local and remote.

Local cluster controllers connect directly to the mainframe via channel connections, which are high speed connections directly into the mainframe's circuitry. Channels offer high performance at high cost over a fairly short range.

Terminals can be connected directly to cluster controllers via links that use the SDLC protocols. Cluster controllers also can support Token Ring attachments.

Token Ring is used increasingly as an alternative for cabling SNA networks. PCs running terminal emulation software can attach to the mainframe via the Token Ring.

A Token Ring also can serve as an SNA backbone, and remote 3174 cluster controllers can be attached to the ring. Cluster controllers that do not attach directly to mainframe channels are called *remote cluster controllers*. Besides attaching to Token Ring networks, remote cluster controllers can be placed at remote sites, connecting through telecommunication links. An example in figure 5.11 is the remote 3174 that is attached to the 3745 front-end processor.

When wide-area networking is required, a front-end processor (also known as a communications controller) such as a 3745 is employed. The 3745 is a powerful computer in its own right, specialized for the purpose of supporting telecommunications networks. A Network Control Program (NCP) relieves the mainframe of much of the responsibility for managing the network wide-area network. At the other end of the telecommunications link, terminals can be serviced by a 3174 remote cluster controller. This cluster controller also can support Token Rings at remote locations. Whenever terminals are situated at remote locations, they must connect to the network through a remote cluster controller at that location.

This has necessarily been a superficial look at the rich SNA network architecture. Not discussed, for example, are recent devices that enable the SNA environment to support Ethernet and TCP/IP protocols. The main intent has been to identify the primary hardware pieces of an IBM network along with key programs that may be running on some of those pieces.

 Study Note Here is a summary of facts that will help you as you examine the remaining material about SNA:

- ◆ SNA is a hierarchical network. Everything branches out from the central Systems Services Control Point (SSCP). Among other functions, the SSCP maps network names to network addresses.

- ◆ An SNA network can be organized in *domains*. Each domain is associated with a separate SSCP.

- ◆ The Virtual Terminal Access Method (VTAM), a program that runs on the mainframe CPU, is the terminal access method most frequently employed on IBM mainframes. VTAM provides SSCP services on the network.

- ◆ Physical Units (PUs) provide physical connectivity on the network and consist of a combination of hardware, firmware (software in Read-Only Memory), and software. Physical units include cluster controllers (3174s) and front-end processors (3745s).

- ◆ Logical Units (LUs) are the end points of network communication and include terminals, printers, and programs that communicate by using SNA.

Physical Unit Types

As mentioned, SNA network devices are called Network Addressable Devices or NAUs, and can be physical devices or programs. Figure 5.12 illustrates the relationship of several types of NAUs. Notice that this figure identifies three types of PUs (types 2, 4, and 5), as well as two types of LUs (2 and 3). These items are defined in this section and in the subsequent section about LU types.

Physical Units, also referred to as *nodes,* are classified by number into types. You already have encountered these devices and have seen how they are organized into a network hierarchy. The PU or node types discussed in the following paragraphs are useful to know.

PU type 5 is a physical unit in a node running the SSCP (VTAM). VTAM uses tables that contain information about the devices on a network along with the services and applications available to each device.

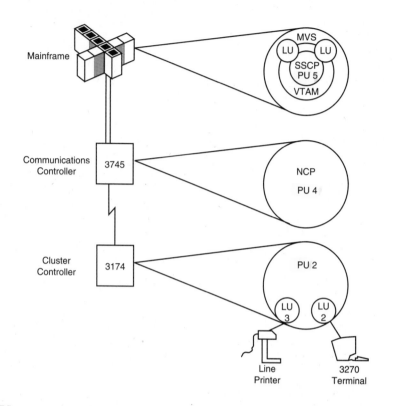

Figure 5.12

Organization and types of Network Addressable Units.

PU type 4 is a physical unit running in a device running NCP. Such devices are called communication controllers or front-end processors. A common example is the 3745. A front-end processor is responsible for managing remote communication resources. Tables utilized by the NCP include information about telecommunication links, remote cluster controllers, and so forth.

PU type 2 is a *peripheral node*, typically a cluster controller such as a 3174.

 Notice that PU (or node) type 5 is located at the host. PU type numbers count down until PU type 2, which is the PU that interfaces with terminal LUs.

Logical Unit Types

Logical Units are similarly classified by types. Table 5.2 summarizes these types.

Table 5.2
Logical Unit Types

LU Type	Communication	Notes
0	Program-to-program	Defined by the implementation.
1	Program-to-device	Master/slave SNA character stream data on printers, hard copy terminals.
2	Program-to-device	Master/slave 3270 data streams to terminals.
3	Program-to-device	Master/slave 3270 data streams to printers.
4	Program-to-program	Master/slave or peer-to-peer or program-to-device SNA character stream to printer.
6 & 6.1	Program-to-program	Peer-to-peer Inter-program communication (such as CICS-CICS, IMS-IMS, CICS-IMS).
6.2	Program-to-program	Peer-to-peer Advanced Program-to-Program Communication (APPC). A generalized task-to-task interface using General Data Stream (GDS).
7	Program-to-device	5250 data streams to terminals on AS/400, System 36, System 38.

You will encounter frequent references to 3270 data streams, which are used to communicate with terminals on IBM mainframes. When a user wants to connect a workstation as a terminal on an IBM mainframe, the PC emulates an IBM terminal by running software (possibly along with additional hardware) that enables it to generate 3270 data streams. This is frequently referred to simply as *3270 terminal emulation*.

Program-to-device LU types are the older types listed. They relate to the origins of mainframes, having powerful CPUs and unintelligent terminals. As peripheral devices have become more powerful, they have gained the capability to participate as peers in the network. The most recent LU types, in particular LU 6.2, enable processes on hosts and workstations to function as peers. Advanced program-to-program communication is a generalized task-to-task interface supporting generalized communication and data transfer.

Sessions

A *session* is a logical connection between two NAUs. Sessions are established to enable NAUs to communicate. When a user connects to a mainframe resource, an LU-to-LU session is established between an LU on the mainframe and the user's terminal LU.

The LU on the host is designated as the primary LU (PLU) and is responsible for error recovery.

The peripheral LU is designated as the secondary LU (SLU).

To establish a session, a user at a terminal LU issues a *bind request* to the host. The host issues a *bind message* that establishes the session. The node that issues the bind message becomes the PLU, whereas the node that receives the bind message is the SLU.

The nature of the session is determined by parameters in the VTAM table, which define the characteristics of the LUs involved. The VTAM table contains information about the types of the LUs (terminal or printer, for example) as well as information about display features and other pertinent characteristics.

A secondary LU accepts a bind only when the characteristics specified in the bind message match the characteristics of the SLU.

 A *bind* is the process of establishing an SNA session.

The SNA Layered Protocol Architecture

Although SNA is a layered protocol suite, it predates the OSI Reference Model and does not map directly to the OSI model's layers. Figure 5.13 illustrates the layers of the SNA protocols with relation to the OSI Reference Model.

Figure 5.13

SNA protocols' layers compared to the OSI Reference Model.

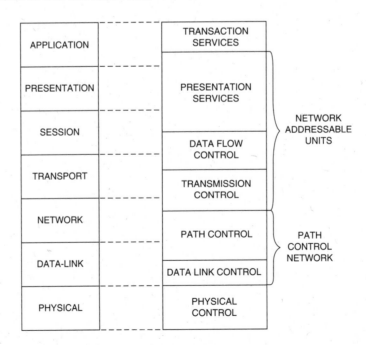

SNA and the OSI Reference Model

Although the SNA architecture does not correspond directly with the layers of the OSI Reference Model, you can make some comparisons.

1. The SNA Physical Control Layer is analogous with the OSI Physical Layer. Both are concerned with the electrical, mechanical, interface, and control characteristics of the physical transmission medium.

2. The SNA Data-Link Control Layer corresponds closely with the OSI Data-Link Layer. SNA utilizes the SDLC protocol to implement master/slave communication links. IEEE 802.5 (Token Ring) also is employed in SNA at the Physical and Data-Link Layers.

   The Data-Link Control Layer constructs link headers and trailers, controls frame transfers, checks for errors, and retransmits frames as required.

3. The SNA Path Control Layer is responsible for routing, datagram fragmentation and reassembly, and flow control. It, therefore, performs functions from the OSI Data-Link and Network Layers.

4. The SNA Transmission Control Layer provides reliable end-to-end communications and is comparable to the OSI Transport Layer. The SNA Transmission Control also performs such presentation layer services as data encryption. It also controls the pacing of data transmission, sequence checking, and error recovery.

5. The SNA Data Flow Layer corresponds to the OSI Session Layer and is responsible for the orderly management of sessions and flow of data.

6. The SNA Presentation Services Layer provides data translation services similar to the OSI Presentation Layer. It also provides services regarding application-to-application communication, sessions, configurations, and network management.

247

7. The Transaction Services Layer is similar to the OSI Application Layer and provides a variety of application services. SNA distribution service (SNADS) is an example of such a service, providing a distribution service for use by applications.

SNA Functional Areas

Figure 5.13 shows how SNA functions are divided into two general classes:

◆ Path Control Network (layers 2 and 3) functions include message routing and data flow through the network.

◆ Network Addressable Units (layers 4, 5, and 6) are responsible for network control and management. These functions are provided by VTAM.

Advanced Peer-to-Peer Networking

The SNA hierarchical structure evolved when peripherals were quite limited in processing power. Under the old terminal-host model, a PC that connects to the mainframe must run terminal-emulation software that relegates it to the role of a terminal; most of the PC's processing power goes dormant.

Intelligent computing devices have become quite common in recent years. Among other things, Advanced Peer-to-Peer Networking (APPN) takes advantage of this fact. APPN enables devices on the network to sidestep the hierarchical network consisting of communication controllers and static VTAM definition tables.

LU type 6.2 and PU type 2.1 are the new node types that enable APPN on an SNA network. The relationship of these node types in APPN is illustrated in figure 5.14. APPN has several characteristics and features as follows:

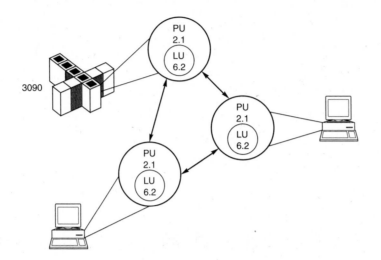

Figure 5.14

Advanced Peer-to-Peer Networking.

◆ Advanced Peer-to-Peer Communications enables nodes on diverse systems to engage in cooperative processing.

◆ Each APPN node is configured as a PU type 2.1, which enables it to participate in dynamic network routing. These devices advertise themselves on the network and update their routing tables dynamically, sidestepping the static tables used by VTAM.

◆ LU 6.2 nodes can engage in multiple sessions with multiple LUs at a given time. They are not limited to single sessions as were prior LU types.

◆ LU 6.2 is more efficient than previous protocols. Prior to LU 6.2, file transfers used the same protocols as were employed to transfer screen formatting data. These protocols were not very robust and block sizes were limited. LU 6.2 file transfers are more robust and efficient, and are many times faster. LU 6.2 sessions exchange display and keyboard information only when required. LU 6.2 terminals, for example, will likely be configured to produce their own displays, transferring to the host only the information required to initiate a transaction.

◆ In a peer-to-peer session, both LU 6.2 nodes can initiate error recovery. Previously, an error at the host aborted the session because the secondary LU could not initiate error recovery.

◆ Cooperative processing means that processing for a task can be spread across two or more nodes. As modern networks grow to encompass more and more intelligent nodes, distributed processing promises to make more efficient use of the processing power available on the entire network.

◆ Improved security procedures can be invoked in mid-process in addition to login security. Auditing processes can be made part of the session.

SNA Network Management

One of the most powerful tools available for network management is Netview, a comprehensive tool that IBM has gradually enhanced to support management of SNA and non-SNA networks. Netview provides the following network management functions:

◆ Problem management collects network problem reports from network devices and manages the process of problem resolution.

◆ Performance and accounting management collects network performance data.

◆ Configuration management records information about the configuration of devices on the network. This information can be cross-referenced during the process of problem resolution.

◆ Change management records information about changes to hardware, firmware, and software systems. In many cases, changes can be downloaded to network devices under central control.

Defining Digital Network Architecture (DNA)

Identify the principal organizations that promulgate and/or champion DNA and its target environments.

Like SNA, the *Digital Network Architecture* (DNA) began life as a proprietary standard for managing terminal-host networks. Both architectures define hardware and protocols for implementing a network and both are widely accepted as a result of the popularity of their respective computer systems.

At one time, Digital Equipment Corporation was happy to refer to itself as DEC. More recently, however, the official preference has been to use Digital as the corporation nickname, and the name Digital is used in this book. However, you frequently will encounter continued use of DEC.

In recent years, pressure has increased to open the architectures of both SNA and DNA. The response of Digital Equipment Corporation has been to base the latest incarnation of DNA on the OSI standard.

DNA Phase V Protocols

Identify the major services provided by DNA.

251

DNA Phase V supports OSI protocols but provides compatibility with older systems by supporting select protocols from earlier DNA phases. Figure 5.15 depicts the relationship of the DNA Phase V protocols to the OSI Reference Model.

Figure 5.15

DNA Phase V protocols related to the OSI Reference Model.

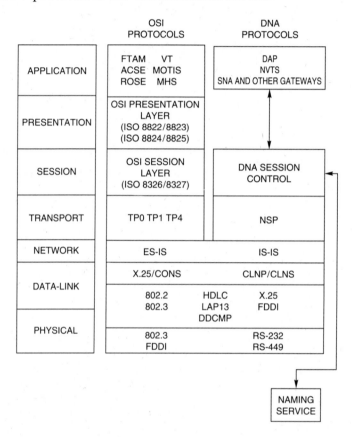

In figure 5.15, you can see that DNA Phase V supports two distinct stacks of protocols above the Session Layer. One stack incorporates OSI-compliant protocols, whereas the other incorporates Digital proprietary protocols.

At and below the Transport Layer, DNA Phase V also supports protocols from the OSI and Digital environments, but the degree of integration is much greater.

Identify the characteristics of DNA.

DNA Physical Layer Protocols

A variety of international standards has been selected for the Physical Layer, including IEEE 802.3, FDDI, and EIA RS-232C and RS-449. Digital has long been a participant in the development of Ethernet. (Digital is among the three manufacturers that contributed their name to the "DIX" connector, the others being Intel and Xerox.)

DNA Data-Link Layer Protocols

The Digital Data Communications Message Protocol (DDCMP) dates from the earliest DNA phases and remains an option in DNA Phase V. DDCMP is a versatile byte-count protocol with the following capabilities:

♦ Operation on synchronous or asynchronous lines.

♦ Point-to-point or multipoint operation with one station operating as a primary and the others operating as secondaries.

♦ Polling mechanisms to arbitrate access in environments where multiple stations can transmit; secondaries must be polled by a primary before they are permitted to transmit.

♦ Acknowledgment of all messages; a CRC mechanism is used to detect errors. Correctly received messages are acknowledged positively; incorrectly received messages result in a negative acknowledgment (NAK).

   DDCMP numbers all messages and permits an acknowledgment to multiple messages. To improve efficiency, DDCMP provides a mechanism that enables message acknowledgments to piggyback on other transmissions.

Other protocols employed by DNA Phase V at the Data-Link Layer are as follows:

◆ IEEE 802.2 and 802.3

◆ HDLC

◆ LAPB

◆ X.25

◆ FDDI

DNA Network Level Protocols

DNA provides connectionless service via the OSI CLNS service and CLNP protocol. DNA Phase V implements the OSI ES-IS and IS-IS routing protocols.

Connection-oriented service is provided by CONS and X.25 PLP (Packet Level Protocol).

Recall from Chapter 3 that a gateway is a device that performs protocol conversion at any protocol layer above the Network Layer. As shown in figure 5.16, DNA X.25 services are examples of such a gateway.

To enable X.25 communication, an X.25 Gateway Access Module is incorporated in the host as an application level service. This module enables user applications to interface with the X.25 gateway.

The gateway incorporates two protocol stacks. On the host side, you will recognize a conventional OSI protocol stack. On the side communicating with the X.25 Public Data Network (PDN), the gateway implements X.25 protocols at levels 2 and 3. A DNA X.25 server module interfaces the OSI protocol stack with the X.25 protocol stack.

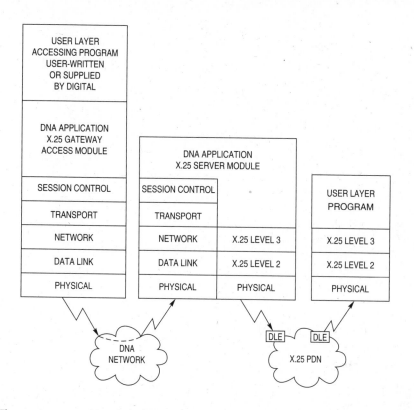

Figure 5.16

Implementation of a DNA X.25 gateway.

The remote system implements the same DNA X.25 protocol stack to interface with the PDN.

X.25 services are implemented through an X.25 gateway. DNA X.25 services are implemented with four modules. These modules are described in table 5.3.

Table 5.3
DNA X.25 Service Modules

Module	Layer	Description
X.25 Gateway	Application	Runs on host. Access module enables host-resident user programs to interface with X.25.

continues

Table 5.3, Continued

Module	Layer	Description
		Communicates as a peer with gateway-based Gateway Access Module.
X.25 Server	Application	Runs on X.25 gateway. Module Enables gateway-resident programs to interface with X.25. Communicates as a peer with host-based Gateway Access Module.
X.25 Level 3	Network	Provides X.25 packet (packet-level) level functions. Module Enables X.25 Server Module to access X.25 Public Data Network (PDN).
X.25 Level 2	Data-Link	Enables connection-(LAPB). Module oriented service with DCE interface with the PDN.

DNA Transport Layer Protocols

DNA Phase V supports TP0, TP2, and TP4 selected from the ISO 8073 standard.

In addition, DNA Phase V supports Digital's own NSP (Network Services Protocol), which is similar to TP4. NSP has the following characteristics:

- Is connection-oriented
- Provides message fragmentation and reassembly
- Provides flow control
- Has two full-duplex, flow-controlled communication subchannels for normal and expedited messages
- Has congestion control to limit traffic on the communication channel

For connectionless service (CLNS) DNA supports NSP and TP4.

For connection-oriented service (CONS) DNA supports TP0, TP2, and TP4.

 Digital's NSP protocol is similar in function to TP4.

DNA Session Layer Protocols

DNA Phase V supports the OSI Session Layer protocol (ISO 8326/8327).

Also supported is the DNA Session Control Layer for support of Digital proprietary application protocols. The DNA Session Control Layer has the following three functional parts:

- **Connection Control** establishes, maintains, and performs the orderly tear down of transport connections.
- **Address Resolution** associates DNA object names with the addresses of the services provided by various protocols. This also interfaces with the DNA Naming Service.

257

♦ **Address Selection** utilizes the addresses provided by the address resolution service and works with connection control to define a protocol stack that matches the requirements of both the local and remote systems.

As you can see, DNA Phase V makes the process of selecting addresses and establishing protocol stacks dynamic. Prior to Phase V, static tables were required that mapped node names to addresses.

This dynamic character is made possible by the DNA Phase V Naming Service, which maintains a directory of the names of all objects with network-wide significance. Each name in the directory is associated with a set of attributes that can be used to make address resolution and address selection determinations.

The DNA Naming Service is provided by *nameservers*, which can be replicated in several locations on the network. The nameservers are continually updated to maintain synchronization of the various replicated copies of the directories.

The operation of DNA Naming Services is illustrated in figure 5.17. All systems must have a *clerk*, which provides the system's interface with the Transaction Agent of the Naming Service. Nameservers advertise themselves to the clerks, and clerks can query an appropriate nameserver for name-to-service mappings. The figure also illustrates the update mechanism whereby the replicated copies of the directories are updated by update senders and update listeners.

DNA Phase V session management is based on a distributed naming service. The services discussed provide functions similar to the SSCP in the SNA architecture. A significant difference exists, however.

SNA is a hierarchical network with a single control point (the SSCP) in any given domain. If the host for that SSCP fails, all network services in the domain fail.

DNA session control is managed by a distributed naming service. To the extent that data is replicated on multiple nameservers, the network is less affected by node failures. No single failure can disable the entire naming service.

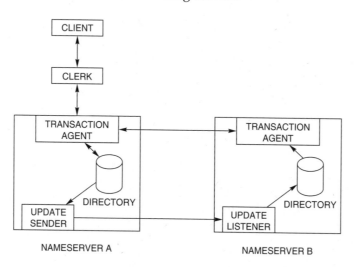

Figure 5.17

Operation of the DNA Session Control Layer.

DNA Presentation Layer Protocols

DNA applications utilize the DNA Session Control Layer. Some Presentation Layer functions are performed by the applications themselves.

OSI applications utilize the OSI Presentation Layer protocols.

DNA Application Layer Protocols

The following applications are supported under DNA Phase V:

- ◆ ACSE
- ◆ ROSE

259

◆ FTAM

◆ VT

◆ MHS

◆ CMIP/CMIS

 DNA supports the OSI ACSE and ROSE protocols at the Application Layer.

DNA Phase V also supports a number of applications specific to the DNA environment:

◆ **Data Access Protocol (DAP)** supports file system operations (file creation, deletion, retrieval, and so on). DAP supports use of indexed files by database applications. DAP also has the capability to execute command files on remote systems.

◆ **Network Virtual Terminal Service** provides terminal services among dissimilar systems. All data is translated into a network terminal command format before being transmitted on the network. Each host translates data from the common command format to suit its own requirements.

◆ **Mail-11** provides electronic mail capability on DEC systems and has gateways into X.400 and other external mail systems.

◆ **SNA Gateway** provides 3270 terminal emulation, *remote job entry* capability (enabling users of the Digital host to submit jobs to be processed by the IBM host), and data transfer between the Digital VMS (Virtual Memory System) and IBM MVS environments. The gateway also enables user-written programs to interface with SNA sessions.

◆ **VMS services for MS-DOS** enable a VMS host to operate as a file server supporting DOS-based PCs.

Digital's approach to network management is called the *Enterprise Management Architecture* (EMA). Not surprisingly, given Digital's commitment to OSI, EMA is based on the CMIP protocol.

EMA consists of *entities* (devices to be managed) and *directors*, which perform network management functions. The director executes in a management console through which a network manager accesses EMA services.

Each entity incorporates an agent that collects information about the entity. This information is forwarded to directors. Agents also can be configured to generate network alarms.

A DNA Maintenance Operations Protocol (MOP) performs software maintenance on network devices. MOP can download system software to devices on the network including workstations and terminal servers. MOP also has the capability of testing communication links and controlling remote stations.

Exploring the Internet Protocol Suite

 Identify the principal organizations that promulgate and/or champion the Internet protocols and their target environment(s).

Transmission Control Protocol (TCP) and Internet Protocol (IP) are simply the best known protocols of a protocol suite referred to here as the Internet protocol suite. The Internet protocols frequently are referred to as TCP/IP despite the fact that many other protocols are also suite components. This section defines the most commonly used protocols in the suite.

As you learn about the Internet protocol suite, you will notice that the lower Data-Link and Physical Layers are not included. The Internet protocol suite deliberately does not define these layers so that the suite can interoperate with many different Link and Physical Layer implementations. In other words, TCP/IP can run over Ethernet, Token Ring, Token Bus, HDLC, and X.25 systems with minor configuration adjustments. This flexibility accounts for the Internet Protocol's successful integration.

The TCP/IP protocols are used to interconnect multiple LANs. TCP/IP is a connection-oriented, end-to-end protocol implemented over a wide range of communication links. This protocol suite provides interconnection service plus a wide range of other services, such as file transfer protocol (FTP), simple mail transfer protocol (SMTP), and terminal services (TELNET). The TCP/IP protocols have been implemented for LANs as well as mainframes. TCP/IP has become a de facto standard for interconnecting LANs and devices by governmental agencies, commercial businesses, and universities.

 Identify the services provided by the major Internet protocols.

TCP/IP offers several services for user connections. These services include facilities to control data transfer, reliability, flow control, multiplexing, connections, and security.

The Origins of the Internet Protocol Suite

At the end of the 1960s, various American universities and research agencies had a great need for a network that would allow nationwide utilization of their existing systems. Among the top priorities was a facility for data exchange. The Advanced Research Project Agency (ARPA) established the ARPANET to develop the design, implementation, and use of a network technology that would provide a means for existing networks to communicate, originally using a packet-switched network with a point-to-point telephone link backbone.

ARPA became known as DARPA (Department of Defense Advanced Research Project Agency) because it was created as a U.S. government organization that promoted primarily projects of military interest. Today, ARPANET is a subnetwork of the world-wide TCP/IP Internet. Currently, hundreds of other large TCP/IP networks in both research and industry are interconnected.

The first proposal for ARPANET included four Internet Message Processors (IMPs) located at the University of California in Los Angeles (UCLA) and the University of California in Santa Barbara (UCSB), the Stanford Research Institute (SRI), and the University of Utah. The contract was won by Bolt, Beranek, and Newman (BBN). BBN has had a strong influence on the development of TCP/IP.

The Internet Activities Board (IAB) was set up by DARPA to organize research for the Internet. The IAB publishes Request for Comment (RFCs), which specifies the protocols that make up the Internet protocol suite. Specific issues regarding protocols are defined in an RFC, and this information often becomes a functional part of the protocol suite. Maintenance of the RFC library is done in the Network Information Center (NIC) of SRI.

Another reason for the success of TCP/IP in the UNIX world was a result of the University of California at Berkeley undertaking an implementation of TCP/IP on behalf of DARPA for its own UNIX systems. This was called 4.2 BSD (Berkeley System Distribution). The source code for this implementation was made available as public domain software in 1983. All research results and developments are available to anyone for a nominal fee.

The U.S. government has decreed that for the parts of Internet under its jurisdiction, all Internet Protocols will eventually be replaced by the Government Open Systems Interconnection Profile suite (GOSIP). However, because the implementation of TCP/IP is so widespread, the conversion is not being forced.

Comparing the Internet Protocol Blueprint

Sticking with the basic comparison to the OSI model, you can see that much of the Internet model maps to the OSI Reference Model. Keep in mind that the OSI model came about almost ten years after the Internet model.

The following sections discuss the four layers in the Internet model.

 Identify the characteristics of the major Internet protocols.

Layer 1: Network

This layer takes its characteristics from previously defined lower-layer protocols, such as Ethernet and X.25.

Layer 2: Internet

The Internet Layer acts much as the Network Layer of the OSI model. Implementation of the IP and ICMP protocols occurs at this level.

Layer 3: Host-to-Host

This layer performs the same functions as the Transport Layer of the OSI model and some functions of the Session Layer as well. TCP and UDP headers are added at this layer.

Layer 4: Process/Application

The topmost layer, Process/Application, compares to the Application and Presentation Layers and most of the Session Layer of the OSI model. TELNET (Virtual Terminal Emulation), FTP and TFTP (File Transfer Protocol and Trivial File Transfer Protocol), and SMTP (Simple Mail Transfer Protocol) are implemented at Layer 4.

Figure 5.18 illustrates the relationship between the OSI model and the Internet model.

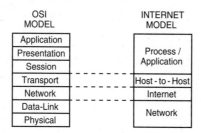

OSI MODEL		INTERNET MODEL
Application		Process / Application
Presentation		
Session		
Transport		Host - to - Host
Network		Internet
Data-Link		Network
Physical		

Figure 5.18

A comparison of the Internet model and the OSI model.

Investigating Internet Packet Architecture

Identify/label the fields and field functions of IP and TCP packets.

Figure 5.19 illustrates the fields that comprise an IP packet. Remember that the packet is a continuous string of ones (1) and zeros (0). The graphic displays the fields in 32-bit segments, also known as *words*.

IP is responsible for routing information across the network. When packets are too large and need to be sent in smaller portions, or *fragments*, the IP is responsible for fragmenting the packets, then reassembling them at the destination. Because multiple routes can be taken to the destination, fragments can arrive at the destination out of order. IP headers (the IP packet) contain information so that fragments can be reassembled in the correct order.

IP cannot perform routing without the help of routing tables. Several protocols maintain and initialize routing tables. One of these protocols, Routing Information Protocol (RIP), is discussed at the end of this section.

Figure 5.19

Format of an IP packet.

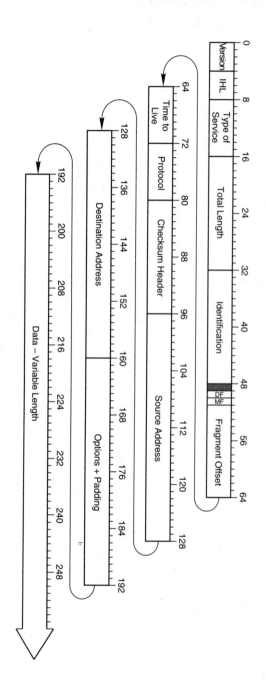

You should be aware of the following characteristics of IP packets:

- ◆ Provide nonguaranteed, connectionless delivery of packets at the Transport (Host-to-Host) Layer
- ◆ Also are called Transport Protocol Data Units (TPDU)
- ◆ Can be fragmented when the message is long
- ◆ Comprise an IP Header for each fragment
- ◆ Also are known as the IP headers

The following sections detail each field of an IP packet.

Version

Length: 4 bits

The Version field contains the revision number of the protocol. Both the sending node and the receiving node, as well as routers, must agree on the version of IP Header they are using.

The current version of IP is four.

IP Header Length (IHL)

Length: 4 bits

The IHL specifies the entire length of the datagram header, measured in 32-bit words. A header that does not use the Options field is five words long.

Type of Service

Length: 8 bits

The Type of Service field is used by upper-layer protocols to tell IP how to handle a datagram.

Figure 5.20 shows the order of the bits in the Type of Service Field. The functions of the bits in this field are summarized in table 5.4.

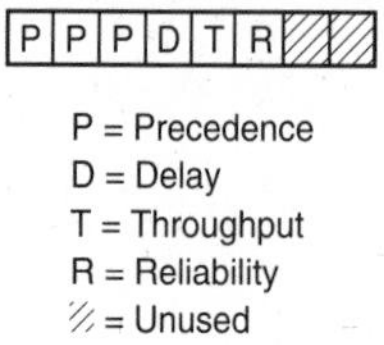

Figure 5.20

Order of bits in the
Type of Service Field.

P P P D T R ///

P = Precedence
D = Delay
T = Throughput
R = Reliability
/// = Unused

Precedence

The first three bits designate the importance of the packet. Zero is normal importance, and seven is the highest priority.

Delay

When set to one, the fourth bit requests a low delay. Voice traffic routes over low delay lines. This bit is set to zero for normal processing.

Throughput

When set to one, the fifth bit requests high throughput. Long file transfers make use of this bit. When set to zero this bit requests normal throughput.

Reliability

When set to one, the sixth bit requests high reliability. Information transfer that relies on data reaching the destination, such as banking transfers, uses this bit. When set to zero, this bit requests normal reliability.

The final two bits are unused and remain set to zero for all transactions. Most commercial versions of TCP/IP do not use Type of Service.

Table 5.4
Type of Service Field

Bits	Description	Values
0-2	Precedence	0 - 7
3	Delay	0 - Normal 1 - Low
4	Throughput	0 - Normal 1 - High
5	Reliability	0 - Normal 1 - High
6-7	Reserved for future use	

Length

Length: 16 bits

This field specifies the size, measured in bytes, of the entire IP packet.

Identification

Length: 8 bits

This field is used to determine which fragments belong together.

Flags

Length: 3 bits

This field is used to determine the order of the current fragment. Bit one is reserved and is always set to zero. Bits two and three are used in several possible combinations as shown in table 5.5.

Table 5.5
Usage of Bits in the IP Packet Flag Field

Bit 1	Bit 2	Bit 3
Reserved	0 - May Fragment	0 - Last Fragment
	1 - Do not Fragment	1 - More Fragments

Fragment Offset

Length: 13 bits

When a router fragments a datagram, each break must be aligned. This field contains the distance of this fragment's data from the start of the original datagram.

Time-To-Live (TTL)

Length: 8 bits

This field designates the length of time that the current datagram can exist on the Internet. Each router to which the packet goes is responsible for decrementing the TTL. The maximum number is 255, which equates to 4.25 minutes. Time is relative to the internetwork, so many routers decrease only one from the total. Slower routes may decrease this number by more than one. The packet must reach its destination before the TTL counter is decremented to a zero value.

Protocol

Length: 8 bits

This field designates the upper-layer protocol to receive the TPDU after IP has finished its processing. TCP has a value of six, and UDP has a value of 17.

Header Checksum

Length: 16 bits

This figure is computed on the entire header to ensure the integrity of the data. This number is recomputed each time it is forwarded because the TTL is updated at each router.

Source and Destination Addresses

These fields contain the software IP addresses for the sender and receiver. IP addresses are expressed in four byte dotted decimal notation. These addressses also are divided into five classes, summarized in figure 5.21.

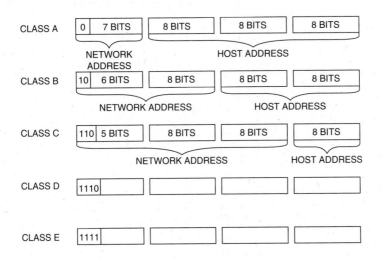

Figure 5.21

Address structures for IP address classes.

Class A

A Class A address starts with the numbers 0 to 127. Expressed in binary form, this is a bit pattern that always starts with zero. In a Class A address, the first byte designates the network address, and the last three bytes designate the host address. Class A addresses are used for networks with a huge number of hosts.

271

Class B

Class B addresses start with the numbers 128 to 191. Expressed in binary form, this is a bit pattern that always starts with one, and then zero. The first two bytes in a Class B address designate the network address, and the second two bytes identify the host address. Medium-to-large sized networks, like those found in universities and large companies, use Class B addresses.

Class C

Class C addresses start with the numbers 192 to 223. Expressed in binary form, this is a bit pattern that always starts with 110. The first three bytes in a Class C address designate the network address and the last byte identifies the host address. Small networks use this class address.

Class D

Class D addresses start with the numbers 224 to 239. Expressed in binary form, this is a bit pattern that always starts with 1110. Class D addresses are used for multicast packets.

Class E

Class E addresses start with the numbers 240 to 255. Expressed in binary form, this is a bit pattern that always starts with 1111. Class E addresses are reserved for experimentation.

Another facet of IP network addressing is the capability to create *subnetworks* from one assigned network address. RFC950 describes the details of subnetting. Subnets allow part of the host address to be used for a broader range of network addresses. NetWare users can equate subnets to Inherited Rights Masks (IRM). Both the subnet mask and the IRMs act as filters, through which items flow.

Options

Length: Variable up to 320 bits

The Options field supports optional services. These services include: source route information, timestamps, and Department of Defense security options.

Studying the Architecture of a TCP Packet

TCP is:

◆ Considered to be the primary Internet transport protocol

◆ Acknowledged, full-duplex, connection-oriented, and flow-controlled

The next item in the internetwork packet is the TCP header. The TCP header is where the information is located for the continuous flow of data between the ULP (upper-layer protocol) and the Host-to-Host Layer where TCP resides. Figure 5.22 shows the actual contents of the TCP header.

Figure 5.22

TCP header format.

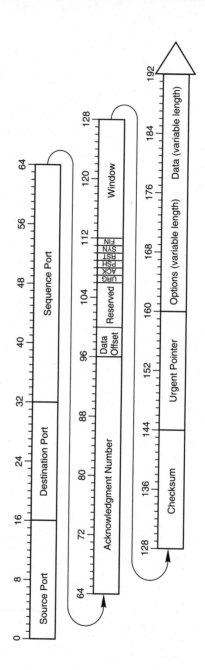

◆ **SYN** (Synchronize) creates a virtual connection between the sender and receiver. The sender sends a packet with the SYN bit set and a sequence number (A). The receiver sends back a packet with the flags SYN and ACK for acknowledgment. The acknowledge field is sequence number (A)+1, and a new sequence number is from this packet (B). The original sender responds only with the ACK and an acknowledge number of (B)+1.

◆ **FIN** (Finish) shows that no more data is to be sent, and the connection can be released.

Window

Length: 16 bits

The window dictates how many bytes the sender is prepared to receive.

TCP uses the Sliding Window Flow Control mechanism to decide how much the node can send or receive.

The Window field also relies on the Sequence Number field and the Acknowledgment Number field to work.

The sender can have an available window of 80 bytes. Another node can send multiple packets that do not exceed 80 bytes before an acknowledgment is sent. As the receiving node is busy with other processes, it can lower its window for accepting data. When busy, the receiver can lower its window temporarily to zero. The sending node is notified of a full buffer if it attempts to send too many bytes.

The Sliding Window is full-duplex.

Checksum

Length: 16 bits

The *checksum* is a calculated field from a portion of the IP header and TCP header along with the TCP header length. This ensures that the packets are sent correctly. If a packet's checksum does not match up, the packet is discarded.

Urgent Pointer

Length: 16 bits

The *urgent pointer* is a data offset pointing to where urgent data is found in the packet.

Options

Length: Variable

The options provide a capability for special options like maximum TCP segment size.

Data

The Data field contains all data being sent and received by upper-layer protocols.

Identifying the Structure of the User Datagram Protocol

The User Datagram Protocol (UDP) is used in place of TCP. It is not connection-oriented and does not acknowledge received data, so it has considerably less overhead. UDP's main function is to accept and move datagrams passed to it from upper-layer protocols. Figure 5.23 shows the fields of a UDP packet.

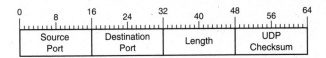

Figure 5.23
UDP Packet fields.

Source Port

Length: 16 bits

The source port is a number assigned to the particular Upper Layer Protocol (ULP), such as TFTP. A list of those assigned numbers is found in RFC "Assigned Numbers."

Destination Port

Length: 16 bits

The destination port is also a number like the source port but comes from the destination host instead.

Length

Length: 16 bits

This field specifies the size, measured in bytes, of the entire TCP packet.

UDP Checksum

This field is optional and covers the entire datagram and a "pseudo-header." This header is obtained by asking the Internet Layer to find the IP address. This is in violation of OSI standards.

TCP provides the following services not provided by UDP:

◆ Controls data flow

◆ Establishes connections

UDP's primary advantage over TCP is that UDP provides a faster data throughput.

IP fragmentation occurs when the TPDU is too large, as can happen when NFS sends a UDP packet over Ethernet. Ethernet allows packets as large as 1.5KB, and NFS sends 8KB UDP datagrams.

Similarly, when internetwork routing paths are of a different nature, packets frequently must be fragmented.

Investigating Additional Protocols for the Internet

You must be aware of additional important protocols within TCP/IP because of their overall effect on TCP/IP. These are discussed in the following sections.

Remote Terminal Emulation—TELNET

TELNET enables a computer to emulate a terminal for connection to a host-based application. Most personal computers have more intelligence than is required by host-based computing systems. TELNET allows the computer to behave like a terminal. More RFCs have been written for TELNET than for any other protocol because virtually hundreds of different input devices exist, each with a complex emulation procedure.

File Transport Protocol (FTP) and Trivial File Transfer Protocol (TFTP)

FTP allows files to be transferred across hosts. It is even possible for Host C to transfer files from host A to host B. FTP requires a login and specific file rights. TFTP does not require a login, therefore the overhead decreases. However, you are only allowed to transfer files that any other user can transfer, which is a specific set of rights in UNIX.

Simple Mail Transfer Protocol (SMTP)

SMTP is the electronic mail engine used between network hosts. A separate user application interface must be used in conjunction with SMTP. SMTP uses UDP and IP to route messages.

Routing Information Protocol (RIP)

RIP is used to update a host's routing information table. Without the RIP function on a network host, systems could not be in contact with each other. RIP broadcasts periodically advertise routing information for a network host. This routing information includes the distance between hosts in terms of hops. A *hop* occurs each time a packet traverses a router. Hop count is a crude estimate of the time required—sometimes called the "cost"—to route a packet by a particular path.

Network File System (NFS)

NFS gives host systems the capability to mount another host's hard drive such that it can be accessed in the same way as a local hard drive directory. NFS was developed by Sun Microsystems on the ONC platform (Open Network Computing). The three protocols associated with ONC are NFS, XDR (External Data Representation), and RPC (Remote Procedure Call). By popular naming, all three protocols have been rolled into the NFS name.

NFS has become a powerful tool in network computing, especially because of hardware pricing over the past few years. Because some larger host systems' hard drive prices are so extreme, people are turning to the NFS solution to centralize their data on a PC-type system or LAN, thereby cutting cost overhead on proprietary disk drives.

eXternal Data Representation (XDR)

XDR is a set of library routines that supports the C programming language. A C programmer can take information from one system to another using XDR without having to worry about one host system platform being different from another host.

 TCP/IP's XDR is comparable to OSI's ASN.1 protocol.

Remote Procedure Calls (RPCs)

RPCs enable systems to search for information from either your system, a client, or from a remote system, a server. After a determination is made of where the call will be processed, the call can be packaged and sent to the server. The server environment is an efficient way to process data, because a server can handle many RPCs simultaneously, unlike the client which handles only one at a time.

RPC-based systems include Novell's NetWare, Microsoft's LAN Manager, Banyan VINES, and Sun's NFS.

 Fitting RPC into the OSI model places it at the Session Layer—Layer 5.

OSI MODEL
Application
Presentation
Session
Transport
Network
Data-Link
Physical

NetWare MODEL

Applications	N C P
NetBIOS Shells	
SPX	
IPX	
Ethernet	802.3	802.5	ARCnet

Figure 5.24

NetWare and the OSI model.

Identify the major services provided by NetWare and related technologies.

The Network and Transport Layers correspond to Internet Packet Exchange (IPX) and Sequenced Packet Exchange (SPX) protocols respectively, both derivatives of XNS. The Session Layer supports the Network Basic Input Output System (NetBIOS) Interface. The Presentation and Application Layers incorporate NetWare Core Protocol (NCP) and NetWare Value-Added Services, to name a few, to be discussed later in this section.

Internetwork Packet Exchange Protocol (IPX)

IPX is a connectionless protocol concerned with routing and addressing from node to destination host or destination node. IPX evolved from XNS's Internetwork Datagram Protocol (IDP). Because IPX's main function is routing, Novell has implemented its own version of Routing Information Protocol (RIP) with IPX. Novell's version of RIP takes on the same ideas as RIP from TCP/IP. NetWare servers and routers broadcast addresses to other servers on the network to provide routing information throughout the internetwork. Figure 5.25 shows IPX packet fields.

Figure 5.25

IPX packet fields.

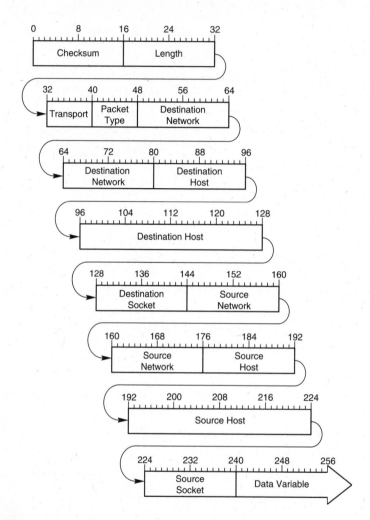

Identify/label the fields and functions of NetWare IPX and SPX packets.

IPX packets are made up of 11 fields, discussed in the following sections.

Checksum

Length: 16 bits

The checksum field conforms with the XNS header.

 The checksum field is disabled on networks that have only one segment. Single segment networks are relatively reliable and do not require this checksum.

Length

Length: 16 bits

The length field gives the length of the entire IPX datagram. The minimum length is 30; the maximum length is limited only by the length of the Link Layer frame unless the packet is routed.

 The theoretical limit to the length of a routed packet is 576 bytes. This limit was set up to use the lowest common denominator, which is the length of an ARCnet frame.

Transport Control

Length: 8 bits

The transport control field is used by NetWare routers by setting the field to zero by IPX prior to sending the packet. Each router to which the packet is passed increments this field by one. By the time the field reaches 16, the packet is discarded.

Sixteen hops through the internetwork in NetWare means a destination is unreachable.

Packet Type

Length: 8 bits

The Packet Type field specifies the upper-layer protocol to which the packet information is being passed. Some possible values of this field are as follows:

- ◆ 0 Unknown Packet
- ◆ 1 Routing Information Packet (RIP)
- ◆ 2 Echo Packet
- ◆ 3 Error Packet
- ◆ 4 Packet Exchange Packet (PEP)
- ◆ 5 Sequenced Packet Protocol (SPP)
- ◆ 17 NetWare Core Protocol (NCP)

Destination Network

Length: 32 bits

The Destination Network field specifies the packet's destination network address. A value of zero indicates that the source and destination are on the same LAN.

Destination Host

Length: 48 bits

The Destination Host field specifies the physical hardware address for the destination node. All bits are used when using IEEE 802.3 or IEEE 802.5. If the address does not need the entire field, such as ARCnet, the remaining bytes are filled with leading zeros.

In a broadcast packet, the Destination Host field is filled with all ones.

Destination Socket

Length: 16 bits

The Destination Socket field specifies the process within the destination node. Xerox defines the values as follows:

- 0451H: File server packet
- 0452H: Service advertising packet
- 0453H: Routing information packet
- 0455H: NetBIOS packet
- 0456H: Diagnostic packet

IPX provides its services to the higher level processes, called *clients*, through the Destination and Source Sockets.

Source Network

Length: 32 bits

The Source Network field is the same as the Destination Network field, except that it holds the network address of the packet's source. A value of zero indicates an unknown network.

Source Host

Length: 48 bits

The Source Host field specifies the physical hardware address for the source or sending node. Use of this field is the same as for the

Destination Host. Addresses not requiring six bytes fill unused bytes with zeros. In a broadcast packet, all 48 bits are ones.

Source Socket

Length: 16 bits

The Source Socket field specifies the address of the source socket, which functions the same as for the Destination Socket.

Data

The Data field contains information designated for the upper layers or carries information from the upper layers down to lower layers.

Sequenced Packet Exchange (SPX)

Identify/label the fields and functions of NetWare IPX and SPX packets.

Sequenced Packet Exchange (SPX) is a connection-oriented, guaranteed delivery service between workstations and servers. Examples of SPX connections are RConsole, remote printing (for NetWare printer services), and SNA gateways. These programs must have SPX to allow for packets to be delivered reliably. Figure 5.26 shows the fields in an SPX packet.

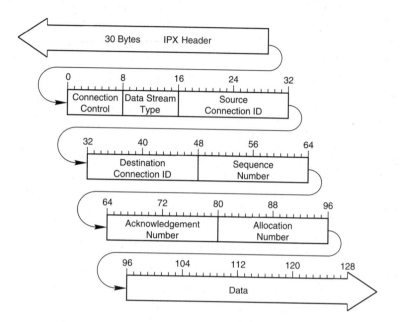

Figure 5.26

SPX packet breakdown.

 TCP and SPX are similar in nature. The two following statements compare and contrast the basic functionality of the two packets:

♦ Both allow several requests to be outstanding.

♦ Only SPX uses Negative Acknowledgments (NAK) to specify that an awaited packet was not received.

SPX uses *virtual circuits*, also referrred to as *connections*. These connections have specific identifiers as defined in the SPX header. These connection identifiers are called *connection IDs*, which are the users of socket services. Multiple connection IDs can be attached to a single socket. These numbers can be viewed in v3.11 through the MONITOR NLM by viewing Connection Information for a user. The connection ID seen is normally 4003.

TCP's source and destination ports are a hybrid of the SPX socket numbers and connection IDs.

SPX packets contain nine fields discussed in the following sections.

Connection Control

Length: 8 bits

The Connection Control field contains four one-bit flags for the control of data flow.

◆ **01H—08H:** Undefined

◆ **10H:** End of message

◆ **20H:** Attention

◆ **40H:** Acknowledgment required

◆ **80H:** System packet

Datastream Type

Length: 8 bits

The Datastream Type is the identifier of the data in the packet, much like that of the Ethernet Type field.

◆ **00H—FDH:** Client defined

◆ **FEH:** End of connection

◆ **FFH:** End-of-connection acknowledgment

Source Connection ID

Length: 16 bits

The Source Connection ID is assigned by the packet source.

Destination Connection ID

Length: 16 bits

The Destination Connection ID is for demultiplexing multiple connections into the same socket.

Sequence Number

Length: 16 bits

The Sequence Number is a numerical identifier for packets sent.

Acknowledgment Number

Length: 16 bits

The Acknowledgment Number identifies the sequence number of the next received packet; this is how SPX attains reliable packet delivery.

Allocation Number

Length: 16 bits

The Allocation Number indicates the number of receive buffers available for the connection. A transmitter can send packets until the sequence numbers and the allocation numbers are equal; this creates end-to-end flow control.

Data

The Data field contains data that has a destination of the upper-layer processes.

NetWare Upper-Layer Services

Novell, Inc. has incorporated many upper-layer services with NetWare, from versions 2.*x* through 4.*x*. These upper-layer services add to NetWare's connectivity and functionality as a network operating system. Several of these upper-layer services are discussed in the following sections.

NetBIOS

Novell's NetBIOS emulation gives those programs specifically written to operate with NetBIOS the capability to run under NetWare.

NetWare Shell

The NetWare Shell gives the workstation the capability to communicate with NetWare servers.

NetWare Core Protocols (NCP)

NCP provides a medium for client/server interaction between a workstation and a file server. Examples of NCP are print services, file locking, and synchronization.

NCP with print services and the workstation shell help users to feel as if printing is a local function connected to their workstation. Users do not realize that the jobs actually travel to the file server, pass through a queue, and are told where to print by a print server.

Information in the bindery is essential to name management, accounting, and security. The bindery builds its database on three levels: object, properties, and values. An example of an object is a user name. Each user has properties such as a password, trustee assignments, and so on. A property has a value. The value of the password property is the text of the user's password, for example.

Note The most common type of data seen on a NetWare LAN is the NetWare Core Protocol (NCP) traffic.

Even the simple process of reading a file requires multiple NCP calls. The user must be acknowledged as a valid network user; a drive must be mapped to the network directory containing the file; the file must be located; rights must be validated; and finally, the file must be opened. Each of these functions requires NCP interaction.

NetWare Remote Procedure Call

NetWare RPC provides the capability for outside resources to make calls to the NetWare file server and transparent access. NetWare RPC works much like Sun RPC for NFS.

Streams, TLI, and Link Support Layer

NetWare Streams works as a direct pipe to the upper-layer services provided by NetWare. It is a direct link between services and device drivers.

TLI functions with Streams to define the function calls passed through the stream.

Link Support Layer links device drivers and transport stacks. This also is known as Open Data-Link Interface (ODI). Link support allows multiple protocols to function with a single driver.

Message Handling Service

MHS is considered a platform. MHS is a generic area where electronic mail can be dropped off and received. MHS does not handle the front-end processing for e-mail; it is only the middle man. MHS enables multiple vendors to send and receive their data at a common post office.

Service Advertisement Protocol (SAP)

NetWare file servers communicate with each other, telling what they have to offer other servers. These communications happen every minute by the broadcasting of Service Identification Packets (SIP). Service Query Packets (SQP) can be used by a SAP user to determine what servers are available. SLIST is one NetWare command that uses SQP.

Value Added Process (VAP) and NetWare Loadable Modules (NLM)

VAPs (used in v2.*x*) and NLMs (used in v3.*x* and v4.0) are NetWare's way of allowing services to run directly from the file server, much like applications running on a workstation. VAP and NLM applications provide services to the entire LAN.

Comparing TCP/IP and SPX/IPX

This section details the similarities and differences of TCP/IP and SPX/IPX.

IP and IPX share the following features:

- ◆ Function at the Network Layer
- ◆ Offer datagram services
- ◆ Use RIP
- ◆ Are connectionless
- ◆ Limit how long a packet can exist on the internetwork

SPX and TCP share these features:

- ◆ Function at the Transport Layer
- ◆ Offer reliable delivery through acknowledgments and virtual circuits
- ◆ Utilize byte streams
- ◆ Offer flow control

TCP/IP has the following features not shared by SPX/IPX:

◆ Has public domain background, developed in the 1970s

◆ Offers flow control using sliding windows

◆ IP uses Time-to-Live for limiting the length of a datagram's life

◆ IP addresses include both the network and node addresses on one element

SPX/IPX differs from TCP/IP in the following respects:

◆ Has vendor's proprietary background, developed in the early 1980s

◆ Offers flow control using free buffer counts

◆ IPX uses the Transport Control field to determine the length of a datagram's life

◆ IPX addresses separate the network and node addresses into two fields

Exploring AppleTalk

 Identify the principal organizations that promulgate or champion the AppleTalk protocols and their target environment.

AppleTalk is Apple Computers' operating system for the Macintosh that has adopted the same theory as the Macintosh itself. Some people call the Mac a "plug and play" machine and in some ways this is true. The Macintosh is delivered with a LocalTalk network interface built in, making the Mac very easy to set up for its own network environment.

The AppleTalk network architecture has grown over the past few years from Phase 1 to Phase 2. Phase 1 supports 254 node connections per network, and now Phase 2 supports up to 16 million unique nodes.

297

AppleTalk and OSI

Identify the major services provided by AppleTalk.

Identify the characteristics of AppleTalk.

This section compares AppleTalk with the OSI Reference Model from the bottom, Physical Layer, up to the Application Layer. Figure 5.27 shows the comparison of AppleTalk and OSI.

Figure 5.27

Mapping between OSI and AppleTalk.

OSI	AppleTalk
Application	AppleShare: Print Server, File Server, PC
Presentation	AFP
Session	PAP / ASP
Transport	ADSP / ATP
Network	DDP / RTMP / ZIP / NBP
Data-Link	AARP
Physical	LocalTalk EtherTalk TokenTalk

The Physical Layer

At the Physical Layer of the OSI model are three major components, two of which already have been discussed in other architectures: Ethernet, Token Ring and LocalTalk. Each has a direct link-up to the Data-Link Layer.

The Data-Link Layer

At the Data-Link Layer, AppleTalk employs three protocols: EtherTalk Link Access Protocol (ELAP), LocalTalk Link Access Protocol (LLAP), and TokenTalk Link Access Protocol (TLAP). In earlier sections of this book, LocalTalk was discussed in detail.

AppleTalk Address Resolution Protocol (AARP) rests across the top of EtherTalk, LocalTalk, and TokenTalk in the Data-Link Layer. AARP is the channel used to translate between the hardware address and the upper-layer protocol addresses. All nodes on the system maintain an Address Mapping Table (AMT) for each higher-layer protocol suite. AARP works basically the same way Address Resolution Protocol works in TCP/IP. If one node knows the software address of another node, then it needs to find that node's hardware address on the network. This is accomplished through AARP. The node makes a broadcast request on the system to resolve the address, and the corresponding node responds.

 AMT is checked before sending an address request. Entries in the AMT expire when they become old. Each AARP implementation has its own selection for this time-out period.

The Network Layer

The Network Layer's main support is from Datagram Delivery Protocol (DDP). DDP is the protocol that all higher layers use. DDP is responsible for the delivery of datagrams between sockets on an internet. All node addresses on the internet consist of a network number followed by the node ID and the socket number. Preceding the DDP is the LLAP type of either one for short header or two for extended header. Short header is used when the source and destination are on the same network. The extended header is used when internet transmission is taking place.

AppleTalk routing is done by DDP, but needs help from Routing Table Maintenance Protocol (RTMP). RTMP is used by Inter-network Routers (IRs) to help establish and maintain routing tables on the Internet and RTMP data packets are sent every ten seconds.

The following five items are in the routing table:

◆ **Network Range** is the actual network segment number.

◆ **Distance** is the number of routers that must be passed through to reach the destination.

◆ **Port** is the actual router port that the packet is exiting onto the segment.

◆ **Next IR** tells the router the numerical identifier of the next IR that the datagram will see.

◆ **Entry State** defines the state of the entry for routing—good, suspect, or bad.

RTMP can specify four types of packets as follows:

◆ **Data packets** are sent as routing updates.

◆ **Request packets** are sent by nonrouting nodes.

◆ **Route data request packets** are sent by end nodes that want to receive RTMP.

◆ **Response packets** follow request packets.

Name Binding Protocol (NBP)

Name Binding Protocol is what the name implies—using an actual name instead of the use of an address. An application sends a request for a name, and the NBP takes over and finds the corre-sponding address to match the name. If the local NBP cannot find the name, DDP looks on the local network to see if the name can be found.

A problem can occur with DDP. DDP cannot support an inter-network. Because of this, AppleTalk supports zones. A *zone* is a set of logically connected nodes on an internet. That internet can span multiple networks, but zones cannot span into each other—a node supports only one zone. For NBP zone support, NBP sends the request to a router, and the router broadcasts the NBP information network-wide with help from Zone Information Protocol (ZIP).

 ZIP holds network number-to-zone name mappings. This information is kept in a table called Zone Information Table (ZIT). Now the NBP can look multi-network-wide for the name-to-address translation with the help of ZIP.

Transport Layer

The Transport Layer of the OSI model maps directly to the following two AppleTalk protocols:

♦ AppleTalk Transaction Protocol (ATP)

♦ AppleTalk Data Stream Protocol (ADSP)

AppleTalk Transaction Protocol (ATP) is much like TCP in the way that it fragments and reassembles data packets, but ATP works with a transaction ID. Transactions are made up of requests from workstations and replies from servers. ATP makes sure that the packets coming in are received correctly. If ATP sees that a packet has errors, it requests a retransmission of only those packets not received properly.

 AppleTalk Data Stream Protocol (ADSP) establishes and maintains full-duplex data streams between AppleTalk sockets. ADSP also uses flow control with sequence numbers to ensure that a system sending data quickly does not overwhelm a slower receiver with too much data.

Session Layer

The Session Layer of OSI maps to AppleTalk protocols as follows:

◆ Printer Access Protocol (PAP)

◆ AppleTalk Session Protocol (ASP)

Printer Access Protocol (PAP) is used for printer-dependent communications. PAP works as a client for both NBP and ATP. This protocol is used for transferring data to and from a server.

AppleTalk Session Protocol (ASP) establishes communication between a workstation and a server. ASP supplies four basic services: opening and closing session connections; session request handling, which handles replies made between workstations and servers; and session management, which determines the current status of the remote and also makes sure that the session packets are reliable.

Presentation Layer

The Presentation Layer maps directly to AppleTalk Filing Protocol (AFP), works as a client of ASP services, and allows control of files located on remote workstations or servers. AFP is similar to NFS in NetWare and UNIX. It allows the files to be translated directly from one system to another. AFP works with Macintosh, Apple II, and MS-DOS files.

AFP also has a security mechanism to prevent unauthorized access of a file system or volume. Three levels of security exist with AFP: user authentication, passwords on volumes, and directory access control. Directory access control has the following three levels of access rights:

◆ **Search** allows the user to search for information in one directory from another.

◆ **Read** allows the user to read the information of a file in that directory.

◆ **Write** allows the user to modify items within a directory.

Application Layer

The Application Layer supports many applications for AppleTalk,
but three of the more popular applications are as follows:

◆ AppleShare Print Server

◆ AppleShare File Server

◆ AppleShare PC

AppleShare Print Server

AppleShare Print Server utilizes NBP and PAP, allowing printers
located on an AppleTalk network to share printing services. Recall
the earlier discussion of NBP searching for logical names on the
network. This is a perfect example of where NBP searches for and
finds the correct area on the network to send the print job. The job
must start at the Application Layer and move down through the
model, but without NBP, this process would not be possible. PAP
also plays a major role in transferring the data going to the
printer.

AppleShare File Server

AppleShare File Server works with AFP services to allow remote
workstation access to files on a volume located on a server.

AppleShare PC

AppleShare PC allows MS-DOS machines to utilize the
AppleShare file services and AppleShare print services.

Review Questions

1. Which statement about OSI Data-Link Layer protocols is false?

   ○ a. CONS uses PLP.

   ○ b. CLNS uses CLNP.

   ○ c. CLNP is run over 802.2 for unacknowledged connection-oriented services.

   ○ d. X.25 PLP can be run over 802.2 for connection-oriented services.

2. Which OSI Transport Layer protocol is comparable to TCP?

   ○ a. TP4

   ○ b. TP3

   ○ c. TP1

   ○ d. TP0

3. Which is an example of a standard data interface between an application and the network in OSI?

   ○ a. TP4 using ASCII

   ○ b. ASN.1 using TP4

   ○ c. ASN.1 using BER

   ○ d. X.409 using ASN.1

4. OSI Directory Services are derived from:

   ○ a. CCITT X.400

   ○ b. IEEE X.400

   ○ c. CCITT X.500

   ○ d. IEEE X.500

5. Which element of SNA is not an NAU?

○ a. PU

○ b. DU

○ c. LU

○ d. SSCP

6. SNA PU types include:

○ a. Type 2 as an FEP

○ b. Type 4 running in the device that runs NCP

○ c. Type 5 as a printer

○ d. Type 5 as a host

7. Which statement about DNA is false?

○ a. The current version is Phase V.

○ b. X.25 services are provided at the Application, Network, and Data-Link Layers.

○ c. NSP is similar to TP4.

○ d. Supports naming services at the Application Layer.

8. The Internet Protocol Suite has ___ layers.

○ a. 3

○ b. 4

○ c. 5

○ d. 7

9. TCP is not:

○ a. An alternative to ULP

○ b. Full-duplex

○ c. Acknowledged

○ d. Connection-oriented

10. NetWare does not use:

    ○ a. IPX for a connectionless protocol

    ○ b. SPX for a guaranteed delivery service

    ○ c. 16 hops as a flag for an unreachable destination

    ○ d. NAK as a negative acknowledgment for IPX

11. The most common type of data on a NetWare LAN is

    ○ a. IPX traffic

    ○ b. NCP calls

    ○ c. SPX traffic

    ○ d. RIP traffic

12. AppleTalk routing is done by

    ○ a. DDP

    ○ b. RTMP

    ○ c. LLAP

    ○ d. ATP

13. Which is not a valid pairing?

    ○ a. IBM—SNA

    ○ b. DEC—DNA

    ○ c. Novell—NetWare

    ○ d. Apple—GOSIP

14. ES-IS and IS-IS are two types of OSI routing protocols that function at the _____ layer.

15. The information unit at the OSI transport level is:

    ○ a. TPDU

    ○ b. TP0

    ○ c. PDU

    ○ d. UDP

16. Which application service element informs applications fo transfer success or failure?

○ a. ACSE

○ b. RTSE

○ c. ROSE

○ d. ASN.1

17. Which Application Service Element is similar to RPC?

○ a. ACSE

○ b. RTSE

○ c. ROSE

○ d. DAISY

18. Which is not a NAU?

○ a. SNA

○ b. SSCP

○ c. PU

○ d. LU

19. MVS, VM and VSE are IBM SNA _____.

20. Cluster Controllers that do not attach directly to mainframe channels are called:

○ a. 3270 Controllers

○ b. Remote Cluster Controllers

○ c. Front End Processors

○ d. SSCPs

21. Cluster Controllers and Front-End Processors are:

  ○ a. PUs

  ○ b. LUs

  ○ c. SSCPs

  ○ d. CPUs

22. Which LU type provides Peer-to-Peer communication using a General Data Stream?

  ○ a. 4

  ○ b. 6.1

  ○ c. 6.2

  ○ d. 7

23. Which is not a characteristic of APPN?

  ○ a. APPN nodes are configured as PU type 2.1.

  ○ b. LU6.2 nodes are not limited to single connections.

  ○ c. LU6.2 nodes can initiate error recovery.

  ○ d. LU6.2 is slightly less efficient than previous protocols.

24. DNA Phase ____ is most closely related to the OSI protocols.

25. DNA uses which of the following Application layer protocols? Pick all that apply.

  ☐ a. RTSE

  ☐ b. ACSE

  ☐ c. ROSE

  ☐ d. MHS

  ☐ e. SMTP

  ☐ f. VMS

26. Which field in the IP packet designates the length of time that the datagram can exist on the Internet?

  ○ a. TTL

  ○ b. TLL

  ○ c. TPDU

  ○ d. IHL

27. TCP uses the _____ _____ _____ _____ mechanism to decide how much information a node can send or receive?

28. Which field in an SPX packet identifies the sequence number of the next packet expected?

  ○ a. Acknowledge Next

  ○ b. Allocation Number

  ○ c. Acknowledgement Number

  ○ d. Sequence Number

29. Which features do SPX and TCP share? Pick all that apply.

  ☐ a. Utilize Byte Streams

  ☐ b. Function at Transport Layer

  ☐ c. Use RIP

  ☐ d. Offer Flow Control

  ☐ e. Use Sliding Window Flow Control

  ☐ f. Reliable Delivery through Acknowledgement

30. The most common type of data seen on a NetWare LAN is _____ traffic.

Answers

1. C
2. A
3. C
4. C
5. B
6. B
7. D
8. B
9. A
10. D
11. B
12. A
13. D
14. Network
15. A
16. B
17. C
18. A
19. Operating Systems
20. B
21. A
22. C
23. D
24. V
25. B,C,D

26. A

27. Sliding Window Flow Control

28. C

29. A,B,D,F

30. NCP

PART 2

Installing, Upgrading, and Troubleshooting Local Area Networks

Working with Network Interface Card Configurations

6

CHAPTER

In this chapter, you learn about several of the network interface components used when configuring a NetWare LAN. Proper planning, research, and verification of certified NetWare-compatible components is an integral part of building an efficient network. The items discussed in this chapter include the following:

◆ ARCnet board settings, cabling, and troubleshooting

◆ Ethernet board settings, cabling, frame types, and troubleshooting

◆ Token Ring board settings, cabling, and troubleshooting

◆ FDDI cabling, advantages, disadvantages, and troubleshooting

During the planning phase of a network implementation project, many hardware choices are available. The verification of component compatibility and confirmation of Novell certification of all hardware and software to be integrated is obtained from several sources. Vendor documentation, FAXBACK phone numbers, technical support lines, and peers are good sources for verification. Novell provides a technical support desk that can be reached by dialing 1-800-NETWARE. Access to the technical bulletins in a NetWare Support Encyclopedia can provide some of the information needed.

Without verification that the hardware you want to use has been tested thoroughly using NetWare, you do not know what compatibility problems may occur. If you do not choose hardware that has been verified at the Novell Labs, you will have a much more difficult time troubleshooting problems. You also will not have Novell support to help fix problems. Spending some time at this phase saves you money in the long run. Novell also offers a service called FAXBACK where you can have certain documents sent to your fax. A master document containing all the titles of the documents on FAXBACK helps you choose which item will provide the information you need. In the U.S. or Canada, call 1-800-233-3382 or 1-801-429-5363.

Diagnose and correct incompatibilities between the network adapter card and the CPU data bus.

After you have obtained the equipment to build your network, you must configure the hardware to avoid conflicts. Conflicts among different pieces of hardware occur when their settings match or overlap. Unless the hardware has special features to avoid conflicts, you must be aware of the areas where conflicts are most likely to occur. The following list contains the most common conflicts that occur when configuring a PC adapter card:

◆ Interrupt conflicts

◆ Base I/O and memory address conflicts

◆ Page memory range conflicts

◆ DMA channel conflicts

◆ Node address conflicts

Keep in mind that conflicts are internal to the individual PC. A common misconception is that all network boards on the same network must share the same settings. This is not true and is impractical to enforce unless all your machines are identical in their components. Look at each client individually for configuration information.

Interrupts are dedicated to certain resources. It is possible to use a dedicated interrupt by disabling an unneeded resource. For example, if you do not need a second COM port, you can disable COM2 by using the PC's configuration program, setting switches or jumpers on the system board, or removing the board that supports COM2. This frees up INT 3 for use with a LAN card.

The following is a list of additional items to research as part of the planning process:

- Cabling specifications and requirements

- Hard drive specifications and requirements

- Software drivers to ensure that they are certified with the version of operating system to be used

Now that you have an idea of what needs to be verified, the next section details information about ARCnet, Ethernet, and Token Ring specifications.

 Differentiate among media types and physical media protocols.

Exploring ARCnet Specifications

ARCnet is an acronym for Attached Resource Computer NETwork, which was founded by the Datapoint Corporation. Novell uses the term RX-Net to denote its form of this architecture and TRX-Net for the Turbo version. ARCnet uses a token-bus packet passing scheme.

 A Turbo version is an updated RX-Net version that hands packets off to the communications buffers rather than attempting to place the NetWare Core Protocol (NCP) packets in a File Server Process (FSP) buffer.

317

ARCnet operates at 2.5 Mbps throughput and can be connected using RG-62/U coax cable or unshielded twisted pair (UTP) wiring. Although ARCnet can support up to 255 node numbers on a single network, systems of this size are not practical.

Figure 6.1 shows the components of a typical ARCnet card. This card is configured for use with twisted pair wiring. ARCnet cards for use with coax cable have a BNC (Bayonet Navy Connector) twist-on connector. You will find jumpers or DIP (Dual In-line Package) switches for setting the following characteristics:

Figure 6.1

Example of an ARCnet NIC.

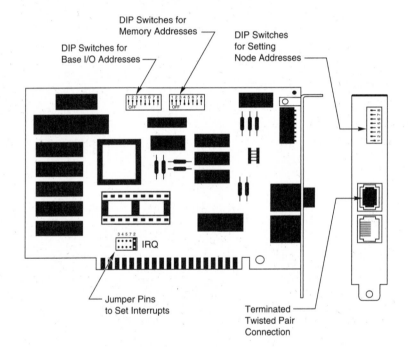

- ◆ Node number
- ◆ Base I/O address
- ◆ Memory address
- ◆ Interrupt
- ◆ Network timeout

The node number and network timeout are unique to ARCnet and are described later in this chapter.

Each network interface card (NIC) on an ARCnet network is assigned a node number. This number must be unique on each network and in the range of 1 to 255.

ARCnet manages network access with a token mechanism. The token is passed from the lowest number node to higher number nodes in ascending order. Lower numbered addresses get the token before the higher numbered addresses.

Traffic is controlled by assigning sequential numbers to nodes using the same order in which they are cabled. Choosing random numbers can create a situation in which a node numbered 23 can be a whole building away from the next number, 46, but in the same room as numbers 112 and 142. The token has to travel in a haphazard manner that is less effective than if you numbered the three clients in the same office sequentially, 46, 47, and 48, and the client in the other building 112. With this configuration, the packet stays within the office before venturing on to other stations.

ARCnet was one of the topologies used early on in networking and is rarely used as the topology of choice in current LAN environments. ARCnet, however, still is a functional and cost-effective means of networking.

ARCnet Board Settings

Depending on the vendor design specifications of your ARCnet card, most base I/O addresses, node addresses, and memory addresses are set by DIP switches. These addresses are set using a binary mode calculation with an on or off setting in the required switch block. Interrupt settings are made by jumper combinations at marked locations on the network interface card (NIC). Many types and brands of ARCnet cards are on the market today. Refer to the MicroHouse Technical Library, the documentation for the NIC or, as a last resort, call the technical support group for the specific vendor of the component.

Most ARCnet cards require a shared memory address. Many manufacturers use the area of D000:0 to DFFF:0 as the default. Standard DOS memory is limited to the first 640KB of a PC's memory. However, extended or expanded memory managers can be used to make memory above 640KB available for use by DOS programs. If memory above the 640KB line (above hex address A000:0) is used for network boards, however, the memory becomes unavailable for use by a memory manager. This makes it difficult to optimize a PC's upper memory area. If a network card requires a memory area such as D000:0-DFFF:0, the memory available for use by DOS memory managers is reduced by 64KB.

ARCnet Cabling

The ARCnet topology uses coax, twisted-pair, or fiber-optic cabling to connect network devices. An ARCnet network is used primarily with either coax or twisted pair cable. Coax is an RG-62/U type cable and is terminated with 93-ohm terminators. Twisted pair uses stranded 24- or 26-gauge wire or solid core 22-, 24-, or 26-gauge type cable and is terminated with 100-ohm terminators. Many ARCnet networks use a mix of both coax and UTP cabling. UTP cable is simple to install and provides a reliable connection to the clients, whereas coax provides a means to span longer distances.

ARCnet can run off a linear bus topology using coax or twisted pair as long as the cards support BUS. The most popular installations of ARCnet run off two types of hubs:

◆ *Active hubs* have active electronic signals that amplify signals and split them to multiple ports. The number of ports on an active hub varies with the manufacturer, but eight is typical. A port on an active hub can be connected to a port on another active device (such as another active hub or an NIC) or to a passive hub.

◆ *Passive hubs* cannot amplify signals. Each hub has four connectors. Because of the characteristics of passive hubs, unused ports must be equipped with a *terminator*, a connector containing a resistor that matches the ARCnet cabling characteristics. A port on a passive hub can connect only to an active device (an active hub or an NIC). Passive hubs can never be connected to passive hubs.

One of the greatest flexibilities of ARCnet is that you can integrate connections from active hubs to a linear bus connection as long as you terminate at the last connection point.

A maximum time limit of 31 microseconds is allotted for an ARCnet signal. This is also called a time-out setting. Signals on an ARCnet can travel up to 20,000 feet during the 31-microsecond default time-out period. You can sometimes extend the range of an ARCnet by increasing the time-out value. However, 20,000 feet is the distance at which ARCnet signals begin to seriously de-grade. Extending the network beyond that distance can result in unreliable or failed communication. Therefore, the time-out parameter and cabling distance recommendations should be increased only with great caution.

The maximum cable distances between individual components in an ARCnet network are dependent on how the components are connected (see table 6.1).

Table 6.1
Maximum ARCnet Cable Distances

Maximum Distance	From	To
2,000 feet	Network node	Active hub
2,000 feet	Active hub	Active hub
100 feet	Active hub	Passive hub
Not supported	Passive hub	Passive hub
100 feet	Network node	Passive hub
2,000 feet	Network node	Network node
20,000 feet	Farthest node	Farthest node

In cabling ARCnet networks with coax cable, you must follow several rules:

◆ Never connect a passive hub to another passive hub directly

◆ Passive hubs should never be used to connect two active hubs

◆ Passive hubs are only used to connect an active hub and a node

◆ Unused connectors on active hubs do not need to be terminated

◆ Unused connectors on passive hubs must be terminated using a 93-ohm terminator

Figure 6.2 shows an ARCnet configuration using active and passive hubs. Active hubs are required to extend the network for long distances and to configure networks that have more than four nodes. Passive hubs are used as an economical means of splitting a port on an active hub to support three devices.

Figure 6.2

Example of an ARCnet topology using active and passive hubs and coax cable.

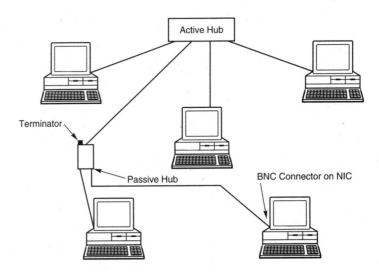

ARCnet Troubleshooting

 Troubleshoot common problems with cards, cables, and related hardware for the three most common networking topologies.

Common sources of problems on ARCnet networks are as follows:

◆ No more than one node can have a given node address on the same network. If two or more nodes share an address, one of the two clients will either lose its network connection or will not be able to find a network.

◆ Missing terminators may not present visible problems on a small network. Missing terminators cause data retransmits on smaller systems, eventually appearing as transmit time-out errors or network errors.

◆ Using a terminator with an incorrect ohm rating. Coax uses 93 ohm; twisted pair uses 100 ohm. A terminator's value in ohms depends on the impedance of the cable. The cable's impedance and the terminator's value should always match.

◆ The ARCnet bus using NICs that do not use the same impedance level. Signals will become attenuated and/or reflected, causing interference with other signals on the wire.

◆ Failed NICs.

◆ Failed active hubs (or a port on that hub).

◆ Cable lengths that exceed specifications (refer to table 6.1). Twisted pair, cabled in a bus rather than a star, cannot have more than ten NICs per segment. This number varies with different manufacturers. ARCnet UTP installed in a bus configuration is generally used only in very small networks of six nodes or less. This configuration has the major draw-back of halting the network if a single cable is disconnected. In an ARCnet bus configuration, the network must be brought down to make any changes or service to the ARCnet cards.

◆ Coax connectors not built and/or crimped correctly. Twist-on connectors are responsible for more intermittent errors on a network than most other failures because of their design.

Twist-on coax connectors became popular in the IBM 3XXX systems. These systems used RG-62 coax cable and operated at 1.5 Mbps throughput. The twist-on connectors are not recommended for use on any modern LAN cable system because of the higher data rates employed.

The primary characteristics of ARCnet are as follows:

◆ The maximum time it takes for the ARCnet signal to travel the length of the network is 31 microseconds.

◆ The maximum distance an ARCnet signal can travel between the two nodes farthest away from each other is 20,000 feet.

◆ The absolute maximum number of ARCnet nodes that can occupy a given network segment is 255. An ARCnet segment consists of all cabling and nodes that share a given network address.

Understanding Ethernet Specifications

Ethernet was originally developed by the Xerox Corporation, Digital Corporation, and the Intel Corporation in the early 1970s. Ethernet is also known as a *spanning tree topology* because the networks expand by branching in tree structures that do not allow redundant paths between nodes. Ethernet uses the CSMA/CD (Carrier Sense Multiple Access/Collision Detection) media contention access method and supports a maximum throughput of 10 Mbps. The Ethernet and 802.3 protocols are described in Chapter 4, "Exploring the Lower Layers," and in the Ethernet Frame Types section of this chapter.

The origins of Ethernet are commemorated in the initials DIX, which is a 15-pin connector used to interface Ethernet components. The acronym DIX is derived from the combination of leading letters of the founding Ethernet vendors: Digital, Intel, and Xerox.

The term Ethernet commonly refers to original Ethernet (which has been updated to Ethernet_II) as well as the IEEE 802.3 standards (see Chapter 2). However, Ethernet and the 802.3 standards differ in ways significant enough to make standards incompatible in terms of packet formats. At the Physical Layer, Ethernet and 802.3 are generally compatible in terms of cables, connectors, and electronic devices.

Today, NetWare 3.11 uses the IEEE 802.3 frame format as a default on its networks. However, a variety of other Ethernet frame formats are supported. NetWare 3.12 and 4.x use the IEEE 802.2 frame format as the Ethernet frame type default. To change this default, change the frame type in the NET.CFG file. Add this frame type if you need to communicate with networks using older Ethernet frame types.

Ethernet is generally used on light-to-medium traffic networks, and performs best when a network's data traffic is sent in short bursts. Ethernet is the most popular network standard. It has become especially popular in many university and government installations.

Ethernet Board Settings

Most older versions of Ethernet NICs are configured using jumpers to set addresses and interrupts. Current models of Network Interface Cards (NICs) can be configured using a diagnostic program that enables changing of interrupt and memory address settings stored in a special memory chip on the NIC.

An example of an Ethernet NIC is shown in figure 6.3. Some of the features of these cards are as follows:

◆ Shared memory selection; most Ethernet cards do not require the use of shared memory

◆ I/O address

◆ Interrupt

◆ Connectors

◆ Active connector selection jumpers

◆ Socket for a remote boot PROM

Figure 6.3

Features of an
Ethernet NIC.

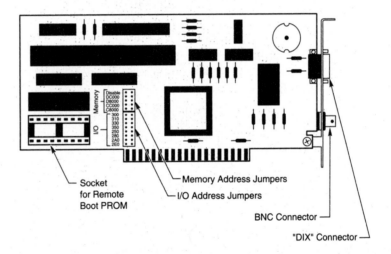

Ethernet cards can have one, two, or possibly all three of the following connectors:

◆ BNC connectors support coax cabling

◆ RJ-45 connectors support 10BASE-T (UTP) cabling

◆ DIX connectors are used to connect to external transceivers

With some cards, DIP switches or blocks of jumpers are used to select the active connector. In many cases, however, the active connector can be selected with configuration software.

A limitation of 1,024 nodes (physical addresses) per network address (see Chapters 3, "Building the Blueprint," and 7, "Using Novell DOS," for network address information) exists on an Ethernet network. Addresses are assigned by IEEE to the vendor for the first three bytes of a six-byte address. The vendor is responsible for assigning the rest of the address and ensuring unique IDs.

As with the Token Ring cards, the card's manufacturer "burns" a unique node address into ROM on each NIC. Unless you override the burned-in address, address conflicts cannot occur on an Ethernet. Vendors sometimes label their cards with the node address. If the address is not visible, use the diagnostic disk supplied by the vendor.

Ethernet Cabling

A variety of cables can be used to implement Ethernet networks. Traditionally, Ethernet networks have been cabled with coaxial cables of several different types. Fiber optic cables are now frequently employed to extend the geographic range of Ethernet networks.

The contemporary interest in using twisted pair wiring has resulted in a scheme for cabling using unshielded twisted pair. The 10BASE-T cabling standard, which uses UTP in a star topology, is described later.

Ethernet remains closely associated with coaxial cable, however. Two types of coaxial cable still used in small and large environments are thin net (also known as cheapernet) and thick net. The Ethernet networks have different limitations based on thin net and thick net cable specifications. The best way to remember the requirements is to use the 5-4-3 rule of thumb for each cable type.

The 5-4-3 Rule

The 5-4-3 rule states that the following can appear between any two nodes in the Ethernet network:

◆ Up to five segments in a series

◆ Up to four concentrators or repeaters

◆ Three segments of (coax only) cable that contain nodes

10BASE2

The 10BASE2 cabling topology, also referred to as thin net, generally uses the on-board transceiver of the network interface card to translate the signals to and from the rest of the network. Thin net cabling can use RG-58A/U or RG-58C/U coaxial type cable, 50 ohm terminators, and T-connectors that directly attach to the BNC connector on the NIC. A grounded terminator must be used on one end of the network segment. The components of a thin Ethernet network are shown in figure 6.4.

Figure 6.4

Thin Ethernet cabling components.

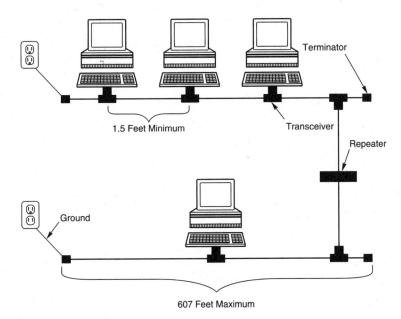

A *transceiver* is a device that takes the digital signal from the node and translates it to communicate on a baseband cabling system (see Chapter 1, "Learning Network Technology Terminology"). NICs that support thin net or 10BASE-T cable generally have built-in transceivers. External transceivers are used for thick Ethernet although they may be used for Thinnet and UTP as well.

Use RG-58A/U cable for Ethernet topology, not RG-58U, which is for use with cable TV setups.

Advantages of 10BASE2

The main advantage of using 10BASE2 in your network is cost. When any given cable segment on the network does not have to be run further than 185 meters, 10BASE2 is often the cheapest network cabling option.

10BASE2 is also relatively simple to connect. Each network node is connected directly to the network cable using a T-connector attached to the NIC.

Troubleshooting 10BASE2

The first step in troubleshooting a 10BASE2 network is to ensure that you have met the rules for using 10BASE2. Several additional rules must be adhered to in 10BASE2 Ethernet environments, including the following:

◆ The minimum cable distance between clients must be 1.5 feet, or .5 meters.

◆ Pig tails, also known as drop cables, from T-connectors should not be used to connect to the BNC connector on the NIC. The T-connector must be connected directly to the NIC.

◆ You may not go beyond the maximum network segment limitation of 607 feet, or 185 meters.

329

◆ The entire network cabling scheme cannot exceed 3,035 feet, or 925 meters.

◆ The maximum number of nodes per network segment is 30 (this includes clients and repeaters).

◆ A 50–ohm terminator must be used on each end of the bus with only one of the terminators having either a grounding strap or a grounding wire that attaches it to the screw holding an electrical outlet cover in place.

◆ You may not have more than five segments on a network. These segments may be connected with a maximum of four repeaters, and only three of the five segments may have network nodes.

Additional troubleshooting tips are found in the Ethernet Troubleshooting section of this chapter.

As mentioned previously, the IEEE 802.3 standard for Thinnet is 10BASE2. This standard describes a 10 Mbps baseband network with a maximum segment length of approximately 200 meters (the actual limit, as stated previously, is 185 meters). Figure 6.5 shows two segments using 10BASE2 cabling.

Figure 6.5

Two segments using 10BASE2 cabling.

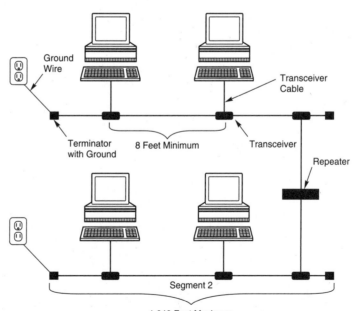

10BASE5

The 10BASE5 cabling topology, also referred to as thick net, uses an external transceiver to attach to the network interface card. The NIC attaches to the external transceiver by an Attachment Universal Interface (AUI) cable to the DIX connector on the back of the card. The external transceiver clamps to the thick net cable. As with thin net, each network segment must be terminated at both ends, with one end using a grounded terminator. The components of a thick net network are shown in figure 6.6.

 Note RG-11 is a 75-ohm cable. 10BASE5 requires 50 ohms.

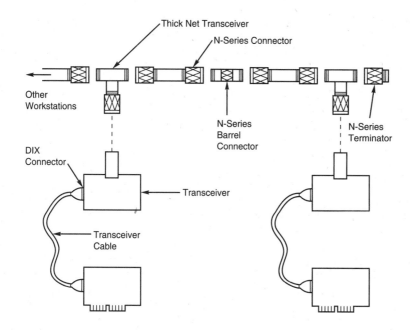

Figure 6.6

Components of a thick Ethernet.

Advantages of 10BASE5

The primary advantage of 10BASE5 is its ability to exceed the cable lengths to which 10BASE2 is restricted. However, it does have restrictions of its own that should be considered when installing or troubleshooting a 10BASE5 network.

Troubleshooting a 10BASE5 Network

As with 10BASE2 networks, the first consideration when trouble-shooting a 10BASE5 network should be the cabling rules and guidelines that have been established. Several additional guidelines, along with the 5-4-3 rule, must be followed in thick Ethernet networks:

- ◆ The minimum cable distance between transceivers is 8 feet, or 2.5 meters.

- ◆ You may not go beyond the maximum network segment length of 1,640 feet, or 500 meters.

- ◆ The entire network cabling scheme cannot exceed 8,200 feet, or 2,500 meters.

- ◆ One end of the terminated network segment must be grounded.

- ◆ Drop cables can be as short as required, but cannot be longer than 50 meters from transceiver to NIC.

- ◆ Cable segments that are cut and connected using a "Vampire Tap" should come from the same cable spool to ensure that each connected piece carries the identical electrical cabling to the other.

- ◆ The maximum number of nodes per network segment is 100. (This includes all repeaters.)

Additional troubleshooting tips are found in the Ethernet Trouble-shooting section of this chapter.

The IEEE 802.3 standard that describes thick net is 10BASE5. This standard describes a 10 Mbps baseband network that can have segments up to 500 meters long. Figure 6.7 shows two segments using thick net and the appropriate hardware.

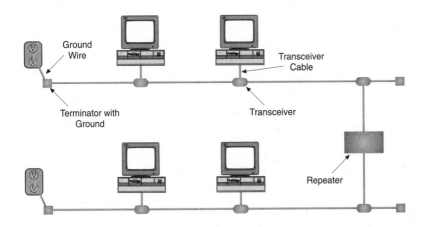

Figure 6.7

Example of thick net Ethernet cabling.

Thin net and thick net cable can be combined to extend the distance of an Ethernet network topology. The following formula can be used to define the maximum amount of thin net cable that can be used in one network segment combination:

> Maximum length of = 1,640 feet
> thin net that can (Length of
> be used new network
> segment to
> be added)

Note   A linear bus topology is more economical than wire because it is not necessary to have a separate cable run for each client. However, some local problems on a linear bus have the capability of bringing the entire network down.

If a break is in the cable or a streaming NIC is in the channel, the entire network can go down. Streaming is more frequently referred to as a broadcast storm. This occurs when a network card fails, and the transmitter floods the cable with traffic, just like a faucet that is stuck open. At this point, the network becomes unusable.

10BASE-T

The trend in wiring Ethernet networks is to use unshielded twisted-pair (UTP) cable. UTP or 10BASE-T cable is one of the three most popular implementations for Ethernet. It is based on the IEEE 802.3 standard.

10BASE-T cabling is wired in a star topology. However, it functions logically like a linear bus. The cable uses RJ-45 connectors, and the network interface card can have RJ-45 jacks built into the back of the cards. External transceivers attached to a DIX connector found in combination with RJ-45 or BNC connectors on the NIC can be used to connect standard Ethernet cards into a twisted-pair topology. Figure 6.8 shows Ethernet cabling using twisted-pair cabling and a hub, also called a concentrator.

Figure 6.8

Example of twisted-pair Ethernet cabling.

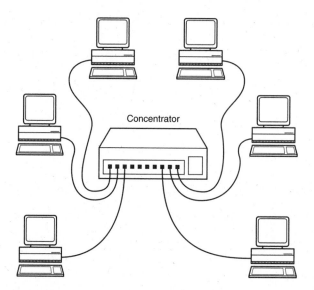

Concentrator

Advantages of 10BASE-T

The star wiring of 10BASE-T provides several advantages, particularly in larger networks. First, the network is more reliable and easier to manage because 10BASE-T networks use a concentrator (a centralized wiring hub). These hubs are "intelligent" in that they can route network traffic around a bad cable segment, and they can detect defective cable segments. This makes it easier for you to locate and repair bad cable segments.

10BASE-T enables you to design and build your LAN one segment at a time, growing as your network needs grow. This makes 10BASE-T more flexible than other LAN cabling options.

10BASE-T is also relatively inexpensive to use compared to other cabling options. In some cases where a data-grade phone system has already been used in an existing building, this cabling can be used for the LAN.

Networks with star wiring topologies can be significantly easier to troubleshoot and repair than bus wired networks. With a star network, a problem node can be isolated from the rest of the network by simply disconnecting the cable and directly connecting it to the cable hub. If the hub is considered "intelligent," management software developed for that hub type, as well as the hub itself, can disconnect the suspect port.

Troubleshooting 10BASE-T

The first step in troubleshooting a 10BASE-T network is to ensure that your network meets the rules for using 10BASE-T. The rules for a 10BASE-T network are as follows:

◆ The maximum number of network segments is 1,024.

◆ The cabling used should be 22, 24, or 26 American Wire Gauge (AWG), and be rated for an impedance of 85 to 115 ohms at 10 MHz.

Unshielded twisted-pair uses a terminator resistance level of 100-200 ohms; shielded twisted-pair uses 150 ohms.

♦ The maximum number of nodes is 512, and they may be connected on any three segments, with five being the maximum number of available line segments.

♦ The maximum unshielded cable segment length is 328 feet, or 100 meters.

You should be able to translate cable segment lengths from feet to meters, or from meters to feet. A meter is equivalent to 39.37 inches.

Additional troubleshooting tips are found in the Ethernet Troubleshooting section of this chapter.

10BASE-T requires that the UTP cable system be compliant with the Level IV standard. Level IV is cable-certified to operate at 10 Mbps throughput.

Ethernet Frame Types

In order for information to be transmitted successfully across an Ethernet network, the sending and receiving network nodes must agree in advance on the structure of the information being transmitted. The sending node must organize the information in an orderly and predictable manner so that the receiving node can find and interpret the transmitted information. This orderly arrangement of information traveling across an Ethernet network is known as an *Ethernet frame*. Different Ethernet frame types describe different standards that specify the protocol structure (configuration of the media).

There are four possible Ethernet frame types. The same Ethernet frame type must be loaded at both the server and accessing clients in order for proper communication to take place. The four available frame types are ETHERNET 802.3 (also known as raw ETHERNET), ETHERNET 802.2, ETHERNET SNAP, and ETHERNET II.

Raw ETHERNET (802.3) was developed before the IEEE 802.3 standard was completed and released. Therefore, ETHERNET 802.3 is not in complete compliance with the IEEE standard. ETHERNET 802.3 is used only on IPX/SPX Novell networks. ETHERNET 802.3 does not contain a field to specify which protocols may be contained within the packet. The lack of this field is one feature of ETHERNET 802.3 that makes it almost exclusively unique to Novell's NetWare 2.2 and NetWare 3.x Operating Systems.

Common features of the ETHERNET 802.3 standard include the following:

- A frame size between 64 and 1,518 bytes

- A preamble in the first line of the header (it contains alternating ones and zeroes to synchronize the communicating stations)

- A one-byte Start Frame Delimiter (SFD) field that follows the preamble and designates the beginning of the frame

- A six-byte field that specifies the address of the station to which the packet is being sent

- An originating address indicating the client, server, or router from where the packet was last sent

- A two-byte field that specifies the length of the data portion of the packet, and which must not have a length greater than 1,500 bytes to be considered valid

- A data field which must be no shorter than 46 bytes and no longer than 1,500 bytes

- A four-byte Cyclical Redundancy Check (CRC) or Frame Check Sequence that helps to ensure that the transmitted data is valid

ETHERNET 802.2 is fully compliant with the IEEE 802.3 standard. ETHERNET 802.2 is the default frame type used in NetWare 3.12 and NetWare 4.x networks. Common features of the ETHERNET 802.2 standard include the following:

◆ All of the same fields as the 802.3 specification

◆ Three additional Logical Link Control (LLC) fields, one byte long, that act much like an 802.3 header

◆ A frame size between 64 and 1,518 bytes

ETHERNET SNAP (SubNetwork Address Protocol) is fully compliant with ETHERNET 802.2 and is actually considered an enhancement to the 802.2 specification. Common features of the ETHERNET SNAP standard include the following:

◆ Two of the LLC fields, which contain fixed data indicating that this is a SNAP packet

◆ A type field as the third of the LLC fields, which enables the packet to carry other high-level protocols within the frame structure, thus ensuring compatibility and making it possible for network operating systems to carry protocols over other types of media, such as Token Ring

ETHERNET II frame types support TCP/IP for NetWare 3.11. Common features of the ETHERNET II frame type include the following:

◆ A packet type field located immediately after the source address field, which is the location of the packet length field in other ETHERNET frame types

◆ A combined preamble and Start Frame Delimiter field that are referred to jointly as the preamble

Although four ETHERNET frame types are available, load only the frame type that you need to use on your network server. If it is necessary in order to support multiple upper-layer protocols, you can load more than one frame type on a server.

Each LAN NIC in the server must have at least one protocol bound to it. To bind a protocol to a NIC, first LOAD the NIC drivers, then bind the protocol to the NIC as in the following:

```
LOAD NE2000 port=320 int=5 frame=ETHERNET_802.3     NAME=ENE5
BIND IPX TO ENE5 NET=BAC1234
```

Ethernet Troubleshooting

Trend measurement and analysis can be applied to all network types and is covered in Chapter 12, "Troubleshooting Concepts and Tools." The use of a sophisticated protocol analyzer, such as LANalyzer for WINDOWS and simpler tools, along with your own experience and knowledge, are two other effective troubleshooting techniques for Ethernet networks. This section covers the latter option.

When troubleshooting an Ethernet network, begin with the more obvious physical problems. For example, check to make certain that all connectors are tight and properly connected. Make certain that ground wires and terminators are used when required. Also, be certain that manufacturer's specifications are met, and that cable lengths, maximum number of nodes, and so on, are correct.

Consider the following when troubleshooting Ethernet networks:

◆ With 10BASE-T, make sure that the cable used has the correct number of twists to meet the data grade specifications.

◆ Check for electrical interference. Electrical interference can be caused by tying the network cable together with monitor and power cords. Outside interference also can be caused by fluorescent lights, electric motors, and other electrical devices.

◆ Make sure that connectors are pinned properly and crimped tightly.

◆ Check the cable lengths to make sure that distance specifications are not exceeded.

◆ If excess shielding on coax cable is exposed, make sure it is not grounding-out the connector.

◆ Make sure that coax cables are not coiled tightly together.

339

◆ Check the grade of the cable being used. For 10BASE2, RG-58/U is required. All 10BASE5 cable must meet Ethernet specifications.

◆ If using a linear bus setup, make sure that the topology rules are followed.

◆ Check for missing terminator or terminators with improper impedance ratings.

◆ Check for malfunctioning hardware, such as a bad NIC, transceiver, concentrator, T-connector, or terminator. Check to make certain that connectors have not been mixed up, such as ARCnet connectors being used on an Ethernet network.

◆ Test the continuity of the cable, using various physical testing devices, such as an Optical Time Domain Reflectometer, or software, such as Novell's COMCHECK utility.

◆ If the Fileserver not found error message appears, check for a mismatch in the Ethernet frame type between the server and the client.

◆ Verify that the LAN card is working properly. Clean the connector fingers (do not use an eraser because it leaves grit on the card); pull the card and replace it with one that you know is in working order; or run the NIC's diagnostics software.

◆ If NIC resource conflicts seem to be a potential cause of network problems, remove all cards except the file server NICs, then replace them one at a time until the conflicting card is found. Then correct the NIC settings and continue checking NICs one at a time. If you are installing new NICs, avoid using the common COM port interrupts of 3 and 4 to prevent potential Ethernet card conflicts.

◆ Make sure that all the component cables in a segment are connected together. A user who moves his client and removes the T-connector incorrectly can cause a broken segment.

Understanding Token Ring Specifications

Token Ring uses a token-passing architecture that adheres to the IEEE 802.5 standard (see Chapter 4). The topology is physically a star, but logically uses a ring to pass the token from station to station (see Chapter 2, "Topologies"). Each node must be attached to a concentrator called a *multistation access unit (MSAU or MAU)*.

Token Ring network interface cards can run at 4 Mbps or 16 Mbps. 4 Mbps cards can run only at that data rate. However, 16 Mbps cards can be configured to run at 4 or 16 Mbps. All cards on a given network ring must be running at the same rate.

As shown in figure 6.9, each node acts as a repeater that receives token and data frames from its *nearest active upstream neighbor (NAUN)*. After a frame is processed by the node, the frame is passed downstream to the next attached node. Each token makes at least one trip around the entire ring. It then returns to the originating node. Workstations that indicate problems send a "beacon" to identify an address of the potential failure. Refer to Chapter 4 for more information about the Token Ring protocol. You will also learn more about this topic later in this chapter.

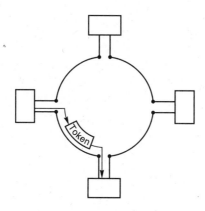

Figure 6.9

Operation of a Token Ring.

To find out if any beacon messages have been sent on your Token Ring network, review your System Error Log, found in SYSCON through Supervisor Options.

Token Ring Board Settings

As with the Ethernet cards, the node address on each NIC is burned in at the manufacturer and is unique to each card. The node address in some cases can be overridden by vendor-specified software instructions. (Check with the vendor of the component.) A maximum of two Token Ring cards can be installed in any node, with each card being defined as the primary or alternate Token Ring card in the machine. A typical Token Ring card is shown in figure 6.10.

Figure 6.10

Features of a Token Ring NIC.

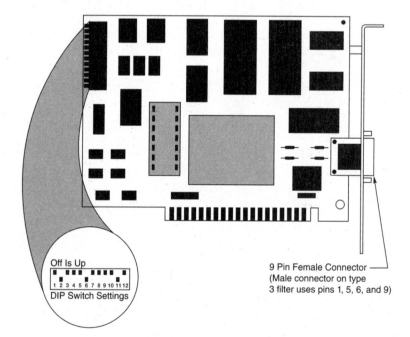

Off Is Up

1 2 3 4 5 6 7 8 9 10 11 12
DIP Switch Settings

9 Pin Female Connector
(Male connector on type
3 filter uses pins 1, 5, 6, and 9)

The following are features of a Token Ring NIC:

- DIP switches (see table 6.2)
- 9-pin female connector
- Remote boot PROM socket

 Note When loading two Token Ring NICs in a NetWare file server, make sure that you configure the primary card at port address of A20. The alternate card must be set at A24. For v3.1x or v4.x, in the AUTOEXEC.NCF file or at the file server console, use the following example commands:

```
LOAD TOKEN PORT=A20 INT=2 MEM=CC000 NAME=CARD1

LOAD TOKEN PORT=A24 INT=3 MEM=DC000 NAME=CARD2
```

The interrupt and base memory address on each Token Ring NIC must be set to avoid conflicts with all other components. Table 6.2 defines the proper DIP switch settings for an IBM 16/4 Token Ring card.

Table 6.2
IBM 16/4 Token Ring Switch Settings

Switch Blk (Off is Up, On is Down)	1	2	3	4	5	6	7	8	9	10	11	12
ADDRESS												
CC000	Off	On	On	Off	Off	On						
DC000	Off	On	Off	Off	Off	On						
INTERRUPT												
2							Off	Off				
3							On	Off				
6							Off	On				
7							Off	Off				
PRIMARY									Off			
ALTERNATE									On			

Table 6.2, Continued
IBM 16/4 Token Ring Switch Settings

Switch Blk (Off is Up, On is Down)	1	2	3	4	5	6	7	8	9	10	11	12
SHARED RAM												
8KB										On	On	
16KB										Off	On	
32KB										On	Off	
64KB										Off	Off	
DATA RATE												
16Mbps												Off
4Mbps												On

Each Token Ring card comes with a diagnostic disk that provides testing for the adapter. Refer to the appropriate documentation for your card for more detailed instructions.

Token Ring Cabling

Traditional Token Ring networks used shielded twisted pair cable. The following are standard IBM cable types for Token Ring:

◆ **Type 1.** A braided shield surrounds two twisted pairs of solid copper wire. Type 1 is used to connect terminals and distribution panels, or to connect between different wiring closets that are located in the same building. Type 1 uses two STPs of solid-core 22 AWG wire for long, high data grade transmissions within the building's walls.

◆ **Type 2.** Type 2 uses a total of six twisted pairs; two are STPs (for networking), four are UTPs (for telephone systems). Additionally, this cable type incorporates two unshielded twisted pairs that can be used for voice circuits. This cable is used for the same purposes as Type 1, but enables both voice and data cables to be included in a single cable run.

◆ **Type 3.** Type 3 has unshielded twisted-pair copper with a minimum of two twists per inch, used as an alternative to Type 1 and Type 2 cable because of its reduced cost. It has four UTPs of 24 AWG solid-core wire for networks or telephone systems. Type 3 cannot be used for 16 Mbps Token Ring networks. It is used primarily for long, low data-grade transmissions within walls. Signals will not travel as fast as with Type 1 cable because Type 3 does not have the shielding used by Type 1.

◆ **Type 5.** With Type 5, fiber optic cable is used only on the main ring. Type 5 can use two 100-um or 140-um optical fibers in one fiber jacket.

◆ **Type 6.** A braided shield surrounds two twisted pairs of stranded copper wire. It is made up of two 26 AWG stranded-core STPs. This cable supports shorter cable runs than Type 1, but is more flexible due to the stranded conductors. Type 6 is the IBM standard for patch cables and extension cables, used also in wiring closets.

◆ **Type 8.** Type 8 uses a single 26 AWG stranded-core STP and is especially designed for use under carpet.

◆ **Type 9.** Type 9 is the same as Type 6 cable except that it is designed to be fire-resistant for use in plenum installations. It uses two STPs of solid-core 26 AWG wire, and is used for long runs within the walls of a building.

Token Ring cabling is used to connect clients to the MSAU, or to connect one MSAU to another. Cables that connect between MSAUs are called patch cables. Patch cables may also be made of IBM Type 6 cable.

 Novell defines Token Ring cabling in terms of two types of systems:

◆ Small movable

◆ Large nonmovable

The small movable system supports up to 96 clients and file servers and 12 MSAUs. It uses Type 6 cable to attach clients and servers to IBM Model 8228 MSAUs. Type 6 cable is a shielded twisted pair cable with stranded conductors. This cable is flexible, but has limited distance capabilities. The characteristics of this cable make it suitable for small networks and for patch cords.

The large nonmovable system supports up to 260 clients and file servers, with up to 33 MSAUs. This network configuration uses IBM Type 1 or Type 2 cable. These are shielded twisted pair cables with solid-wire conductors suitable for carrying signals greater distances than are possible with Type 6. The large nonmovable system also involves other wiring needs such as punch panels or distribution panels, equipment racks for MSAUs, and wiring closets to contain the previously listed components.

The MSAU is the central cabling component for IBM Token Ring networks. The 8228 MSAU was the original wiring hub developed by IBM for Token Ring networks. Figure 6.11 shows 8228 MSAUs. Each 8228 has ten connectors, eight of which accept cables to clients or servers. The other connectors are labeled RI (ring in) and RO (ring out). The RI and RO connectors are used to connect multiple 8228s to form larger networks.

8228s are mechanical devices that consist of relays and connectors. Their purpose is to switch clients in and out of the network. Each port is controlled by a relay powered by a voltage sent to the MSAU from the client. When an 8228 is first set up, each of these relays must be initialized with a setup tool shipped with the unit.

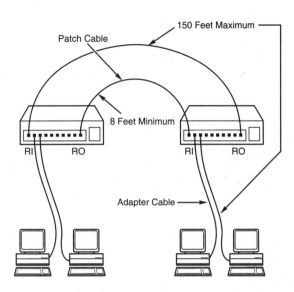

Figure 6.11

An example of Token Ring cabling using MSAUs.

The setup tool is inserted into each port and held there until a light indicates that the port is properly initialized.

IBM Token Ring networks use two types of connectors. NICs are equipped with a nine-pin D-connector. MSAUs, repeaters, and most other equipment use a special IBM data connector. Two types of cables are employed:

♦ *Patch cables* have IBM data connectors at both ends. These cables interconnect MSAUs, repeaters, and most other Token Ring components.

♦ *Token Ring adapter cables* have an IBM data connector at one end and a nine-pin connector at the other. Adapter cables connect client and server NICs to other network components that use IBM data connectors.

Figure 6.11 shows an example of a network cabling several clients and MSAUs. The distances noted in the figure are based on the rules for the small movable cabling system.

When you are connecting a Token Ring network, make sure that you do the following:

1. Initialize each port in the 8228 MSAU by using the setup tool shipped with the MSAU (wait for the click) before connecting a cable.

2. If using more than one MSAU, connect the ring out (RO) port of each MSAU with the ring in (RI) port of the next MSAU in the loop. This must physically complete a circle or ring.

A variety of rules must be observed when configuring Token Rings. The following rules apply to small, movable Token Ring networks:

◆ The minimum patch cable distance between two MSAUs is eight feet.

◆ The maximum patch cable distance between two MSAUs is 150 feet. Patch cables come in standard lengths of 8, 30, 75, and 150 feet for Type 6.

◆ The maximum patch cable distance connecting all MSAUs is 400 feet.

◆ The maximum adapter cable distance between an MSAU and a node is 150 feet.

A small movable IBM cable system consists of the following:

◆ Maximum 96 nodes

◆ Maximum 12 MSAUs

◆ Uses Type 6 cable

A large nonmovable IBM cable system consists of the following:

◆ Maximum 260 nodes

◆ Maximum 33 MSAUs

◆ Uses Type 1 or Type 2 cable

Note Token Ring networks also can be cabled using UTP cabling, which IBM calls Type 3 cable. The IEEE 802.5 standard describes 4 Mbps Token Ring using UTP cable. However, level 5 UTP is currently used for 16 Mbps Token Ring.

When using UTP wiring, a media filter must be installed between the NIC and the UTP cable. Some newer Token Ring NICs have built-in media filters and RJ-45 jacks ready to interface with UTP wiring.

Token Ring Troubleshooting

When troubleshooting a Token Ring network, as with trouble-shooting other types of networks, begin with the more obvious physical problems, checking such things as connectors to see if they are tight and properly connected. You also should check to see that manufacturer's specifications are met, and that cable lengths, maximum number of nodes, and so on, are correct.

When troubleshooting Token Ring networks, you also should look for the following:

◆ Any base I/O, DMA shared memory, or interrupt conflicts with other boards.

◆ The version of the client or server software driver, to make sure that its revision level is compatible with your NIC (drivers are different for file servers and clients).

◆ Proper connections of MSAUs, with ring out ports connecting to ring in ports throughout the ring. In troubleshooting problems that you have first isolated to a particular area of the network, if you suspect the MSAU, isolate it by changing the ring in and ring out cables to bypass the MSAU. If the ring is now functional again, consider replacing the MSAU. You may also find that if your network has MSAUs from more than one manufacturer, they are not wholly compatible. Impedance and other electrical characteristics may show slight differences between manufacturers, causing intermittent network problems.

◆ Other MSAU problems. Some MSAUs other than the 8228 are active and require a power supply. These MSAUs fail if they have a blown fuse or a bad power source.

◆ Correct attachments of patch cables and the adapter cable. Remember, patch cables connect MSAUs together, and the adapter cable connects the NIC to the MSAU. Patch cables, adapter cables, and MSAUs are common sources of problems. Isolating the problem is easier to do if you have a current log of your network's physical design. Once you have narrowed down the problem, you can isolate potential problem areas on the network from the rest of the network, and then use a cable tester to find the actual problem.

◆ A failed NIC. Try substituting another one known to work properly. NICs that have failure rates that exceed a preset tolerance level may actually remove themselves from the network.

◆ A bad MSAU or MSAU port. Ports may need to be reinitialized with the setup tool. Removing drop cables and reinitializing each MSAU port is a "quick fix" that is useful on relatively small Token Ring networks.

◆ Incorrect card speeds; for example, a 16 Mbps card is inserted into a 4 Mbps ring or vice versa. Neither situation is correct. The speed of the NIC is displayed when the Token Ring driver is loaded at the client.

◆ The wrong type of cable for the speed of the network.

◆ Bent or broken pins on the adapter cable.

◆ Duplicate node addresses. If you are overriding the burned-in network addresses, it is possible that duplicate node addresses may be set.

◆ The Type 3 media filter, if connecting to a 4 Mbps twisted pair network.

One of the advantages of a Token Ring network is its built-in ability to monitor itself. This process provides electronic trouble-shooting and, when possible, repair processes. When it is not possible for the Token Ring network to make its own repairs, a process called *beaconing* is helpful. Beaconing narrows down the portion of the ring where the problem is most likely to exist. This potential problem area is referred to as the *fault domain*.

The Beaconing Process

The design of the Token Ring network itself contributes greatly to the ability of the beaconing process to troubleshoot its own network. The design includes two types of network stations known as Active Monitors and Standby Monitors. Only one Active Monitor can exist on a network at a time. All other stations are Standby Monitors.

Generally, the first station that is powered-up and becomes part of the network is automatically the Active Monitor station. The responsibility of the Active Monitor station is to announce itself to the next active downstream station as the Active Monitor station, and request that station to announce itself to its next active downstream station. The Active Monitor station sends out this beacon announcement every seven seconds.

Once each station has announced itself to its next active downstream neighbor, the announcing station becomes the nearest active upstream neighbor (NAUN) to the downstream station. Each station on a Token Ring network has an upstream neighbor as well as a downstream neighbor.

Once each station is aware of its NAUN, the beaconing process continues every seven seconds. If for some reason a station does not receive one of its expected seven-second beaconed announcements from its upstream neighbor, it attempts to notify the network of its lack of contact from the upstream neighbor. It sends a message out onto the network ring, which includes the following:

◆ The sending station's network address

◆ The receiving NAUN's network address

◆ The beacon type

From this information, the ring can determine which station may be having a problem and attempt to fix the problem without disrupting the entire network. This problem fix is known as *autoreconfiguration*. If the autoreconfiguration is unsuccessful, manual correction is required. Figure 6.12 shows a Token Ring network utilizing the beaconing process.

Figure 6.12

Token Ring beaconing.

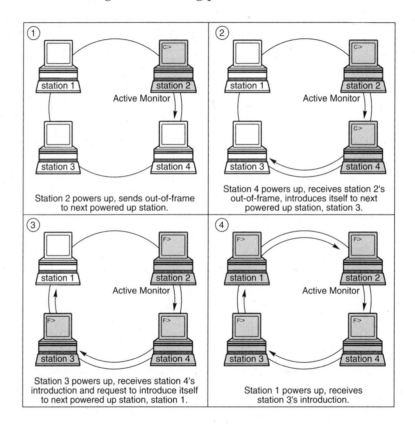

① Station 2 powers up, sends out-of-frame to next powered up station.

② Station 4 powers up, receives station 2's out-of-frame, introduces itself to next powered up station, station 3.

③ Station 3 powers up, receives station 4's introduction and request to introduce itself to next powered up station, station 1.

④ Station 1 powers up, receives station 3's introduction.

The preceding section detailed common characteristics of ARCnet, Ethernet, and Token Ring. Other components also must be examined for conflicts and proper configuration. The next section describes these items.

Understanding FDDI

 Decide when it is appropriate to consider the installation of FDDI.

Fiber Distributed Data Interface (FDDI) is a LAN standard that, like Token Ring, follows the IEEE 802.5 standard (see Chapter 4) for accessing the network. FDDI carries both LED and laser-generated LAN communications through fiber-optic cables.

Fiber optic cable is primarily made of pure glass that is pulled into very thin wires or fibers. Many of these fibers are bundled together to form a core. This core is surrounded by another layer of glass called *cladding*. The LED sends the signals through the core of this cable, and the cladding contains these signals to the core. The signal on each fiber can go in only one direction at a time. The bundle of fibers enables the LED to send multiples of signals at a time.

Unlike Token Ring and its related network interface cards that transfer data across the network at speeds of 4 or 16 Mbps, FDDI transfers information at a rate of 100 Mbps. In addition, FDDI is structured to take advantage of two rings, rather than one. This Dual Counter Rotating Rings structure enables FDDI to transfer data across one ring while it performs backup and other services on the second ring.

In addition, FDDI uses multiple tokens and has the ability to bypass network stations designated as low priority, so it can provide faster service to high-priority network stations.

Like a Token Ring LAN, FDDI uses a token to transfer data frames around the network. After the data frame is processed by the correct network station, the token is passed on to the next attached network node.

The second ring in the FDDI network rotates in the opposite direction of the first ring. This counter-rotation enables the network to compensate for a break in the fiber. If one ring in the network becomes broken due to a problem at one of the network stations, those stations located on either side of the break can isolate the break in the fiber by forming a single ring (wrapping) from their own ports, as shown in figure 6.13.

Figure 6.13

Isolated cable break in an FDDI network.

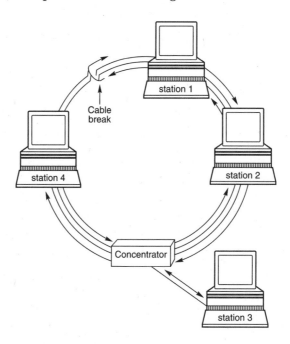

Each network station can be attached to either one ring or to both rings, depending on the class of the connected station. There are two types of station classes: Class A and Class B.

Class A stations, also called Single Attached Stations (SAS), can be attached to only one ring at a time. Only Class B stations, or Dual attached Stations (DAS), can be connected to both rings simultaneously. This designation of station classes helps to keep unstable network devices from breaking both network rings.

Another method of isolating faulty nodes in the network is through the use of wiring concentrators. Wiring concentrators function in theory much like the Token Ring MSAU. They act as centralized cabling connection devices for network stations. Unlike MSAUs, however, wiring concentrators are capable of communicating with stations and verifying the integrity of the station-to-concentrator connection.

Advantages of Using FDDI

The ability to isolate a break in the cable and continue network communication makes FDDI an extremely reliable cabling option. FDDI has several other advantages.

FDDI overcomes some of the performance problems experienced by traditional Token Ring networks. It accomplishes this by implementing a standard that provides fair and timely access to the network.

Increased reliability is another advantage of using FDDI. That reliability comes in several forms, including the following:

◆ **Information security.** Fiber-optic cable is difficult to wiretap.

◆ **Physical security.** Fiber-optic cable is more resistant to cable breakage than are other types of cabling.

◆ **Electrical security.** Fiber-optic cable is not susceptible to electrical interference, and does not conduct electricity.

FDDI also can transmit network packets over its cable for distances that are significantly longer than other types of cabling. For example, on a fiber-optic cable with no cable bends or breaks that would otherwise reduce the integrity of the transmission, information theoretically can travel hundreds of miles.

FDDI also has built-in management of three aspects of the network, including the following:

◆ Ring Management (RMT) is responsible for finding and resolving faults in the network ring.

◆ Connection Management (CMT) is responsible for controlling stations that are inserting themselves into the network, or removing themselves from the network.

355

◆ Station Management (SMT) makes it possible for special high-level programs to monitor the ring.

As noted earlier, FDDI networks are substantially faster than Token Ring networks, capable of communicating at a rate of 100 Mbps. They accomplish this speed not only as a result of the type of cable (fiber optic) that they use, but also as a result of their use of multiple tokens and their ability to service only the high-priority network stations, bypassing the low-priority stations whenever necessary.

A fiber optic cable is also significantly lighter in weight than is, for example, twisted pair cabling with an equivalent bandwidth.

 Don't look directly at fiber-optic cable without eye protection. To check to see whether a fiber-optic port is transmitting, darken the room and place a piece of paper in front of the port. If it is transmitting, a light will be reflected onto the paper.

Disadvantages of Using FDDI

There are two primary disadvantages of using FDDI in your network. First, because of the complexity and newness of FDDI technology, you need a great deal of expertise to install and subsequently maintain an FDDI network.

Second, although the cost of the cable itself is comparable to that of Unshielded Twisted Pair (UTP) cabling, the concentrators and LAN adapters are relatively expensive. For example, a typical FDDI concentrator runs between $1,000 and $1,500 per network node. Therefore, the overall cost of an FDDI network for a LAN of any size can quickly become quite costly.

FDDI Cabling

Various types and wavelengths of fiber-optic cables are available. A typical fiber-optic cable consists of a core made from silica, surrounded by a primary and secondary buffer, and then enclosed in a jacket. Kevlar may be added to provide strength.

The important thing to remember about choosing a fiber-optic cable is to select one based on its intended use, and to match the cable to its appropriate connectors. Figure 6.14 shows a typical duplex fiber-optic cable.

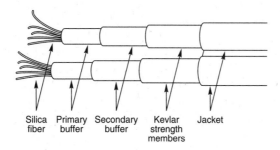

Silica Primary Secondary Kevlar Jacket
fiber   buffer   buffer   strength
                            members

Figure 6.14

Fiber optic duplex cable assembly.

FDDI Troubleshooting

As with troubleshooting all types of networks, begin by looking for the obvious problems, such as loose connectors, damaged cables, and so on. After ruling out these types of problems, consider other possible causes. Look first at those problems considered typical of FDDI networks:

◆ Incorrect cable type for actual distance between nodes. On an FDDI network where network information must travel thousands of feet, Multimode Fiber should be used. When distances between nodes begin to reach tens of thousands of feet, or exceed distances of two kilometers, Single-Mode Fiber is necessary.

357

◆ Problems with communicating between network nodes. Even small breaks in a fiber-optic cable can result in network communication problems. There are several ways to detect cable problems, all except one requiring special equipment. If a break in a segment of the cable is a complete break, you can detect the break using a flashlight. Otherwise, you can use an optical power meter and a source of light energy to test the cable. If either of these methods is insufficient, you can use the most expensive method, an Optical Time Domain Reflectometer (OTDR).

◆ Dirt on connectors is another cause of communication problems between network nodes. Data is transmitted through fiber-optic cables using light. Therefore, it is important that you keep connectors free from dust and dirt. You can clean connectors using any type of lint-free cloth dampened with alcohol. Do not use water or any type of cleaning fluids other than alcohol.

◆ Communication problems also can be caused by bad connectors or by a segment of the cable that is open (incorrectly terminated). A loss of optical power that exceeds 13.0 decibels is an indication that cable problems of this nature may exist. To correct these problems, replace faulty connectors and/or properly close any open cable segment.

◆ A delay of up to four milliseconds in communication is not unusual for fiber-optic cable. If communication delays are a problem, consider using NetWare's Packet Burst Protocol to send multiple rather than single frames across the network, thus reducing transmission delay.

◆ When the network does not efficiently handle transmissions across cable that exceeds 50 meters, or which requires 10 Mbps or more throughput, this problem may be directly related to the type of fiber-optic cable. If you are using plastic fiber optic cable in your network, consider replacing all or at least some of this cable with glass cable. Speed can be affected by the type of fiber-optic cable used.

◆ The path that network information must travel should be the most efficient. If you are using bridges instead of routers in your network, consider switching to network routers. NetWare network routers, or routers such as CI500 and Wellfleet that are certified by Novell, can choose the best path for any given packet. They are somewhat slower than bridges, however, because of the increased processing that they perform. The design of FDDI translation bridges makes routers the preferred choice for FDDI networks running NetWare.

Which Topology Should I Use?

As a network administrator or support engineer, you have to make some tough decisions on the best type of topology to incorporate into your network environment. It is similar to choosing what type of vehicle and size of engine you need to drive your loads on local streets, freeways, or highways. You need to consider using Token Ring (4 Mbps or 16 Mbps) or Ethernet (10 Mbps). You also need to consider which type of cabling system you need for your network.

The factors that are involved in your choice include the following:

◆ Type of applications and their percentage of overall use

◆ Flexibility of setup

◆ Cost

◆ Knowledge level of your support or vendor source

◆ Availabilty of replacement or add-on components

No one topology is better than another. Your choice is dependent on how the factors affect your network environment.

Choose the Ethernet topology for those types of networks with a light-to-medium workload. If you are using standard applications, such as word processing, spreadsheets, gateway host sessions, electronic mail, and calendaring packages, Ethernet will work efficiently.

Ethernet has a maximum throughput of 10 Mbps. (Standard loads usually are working around 8-9.1 Mbps.) The cost is nominal, and interchangeable components are readily available. Clients can attempt to transmit more quickly rather than waiting their turn, as is done with the Token Ring topology.

The disadvantage of Ethernet is that the size of the data frames in the packets may require more traffic to pass along the data files on the media. Also, the collision-oriented system can be degraded with the heavy use of database, imaging, multimedia, or CAD/CAM applications.

Token Ring topology is a choice for networks that tend toward heavy workloads. The size of the data frame in the packet is larger than in Ethernet. Token Ring can handle large file transfers—such as database, CAD/CAM, and multiple accesses to imaging files—more easily. Token Ring runs at 4 Mbps or 16 Mbps on many types of media. Some applications of 16 Mbps Token Ring speed are not always as efficient as using the 4 Mbps or the Ethernet 10 Mbps.

Token Ring is more reliable because no collisions occur with the token passing scheme. The disadvantages of Token Ring are cost, station transmission capabilities, and the overhead for management of the token scheme. Also, the more clients you add to a ring, the more that performance can be degraded. Consider splitting the ring into smaller rings with fewer clients attached.

Use your best judgment on your network setup. Where your applications reside, the location of your workloads, and the availability of your network components will determine whether you should use one topology or perhaps mix them.

Review Questions

1.   Which is the least important when configuring a client?

   ○   a.   Avoiding conflicts

   ○   b.   How other clients are configured

- c. Checking that cables meet specifications for their intended topology
- d. Matching drivers to operating system revisions

2. Which statement about ARCnet is false?

- a. ARCnet can be cabled in star or bus.
- b. ARCnet uses RG-62/U for coax.
- c. ARCnet has the unique feature time-out setting of 31 microseconds.
- d. ARCnet can span a distance of 25,000 feet.

3. Which combination is not supported?

- a. Passive hub to passive hub
- b. Active hub to passive hub to active hub
- c. Active hub to passive hub
- d. Network node to passive hub

4. Which is not a feature of an Ethernet board?

- a. Ethernet boards usually have DIX connectors.
- b. Ethernet boards can have thick (DIX), thin (BNC), or twisted pair (RJ-45) connectors.
- c. Ethernet boards have internal transceivers for thin net.
- d. Ethernet boards have a time-out setting.

5. Which level cable is correct for 10BASE-T?

- a. Level I
- b. Level II
- c. Level IV
- d. Level VI

6. Which statement about Token Ring cabling is true?

   ○ a. Small, movable systems support up to 96 clients and 12 MSAUs. Token Ring networks cannot use UTP cabling.

   ○ b. The maximum patch cable distance between two MSAUs is 75 feet.

   ○ c. The minimum patch cable distance is 2.5 feet.

   ○ d. Token Ring uses Type 2, Type 4, and Type 6 cabling.

7. Which two of the following statements regarding FDDI are true?

   ☐ a. It follows the IEEE 802.5 standard.

   ☐ b. Like Token Ring, it uses only a single token.

   ☐ c. FDDI can transfer data at speeds of 100 Mbps.

   ☐ d. Stations must attach to the cable by a concentrator.

8. FDDI stands for

   ○ a. Fiber-based Data Distribution Interface

   ○ b. Fiber Distributed Data Interface

   ○ c. Fiber optic Data Distributed Interface

   ○ d. Fiber Data Distribution Interface

9. Plastic and glass fiber optic cables can be used equally well in all situations except

   ○ a. When the cable distance is less than 50 meters.

   ○ b. When the cable has an open condition.

   ○ c. When stations are attached using a concentrator.

   ○ d. When throughput of 10 Mbps or greater is required.

10. Which of the following is one advantage that FDDI has over Token Ring?

   ○ a. Fiber optic cable is difficult to wiretap.

   ○ b. FDDI is capable of isolating cable breaks.

   ○   c. FDDI provides fair and timely access to the network.

   ○   d. FDDI has built-in ring management.

11. What is the main advantage of using 10BASE2 when network segments do not have to exceed 185 meters?

   ○   a. It is relatively simple to connect.

   ○   b. Drop cables can be used, making it easier to troubleshoot.

   ○   c. Each node connects directly to the cable.

   ○   d. It is the least expensive of the cabling options.

12. Which of the Ethernet cabling options requires that each end of the bus be terminated?

   ☐   a. 10BASE2

   ☐   b. 10BASE5

   ☐   c. 10BASE-T

   ☐   d. Thin net

13. Which of the cabling options is considered the trend for wiring Ethernet networks?

   ○   a. 10BASE2

   ○   b. 10BASE5

   ○   c. 10BASE-T

   ○   d. Thick net

14. Which of the following is not an advantage in using 10BASE-T for cabling a network?

   ○   a. It is easier and more reliable to manage.

   ○   b. Centralized hubs make it easier to detect bad cable segments.

   ○   c. Beaconing helps to isolate cable breaks.

   ○   d. It is relatively inexpensive to use.

15. Which of the following Ethernet frame types is designated as raw Ethernet?

   ○ a. ETHERNET_802.2

   ○ b. ETHERNET_802.3

   ○ c. ETHERNET_SNAP

   ○ d. ETHERNET_II

Answers

1. B

2. D

3. A

4. D

5. C

6. C

7. A, C

8. B

9. B

10. A

11. D

12. B, A

13. C

14. C

15. B

Using Novell DOS

Although many network clients run Microsoft DOS as their local operating system, many individuals and companies are discovering the benefits that Novell's DR DOS 6.0 offers them over Microsoft DOS 5.0. This chapter discusses Novell's DR DOS 6.0. It also discusses some aspects of Novell DOS 7.0, the next released version of DR DOS 6.0.

After reading this chapter, you will be able to do the following:

- ◆ Understand the benefits and features of DR DOS 6.0

- ◆ Run DR DOS 6.0 setup

- ◆ Use MemoryMax to increase available application memory

- ◆ Enhance disk performance with DISKMAP

- ◆ Switch between applications using TaskMAX

- ◆ Get help using DOSBook and /H

- ◆ Troubleshoot a DR DOS 6.0 client

Understanding the Benefits and Features of DR DOS 6.0

DR DOS 6.0 and Novell DOS 7.0 are excellent alternatives to and replacements for Microsoft DOS 6.x, because they are both fully compatible with NetWare and provide several useful enhancements:

♦ Disk compression and defragmentation abilities that enable you to double the client's available hard disk storage space and maximize actual disk space by defragmenting and resaving fragmented files.

♦ Increased conventional memory space for application programs, which is accomplished by moving part of the DR DOS operating system, drivers, and other *terminate-and-stay-resident* (TSR) programs into other areas of memory.

♦ DISKMAP, DELWATCH, and UNDELETE utilities, which together enable you to recover files that you previously deleted.

♦ Data protection and system security that is enhanced through the use of a BACKUP utility, and the ATTRIB command that enables you to flag specific files to keep them from being copied or accidentally deleted. Figure 7.1 shows the successful backup of a single directory on the local hard disk to a network drive.

Figure 7.1

Backup of a local directory.

```
C:\>backup c:\collage\*.* k:

Backing-up from C:\COLLAGE to K:\BACKUP
All files in K:\BACKUP will be deleted.

Strike a key when ready.


Backing up to K:\BACKUP
\COLLAGE\ALTOFF.EXE
\COLLAGE\ALTON.EXE
\COLLAGE\CLEANUP.BAT
\COLLAGE\COLLAGE.EXE
\COLLAGE\COLLAGE.HLP
\COLLAGE\INSTALL.EXE
\COLLAGE\READ.ME
\COLLAGE\S.EXE
\COLLAGE\SAMPLE.PCX
\COLLAGE\SAVE.EXE
\COLLAGE\SHOW.EXE
\COLLAGE\SHOWLITE.EXE
\COLLAGE\SNAP.EXE
\COLLAGE\VIEW.EXE
```

♦ Application switching that does not require the additional purchase and use of Microsoft Windows, but uses TaskMAX to provide this ability.

◆ Built-in online help through DOSBook and for command-line utilities using the /? or /H options.

◆ Installation procedures and a SETUP program that enable you to customize your startup files interactively, reducing the amount of manual editing you must do in order to optimize your computer system.

◆ The UNINSTALL command that enables you to save your old operating system when you install DR DOS 6.0 so if it ever becomes necessary, you can remove DR DOS 6.0 and reactivate your previous version of DOS.

◆ Full-screen and command-line editing capabilities, which are configurable.

◆ Capability of transferring files and programs from one computer to another through the computer's serial ports and the DR DOS 6 FileLink file transfer utility. Figure 7.2 shows the initial screen for the FileLink utility.

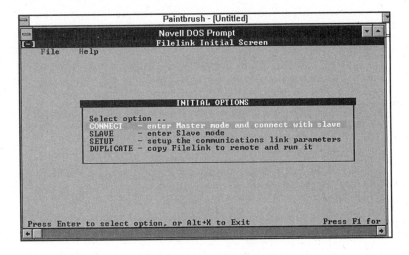

Figure 7.2

The FileLink Initial Options screen.

◆ Disk caching to increase the speed of read and write disk (or disk) requests.

Understanding how DR DOS works can help you make the best use of DR DOS features. As with Microsoft DOS, DR DOS functions by executing different internal and external commands. However, improvements have been made to the DR DOS versions of many of the regular Microsoft DOS commands with which you may be familiar. In addition, commands that are not included in Microsoft DOS have been added to DR DOS. These are some of the improved and added commands:

♦ CHKDSK checks fixed and floppy disks for errors and shows you information, such as the volume name, create date, errors (if found), and total bytes in different areas (hidden files, directories, and files that are pending deletion).

♦ DISKCOPY makes a complete image copy of one nonfixed disk to another nonfixed disk using the same format. DISKCOPY formats the target disk to match the source disk. Use XCOPY between disks that have incompatible formats (3.5-inch to 5.25-inch).

♦ MEM displays information about the current configuration of your client's memory, including memory type, total bytes, and, if the correct switches are used, exact memory location. Figure 7.3 shows the switches that can be used with the MEM command.

Figure 7.3

Help screen for memory usage utility.

```
C:\>mem /?
MEM R1.08    Memory usage utility
Copyright (c) 1990,1993 Novell, Inc.  All rights reserved.

MEM [/Help] [/switches]

    /A          show all information
    /B          show memory blocks in conventional memory only
    /CLASSIFY   show a summary of loaded programs
    /DEBUG      show loaded programs and internal drivers
    /F          show memory blocks in segment FFFF (high memory) only
    /I          show internal and loaded device drivers
    /M          show system memory map
    /P          list one page at a time
    /PROGRAM    show currently loaded programs
    /S          show system structures
    /U          show memory blocks in upper memory only

If no parameter is specified the total amount of memory available is show

C:\>
```

♦ UNDELETE enables you to restore files that you previously deleted, if you had DELWATCH activated before deleting the files.

♦ XDIR provides additional options for listing files and directories on your disk drive. Additional information that it displays includes a computed checksum for each file, a reversed sort order, and a display of files in subdirectories and in the current directory.

♦ CURSOR changes the way the cursor is displayed on the monitor to make it easier to see on special monitors, such as the *Liquid Crystal Display* (LCD) screens used on laptops and other portable computers.

♦ REPLACE enables you to update older files with newer copies in the current directory or across different subdirectories. Figure 7.4 shows the help screen for the REPLACE utility, listing the options that can be used with this utility.

```
C:\>replace /?
REPLACE R1.46 Selective file copy
Copyright (c) 1987,1993 Novell, Inc.  All rights reserved.

REPLACE [/Help] [@][d:][path][filename[.ext]] [d:][path] [/options]

The first file specification is the drive, path and name of file(s) to be
copied (wildcard filenames allowed). This specification must be present.
Use '@' to specify that the given file contains a list of files to be copied.

The second file specification is the destination drive and path to which files
will be copied. The default is the current drive and path.

    /A          only copy files that do not exist on the destination
    /H          don't ignore files with hidden or system attributes
    /M          merge changed files on source with unchanged files on dest.
    /N          preview operation - do not actually copy any files
    /P          prompt before copying each file
    /R          overwrite read-only files
    /S          copy files in subdirectories
    /U          only replace files older on the destination than the source
    /W          wait for disks to be changed

C:\>
```

Figure 7.4
The REPLACE help screen.

♦ TOUCH enables you to change the time and date stamps assigned to one or more files.

♦ XDEL enables you to delete several or all files in a subdirectory without having to respond to a prompt before each file is deleted. XDEL also enables you to remove any empty subdirectories.

♦ TREE provides a list of all directories and subdirectories on the disk and shows the number of files in each directory, as

well as the total bytes of space used by each directory.
Figure 7.5 shows a portion of a TREE.

Figure 7.5

Result of a TREE
command.

```
C:\>TREE
        bytes  files   path
   13,522,239    53   c:\
    1,905,111    99   c:\drdos
            0     0   c:\drdos\tmp
      256,666     5   c:\temp
            0     0   c:\temp\backup
    7,458,073   180   c:\nwclient
    1,091,118     9   c:\nwclient\tutor
      248,585    98   c:\nwclient\nls
      232,096    32   c:\nwclient\nls\english
            0     0   c:\nwclient\ins
       84,579     9   c:\nwclient\rpl
      347,258     4   c:\mobile
            0     0   c:\complib
      633,073     8   c:\complib\cs
    8,099,190   149   c:\windows
    8,159,799   151   c:\windows\system
      248,585    98   c:\windows\nls
            0     0   c:\windows\temp
    4,326,536   136   c:\wp51
       83,509     4   c:\wp51\styles
      730,133    31   c:\flexware
```

◆ SCRIPT translates text files into usable PostScript format.
SCRIPT can be used either from the command line or as a
TSR. Using it from the command line requires input from a
file, a program, or the system console. Using SCRIPT as a
TSR automatically translates all data specified for printing
into PostScript format.

 SCRIPT can be a benefit for screen prints from
clients sent to a laser printer.

There are other advantages to and options for using DR DOS 6.0.
However, only the major ones are covered in this chapter. You can
get more information about any of these as well as other options
and commands by using DOSBook and the command-line help
switches /? and /H.

Running DR DOS Setup

The DR DOS 6.0 and Novell DOS 7.0 setup programs are similar.
SETUP is a menu-based utility used to configure most of the DR
DOS options.

Start SETUP by typing **SETUP** at the DOS prompt and pressing Enter. Several initialization files are read into memory, then the main SETUP window appears.

You can choose to perform various setup options from the main setup screen. For example, you can set up disk compression, data protection and security, or task management. In Novell DOS 7.0, you also can set up networking because Novell DOS 7.0 includes Personal NetWare, Novell's peer-to-peer network operating system. In Novell DOS 7.0, the SETUP main screen appears as shown in figure 7.6.

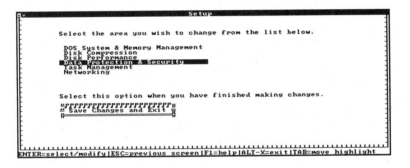

Figure 7.6

Novell DOS 7 setup screen.

One of the best reasons for using SETUP is its ability to help you maximize memory available for running application programs. By using the SETUP utility to optimize memory, you do not have to modify your configuration files manually using a text or other type of editor.

However, with SETUP (particularly the Novell DOS 7 version), you can perform several configuration and setup tasks, including the following:

◆ Create and reconfigure disk compression

◆ Establish an area in memory to act like a fast disk (VDISK.SYS)

◆ Turn on and define the parameters of NWCACHE (*disk caching software*)

◆ Activate DELWATCH and DISKMAP (file recovery utilities), Search & Destroy (Novell DOS 7's Anti-Virus software), screen saver (Novell DOS 7's security for unattended computers program), and LOCK (also a security program for unattended computers that works with both DR DOS 6.0 and Novell DOS 7.0)

◆ Load MultiTasking and TaskSwitching software

◆ Set up and configure Personal NetWare from Novell DOS 7.0

As mentioned previously, one of the key advantages of DR DOS 6.0 and Novell DOS 7.0 is the ability to manage memory to ensure that the maximum amount of memory is available for running application programs. MemoryMax is a collection of software that provides additional memory management capabilities.

Using MemoryMax To Increase Available Application Memory

MemoryMax, activated by typing **MEMMAX** (and related command switches) at the DOS prompt and pressing Enter, utilizes several device drivers and DOS commands to maximize the RAM memory in your client. Figure 7.7 shows the command-line help screen for MEMMAX, which displays and defines the available MEMMAX command switches.

Figure 7.7

MEMMAX help screen showing command switches.

```
C:\>MEMMAX /?
MEMMAX R2.0   Memory extension control
Copyright (c) 1990,1993 Novell, Inc.  All rights reserved.

MEMMAX [/?!/Help] [+!-U] [+!-L] [+!-V] [/U] [/L] [/V]
  +U    opens upper memory for programs (-U closes it)
  +L    opens lower memory for programs (-L closes it)
  +V    maps memory into video memory space (-V unmaps it)
  /U    displays upper memory status
  /L    displays lower memory status
  /V    displays video memory status
Upper memory is memory between 640 Kb and 1 Mb.
Lower memory is memory in the first 64 Kb.

C:\>
```

The primary method of freeing conventional memory for use by applications used by MEMMAX is to move the local operating system out of conventional memory and into extended or expanded memory. This requires two specific device drivers, and two specific DOS commands. The device drivers used are the following:

◆ EMM386.SYS, which is used with Intel-based 80386 and 80486 computers

◆ HIDOS.SYS, which is used with Intel-based 80286 computers that have extended memory

The DOS commands used are the following:

◆ HIDOS=ON (OFF is the default), which is used after either the EMM386.SYS or HIDOS.SYS device driver is loaded and which relocates most of the DR DOS 6.0 operating system kernel (*base data structure*) into upper memory

If you are already using a third-party memory manager such as QEMM in your computer, do not use HIDOS because it may cause a conflict. DR DOS 6.0 uses a different technique for mapping the upper memory areas than other third-party memory managers.

◆ HIBUFFERS=## (where ## represents a given number such as 20), which specifies memory buffers but locates them in upper memory, freeing otherwise unavailable conventional memory (assuming that either the EMM386.SYS or HIDOS.SYS device driver has been loaded)

High memory is very limited. If HIDOS has been set to ON, and if there is an insufficient amount of high memory for setting up the requested number of buffers, the remaining buffers are allocated from upper memory. If HIDOS is not set to ON and

continues

373

remains at the default of OFF, the remaining buffers are allocated from conventional memory. Therefore, it is important to place the HIDOS=ON command in the CONFIG.SYS file before the HIBUFFERS=## command.

EMM386.SYS

Some of the features provided by the EMM386.SYS device driver include the following:

- ◆ LIM 4.0 expanded memory support

- ◆ Upper memory relocation of the operating system kernel

- ◆ An additional 64-96KB of conventional memory, depending on the video adapter being used and whether or not the /VIDEO option is activated

- ◆ Full XMS support

- ◆ Microsoft Windows 3 Real, Standard, and Enhanced Mode support

The EMM386.SYS device driver also enables code and data to be copied from ROM to RAM. This reduces the execution time required for some processes.

For details on the proper syntax to use with the EMM386.SYS device driver, run DOSBook as follows:

1. Type **DOSBOOK** at the DOS prompt and press Enter.

2. Choose Contents from the DOSBook Welcome screen.

3. Press Page Down until Chapter 10 Managing Memory appears on the screen.

4. Press the down and right arrows until EMM386 is highlighted.

5. Press Enter.

The information that appears shows the exact syntax needed when loading the EMM386.SYS device driver, as well as a list of all available options and their descriptions. Some of the available options are shown in table 7.1.

Table 7.1
EMM386.SYS Options

Option	Description
/AUTO	Turns the memory manager on and off automatically
/EXCLUDE	Sets aside a particular area in memory and makes it off-limits to the memory manager when it looks for usable memory
/FRAME	Emulates expanded (EMS) memory
/INT15=KB	Sets aside the specified kilobytes of extended memory for non-XMS/EMS-compatible third-party programs
/MULTI	Supports the multitasking capabilities of DOS
/ROM	Copies slower ROM memory into RAM
/VIDEO	Tells the computer to use all unused video memory for applications
/WINSTD	Supports Windows 3 Standard (80286) mode

Enhancing Disk Performance with DiskMAX

DiskMAX is DR DOS 6.0's term for a series of utilities that are used to enhance the performance of your disk. These utilities include the following:

◆ SSTOR, software that is used to compress data on a disk so that more data can be stored

◆ Super PC-Kwik, software that sets up an area in memory so that frequently accessed files can be read or stored more quickly

◆ DISKMAP, software that copies the current file allocation table (FAT) to enable use of UNDELETE

◆ DELWATCH, TSR software that marks for deletion instead of actually deleting files so that UNDELETE can be used to restore the files at a later date

◆ UNDELETE, software that is used to recover deleted files that were marked with DELWATCH or temporarily saved by DISKMAP and not yet written over

◆ DISKOPT, software that optimizes the hard disk by repositioning data so as to make all files contiguous and provide additional free disk space

SSTOR

Typing **SSTOR** at the DOS prompt and pressing Enter activates the SuperStor Data Compression Utilities. These utilities enable you to compress files on a disk.

When you activate SuperStor, a list of system devices appears, along with a Main Menu. The Main Menu options include the following:

◆ Prepare, which creates a file on the disk you specify to be the disk that holds the SuperStor compressed disk

◆ Remove, which eliminates the compressed disk *and eliminates all data on that disk*

◆ Statistics, which displays various items of information regarding the SuperStor compressed disk

◆ Help, which provides online help regarding SuperStor that is available during different SuperStor prompts

- ◆ E<u>x</u>it, which enables you to exit from the SuperStor Data Compression Utilities

The following are compression rates for SSTOR:

Word processing files	2:1—4:1
Spreadsheet files	2:1—4.1
Database files	2:1—8:1
Video image files	2:1—8:1
CAD/CAM	3:1—8:1
Executable program files	1.4:1—2:1

In Novell DOS 7.0, data compression is achieved through a utility called Stacker. Once created, Stacker volumes can be mounted or dismounted, much like NetWare volumes. Unmounted Stacker disks cannot be accessed. As with SuperStor, both floppy disks and fixed disks can have data compression applied using Stacker.

Super PC-Kwik

Super PC-Kwik is DR DOS 6.0's disk caching software. Novell DOS 7.0 uses NWCACHE.

Super PC-Kwik is activated by issuing the **SUPERPCK** command. SUPERPCK is a TSR program. Its responsibility is to reduce disk read and write times by storing the most-used information in memory for quicker access.

Disk caching can be installed using INSTALL or SETUP, or it can be activated from the DOS prompt. It also can be unloaded by typing **SUPERPCK /U** at the DOS prompt and pressing Enter.

DISKMAP, DELWATCH, and UNDELETE

The three utilities, DISKMAP, DELWATCH, and UNDELETE, together are used to restore previously deleted files.

DISKMAP copies the FAT for the specified disk, then saves that copy until you rerun DISKMAP. Whenever you rerun DISKMAP, a new copy of the FAT is saved.

The DISKMAP FAT copy provides a pointer so that the UNDELETE utility can find the original location of a deleted file. As long as the space on the disk that the original file occupied has not been overwritten by another file, UNDELETE is able to find and restore the deleted file by using the copy of the FAT that DISKMAP makes available.

You can erase the DISKMAP copy of the FAT at any time by typing **DISKMAP /D** at the DOS prompt and pressing Enter. The name of the file that is created, or subsequently deleted, is DISKMAP.DAT.

DISKMAP can be run automatically for you each time you boot your computer by including the DISKMAP command, followed by the drive letter, in your AUTOEXEC.BAT file. You can do this manually using a DOS editor, or you can have the command added to your AUTOEXEC.BAT file for you when you run the SETUP program. Using DISKMAP over DELWATCH to cover deleted files does not affect the application memory in the client.

DELWATCH does not copy the FAT. Instead, DELWATCH runs as a TSR and flags any deleted file as pending instead of actually deleting it, once DELWATCH has been activated.

To activate DELWATCH type **DELWATCH /drive / optional_switches** at the DOS prompt and press Enter. As with DISKMAP, DELWATCH can be added to the AUTOEXEC.BAT file to automate its use as well.

Because DELWATCH is a TSR, it takes memory space that otherwise would be used for application programs. You may need to choose between using this TSR and running a more memory-intensive application.

DELWATCH also can take up a large amount of file storage space. By default, the maximum number of files that DELWATCH will save is 200. However, this is quite a large number. You may find that you begin seeing insufficient-space errors when trying to save regular files, because DELWATCH has taken up so much of your hard disk. DELPURGE is used to eliminate stored deleted files.

If you want to retrieve any of the pending deleted files, use the UNDELETE command. UNDELETE is run from the command line. It enables you to retrieve files that have been deleted but saved using either the DISKMAP or DELWATCH commands.

Using UNDELETE, you can specify which files to UNDELETE (including using a wild card to specify them) (/A), see what files have been deleted (/L), recover only files saved using either the DISKMAP or DELWATCH method (UNDELETE /R:method), and recover files in a specific subdirectory (/S). Other options are available as well. To see all available options, type **UNDELETE /h** at the DOS prompt, and press Enter.

DISKOPT

DISKOPT helps you get the most out of your PC by defragmenting files and relocating free space to an area on the disk where access is quicker.

When a file or free disk space is defragmented, the files or free space that are scattered around the hard disk are reorganized to put all of those individual pieces together. Doing so makes subsequent access of a single file or a single portion of free space much faster.

DISKOPT can be used on fixed or floppy disks. Start DISKOPT by typing **DISKOPT** at the DOS prompt and pressing Enter. Choose which disk you want to optimize. Once the Disk Optimizer screen appears, you can choose to **O**ptimize the disk, to **S**ort the files on it, or **H**elp for the help menu.

Once you start the optimization process, you can interrupt it by pressing Esc. Pressing Esc returns you to the DOS prompt.

You also can sort files on the disk using the <u>S</u>ort option. Once you open the Sort pull-down menu, you can choose to sort by any of the following:

- ◆ <u>N</u>ame
- ◆ <u>E</u>xtension
- ◆ <u>D</u>ate
- ◆ <u>S</u>ize
- ◆ <u>C</u>luster
- ◆ <u>N</u>o sort

If DISKOPT finds lost clusters when you run it, you must exit DISKOPT and run CHKDSK /F to first convert the lost clusters to FILEnnnn.CHK files. Then you can run DISKOPT.

Novell DOS 7.0 offers you more flexibility with DISKOPT. With Novell DOS 7.0, you can choose the <u>M</u>ethod for optimization, as well as choosing to <u>O</u>ptimize or <u>S</u>ort the disk. The <u>M</u>ethod choices include the following:

- ◆ Full <u>O</u>ptimization
- ◆ Full with File <u>R</u>eorder
- ◆ <u>F</u>ile Defragment Only
- ◆ Free <u>S</u>pace Defragment Only
- ◆ Sort <u>D</u>irectories Only

Several switches can be used when running DISKOPT. Figure 7.8 shows the help screen for the Novell DOS 7.0 version of DISKOPT, including the available switches.

```
DISKOPT [drive:] [/B][/O][/Sx][/Mx][/H]

 /B              Force monochrome attributes on the display.

 /N              Do not redefine characters of EGA or VGA systems.

 /O              Start optimization immediately without user intervention

 /Sx             Selects directory sorting method.
                   x = a - Sort by name        (default with option /M5)
                       e - Sort by extension
                       d - Sort by date
                       s - Sort by file size
                       n - No sort             (default in all other cases)

 /Mx             Selects the disk optimization method.
                   x = 1 - Full Optimization
                       2 - Full with File Reordering
                       3 - File Defragment Only
                       4 - Free Space Defragment Only
                       5 - Sort Directories Only
                       (Default method depends on the selected disk layout.)
 /H or /?        Display help (this screen).
[RUBY_3] C:\>
```

Figure 7.8

DISKOPT available command-line switches.

Switching Between Applications Using TaskMAX or TaskMGR

Keeping software applications in memory so that they can be readily accessed when needed is one of the advantages of using Windows. DR DOS 6.0 and Novell DOS 7.0 provide that ability through multitasking software called TaskMAX in DR DOS 6.0 and TaskMGR in Novell DOS 7.0.

TaskMAX and TaskMGR are task switchers. Once TaskMAX or TaskMGR is installed and running, you can switch between applications that you already have up and running.

Note

SHARE.EXE must be loaded before the task switching program in order for the task switching to function. Therefore, if you are loading task switching automatically, place the command to load SHARE.EXE in the configuration file before the command to start task switching.

381

If you do not load SHARE.EXE first, you receive an error message when you try to load the task manager.

You can use task switching to accomplish different types of tasks. For example, you can run a graphics program to create graphic designs for a document, then switch to a word processing package and write the accompanying text. You can switch back and forth between the graphics program and the word processing program as needed. Then when you are ready, you can copy the graphic into the text document.

 Be careful about blocking text to be copied between documents because you may inadvertently bring in characters that you did not intend to copy.

Multitasking requires an 80386 or newer processor to enable multiple tasks to run simultaneously in the background. However, if your PC has an 80286 or earlier microprocessor, you still can load more than one application and switch between applications. The difference is that the actual processing takes place only during the time a specific application is being accessed. Processing for other background applications is temporarily suspended.

To use the DR DOS 6.0 Task Manager application switcher, load TaskMAX from INSTALL. Then you can activate TaskMAX from the DOS prompt. Once loaded and set up, you can call up the Task Manager menu whenever you need to and switch from one task to another using the hot key. If you accept the defaults during installation, the hot key is Esc.

There are several installation switches and options that can be used when TaskMAX is already resident in memory available. The help screen for TaskMAX shown in figure 7.9 lists the installation options as well as the memory-resident options.

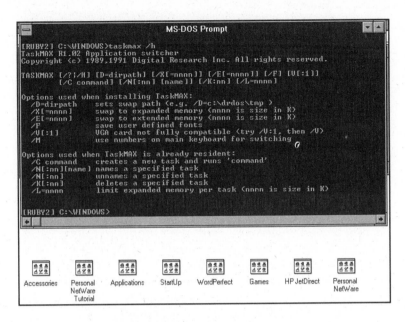

Figure 7.9
TaskMAX help screen.

To set up the Novell DOS 7.0 Task Manager, you must run the Setup program and choose Task Manager from the main Setup screen. You then can choose between loading MultiTasking software or Task Switching software, depending on the Intel microprocessor installed in your PC.

To install the Novell DOS 7.0 Task Manager manually once you have booted your PC, type **TASKMGR** at the DOS prompt, and press Enter. You can install it using one or more of several installation switches. Some of the more common installation switches are shown in table 7.2.

Table 7.2
Common Task Manager Install Switches

Switch	Usage/Description
/D=dirpath	Replace dirpath with the disk drive and path where you want the swap file to be stored.

continues

383

Table 7.2, Continued
Common Task Manager Install Switches

Switch	Usage/Description
/E[=*nnnn*]	Replace *nnnn* with the number of kilobytes of extended memory that you want to have set aside for the swap file.
/S	Install the Task Switcher instead of the Task Manager, if you are running on a PC that has a 286 processor rather than a 386 or higher processor.
/X[=*nnnn*]	Replace *nnnn* with the number of kilobytes of expanded memory that you want to have set aside for the swap file.

There are other options that you can use with TaskMGR once you have loaded it. The commands associated with these options are shown in table 7.3.

Table 7.3
TaskMGR Usage Command Switches

Switch	Usage/Description
/C command	Create a new task and load another copy of Novell DOS 7's COMMAND.COM file (to load task, such as WordPerfect, replace command with the name of the file that starts the task).
/K[:nn]	Delete a task that you specified earlier.
/L=*nnnn*	Replace *nnnn* with the number of kilobytes of expanded memory you want to set as the limit for each task.

Switch	Usage/Description
/N[nn]	Replace nn with the previously assigned number of a specific task that you want to remove (the number is found on the menu that Task Manager creates when you load different tasks).
/N[nn][name]	Replace nn with the number that the task switcher assigned to a loaded task (this number is found on the Task Manager menu).

Once the Task Manager is loaded, you can open the menu with the hot key by pressing Ctrl+Esc.

The Task Manager menu contains two separate menus with entries in each, even though you have not yet added any applications. One menu is titled Tasks, and the other menu is titled Functions (or Task Switcher Functions).

The entries under the Functions menu include the following:

◆ About TaskMGR or About TaskMAX

◆ Create new task

◆ Remove TaskMGR or Remove TaskMAX

Under the Tasks menu, only one entry appears initially. That entry is the COMMAND 1 entry, the entry that enables you to choose the DOS command prompt. Other entries appear as you start applications and use TaskMAX or TaskMGR to switch between them.

To learn more about either TaskMAX or TaskMGR, use DOSBook, or run TaskMAX or TaskMGR and experiment with it.

Getting Help Using DOSBook and /H

DOSBook is the DR DOS 6.0 and Novell DOS 7 on-line reference manual. It contains just about everything that is in the hard-copy manual, and in many instances, much more. DOSBook puts the procedures for the tasks you need to accomplish at your fingertips. It also provides conceptual information. DOSBook can be run directly from the DOS prompt or from inside a Microsoft Windows DOS box.

To open DOSBook, type **DOSBook** and press Enter. If you are running Windows, first open a DOS box. Then type **DOSBook** and press Enter.

DOSBook's first screen provides a list of options from which to choose. It also instructs you to press the F1 key for information on how to use DOSBook, or to press the Esc key to exit DOSBook.

When you first open the DR DOS 6.0 version of DOSBook, the initial screen contains three main categories:

♦ DR DOS BASICS, which provides access to a list of basic DOS commands (internal and external), command syntax, help on accessing drives, and other basic DOS operations

♦ COMMANDS AND UTILITIES, which provides access to information about basic DOS syntax, editing commands, control key combinations, and an alphabetical list of DR DOS 6.0 commands

♦ TROUBLESHOOTING, which provides access to an alphabetical list of error responses and, subsequently, to an explanation of the origin, potential cause, and correction procedure for each error

When you first open the Novell DOS 7.0 version of DOSBook, the initial screen contains five main categories:

♦ CONTENTS, which provides a full table of contents for the Novell DOS 7 DOSBook

♦ INTRODUCTION, which provides an introduction to Novell DOS 7 and its features and functions

- ◆ COMMANDS, which provides an alphabetical list of the commands that you can use in Novell DOS 7, subsequently providing detailed information about each command

- ◆ CONFIGURING, which provides access to the Novell DOS 7 book, Chapter 9, "Configuring the System," to give you access to topics related to running SETUP and fine-tuning your Novell DOS 7 operating system

- ◆ INDEX, which provides an alphabetical index for cross-referencing available DOSBook topics so that you can search for a specific topic

Choose one of the categories from the main DOSBook screen and additional screens appear to help you narrow your search. Figure 7.10 shows the Abort, Retry, Ignore, Fail ? help screen chosen from TROUBLESHOOTING in the DR DOS 6.0 version of DOSBook as opened inside a Microsoft Windows DOS Box.

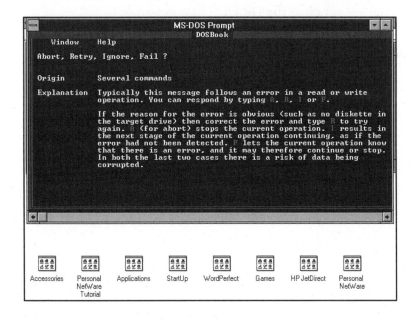

Figure 7.10

DOSBook Troubleshooting Help Screen.

Troubleshooting a DR DOS 6.0 Client

 Do basic troubleshooting on DR DOS workstations.

Troubleshooting problems on any piece of computer hardware can be a major task. When you take that computer and make it part of a network, you add a layer of potential problems. Troubleshooting becomes even more complex. This section covers basic troubleshooting methods for DR DOS 6.0 clients; additional basic troubleshooting information can be found on both the DR DOS Host BBS and the Novell Desktop message section of NetWire. To access the NetWire troubleshooting section, type **Go NOVDESKTOP** once you have accessed NetWire.

The following are the most common problems you may have when using your DR DOS 6.0 client as a network node:

◆ Network hardware conflicts

◆ HILOAD errors with the network shell

◆ Incompatibility between the NetWare Shell and drivers

◆ Client hanging during bootup

Network Hardware Conflicts

Hardware conflicts may occur between the NIC and the MemoryMax driver if a specific area of ROM already is being used by the NIC when the MemoryMax driver attempts to load.

If such conflicts occur, you need to load the MemoryMax driver, either EMM386.SYS or HIDOS.SYS using the /EXCLUDE option. This enables you to tell the driver not to use the areas of memory that the NIC is using.

HILOAD Errors with the Network Shell

The HILOAD command puts the network shell programs into upper memory whenever possible, thus freeing up more space in conventional memory for application programs. However, sometimes there is insufficient upper memory to load the network shell files.

More memory can be added to upper memory by including the /FRAME=NONE option when you load the EMM386.SYS driver.

You also can open up more upper memory before HILOADing the network shell files by using the MEMMAX +U option. If you use this option before loading the network shell files, be sure to close upper memory after HILOADing the network shell files by issuing MEMMAX again, followed by the -U option.

Incompatibility Between the NetWare Shell and Drivers

Only NET3, NETX, EMSNETX, XMSNETX, or BNETX can be run with DR DOS 6.0. Run the NetWare DOS Requester, including the VLM files with Novell DOS 7.0.

Client Hangs During Bootup

There can be many causes for a client to hang during bootup. When troubleshooting this type of problem, the first thing to do is to put a question mark at the beginning of any CONFIG.SYS lines that you think might be the cause of the client hanging problem.

Putting a question mark in front of a CONFIG.SYS line causes the client to pause and question whether or not you want to run that line. It enables you to see each line one at a time before it is run. That way you can tell if the command being executed in that particular line is causing the computer to hang. Each line executes one at a time.

389

The question mark also must offer you the option of running (Y) or not running (N) that particular CONFIG.SYS line. To allow this option, you also must put a YES/NO option in the same line that you place the question mark. The following CONFIG.SYS file shown includes one of these lines. The line with the question mark enables you to choose to either load or not load the NetWare client files that provide connections to the network:

```
DOS=HIGH
DEVICE=C:\DRDOS\EMM386.SYS /F=AUTO /VIDEO
HIDOS=ON
BREAK=ON
HIBUFFERS=30
FILES=45
LASTDRIVE=Z
?"Load Networking Software (Y/N)"C:\NWCLIENT\STARTNET.BAT
```

The CONFIG.SYS file is not usually where you specify the loading of network software. The last line shown in the CONFIG.SYS file is more likely to be found in the AUTOEXEC.BAT file, which executes after the CONFIG.SYS file. However, this example shows you how to use the question mark and Y/N choice to troubleshoot a CONFIG.SYS file.

Of course, these are just some of the potential DR DOS client troubleshooting options. The DR DOS manual and DOSBook provide more troubleshooting information as well.

Review Questions

1. Which of the following is not a feature of DR DOS 6.0?

   ○ a. Increased conventional memory

   ○ b. Disk compression and defragmentation utilities

   ○ c. Enhanced data protection and system security

   ○ d. NDIR for listing local files

2. CHKDSK is a DOS command used to

   ○ a. increase conventional memory for applications

   ○ b. update older files with newer copies

   ○ c. find out a volume's name

   ○ d. display client memory configuration

3. One reason you might use the XDIR command instead of the DIR command is

   ○ a. to see a file's checksum

   ○ b. to change the display order of files

   ○ c. to pause after each screen

   ○ d. to see files on the network

4. If you are having difficulty seeing the cursor on your laptop computer, one DR DOS 6.0 command that might help is

   ○ a. MEM

   ○ b. CURSOR

   ○ c. XDIR

   ○ d. REPLACE

5. The DR DOS 6.0 command that enables you to change the date and time stamp of a file is

   ○ a. MEM

   ○ b. CURSOR

   ○ c. XDIR

   ○ d. REPLACE

6. One of the best uses for the Setup program is

   ○ a. maximizing available application memory

   ○ b. defining NWCACHE parameters

○ c. loading MultiTasking software

○ d. configuring Personal NetWare

7. Which two of the following MEMMAX commands make more memory available for programs?

☐ a. +U

☐ b. +L

☐ c. +C

☐ d. +X

8. If you already are using a third-party memory manager, one DR DOS 6.0 command that you cannot use is

○ a. HIBUFFERS=

○ b. LOADHIGH=

○ c. HIDOS=

○ d. HIMEM=

9. Of the features provided by EMM386.SYS, which feature reduces the execution time for some processes?

○ a. Copying code and data from ROM to RAM

○ b. Support for XMS

○ c. LIM 4.0 expanded memory support

○ d. Microsoft Windows 3 Real support

10. Which of the following utilities is not used by DiskMAX to enhance disk performance?

○ a. SSTOR

○ b. DISKMAP

○   c. UNDELETE

○   d. SHARE

11. Removing compression from a disk using SuperStore requires that you choose which one of the following main menu options when you issue the SSTOR command?

○   a. **P**repare

○   b. **R**emove

○   c. **S**tatistics

○   d. **C**luster

12. Which of the following statements regarding disk caching software is true?

○   a. SUPERPCK activates Novell DOS 7.0's disk caching.

○   b. NWCACHE can be removed by typing **NWCACHE /R**.

○   c. Disk caching software reduces disk access time.

○   d. Disk caching software is not a TSR.

13. Which one of the following utilities does *not* restore deleted files?

○   a. DISKMAP

○   b. DELWATCH

○   c. UNDELETE

○   d. DELETE

14. Which of the following utilities makes a copy of the FAT?

○   a. DISKMAP

○   b. DELWATCH

○   c. UNDELETE

○   d. DELETE

15. If memory for running applications is particularly limited on your computer, which utility should you avoid loading because it is a TSR?

   ○ a. DELWATCH

   ○ b. DISKOPT

   ○ c. CLUSTER

   ○ d. COMMAND

16. Which of the following statements is not true regarding DELWATCH?

   ○ a. It is a TSR.

   ○ b. You cannot interrupt it once you have started it.

   ○ c. Lost clusters must be corrected before running it.

   ○ d. All of the above statements are untrue.

17. TaskMGR's default hot key is

   ○ a. Ctrl+Home

   ○ b. Ctrl+Del

   ○ c. Ctrl+Esc

   ○ d. Ctrl+End

18. If you are attempting to switch between tasks and encounter problems, which is the least drastic approach you should take?

   ○ a. Open DOSBook and search for help on TaskMGR.

   ○ b. Open the TaskMGR menu and Remove TaskMGR, then reload it.

   ○ c. Press Alt+Esc and exit TaskMGR.

   ○ d. Contact someone at your company who is familiar with TaskMGR.

19. Which of the following is not a common problem with using a computer as a network client with DR DOS 6.0 loaded?

○ a. HILOAD errors with the network shell.

○ b. Client hanging during bootup.

○ c. Conflicts on network hardware.

○ d. VLMs that cannot be unloaded.

Answers

1. D
2. C
3. A
4. B
5. D
6. A
7. A, B
8. C
9. A
10. D
11. B
12. C
13. D
14. A
15. B
16. B
17. C
18. A
19. D

Addressing Your Network

In this chapter, you learn how to differentiate between multiple-server networks and internetworks. You also learn to identify and configure different types of network addresses. When setting up a network, proper addressing of all network components is essential.

Items covered in this chapter are as follows:

◆ Node addresses

◆ Network addresses

◆ Multiple-server networks

◆ Internetworks

◆ IPX internal network addresses

Defining Node Addresses

Every node on a network must be identified by a unique address. This address usually is determined either by a ROM or by switches or jumpers on the network interface card. It also can be determined by configuration parameters associated with the workstation's NetWare shell.

With Ethernet and Token Ring, addresses for workstation and server NICs are seldom a problem. When the NICs are made, the manufacturer identifies each card with a physical address guaranteed to be unique among all cards manufactured worldwide. Unless these burned-in addresses are overridden, address conflicts cannot occur.

An AppleTalk node determines its node address by a system of organized trial and error. No intervention on the part of the network administrator is required.

The addresses of ARCnet NICs are configured with DIP switches or jumpers on each network card. The network installers are responsible for ensuring that no two ARCnet NICs share the same address on a given physical network. Errors in setting NIC addresses are common causes of problems on ARCnet networks.

Understanding Network Addresses

In understanding network addresses, you must first understand what a network is comprised of. In Chapter 3, you learned about network addresses and physical node addresses. A network consists of the cabling and components that occupy a given physical cabling scheme. All devices on the network share a common network address. Networks can be combined with other networks using bridges, routers, and gateways. A large network that combines multiple networks is commonly called an *internetwork*. An internetwork comprises several subnetworks, each of which has a unique network address. An internetwork is illustrated in figure 8.1. This internetwork uses an internal router (a router running in a NetWare server).

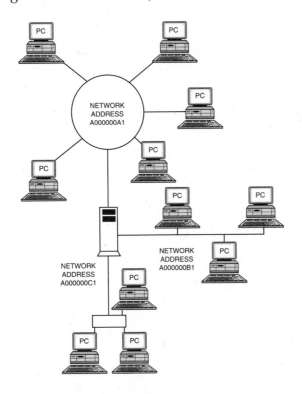

With NetWare, a network address is a positive eight-digit hexadecimal number that must be in the range of 1 to FFFFFFFE.

Long series of ones and zeros are difficult for humans to scan, and decimal conversions of some values are awkward. This is where hexadecimal numbers (hex for short) become useful. Hex uses base 16, as compared to base 2 for the binary system, or base 10 for the decimal system. The hexadecimal system uses the numbers 0 through 9 to represent the binary numbers 0000 through 1001 (decimal 0 to 9), and the letters A through F to represent binary 1010 through 1111 (decimal 10 to 15). Thus, a hexadecimal number is easier than a decimal number for a computer to read, and easier than a binary number for most humans to read.

The network address cannot contain commas, decimal points, or any other non-numeric characters (except, of course, A through F). Hex addresses of 0 and FFFFFFFF cannot be used (FFFFFFFF is a network broadcast address identifier).

Basically, each network cable that connects to a server is identified with a unique network address. Several servers can be attached to the same network. All will identify the network using the same network address. When you install a network card and configure NetWare to use the card, you will specify the network address as part of the card's configuration information.

If you are using multiple frame types with the LAN drivers in v3.11, you must assign a unique network address for each frame type.

NetWare 2.x versions maintain the record of this address in the CONFIG.DAT file and 3.x versions maintain the address in the AUTOEXEC.NCF file.

NetWare 3.11 servers can support more than one protocol on the same physical network through the same network interface card. If this is done, a separate network number must be assigned for each protocol.

Multiple-Server Networks

A multiple-server network (see fig. 8.2) has more than one file server on the same physical cabling system. One network interface card is in each file server on the single cabling scheme. The network address is the same on each file server. NetWare 2.x and 3.x can exist on the same cabling system.

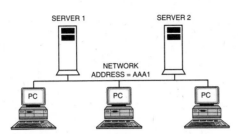

Figure 8.2
Example of a multi-server network.

Internetworking

An *internetwork* consists of two or more networks not on the same physical cabling system. The various networks can be of the same or different topologies. NetWare uses various combinations of internal and external routers to integrate the various networks into an internetwork.

An *internal router* consists of two or more network interface cards installed in the file server. All NetWare servers can function as routers. This feature is activated simply by installing two or more NICs in the server. The NetWare router function automatically routes network traffic, performing any conversions required to move traffic from one network topology to another. In figure 8.3, the server is functioning as an internal router, routing traffic between network 3022 and 3023.

A NetWare external router is a stand-alone PC running NetWare router software. The router has one or more network boards installed and runs software configured with the ROUTEGEN utility. Chapter 6 explains how to configure NetWare routers. Figure 8.3 illustrates an external router routing traffic between network 3022 and 3024.

When configuring routers, all server and router NICs attaching to a given physical cabling scheme must be configured with the same network address. Traffic cannot be routed properly if this rule is violated, and NetWare servers generate frequent error messages if they detect attempts to use more than one address on a cable segment.

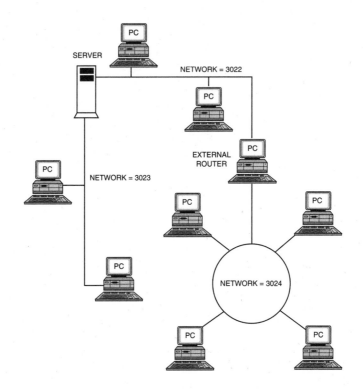

Figure 8.3

Internal and external
NetWare routers in an
internetwork.

Internal IPX Network Number

Each NetWare 3.x server must be configured with an internal
network number, which provides an address for routing traffic
inside the server itself. No hardware is associated with the internal network number. However, a line such as the following must
appear in the server's AUTOEXEC.NCF file:

```
IPX INTERNAL NET B0001
```

The IPX internal network number must be unique for each
NetWare 3.11 file server on the internet. It cannot duplicate any
other internal network number or external network address. The
internal network address is a number of up to eight hexadecimal
digits in the range of 1 through FFFFFFFE. As part of the file
server installation process in v3.x, a prompt appears asking for an

IPX internal network number. This address is recorded in the AUTOEXEC.NCF file as the second entry in the script (after the file server name; see fig. 8.4).

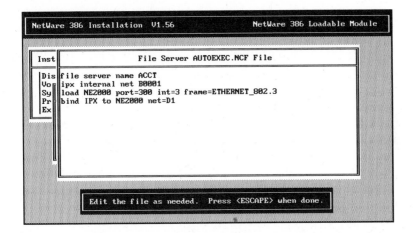

Figure 8.4

An AUTOEXEC.NCF file showing the internal network number.

Using Internal Addresses for Non-Dedicated NetWare 2.*x* Servers

When the server also must support a DOS workstation, you can configure NetWare 2.*x* servers to operate in non-dedicated mode. The DOS process functions as a logical network and must be assigned an address so that traffic can be routed to and from it.

When you configure a non-dedicated NetWare 2.2 server, you need to specify a DOS process address. This address must not duplicate any network addresses on the internetwork.

403

Summarizing Network Addressing Rules

Follow these rules for configuring addresses on your networks:

1. Each node on a given physical network must have a unique physical address.

2. Each physical network must be assigned a network address that does not duplicate any other network address on the internetwork.

3. All servers that attach to the same physical network using the same protocol must be configured to reference the network with the same network address.

4. All NetWare 3.11 servers must be configured with an internal network address. This address must not duplicate any other network, internal network, or DOS process address on the internetwork.

5. All non-dedicated NetWare 2.2 servers must be configured with a DOS process address. This address must not duplicate any other network, internal network, or DOS process address on the internetwork.

6. If a NetWare 3.11 server is configured to support more than one protocol on a given physical network, a separate network address must be assigned to each protocol.

Review Questions

1. Which statement about node addresses is false?

   ○ a. Every node on a network must have a unique address.

   ○ b. Conflicts can be safely ignored.

   ○ c. ARCnet board node addresses are set by DIP switches.

   ○ d. Ethernet boards have preset addresses.

2. Internetworking devices include:

  ○ a. Bridges

  ○ b. Routers

  ○ c. Gateways

  ○ d. All of the above

3. Which is not a valid network address?

  ○ a. BABE

  ○ b. FFFFFFFE

  ○ c. ABC-123

  ○ d. BA5EBA11

4. Which statement is most false?

  ○ a. NetWare can support multiple protocols on the same NIC.

  ○ b. Each frame type requires a unique address.

  ○ c. Network addresses also are called cable addresses.

  ○ d. v2.x holds addresses in its CONFIG.SYS; v3.x holds addresses in AUTOEXEC.NCF.

5. Internal IPX numbers:

  ○ a. Are an internal routing address

  ○ b. Are a common factor among servers connected on the same segment.

  ○ c. Are chosen automatically by NetWare 3.11

  ○ d. Must be registered

6. Which statement is false?

  ○ a. Non-dedicated v2.2 must have a DOS process address.

  ○ b. Each protocol on the server must have a unique address.

   ○   c. Node addresses cannot match the file server's internal
         IPX number.

   ○   d. Internal IPX numbers must be unique on the network.

7. Which protocol uses an organized trial-and-error method of
   node assignment?

   ○   a. Token Ring

   ○   b. AppleTalk

   ○   c. ARCnet

   ○   d. Ethernet

8. Multiple-server networks:

   ○   a. All have a common cable segment

   ○   b. Cannot be a part of an internetwork

   ○   c. Must have unique network addresses

   ○   d. Are made up of gateways

Answers

1. B

2. D

3. C

4. D

5. A

6. C

7. B

8. A

Installing the Client

9

CHAPTER

In this chapter, you learn about several of the methods used to interface a client to a file server. The type of operating system and the communication protocols enabled with the network determine the proper method to choose. The topics discussed in this chapter include the following:

♦ Using IPX/NETX

♦ Using ODI drivers

♦ Using the VLM DOS Requester

♦ Using the remote boot client

♦ Using Windows on a client

Using IPX/NETX

Historically, the most common tools for connecting DOS workstations to NetWare networks were the IPX.COM program in combination with one of several programs that were generically called NETx. IPX.COM implemented the IPX protocols for the network. NETx enabled DOS applications on the workstation to communicate with the network.

Although the IPX/NETx combination is no longer the preferred method for networking DOS PCs, the approach still works with NetWare 2.*x* and 3.*x*. The popularity of these programs practically ensures that you will encounter them on NetWare networks for quite some time in the future.

IPX.COM

Novell has used the generation of the Internet Packet Exchange (IPX) protocol in its history of attaching clients to the network to request services. Historically, Novell has relied on IPX as the major protocol for NetWare network communication. Until recently, with the introduction of the Open Data Interlink drivers, the IPX protocols were installed on the workstation using a command file named IPX.COM. The IPX.COM file must be custom-generated for each different workstation configuration using the WSGEN disk found in the NetWare 3.11 installation package. The IPX.COM file that is customized from the WSGEN disk must be configured for each type of Network Interface Card (NIC) in each client; along with the board's interrupts, DMA channels, and other configuration data. The information in the IPX.COM file generation process includes the following:

♦ The module for the type of NIC driver by vendor

♦ The configuration option that is chosen by IRQ, I/O Base, or RAM Buffer Setting, or whether it is a self-configurable card

During the generation process, the information is linked to form the connections between the NIC and the network communication protocol.

IPX.COM also performs other communication-related services. These include the following:

♦ Assigning source and destination addresses to data packets to create an internetwork address

◆ Managing packet routing to the correct socket location (the program having that specific socket, or post office box, open for use)

Management of IPX Communication

Novell NetWare developed several protocols specifically for its use with NetWare before the definition of the OSI reference model was finalized. The NetWare protocols use the IPX.COM file to support various communication protocols for use on the network. These communication protocol fields include the following:

◆ Routing Information Protocol (RIP)

◆ Service Advertising Protocol (SAP)

◆ NetWare Core Protocol (NCP)

On the network, RIP is enveloped in the data area of IPX packets. The RIP protocol provides the following services:

◆ Assists clients in locating the fastest route to a network device by broadcasting a route request

◆ Routers perform broadcasts when they detect a change in the configuration of the internetwork

◆ Routers respond to requests from clients

◆ Routers request information from other routers to update their own tables

The SAP enables the advertising of services and addresses by offering nodes such as gateways, file servers, and print servers to advertise themselves on the network. Clients need to know the availability and the address of these services before they can initiate a session with these nodes. The SAP is used to perform the following functions:

◆ Respond to a request such as a "Get Nearest Server" or "Give Nearest Server" entry that can be seen on a TRACK ON file server screen

♦ Handle periodic broadcasts by routers and servers

♦ Request names and addresses of all or specific types of servers

The NCP monitors connection control and service requests. NCP packets are handled by the NetWare shell. The NCP provides its own session control and packet-level error checking capabilities. Each NCP packet that a client sends to a file server must have a sequence and connection number assigned to it. The sequence number of the packet identifies each packet so that the error-checking capabilities between the file server and the client will know when a packet is lost. The connection number is assigned by the file server to the client when a connection is established. Requests for this information are contained in the service code field of the NCP packet.

IPX uses medium-access protocols, such as 802.5 Token-Ring, ARCnet, and Ethernet, to define the unique addresses of the clients on the network. The packets sent on the network must be delivered to the proper node. Each packet contains a Medium Access Control (MAC) header field that contains the source and destination address for the packet.

IPX contains RIP, SAP, NCP, and MAC header information to manage the delivery of packets for proper communication on the network.

To use a client with Windows on NetWare, updating files from NetWire or the Microsoft Windows Setup Disk #2 is required. A special IPX.OBJ file is linked into IPX.COM, and files with .DLL and .DRV extensions for NetWare are included in the Windows directory.

Running WSGEN To Generate IPX

The WSGEN utility configures a file that DOS workstations must use to gain access to the network. When you use WSGEN, you generate a file called IPX.COM. IPX stands for *Internetwork Packet Exchange*.

You can run the WSGEN program from a floppy drive or hard disk. If you run the program from a floppy drive, you first must create a copy of the original disk. The original Novell disk is write-protected, and WSGEN needs to create a new IPX.COM file for you. Novell supplies a number of network card drivers with the WSGEN program. If the driver you need is not included with the Novell disks, you also need a driver disk from the hardware manufacturer. Network card drivers generally are located on a disk shipped with the interface card and need to be placed on a floppy disk with the volume label LAN_DRV_*xxx*, in which *xxx* is a three-digit number designated by the manufacturer.

 Note The syntax for the DOS LABEL command is LABEL A:LAN_DRV_*xxx*.

When WSGEN runs, it searches all floppy drives for disks with these labels and includes the appropriate drivers in the lists presented to you for selection.

System administrators can set up a directory on their local hard drive or on the network to provide a fast method for creating network shells when needed. To set up the required directories, you need a main directory. You can name this directory SHELLS, for example.

After you use the DOS MD command to create a SHELLS directory, create a subdirectory named WSGEN. Then copy the contents of the Novell WSGEN disk into the \SHELLS\WSGEN directory. If any optional LAN drivers are required, you must copy them into directories that have the same name as the floppy

411

disk that contains the drivers. To allow for a floppy name with more than eight characters, place a period (.) before the last three characters or numbers as in the following example:

```
\SHELLS\WSGEN\
              ┊
              ┊-LAN_DRV_.001
              ┊
              ┊-LAN_DRV_.002
```

Novell's WSGEN program looks for this label to locate the driver files.

Next, copy the WSGEN.EXE file into the SHELLS directory. You then can execute the WSGEN program from this directory by typing WSGEN and pressing Enter. NetWare displays a screen like the one shown in figure 9.1. When this screen appears, press Enter to continue.

Figure 9.1

The WSGEN opening screen.

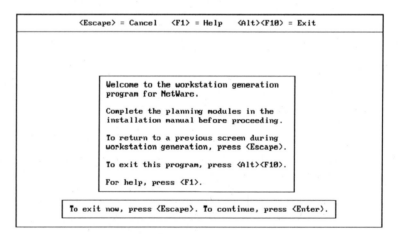

```
        <Escape> = Cancel    <F1> = Help    <Alt><F10> = Exit


                Welcome to the workstation generation
                program for NetWare.

                Complete the planning modules in the
                installation manual before proceeding.

                To return to a previous screen during
                workstation generation, press <Escape>.

                To exit this program, press <Alt><F10>.

                For help, press <F1>.

        To exit now, press <Escape>. To continue, press <Enter>.
```

Practical TIP

If WSGEN appears to lock up while searching the floppy drives, reboot the computer and check your directory structures. This problem is common when you are running the WSGEN program from the wrong directory.

412

The next screen that appears is the driver-selection screen (see fig. 9.2). At this screen, you select the appropriate NIC driver required by your network interface card. Simply use the arrow keys to scroll up or down until you find the correct driver.

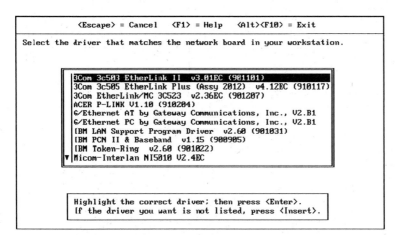

```
     <Escape> = Cancel    <F1> = Help    <Alt><F10> = Exit

Select the driver that matches the network board in your workstation.

    ┌─────────────────────────────────────────────────────┐
    │3Com 3c503 EtherLink II  v3.01EC (901101)            │
    │3Com 3c505 EtherLink Plus (Assy 2012)  v4.12EC (910117)│
    │3Com EtherLink/MC 3C523  v2.36EC (901207)           │
    │ACER P-LINK V1.10 (910204)                          │
    │G/Ethernet AT by Gateway Communications, Inc., V2.B1 │
    │G/Ethernet PC by Gateway Communications, Inc., V2.B1 │
    │IBM LAN Support Program Driver  v2.60 (901031)      │
    │IBM PCN II & Baseband  v1.15 (900905)              │
    │IBM Token-Ring  v2.60 (901022)                     │
   ▼│Micom-Interlan NI5010 V2.4EC                        │
    └─────────────────────────────────────────────────────┘

    Highlight the correct driver; then press <Enter>.
    If the driver you want is not listed, press <Insert>.
```

Figure 9.2

The driver-selection screen.

If the driver you need does not appear in the selection window, the driver may not be included with NetWare, or the driver disk may not be installed correctly. If you install a LAN_DRV_.xxx directory, make sure that the underscores (_) and the period (.) are correct. If you create a LAN_DRV_.xxx directory, be sure not to confuse the underscore character (_) with the hyphen character (-).

Another way to handle the addition of new drivers is to press Ins while the driver-selection screen is visible. NetWare then prompts you to insert the disk that contains the additional drivers. The new drivers are then added to the list of available drivers.

When you locate the desired driver, press Enter. The screen shown in figure 9.3 appears.

Figure 9.3

The hardware-configuration screen.

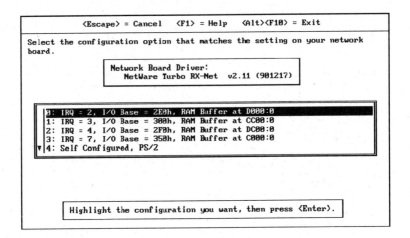

```
        <Escape> = Cancel    <F1> = Help    <Alt><F10> = Exit

Select the configuration option that matches the setting on your network
board.

              Network Board Driver:
                 NetWare Turbo RX-Net   v2.11 (901217)


  ┌──────────────────────────────────────────────────────────┐
  │0: IRQ = 2, I/O Base = 2E0h, RAM Buffer at D000:0           │
  │1: IRQ = 3, I/O Base = 300h, RAM Buffer at CC00:0           │
  │2: IRQ = 4, I/O Base = 2F0h, RAM Buffer at DC00:0           │
  │3: IRQ = 7, I/O Base = 350h, RAM Buffer at C000:0           │
  ▼│4: Self Configured, PS/2                                    │



       ┌────────────────────────────────────────────────┐
       │ Highlight the configuration you want, then press <Enter>. │
       └────────────────────────────────────────────────┘
```

 Avoid and repair workstation conflicts based on resources such as memory, IRQ, and DMA.

You need to know a few things about the particular workstation with which you are working. This screen provides you with the hardware options supplied by the interface manufacturer. These options include interrupts, base memory address, I/O address, and DMA channels. The default option zero is usually a good choice for a standard workstation configuration. If your workstation has a modem, terminal emulator, or other special hardware, you need to have all the equipment settings available. When selecting a configuration option, be aware of all the additional interface card settings in the computer.

 You should make a list of all card settings. This list can help you locate unused hardware settings that your network interface can use.

If none of the available choices appears to provide all the settings, select option zero. From here, you can install a customized configuration with the JUMPERS utility.

After selecting a configuration option, press Enter to begin the linking process. After you select the hardware option, NetWare displays your choice and prompts you for confirmation. Select Yes to confirm your selection or No to abort (see fig. 9.4).

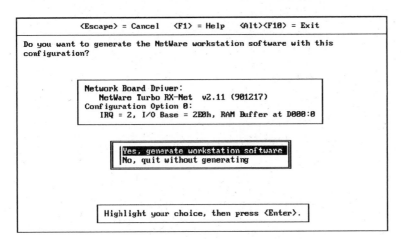

```
  <Escape> = Cancel    <F1> = Help    <Alt><F10> = Exit

 Do you want to generate the NetWare workstation software with this
 configuration?

        Network Board Driver:
            NetWare Turbo RX-Net  v2.11 (901217)
        Configuration Option 0:
            IRQ = 2, I/O Base = 2E0h, RAM Buffer at D000:0


            ┌─────────────────────────────────────────┐
            │Yes, generate workstation software        │
            │No, quit without generating               │
            └─────────────────────────────────────────┘


        Highlight your choice, then press <Enter>.
```

Figure 9.4

Confirming your selection.

If the link process runs without error, NetWare displays a screen informing you that workstation software generation is complete. At this time, you can copy the IPX.COM file from the \SHELLS\WSGEN directory to your workstation boot disk along with the appropriate shell: NETX.COM, XMSNETX.EXE, or EMSNETX.EXE.

Logging In through DOS

After you successfully generate your workstation files and copy them to your boot disk, you are ready to attach to the NetWare file server.

You can issue the following commands manually or place them in a batch file in the order listed (you can replace NETX with the optional XMSNETX or EMSNETX):

```
IPX
NETX
F:
LOGIN fileserver name/username
```

415

When you issue the IPX and NETX commands, NetWare displays the information shown in figure 9.5.

Figure 9.5

A sample screen that appears after you successfully attach to the file server.

```
[DR DOS] C:\SH386>ipx
Novell IPX/SPX v3.04 (910703)
(C) Copyright 1985, 1991 Novell Inc.  All Rights Reserved.

LAN Option: NetWare Turbo RX-Net  v2.11 (901217)
Hardware Configuration: IO: 350; MEM: D800; IRQ: 5 (Jumpers Config)

[DR DOS] C:\SH386>netx

NetWare V3.22 - Workstation Shell (910731)
(C) Copyright 1991 Novell, Inc.  All Rights Reserved.

Running on DOS V3.31

Using configuration file SHELL.CFG
SHOW DOTS ON

Attached to server CDI
09-30-91    5:06:13 pm

[DR DOS] C:\SH386>
```

The IPX, NETX, XMSNETX, and EMSNETX programs each have optional command-line switches that can simplify the network administrator's job.

IPX

IPX.COM provides these options (see fig. 9.6):

Figure 9.6

The IPX options.

```
C:\SH386>ipx ?
Novell IPX/SPX v3.04 (910703)
(C) Copyright 1985, 1991 Novell Inc.  All Rights Reserved.

LAN Option: NetWare Turbo RX-Net  v2.11 (901217)
Hardware Configuration: IO: 350; MEM: D800; IRQ: 5 (Jumpers Config)

Usage: IPX [options]
valid options:
        -I or /I                   Display version information
        -D or /D                   Display hardware options
        -O or /O<num>              Load using hardware option <num>
        -C or /C=[path]<filename>  Use an alternate configuration file

        -? or /?                   Display this help screen

C:\SH386>
```

◆ **-I or /I.** Use this option to display an information screen. This option is handy for determining the version and hardware settings of the IPX you are using (see fig. 9.7).

◆ **-D or /D.** Use this option to display available hardware settings.

◆ **-O or /Ox.** Use this option to set IPX to use a hardware setting displayed with the D option.

◆ **-C or /C.** This option enables advanced users to use a special configuration file rather than the Novell default SHELL.CFG or NET.CFG.

◆ **-? or /?.** Use this option to display all available options as shown in figure 9.6.

```
C:\SH386>ipx i
Novell IPX/SPX v3.04 (910703)
(C) Copyright 1985, 1991 Novell Inc.  All Rights Reserved.

LAN Option: NetWare Turbo RX-Net  v2.11 (901217)
Hardware Configuration: IO: 350; MEM: D000; IRQ: 5 (Jumpers Config)

C:\SH386>
```

Figure 9.7

Displaying version information.

 The /D and /Ox command-line switches are handy when you need to test a shell or when a shell is included in the batch file. These switches enable you to use any standard configuration without the need to relink the IPX program.

Permanently configuring the IPX program for normal use is still a good idea. Doing so saves confusion if the user attempts to load IPX without the batch file.

417

NETX, XMSNETX, and EMSNETX

NETX, XMSNETX, and EMSNETX provide the following three options:

◆ **-I or /I.** Use this option to display an information screen (see fig. 9.8).

◆ **-U or /U.** Use this option, Uninstall, to remove the shell from memory.

◆ **-PS or /PS.** Use this option, Preferred Server, to specify the server from which you get the LOGIN command.

Figure 9.8

Displaying version information.

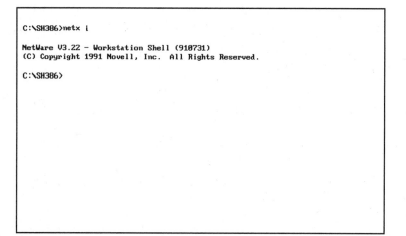

```
C:\SH386>netx i

NetWare V3.22 - Workstation Shell (910731)
(C) Copyright 1991 Novell, Inc.  All Rights Reserved.

C:\SH386>
```

NetBIOS

NetBIOS provides the following two options:

◆ **-I or /I.** Use this option to display an informational screen.

◆ **-U or /U.** Use this option, Uninstall, to remove NetBIOS from memory.

When using the /U command-line switch, make sure that the programs are removed in the opposite order from which they are installed. Also, be aware that you may receive unpredictable results when unloading any memory-resident program that may have another program loaded in after it.

Using JUMPERS

The JUMPERS utility is designed to patch an IPX program to the selected hardware settings without requiring you to rerun WSGEN. JUMPERS also enables you to mix and match options so that you can create custom options for tightly configured workstations.

Not all network card drivers are compatible with the JUMPERS utility. Currently, the best method to determine compatibility is the trial and error method. JUMPERS informs you if you choose a driver that cannot be configured.

The JUMPERS utility is in the WSGEN directory, and you can use it to change the option setting of IPX files linked with JUMPERS-compatible drivers.

To start JUMPERS, type JUMPERS at the DOS prompt and press Enter. The JUMPERS opening screen appears as shown in figure 9.9.

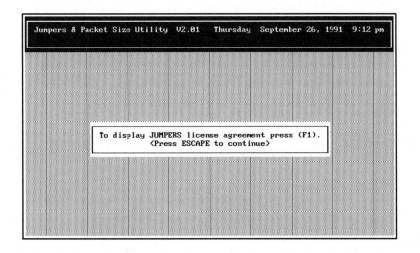

Figure 9.9

The JUMPERS opening screen.

When you press F1, NetWare displays the license agreement. To see the next screen, which enables you to specify the file to be modified, press Esc. When JUMPERS prompts for the file to modify (see fig. 9.10), enter **IPX.COM**. Remember to include the COM file extension.

Figure 9.10

Specifying the file to modify.

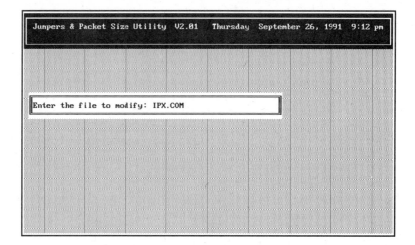

The JUMPERS utility then reads in the current hardware settings and displays a list of these settings in a menu format. Figure 9.11 shows an example of an ARCnet IPX using I/O port 2E0, interrupt 2, and memory address D000:0. This driver also is configured for large packets with the setting 4,096.

Figure 9.11

The current configuration.

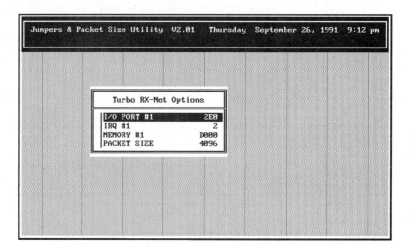

Currently, a de facto standard referred to as ARCnet TURBO-II exists. This standard enables ARCnet cards to use packet sizes other than the standard 512 bytes. You can set these to larger sizes provided that the file server accepts them to increase performance.

When configuring a JUMPERS-compatible Ethernet driver, you also have the option of changing the packet frame type. This option enables you to change between the standard 802.3 frame and the Ethernet II frame, which is common in UNIX and DEC environments. This feature is important in systems with both Novell and UNIX users.

To make changes to any of the individual settings, select the desired option and press Enter. NetWare then provides you with a list of supported values from which you can choose. Continue this procedure for each option that requires changes. Figure 9.12 shows an example of an ARCnet driver being changed to memory address DC00:0.

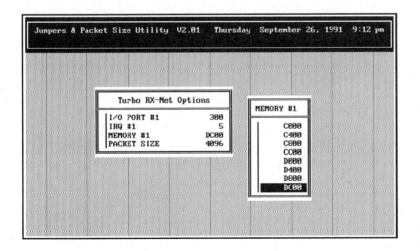

Figure 9.12

Changing memory addresses.

After you make all the changes, press Esc. NetWare prompts you to save your choices. Depending on your selection, JUMPERS exits, saves your choices, and modifies the hardware setting. You then can check the configuration of IPX.COM by using the /I command-line switch after the IPX command.

The NETX Shell

To enable applications on a PC to communicate with NetWare servers, a mechanism must be in place to decide whether a service request can be fulfilled by the local PC or whether the request must be sent on to a server. Prior to NetWare 4, the technology for performing this task was called the NetWare *shell*. The term shell is used because a special program surrounds DOS and intercepts all DOS service requests. The shell decides whether each request for file or print services should go to DOS or to the network.

Over the years, the workstation shell has been implemented by a series of command files. The file that is considered the actual "shell" for client communication is called NETX.EXE. This file is the "traffic cop" between applications and the operating system. The NETX file translates requests initiated at the keyboard and determines if the function is handled on the local client by DOS or is sent to the file server for processing.

 Over the years, several different command files have been used to provide shell services. For many years, a different file version was required for each DOS version, and DOS versions 2, 3, 4, and 5 required the files NET2.COM, NET3.COM, NET4.COM, and NET5.COM, respectively. These file versions were collectively referred to as NETx.COM.

A universal shell file named NETX.COM was developed after the release of DOS 5. When DOS 6 was released, the file was updated and changed from a COM to an EXE file. The new file, NETX.EXE, worked with DOS versions 2 through 6.

There is a trick to upgrading to NETX.EXE when NETX.COM is already on your system. The NETX.COM file is an older version of the shell. The EXE file also works with DOS 6.0 and above. DOS rules state that the command file (COM) will be executed first. If you upgrade to NETX.EXE, you should rename the COM file and save it until you are sure the newer file is working properly.

The NETX.EXE file works with both IPX.COM and ODI drivers. The NETX file is a terminate–and–stay–resident (TSR) program. This shell file will take the place of the following:

◆ **NETx.COM.** The x is sometimes replaced with the DOS version number on top of which it is running. This file affects conventional memory.

◆ **EMSNETX.COM.** This loads into expanded memory and uses the LIM 4.0 memory manager.

◆ **XMSNETX.COM.** This loads into extended memory and is located above the 1MB linear memory limits of DOS.

You should check NetWire in the NOVLIB section for driver updates. The file names to look for are DOSUPx.ZIP and WINUPx.ZIP. Novell updates NetWire on a regular basis with any enhancements.

The NETX.EXE file is loaded after the IPX.COM file is executed. When the NETX shell is loaded, it responds to the preferred server designated in the SHELL.CFG file. If the PREFERRED SERVER statement is not specified in the SHELL.CFG, the client attaches its connection to the fastest responding server.

Using the SHELL.CFG File

The SHELL.CFG file is a network configuration file that is located in the client directory. It is included in the directory from where the IPX.COM and NETX.EXE files are initiated. You can change the SHELL.CFG default parameters or add more parameters for performance tuning. A detailed listing of the available parameters are found in Appendix B of the NetWare 3.11 Installation Guide.

Troubleshooting Tips for IPX/NETX Clients

 Troubleshoot malfunctioning installations of IPX and ODI based DOS workstations.

The following tips will help you when troubleshooting IPX/NETX clients:

♦ Make sure the IPX option settings match the configuration of the LAN board.

♦ Make sure the NIC drivers work with the Revision numbers on the chipset of the LAN board.

♦ Make sure all cables are attached properly and are made to correct specifications.

♦ Reseat the board or move to another working slot in the CPU.

♦ Use the COMCHECK diagnostic utility provided by Novell as part of the installation package.

♦ Add the PREFERRED SERVER = statement in the SHELL.CFG file to point to the correct server.

♦ Point a login to a particular server by adding the server name to the LOGIN command. Use the following as an example:

```
LOGIN PLANODCW_FS/SUPERVISOR
```

Then press Enter.

◆ Use the PREFERRED SERVER = parameter with the NETX file. Use the following as an example:

```
NETX PS=PLANODCW_FS
```

You can monitor potential NIC bottlenecks in the file server by using the MONITOR utility to view LAN INFORMATION. To use an Ethernet card as an example for monitoring, look at the ENQUED SEND COUNTS statistic. This statistic shows the number of packets buffered by the NIC in the file server because the driver is too busy to send the packets to the processor. If it reaches two percent of the total packets transmitted on a regular basis, the NIC driver cannot keep up with the server. You may need to upgrade the NIC from an 8-bit card to a 16-bit card or a 16-bit card to a 32-bit card if the CPU can handle either. You may also need to check to see whether your LAN board driver is the latest version available.

The WATCHDOG Process

A client takes a connection slot at the file server when it initiates the shell (NETX). The NetWare operating system limits user connection slots based on the user limit license that the SERVER.EXE file in v3.1x establishes. There can be more users created on the system than the maximum number of connection slots licensed for in the operating system. Unused connection slots need to be cleared periodically.

It is a major security risk to leave a client logged in and unattended. NetWare does not provide a utility that logs a client out after an extended period of inactivity. These tools are provided by third-party vendors to perform the automatic logout functions. An example of this type of software is NETOFF, developed by Citadel Computer Systems.

425

The server uses the watchdog process to monitor connections that the server has not had a response from for a predetermined period. This watchdog process polls the clients to check the response from shell activity. If it does not receive response from the shell, it resets the connection's WATCHDOG TIMER field to 0 and then increments the WATCHDOG COUNTER field by one. The watchdog process then sends a packet to poll every minute—if the shell does not respond, the timer is again set to 0 and the counter is incremented by 1, for a maximum default of 11 times. The file server clears the client's connection after the maximum count is reached.

A NetWare 3.*x* server uses a parameter that enables administrators to monitor the WATCHDOG PROCESS at the file server. The following command is set in the AUTOEXEC.NCF file or typed at the console screen to view the WATCHDOG PROCESS messages:

```
SET CONSOLE DISPLAY WATCHDOG LOGOUTS = ON
```

Using ODI Drivers

There is a need for standards in communications with multiple types of emerging technologies arriving daily in the market. In order to communicate with existing LAN environments, Novell has been a leader in establishing rapport with other vendors to build a foundation for these needed standards. This is the reason Novell pushed the use of Open Data-Link Interface (ODI) drivers and dropped support of discontinued further IPX.COM development in June 1992.

Why Use ODI Drivers?

Open Data-Link Interface (ODI) development was first published in 1989. ODI first evolved in partnership between Novell and Apple Computer to provide support for multiple protocols on a single network. ODI enables LAN administrators to easily add or change protocols used on an existing or new network.

You must confirm that your NIC is certified to run with ODI drivers before it can be used in the network. Review the documentation that comes with the NIC, check NSEPRO, call 1-800 NETWARE, or contact the NIC vendor.

To access services on a multiple protocol network, only one Network Interface Card (NIC) is required. To use this function, an optional product is added and adjustments are made to the NET.CFG file. Clients also can communicate across network segments with different frame types by including additional frame types in the NET.CFG file.

One file server NIC card can also use multiple frame types. The ODI LAN driver in a file server can establish communication with any protocol stack by BINDing multiple types of protocols to the same LAN server NIC. You will need to load additional NetWare Loadable Modules (NLM) at the file server to interact with multiple protocols.

Novell literature uses the term *network board* to describe the cards that connect PCs to networks. You also will encounter the term *network interface card*, frequently abbreviated as *NIC*, to describe these devices. Both names describe the same pieces of hardware, but the term in the Novell red books is *network board*.

ODI Components

There are three components in the ODI architecture that further define the functionality of the flexible communication services:

- The Link Support Layer (LSL)
- The Multi-Link Interface Driver (MLID)
- The Protocol Stacks

The Link Support Layer (LSL) is a piece of software that offers a protocol to use multiple driver types and also offers a single driver to support multiple protocol types. The LSL acts as a "mailman" to determine which protocol stack should receive the packet (letter) when it receives the packet from the Multi-Link Interface Driver (MLID). The development of this one file eliminates the need for drivers for each frame and/or protocol combination.

The MLID controls the communication between the LSL and the LAN network interface card. The following are the two components built into the MLID:

◆ **Media Support Module (MSM).** This is the source code provided by Novell to help developers who are writing drivers to access multiple types of media. The access to this code enables the developer to speed up delivery and emphasize development of hardware options in a vendor's product.

◆ **Hardware-Specific Module (HSM).** This is the actual code written by the developer for that vendor of the LAN network interface board.

The design of the MLID is hardware-specific to the NIC and enables the interaction with the LSL to be very flexible. The MLID will remove the MAC header of the packet of data it receives and pass it on to the LSL as though the difference in media is invisible.

A protocol stack is a communication protocol that contains all protocols used above the Data-Link layer of the OSI reference model. Protocols have been developed by many different companies and use their own rules for data transmission. The protocol stack will provide its own information to the packets such as connection services and routing information. The protocol stack will receive information from the LSL, unaware of NIC type or media used, and pass it on up to higher layer protocols (i.e. the Application Layer—see fig. 9.13).

ODI Architecture

| IDX | TCP/IP | APPLETALK | OSI |

Link Support Layer (LSL)

Multiple Link Interface Driver
(MLID)

Network Interface Card
(NIC)

Figure 9.13
ODI Architecture.

Note Some applications are protocol-dependent and cannot be used by any other types of protocol stacks. It is better if you research functions to ensure functionality of all applications working together on a network.

Study Note Popular types of protocol stacks include the following:

- ◆ IPX/SPX
- ◆ TCP/IP
- ◆ AppleTalk
- ◆ OSI

429

A client using ODI can access several services and applications concurrently. One NetWare ODI example is IPXODI.COM with Sequenced Packet Exchange (SPX). The IPXODI.COM file contains three parts:

- ◆ IPX
- ◆ SPX
- ◆ Remote Diagnostics Responder

IPX packages the information that the shell (NETX) has determined for the network and passes it on to the LSL. SPX handles acknowledgments, requests, and packet sequencing between the client and the network. Third-party vendors use the Remote Diagnostics Responder to gather diagnostic information for their network support applications. You can unload some of the components of the IPXODI.COM file to save memory. To load IPX and SPX only and save 4KB of memory, type:

```
IPXODI d
```

To load IPX only and save 8KB of memory, type the following:

```
IPXODI a
```

 NetWare utilities such as RCONSOLE require that SPX and the Remote Diagnostics Responder must remain loaded.

In order for the ODI drivers to work, load the drivers in the following sequence:

```
LSL.COM

MLID

IPXODI.COM

NETX.EXE
```

Type the drivers at the DOS prompt or load in an AUTOEXEC.BAT file as shown below:

1. **LSL** (press Enter)

2. **3C509** (press Enter)

3. **IPXODI** (press Enter)

4. **NETX** (press Enter)

You can unload these from memory for troubleshooting purposes or to change the protocol stack needed. Unload the drivers in the reverse order as shown below:

1. **NETX /U** (press Enter)

2. **IPXODI /U** (press Enter)

3. **3C509 /U** (press Enter)

4. **LSL /U** (press Enter)

Using the NET.CFG File with ODI

The NET.CFG file is a configuration file used specifically with ODI drivers. It uses defined rules for loading information:

◆ The main section headings are not case-sensitive and must be left-justified. The heading must precede the options you want to include in each type of section.

◆ Options must appear under a heading and be preceded by a tab or hard spaces. Options are not case-sensitive.

◆ The common section headings used are the following:

LINK SUPPORT

PROTOCOL

LINK DRIVER

◆ All comments must be preceded with a semicolon (;).

◆ Each line must end with a hard return.

431

◆ Numbers must be written in decimal notation except when noted otherwise. (Port addresses are examples of numbers that are specified in hexadecimal notation.)

◆ If using SHELL.CFG parameters, they must be placed at the top of the NET.CFG file and left-aligned.

If a SHELL.CFG file exists when upgrading from IPX to ODI drivers, you may keep all SHELL.CFG parameters in the SHELL.CFG file. If a SHELL.CFG does not exist, create a NET.CFG file. If a SHELL.CFG file exists and you place SHELL.CFG parameters in a NET.CFG file, the SHELL.CFG parameters in the NET.CFG file will not be executed.

It is easier to administer when you combine SHELL.CFG options into a NET.CFG file and delete the old SHELL.CFG file.

The following is an example of a NET.CFG file used with the NETX.EXE shell and ODI drivers:

```
Preferred Server = PLANODCW_FS
Show Dots = On
LINK DRIVER 3C509
        ; Change the interrupt (IRQ) to 9
        INT 9
        ; Change the port to 310 hex
        PORT 310
        FRAME ETHERNET_802.3
```

NetWare 4.*x* includes a file named WSUPGRD.EXE that replaces the WSUPDATE.EXE utility that assists in upgrading dedicated IPX drivers with ODI drivers on a local drive. WSUPGRD.EXE will also work with NetWare 3.*x*. The documentation in the manuals for WSUPGRD.EXE is not as reliable as the document #TID013780, found in the NSEPRO.

Advantages of ODI over IPX

You should be aware of several advantages of the ODI drivers over the older IPX.COM driver file:

◆ ODI supports LANalyzer for Windows.

◆ ODI has improved flexibility for memory management. You can load and unload them as necessary.

◆ ODI is easier to configure. No regeneration is required with NIC card changes.

◆ Each client can have up to four active NICs.

◆ ODI supports multiple protocols and frame types on a single network.

Troubleshooting Tips for ODI

Troubleshoot malfunctioning installations of IPX and ODI based DOS workstations.

Here are some tips for troubleshooting ODI workstation drivers:

◆ Unload the drivers in reverse order and load them back one at a time. As you load them, read the messages displayed on the screen to monitor conflicts.

◆ Type a question mark after each ODI executable to see specific information on each one as in the following:

```
IPXODI /?
```

◆ Make sure the settings in the NET.CFG file do not conflict with NIC settings or other network specifications.

◆ Make sure the NIC is certified to work with ODI drivers.

- Check the frame type running on the network. Newer drivers on Ethernet (all NetWare 4.x and NetWare 3.12) use the Ethernet 802.2 frame by default. Older drivers defaulted to Ethernet 802.3.

- Check NetWire for the latest enhancements to ODI components.

Using the VLM DOS Requester

The NetWare Directory Service feature of NetWare 4.01 cannot be accessed by workstations running the NetWare Shell. Beginning with NetWare 4.x, Novell has replaced the Shell with an interface called the DOS Requester. The new Requester technology works more smoothly with DOS, but the purpose of the Requester is the same as the purpose of the Shell: to ensure that local service requests go to the local PC and network requests are directed to the appropriate NetWare server.

What Are VLMs?

The latest NetWare client software is the DOS Requester that contains several components called Virtual Loadable Modules (VLMs). The DOS Requester no longer uses a file similar to NETX.EXE. Instead, the Requester uses Virtual Loadable Modules (VLMs). These files have an extension of .VLM. The DOS Requester uses a VLM manager called VLM.EXE that manages incoming requests and outgoing replies delivered by these modules.

 The newer VLMs are part of the v3.12 and v4.x installation packages. You can acquire these VLMs from NetWare to run on v3.11.

There are two types of VLMs:

◆ **Child VLMs.** These handle logical groupings for particular types of NetWare servers and transport protocols, for example:

  ◆ IPXNCP.VLM handles IPX services.

  ◆ BIND.VLM is used for v3.*x* bindery servers.

  ◆ NDS.VLM is used for v4.*x* NetWare Directory Services.

  ◆ FIO.VLM handles file input/output when accessing the network. This module uses Large Internet Packets (LIP), Packet Burst, and File Caching functions.

  ◆ NETX.VLM is used with bindery services for backward compatibility for the applications expecting NETX.COM or NETX.EXE instead of the VLM.EXE manager.

◆ **Multiplexors.** These route calls to the correct child VLM and also can be called parent VLMs, for example:

  ◆ NWP.VLM coordinates requests to the network modules, such as BIND.VLM and NDS.VLM, to perform connecting and logging in and out functions, and handling broadcasts.

  ◆ CONN.VLM allocates the number of connections the DOS Requester can have, and supplies APIs and table information to other VLMs.

  ◆ TRAN.VLM manages communication at the transport layer when protocols are loaded. As an example, it uses IPXNCP.VLM when handling packets for transmission over the media.

435

Advantages of the DOS Requester over NETX

The DOS Requester has many advantages over the NETX Shell, including the following:

◆ It uses Large Internet Packet (LIP) technology as a default. This enables NetWare networks using topologies such as Ethernet and Token Ring to increase their default packet size from 576 bytes to a larger packet size. Increasing to a larger packet size can increase the throughput on routers and bridges that can distinguish changes in packet sizes.

◆ It uses Packet Burst protocol technology as a default. This enables transmission of multipacket messages across the internetwork. Maximum packet burst sizes are negotiated between the client and the server at connection time.

◆ It enables use of only the VLM modules that are necessary for your network. This could reduce memory requirements in the client. VLM.EXE takes advantage of memory swapping by selecting the best possible place to work from when loading—extended first, expanded second, and conventional if the other two memory locations are not available.

◆ It supports the use of NetWare Directory Services used in NetWare 4.*x*.

Using the NET.CFG File with VLM.EXE

The VLM Installation Program adds one entry to the NET.CFG file that is different from the standard ODI setup. The NET.CFG file includes a new heading section called NETWARE DOS REQUESTER. The following is an example of a NET.CFG file using VLMs:

```
SHOW DOTS = ON
LINK DRIVER 3C509
     INT 9
     PORT 310
```

```
        FRAME ETHERNET_802.3
NETWARE DOS REQUESTER
      FIRST NETWORK DRIVE = F
      USE DEFAULTS = OFF
      VLM=CONN.VLM
      VLM=IPXNCP.VLM
      VLM=TRAN.VLM
      ;VLM=SECURITY.VLM
      ;VLM=NDS.VLM
      VLM=BIND.VLM
      ;VLM=RSA.VLM
      VLM=NWP.VLM
      VLM=FIO.VLM
            VLM=GENERAL.VLM
            VLM=REDIR.VLM
            VLM=PRINT.VLM
            VLM=NETX.VLM
            ;VLM=AUTO.VLM
```

The USE DEFAULTS = OFF line tells the VLM.EXE not to execute all the VLMs included in the NWCLIENT directory. You can turn them off as shown by marking them with a semicolon.

Installing VLMs

The DOS REQUESTER software is available in the v3.12 and v4.x installation packages. The NetWare client software comes on four disks:

◆ WSDOS_1 contains the installation files.

◆ WSDRV_1 and WSDRV_2 contain DOS ODI drivers.

◆ WSWIN_1 contains drivers to run WINDOWS with NetWare on a client.

To begin the installation process, insert the WSDOS_1 disk in the local drive on the client, change to that drive (A:, Enter), then type **INSTALL**. Press Enter. The screen shown in figure 9.14 provides entry points for all five steps required for the installation process:

Figure 9.14

The DOS Requestor installation opening screen.

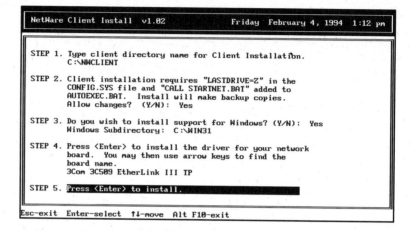

```
NetWare Client Install  v1.02              Friday  February 4, 1994  1:12 pm

   STEP 1. Type client directory name for Client Installation.
           C:\NWCLIENT

   STEP 2. Client installation requires "LASTDRIVE=Z" in the
           CONFIG.SYS file and "CALL STARTNET.BAT" added to
           AUTOEXEC.BAT.  Install will make backup copies.
           Allow changes?  (Y/N):  Yes

   STEP 3. Do you wish to install support for Windows? (Y/N):  Yes
           Windows Subdirectory:  C:\WIN31

   STEP 4. Press <Enter> to install the driver for your network
           board.  You may then use arrow keys to find the
           board name.
           3Com 3C509 EtherLink III TP

   STEP 5. Press <Enter> to install.

Esc-exit   Enter-select   ↑↓-move   Alt F10-exit
```

1. This is the directory path in which the install process intends to install the VLM files and the ODI drivers. As a default, C:\NWCLIENT is used.

2. This step discusses the changes that will be made to the CONFIG.SYS and AUTOEXEC.BAT files. Answer **YES**.

3. If you are using Windows on your client, answer **YES** and type in the directory on the client where Windows is located.

4. This enables you to update your drivers to support an ODI interface. The DOS directory on the WSDRV_2 disk contains the drivers provided by NetWare. You may need to insert another vendor's disk with the ODI drivers if your NIC is not included in the default list.

5. Once this step is selected, all the processes selected in the prior steps will make changes to file names and store files in the appropriate directories on the client. The display screen in figure 9.15 is shown when the install utility finishes.

Read each item on the screen, make notes, then press Enter to exit. From your notes, reboot your client now for the VLM drivers to take effect and observe the changes noted.

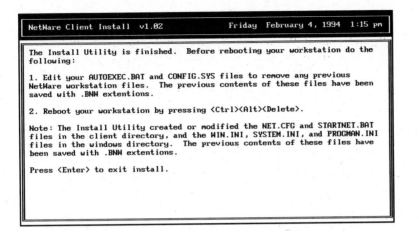

Figure 9.15

The DOS Requestor installation finishing screen.

Troubleshooting VLM Clients

Here are some suggestions for troubleshooting VLM clients:

◆ When VLM.EXE is executed, be sure the default directory is set to your directory pointer.

◆ Check the NET.CFG file for the load order of the VLMs—child VLMs must be loaded before Multiplexor VLMs. Comment– out those VLMs not needed by using a semicolon in front of the file name.

◆ If you are using IPX as the transport protocol, make sure the IPXNCP.VLM is being loaded.

◆ Do not run NETX.COM or NETX.EXE with VLMs. Use NETX.VLM in the NET.CFG file and VLM.EXE.

◆ If you are removing VLM.EXE, edit the NET.CFG file and remove the LASTDRIVE=Z statement from the CONFIG.SYS file.

◆ Make sure you have enough memory on the client to run VLMs.

◆ Use the /? command line option to view other available options. Type **VLM /?** and press Enter.

Using the Remote Boot Client

Networks can interface with clients that do not have a floppy or hard drive. This is handled by a virtual drive called remote boot. Clients with remote boot are used for cost savings, security, speed, and convenience. There is less maintenance or access to sensitive files on clients without hard drives or floppy disks.

The client contains a network interface card (NIC) that includes a ROM chip that provides connection services to the file server. The file server uses the information from a boot disk image file called NET$DOS.SYS. This file includes details about the system sectors, FAT and directory tables, and the files needed for attaching a connection to the network. These files include the ODI drivers, a LOGIN program, and a unique ID batch file. The NET$DOS.SYS file must be flagged with the "shareable" attribute.

The client will send a read request to a floppy when it is booted. The ROM chip on the NIC will intercept the read request and relay the request to the network. The boot disk image file is then used as the resource for client information. If there are multiple clients using remote boot, a file named BOOTCONF.SYS is created on the file server to manage the multiple remote boot image files.

Using Remote Boot with ODI Drivers

The following are the steps for using a remote boot with ODI drivers:

1. At the file server console type the following:

   LOAD RPL

   The RPL.NLM replaces the v3.11 modules_PCN2LRPL.NLM, ETHERRPL.NLM, and TOKENRPL.NLM. The RPL.NLM comes with the v3.12 and v4.x installation packages. You can get this file from NSEPRO or NetWire.

2. Ensure that the bootstrap programs that have the extension of .RPL are installed in the SYS:LOGIN directory. These files come with the RPL.NLM program.

3. RPL.NLM is a protocol stack and must be bound to the file server NICs that have remote boot clients attached to their segments. At the file server console (and or the AUTOEXEC.NCF) type the following:

   BIND RPL TO [LAN driver]

4. Create a NET$DOS.SYS remote boot disk image file. There is a separate process for single and multiple remote boot image files.

To create a single NET$DOS.SYS file:

1. Boot a client and log in as **SUPERVISOR**.

2. Insert a boot disk containing the files that attach the remote boot client: COMMAND.COM, LSL.COM, RPLODI.COM, MLID driver, IPXODI.COM, NETX.EXE, and the AUTOEXEC.BAT file. The following is an example of an AUTOEXEC.BAT file:

```
PROMPT $P$G
LSL
RPLODI
3C509
IPXODI
NETX
```

3. MAP drives to the directories that DOSGEN will write to:

   map f:=sys:system

   map g:=sys:login

   Change to the SYS:LOGIN directory by typing **g:**. Press Enter.

4. Run DOSGEN by typing **f:dosgen**. Press Enter.

   DOSGEN creates the NET$DOS.SYS disk image file in the SYS:LOGIN directory.

5. Copy the AUTOEXEC.BAT file from the boot disk into the SYS:LOGIN and the user's default home directory.

6. Flag the NET$DOS.SYS file in the SYS:LOGIN directory with the "shareable" attribute by typing the following:

   flag net$dos.sys s

   Press Enter.

To create multiple remote boot image files:

1. Boot a client and log in as **SUPERVISOR.**

2. Rename the AUTOEXEC.BAT file on each boot disk with a unique name, such as WS1.BAT.

3. Copy the renamed WS1.BAT file into the SYS:LOGIN and the default directory specified from the system login script.

4. Create a new AUTOEXEC.BAT file on each boot disk to execute the batch file that was renamed.

5. MAP drives to the directories that DOSGEN will write to:

   map f:=sys:system

   map g:=sys:login

   Change to the SYS:LOGIN directory by typing **g:.** Press Enter.

6. Create a uniquely named .SYS file in the SYS:LOGIN directory for each boot disk. Use the DOSGEN file from the WSDOS_1 disk, for example, WS1.SYS.

7. With the boot disk in drive A:, from the G: directory type the following:

   f:dosgen a: ws1.sys

   Press Enter. This file will be created in the SYS:LOGIN directory.

8. Create a file named BOOTCONF.SYS in the SYS:LOGIN directory with each remote boot client's information, for example:

0xNET10,260123456=WS1.SYS

0xNET10,260198734=WS2.SYS

A line must be created for each remote boot image file with the following information:

- ◆ 0x (the number zero plus x)

- ◆ The network address

- ◆ A comma

- ◆ The node address

- ◆ The boot disk image file name

9. Flag the .SYS files in the SYS:LOGIN directory with the "shareable" attribute:

flag *.sys s

Press Enter.

Troubleshoot problems with remote workstations booting.

The transient portion of the COMMAND.COM file is larger in MS-DOS 5.0 than in other DOS versions. To use a remote boot with MS-DOS 5.0, you use a file named RPLFIX to be run with the NET$DOS.SYS file. COMMAND.COM overwrites part of the remote boot image file if RPLFIX is not used.

Some revisions of boot ROMs do not work with ODI drivers and MS-DOS 5.0. Check with that manufacturer for updated chips.

443

Using Windows on a Client

Windows is a graphical user interface (GUI, pronounced goo-ey) that is used in a networking environment. Windows can enhance network functionality—training time is reduced, user comfort level is higher, and support costs can be reduced. Consistency in network access can become a big issue, taking up a lot of a network administrator's time. Using a Windows-type front end can enhance the overall network environment.

The VLM installation process will load the appropriate Windows .DLL, .DRV, and .INI information to work with NetWare. After the VLM installation utility is complete, reboot the client for the changes to WINDOWS to take effect.

If you are using IPX.COM or ODI drivers, you can load Windows support with the Windows Disk #2. Setting up the basic Windows 3.1 package to work with NetWare is a simple process. It is more efficient to have the NetWare drivers loaded before you begin this process. To begin this process, bring up Windows, select the MAIN.GRP icon, then select WINDOWS SETUP as shown in figure 9.16.

Figure 9.16

Location in Windows for network definitions designation.

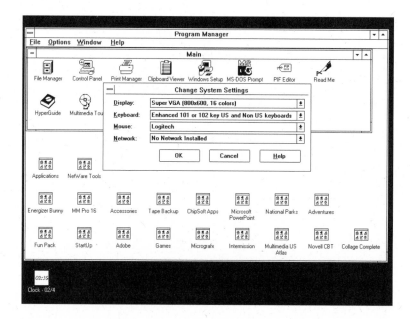

Note The set-up process for Windows for Workgroups 3.11 is different than the basic Windows 3.1 package. Please refer to the documentation supplied with software. Use NSEPRO or NetWire for enhancement references.

Click on the down arrow of the NETWORK selection and select the shell version that best fits the one in your client directory. The selection will display as shown in figure 9.17.

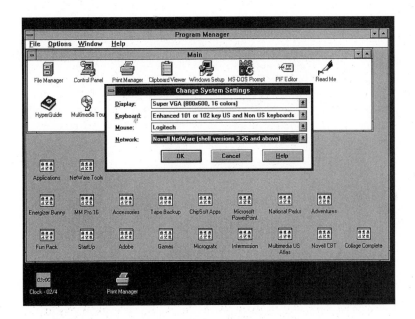

Figure 9.17

Selection for use with NetWare 3.1*x*, using Shell 3.26 and later.

Click on OK, and the screen will then ask you to insert the Microsoft Windows 3.1 Disk #2 as shown in figure 9.18.

Figure 9.18

The Windows set-up screen to load needed NetWare files.

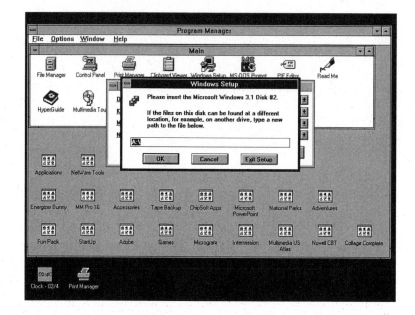

Click on OK. When this process is complete, reboot Windows. Windows will now recognize that the client is using NetWare. You now can set Print Manager to make network connections for queues (see Chapter 11, "Printing with NetWare"). You can refer to the "Windows Resource Kit" for more details about using Windows on a network.

Review Questions

1. Which of the following is not a true statement regarding the IPX.COM file?

   ○ a. It is generated using the WSGEN disk.

   ○ b. It is part of the NetWare 3.11 Install package.

   ○ c. It includes the IRQ, I/O address, and RAM buffer setting.

   ○ d. One file is created for all network clients, regardless of how many different NICs are included on the network.

2. Which two of the following statements are true regarding the IPX.COM file?

   ☐ a. It assigns source and destination addresses to data packets to create an Internetwork address.

   ☐ b. It manages packet routing to the correct socket location.

   ☐ c. It acts as a "traffic cop" between applications and the operating system.

   ☐ d. It is the older version of the shell.

3. Which of the following is not one of the communication protocol fields enveloped by the IPX.COM file for use on the network?

   ○ a. Systems Inventory Protocol (SIP)

   ○ b. Routing Information Protocol (RIP)

   ○ c. Service Advertising Protocol (SAP)

   ○ d. NetWare Core Protocol (NCP)

4. The RIP protocol allows several types of information to be exchanged. Which of the following is not a type of information that RIP allows to be exchanged?

   ○ a. Router requests for fastest route to a network number

   ○ b. Router broadcasts when changes in internetwork configuration are detected

   ○ c. Request for names and addresses of all servers

   ○ d. Router table updating information

5. Which of the following protocol communication fields handles periodic broadcasts by routers and servers?

   ○ a. SIP

   ○ b. RIP

   ○ c. SAP

   ○ d. NCP

6. The NCP monitors connection control and service requests and provides which of the following?

   ○ a. Control of the NetWare shell

   ○ b. Packet-level error checking

   ○ c. Advertising of services and addresses

   ○ d. Responses to "Get Nearest Server" requests

7. The purpose of a packet sequence number is

   ○ a. to provide medium-access protocols such as 802.2 and 802.3.

   ○ b. to manage the delivery of packets for proper communication on the network.

   ○ c. to translate requests initiated at the keyboard into functions to be handled by the OS.

   ○ d. to enable the error-checking capabilities between the file server and client to know when a packet is lost.

8. The file that is considered the actual shell for client communication is called

   ○ a. IPX.OBJ

   ○ b. IPX.COM

   ○ c. NET.EXE

   ○ d. NETX.EXE

9. Which of the following is not one of the files replaced by the client communication shell?

   ○ a. NETx.COM

   ○ b. IPX.ODI

   ○ c. EMSNETX.COM

   ○ d. XMSNETS.COM

10. Which of the following files can be modified to change default parameters or add more parameters in order to fine-tune the performance of your workstation on the network?

   ○ a. IPX.COM

   ○ b. NETX.EXE

   ○ c. SHELL.CFG

   ○ d. CONFIG.SYS

11. Unused connection slots need to be cleared periodically because

   ○ a. third-party logout functions must be used occasionally.

   ○ b. it is a security risk to leave a logged-in and unattended client.

   ○ c. too many packets sent to poll the clients causes congestion on the network.

   ○ d. all network users should have equal access to the network.

12. Which of the following is not a reason to use ODI drivers?

    ○ a. They provide support for multiple protocols on a single network.

    ○ b. Only one NIC is required to access services on a multiple protocol network.

    ○ c. Novell is a leader in pushing for network standards.

    ○ d. Clients can communicate across network segments with different frame types if ODI drivers are used.

13. As a NetWare 3 administrator, in which of the following files would you set the CONSOLE DISPLAY WATCHDOG LOGOUTS = ON parameter in order to monitor the WATCHDOG PROCESS?

    ○ a. AUTOEXEC.NCF

    ○ b. AUTOEXEC.BAT

    ○ c. CONFIG.NCF

    ○ d. CONFIG.SYS

14. If you were the component of the ODI architecture responsible for acting as the "mailman" to determine which protocol stack should receive the packet, you would be the

    ○ a. Media Support Module (MSM)

    ○ b. Multi-Link Interface Driver (MLID)

    ○ c. Hardware-Specific Module (HSM)

    ○ d. Link Support Layer (LSL)

15. Which of the following are true statements regarding the MLID (choose two)?

    ☐ a. Its design is hardware-specific to the NIC.

    ☐ b. It contains the LSL and protocol stacks.

    ☐ c. It determines which protocol stack receives the packet.

    ☐ d. It removes MAC headers from packets of data it receives and passes them on to the LSL.

16. A protocol stack can best be defined as

   ○   a. functions that ensure that all applications work together on a network.

   ○   b. a type of communication protocol containing all protocols used above the Data-Link layer of the OS reference model.

   ○   c. a grouping of connection services and routing information.

   ○   d. packages that help the shell determine whether or not acknowledgments, requests, and packets should be passed on the LSL.

17. In order to save 8KB of memory when loading IPX, which switch should you use when loading the IPXODI.COM file?

   ○   a. A

   ○   b. D

   ○   c. U

   ○   d. S

18. Which load sequence enables ODI drivers to function properly?

   ○   a. LSL.COM, MLID, IPXODI.COM, NETX.EXE

   ○   b. LSL.COM, MLID, IPXODI.COM, NETX

   ○   c. LSL.COM, IPXODI.COM, MLID, NETX.EXE

   ○   d. NETX.EXE, LSL.COM, MLID, IPXODI.COM

19. What is the NetWare 4 file called that replaces the WSUPDATE.EXE utility and used to assist in upgrading dedicated IPX drivers with ODI drivers?

   ○   a. WSUPGRD.EXE

   ○   b. UPGRDEWS.EXE

   ○   c. WSUPDT4.EXE

   ○   d. WSUPGRD4.EXE

20. Which of the following is *not* an advantage of using ODI over IPX?

   ○ a. No regeneration is required when a NIC is changed.

   ○ b. ODI supports multiple protocols and frame types on a single network.

   ○ c. Memory management is improved because you can load and unload files as needed.

   ○ d. Each client can have up to eight active NICs.

21. VLMs are *not*

   ○ a. files that have a .VLM extension.

   ○ b. part of the latest NetWare client software.

   ○ c. used for troubleshooting IPX-based network problems.

   ○ d. part of the NetWare 3.12 and 4.*x* installation packages.

22. As the administrator for your NetWare network, you need to remove the VLM.EXE file temporarily in order to correct a problem. What else must you do when you remove the VLM.EXE file?

   ○ a. Make sure you have enough memory on the client to correctly unload the VLMs.

   ○ b. Remove the LASTDRIVE=Z statement from the CONFIG.SYS file.

   ○ c. Change the load order of the VLMs in the NET.CFG file.

   ○ d. Add the NETX.VLM line to the NET.CFG file and reboot the computer.

23. Remote boot can also be defined as

   ○ a. a RAM chip that provides connection services to the network.

   ○ b. a Virtual Drive.

    ○   c. a disk image file called NET$DOS.SYS.

    ○   d. a file that includes information about logging in to the network.

24. Which file must be created on the file server when multiple remote boot image files need to be managed?

    ○   a. BOOTCONF.SYS

    ○   b. BOOTNAME.COM

    ○   c. NET$DOS.SYS

    ○   d. AUTOEXEC.NCF

25. Which Windows disk contains the appropriate files to add NetWare to its functionality?

    ○   a. Disk #6

    ○   b. Disk #1

    ○   c. Disk #2

    ○   d. Disk #5

Answers

1. D

2. A, B

3. A

4. C

5. C

6. B

7. D

8. D

9. B

10. C

11. B
12. C
13. A
14. D
15. A, D
16. B
17. A
18. A
19. A
20. D
21. C
22. B
23. B
24. A
25. D

Working with Storage Devices on a Network

In this chapter, you learn about the advantages and disadvantages of different types of storage devices that can be used on the network. There are many types of storage devices that have evolved throughout the history of the computer industry. Understanding how these devices operate and what their limitations are is an important function of a network administrator's job. The following are the types of storage devices that will be discussed in this chapter:

◆ Hard drives

◆ CD-ROM players

◆ Magneto-optical drives

Hard Drives

The hard drive is perhaps the most important storage device on your network. Great care and attention must be given to the hard drive because it is the core of the file server. The operating system that gives a network its functionality must reside on that core drive. If that core drive fails, the entire network will go down. A network administrator is responsible for developing a design for fault tolerance in protecting the core of the network. You also must be able to diagnose potential failure points and be proactive in preventative maintenance. An experienced network administrator must be able to do capacity planning and know how to react in a contingency management mode.

The terminology in the computer industry uses the term *fixed disk* to mean *hard disk*. The fixed disk or the *platters* are contained in the hard drive casing, as opposed to inserting a removable disk in the floppy drive (see fig. 10.1). The technology of a hard drive enables it to provide speed, reliability, and a lot of storage in a small space in one location.

The device that enables the communication between the hard drive and the CPU is called the *disk controller card*. The disk controller card can be built into the motherboard, as part of the drive or as a separate component. The controller interprets the commands from the CPU and sends the interpreted signals to either seek, read, or write data to the hard drive.

 The drive casing is sealed by the manufacturer in a dust- and moisture-free environment. Do not open this drive casing for any reason—dust particles can scratch your platters. They can become inoperable and you could lose valuable data.

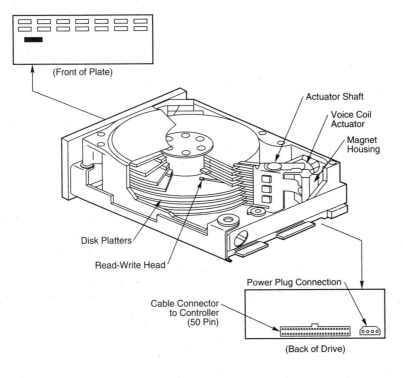

(Front of Plate)

Actuator Shaft

Voice Coil
Actuator

Magnet
Housing

Disk Platters

Read-Write Head

Power Plug Connection

Cable Connector
to Controller
(50 Pin)

(Back of Drive)

Figure 10.1

Internal components
of a hard drive.

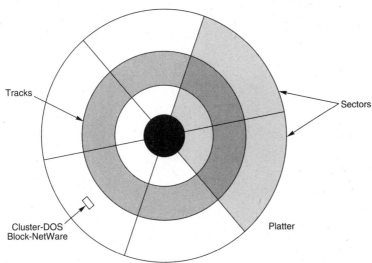

Tracks

Sectors

Cluster-DOS
Block-NetWare

Platter

457

The hard drive is made up of many components that work in unison and can be described as an electronic wonder. The drive contains a spindle motor that rotates the platters inside the drive casing. The voice coil actuator moves the read/write heads to the needed position on the disk platter. The time it takes for the read/write heads to find the correct track is called *seek time*.

After the track has been located, the amount of time it takes for the needed piece of data to rotate under the read/write head is called *drive latency*. The combination of seek time and drive latency (the total amount of time it takes to get to the data on the platter) is called *access time*. To "settle" a drive is the time it takes for the head to stabilize above the track after the process or the motion for seeking data has stopped.

The *data transfer rate* is the speed at which data is moved from the disk to the electronic "brains" of the CPU. The amount of data moved is measured in megabytes per second. All these timing features in a hard drive are important to how quickly data can be accessed on the network.

A cluster is the minimum unit of space for the storage of a file allocated by DOS. A block is the minimum unit of space (usually 4KB) for the storage of file information by NetWare.

Types of Hard Drive Interfaces

Differentiate among standard hard drive types.

There are several types of hard drive interfaces and encoding schemes used with these interfaces in the networking environment. As a network administrator or support engineer, you should become familiar with each type because of the varied install base that still exists. An early example of a type of a hard drive is an ST-506 model manufactured by Seagate. The ST-506 originally was built for 5MB size drives. The Run Length Limited (RLL) or the Modified Frequency Modulation (MFM) encoding scheme is used for the larger ST-506 drives.

MFM is referred to as double-density recording and is used as a coding system to pack more information on hard disks. MFM is still used today on floppy disks and small hard drives.

RLL has increased data density capabilities over MFM by the way it manipulates electronic flux transitions. Fluxes are defined as the way the magnetic field handles the 0's and 1's of digital information. The RLL handles a higher data throughput over the MFM encoding scheme.

IDE Drives

The Integrated Drive Electronics (IDE) drive uses the mechanics of having the controller interface integrated with the electronic controls of the hard drive. The IDE terminology often is identified as an AT-type interface with the cable connector for the controller built into the CPU's motherboard. The IDE drive is a cost-effective solution that uses the RLL encoding scheme. Even though the IDE solution has widely replaced the ST-506 drives, there are some limitations on using IDE drives with NetWare:

◆ Unless a special nonstandard BIOS is used, there is a maximum drive capacity of 528MB.

◆ IDE does not support drive command overlapping nor can it multitask I/O. If you are mixing IDE drives in a file server with other types of drives, the network operating system must wait for the IDE to complete any commands issued before the network operating system can issue any commands to any other drives.

459

◆ IDE does not support any optical or tape drives (the SCSI interface does).

◆ IDE does not support bus-mastering.

 It is recommended that you never do a low-level format on an IDE drive. If you do this repair task, you could erase the manufacturer's bad block information that is written in a special format on the IDE drive.

ESDI Drives

The Enhanced Small Device Interface (ESDI) uses one cable for floppy control, one for hard drive control, and one for data. The ST-506 drive uses the same cabling system, but it is not interchangeable with the ESDI drive. The ESDI drive became more popular than the ST-506 because of its capability of having a higher performance level and using a larger storage capacity. The ESDI also can store information about bad tracks onto the disk, and the interface is designed to work with tape systems. The popularity of ESDI was fairly short-lived, however, and SCSI drive systems have replaced ESDI as the drives of choice on network servers.

Older ESDI drives are supported by the computer's BIOS. Newer drives that have 1,024 or more cylinders do not work well in older ESDI machines. Drives that have more than 1,023 cylinders and 33 sectors per track are not likely to be supported by DOS versions before v3.3. The controllers of XTs, ATs, and Western Digital WD1002 controllers cannot recognize the cylinder count above 1,023 in larger drives.

 If you are using PS/2 CPUs as file servers (older ones came with ESDI drives) and early versions of NetWare, be careful in updating disk information with the reference disk after NetWare has been loaded. The older operating systems wrote the Cold Boot Loader to part of the track 0 on the ESDI drive.

When the reference disk updates drive information, it writes to track 0 and it will write on top of the cold boot loader. You will have to use your backup copy of the NET$OS.EXE file and boot from a floppy drive to get the server back up. If you want to boot from the hard drive again, you have to rebuild the file server from scratch.

SCSI Drives

The Small Computer Systems Interface (SCSI) provides an expansion bus architecture that allows up to seven SCSI-type devices (hard drives, CD-ROM, tape units). These can all be the same tape device, be used in combination, or be only one device on one bus slot (see fig. 10.2). These devices are attached to the cable chain that is attached to the SCSI controller card installed in a server or a client.

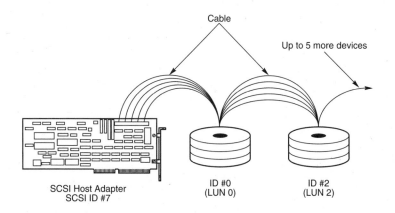

Figure 10.2

SCSI drive device addressing.

The devices that are installed internally in the CPU use ribbon cables designed for SCSI. External devices attach by cables that are built with the appropriate connectors for each of the devices attached to the SCSI chain.

The SCSI arbitration scheme allows a faster data transfer rate among the devices attached to each bus slot chain. The advantage in using SCSI is that the CPU does not have to intervene with the processing on the chain in order for the SCSI devices to complete their operations. The SCSI controller has its own BIOS that will run in the upper memory area of the CPU. It also uses hardware port addresses, memory addresses, and DMA channels to ensure compatibility with other components in the CPU.

Each SCSI address can support a controller that provides access to one or two hard drives. An advanced SCSI programming interface (ASPI) device driver is provided by the manufacturer and is needed to coordinate communications between different types of devices. There are SCSI controllers that are available with connector ports for use with floppy disk drives. If you want to use the floppy controller already built into your CPU, you can disable the floppy controller on the SCSI board.

The SCSI bus must be terminated at both ends (see fig. 10.3). A SCSI device driver cannot interpret the difference between the original signals or returned signals as an Ethernet bus does. To prevent confusion caused by reflected signals, terminators are used to absorb or prevent signals from becoming unstable. Each SCSI device connected to this terminated bus must have a unique address. This unique address is called a Logical Unit Number (LUN).

The American National Standards Institute (ANSI) X3T9.2 committee sets the standards for the SCSI interface. The newest SCSI standard, SCSI-2, defines the protocols, hardware, and command set to run devices other than hard disks. The older SCSI standard could not reliably control the devices beyond the hard drive setup. It is not recommended that you mix SCSI-1 and SCSI-2 standards in the same host, unless the SCSI adapter provides a method of handling both standards. The ISA bus has a transfer data rate maximum of 2MB per second, whereas the SCSI-2 can transfer data at 4MB, and during the FAST operation, can transfer data up to 10MB per second. You should use the EISA, MCA, or PCI bus with the appropriate SCSI interface cards for the FAST SCSI-2 operation to work efficiently.

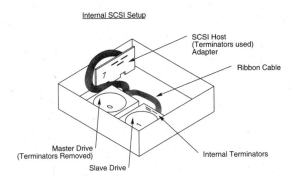

Internal SCSI Setup

SCSI Host
(Terminators used)
Adapter

Ribbon Cable

Master Drive
(Terminators Removed)

Slave Drive

Internal Terminators

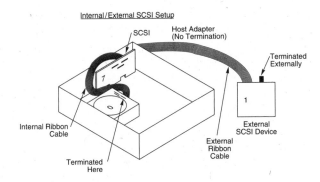

Internal/External SCSI Setup

SCSI
Host Adapter
(No Termination)

Terminated
Externally

Internal Ribbon
Cable

1

External
SCSI Device

External
Ribbon
Cable

Terminated
Here

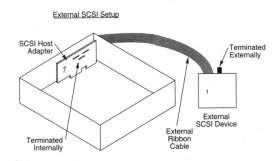

External SCSI Setup

SCSI Host
Adapter

Terminated
Externally

1

External
SCSI Device

Terminated
Internally

External
Ribbon
Cable

Figure 10.3

Termination of SCSI internal/external setups.

463

There is an implementation of SCSI called WIDE SCSI-2 that is not used as much as the FAST SCSI-2 standard, as WIDE SCSI-2 is fairly new. WIDE SCSI-2 uses a second data path that offers the capability of 20MB per second data transfer rate. The WIDE SCSI-2 controller integrates the 68-pin SCSI cable and the differential signaling process. Standard SCSI devices use a 50-pin cable and the single-ended signaling process. There are SCSI host adapters that have a combination of connection slots for a SCSI internal bus with both 68-pin and 50-pin cables. These combination type adapters use either the differential or single-ended signaling process, but not both.

You cannot mix the differential and single-ended devices on the same SCSI bus—they are electronically incompatible. If you have both types of SCSI devices, use one adapter for WIDE SCSI using differential signaling, and another adapter that uses the single-ended devices. Future implementations for the WIDE SCSI devices will develop enhancements for using single-ended signaling.

Tips for Working with SCSI Devices

 Diagnose and correct common hard drive problems.

The use of SCSI devices is rapidly becoming an industry standard. These devices are flexible, affordable, and are relatively easy to install. As a network administrator or support engineer, you should use the following tips in setting up a SCSI environment:

◆ When selecting your hardware and software, make sure the revision levels are current and that each can work within the same bus with the other devices.

◆ Use all SCSI-2 devices when designing a network. Older SCSI-1 hard disks will mix with SCSI-2 equipment if you have to use available resources.

◆ Use SCSI host adapters that use a software setup for jumper and termination settings. Then you do not have to remove the card from the CPU each time you need to change the settings.

◆ Make sure that you use the proper pin number and connector size for the SCSI host adapter and the devices attached to complete the bus. Watch for cables with FAST SCSI-2 adapter connections attaching to the standard Centronics connector on the external SCSI devices. Unfortunately, the proper SCSI connector cables are not always shipped to meet the needs in your environment.

◆ Always confirm that each SCSI bus is properly terminated and that the cables are fitting snugly into the connector slots. The maximum length for a SCSI bus is 19 feet, 10 inches. Make sure that the external disk subsystems are using cables that match the proper impedance level.

◆ The SCSI bus requires a stable current for the signals to operate properly. Verify that your host adapter and other SCSI devices are supplying the necessary terminating power.

◆ Make sure your SCSI host adapter's BIOS, port address, IRQ, and DMA channel addresses do not conflict with other components in the CPU.

◆ Make sure that each SCSI device has a unique identifier number (LUN). Each SCSI adapter has a default address of 7 set by the manufacturer. The first bootable hard disk must have a SCSI LUN of 0. Other standard SCSI devices on the bus should be numbered 1-6 in the sequential order that the devices are located in the SCSI chain. Some Hewlett-Packard and IBM PS/2 CPUs use a SCSI adapter with an ID of 7 and the devices on the bus start at LUN 6; then each device is numbered sequentially downward to 0.

◆ It is best not to mix models of SCSI adapters if they are being used in the same computer. The ASPI software manager that is used by the adapter is written uniquely for that card. Mixing ASPI managers—even by the same manufacturer but different models—can cause operating conflicts.

◆ SCSI host adapters can coexist with other types of hard disks and their controllers. Still, it is best to keep device models consistent in the computer.

 There are many third-party software utilities that can be used to determine what drive interface is used in a client or file server. Tools such as CHECKIT PRO, as shown in figure 10.4, can assist a network administrator in determining the needed details.

Figure 10.4

CHECKIT PRO Hard Drive information screen example.

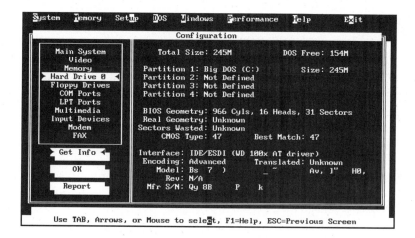

Disk Coprocessor Boards

Disk Coprocessor Boards (DCBs) are controller cards that offload the I/O from the CPU onto the DCB's own coprocessor chip. This frees up the CPU's processor to assist in improving network performance. DCBs also are referred to as Host Bus Adapters (HBAs) in Novell literature.

A file server can handle up to four DCB channels. A *disk channel* is a DCB and its disk subsystems. Each DCB can handle a maximum of eight SCSI controllers, with each controller supporting up to two disk drives. SCSI external disk subsystems can be daisy-chained off the DCB port on the end of the card (see fig. 10.5). DCBs are developed for the ISA (AT bus), EISA, and Microchannel architecture. Development of DCBs today is done by third-party vendors.

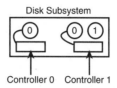

File Server   Disk Subsystem

DCB

Controller 0   Controller 1

Figure 10.5

Disk Coprocessor Board configuration.

The original DCBs were developed by Novell and had an 80188 on-board processor. The DCB also served as a UPS monitor that could gracefully down a server in the event of a UPS "battery low" condition. DCBs also were used as a keycard for serialization of early versions of NetWare 2.*x*. The DISKSET utility is required for using Novell's DCBs to send disk and drive configuration information to the EEPROM on the DCB. Any physical adds or deletions to the controller or disk drive setup required the use of DISKSET. Current DCBs by third parties use the utilities provided by the vendor. Most extended channel disk subsystems or internal multiple drives today use internal SCSI cards in the file server instead of DCBs.

Although the DCB was at one time the preferred method for constructing high-performance disk storage systems, many current SCSI controllers offer much higher performance.

Study Note

◆ A file server can handle up to 4 DCB channels.

◆ A disk channel consists of a DCB and the disk subsystems that attach to it.

◆ Each DCB can handle a maximum of eight SCSI controllers.

Proper integration of hardware components in a network is integral for efficient LAN performance. Verification from vendors and Novell Technical Support can help in your network planning. You must pay attention to potential conflicts for interrupts, memory addresses, and node addresses. Cabling limitations, hard drive requirements, addressing and termination, and certified software drivers also must be considered. If you do the proper homework and planning, you will reduce the chances of cost overruns and unplanned down time.

Setting Up Hard Drives

The hard disk is the most important device in a file server for storing both data and the applications that provide the glue for the network to function. The speed, the capacity, and the reliability of the hard disk can make or break your everyday operations (and maybe your sanity!). Understanding the hard disk, using the proper setup features, and performing proactive maintenance is an important function of a network administrator.

Working with Jumpers on the Hard Drive

When the hard drive arrives from the manufacturer and is unpacked from the box, all the jumpers on the drive are set at default options. These settings may or may not work in your computer. As a network administrator or support engineer, you must confirm that the settings on the drive will work for the interface type and encoding scheme required for that computer. Depending on your drive type, the following jumpers may need to be set directly on the drive:

- ◆ **ACT.** Set primarily on IDE and SCSI drives, and lights an external LED to indicate that the drive is active.

- ◆ **Drive Select.** Used primarily by ESDI, MFM, and RLL drives, depending on the number of drives and if you are using a flat or twisted cable.

- ◆ **C/D or DS.** Used by IDE to determine if the drive is to be a C or a D drive.

- ◆ **SCSI Address.** A unique address set by three jumpers that define a binary number. The manufacturer sets this address at 0. Check your drive documentation for all SCSI drives—this setting can vary with different vendors.

◆ **DSP.** Used by IDE to designate when a cable is being shared or which one of the drives is the master drive.

The controller card (if used by the drive) may need to have the following jumpers set:

◆ **Controller Interrupt.** You also may need to establish this setting in the STARTUP.NCF file on your file server when the .DSK file is loading. Usually, this setting is made by the manufacturer and should be left at this default setting.

◆ **Base I/O.** This should not conflict with any other device in the computer. This is set as a default from the manufacturer and rarely is changed unless there is a conflict.

◆ **DMA Channel.** NetWare does not recommend sharing a DMA channel between two devices. There are some ESDI and SCSI controllers that may need to have this setting verified.

◆ **Base BIOS Address.** Some controller cards use ROM BIOS and may need to have this set. Addresses over E000h may not be supported by some motherboards. Conflicts may arise with this setting and network interface cards or VGA cards.

Types of Cables Used with Hard Drives

The cable setup is important; it should be installed so that the pins in the connectors on the cable can receive and transmit the proper signals for data transfer. As a network administrator or support engineer, you must be aware of different cable types and proper installation of these cables. Improper installation can cause the loss of data and the potential destruction of drive components. Use the following recommendations when working with drive cables:

◆ Make sure that the colored stripe (usually red) is attached to Pin 1 on the controller card and to the hard drive (see figure 10.6).

469

Figure 10.6

Proper connection of Pin 1 between a hard drive and a disk controller card.

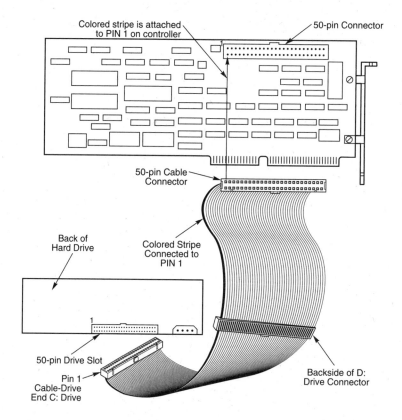

◆ In an AT standard computer, the floppy and hard drive cables have different twists and cannot be interchanged.

MFM and RLL hard drive cables have five twisted lines, and a floppy cable has seven twisted lines.

Floppy cables have the twists in the lower pin numbers.

◆ Small–numbered wires: twisted, smaller drive, i.e. floppy.

◆ High–numbered wires: twisted, larger drive, i.e. hard drive.

◆ A SCSI cable may have 25 or 50 pins on the connector, and the bus it is attached to must have exactly two terminated ends. Terminators may be found near the connector slot on the SCSI device in packs of three resistors.

◆ An IDE cable must not be longer than 18 inches, and it uses a 40-pin cable.

◆ You need three cables to connect two RLL or MFM drives to one controller—two data cables and one control cable. The control cable regulates the way the disk functions. If you are using two drives, remove the terminator that is on the drive in the middle of the chain (see fig. 10.7).

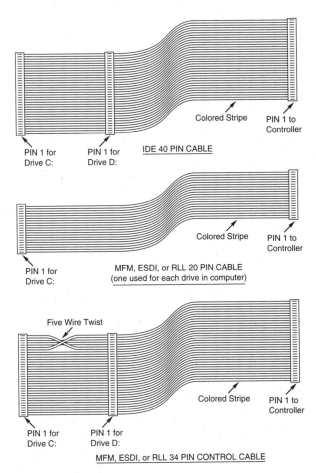

Figure 10.7
Types of drive cables.

Colored Stripe   PIN 1 to Controller

PIN 1 for Drive C: PIN 1 for Drive D: IDE 40 PIN CABLE

Colored Stripe   PIN 1 to Controller

PIN 1 for Drive C: MFM, ESDI, or RLL 20 PIN CABLE (one used for each drive in computer)

Five Wire Twist

Colored Stripe   PIN 1 to Controller

PIN 1 for Drive C: PIN 1 for Drive D: MFM, ESDI, or RLL 34 PIN CONTROL CABLE

471

Formatting the Hard Drive

Physical installation of a hard drive into a computer, setting the jumpers, and connecting the cables are the initial necessary tasks in preparing the drive for network use. When you receive a new hard drive or you are reusing an existing drive, you must prepare these drives in the required format so that data can be stored on them.

There are four important steps in preparing a hard drive to operate as it is designed:

1. Low-level formatting

2. Entering CMOS setup information

3. Establishing partitions

4. Performing a high-level DOS format

 Diagnose and correct hard drive installation problems, including those concerning volumes, partitions and segments.

Low-Level Formatting

Low-level formatting usually is done by the manufacturer of the drive at the factory. It is a destructive process and should only be done as the last resort in attempting to repair a drive. A low-level format is the process of defining sectors and the bad spots on the hard drive. Sectors provide the marking points (or indexes such as in a phone book) where information can be read, retrieved, or written.

There are third-party programs such as CKLLFMT in the CheckIt PRO software package. Some versions of DOS or the advanced drive diagnostics disk for the drive include low-level format utilities. You should check with the manufacturer of your drive for the proper procedure and program to do a low-level format.

A low-level format not only establishes sector IDs, it marks off bad sectors, tests the disks by performing a surface analysis, temporarily fills each sector, and sets the interleave ratio entered. Besides using a low-level format to give a new hard drive the directions on getting started, a low-level format can be done to remark the sectors of a drive that have been previously used, make an attempt at repairing a drive that is exhibiting a large number of errors, or change the interleave ratio.

If for some reason you have to low-level format a drive, make sure you format the drive in the same temperature and in the same position it will be used—flat or sideways. The temperature and gravity environment are very important to disk drives.

Setting the Interleave Ratio

Establishing the interleave ratio helps the drive to manage the flow of information between the computer and the disk better. Setting the interleave factor is not as necessary a concern for newer drives. Older drives used to be faster than what the CPU's microprocessor could handle; therefore, the interleave factor was developed to slow the drive down but still make it functional. The interleave ratio can help prevent bottlenecks if it is set properly.

Technology has enabled newer drives to set sector sparring, which is similar to NetWare's hot fix. This new feature will reserve one sector on every track for the remapping of bad sectors. This reduces the capacity of your new drive and should only be used if there are a lot of problems with the drive.

The physical sector arrangement and the logical arrangement of how the sectors are numbered in a track determines the interleave ratio (see fig. 10.8). An interleave factor is chosen by setting a ratio for the computer to use in determining how it is to read disk information. A ratio is defined as the length of a sector and the distance between two logical sectors. One sector is used as the starting point for measuring the length of an interleave. Setting an interleave factor too low or high can impede performance.

Figure 10.8

Sector reading by a hard drive set at a 2:1 interleave ratio.

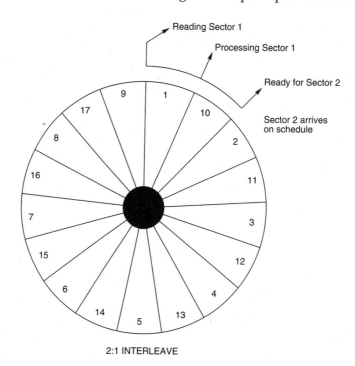

IDE drives use cache and really have no need for an interleave setting. Some SCSI drives and all MFM encoded drives can manage interleave ratios. The following interleave ratios are recommended:

◆ 1:1 for machines running NetWare that are 10 Mhz or faster, using 286 or 386 system boards. DOS machines at 20 Mhz or faster using 286 or 386 motherboards use this interleave. All 486 machines use 1:1.

474

- ◆ 2:1 for machines running DOS that are 10–16 Mhz and are using 286 or 386 motherboards.

- ◆ 3:1 for 6–8 Mhz AT class computers and for XT type machines running DOS applications.

- ◆ 4:1 for all 4.77 Mhz XT class machines.

Establishing Partitions

The hard drive must be partitioned after a low-level format has been completed. Modern drives that are new out of the box are already low-level formatted and ready to be partitioned. The operating system must be compatible with the format of the logical structure of the hard disk. The logical structure is set up with a DOS program called FDISK (see fig. 10.9). FDISK sets the partitions needed on a hard drive. Information about partitioning hard drives appears in Chapter 2.

```
Current fixed disk drive: 1

Choose one of the following:

1. Create DOS partition or Logical DOS Drive
2. Set active partition
3. Delete partition or Logical DOS Drive
4. Display partition information

 Enter choice: [1]

Press Esc to exit FDISK
```

Figure 10.9

Opening screen using an FDISK program to partition hard drives.

Note For NetWare 3.*x* and above file servers, a DOS partition of only 10MB is recommended. DOS must be installed in a Primary DOS partition, which must be configured as the drive's Active partition. This can be done with an FDISK program.

475

The DOS operating system recognizes the rest of the NetWare-ready hard drive as a non-DOS partition. After the NetWare operating system is loaded, NetWare identifies the DOS partition as *Physical partition #0* and the NetWare partition as *Physical partition #1.*

 The low-level format utility that is shipped with a SCSI drive is the best program to use if you need to perform the low-level format process. Generic-type low-level format utilities usually will not work with the SCSI drives.

Entering CMOS Setup Information

The Complementary Metal-Oxide Semiconductor (CMOS) is a battery-operated chip that is found on the motherboard of the computer. The CMOS chip is an important microprocessor found primarily in the newer generation of personal computers. This chip is important to the operation of the computer because it is responsible for telling the electronics of the PC what is contained in the CPU and the location of these components in the scheme of being able to operate together. The CMOS chip provides the electronic current management for the positive and negative electrons that provide the flow of electrical signals to the components.

 If your computer shows unexplained erratic behavior or is losing the date or time, replace the battery with a new one that meets the same voltage requirements. This voltage number is printed or stamped on the battery.

The CMOS must be told what type of components the computer has and where they are located. The information about the hard drive is an important setup requirement in CMOS. You can get to CMOS with most computers during the power-up process by

476

pressing Ctrl+Alt+Esc. You also can view CMOS information through third-party utilities such as CheckIt PRO, as shown in figure 10.10. The CMOS setup characteristics require the TYPE number of the drive, which is found marked on the drive or in the manufacturer's documentation. The type information includes the number of cylinders, heads, sectors, and the size of the hard drive. If the drive requires write precompensation information, the CMOS asks for this detail also.

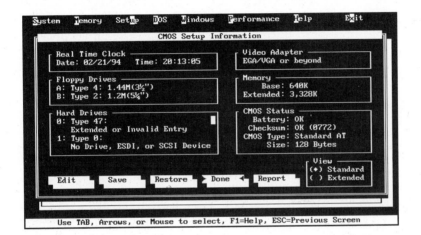

Figure 10.10

CMOS Setup Information found by CHECKIT PRO.

The drive you install does not have to match one of the CMOS drive types perfectly. IBM's CMOS Type 1 is used for most ESDI drives. The Type 1 represents a 10MB drive, and at power-up the BIOS from the ESDI controller card overwrites this information to what is needed for ESDI operations. SCSI drives use the Type 0 or Not Installed parameter. The MicroHouse Technical Library has an extensive listing of drive types from which to find a type that closely represents your drive (see Appendix D). Choose a type that has the cylinder count that is equal to or less than the number of cylinders available on your drive. Do not use a type that exceeds the megabyte size or the number of heads on your physical drive.

Note Write precompensation is used primarily by older drives. This process manages the timing of retrieval of information from the platters as the sectors get closer together toward the center of the drive. The magnetic field that is passed to the read/write heads on a hard drive is made stronger to handle the changes in the geometric division of the drive as the read/write heads move to the center of the disk. As a default, write precompensation is determined by taking the maximum number of cylinders on that individual drive and dividing that number by two.

High-Level DOS Format

The fourth part in setting up a hard drive is performing a high-level format. The DOS program, FORMAT, accomplishes this task on a new or used drive. The high-level format can be used to erase all the files in an entire DOS partition.

In order for a file server to have a bootable partition, you must format the primary DOS partition with the following command:

```
FORMAT /S
```

The /S parameter places the hidden DOS system information files and the COMMAND.COM in the DOS partition. The format process also accomplishes the following tasks:

- ◆ Creates a blank root directory (except when using the /S parameter)

- ◆ Creates a DOS boot sector and a DOS file allocation table (FAT)

- ◆ Scans the disk and notes the bad sectors

It is a benefit to have a DOS bootable partition on a NetWare 3.x and above file server. The server boots up faster from the hard disk. You can set the necessary statements to remotely reboot a server. You also can load a communication package on the DOS partition, down the server, then have an on-site person set the server as a host. Then you could dial in to copy updated files, such as .DSK or .NLM drivers, or maybe run CheckIt PRO to investigate server details.

Before you format a used drive that already contains data, make sure you back up all the files you need to protect. Low-level formats never allow the data to be recovered by an unformat utility. There are some third-party utilities that can recover high-level formats, provided the hard drive has not been written to since the format was performed. Professional data recovery services such as On-Track can assist in recovering data from a destroyed drive. As a network administrator or support engineer, you should be aware that most disks have bad sectors—don't panic if you see a few. A manufacturer considers a hard drive to be acceptable to be shipped if the bad sectors are less than 1 percent of the total size of the drive.

NetWare Drive Information

NetWare calculates a unique device code for each device on the bus or for each hard drive. System error messages use this code to display failure messages. As an example, the device code 20010 refers to the first drive (0) on the second controller (1) on the first host bus adapter (0) on the first instance the ISADISK.DSK driver (20) is found. NetWare uses the ISADISK device driver for ST-506 drives using RLL or MFM encoding schemes. These types of drives have the disk controller and the host bus adapter on the same physical drive. The controller digit found in the device code always is zero. The IDE type drives can use the ISADISK.DSK file or preferably the IDE.DSK device drivers. The SCSI drivers are provided by the manufacturer of the host adapter card. The device code for SCSI is always set to 0.

 The device drivers that come in the core package of a new 3.11 operating system box are slightly outdated. Although they are operational, enhanced ISADISK and IDE drivers are available on NetWire or on NSEPRO.

479

When a 3.x server is setting up the operating system, it establishes the Hot Fix redirection area first. NetWare considers the location from the beginning of the NetWare data area to the end of the NetWare data area as a *logical partition*. A NetWare logical partition holds the NetWare operating system files and the data that is loaded to be accessed by the network users. Each logical partition has its own identifying number. A NetWare logical partition can be made up of more than one physical partition, contiguous with a physical partition, or be made as part of a physical partition. NetWare uses physical partition numbers for housekeeping tasks performed by the operating system. Logical partition numbers are used for mirrored drive designation.

After you set up NetWare partitions through the INSTALL.NLM, you also must establish volume information. NetWare 3.x (20) enables volumes to be spanned across multiple hard drives. Volume segments are made up of the same volume information on different hard disks. There can be up to 8 segments on a hard drive and 32 segments per volume. Performance can be improved by spanning volumes. The disadvantage to spanning is that the loss of one drive and its partial volume segment can cause the loss of access to the entire volume. RAID, mirroring, or duplexing can help prevent the loss of an entire volume from happening.

Working with RAID Drives

Identify the unique role of RAID hard drives in relation to NetWare data security.

The network environment of today has evolved from having only a file server, a printer, and a few client stations, to having large enterprise designs requiring unlimited availability. The critical nature of data accessibility requires that network administrators or support engineers provide the best storage and recovery solutions as cost effectively as possible. The reliability of the network is not required for just the file server, but for the client also. The early history of the computer environment lacked the flexibility of the PC world, and the critical data needed was kept on a mainframe machine. Data manipulation on a mainframe requires many lines of code and cooperation from several differently skilled computer technicians. With the flexibility of the PC environment, extra precautions must be made in protecting against human or mechanical error.

The Redundant Array of Inexpensive Drives (RAID) can work with NetWare's System Fault Tolerance (SFT) features to protect data in a network environment. The use of RAID enables you to set up the best disk array design to protect your system. RAID is defined in detail as the architecture of combining two or more disks to create a large virtual disk structure to develop a source for redundancy of data. In a disk array, the drives are coordinated into different levels of RAID to which the controller card distributes the data as it is designed to do.

RAID uses a format of splitting data among drives at the bit, byte, or block level. The term *data striping* refers to the capability of arranging data in different sequences across drives. An example demonstration of this data splitting is shown in figure 10.11.

Your input in designing the most reliable drive setup for your network is an important responsibility. You must choose the best RAID implementation level that will meet your users' requirements in data integrity and cost. There are seven levels of RAID available on the market today. The numbers that represent RAID levels are 0, 1, 2, 3, 4, 5, and 10. A higher number does not necessarily mean that it is a better choice than the lower number. You must select the best for your environment. The following paragraphs present a brief discussion of each of the seven available levels.

Figure 10.11

Examples of data striping.

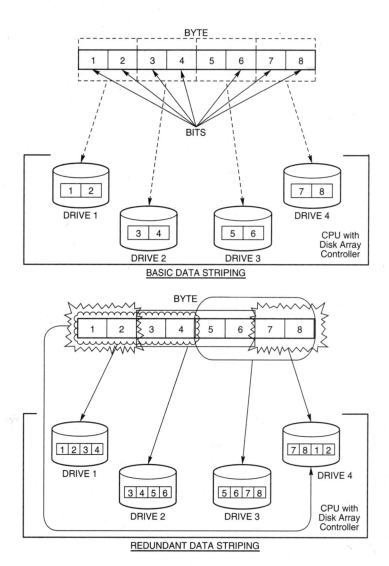

RAID 0. Level 0 uses data striping and block interleaving. This level distributes the data block-by-block across the disk array in the same location across each drive. Data can be read or written to these same sectors from either drive, improving performance. The failure of a single drive can bring down the system. Redundancy of data is not provided.

RAID 1. Drives are paired or mirrored with each byte of information being written to each identical drive. You can duplex these devices by adding a separate host adapter for each drive. Mirroring provides a better performance benefit than that of RAID 0. If one drive in the pair fails, the other drive can continue to operate. This level can get expensive with the cost of drives to meet your needs for capacity. You will need to make sure your power source has enough wattage to handle the additional devices.

RAID 2. This level uses data striping with bit interleave. This means that data is written across each drive in succession, one bit at a time. Faulty bits are isolated by using checksum-capable drives. This level does not require total data redundancy. RAID 2 drives are transmitting in a parallel mode, enabling a faster data transfer rate. The write mode can be slower because each drive is working on every write attempt. The data used for checksum information is redundant. This level is not effective or cost-efficient for use in personal computers.

RAID 3. This level uses bit interleave data striping with parity checking capabilities. Data striping is done across the drives, one byte at a time. There usually are four or five drives at this level, with one drive dedicated for parity information to ensure the integrity of the data. RAID 3 has a very high data transfer rate and can handle long data transfers. This level is more reliable than RAID 2. Parity maintenance can be an overhead problem and cause the write performance to slow because the parity drive must be accessed for every write. There also could be major system problems if any two drives fail. The failure of a single drive will not affect the availability of data—the array controller will use the parity drive to reconstruct the contents of the failed disk. RAID 3 is not ideal for NetWare 3.*x.* As a default, NetWare accesses data in 4KB blocks, which is not considered a long transfer rate.

RAID 4. This level uses block interleave data striping with parity checking. This means that this level uses a single parity drive, as does RAID 3, and uses block data striping, as does RAID 0. The drives in this RAID level function individually, with an individual drive reading a block of data. The combination of multiple drives has the ability to do multiple simultaneous reads. The block-level striping process is more efficient than RAID 3 byte-level striping. The downfalls of this level are the same as RAID 3, with the addition of the parity drive not being used to store data. If the array controller fails, the entire array cannot function.

RAID 5. This level uses block interleaved data striping with distributed check-data on all drives in the array. RAID 5 is efficient in handling small blocks and has quicker transfer rates because reads and writes can happen in parallel mode. The capability of virtual redundancy at an inexpensive cost is a benefit of RAID 5. This level is not as fast as RAID 0 or RAID 1 because it distributes parity information across all drives. Large file transfers are done in blocks and can be slower than RAID 3, which uses parallel bytes. RAID 5 efficiency goes up as the number of disks in the array increases. You can use hot spares mounted in the array cabinet. These extra drives can be picked up by the array automatically, replacing the failed drive. The data will be rebuilt to the added drive to function in sequence with the rest of the array as if nothing happened. This failed drive can then be replaced "on the fly."

RAID 10. This level is defined as data that is duplicated across two identical RAID 0 arrays or hard disk drives. All data that is contained on a physical drive in one array is mirrored on a drive in the second array. RAID 10 uses the similar concept that NetWare's SFT III mirrored file servers use.

When you are choosing RAID for the customer, consider the following factors to make the best selection:

- The importance of the applications and data to the cost of downtime and lost business

- The number of users and the amount of drive capacity needed

- The size of the data blocks and whether they require direct or sequential access on the drives

- The proportion of reads to writes to the I/O activity and the maximum transfer rate needed

There are many vendors that offer RAID solutions. Some examples of these vendors include AST, Compaq, Dell, IBM, and

Storage Dimensions. Dell Computer offers a reliable high-end file server that uses RAID 10, PCI bus architecture, a Pentium processor, and FAST SCSI-2 host adapters. This combination can be used for the mission-critical environment using NetWare.

Understanding Disk Mirroring and Disk Duplexing

Disk mirroring and disk duplexing are two important system fault tolerance features added in SFT II to protect information in the event of hardware failure.

Disk Mirroring

Disk mirroring is defined as two hard drives—one primary and one secondary—using the same disk channel (controller cards and cable). The process is illustrated in figure 10.12. Disk mirroring is most commonly configured using disk drives contained in the server. You soon see that duplexing enables you to configure a more robust hardware environment.

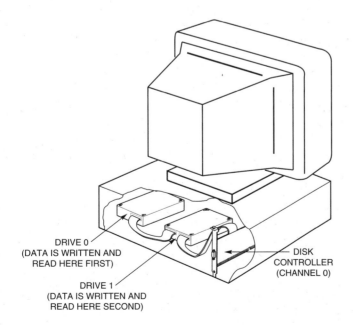

Figure 10.12

How disk mirroring works.

DRIVE 0
(DATA IS WRITTEN AND READ HERE FIRST)

DRIVE 1
(DATA IS WRITTEN AND READ HERE SECOND)

DISK CONTROLLER (CHANNEL 0)

485

All changes to the primary disk are duplicated on the secondary so that the secondary is a mirror image of the primary. In the event that the primary drive fails, users can access data on the secondary drive as if nothing happened. Disk mirroring can be done internally in a file server if enough drive and card slots are available. A DCB can be used to provide access to an external disk subsystem. Disk drives must be the same logical size, terminated properly, and addressed correctly.

Disk Duplexing

In the event of a disk channel failure (controller card or cable), access to all data on the channel is stopped. A message is displayed on the file server console screen (if your users do not let you know about it first). Even though drives can be mirrored, if they are connected to the same disk controller, all disk activity on the mirrored pair ceases.

Disk duplexing performs the function of simultaneously writing data to disks located on different channels. As figure 10.13 illustrates, each hard disk in a duplexed pair is connected to a separate hard disk controller. This figure shows a configuration in which the drives are housed in separate disk subsystems. Each subsystem has a separate power supply. This is a more reliable setup than is possible with mirroring, because a failure of one disk drive power supply does not disable the server, which continues to work with the system that remains under power.

A duplex configuration has two disk channels. In this example, each channel has two disks. NetWare identifies the drives by their channel and drive numbers, as shown in figure 10.13.

Duplexing enables NetWare to perform split seeks, in which NetWare seeks with both drives of a duplexed pair and retrieves data from the first drive on which the data is found. Split seeks are a distinct advantage of duplexing when compared to mirroring and can significantly improve a server's file access time.

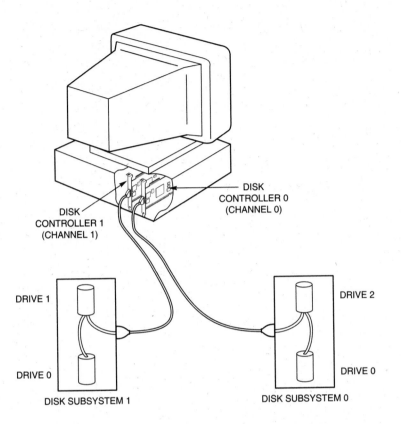

Figure 10.13
How disk duplexing
works.

Working on the same channel is analogous to going to a baseball game when only one gate is open to the stadium. You can enter or exit through only one gate (channel) at the stadium (file server), and the crowd (data) can get backed up on both sides. If more than one gate (another channel) is open, the crowd (data) does not get backed up on both sides of the fence (file server or workstation).

Duplexing protects information at the hardware level with duplicate channels (controller cards and cables) and duplicate hard drives (refer to fig. 10.12).

Mirroring uses one controller card and two hard drives (refer to fig. 10.13). The point of failure for this setup is primarily the controller card or the cable connecting the drives to the controller card. Disk duplexing uses two controller cards and a minimum of one drive per controller card. The point of contention for failure is reduced with duplicate hardware.

Disk Mirroring or Duplexing in v3.*x*

Use the INSTALL.NLM to mirror or duplex in v3.*x*. The following example is done on a network drive after the original operating system installation was completed. The following steps must be completed to install a disk pair as mirrored or duplexed:

1. Install the hardware components with the correct termination and hardware addresses. Document the model of the controller card and drives.

2. Bring the sever up and at the file server console (or through RCONSOLE) load the INSTALL.NLM. From the Installation Options menu, select Disk Options. The screen shown in figure 10.14 displays the Available Disk Options menu.

3. Select Mirroring and press Enter. The Partition Mirroring Status screen appears as shown in figure 10.15. This screen contains the status of all the drives in the v3.*x* file server to be edited. Select the drive designated as Logical Partition #1 to be the primary drive and press Enter.

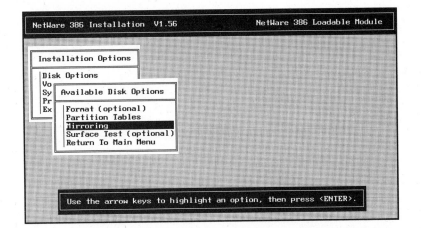

Figure 10.14

The Available Disk Options menu in INSTALL.

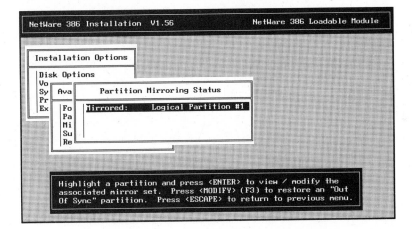

Figure 10.15

The Partition Mirroring Status display in INSTALL.

4. The screen displays the Mirrored NetWare Partitions menu as shown in figure 10.16. Press Ins to add another partition to the Mirrored NetWare Partitions screen. The menu screen shown in figure 10.17 then displays the Available Partitions from which to choose.

Highlight an available partition and press Enter. The Device numbers come from the addressing and termination of the SCSI drive installation.

Figure 10.16

The Mirrored NetWare Partitions display in INSTALL.

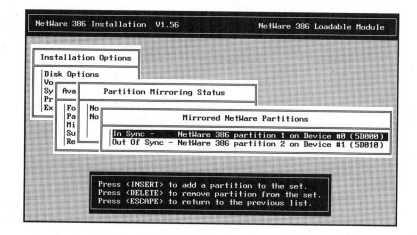

Figure 10.17

Display of partitions available for assignment as mirrors.

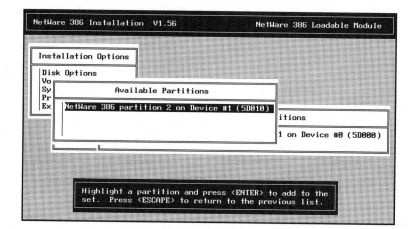

5. The Mirrored NetWare Partitions screen menu (see fig. 10.18) displays the In Sync status of the primary mirrored partition. In Sync means that the designated partition is unmirrored and has no data problems. The Partition 2 shows an Out Of Sync status. Within ten seconds, the Partition 2 drive begins synchronizing with Partition 1.

 To check the status of the remirroring process, press Alt+Esc to get to the colon prompt. The message `Remirroring partition #` appears, indicating that the process has begun.

The synchronization process takes several minutes, depending on the size of the drive being mirrored.

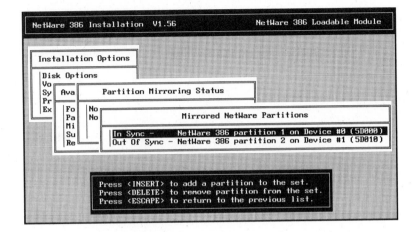

Figure 10.18

The Mirrored NetWare Partitions box displaying information about an out-of-sync mirrored pair.

6. The Partition Mirroring Status menu screen (see fig. 10.19) then shows confirmation of the logical partition as being mirrored when the synchronization process from step 5 is completed. The partitions are now mirrored and in operation.

   Press Esc until you exit from the INSTALL.NLM. You now can continue to do normal processing.

 The mirroring process should be performed during nonproduction hours, and all user logins should be disabled.

491

Figure 10.19

Mirrored drives in process of synchronization.

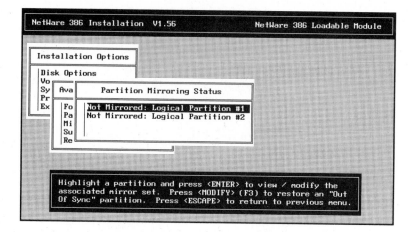

Tips for Working with Mirrored/Duplexed Drives

As a network administrator or support engineer, you must plan appropriately the use of mirrored/duplexed drives in your file server. Improper setup or lack of monitoring these types of hard drive setups can cause loss of data and destruction of hardware. As part of your maintenance process, use the following recommendations in your planning design:

◆ Mirroring and duplexing should not take the place of backups—keep doing them on a regular basis.

◆ Always load the disk drivers in the same order—the internal controllers should be loaded first, in the order they are to be addressed.

◆ NetWare does not differentiate between mirroring or duplexing in its system messages.

◆ Periodically check the status of your mirrored or duplexed drives to see if they are still "in synch." Check the physical and the logical window using the INSTALL.NLM on the file server.

◆ As part of your network documentation, keep a record of the device codes of your hard drives. This could help you troubleshoot the load order of your disk drivers using system messages.

◆ IDE drives should not be used as duplexed drives because of how the built-in controllers piggyback each other in a master/slave relationship. If the primary drive goes down, the second drive will also. Exceptions to this rule are the use of a motherboard that has dual IDE ports or the use of paddle boards.

 Differentiate the characteristics and uses of storage devices that can be networked other than standard hard drives.

Working with CD-ROM Drives

CD-ROM players can enhance your network environment by adding flexibility to your resources for multitudes of information. You can have a CD-ROM player attached as a device on your SCSI bus that is connected to your file server. A CD-ROM drive can be found that has multiple drive bays, with each bay recognized as a volume on the server. For v3.1x, software packages such as SCSI-Express and Corel SCSI can do this volume setup. NetWare 3.12 has a CDROM.NLM that enables the CD-ROM to be seen as a built-in volume. The client can use a locally attached CD-ROM player with the proper MSCDEX driver extensions and parameters loaded in the CONFIG.SYS and AUTOEXEC.BAT files. The CD-ROM unit in the NetWare environment must be ISO-9660-compliant.

The following are the advantages of a CD-ROM player in a networked environment:

- ◆ The file formats are standardized and can be accessed easily.

- ◆ There is access to more volumes of information. Keyword searches on some applications increase data resources in one setting.

- ◆ Media is lightweight, can be stored easily, and costs for duplication are low.

The following are the disadvantages of a CD-ROM player:

- ◆ CD-ROM players can get expensive, but continually are coming down in price.

- ◆ CD-ROM players are slower than hard disks. Modern hard drives are 20 times faster than the 200—300-millisecond seek rate of the CD-ROM. Newer CD-ROM players coming to the market that are available for networks will have 3X and 4X speed capabilities.

Tips for Working with CD-ROM Players

CD-ROM players can be an enhancement to any network. A network administrator or support engineer must be knowledgeable in this hardware arena. As with any other device included in your network environment, improper planning can cause expensive data recovery and troubleshooting delays. Use the following tips when using CD-ROM players in your network:

- ◆ Check for incompatibilities by having the CD-ROM player and the hard drive on the same SCSI controller. Review the manufacturer's documentation and check the software vendor's requirements.

- ◆ Some CD-ROM players require a "caddie" box for the CD-ROM platter to be placed in before it can be inserted into the player. Make sure your users know about this–failure to properly use a caddie box can result in severe damage to your CD. (*Please* read your documentation before using the player!)

- ◆ Do not install a CD-ROM player in a drive bay in the CPU that is located directly above a hard drive in the CPU casing.

The magnetic fields created by the CD-ROM unit can erase data from the hard drive.

♦ The error message `Invalid drive specification` means that the MSCDEX file is loaded too low in your AUTOEXEC.BAT file. The error message `Disc not High Sierra Format` means you need to upgrade the version of your currently installed MSCDEX extension drivers to work with the newer ISO-9660 CD-ROM format.

Working with Magneto-Optical Drives

Magneto-optical Drives (M-O) are used to capture text, audio, video, and other types of integrated media in a combined format on the optical platter. M-O drives are used as a compromise between digital access tape (DAT) drives which are an inexpensive, slower medium, and hard drives which are expensive, yet faster in speed. M-O drives are faster than tape and more expensive than hard drives.

The use of optical drives can replace the standard tape and hard drives for backup, archiving (which is the best use for M-O), and for storage of data-intensive applications such as CAD/CAM type programs. The setup of M-O drives is similar to tape backup units—they can be jukeboxes, external, or internal devices. M-O should not be confused with Write Once Read Many (WORM) systems because WORM drives cannot have the data changed on the optical-type disk after it has been written.

A magneto-optical drive operates with the use of laser beams and magnetism. An M-O disk is coated with layers on which spiral grooves have been molded. To write data, a polarized laser beam is reflected onto the surface of the M-O platter. The reflection is measured for its rotation on the plane of the disk that has been polarized magnetically. The data is then interpreted from how the rotation is magnetically oriented. Reverting the magnetic orientation to the way it was directed prior to the M-O disk being written to will erase data.

495

The following are the advantages of magneto-optical disks:

◆ **Removable Media.** Disks can be removed and are capable of being changed with another M-O disk.

◆ **Capacity.** M-O can handle capacities from 650MB to 1,000GB and can be loaded into jukeboxes for increased capacity of data accessibility.

◆ **Random Access.** M-O supports many read/write operations, unlike streaming tape cartridges.

◆ **Durability.** Head crashes are impossible because of the use of laser beams.

◆ **Backup.** It can be used for large unattended backups and archiving of data.

The following are the disadvantages of magneto-optical disks:

◆ **Cost.** Very expensive currently. Drive prices range from $3,500 to $5,000, and the optical disk platter ranges in price from $180 to $300.

◆ **Speed.** Magneto-optical drives are not as fast as SCSI drives. M-O drives need a double pass to the platter to write any data.

◆ **Size.** These drives are too big to fit inside laptops. This may interfere with the requirements for the mobile network of today.

Review Questions

1. The most important storage device on the network is

  ○ a. Fixed disk

  ○ b. CD-ROM

  ○ c. Magneto-optical disk

  ○ d. Floppy disk

2. Communication between the hard drive and the CPU is handled by which device?

    ○   a. NIC

    ○   b. Fixed disk cable

    ○   c. Disk controller card

    ○   d. Floppy drive cable

3. The time it takes for the read/write heads to find the correct track on a fixed disk is known as:

    ○   a. Access time

    ○   b. Transfer rate

    ○   c. Megabytes per second

    ○   d. Seek time

4. Which of the following is *not* one of the components of a hard drive?

    ○   a. Spindle motor

    ○   b. Voice coil actuator

    ○   c. Platter

    ○   d. Cluster block

5. The term _____ refers to the way the magnetic field handles the 0's and 1's of digital information.

6. Which of the following is *not* a limitation of an Integrated Drive Electronics (IDE) drive?

    ○   a. It cannot multitask I/O.

    ○   b. It has a maximum drive capacity of 528M even when a special nonstandard BIOS is used.

    ○   c. It does not support any optical or tape drives, as does the SCSI interface.

    ○   d. It does not support bus-mastering.

7. The main reason that you should never do a low-level format on an IDE drive is:

    O   a. You might erase the manufacturer's bad block information.

    O   b. You might be unable to access the IDE drive again to reestablish it.

    O   c. It removes the drive's ability to support overlapping and multitasking of I/O.

    O   d. Electronic flux transitions of the drive may be reversed.

8. Which two of the following are cited as reasons why ESDI drives have become more popular than ST-506 drives that use the same cabling system?

    ☐   a. ESDI drives are interchangeable with ST-506 drives.

    ☐   b. ESDI drives are capable of performing at higher levels.

    ☐   c. ESDI drives allow the Cold Boot Loader to be written to track 0, freeing disk space for data storage.

    ☐   d. ESDI drives have a larger storage capacity.

9. Which drive type provides an expansion bus that allows up to seven types of devices to be connected?

    O   a. IDE

    O   b. ESDI

    O   c. SCSI

    O   d. ASPI

10. Which of the following is *not* true of the WIDE SCSI-2 implementation of SCSI?

   ○ a. It uses a 50-pin cable and the single-ended signaling process.

   ○ b. It uses a second data path offering up to 20M-per-second data transfer rate.

   ○ c. It implements a 68-pin SCSI cable with the differential signaling process.

   ○ d. It is not used as much as the FAST SCSI-2 standard.

11. Which drive device is rapidly becoming the industry standard?

   ○ a. ASPI

   ○ b. ESDI

   ○ c. SCSI

   ○ d. IDE

12. If you do not want to remove the SCSI host adapter each time you need to change its settings, you should:

   ○ a. Make sure that the same cabling is used for all SCSI devices on the network.

   ○ b. Make sure that you use a SCSI host adapter that uses software for setup of jumpers and termination settings.

   ○ c. Make sure that each SCSI device has a unique identifier number.

   ○ d. Make sure that all SCSI devices are the same, using either all SCSI-1 or all SCSI-2 devices.

13. The SCSI LUN required for the first bootable hard disk on all except for some HP and PS/2 machines is:

○ a. 0

○ b. 1

○ c. 6

○ d. 7

14. One primary use of the third-party tool called CHECKIT PRO is:

○ a. To set up hard drives for storage

○ b. To modify jumpers on the drive

○ c. To allow you to mix SCSI devices

○ d. To determine a workstation's drive interface

15. Which of the following is not a jumper that may have to be set on the hard disk?

○ a. ACT

○ b. IDE

○ c. DS

○ d. DSP

16. Although usually set for the controller card by the manufacturer, you may need to put which setting into the STARTUP.NCF file of a network server?

○ a. Controller interrupt

○ b. Base I/O

○ c. DMA channel

○ d. Base BIOS address

17. The last step involved in preparing a hard drive to operate is:

○ a. Performing a low-level format

○ b. Performing a high-level format

○ c. Establishing partitions

○ d. Entering CMOS setup information

18. Setting the interleave factor on older drives is done primarily to:

○ a. Prevent newer drives from affecting older drives and causing network congestion

○ b. Speed up the drive to match the CPU's microprocessor

○ c. Help the drive better manage the flow of information between the computer and the disk

○ d. Improve the speed of machines running DOS on 286 system boards

19. To set up the logical structure of the hard disk, use:

○ a. CMOS

○ b. CKLLFMT

○ c. FDISK

○ d. CHECKIT PRO

20. Which statement is *not* true regarding CMOS?

○ a. CMOS stands for Complementary Metal-Oxide.

○ b. It is used only in older PCs.

○ c. It is battery-operated.

○ d. It tells the PC what is in the CPU.

21. The process that manages the timing of retrieval of information from the platters as the sectors get closer together is called:

   ○ a. Write precompensation

   ○ b. Read/Write definition

   ○ c. BIOS setup

   ○ d. Microhouse technical analysis

22. In a NetWare 3.x environment, once you set up NetWare partitions through INSTALL.NLM, the next step is to:

   ○ a. Set up the operating system

   ○ b. Establish the hot fix redirection area

   ○ c. Establish volume information

   ○ d. Assign each logical partition an identification number

23. Which level of RAID mirrors bytes of information written to identical drives?

   ○ a. 1

   ○ b. 3

   ○ c. 5

   ○ d. 10

24. When working with mirrored or duplexed drives, you should:

   ○ a. Discontinue doing backups (they no longer are needed because you cannot lose information)

   ○ b. Replace all drives with IDE drives because their master/slave relationship reduces the chance that one or the other drive will go down

○ c. Periodically reorder the load order of the disk drives so that you reduce the chance of wearing out the internal CPU's controller by overuse

○ d. Regularly record device codes for your hard drives to troubleshoot the load order of your disk drivers using system messages

25. Which of the following is true regarding CD-ROM players?

○ a. If you receive the Invalid drive specification error message, you must upgrade the MSCDEX extension drivers to work with the newer ISO-9660 CD-ROM format.

○ b. They should not be installed in a drive bay directly above a hard drive because they can erase data from the hard drive.

○ c. They should not be installed in the same network as a magneto-optical disk driver because the two are incompatible.

○ d. You can insert CDs in players that usually use a "caddie" box, as long as the CD-ROM drive is an internal rather than an external drive.

26. Which statement about DCBs is false?

○ a. Novell developed the original DCB.

○ b. DCBs still offer better performance than current SCSI controllers.

○ c. A file server can handle up to four DCB channels.

○ d. Each DCB can handle a maximum of eight SCSI controllers.

Answers

1. A
2. C
3. D
4. D
5. FLUX
6. B
7. A
8. B, D
9. C
10. A
11. C
12. B
13. A
14. D
15. B
16. A
17. B
18. D
19. C
20. B
21. A
22. C
23. A
24. D
25. B
26. B

Printing with NetWare

11
CHAPTER

Network printing service is one of the most heavily used aspects of networking. Because printing is dependent upon correct mechanical functioning, it also is one of the areas that provides the network administrator with the most troubleshooting opportunities.

One way to reduce network printing troubleshooting opportunities is to choose and install the correct printing software based upon your network needs. Once installed and running, troubleshooting network printing becomes an important part of a network administrator's job.

This chapter discusses several aspects of network printing, from basic information and installation to troubleshooting. After reading this chapter, you will be able to do the following:

- ◆ Understand the basics of printing with NetWare
- ◆ Set up network printing using PCONSOLE, PSERVER.NLM, PSERVER.EXE, and RPRINTER.EXE
- ◆ Maintain laser and dot-matrix printers
- ◆ Connect to network printing through Windows
- ◆ Troubleshoot network printing problems

Understanding Basic Printing with NetWare

Printing on a printer that is attached to your computer is a simple process. The application program you are running sends the request for a print job to the specified port (usually an LPT port) on the back of your computer. From there, the print job passes through the printer cable to the buffer in the printer. When the printer is ready to print (has enough paper and toner, and is online), the print job is printed. The printer's buffer holds portions of the print job that are too large to keep up with the speed of the printer until the printer is ready for additional lines to print. The printer's buffer is limited, but its availability frees your computer quicker so that it can perform other tasks.

If you are using laser printers on your NetWare 3.11 network, you should obtain the updated PSERVER.NLM file from NetWire. The updated PSERVER.NLM file improves the performance of laser printers on a NetWare 3.*x* network.

The operation of printing changes a little when you print on a network. When a request for network printing is made, the print job is not sent out through the print port to the printing cable. Instead, it is sent out through the network cable attached to your computer. The print request is then sent to be stored temporarily in a print queue on the specified print server. (A *queue* is a file on the network where jobs wait until a printer becomes available to service them. It works just like the ticket queue at a movie theater.) The queue is then responsible for assigning the print job to a printer. Jobs are printed in the order in which they are received, unless a priority has been given to either the print job or the print queue.

Print jobs are held in a queue until they can be sent to either the designated printer or the first available printer. Where a print job is sent is determined at least in part by the set-up of network printing.

Network printing is set up based on the needs of the users and the configuration of the network. Four common NetWare utilities/ programs are used to set up and control network printing:

- ◆ PCONSOLE
- ◆ PSERVER.NLM
- ◆ PSERVER.EXE
- ◆ RPRINTER.EXE

Each of these utilities or programs are discussed in the following section.

Setting Up Network Printing Using PCONSOLE, PSERVER.NLM, PSERVER.EXE, and RPRINTER.EXE

Diagnose and resolve printing problems related to physical connections, print queues, print servers, remote printing, configuration, print utilities and PostScript files.

Whether you use PCONSOLE, PSERVER.NLM, PSERVER.EXE, RPRINTER.EXE, or a combination to set up print services on your network depends on the needs of your network users, as well as on the physical location of the available network printers.

You run PCONSOLE on a network client to create and define print queues and print servers, as well as to control network printing or view information related to network printing.

You load PSERVER.NLM on a network file server to link the file server to the print servers and send print jobs assigned to various print queues.

You use PSERVER.EXE on a dedicated DOS client to send print jobs from the file server's print queues to the printers assigned to those print queues.

You run RPRINTER.EXE to connect and set up a remote printer (one that is connected to a client somewhere on the network) to a print server to extend the network's printing services.

 Make sure that you are using the latest enhancements to the PSERVER series. The NetWare 3.11 original core package PSERVER has many bugs that affect laser printers (v3.12 is okay). Check NetWire or the NSEPro if you have any problems with garbage being printed.

PCONSOLE, PSERVER.NLM, PSERVER.EXE, and RCONSOLE.EXE are discussed in the following sections.

PCONSOLE

PCONSOLE is the main utility used to set up and test network printing that includes print queues and print servers. Most of the setup is accomplished using the PCONSOLE utility. However, the testing is accomplished using other utilities.

To run PCONSOLE, type **PCONSOLE** at the prompt and press Enter. This action starts PCONSOLE and brings up the Available Options menu. You must have Supervisor or Supervisor–equivalent security rights to create or delete print queues and print servers.

Three choices are provided on this first menu. The three choices enable you to change to a different network server, view or set up print queues, and view or set up print servers. The last two options

are the ones that you use in order to set up printing for a printer
that is connected directly to the network file server. Figure 11.1
shows the initial PCONSOLE menu

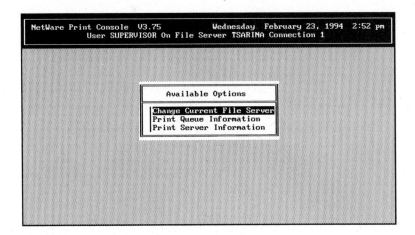

```
NetWare Print Console  V3.75            Wednesday  February 23, 1994  2:52 pm
                   User SUPERVISOR On File Server TSARINA Connection 1



                        Available Options
                     ┌─────────────────────────┐
                     │Change Current File Server│
                     │Print Queue Information   │
                     │Print Server Information  │
                     └─────────────────────────┘
```

Figure 11.1
PCONSOLE's first
menu screen.

Setting up network printing services, including print queues and
print servers, requires that you complete several steps, most of
which use the PCONSOLE utility. However, PCONSOLE is not
the only utility that you use. Table 11.1 shows the basic steps and
tells you which utility you must use in order to accomplish each
step. More detailed instructions for setting up print queues and
print servers follow·table 11.1.

Table 11.1
Steps to Set Up Print Queues and Print Servers

Step	Utility to Use
1. Set up a print queue.	PCONSOLE
2. Create a print server.	PCONSOLE
3. Attach printer to print queue.	PCONSOLE
4. Set up notification.	PCONSOLE
5. Test printer setup.	PSERVER & CAPTURE

Setting Up a Print Queue

Once you start PCONSOLE and the main Available Options menu appears on the screen, you set up a print queue by completing the following steps:

1. Choose Print Queue Information from the Available Options menu. The Print Queues screen appears showing a list of existing print queues, if any.

2. Press Ins.

3. Type a name for the new print queue in the New Print Queue Name box, and press Enter. Figure 11.2 shows the screens that appear when adding a print queue. The name of the print queue being added is TEST_Q.

4. Press Esc. This returns you to the Print Queues screen.

5. Press Esc a second time. This returns you to the Available Options menu and positions you to create and configure a print server to work with the print queue that you just created.

Figure 11.2

Screens to add a new print queue.

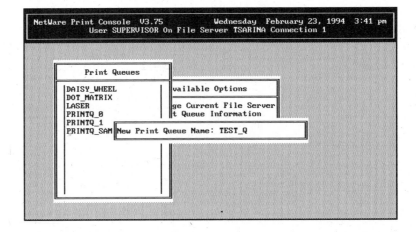

Creating a Print Server

Once you set up the print queue and return to the Available Options menu, you can set up a print server by completing the following steps:

1. Choose Print Server Information.

2. When the Print Servers screen appears, press Ins.

3. Type a name for the new print server in the New Print Server Name box, and press Enter. Figure 11.3 shows the screens that appear when adding a print server. The name of the print server being added is TEST_S.

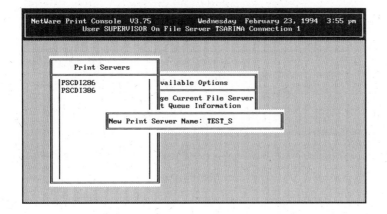

Figure 11.3

Screens to add a new print server.

4. Press Esc. This returns you to the Print Servers screen with the highlight on the print server you just created.

5. Press Enter. This opens the Print Server Information screen.

6. Choose Print Server Configuration from the list of available options.

7. Choose Printer Configuration from the Print Server Configuration menu.

8. When the Configured Printers screen appears, choose the next available printer number, which is 0 (zero) if you have not yet configured any print servers.

Note In NetWare 3.*x*, you can have up to 16 available printers per print server (numbered 0–15). You can be attached to a maximum of 8 file servers to select printing resources.

9. When the Printer configuration screen appears, as shown in figure 11.4, set the configuration options for your particular printer. This figure shows configuration options set for a printer that is connected to the LPT1 parallel port of the file server.

Figure 11.4

The printer configuration screen.

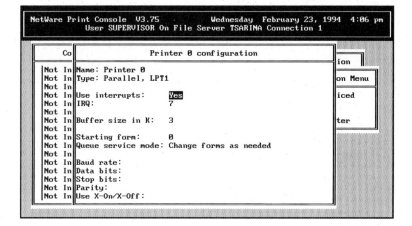

```
NetWare Print Console  V3.75          Wednesday  February 23, 1994  4:06 pm
              User SUPERVISOR On File Server TSARINA Connection 1

        ┌─────┬──────────────────────────────────────────────────┐
        │  Co │            Printer 0 configuration               │ ion
        │     │                                                  │
   Not In│Name: Printer 0                                        │
   Not In│Type: Parallel, LPT1                                   │ on Menu
   Not In│                                                       │
   Not In│Use interrupts:       Yes                              │ iced
   Not In│IRQ:                  7                                │
   Not In│                                                       │
   Not In│Buffer size in K:     3                                │ ter
   Not In│                                                       │
   Not In│Starting form:        0                                │
   Not In│Queue service mode: Change forms as needed             │
   Not In│                                                       │
   Not In│Baud rate:                                             │
   Not In│Data bits:                                             │
   Not In│Stop bits:                                             │
   Not In│Parity:                                                │
   Not In│Use X-On/X-Off:                                        │
        └──────────────────────────────────────────────────────┘
```

10. Press Esc and choose Yes when prompted with Save changes.

11. Press Esc a second time. This returns you to the Print Server Configuration menu and positions you to attach a printer to the queue that you created previously.

Note Figure 11.4 shows configuration information for a printer connected to a parallel port on a file server or a dedicated print server. If the printer were connected to a serial port instead, other information such as Baud rate, Data bits, Stop bits, Parity, and Use X-On/X-Off, would need to be filled in as well. These fields are not completed in figure 11.4.

Attaching the Printer to the Print Queue

Once you set up the print queue and the print server and have
returned to the Print Server Configuration menu, you can attach a
printer to the designated queue by completing the following steps:

1. Choose Queues Serviced by Printer from the Print Server
   Configuration menu.

2. When the Defined Printers screen appears, choose the
   printer number that you just set up. In figure 11.4, Printer 0
   was the printer number that was set up.

3. A screen empty of any entries appears. Press Ins to bring up
   the Available Queues screen.

4. Choose the queue that you created earlier. In figure 11.2, the
   print queue that was created was called TEST_Q. Figure 11.5
   shows the results of choosing TEST_Q from the list of
   Available Queues.

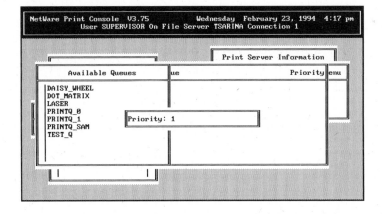

Figure 11.5

Print queue named
TEST_Q being added
to print server
TEST_S.

5. When prompted as shown in figure 11.5, enter a priority for
   this print queue. The priority is specified using any number
   1 through 10. Choosing number 1, the default priority, gives
   this queue the highest available priority for servicing print
   jobs.

6. With the File Server, Queue, and Priority now showing,
   press Esc.

513

7. Press Esc a second time. This returns you to the Print Server Configuration menu and positions you to set up printer notification.

 You can have multiple queues with the same or different priorities talking to the same printer. You can also have multiple printers talking to the same queue.

Setting Up Notification

Once you set up the print queue and the print server, attach the new print queue to the new print server and return to the Print Server Configuration menu. You can designate who should be notified when the printer experiences any problems, such as out of paper, toner low, and so on. To set up notification, complete the following steps:

1. Choose Notify List for Printer from the Print Server Configuration menu.

2. Choose the printer number. As shown in figure 11.4, Printer 0 is the chosen printer.

3. A blank list of users to notify appears. Press Ins to open the Notify Candidates list and begin adding users to this list.

4. Scroll through the list of Notify Candidates. To add more than one user, mark each user's name by highlighting it and pressing the F5 key. To add only one user, highlight the user's name, then complete the next step. Press Enter.

5. Specify the interval at which users or groups should be notified of printer problems. The First Notify Interval states how many seconds are to pass before someone is notified of a printer problem. If the problem is not immediately corrected, the Next Notify Interval states how many seconds are to pass before users are notified a second and subsequent times until the problem is corrected.

6. Press Esc, then choose Yes when prompted with Save Changes to accept the Notify Intervals and add the user(s) and/or group(s) to the list of Notify Candidates. Figure 11.6 shows user Supervisor and group Techs as Notify Candidates for File Server Tsarina

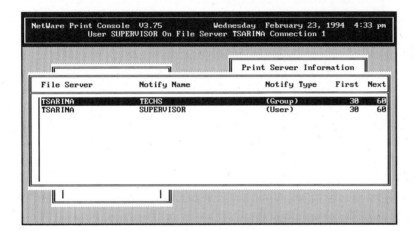

```
NetWare Print Console  V3.75            Wednesday  February 23, 1994  4:33 pm
                User SUPERVISOR On File Server TSARINA Connection 1


                                          Print Server Information

       File Server        Notify Name            Notify Type    First  Next

       TSARINA            TECHS                  (Group)          30    60
       TSARINA            SUPERVISOR             (User)           30    60
```

Figure 11.6
Printer Notify list.

7. Press Esc repeatedly until you are prompted with Exit PConsole, then choose Yes.

Now that you have created a print queue and a print server, attached a queue to a server, and specified users and/or groups to notify in the event of printer problems, you can test your printing setup to ensure that it is working properly.

PSERVER.NLM

PSERVER.NLM is a NetWare Loadable Module used to load a print server on a NetWare file server. Loading PSERVER.NLM is one aspect of establishing print services for a network. With PSERVER.NLM loaded, PSERVER.NLM enables NetWare 3.*x* users to access up to 16 printers being serviced by print queues on up to 8 file servers.

Loading PSERVER.NLM is done only after preparations are made for users to access the print server. The required steps and the point at which PSERVER.NLM is loaded can be seen in table 11.2, which outlines the steps required to set up print services when the print server is a network file server.

Table 11.2
Steps to Set Up Print Services Using PSERVER.NLM

Step	Utility to Use
1. Create print queues and print servers.	PCONSOLE
2. Attach printers to print queues and set up notification.	PCONSOLE
3. Load the print server NLM.	PSERVER.NLM
4. Test printer setup.	CAPTURE

Testing Printer Setup

Prevent, diagnose, and resolve common problems with printers.

The following steps walk you through the process of testing the print queue and server that you just set up:

1. If you have not already done so, physically connect the printer to the LPT port on the file server.

Before connecting or disconnecting any hardware, it is always safer to power off the involved equipment. Parallel ports are often particularly sensitive to having cables attached and disconnected while the power to the computer is still on. Be sure to down the file server before powering it off. Reload the server once you have connected the print cable and powered the computer back up.

2. At the file server's console prompt, type **LOAD PSERVER** *pserver_name*, replacing *pserver_name* with the name of the print server that you created. For example, to load a print server called PSCDI386, type **LOAD PSERVER PSCDI386** and press Enter. Figure 11.7 shows the Novell NetWare Print Server PSCDI386 screen that appears after loading this print server.

```
                    Novell NetWare Print Server V1.21
                         Server PSCDI386 Running

  0: Laser                          4: Not installed
     Printing
     Job #: 7, 000991.RPT
     Queue: CDI286/LASER

  1: Dot Matrix                     5: Not installed
     Not connected

  2: Daisy Wheel                    6: Not installed
     Not connected

  3: Not installed                  7: Not installed
```

Figure 11.7

Print server PSCDI386 Information screen.

3. From a client, log in to the file server with an attached printer.

4. Type **CAPTURE /Q=***queue_name* and press Enter. Replace *queue_name* with the actual name of the queue, such as **TEST_Q**.

You can verify the status of the capture command on your client at any time by typing **CAPTURE /SH** at the prompt and pressing Enter. This command shows you the status of capture for each of your computer's printing ports.

5. Verify that printing actually is functioning by typing a couple of lines of nonsense onto your computer's screen at the DOS prompt, then press either Print Screen or Shift+Print Screen, depending on your particular computer.

6. Type **ENDCAP** and press Enter.

If the printer is installed successfully, your screen dump appears on the printer. If the screen dump does not appear, repeat the steps explained previously. You also can do some troubleshooting as described later in this chapter.

If you make any changes through PCONSOLE to queues or print server information after PSERVER has been loaded, you must down and reload PSERVER before they will take effect.

Creating Print Queues and Print Servers

Print queues and print servers are created using the PCONSOLE utility. Log in to the network file server, then start PCONSOLE by typing **PCONSOLE** at the prompt and pressing Enter. Then complete the following steps to create print queues and print servers:

1. Choose Print Queue Information from the Available Options menu.

2. Press Ins.

3. Type a name for the new print queue in the New Print Queue Name box, and press Enter.

4. Press Esc. This returns you to the Print Queues screen. Figure 11.8 shows the Print Queues screen to which the print queue CDI286_LASER has been added.

5. Press Esc a second time. This returns you to the Available Options menu and positions you to create and configure a print server to work with the print queue that you just created.

6. Choose Print Server Information.

7. When the Print Servers screen appears, press Ins.

8. Type a name for the new print server in the New Print Server Name box, and press Enter.

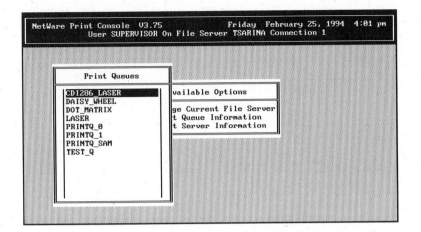

Figure 11.8
Print Queues screen
with CDI286_LASER
print queue added.

9. Press Esc. This returns you to the Print Servers screen with
   the highlight on the print server that you just created.

10. Press Enter. This opens the Print Server Information screen.

11. Choose Print Server Configuration from the list of available
    options.

12. Choose Printer Configuration from the Print Server
    Configuration menu.

13. When the Configured Printers screen appears, choose the
    next available printer number. Figure 11.9 shows the
    Configured Printers list with a LASER, DOT MATRIX, and
    DAISY WHEEL printer already configured.

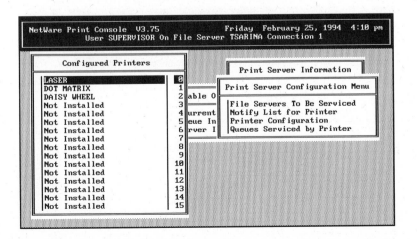

Figure 11.9
The Configured
Printers screen.

14. When the Printer Configuration screen appears, choose the Type field, then choose the printer type.

15. Press Esc and choose Yes when prompted with Save changes.

16. Press Esc a second time. This returns you to the Print Server Configuration menu and positions you to attach a printer to the queue that you created previously.

Attaching Printers to Print Queues and Setting Up Notification

Once you set up the print queue and the print server, and return to the Print Server Configuration menu, you can attach a printer to the designated queue and then set up printer notification by completing the following steps:

1. Choose Queues Serviced By Printer from the Print Server Configuration menu.

2. When the Defined Printers screen appears, choose the printer number that you just set up.

3. A screen opens showing all previously defined queues and the file server to which they are assigned. Press Ins to bring up the Available Queues screen.

4. Choose the queue that you created earlier. Figure 11.10 shows the CDI286_LASER queue highlighted.

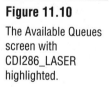

Figure 11.10

The Available Queues screen with CDI286_LASER highlighted.

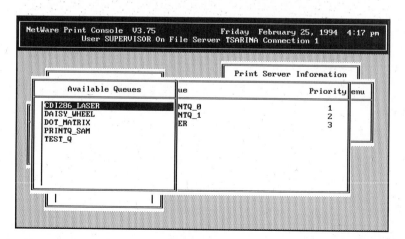

5. When prompted, enter a priority for this print queue.

6. With the File Server, Queue, and Priority now showing, press Esc.

7. Press Esc a second time.

8. Choose Notify List for Printer from the Print Server Configuration menu.

9. Choose the printer number.

10. Press Ins to open the Notify Candidates list and begin adding users to this list.

11. Scroll through the list of Notify Candidates, marking users and groups with the F5 key.

12. Press Enter.

13. Specify the interval at which users or groups should be notified of printer problems.

14. Press Esc, then choose Yes when prompted with Save Changes to accept the Notify Intervals and add the user(s) and/or group(s) to the list of Notify Candidates.

15. Press Esc repeatedly until you are prompted with Exit PConsole, then choose Yes.

Now that you have created one or more print queues and print servers, attached queues to servers, and specified users and/or groups to notify in the event of printer problems, you can load the print server using PSERVER.NLM.

Loading the Print Server NLM

You load PSERVER.NLM onto a network file server in order to offer users access to a printer that is connected to that file server.

To load the PSERVER.NLM, complete the following steps:

1. Verify that the printer connected to the file server is on and properly functioning.

2. At the file server's console prompt, type **LOAD PSERVER** *pserver_name* and press Enter. Replace *pserver_name* with the name of an existing print server.

While PSERVER.NLM is being loaded, you can expect to see a system response similar to the following, although the response on your computer may be shortened:

```
Loading module PSERVER.NLM
NetWare 386 Print Server
Version 3.76   August 11, 1993
Copyright 1993 Novell, Inc.   All rights reserved.
Auto-loading module NUT.NLM
NetWare 386 Utility User Interface
Version 1.13   December 20, 1990
Copyright 1990 Novell, Inc.   All rights reserved.
Auto-loading module CLIB.NLM
NetWare  C NLM Runtime Library 3.12
Version 3.12   May 19, 1993
(C) Copyright 1989-1993, Novell Inc. All rights reserved.
        Patent Pending - Novell, Inc.
Auto-loading module STREAMS.NLM
NetWare STREAMS
Version 3.12   April 19, 1993
(C) Copyright 1989-1992 Mentat, Inc.
Portions (C) Copyright 1989-1993 Novell, Inc.
All Rights Reserved.
826 functions exported
```

Once PSERVER.NLM is loaded, the Novell NetWare Print Server screen opens. This screen initially displays the status of eight print servers, numbered 0 through 7.

Practical TIP To see the next group of printers, numbered 8 through 15, press any key. You can use the Alt+Esc key combination to view other screens on the file server.

If only one print server is installed, the remaining seven print server sections show a Not Installed status.

Figure 11.7 shows the Novell NetWare Print Server screen for print server PSCDI386. This figure shows that three printers are installed, although two of the printers are not connected.

The first printer, printer 0, is a laser printer. Print job number 7 is currently active. It is printing a file called 080991.RPT. This print server, PSCDI386, received print job number 7 from the print queue called CDI286/LASER.

Once a print job has been submitted, it is displayed in the Novell NetWare Print Server screen until it has been printed. When testing the printer's setup, you should see your print job displayed on this screen.

Testing Printer Setup

Testing the printer setup is done as described previously under the PCONSOLE section. The difference is that PSERVER.NLM has already been loaded. Therefore, you have to perform only the following steps to test your printer setup.

1. Verify that the printer is connected to the print server and that the PSERVER.NLM has been loaded.

2. From a client, log in to the network file server.

3. Type **CAPTURE /Q=***queue_name* and press Enter. For example, the user who submitted the job shown as printing in figure 11.7 would have typed **CAPTURE /Q=CDI286/ LASER** and then pressed Enter.

4. Make a print request. This can be done in one of several ways. You can make a print request through an application program by doing a screen capture or by using the Windows or a NetWare print utility.

If printing has been correctly set up and the PSERVER.NLM loaded properly, your print job should print on the printer serviced by the attached print queue.

You can also test printing by using the Print Screen command at the system prompt. Figure 11.11 shows the help screen associated with the Print Screen command. This help screen displays the required command syntax and describes each option.

Figure 11.11

The Print Screen command help screen.

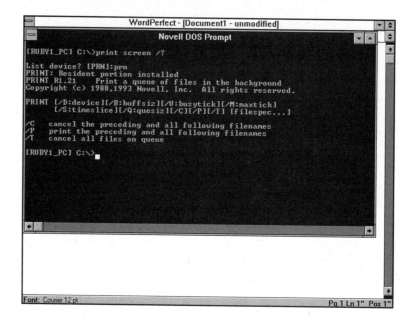

Figure 11.11

The Print Screen command help screen.

If you experience any problems with printing, refer to the "Tips for Troubleshooting Network Printing" section of this chapter.

PSERVER.EXE

PSERVER.EXE is an executable program that, when run on a client with a printer connected, causes the client to become a dedicated print server.

In order to establish a client as a dedicated print server, print services must first be set up on the network. The required steps for setting up print services, including the point at which PSERVER.EXE is loaded on the dedicated client, are outlined in table 11.3.

Table 11.3
Steps to Set Up Print Services Using PSERVER.EXE

Step	Utility to Use
1. Create print queues and print servers.	PCONSOLE
2. Attach printers to print queues and set up notification.	PCONSOLE
3. Modify client's NET.CFG file.	Any text editor
4. Load the print server software.	PSERVER.EXE
5. Test printer setup.	CAPTURE

Creating Print Queues and Print Servers

As explained previously, print queues and print servers are created using the PCONSOLE utility.

To create print queues and print servers, log in to the network file server, type **PCONSOLE** at the prompt, and press Enter. Then complete the following steps to create print queues and print servers:

1. Choose Print Queue Information from the Available Options menu.

2. Press Ins.

3. Type a name for the new print queue and press Enter.

4. Press Esc.

5. Press Esc again.

6. Choose Print Server Information. Figure 11.12 shows the Print Server Information screen.

Figure 11.12

Print Server
Information screen.

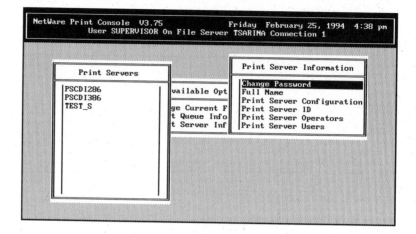

 Note The Print Server Information screen enables you to do more than just set up and configure a print server. You also can complete the following related tasks from this menu:

- Change the print server's password.
- Enter a descriptive full name.
- Configure several aspects of the print server.
- Display the print server's object ID.
- Display users and groups who are operators.
- Display users who are authorized users.
- View print server status if it is operational.

7. When the Print Servers screen appears, press Ins.

8. Type a name for the new print server and press Enter.

9. Press Esc.

10. Press Enter.

11. Choose Print Server Configuration from the list of available options.

12. Choose Printer Configuration from the Print Server Configuration menu.

13. Choose the next available printer number.

14. When the Printer Configuration screen appears, choose the Type field, then choose the printer type.

15. Press Esc.

16. Choose Yes when prompted with Save changes as shown in figure 11.13.

17. Press Esc a second time.

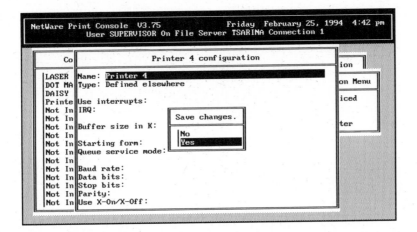

Figure 11.13

Save changes prompt screen.

Attaching Printers to Print Queues and Setting Up Notification

Now that you have created print queues and print servers, you can attach printers to print queues and set up printer notification by completing the following steps:

1. Choose Queues Serviced By Printer from the Print Server Configuration menu.

527

2. When the Defined Printers screen appears, choose the appropriate printer number. A screen opens showing all previously defined queues and file server to which they are assigned.

3. Press Ins to bring up the Available Queues screen.

4. Choose the appropriate queue.

5. When prompted, enter a priority for this print queue.

6. Press Esc.

7. Press Esc a second time.

8. Choose Notify List for Printer from the Print Server Configuration menu.

9. Choose the printer number.

10. Press Ins to open the Notify Candidates list and begin adding users to this list.

11. Scroll through the list of Notify Candidates, marking users and groups with the F5 key if you want to select more than one user or group. Figure 11.14 shows a Notify Candidates list for a print server.

Figure 11.14

Notify Candidates list.

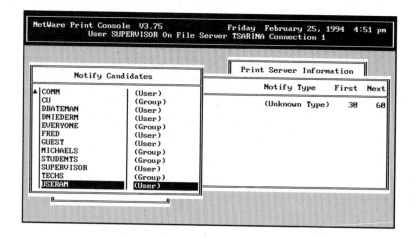

528

12. Press Enter.

13. Specify the interval at which users or groups should be notified of printer problems.

14. Press Esc, then choose Yes when prompted with
    `Save Changes`.

15. Press Esc repeatedly until you are prompted with Exit PConsole, then choose Yes.

Now that you have created one or more print queues and print servers; attached queues to servers; and specified users and/or groups to notify in the event of printer problems, you must modify the client's NET.CFG file to include the correct number of SPX connections.

Modifying Client's NET.CFG File

When a client is going to be used as a dedicated print server, the client's NET.CFG file must be modified in order to accommodate the need for an increase in the number of SPX connections that is required when PSERVER.EXE is loaded. The NET.CFG file is located in the NWCLIENT directory if the default directory was used during installation of the client software.

You can use any text editor to modify this file as long as the text editor saves the file as a basic text file. You also can use various application programs such as WordPerfect or Microsoft Word to edit this and other client text files, providing the application program has the option of saving the file as an ASCII text file.

 Note The NetWare 3.11 Print Server manual indicates that the SPX CONNECTIONS= line in the CONGIF.SYS file should specify 50. This number has proven to be insufficient. The NetWare 3.12 Print Server manual correctly specifies the number of SPX connections as 60 in the NET.CFG file. The entry should read as follows:

```
SPX CONNECTIONS = 60
```

529

If you do not have an SPX connections line in the client's NET.CFG file, you must add one. This line is placed as a left-justified line at or near the beginning. It must not be indented. If you do not add this line to the NET.CFG file, or you do not left-justify the line, the computer assumes a default of 15 connections, which is insufficient to run PSERVER.EXE.

After modifying and saving the NET.CFG file, reboot the client to cause the changes to become effective. Then you can load the print server software.

Loading the Print Server Software

To load the print server software from the client that has been selected to be the dedicated print server, log in to the network. You must have at least Read and File Scan rights to the SYS:PUBLIC directory.

At the prompt, type **PSERVER** *print_server_name* and press Enter. The Novell NetWare Print Server information screen is opened.

 The Novell NetWare Print Server information screen looks and acts the same way as the Novell NetWare Print Server information screen that opens when you load the PSERVER.NLM on a file server, with one exception: Once the former comes up on the dedicated PSERVER, it is not removable unless powered off.

As with the other print servers, once you have loaded the print server software, you should test it to make certain that it is functioning properly.

Testing Printer Setup

Printer setup for a dedicated-client printer is tested the same way that you test printing for a printer attached to a network file server.

You can print from applications that are designed for network printing, providing that application is first set up to print to a network printer. You can also print from applications that were not designed originally for network printing. You can use one or more of several NetWare printing utilities to print files on the network, including the following:

◆ CAPTURE/ENDCAP

◆ NPRINT

◆ PCONSOLE

You use CAPTURE and ENDCAP primarily to print screen displays. These utilities begin and end the directing of print commands that otherwise would go to the printing port on your computer or to a print queue on a network print server.

You use NPRINT and PCONSOLE to print basic ASCII text files. The main difference between these two utilities is that NPRINT is a command-line utility and PCONSOLE is a menu-based utility.

 CAPTURE and NPRINT can also be used to print graphics to a printer. However, if you use CAPTURE or NPRINT to send graphics to a printer, you must use byte stream mode instead of ASCII text mode. In order to accomplish this successfully, use the /NT (No Tabs) switch. Otherwise, use PRINTCON to define print job configurations and specify byte stream when printing graphics.

PCONSOLE enables you to choose your way through various menu options in order to print your ASCII text files. You can also insert a print job for an ASCII text file through the Print Queue Information and Job Entries In Queue menu options.

NPRINT requires that you specify several parameters in order to print successfully. Figure 11.15 shows the NPRINT help screen, which displays available NPRINT parameters.

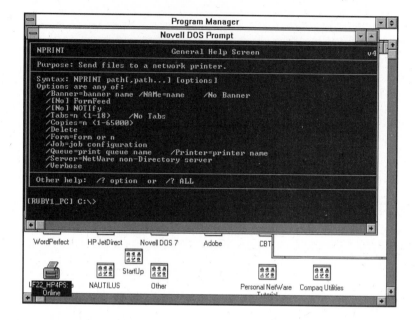

RPRINTER.EXE

Use RPRINTER.EXE to connect to or disconnect from a remote
printer (a printer connected to a nondedicated client) on your
network. Clients with a printer connected can be set up to enable
network users to have access to that printer without interfering
with that client's user processes.

Three types of remote printers can be configured:

◆ Remote serial

◆ Remote parallel

◆ Remote unknown

The three types listed refer to the type of port to which the printer
is connected. A remote serial printer is a printer that is attached to
the client through the serial port.

The remote parallel printer is a printer that is attached to the client
through the parallel port.

A remote unknown printer is a printer that may be connected to the client through either a serial or a parallel port, but the connection is currently unknown or may be subject to change, such as when you are in the process of testing a printer.

Before installing a remote printer, there are several things to keep in mind.

◆ You can run RPRINTER in either command-line or menu mode.

◆ You must load the NetWare DOS Requester before you run RPRINTER.

◆ You can load RPRINTER automatically by putting the RPRINTER command into the client's AUTOEXEC.BAT file.

◆ You need to increase the SPX CONNECTIONS= command in the client's configuration file to 60, or add the line if it does not exist.

The required steps for setting up print services, including the point at which RPRINTER.EXE is loaded on the nondedicated client, are outlined in table 11.4.

Table 11.4
Steps to Set Up Print Services Using RPRINTER.EXE

Step	Utility to Use
1. Create print queues and print servers.	PCONSOLE
2. Attach printers to print queues and set up notification.	PCONSOLE
3. Load the print server software.	PSERVER.EXE
4. Run client's printing software.	RPRINTER.EXE
5. Test printer setup.	CAPTURE/Other Utilities

533

Loading the Print Server Software

To run a remote printer, you must set up a print server to service the remote printer. Set up the print server by loading the print server software. The print server that is to service the remote printer can be either a file server with a print server loaded (PSERVER.NLM) or a dedicated client with a print server loaded (PSERVER.EXE).

To load the print server software, type **LOAD PSERVER** *print_server_name* at the DOS prompt of the file server, then press Enter. Or, load the print server software by typing **PSERVER** *print_server_name* at the DOS prompt of the dedicated client and press Enter.

Both of these actions start the print server and open the Novell NetWare Print Server information screen.

The print server information screen looks and acts the same way regardless of whether it is running as an NLM on a Novell NetWare file server or as an EXE on a dedicated Novell NetWare client. Figure 11.16 shows the relationship among various print server options, as well as remote and local printer options on a NetWare network. (A local printer is connected to a client on a network, but does not run RPRINTER and does not provide print services to other network clients.)

Figure 11.16

Relationship of NetWare network printing services.

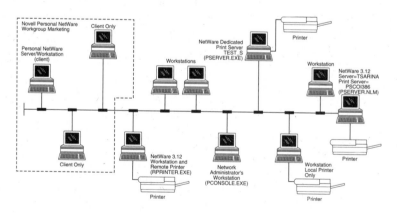

Running Client's Printing Software

RPRINTER.EXE is the TSR (terminate-and-stay-resident) program that is loaded into the memory of the client with a remote printer attached. It takes a maximum of 9KB to run. Once loaded, it enables the client to provide the network with printing resources through its attached printer. This printing resource then is commonly referred to as a remote printer.

Remote printing services can be made available to the network at anytime by loading RPRINTER.EXE on a network client that has a printer attached. Remote printing services can also be removed temporarily or permanently from the network by unloading RPRINTER.EXE from the client.

A remote printer differs from a print server in one primary way. A remote printer is not physically attached to a client or file server that has the actual print server software loaded. Instead, it is physically attached to a client that has an executable program (RPRINTER.EXE) running in the background. This program enables network users to have access to the printer. Without this program loaded on the client, the attached printer is a local printer only.

Before loading RPRINTER.EXE at the client, you must first load the NetWare DOS Requester software, including the following files:

- ◆ LSL.COM
- ◆ Network interface card (NIC) driver, such as NE2000
- ◆ IPXODI.COM
- ◆ VLM.EXE

 Note Although you can run RPRINTER.EXE with the older NetWare shell, you may want to consider upgrading your client to the newer DOS Requester files because of the additional services and benefits that the NetWare DOS Requester provides.

535

Before running RPRINTER.EXE on a client, you should check the client's NET.CFG file to see if it includes the following line:

```
LOCAL PRINTERS=0
```

If the NET.CFG file does include this line, delete the line from the file so that the locally attached printer will be recognized, or change it so that it shows the correct number. Then you must reboot the client in order for your change to take effect.

To load remote printing services at a nondedicated network client, type **RPRINTER** *print_server_name print_server_number*, then press Enter. Replace *print_server_name* and *print_server_number* with the name and number of the print server you set up to serve this remote printer.

Once you have set up your client for remote printing, you and other network users can access and print to your printer. You print to your client's printer as if it were any other printer on the network.

 Insert **RPRINTER** *print_server_name print_server _number* after you load your NetWare Shell or DOS Requester and change to the F: drive (or your first network drive letter).

Testing Printer Setup

Printer setup for a remote printer is tested the same way that you test printing for a printer attached to a network file server or to a dedicated client.

You can print to your remote printer from applications that are designed for network printing, if they have been first set up to print to a network printer.

You can also print to the remote printer from applications that were not designed originally for network printing. As mentioned previously in this chapter, you can use one or more of several NetWare printing utilities to print files on the network.

One other printing option is available to you. You can print to NetWare network printers using software provided within Microsoft Windows.

Printing through Windows

You can connect and print to a network printer using Microsoft Windows utilities. In addition, Hewlett-Packard (HP) provides a program called JetAdmin that enables you to install and administer any HP JetDirect interface remotely.

This section describes how to use Windows to make a network printer connection before you attempt to print, how to print to a network printer without using Print Manager, and how to print to a network printer using Print Manager.

In addition, this section briefly discusses JetDirect, including its benefits and configuration steps.

Connecting to a Network Printer Using Microsoft Windows

Before you can connect to a network printer to print, you must have completed two tasks. First, you must have installed Microsoft Windows for use with a network. (See Chapter 9, "Installing the Client.") Second, you must have a network currently up and running. You cannot connect to a network printer if the network does not already exist or is not up and running.

To connect to a network printer using Microsoft Windows, complete the following steps:

1. Log into the network using your assigned user name.

2. Open Microsoft Windows and bring up Program Manager.

3. Open the Main Window.

4. Open the Control Panel.

537

5. Choose the Printers icon.

6. Choose Connect from the Printers window.

7. Choose Network from the Connect box.

   Figure 11.17 shows the progression of screens that occur when you complete steps 4 through 6.

   When you choose Network from the Connect box, the NetWare Printer Connections Window opens. This window enables you to perform several network operations, including that of capturing a network printer to one of your client's available ports.

8. If you are running a 3.12 client, continue with this step. From the NetWare Printer Connections window, scroll through the list of available resources. Select a printer by pressing and holding the left mouse button, then drag and drop the printer to one of the available ports.

Figure 11.17

Windows screens to begin a network printing connection.

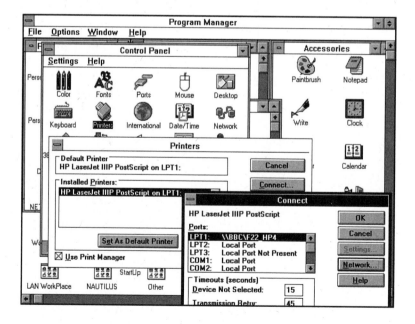

Figure 11.18 shows the NetWare Printer Connections window with the RUBY1_PC\FFF printer now captured to port LPT1 on the client.

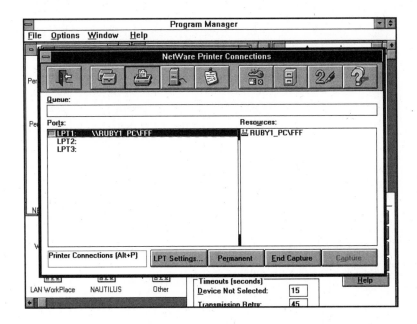

Figure 11.18

NetWare Printer Connections window.

Note The connection is only temporary and will be lost when you close Windows unless you choose the Permanent button in the NetWare Printer Connections window. This action causes the CAPTURE command to this network printer to be re-established each time you log into the network and run Windows. However, you don't always have to use a CAPTURE command set in NetWare for Windows to find queues to print.

Network printing is now set up. Every time you request that a document be printed, it will print directly to the network printer. You now can print to this network printer with the Windows Print Manager running in the background, or without it.

Printing to the Network without Using Print Manager

You can allow Windows Print Manager to run in the background. If you do, the Print Manager enables you to continue to work while printing requested documents. However, you can print from Windows applications without using Print Manager by disabling its use.

To prevent Windows Print Manager from running as a background process, which may help to speed up network printing, complete the following steps:

1. Log into the network using your assigned user name.

2. Open Microsoft Windows and bring up Program Manager.

3. Open the Main Window.

4. Open the Control Panel.

5. Choose the Printers icon.

6. Unmark Use Print Manager, found in the lower left corner of the Printers window. Figure 11.19 shows the Printers window with the Use Print Manager box marked.

7. Choose Close to close the Printers window.

8. Print to the network using the windows application program that you are working with.

Printing to the Network Using Print Manager

You can send print jobs directly to the network printer by running the Windows Print Manager. Of course, to accomplish this, you must either not have unmarked the Use Print Manager box in the Printers window, as described previously, or you must go back into the Windows Printers window and re-mark the Use Print Manager box. Then you can print to a network printer using Print Manager and the Windows application in which you created the document.

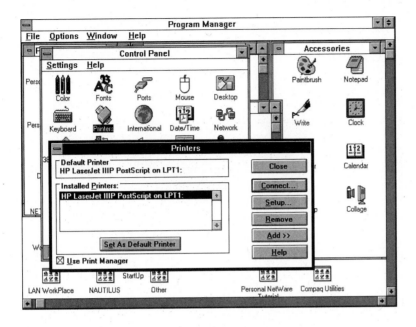

Figure 11.19

Removing Print Manager from background control.

To print from a Windows application, follow the printing procedure required by the application. Because Print Manager is running, it controls the print job. You control Print Manager by specifying various options within Print Manager. You can accomplish several print job tasks inside Print Manager including the following:

◆ Changing the priority of print jobs

◆ Viewing the print jobs in a queue

◆ Displaying printing messages

◆ Performing other Print Manager tasks

To perform any of these tasks, you must first complete the following steps:

1. Log in to the network

2. Start Windows

3. Open the Main Window

4. Choose Print Manager

541

You can then perform a variety of tasks, each of which are explained in detail in Window Print Manager help. Open help by choosing Help from the Print Manager menu bar. You then can choose Contents and see the available How To help options as displayed in figure 11.20.

Figure 11.20

Print Manager Help displaying list of How To options.

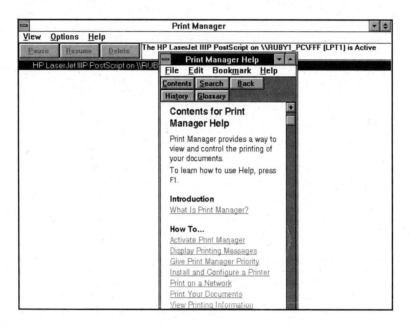

Remote Administration of HP Network Printers

Network administrators can remotely install, configure, troubleshoot, monitor, and otherwise manage HP printers on a network by using the HP JetAdmin utility from any client running Microsoft Windows 3.*x*.

> **Note** JetAdmin is Hewlett-Packard's proprietary product and must be purchased from HP or a distributor. This is a good example of a third-party vendor working well with NetWare printing functions.

Using the JetAdmin utility, you can display the current status of the printer and see up to 38 status messages, including some of these more common ones:

◆ Door open

◆ Manual feed

◆ Offline/Online

◆ Paper tray empty

◆ Toner low

You also can use the HP JetAdmin utility in place of the NetWare PCONSOLE utility to create, delete, and configure print queues. In addition, you can configure various printer settings using JetAdmin, such as IPX/SPX and other protocol support.

JetAdmin also provides features that otherwise are provided through Novell's NetWare utility (PCONSOLE), such as choosing users and/or groups to be notified when the printer is experiencing a problem.

These are some of the other benefits of using the HP JetAdmin utility:

◆ The capability of connecting to the NetWare server itself, bypassing the NetWare print server

◆ A NetWare Protocol Restart option that enables you to disconnect and restart all server connections and reload the configuration files

◆ The option to select the frame types that the NetWare protocol stack sends and receives

Before you can benefit from any of the features that HP JetAdmin provides, you must first configure the HP JetDirect interface.

In order to configure the HP JetDirect interface, you must first log in to the NetWare server from a client as a user with Supervisor or equivalent rights. Then, you must create a print queue and a print server (if they do not already exist), create a printer definition for a remote printer, assign the print queue to the remote printer, and load PSERVER.NLM at the server console. All of these preliminary steps, except for loading PSERVER.NLM, can be done using PCONSOLE.

Now you can complete the process of configuring remote printer mode using JetAdmin:

1. Start Microsoft Windows.

2. Create an icon that will execute the JetAdmin program from where it has been loaded.

3. Choose the JetAdmin icon from the HP JetDirect program group.

4. Choose Configuration.

5. Choose Operating Mode.

6. Choose Remote Printer.

7. Type in a descriptive name for the remote printer.

8. Using the down arrow gadget under the Print Server Name line, scroll through the list of print servers and choose the appropriate print server.

9. Using the down arrow gadget under the Printer Number line, scroll through the printer numbers and choose a printer number.

10. Choose OK, then choose OK again.

11. Choose Exit.

In addition to configuring the HP JetAdmin to assign a network printer to a print server in remote printer mode, you can configure the HP JetDirect interface in queue server mode. To accomplish this task, complete the following steps:

1. With the JetPrint main menu open, select the printer to configure.

2. Choose Configuration.

3. Choose Operating Mode.

4. Choose Queue Server Mode.

5. Type in a descriptive name for the printer.

6. Choose Add Queue.

7. Select NEW_QUEUE.

8. Choose Add.

9. Choose OK three times.

10. Choose Exit to close JetAdmin.

11. Test the printer by sending a print job to the print queue that you just added.

Although this section touches only briefly on the HP JetAdmin utility, you can see that HP JetDirect is designed to help you remotely manage your HP printers on a Novell NetWare network.

Maintaining Laser and Dot-Matrix Printers

No matter how careful you are at setting up your network printing, you may occasionally have network printing problems. Whether you are the network administrator or just trying to figure out why you cannot get your print job to print, you can benefit from knowing how to care for your network's laser and dot-matrix printers, as well as how to troubleshoot possible printing problems. This section and the following one help you get the most out of network printing.

Troubleshooting network printing is made easier by keeping your printers in top shape. This requires regular and periodic maintenance of your network printers.

The two most common types of printers used on networks today are dot-matrix and laser printers. While both of these printers have their own printing mechanisms, they do have some things in common when it comes to maintenance, including the following:

◆ You should first and foremost follow the directions given by the printer's manufacturer. That includes directions for setup and connection of the printer, as well as for its regular maintenance.

◆ Areas around printers should be kept as free from dust and dirt as possible. Particularly troublesome are paper shreds and paper dust. Loose paper particles accumulate not only around printers but inside as well. Therefore, you should vacuum around the inside of the printer as well as around the outside area.

◆ Regular dust as well as paper dust is a problem source for printers. Paper jams, as well as printing ribbon and ink smudges, are often the result of dirty paper and ribbon paths. Clean these paths regularly using a lint-free cloth. Do not spray any liquid cleaners into the printer because they may cause an electrical short. Wipe with dry cloths only.

◆ Belts should be checked to make certain they are properly tightened. Instructions are often provided in the manufacturer's documentation. However, if you do not want to perform this type of maintenance yourself, sending the printer out for regular service at a depot maintenance facility often includes this type of maintenance.

◆ In addition to not spraying any chemicals or cleaners into the printer, you should not add lubricants of any type unless specifically instructed to do so by the manufacturer's documentation.

◆ Printers also are troubled by other environmental factors that, if carefully controlled, may reduce the number of troubleshooting incidences. For example, static electricity can cause your printer to have intermittent problems. Other environmental factors include temperature and humidity. Keeping both of these as stable as possible helps to prevent problems with your printer.

In addition to following these general recommendations for printer maintenance and care, see that both laser and dot-matrix printers benefit from maintenance that is specific to their individual needs.

Maintenance for Laser Printers

The following tips may prove useful when trying to maintain a laser printer properly and may help to reduce the number of troubleshooting incidences:

◆ Take great care when cleaning all parts of a laser printer, particularly the corona wires so that you do not break them.

◆ To prevent buildup, clean the corona wire (a thin wire stretched across the width of the printer that attracts toner to the paper with an electric charge) each time you put in a new print cartridge. Fuzzy printed pages may indicate that the corona wire needs cleaning. Totally black pages may mean that the corona wire is broken or severely fouled with toner.

◆ Use only new print toner cartridges if that is what the manufacturer specifies. Some printers can use a toner cartridge that has been refilled once, but an improperly refilled toner cartridge can cause you more problems than the money you saved. Therefore, use them only if you get them from a trusted and reliable source, and only if the manufacturer of the printer does not tell you not to use them. Speckled documents indicate a problem with the primary corona grid. This grid is part of the toner cartridge. Therefore, replacing the toner cartridge may correct this problem.

◆ Always handle toner cartridges with great care, being certain not to tip, shake, spill, or otherwise improperly store them.

◆ When changing the toner cartridge, also change the fuser bar. You recognize it as a blackened cotton bar. It usually lifts out of the laser printer. It is located next to the corona wire and may be hidden under a liftable door that indicates a danger of high temperatures. Therefore, you may also want to let the printer cool before removing the fuser bar or cleaning the corona wire.

◆ Parts of the printer may become gummed up when using envelopes or address labels. Therefore, use only envelopes and address labels that are designed for use in a laser printer.

◆ Because high temperatures are generated with laser printers, be certain that the printer is positioned so as to allow an ample flow of cool air when the printer is in operation. Do not stack printer reference manuals or other items next to the printer. Position the printer several inches from anything that may interfere with air circulation. Also, keep the printer away from sunny windows because they may cause the air around the printer to become overheated.

◆ Cheap paper causes many paper jams. Use paper that has at least a 20 lb. grade or is marked specifically for laser use.

Maintenance for Dot-Matrix Printers

The following tips may prove useful when trying to maintain a dot-matrix printer properly, and may reduce the number of troubleshooting incidences:

◆ As with laser printers, adequate heat dissipation is important. Therefore, do not set anything too close to the printer, and keep it away from all potential heat sources such as sunny windows or space and room heaters.

◆ Quality output depends on the use of quality ribbons. Damage to the printer's print head can result from poor quality ribbons. Ribbons that are not used frequently eventually dry out and have to be replaced even though they have not yet produced the number of pages that they were designed to print.

◆ Quality of multipart forms depends heavily on the quality of the printer itself; some dot-matrix printers cannot success-fully print multipart forms. The impact strength of lower-quality printers may be insufficient to print more than two- or three-part forms successfully.

◆ Dot-matrix printers have stepper motors that advance the paper in the printer. You can advance the paper manually using the platen head knob. However, you can damage the stepper motor if you turn the platen head knob while the printer is turned on. Removing the knob after a new box of paper has been loaded can prevent accidental damage of the stepper motor.

Tips for Troubleshooting Network Printing

 Given a set of symptoms, determine whether a problem concerns NetWare printing or the printer itself.

Printer maintenance is an important aspect of reducing printing problems on your network, but even the most meticulous network administrator eventually will experience network printing problems that must be figured out and then corrected. This section is intended to give you an overview of troubleshooting techniques useful when network printing problems occur.

Decision Trees

Many network problems can be figured out by following a troubleshooting decision tree. A decision tree gives you a graphical path to follow in order to narrow your search by systematically eliminating options.

A decision tree for troubleshooting network printing might look similar to the one shown in figure 11.21. You may want to create your own printing troubleshooting decision tree, based on the information that you read in this chapter and on your personal troubleshooting experiences.

Figure 11.21

Sample network printing troubleshooting decision tree.

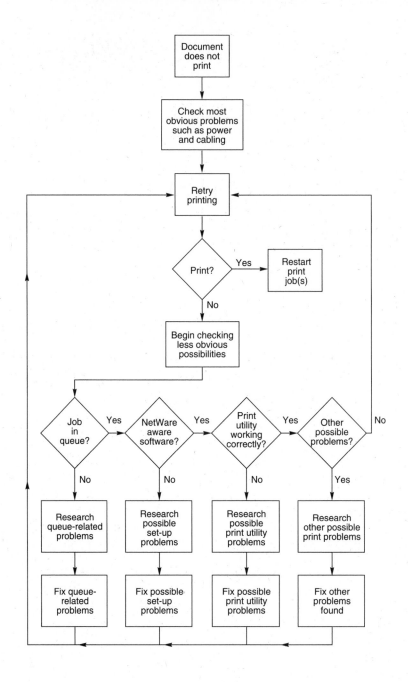

The decision tree shown in figure 11.21 is simplified and basic, and should not be viewed as a complete network printing trouble-shooting decision tree. You can and probably should create a decision tree of your own by reviewing all possible potential printing problems, including those discussed in this chapter, those in Novell's Print Server manuals, and those in the user manual for each network printer. Having your own decision tree to guide you when troubleshooting network printing problems may well be worth the time invested in its creation.

Print Queues

Recall that print queues temporarily hold the jobs that have been sent for printing. Print queues are directories on file servers, and as such, are subject to file server problems as well as to problems specific to the print queue itself.

For example, if the file server has an insufficient amount of available disk space to store a print job temporarily, an error message such as the following may be generated:

```
WARNING_CANNOT CREATE SPOOL FILE
```

The cure for this type of an error is to increase the available disk space on the file server. You can use utilities such as VOLINFO or CHKDSK to verify that the problem is an insufficient amount of disk space, and make adjustments accordingly.

Figure 11.22 shows VOLINFO being run on file server GENERAL. As you can probably conclude from the fact that the logged-in user in figure 11.22 is user GUEST, only minimum network rights are required to run the VOLINFO utility.

Figure 11.22

VOLINFO run for file server GENERAL.

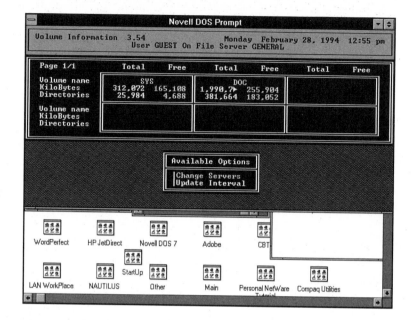

Print Servers

Two types of print servers exist on Novell NetWare networks: those that run at the file server through PSERVER.NLM, and those that run at a dedicated client through PSERVER.EXE. Therefore, although there are some common suggestions for troubleshooting print servers, there are also troubleshooting suggestions that are specific to each type of print server.

Common Print Server Troubleshooting Techniques

Regardless of whether you are running PSERVER.NLM or PSERVER.EXE, you should make certain that you have the *latest version* of the print server as well as the latest version of any drivers that are compatible with your version of NetWare.

There is an updated version of PSERVER.NLM that is available from the NetWire Novell Library. The file to download is called PSERVx.EXE. It corrects problems with earlier versions of PSERVER.NLM related to the rewind function, printing large graphics, and notification messages.

Before removing the print server, be certain that it has completed servicing all of the jobs submitted to it. PCONSOLE's Print Server Information and Status/Control options are useful in this effort.

If you are receiving complaints that printing is too slow on the network, consider whether or not a specific print server may be servicing too many printers. If you are close to the maximum of 16 printers on one print server, consider setting up another print server and splitting the printers between the two.

Print server definitions also can become corrupted. Slow printing is an indication of this type of problem. If you do not have anywhere near the maximum number of printers on a given print server, but printing is still slow on the network, you may need to delete the current print server definitions and re-create them. You can use DOS commands or FILER to remove current print server files and related subdirectories. Run BINDFIX.EXE after production hours to delete old queue information. Print queues and server directories are hidden in the SYS:SYSTEM directory.

Bottlenecks on the network can contribute to slow printing response as well as to other network printing problems. In addition, the type of documents being printed (graphics versus text) and the hardware used on your network can affect printing. Therefore, you should consider and look at each of these possibilities when troubleshooting.

 The greatest hardware-related factor that can have a negative effect on network printing is the processor of the computer. If you can avoid it, do not run NetWare core printing services on an 80286 file server. Printing performance is greatly affected when using a computer with an 80286 processor.

553

Do not use an 8086 or 8088 CPU as a print server with a laser printer. The older microprocessors pulled interrupts, were slow in buffering traffic, and hinder the faster laser printer I/O needs.

The following are additional factors that might affect printing performance:

◆ Third-party products

◆ Multiple jobs in the print queue

◆ Network work load

PSERVER.NLM Troubleshooting Techniques

In the case of PSERVER.NLM, unloading it before first downing the print server through PCONSOLE may cause printing problems or false printing problems on your network. To warn other users before you bring the print server down, you might broadcast a message that you are doing so temporarily.

For example, if you unload PSERVER.NLM before it finishes serving a print request, the user who made the request may believe that there is a network printing problem when the print job is not received. This may result in the user submitting the print job several more times, clogging the print queue with redundant requests that cannot be serviced currently.

In addition, the user may decide that the problem is serious enough to warrant reporting. The network administrator or someone else attempting to troubleshoot the printing problem may not be immediately aware of the cause of the false problem, and may waste a good deal of time trying to figure it out.

PSERVER.EXE Troubleshooting Techniques

Although it is not technically considered a problem, a print server that does not reboot automatically after an interruption can increase a network administrator's work load. This type of a problem can be solved by using special utilities that are available from NetWire through the Novell Library. These utilities can be obtained by downloading a file called NETERR.ZIP.

NETERR.ZIP contains utilities provided by a company called Infinite Technologies. They are designed for gateways, mail, print servers, and other tasks performed by dedicated NetWare clients. The utility of benefit for printing problems causes the dedicated print server client to reboot automatically when it detects the Abort, Retry message.

Be sure to use the most recent version of the NetWare DOS Requester that is compatible with your version of NetWare to prevent problems such as print servers that hang. Rebooting the computer provides an immediate correction to the problem of the client hanging, but it is only a temporary and limited fix for the problem.

A minimum of 266KB of conventional memory is needed to run one network printer or a dedicated print server. (Add 10KB for each additional printer.) Insufficient available conventional memory can be corrected by using memory managers, such as DR DOS 6.0 and Novell DOS 7.0's Memory Manager, to move the local operating system out of conventional memory and into extended or expanded memory. This frees more conventional memory for network printing.

Remote Printers

Most network printing services are as fast as or faster than printing to a local printer. Occasionally, printing to a remote printer is an exception. Sometimes problems such as IRQ conflicts, unsupported hardware interrupts, and problems with cables (particularly standard cables) may result in slower printing on remote printers.

When working with remote printers on your network, the following tips may be useful:

◆ Be certain that the configuration you set for a remote serial printer is the same for both the printer's DIP switches and for PCONSOLE's configuration entries.

◆ Run RPRINTER.EXE at the client whenever a message is received indicating that the printer is not connected. Also, update your RPRINTER.EXE to the latest compatible version, available as PSERVx.EXE through NetWire or NSEPro.

◆ In addition to running a current version of RPRINTER.EXE, client initialization problems can be corrected by making certain that the client has sufficient memory and that the client being used is an IBM-compatible clone, because RPRINTER.EXE does not run on some incompatible clones.

◆ If RPRINTER.EXE cannot be installed successfully on a client, check to make certain that PSERVER is loaded for the print server that will be servicing this remote printer.

◆ If RPRINTER.EXE hangs the client when it is being loaded, try changing the settings on the NIC card, because there may be a conflict. Another option is to make certain that you are using at least v1.22R or above; earlier versions hang a client when run with Microsoft DOS 5.0.

Users sometimes experience problems when attempting to use RPRINTER.EXE and its related help file, RPRINTER.HLP. Because some users may try to run RPRINTER.EXE without first logging in to the network, you may avoid unnecessary calls from your users if you load these two files into the file server's login directory. Then these files are accessible by network users even if they have not first logged in to the network.

You also can load these two files onto the local drive. However, updating these files may prove to be more difficult in a large network.

If remote users of the client with RPRINTER.EXE loaded complain of ruined print jobs, the client's local user may be attempting to print to their attached printer without having first issued the CAPTURE statement, or without using PSC to designate temporarily their printer as private. To correct this problem, show the user of the client running RPRINTER.EXE how to use the PSC command.

The Usage help screen for the PSC command-line utility is shown in figure 11.23.

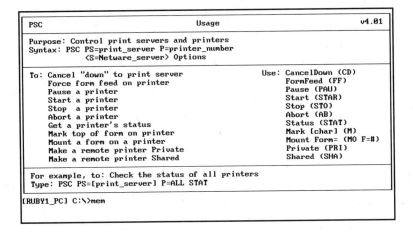

Figure 11.23

PSC Usage help screen.

When running PSERVER, the SPX CONNECTIONS = line in the client's NET.CFG file needs to be set to 60. This is not true for RPRINTER. The default of 15 SPX connections is often sufficient, because RPRINTER uses only one SPX connection each time that it is run. Fewer SPX connections may help with limited conventional memory as well.

Another way to help increase available conventional memory on a client that runs RPRINTER.EXE is to change the buffer size to approximately 6KB. This reduces the size of the RPRINTER.EXE TSR and can improve printing throughput. Of course, if you require a larger buffer size to perform other client tasks besides running RPRINTER.EXE, then you may have to set the buffer to a larger size anyway.

The following are additional troubleshooting tips to keep in mind when working with remote printers:

♦ RPRINTER.EXE should be loaded after loading the Microsoft STACKER compression utility, if you are using STACKER, because problems with STACKER overwriting RPRINTER.EXE have been reported.

♦ If there is a router between the remote printer and the print server that services it, increase the SPX ABORT TIMEOUT and IPX RETRY COUNT parameters in the NET.CFG file of the remote printer's client. This should reduce the number of periodic or random printer hangs.

♦ Older computers, such as those using an Intel 80286 processor, although not recommended for use as print servers, may be useful as remote printers, particularly if the client's user does not need to have an 80386 or higher processor for performing daily tasks on their nondedicated client.

Physical Problems

Part of testing a printer setup is to send a print job to the printer. If that print job does not print out, the problem may be related to the setup. However, it also may be related to physical printer problems. Once you have verified that the setup is correct, you can consider the following potential physical problems with network printers:

♦ The printer itself may have been turned off, or the Online/ Offline button may have been set to Offline.

♦ Toner cartridge may be too low to allow printing, or the ribbon may be out of its path and causing a printer jam.

♦ Paper, envelopes, or labels may be stuck in the print path, causing a paper jam.

♦ The print cable may be loose or disconnected from either the printer itself or from the computer to which it is connected.

◆ A frayed or damaged cable also may prevent a document from printing.

◆ Pinouts for the cable may be incorrect for this particular printer; different printers can have different pinout configuration requirements.

◆ Ungrounded printers may take themselves offline when excess static from special types of paper or carbonless forms is generated inside the printer.

Other things to consider when physical printing problems seem apparent include whether or not the printing setup is correct (check print queues, print servers, and so on) and problems with the network cabling and connection (check concentrators, hubs, MAUs, NICs, and so on).

Application programs that handle printing differently from NetWare can be a problem. For example, some application programs print to COM ports. However, NetWare generally captures to LPT ports. Special arrangements may have to be made to handle problems with application programs.

Serial printing may pose special problems of its own. Novell recommends that parallel printing be used on the network whenever possible, to help eliminate printing problems. Problems that you may encounter with serial printing include the following:

◆ Slower printing, which is further compounded by parity checking

◆ Additional participation at installation by the installer, which compounds the potential for setup errors

◆ Lack of universal compatibility

Although serial printers can handle longer cable distances than parallel printers (serial cables can average up to 50 feet and parallel cables generally average up to 10 feet), the longer cabling distances can compound troubleshooting errors and efforts.

Printer Configuration

As printers become more and more advanced, those advances are likely to result in applications that are unprepared to manage these complex printers. The more complex print drivers now available often prevent or resolve potential problems related to such advanced printers as laser and thermal transfer printers.

In order to accommodate these more advanced printers when the applications are not capable of handling them, NetWare applications such as PRINTDEF and PRINTCON can be used to create associated printer and job definitions.

This customizing and defining of printer and job definitions is accompanied by an increased need for buffer space. To accommodate this increase in requirements, you can modify the NET.CFG file to include the following two statements:

```
PRINT HEADER = n

PRINT TAIL = n
```

In these statements, *n* is replaced with a number that specifies how many bytes of space should be set up for the print header or the print tail. The default for print header is 64 bytes. The default for the print tail is 16 bytes. Using print header and print tail control codes is particularly important for printing to PostScript printers.

If users are complaining about the print quality of their graphics files, it may be the result of several possible conditions:

- ◆ The application program is incorrectly configured for working in a network printing environment.

- ◆ Users are capturing to a print queue that is not configured to handle the printer to which they are printing.

- ◆ Users are printing to a network printer that is not configured for that particular software.

Correcting any of these problems is more a matter of network management than of the printers themselves; however, if you are aware of these potential problems, they may be easier to correct when they occur.

If network printing is slow, particularly when graphic files are involved, it may be that the file server does not have sufficient cache buffers to handle the large files quickly. Adding memory to the file server can increase the number of buffers, which may in turn increase the printing speed.

Printer Utilities

Several print service utilities are involved in printing. Newer versions of these utilities already correct some of the problems associated with ever-improving and changing printers.

One way to correct many little but troublesome printing problems may be to update to the latest print services files. If you have access to NOVLIB on CompuServe, you can copy all updated files by copying over and then uncompressing the following files:

◆ PSERVx.EXE

◆ PUTILx.EXE

◆ PRINTx.EXE

The printer utilities that significantly impact network printing include PCONSOLE, PRINTCON, CAPTURE, and NPRINT.

PCONSOLE

PCONSOLE is used to set up print servers and print queues, as well as to view information about network printing or to manage printing on the network. Instructions for using PCONSOLE to set up print servers and print queues is provided earlier in this chapter. Tasks that you can perform with PCONSOLE include the following:

◆ Attach to a file server

◆ Log out of other file servers

◆ Choose the current file server

561

- ◆ Log into a file server under a different user name
- ◆ Create, delete, and rename print queues
- ◆ Assign or remove queue operators and users
- ◆ Change queue operator flags
- ◆ Set up a print server to service a print queue
- ◆ Remove a print server from servicing a print queue
- ◆ View attached print servers and jobs in a queue
- ◆ Print files and delete or reorder print jobs
- ◆ Change parameters of a print job
- ◆ Put print jobs on hold and restore held print jobs
- ◆ View the object ID of a print queue
- ◆ View the servers assigned to a print queue
- ◆ Create, delete, rename, and set print server passwords
- ◆ Name a print server
- ◆ Attach file servers to print servers
- ◆ View a print server's object ID and information
- ◆ Down a print server
- ◆ Add or remove printers to or from the print server
- ◆ Set a printer's service mode or change its configuration
- ◆ Set form numbers and notify lists for printers
- ◆ List printers and queues serviced by the print server
- ◆ Assign or remove print server operators and users
- ◆ Assign or remove queues to or from printers

Because PCONSOLE provides such a variety of printing services tasks, there are more things that can be forgotten when it comes to configuring your print queues and print servers. Therefore, configuration errors (or lack of proper configuration) often can be associated with this utility.

Two common problems related to PCONSOLE include an insufficient buffer size set in memory, which causes words or characters to be dropped from the printed document, and a problem with asynchronous routers that do not support SPX.

Correct the first problem by increasing the buffer size that is set when you configure the printer using PCONSOLE. Correct the second problem by increasing the SPX Timeout and IPX Retry counts.

 Note PRINTCON and PRINTDEF use are not necessary if you are running strictly in a Windows environment.

PRINTCON

PRINTCON is used to define print options so that you can establish standard print configurations. It acts like a database from which CAPTURE, NPRINT, and PCONSOLE access configuration information. Tasks that you can perform with PRINTCON include the following:

◆ Creating, deleting, editing, or renaming a print job configuration

◆ Selecting configuration for default

◆ Copying print job configurations so that multiple users can use the same print job configuration

Three particular printing problems can be corrected using PRINTCON. First, graphic files that time out early due to lengthy calculations can result in premature page breaks. This can be corrected by lengthening or disabling the Timeout Count in the PRINTCON job definition.

Second, print job configurations that could be the same for all users but which are not, causing extra configuration maintenance work, can be replaced easily by choosing the best configuration,

563

then copying it into the PRINTCON.DAT file in SYS:PUBLIC. This gives all users access to this common print configuration.

Third, if you have users who require more than 37 print job configurations, give those users a second login identification so that they can have up to 37 more print job configurations.

CAPTURE and NPRINT

CAPTURE is used to enable you to print in special circumstances. Those special circumstances include the following:

- ◆ Printing screen captures or displays
- ◆ Printing data to a file on the network
- ◆ Printing from a non-network-compatible application to a network printer

Problems with using the CAPTURE command are often associated with the incorrect use or the lack of use of available CAPTURE options. Figure 11.24 shows the options available for use with the CAPTURE command.

Figure 11.24

CAPTURE utility options.

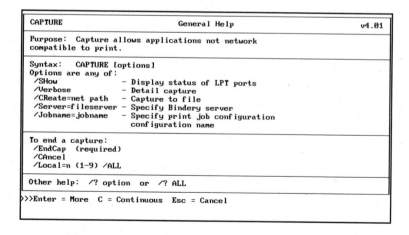

```
CAPTURE                        General Help                        v4.01

Purpose:  Capture allows applications not network
compatible to print.

Syntax:   CAPTURE [options]
Options are any of:
  /SHow              - Display status of LPT ports
  /Verbose           - Detail capture
  /CReate=net path   - Capture to file
  /Server=fileserver - Specify Bindery server
  /Jobname=jobname   - Specify print job configuration
                       configuration name

To end a capture:
  /EndCap  (required)
  /CAncel
  /Local=n (1-9) /ALL

Other help:  /? option  or  /? ALL

>>>Enter = More   C = Continuous   Esc = Cancel
```

NPRINT is used to print DOS text files or files which have been formatted for a specific printer by an application program. As with the CAPTURE command, problems with using NPRINT are often associated with the incorrect use or the lack of use of available NPRINT options. Figure 11.25 shows the options available for use with the NPRINT command.

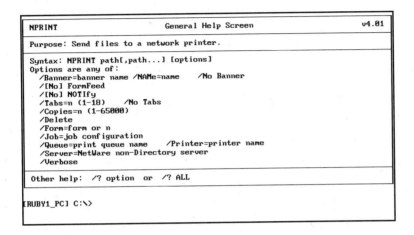

```
NPRINT                    General Help Screen                    v4.01

Purpose: Send files to a network printer.

Syntax: NPRINT path[,path...] [options]
Options are any of:
    /Banner=banner name /NAMe=name      /No Banner
    /[No] FormFeed
    /[No] NOTIfy
    /Tabs=n (1-18)      /No Tabs
    /Copies=n (1-65000)
    /Delete
    /Form=form or n
    /Job=job configuration
    /Queue=print queue name      /Printer=printer name
    /Server=NetWare non-Directory server
    /Verbose

Other help:  /? option  or  /? ALL


[RUBY1_PC] C:\>
```

Figure 11.25

NPRINT utility options.

There are two other troubleshooting tips related to CAPTURE and NPRINT. First, both CAPTURE and NPRINT interpret the ASCII tab character (09) as meaning eight spaces. However, the same ASCII character is interpreted by laser printers to mean font and graphic information, often resulting in misinterpretation in printed documents. Therefore, when using either the CAPTURE or NPRINT command to print to a laser printer, also use the /NT (No Tabs) switch.

Second, use the /KEEP switch with CAPTURE and NPRINT to keep print jobs that are in the process of being added to a queue from being dropped if your network connection is severed, particularly if done so by a backup program that may be running automatically after normal hours.

PostScript Printers

Because the PostScript language handles information differently from that of other printers, you should be aware of these differences in order to prevent quirky printing problems.

565

The following troubleshooting tips should be helpful when your network includes one or more PostScript printers:

♦ Be sure that you are using the latest PostScript drivers for applications, including Windows.

♦ Increase the PRINT HEADER and PRINT TAIL parameters in the NET.CFG file, as discussed previously in this chapter.

♦ Set the appropriate PostScript switch on printers that require it, or make certain that the printing cartridge for PostScript support is loaded properly and seated tightly, if printed documents are not recognizable or PostScript printing is not functioning.

♦ PostScript print jobs use the byte stream mode, so always use the /NT (No Tabs) and /NB (No Banner) switches with print jobs. Use the /NFF (No Form Feed) switch if printing using the NPRINT or CAPTURE command.

Review Questions

1. Which of the following is the main utility used to set up print queues?

○ a. PCONSOLE

○ b. PSERVER

○ c. RPRINTER

○ d. CAPTURE

2. Software for a remote printer should not be loaded onto a client until which two utilities have been used to set up print services?

☐ a. PCONSOLE

☐ b. PSERVER

☐ c. RPRINTER

☐ d. CAPTURE

3. Which of the following is not a function of the PCONSOLE utility?

○ a. Set up print queues.

○ b. Establish users to notify of printer problems.

○ c. Test printer setup.

○ d. Attach printers to print queues.

4. Of the following steps required to set up network print services, which one must be completed before the others?

○ a. Set up print queues.

○ b. Establish users to notify of printer problems.

○ c. Test printer setup.

○ d. Attach printers to print queues.

5. Which of the following statements is *not* true regarding print queues?

○ a. Queues are added after print servers are defined.

○ b. Print queues are assigned a priority from 1 to 5.

○ c. Print servers must be attached to print queues.

○ d. New queues are added by pressing Ins from the Print Queues screen and typing in a name.

6. The Printer Notify List is accessed by running the _____ print services configuration utility.

7. Of the following print services utilities, which one provides printing services for a printer connected to a network file server?

○ a. PCONSOLE.EXE

○ b. PSERVER.EXE

○ c. PSERVER.NLM

○ d. RPRINTER.EXE

8. ENDCAP is a companion command to the _____ utility.

9. Which of the following options enables you to see the current status of your captured LPT ports?

    O   a.   /SH

    O   b.   /S

    O   c.   /CA

    O   d.   /S

10. Which of the following print services utilities must be used with the LOAD command?

    O   a.   PCONSOLE

    O   b.   PSERVER

    O   c.   ENDCAP

    O   d.   RPRINTER

11. In order to use a client as a dedicated print server, which utility must be run at that client?

    O   a.   PCONSOLE.EXE

    O   b.   CAPTURE.EXE

    O   c.   PSERVER.EXE

    O   d.   RPRINTER.EXE

12. Which of the following utilities, when run on a client, does *not* require that the SPX CONNECTIONS statement in the NET.CFG file of that client be changed to 60 connections?

    O   a.   PCONSOLE.EXE

    O   b.   CAPTURE.EXE

    O   c.   PSERVER.EXE

    O   d.   RPRINTER.EXE

13. You can automate the loading of a remote printer on a client by putting the RPRINTER command into the client's _____ file.

14. Which is the primary difference between a print server and a remote printer?

   O   a.   RPRINTER.EXE is a TSR, PSERVER.EXE is not a TSR.

   O   b.   The physical attachment of the printer is different.

   O   c.   Only RPRINTER can be run with the NetWare Shell.

   O   d.   You cannot print to a remote printer using Microsoft Windows' print software.

15. Which two tasks must you complete before connecting a network printer using Microsoft Windows?

   ☐   a.   Choose Network from the Windows Connect box.

   ☐   b.   Install Microsoft Windows for network use.

   ☐   c.   Be certain you can attach to a network that is up and running.

   ☐   d.   Load RPRINTER on your client.

16. What must you do to prevent a network printer connection from being lost when you close Windows?

   O   a.   Leave the connection window running as a TSR.

   O   b.   Choose the Permanent button after connecting a port to a network printer.

   O   c.   Run CAPTURE at your client before loading Microsoft Windows and connecting a port to a network printer.

   O   d.   Log in to the network.

17. If a network printer is experiencing intermittent and indeterminate problems, one possible cause may be

   ○   a.   paper jammed into the feed roller.

   ○   b.   rPRINTER.EXE improperly loaded at the client.

   ○   c.   a printer belt that is improperly tightened.

   ○   d.   an undetected source of static electricity.

18. Which of the following is not a regular maintenance technique for a dot matrix printer?

   ○   a.   Clean the corona wire whenever you change the toner cartridge.

   ○   b.   Turn the printer off before using the knob to advance the platen head.

   ○   c.   Replace printing ribbons with good quality ones.

   ○   d.   Check and remove the printer from potential heat sources.

19. The WARNING_CANNOT CREATE SPOOL FILE error message may indicate that

   ○   a.   pSERVER.EXE needs to be reloaded after rebooting the computer.

   ○   b.   too many printers are being serviced by a single print server.

   ○   c.   the file server has an insufficient amount of disk space.

   ○   d.   the latest version of PSERVER.NLM should be obtained from NetWire and loaded onto the file server.

20. If your network setup has close to the maximum number of printers connected to a single print server, you can expect to hear users complain that

   ○   a.   printing on the network is too slow.

   ○   b.   printing quality is substantially reduced.

   ○   c.   remote printers periodically take themselves offline.

   ○   d.   print jobs are delivered to the wrong printers.

21. As a network administrator, if network printing suddenly becomes too slow, you might suspect that the problem may be due to

    ○   a.   print queues that are assigned to the wrong print servers.

    ○   b.   print server definitions that have become corrupted.

    ○   c.   users who are printing too many graphic files.

    ○   d.   an incompatible third-party software program that you added to the network last year.

22. If users complain that their print jobs sent to remote printers are occasionally ruined, you might suspect that

    ○   a.   too many print jobs are being simultaneously submitted to the remote printer.

    ○   b.   the user on the remote printer's client is occasionally sending print jobs to the local printer without first issuing the CAPTURE command.

    ○   c.   rPRINTER.EXE is occasionally hanging the client at bootup because of a conflict on the client's NIC.

    ○   d.   the user has not first logged into the network, even though your configuration placed RPRINTER.EXE and RPRINTER.HLP in the login directory.

23. Which two NET.CFG file parameters need to be increased when there is a router between the remote printer and the print server?

    ☐   a.   SPX CONNECTIONS

    ☐   b.   BUFFER SIZE

    ☐   c.   SPX ABORT TIMEOUT

    ☐   d.   IPX RETRY COUNT

24. Which physical print problem may cause a printer to take itself offline?

    ○   a.   A frayed or damaged cable

    ○   b.   Incorrect cable pinouts

    ○   c.   Jammed paper, envelopes, or labels

    ○   d.   Lack of a ground wire

25. Because PostScript printers use the byte stream mode, which two switches must be used when sending a graphic to a PostScript printer?

    ☐   a.   /NT

    ☐   b.   /CR

    ☐   c.   /NN

    ☐   d.   /NB

Answers

1. A

2. A, B

3. C

4. A

5. B

6. PCONSOLE

7. C

8. CAPTURE

9. A

10. B

11. C

12. D

13. AUTOEXEC.BAT

14. B

15. B, C

16. B

17. D

18. A

19. C

20. A

21. A

22. B

23. C, D

24. D

25. A, D

Troubleshooting Concepts and Tools

This chapter examines some tools and methods used in troubleshooting the components of your network. Careful monitoring of the different components that make up your network enables you to prevent many problems. Taking precautions and performing proactive maintenance can help eliminate problems long before the critical stage.

The network administrator's main responsibility is to monitor and record any network-related problems. In most cases, if the administrator does not do anything to prevent or watch out for these problems, no one will. System monitoring and troubleshooting is enhanced by a wide range of third-party and Novell NetWare diagnostic and monitoring utilities. These utilities can give both users and network administrators the data required to maintain and efficiently operate a network.

The network administrator has to know a lot about many different components and how to deal with people before and after a problem occurs. A good administrator will always be looking for ways to become more aware of technical and people issues. As you investigate this chapter, you will learn about problem prevention and troubleshooting in a NetWare environment. The topics discussed include the following:

- The troubleshooting process

- Troubleshooting tools

- Problem prevention

Understanding the Troubleshooting Process

Learning to troubleshoot and prevent network problems cannot always be learned from a book. Experience in dealing with different types of network issues is the best teacher. Even though you may have been working with networks and dealing with people for a long time, there is always a potential for new experiences.

As you learn from research and with experience, you can break the problem down and isolate the component that is causing the problem. You can develop your own strategy on the most efficient way to deal with finding reliable solutions. You can develop your own "troubleshooter's mind" with experience and by applying the following process used by many experts.

Before You Get Too Involved

As you are developing your "troubleshooter's mind," you should log and document what process you went through to solve the problem. You can use this documentation to refer to later, reminding yourself of what did or did not work to solve the problem.

There are some common issues you should look at before you get too involved. Try the following, depending on the type of problem:

- ◆ Check for and eliminate user or operator error:

    What was the user doing when the problem occurred?

    Was the problem real or just a perception?

    Was the problem an issue of education? Could the user be trained to do the process right?

- ◆ Check the equipment:

    Are all the parts present? Are the components the right ones to work together?

    Are all the components connected properly?

- ◆ Power all components off and then turn them back on in the proper order.

- ◆ Back up your data for safety, security, and restoring ability if hard disks are involved. Be sure you can restore the backup files you have created. Many administrators have discovered too late that their backup system was not functioning properly!

- ◆ Remove any unneeded components, such as terminate-and-stay-resident programs (TSRs), devices causing interference (fans or heaters located close by), and extra interface cards.

- ◆ Edit the CONFIG.SYS or AUTOEXEC.BAT files for any potential conflicting statements.

- ◆ Ask "What's changed?" Check your administration records. If you work with other administrators, ask them what they've changed recently. Ask the user or operator about changes to the environment.

Executing the Troubleshooting Process

Use a step-wise troubleshooting model to analyze and act upon problems.

As a network administrator or support engineer, you should develop a consistent logical process for performing troubleshooting (see fig. 12.1). Planning is the key to making you a more efficient network technician and enabling you to find solutions more quickly. Try the following steps in developing your plan and your solutions:

Figure 12.1

Step order in the troubleshooting process.

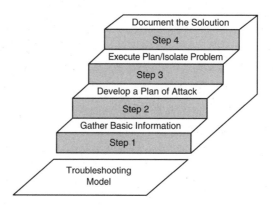

Step 1: Gather Basic Information

1. Find out who is being affected by the problem and what the symptoms of the problem are.

2. Check documentation for problem history and configuration information. Also check logs for "baseline" or normal performance utilization for the network. You need to understand what the standard performance expectations are for this network.

3. Determine what is being done and when the problem occurs on the network. Does the problem happen at certain times of the day, week, or month?

Step 2: Develop a Plan of Attack and Isolate the Problem

1. Take the information you have gathered about the network and make an educated guess as to the source of the problem—is it the hardware, the software (operating system or application), or is it user error?

2. Use the items that could be the source of the problem and prioritize their effect on the solution process. Take your hypotheses about the solution process and determine which is probably the right one and the cost in trying it. Choose the one that is most effective for the solution; if it does not work, try your second hypothesis, and so on.

 A problem is not solved unless users are convinced that their productivity is no longer being impacted by the network.

Step 3: Execute the Plan

1. Break your hypothesis process into smaller reasonable concepts that can be tested.

2. Test each of these smaller concepts and change one thing at a time when doing the testing. After you make the change, test the network to see if the condition of the problem has been affected.

3. Use only known good software, components, and test equipment when you are executing the plan.

4. Use other resources for troubleshooting help—other utilities, your peers, or other experts. Do not let yourself get too tired to think. Also, do not let your ego get in the way. You may learn something from someone else that could make you look good next time the problem occurs.

5. Use the *forward chaining* method when you are dealing with network communications. Forward chaining is the process of starting troubleshooting at the source component (using the testing concepts) and moving toward the destination component while testing.

579

Step 4: Document the Solution

1. Log the problem and the solution in the network documentation.

2. Perform preventative processes for problem resolution. Take the steps necessary to solve the problem if it occurs again (keep hot spares available).

The four steps in the troubleshooting model are the following:

♦ Gather basic information

♦ Develop a plan of attack

♦ Execute the plan and isolate the problem

♦ Document the solution

Records of Activity and Documentation

To use appropriate recordkeeping to keep LANs running smoothly and support troubleshooting.

Each network administrator must maintain a type of site administrator's manual. Quality documentation can save many hours of troubleshooting. Maintaining these logs and network documentation takes time, but it's worth it. The types of documentation that should be kept are divided into the following categories:

♦ The Network System

♦ The History and Use of the Network

♦ Resources for Working with the Network

The Network System

The Network System documentation includes the following items:

- A detailed graphic representation of the network layout that identifies wiring centers, file and print servers, routers and bridges, gateways, and user locations

- An inventory of all components and the software settings for each

- Documentation of cabling distances, types, limitations, and locations

- Documentation on client configuration, software, and hardware, and the importance of its use on the network

- A change log for hardware and software upgrades, and for network configuration changes

The History and Use of the Network

The documentation that is included for the history and use of the network is as follows:

- A log of past problems and solutions, the amount of downtime incurred, and an ongoing performance analysis of printers and routers (keep for at least two years)

- Information on usage patterns, statistics, bandwidth utilization, and network performance in the normal operating mode

- User profiles on what each one does and the potential training needs

- What the entire business enterprise is and how it is related to the network—this involves human factors as well as technological factors

Resources for Working with the Network

Use the following list to keep track of resources you might need:

- ◆ Who are you going to call at the needed level of priority?

- ◆ Who is it that you escalate to: another technical support level, the vendor, or your manager?

- ◆ Current phone numbers and escalation levels posted in a visible location to the network administrator (a current list of phone numbers, addresses, and contact names also should be kept in the site administrator's manual).

- ◆ Keep copies of documentation that comes with any software package or hardware component in the same secure location.

 There are forms in the back of the NetWare 3.1x Installation manual that a network administrator can use to document file servers, clients, and operating system details. These can be enlarged on a copier and placed in the site administrator's manual when completed.

Using Troubleshooting Tools

 Choose which research tools are most likely to provide a solution when tackling specific problems.

There are many types of diagnostic utilities that are available on the market today. These can be found by attending trade shows, reviewing trade magazines, or by word of mouth. You may have to use combinations of packages to provide all the modules you need to troubleshoot different parts of the network. There are some software utilities that do not work with certain hardware types or combinations of hardware. When you search for the utilities to use on your network, choose the package or combination that best meets your overall requirements.

The tools shown in this chapter are only representative of what is available for NetWare that can be used as resources for troubleshooting.

CHECKIT PRO

CHECKIT PRO is developed by TouchStone Software Corporation. CHECKIT PRO comes in two volumes—SysInfo and TEST & TOOLS. The SysInfo volume enables you to find out configuration information about your MS-DOS-compatible PC (see fig. 12.2). This system information can be displayed in graphic format or in a detailed report.

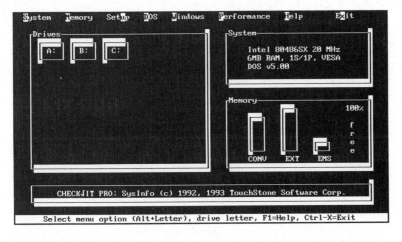

Figure 12.2
CHECKIT PRO's SysInfo opening screen.

Other tasks you can use SysInfo for include the following:

♦ Provide information on components to determine any potential conflicts in IRQs and I/O or memory addresses

♦ View CMOS, take an inventory of internal components, and print reports to include in your network documentation

583

◆ Execute benchmark readings of system performance, then compare these to earlier tests and perform proactive maintenance if necessary

As you can see in figure 12.3, the report on IRQ usage shows a conflict at Interrupt 7 between LPT1 and a sound card.

Figure 12.3

CHECKIT PRO's SysInfo IRQ Usage screen.

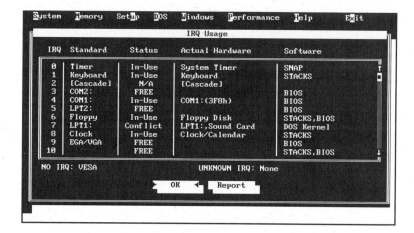

The Test & Tools volume is a separate software package that works on an individual client. This volume is not only for machines that are in need of repair, but for burn-in of new machines and the testing of upgrades (see fig. 12.4).

Figure 12.4

CHECKIT PRO's Test & Tools screen.

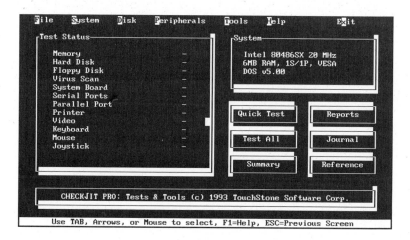

TouchStone provides a software package called CHECKIT LAN that will perform diagnostics for the network.

The TEST & TOOLS volume also enables you to perform the following tasks:

- ◆ Check for viruses

- ◆ Create backup disks of CMOS information for disaster recovery of the client

- ◆ Check the alignment of floppy drives

The Micro House Technical Library

 Use the Micro House Technical Library as an information resource on system boards, shared drives, and interface cards.

The Micro House Technical Library (MTL) is an excellent source of technical information that can be used as a definitive research tool. The MTL comes on CD-ROM, and it is available on a yearly subscription that is updated on a monthly basis. The MTL comes with the following three volumes of information:

- ◆ **The Encyclopedia of Hard Drives.** The listing of available details is shown in figure 12.5.

- ◆ **The Encyclopedia of Main Boards.** The listing of available details is shown in figure 12.6.

- ◆ **The Network Interface Technical Guide.** The listing of available details is shown in figure 12.7.

Figure 12.5

MTL opening screen for hard drive information.

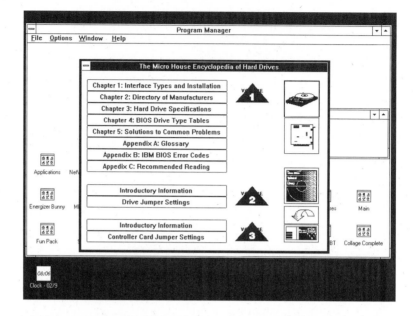

Figure 12.6

MTL opening screen for main board information.

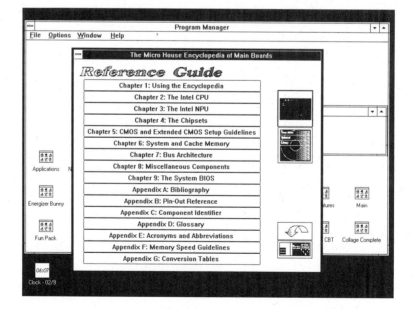

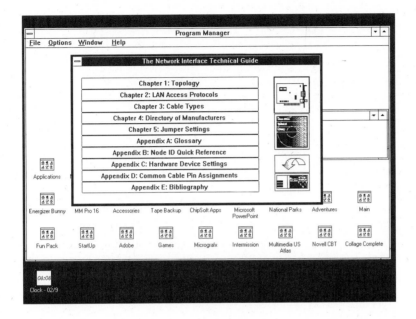

Figure 12.7

MTL opening screen for network interface information.

As you can see in the preceding figures, there is an expanded resource of technical information available for a network administrator. You can search for documents quickly with the MTL using a Boolean keyword search process.

During your certification examination, you will be required to perform an information search in a Micro House Technical Library. To ensure that you gain hands-on experience with MTL, New Riders Publishing and Micro House have provided a copy of MTL on CD-ROM with this book. Refer to Appendix D, "Using Netware Troubleshooting Tools," for details on how to load and learn from the Micro House Technical Library.

The NSEPro

 Use NSEPro as an information source to get the best possible solutions to problems in the shortest possible time.

The Network Support Encyclopedia—Professional Edition (NSEPro), comes on CD-ROM and is available on a yearly subscription basis, updated monthly. When you call 1-800-NETWARE for technical support, your phone call is answered by the help desk people using the NSEPro as their first source of information. You can resolve potential or existing problems more quickly if you have this tool on site. Included as topics in the NSEPro are the following (see fig. 12.8):

- What's New
- Service and Support
- Sales and Marketing
- Novell Programs
- NetWare Update
- Novell Product Manuals
- About NetWire
- New User Information

The NSEPro is built on FOLIO Previews, a type of text retrieval system. The NSEPro divides information into "folios" and "views" sections. A main menu is a folio and a view is a collection of component folios. You can search views for topics of interest. Future versions of NSEPro will have a Windows-based folio.

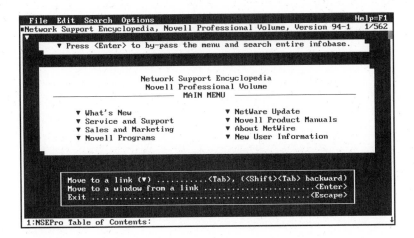

```
 File  Edit  Search  Options                              Help=F1
■Network Support Encyclopedia, Novell Professional Volume, Version 94-1   1/562
▼
     ▼ Press <Enter> to by-pass the menu and search entire infobase.



                      Network Support Encyclopedia
                       Novell Professional Volume
                    ─────────── MAIN MENU ───────────

           ▼ What's New              ▼ NetWare Update
           ▼ Service and Support     ▼ Novell Product Manuals
           ▼ Sales and Marketing     ▼ About NetWire
           ▼ Novell Programs         ▼ New User Information



       ┌────────────────────────────────────────────────────────┐
       │ Move to a link (▼) ..........<Tab>, (<Shift><Tab> backward) │
       │ Move to a window from a link .......................<Enter> │
       │ Exit ...............................................<Escape> │
       └────────────────────────────────────────────────────────┘

 1:NSEPro Table of Contents:
```

Figure 12.8

The NSEPro main menu screen.

Practical TIP

To download NetWire files that are on the NSEPro CD-ROM easily, make sure you set the NSE_DOWNLOAD statement from the login script or the client's AUTOEXEC.BAT file, for example:

```
SET NSE_DOWNLOAD = D:DOWNLOAD
```

The **D:** prompt represents the drive where you would have the NSEPro loaded.

Start the NSEPro from your local drive or default network home directory. Include the NSEPro drive location in your AUTOEXEC.BAT path or as a SEARCH mapping in the file server login script.

NSEPro Topics

There are many places in the NSEPro from which you can gather details. The following is a list of available sources of information:

◆ **What's New.** This section covers all the new items added to the NSEPro since the last update.

◆ **Service and Support.** This section is the most important area for network administrators and technical support people.

589

Details included in this section are the following:

Technical Information Documents

Files, Patches, and Fixes (from NetWire)

NetWare Application Notes

Novell Professional Developer Bulletins

Novell Lab Bulletins

Software Testing Program Reports

Top Issues

Printing Decision Trees

◆ **Sales and Marketing.** This section includes the Novell Buyer's Guide, sales tools, and brief descriptions of Novell products.

◆ **Novell Programs.** This section includes information on Novell Education and Certification programs (CNA, CNE, CNI) and the Novell Authorized Service Center program. There also is information on the CNE Professional Association (CNEPA) and the NetWare Users International (NUI) organizations.

◆ **NetWare Update.** This section is used to categorize all available files, patches, fixes, and enhancements for NetWare. You should use this listing to check the files running in your network operating system to make sure they are the most current.

◆ **NetWare Product Manuals.** This section includes complete copies of various Novell products.

◆ **About NetWire.** This section includes information and communication access tools for Novell's electronic bulletin board.

◆ **New User Information.** This section includes NSEPro documentation and information about the NSEPro.

When searching for information in the NSEPro, you should search within each folio where the information might be found. Searching the entire database from the TABLE OF CONTENTS screen does not always yield the best results.

NetWire

Use NetWare as an information resource and peer communications tool to get the best possible solutions to problems in the shortest possible time.

NetWire is an electronic information resource that is available through the CompuServe Information Service. To access NetWire, you must have an account on CompuServe, communications software, and a modem. The communications software can be NovCIM, which will work with DOS, Macintosh, and Windows. There is a graphical user interface that is tailored to work with NetWire called WinCIM (shown in fig. 12.9).

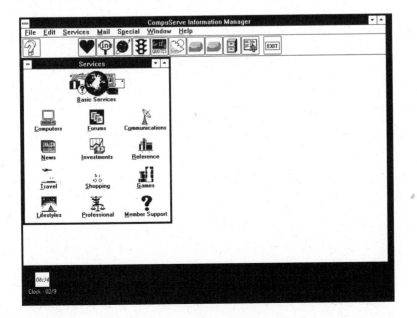

Figure 12.9

WinCIM opening screen for CompuServe.

You can use WinCIM from Windows to dial directly into CompuServe to attach to NetWire, as shown in figure 12.10. WinCIM can be acquired through CompuServe by typing **GO WINCIM** after entering CompuServe.

Figure 12.10

WinCIM connection screen for dialing into CompuServe.

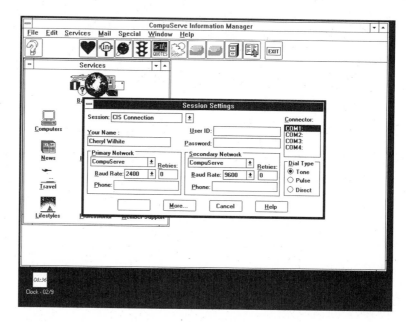

Through NetWire you can find information and help on NetWare issues. These information forums include the following:

◆ **Technical Answers.** System Operators (SysOps) and other knowledgeable NetWire users can answer questions posted here. About 97 percent of the questions are answered within 24 hours.

◆ **Colleague Communication.** You can communicate throughout the world with over 90,000 NetWare users. This area is divided into sections based on product and troubleshooting categories.

◆ **Available Technical Information.** There is an extensive library of downloadable files. These files are updated daily and include the most recent patches and drivers as well as shareware and third-party applications. All files have been scanned for viruses before they are made available to the public. The latest Novell product information, technical bulletins, tips, and press releases also are accessible.

◆ **Corporate Information.** This section includes a calendar of NetWare-related conferences and trade shows. There also is a list of all Novell offices and Novell Authorized Education Centers (NAECs).

NetWire has a list of forums with which you can post and answer messages. To access a list of forums, type **GO NOVFORUM**. The following is a chart of NetWare forums:

 NetWire changes FORUM and LIBRARY information on a regular basis. You should check for these changes often. To study for this CNE test, know what is available from which type of FORUM or LIBRARY structure.

Using MONITOR.NLM for Management Operations

The file server console utility, MONITOR, is one of the primary NetWare troubleshooting tools. To view the MONITOR screen, type **LOAD MONITOR** at the file server. The MONITOR.NLM also provides a full set of statistics used with advanced diagnostics procedures. Notice that MONITOR's main menu, as seen in figure 12.11, displays many statistical summary parameters.

Figure 12.11

The MONITOR.NLM main menu.

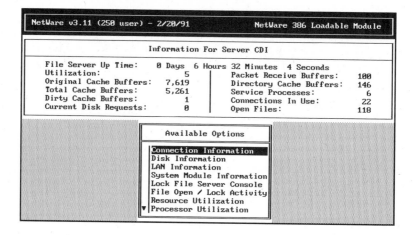

Connection Information

The first item on the Available Options menu is the Connection Information option (see fig. 12.12). This screen shows everyone currently logged in to the network, as well as any clients that have IPX and the shell loaded but are not logged in. Client connections can be cleared by highlighting the connection and pressing Del.

Figure 12.12

MONITOR's Connection Information screen.

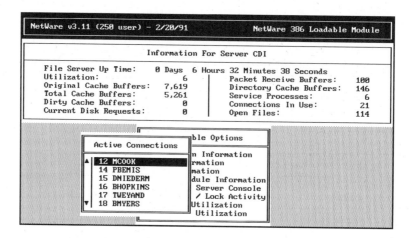

Disk Information

The next option, Disk Information, displays a Drive Status screen for all drives (see fig. 12.13). The Drive Status screen includes Hot Fix Status information.

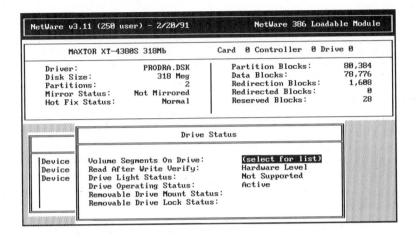

Figure 12.13

System disk drive information.

LAN Driver Information

Each LAN driver loaded at the file server is displayed after accessing the LAN Information option (see fig. 12.14). LAN Driver information shows packet information, addresses, and protocol information. Figures 12.15 and 12.16 show the information available for each of the system's LAN drivers.

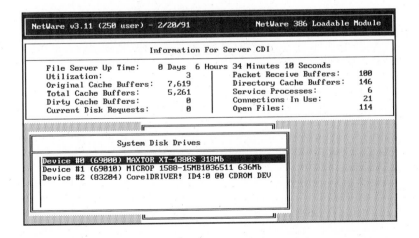

Figure 12.14

LAN Driver Information's screen.

595

Figure 12.15

LAN Driver
Information.

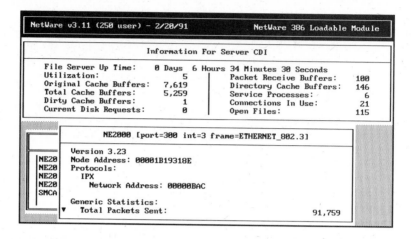

Figure 12.16

LAN Driver
Information.

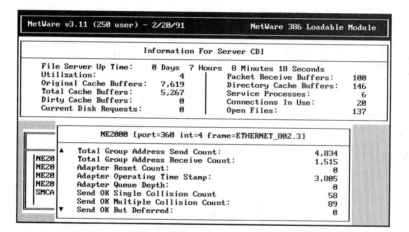

Another important screen to watch is the Resource Utilization option. This MONITOR.NLM window provides information on system memory. The statistics shown in figure 12.17 summarize the memory usage. A detailed explanation of each item can be found in the NetWare 3.1x System Administration reference. As illustrated, 38 percent of server memory is currently free as cache buffers. When this number drops below 20 percent, memory should be added to the file server. The amount of memory needed depends on the circumstances but should be added in increments of 1-2MB.

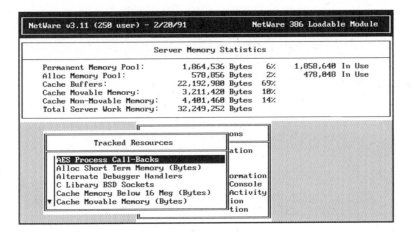

Figure 12.17

The Resource
Utilization menu.

Other related commands that should be checked from time to time enable administrators to check for duplicate node addresses, repair volumes, format a NetWare hard drive, and fix and recover binderies.

Many other programs are available on the market. The NetWare commands discussed in the following sections are a great place to look for solutions to network problems. If these commands do not fix the problem, you may have a hardware-specific problem. If this is the case, test the equipment and look for specialized diagnostic programs.

Checking Connections with COMCHECK

COMCHECK enables the administrator to check client communication and node addresses without being logged in to the network. Figure 12.18 shows the main screen as each workstation calls up COMCHECK.

Figure 12.18

COMCHECK's main screen.

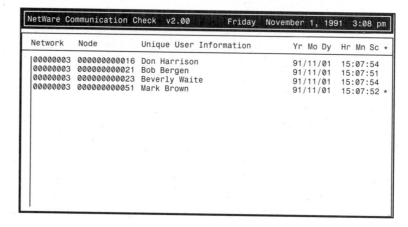

Before using COMCHECK, each client that you want to test must have IPX loaded. COMCHECK asks for unique user information so that each client can be tracked as it is attached.

Pressing Esc brings up an optional menu from which the administrator can modify the Broadcast Delay Period and the Dead Timeout Period. Figure 12.19 shows that the default Broadcast Delay Period is 15 seconds, which is how often this client broadcasts its capability to talk on the cable.

Figure 12.19

COMCHECK's Broadcast delay period.

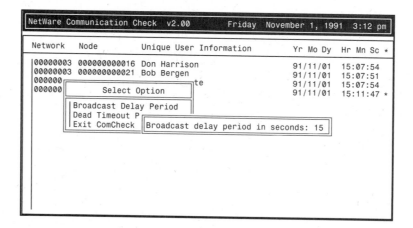

The Dead Timeout Period, as shown in figure 12.20, by default, is 60 seconds. The Dead Timeout Period shows how long a workstation waits for another client to broadcast. If no new broadcasts are received, the client is considered "dead" or unable to respond.

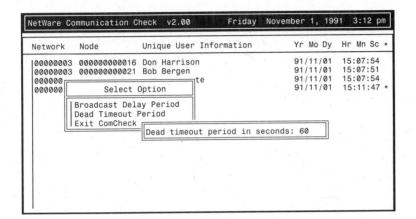

Figure 12.20
COMCHECK's Dead
Timeout Period.

Troubleshooting Utilities BINDFIX and VREPAIR

Included with NetWare are several utilities that enable system administrators to diagnose and repair network problems. These utilities are designed to be used in the event of specific difficulties. In this section, you learn about repairing the binderies with BINDFIX and fixing volumes with VREPAIR.

As a system supervisor, you need to be aware of the items in a network that frequently have problems. Even more important, you need to know where to check for information to prevent system downtime and performance problems.

Repairing the Binderies Using BINDFIX

Bindery files contain all the security information about users and groups on the system. Password requirements, station and time restrictions, and security equivalencies are all kept in these files, which are flagged as Hidden and System files residing in the SYS:SYSTEM directory.

NetWare 3.1x provides three bindery files: NET$OBJ.SYS, NET$PROP.SYS, and NET$VAL.SYS. When a user logs in to the network, the system first checks the NET$OBJ.SYS file to see if the login name is recognized by the file server. After verifying that the login name is valid, the system looks into the NET$PROP.SYS file to see if any account restrictions are on the login ID. If restrictions are there, the final step is to check the NET$VAL.SYS file to find the actual value of the restrictions.

One of the system supervisor's responsibilities is to change the rights for a user. As a manager, you usually make modifications to a user's account from the SYSCON menu or with the GRANT command-line utility, and then exit. Outside of SYSCON, you may notice that it appears as though the change did not take place, and upon reentering SYSCON, you find that the modification has disappeared. This scenario indicates a possible corruption of the bindery files. The BINDFIX utility is designed to examine the bindery files and to mend defects.

The rules for running BINDFIX are simple but should be followed exactly for the most accurate results:

1. Make sure that you are the only user logged in to the system as the user supervisor.

2. Secure the file server with the DISABLE LOGIN command so that no one can log in while you are performing the BINDFIX operation.

3. Place yourself in the SYS:SYSTEM directory and type **BINDFIX**.

BINDFIX is one of the supervisory commands found in the SYS:SYSTEM directory. By default, only supervisor equivalents have rights to this directory.

The program asks two questions: `Would you like to delete mail directories for users that no longer exist?` and `Would you like to delete trustee assignments for users that no longer exist?` BINDFIX attempts to repair the binderies so that users no longer on the system are no longer part of the current security setup.

BINDFIX also attempts to match common network elements on the system. For example, if a user is a member of a group, it checks to see that the group really exists. Likewise, if a user is a member of a group, BINDFIX attempts to verify the existence of that user on the system (see fig. 12.21).

```
Buffers: 40
LAN A Configuration:
  Network Address: 00000003
  Node address is determined automatically.
  Hardware Type: NetWare RX-Net  V1.00 (881010)
  * 0: IRQ = 2, I/O Base = 2E0h, RAM Buffer at D000:0
    1: IRQ = 2, I/O Base = 350h, RAM Buffer at C000:0
    2: IRQ = 2, I/O Base = 300h, RAM Buffer at CC00:0
    3: IRQ = 2, I/O Base = 2F0h, RAM Buffer at DC00:0
    4: IRQ = 3, I/O Base = 2E0h, RAM Buffer at D000:0
    5: IRQ = 3, I/O Base = 350h, RAM Buffer at C000:0
    6: IRQ = 3, I/O Base = 300h, RAM Buffer at CC00:0
    7: IRQ = 3, I/O Base = 2F0h, RAM Buffer at DC00:0
    8: IRQ = 4, I/O Base = 2E0h, RAM Buffer at D000:0
    9: IRQ = 4, I/O Base = 350h, RAM Buffer at C000:0
   10: IRQ = 4, I/O Base = 300h, RAM Buffer at CC00:0
   11: IRQ = 4, I/O Base = 2F0h, RAM Buffer at DC00:0
   12: IRQ = 7, I/O Base = 2E0h, RAM Buffer at D000:0
   13: IRQ = 7, I/O Base = 350h, RAM Buffer at C000:0
   14: IRQ = 7, I/O Base = 300h, RAM Buffer at CC00:0
   15: IRQ = 7, I/O Base = 2F0h, RAM Buffer at DC00:0
Disk Driver: Industry Standard ISA or AT Comp. Disk Cont. V2.01 (890810)
  Channel 0 Configuration:
  * 0: ISADISK    PRIMARY      Verify=ON     I/O=1F0h    IRQ=14
-- More --
```

Figure 12.21

The BINDFIX utility.

When BINDFIX is complete, it returns a message telling you if it was successful or unsuccessful. If unsuccessful, you might have to rely on a version of the binderies previously backed up before the corruption occurred.

If BINDFIX is successful, the next step is to verify that the problem is gone. In this example, go back into SYSCON and try to modify the trustee assignments. BINDFIX creates new bindery files and renames the previous files with OLD extensions. If the problem is gone, the OLD files can be deleted.

NetWare also provides a utility called BINDREST. This utility is intended to restore the "old" bindery files if a problem occurs. To run BINDREST, follow the rules used with BINDFIX and run the BINDREST command. BINDREST replaces the binderies with the OLD extension.

The only time to use BINDFIX, when no problems are evident, is if you have deleted a large number of users from the system. BINDFIX makes sure that the binderies are purged of any information pertaining to the deleted users.

Using VREPAIR

VREPAIR is used to repair NetWare server volumes that have been corrupted, which may result from hardware or power failures. VREPAIR can correct many errors in directories and FATs without damaging data on the volumes.

Use VREPAIR to repair a volume that produces read errors, mirroring errors, or that cannot be mounted. VREPAIR also can correct problems that occur when an attempt is made to add a name space with insufficient memory.

Using VREPAIR on NetWare 3.1*x* Servers

The volume to be tested must be dismounted. In order to test the SYS: volume, you will need to place a copy of VREPAIR.VLM in your DOS boot drive. It then will remain available when the SYS: volume is dismounted.

To run VREPAIR, follow these steps:

1. Dismount the volume by entering the command **DISMOUNT** followed by the volume name.

2. Type **LOAD VREPAIR** (or **LOAD C:\VREPAIR** if you are repairing the SYS: volume).

3. Check the VREPAIR options presented. The options are fully described in the File Server Utilities manual. The default choices are generally acceptable. These choices do the following:

   ◆ Quit if a VREPAIR name support NLM is not loaded. This choice retains name space information on the volume.

♦ Write only changed directory and FAT entries out to disk.

♦ Keep changes in memory for later update.

4. Select Repair a Volume from the Options menu.

5. You will be given the option of having VREPAIR stop for each error or log errors in a text file.

6. When VREPAIR is done, examine the report.

If VREPAIR cannot repair a volume so that it can be remounted, you will need to delete the volume, recreate it, and restore the files from your backup tape archive.

NetWare LANalyzer for Windows

Novell's newest LANalyzer product is based on Microsoft Windows and does not require a specialized interface card. LANalyzer for Windows requires that the LAN adapter use Novell ODI Drivers, and Token Ring interfaces must provide operation in the promiscuous mode. Promiscuous mode enables all network traffic, including errors, to be passed on to the LANalyzer. Many LAN adapters do not support this mode and do not function as a protocol analyzer.

As shown in figure 12.22, Novell's newest protocol analyzer uses the Microsoft Windows environment to provide the user a simple GUI interface. The speedometer-like gauges represent real-time indications of the packet activity currently on the cable.

LANalyzer for Windows also enables you to capture data and save the information to a file for later diagnosis. Although the Windows version does not provide you with the complete flexibility of the DOS version, it does enable you to diagnose most of the problems at a much lower cost.

Figure 12.22

NetWare LANalyzer
for Windows.

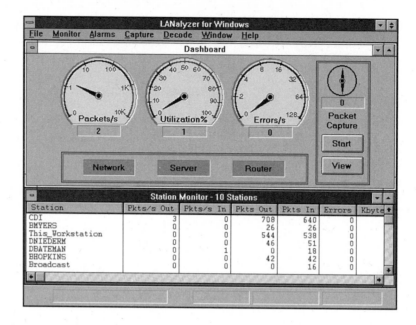

Both versions of the LANalyzer can determine true network utilization and can be used to monitor data of servers, gateways, routers, and bridges along with data to and from a client. The original DOS-based LANalyzer can assist a network administrator in determining how to expand the LAN efficiently by providing a means of stress testing and simulating network traffic.

Both LANalyzer products provide information on the following:

◆ Collisions

◆ Short packets

◆ CRC errors

◆ Network addresses

◆ Packet size

◆ Data patterns

◆ Protocol-related errors and information

The protocol analyzer can be a useful tool if you take time to learn its operation. Protocol analyzers also require a working knowledge of the packet structures for the protocols being examined. The knowledge of the protocol packet structure along with an analyzer, such as the LANalyzer, enables you to inspect your network data with great accuracy.

A product such as a protocol analyzer can be difficult to understand and use without a working knowledge of communications protocols. The protocol analyzer is a high-level tool and is used mostly in large networks to diagnose difficult problems. More details about using the LANalyzer for Windows can be found in Chapter 13, "Optimizing the Network."

NetWare System Messages Manuals

The Novell NetWare System Messages manuals are designed to assist you when problems occur. These manuals are a reference to the messages generated by the operating system, shells, LAN drivers, or ODI drivers. These manuals help you understand what a particular message means and why it occurs.

The System Messages manuals included with NetWare contain three different types of messages. Error messages indicate that a critical problem has occurred and further operation is not possible. Warning messages mean that a problem has occurred, but normal operation should be possible. Status messages simply inform the user or administrator about a particular process.

Each entry in the System Messages manuals contains four separate sections that provide the following information:

- The message as you received it on your client or file server screen; be sure to confirm the exact syntax of the message because many messages are similar

- The source of the message, including information that enables you to determine which program or process sent the message

- ◆ The reason or explanation for why the message occurred

- ◆ The course of action to take; a solution to the problem

When researching a problem in the System Messages manuals, remember that each problem has many variables. These manuals attempt to give possible solutions to the most common problems. Although the Novell NetWare System Messages manuals are very informative, do not consider them the absolute solution. Any and all problems or errors should be examined closely. It also is common that the message you receive is not the primary problem, but the result of yet another problem.

Using Problem Prevention

Being proactive in problem prevention is one of the most important aspects of a network administrator's job. The types of environmental concerns that affect the functionality of a network can include the following:

- ◆ Viruses

- ◆ Security protection

- ◆ Physical dangers

- ◆ Electrical problems

It is difficult to get users, their managers, the person who pays for the network components, or a network administrator who has not experienced the effects of environmental hazards to be proactive in preventing these type of problems. These hidden potentials can cause immediate damage or produce a slow breakdown of the network. With either damage factor, the cost can be great—whether it is in equipment cost or the integrity of data that has been corrupted.

Viruses

 Discuss the role of good backups and virus protection software in preventing and repairing problems generated by viruses.

A virus is a type of computer program that will make changes to the file structure located on a floppy or a hard disk. The virus can copy itself between the hard disk and the floppy—with the potential of being copied to other clients or networks. Viruses can lay dormant for a period of time and then later show their destructive natures. Viruses also can have an immediate effect on your computer.

Viruses can be transferred through modems by accessing other affected networks, computers, electronic bulletin board services, or software bought from a reseller. The files that have the potential to be affected most have the OVL, COM, BAT, or EXE extensions. Boot sectors, file allocation tables, used disk sectors, and memory also can be affected by virus attacks.

To protect your clients from virus infections, try the following precautions:

♦ If you detect a virus, stop work right away (it is not recommended that you save the data that is loaded currently), and remove the virus with the appropriate licensed software.

♦ Scan every floppy you use for viruses. Reminders should be given to users to do this on a consistent basis.

♦ The majority of viruses will attack data-related files. Always make scheduled backups and test them on a regular basis.

♦ Monitor your client for viruses on a regular basis with up-to-date virus-checking software. Make sure your virus disk does not have a virus before and after you use it.

607

♦ When you download a file from a remote source (a bulletin board service or another network), do so to a floppy—then check the floppy for viruses. After you are sure it is clean, transfer the file to a hard drive.

Viruses on the NetWare network are more difficult to acquire. The way the NetWare shell handles DOS calls and access to the file server's FAT tables and disk sectors (must have Supervisor rights) restricts the infections made by viruses. Files on the server have the potential of being affected, but the access to these files can be controlled with setting passwords, directory rights, and file attributes. To protect your network from virus infections, use the following recommendations as needed for your network:

♦ Initiate virus protection programs from the login script.

♦ Inform and educate your users about virus prevention and about the different types of viruses and their symptoms.

♦ Use virus protection software packages that are made to work with NetWare environments such as NetSheild (McAfee Associates), LANProtect (Intel), Inoculan (Cheyenne), and Central Point's Anti-Virus for NetWare.

♦ Always boot up your file server from the same drive— whether it is from the hard drive or the floppy drive.

♦ Certain executable files have configuration files that are required for operation. Because of security restrictions for the executables directory, an administrator should log in as a Supervisor. As part of the login process, the LOGIN_ID identifier variable (Supervisor) in the login script should be set to initiate a virus checker program. That way, editing of network-critical files is covered by security and administrator control.

Security Protection

Compose a realistic and workable plan for environmental security.

Security of the network environment involves more than monitoring access rights to the operating system. In problem prevention, as a network administrator, you must think about all the components that make up the network. A plan must be made to control the risks of all the integrated variables. Problem prevention in the security arena involves the following components:

- ◆ Organizational policy

- ◆ Human resources

- ◆ Environmental components

- ◆ Communications

- ◆ Operation functions

- ◆ Peripheral management

- ◆ Applications and operating system access

There are many types of threats to security that can be a risk to a network. These types of threats can include the following:

- ◆ Interruption—extended periods of downtime can cost a business critically needed productivity.

- ◆ Corruption—files and data could become corrupted and therefore unusable.

- ◆ Disclosure or eavesdropping—passwords or confidential data could be captured and made public to be used by thieves.

- ◆ Destruction—negligence or sabotage can cause the loss of data or important hardware components.

An environmental security plan should be developed in order to prevent these threats from becoming a reality. Creating a plan for security can involve the following functions:

◆ Implement controls that are necessary and cost-effective.

◆ Monitor the system of controls. As a network administrator, you should strongly support these controls.

◆ Evaluate what each network segment does and how a malfunction would affect the organization.

◆ Evaluate the potential threats for this segment by determining the consequences, what is likely to happen, potential overuse, or what possibly could go wrong.

◆ Evaluate the controls that monitor acknowledged threats. As an example, look at the locks to doors and cabinets. Check to see if the control can be defeated easily or potentially over a period of time.

There are many controls you can use as a network administrator that have been proven by others. If you discover a better or new way to ensure environmental security, share it with your peers as soon as possible. This sharing of information can be through phone calls, user groups, or postings on NetWire. The following is a sample listing of types of controls that can be used:

◆ Build into your network a systematic redundancy of critical network components.

◆ Enforce password use, length of password, unique settings, and frequency of password changes.

◆ Monitor and control access to all network components by vendors and maintenance staff.

◆ Change phone numbers on dial-up lines and provide proper security on these lines.

◆ Make sure your hardware error-detection functionality is working on a regular basis.

◆ Restrict access to computer facilities to a "need-to-be-there" basis.

- Monitor your hubs and concentrators for any tapping devices.

- Have your backup tapes and disks stored in a secure, off-site storage facility.

- Have your disaster recovery plans documented and tested in case of an earthquake, fire, flood, or terrorist activity.

- Use software and security applications that use encryption schemes.

- Use devices such as a UPS to protect critical computer equipment and air conditioning for these components.

 Be careful when using the SET UNENCRYPTED PASSWORDS = OFF setting with your operating system. Certain backup programs and older NetWare versions do not recognize newer versions of NetWare client requirements.

 Arrange the physical setup and location of the LAN to minimize the possibility of problems caused by environmental factors.

Physical Dangers

 Determine the vulnerability of existing NetWare sites to environmental damage and take steps to minimize that vulnerability.

Take steps to minimize the vulnerability of new NetWare installations to environmental damage.

There is a cumulative effect of many types of physical problems that can affect how a network operates. A damaging problem to a component does not have to involve an immediate visible effect. The problem can cause intermittent error messages or cause degradation over a period of time that will cause a network to crash. There are certain precautions you can take that can add years to the life of your equipment. The following is a list of physical precautions that can be monitored:

◆ **Air Quality.** Pollutants can be brought into your machine by the cooling fan in the power supply. These pollutants can build up and act as thermal insulation and cause overheating. Nicotine from cigarette smoke, dust, and rubber erasure grit are types of pollutants. Humidifiers can be used to eliminate some static electricity (dry air causes more static electricity).

◆ **On and Off Cycling.** You can eliminate the stress on the components of heating up and cooling off by keeping the equipment turned on in a properly air-conditioned environment.

◆ **Temperature.** Make sure the equipment that has been received in shipment has had time to adjust to the room temperature. Extreme temperature differences inside the hardware components can cause condensation and, later, disaster. Contraction from heat differences can cause chips and other components to "creep" out of their sockets.

◆ **Magnetism.** Do not use magnetic screw drivers, magnetic paper clips, and note posters on or in the CPU. Also, do not leave disks near telephones and stereo speakers.

◆ **Power Failures.** When power is removed abruptly from a running network server, open files can be corrupted beyond repair. Every network server should be protected by an uninterruptible power supply (UPS) that will keep the server running in the event of power failure. This enables the network administrator to shut down the server smoothly.

Electrical Problems

Preventing problems in the electrical environment can be done by taking some simple precautions. Although as a good network administrator you have taken all possible precautions, some problem prevention must be done after an unexpected problem occurs. There are four potential areas of problems that can involve network-related components:

◆ Electro-Static Discharge (ESD)

◆ Noise

◆ Transients

◆ Crosstalk

ESD

Static electricity damage to the newer components in today's network environment can be the most dangerous factor in component loss and network cost. The smaller the components become, the more susceptible they are to static damage. When the risk is not visible, users are less likely to pay to ensure protection.

Static charges can develop in many different ways. One of the most common examples is when you walk across the carpet. Your shoes rubbing on the carpet can build up an electrostatic charge in your body. You often find out about this electrostatic build-up when you touch another person or a doorknob. The human body will not feel a charge until build-up from the charge reaches approximately 3,000 volts. Normal movements such as moving a chair or your foot can generate charges in the 1,000 volt range. We may not feel these charges, but computer components can be damaged or destroyed with static discharges as low as 20 volts. Also, static problems are more likely to happen in low humidity conditions.

Styrofoam cups are one of the biggest conductors of static electricity. Don't place styrofoam items such as coffee cups near network components. Have reusable mugs available. (Besides—it's more environmentally safer!)

There are aspects of your network environment in which ESD protection is very important. Be sure to monitor these closely:

♦ The way you store your spare parts

♦ What the field service technician is wearing (ties not tucked in, jewelry, and so forth) and if the technician is grounded properly

♦ The shipping and receiving areas where network components will be boxed or unboxed

♦ The site where the service call is made

Packaging for components comes in many different types. The shields for ESD protection are static-shielding bags that have a silver-gray tint. Bags with holes of any kind in them are not effective in protection.

There are advantages to investing in a control program. The cost of practicing control can save an estimated 300—4,000 percent on equipment and lost productivity! The benefits of an ESD control program include the following:

♦ Less need for expensive spare hardware

♦ Fewer unexplained intermittent problems

♦ Reduced downtime

♦ Fewer disgruntled users or customers

There are certain rules you should follow in preventing ESD problems. The following are a few recommendations from those who have practiced ESD control:

- Do not place components on a conductive surface such as a metal tabletop.

- Do not touch components by the electrical leads. As an example, do not hold a network interface card by the extension area that you plug into a slot in the CPU.

- Ground yourself properly.

- Do not let anyone touch you when you are working with NICs or inside a CPU; they may cause a static charge event.

Crosstalk

Crosstalk is a type of electrical interference that often does not receive sufficient attention in a network environment. Crosstalk exists when the magnetic fields of two wires transmit interference between each other. The data signals can become distorted and not pass the proper number of packets along the medium. You should use the proper level of wire for your topology, making sure the number of twists per foot meet technical specifications. You also should make sure your data cables are not coiled tightly, that they do not cross fluorescent lights, and that they are not bundled with power cables.

Noise

Noise is a low-current, high-frequency, low-voltage electrical signal that will occur in an observable pattern on diagnostic equipment. Noise can be caused by radio frequency interference (RFI) or electromagnetic interference (EMI) signals. RFI can be sent by cordless telephones, motors, transmitters, and intercoms. EMI can occur from power supplies or large motors. Your computer also can be a source of RFI; this usually is confirmed with an oscilloscope. To reduce the risk of noise interference, you should take the following precautions:

- Make sure your equipment has the proper FCC rating for noise emissions.

- Watch for sources of EMI and RFI emissions and plan accordingly as to where the installation will be located. Observe your local neighborhood for major overhead power lines, radio station towers, or electrical distribution plants.

- Make sure that your equipment and building are properly grounded.

- Do not run cables near fluorescent lighting.

- Put shielding in doors, walls, floors, and ceilings of the area where your network components exist if you are located near radio transmitters.

Transients

Transients are hard to detect because they can occur randomly. Transients involve high voltages and the energy level consists of high current bursts. Your computers are easily susceptible to transient-related problems. Lightning strikes near a cable, an event at a power station, or a sudden large burst of power down the line can create transients.

You should take the following steps to control the risk from transients:

- Consider acquiring a hardware transient suppressor if your neighborhood grid is susceptible to transients.

- Maintain the ground plug in the power cable for your components. Do not convert a three-prong plug to a two-prong plug.

- Do not allow devices such as copy machines, coffee makers, fans, and heaters to be plugged into the same outlets where your network system is attached.

- Use a separate dedicated type outlet (orange plug) for the computer network. This separate circuit should have its own low-resistance ground and circuit breaker.

Study Note

A *transient* is a high-voltage, high-current burst of energy.

A *noise* is a low-voltage, low-current, high-frequency signal.

Review Questions

1. Which of the following is not a troubleshooting technique for eliminating common problems before troubleshooting for more complicated problems?

   ○ a. Checking that all of the computer and network equipment is properly connected.

   ○ b. Making certain that the problem is not just a user's perception of a problem but is a true network problem.

   ○ c. Checking documentation for problem history and configuration information.

   ○ d. Backing up your data for safety, security, and restoring abilities if hard disks are involved.

2. When troubleshooting your network, which three are part of the first steps to take?

   ☐ a. Check documentation for problem history and configuration.

   ☐ b. Find out who is being affected and what are the symptoms of the problem.

   ☐ c. Make an educated guess as to the source of the problem based on the information you have gathered.

   ☐ d. Determine what is being done and when the problem occurs.

3. Starting your troubleshooting at the source component and then checking components until you have reached the final destination component is known as

   ○ a. forward chaining.

   ○ b. hypothesizing.

   ○ c. isolating the problem.

   ○ d. documenting the solution.

4. Which of the following is *not* one of the steps in the troubleshooting model?

   ○ a. Gather basic information.

   ○ b. Develop a plan of attack.

   ○ c. Execute the plan.

   ○ d. Reboot the network file servers.

5. A detailed graphic representation of the network layout is which type of network documentation?

   ○ a. The Network System.

   ○ b. The History and Use of the Network.

   ○ c. Resources for Working with the Network.

   ○ d. The Plan of Attack in Isolating Problems.

6. A current list of phone numbers and escalation levels posted so as to be readily visible is which type of network documentation?

   ○ a. The Network System.

   ○ b. The History and Use of the Network.

   ○ c. Resources for Working with the Network.

   ○ d. The Plan of Attack in Isolating Problems.

7. Which type of network documentation should be kept for a minimum of two years in order to expedite troubleshooting and track network use?

   O a. Cabling documentation of distances, types, and limitations.

   O b. A log of past problems and solutions.

   O c. Client configuration and software documentation.

   O d. Hardware and software upgrade logs.

8. Of the various software tools available, which tool enables you to find out configuration information about your MS-DOS-compatible PC?

   O a. CHECKIT PRO

   O b. Test & Tools

   O c. MTL

   O d. NSEPro

9. When doing a burn-in of new machines or testing upgrades, one particular software package that is useful is

   O a. CHECKIT PRO.

   O b. Test & Tools.

   O c. MTL.

   O d. NSEPro.

10. Which of the following is *not* one of the volumes provided by the Micro House Technical Library?

   O a. The Encyclopedia of Hard Drives.

   O b. The Encyclopedia of Main Boards.

   O c. The Network Interface Technical Guide.

   O d. The Encyclopedia of Backup Devices.

11. Technical information documents, files, patches, fixes, NetWare Application Notes, and Novell Professional Developer Bullets can all be found in

    ○ a. CHECKIT PRO.

    ○ b. Test & Tools.

    ○ c. MTL.

    ○ d. NSEPro.

12. In which section of NSEPro would you find the Novell Buyer's Guide?

    ○ a. Service and Support

    ○ b. Sales and Marketing

    ○ c. Novell Programs

    ○ d. NetWare Product Manuals

13. An electronic information resource that is available through the CompuServe Information Service is called

    ○ a. DOWNLOAD.

    ○ b. NSEPro.

    ○ c. NetWire.

    ○ d. NetWare Update.

14. If you wanted to find a NetWare-related conference to attend, you might search for one on

    ○ a. NSEPro.

    ○ b. NetWire.

    ○ c. WINCIM.

    ○ d. NovCIM.

15. One of the primary NetWare troubleshooting tools is

    ○ a. MONITOR.NLM.

    ○ b. NetWire.

    ○ c. BINDFIX.

    ○ d. VREPAIR.

16. Which of the following is not an option on MONITOR's main menu?

    ○ a. Connection Information

    ○ b. Disk Information

    ○ c. Backup Device Information

    ○ d. LAN Driver Information

17. One of the main uses for the COMCHECK utility is to

    ○ a. administer client communication.

    ○ b. change network node addresses.

    ○ c. broadcast user messages.

    ○ d. check client connections.

18. Which two utilities included with NetWare enable the system administrator to diagnose and repair network problems?

    ☐ a. BINDFIX

    ☐ b. MONITOR

    ☐ c. VREPAIR

    ☐ d. COMCHECK

19. A new employee has been hired in your department. As the system administrator, you set up the user's account and then grant the appropriate rights. Outside of SYSCON, it appears as though your actions did not take effect. What should you consider doing?

    ○ a. Reboot the file server.

    ○ b. Run BINDFIX.

    ○ c. Delete then recreate the user.

    ○ d. Manually modify the NET$PROP.SYS file.

20. If the bindery has become corrupted and you have run BINDFIX, but BINDFIX returned a message indicating that it was unsuccessful, what is the next step that you should consider taking?

    ○ a. Run BINDREST and restore the old bindery files.

    ○ b. Verify that the problem still exists.

    ○ c. Restore an older version of the bindery files that you backed up before the corruption occurred.

    ○ d. Go into SYSCON and modify the trustee assignments for the user who was having problems.

21. VREPAIR can be used to repair a NetWare server volume that has been corrupted under all except which of the following circumstances?

    ○ a. When the volume is producing read errors.

    ○ b. When mirroring errors are being reported.

    ○ c. When a user cannot log in to the network.

    ○ d. When name space cannot be added due to insufficient memory.

22. Which of the following statements about VREPAIR is *not* true?

    ○ a. The volume must be dismounted before loading VREPAIR.

    ○ b. To prevent accidental destruction of a good volume, VREPAIR has no default options.

    ○ c. You should quit VREPAIR if a VREPAIR name support NLM is not loaded.

    ○ d. VREPAIR can write only changed directory and FAT entries out to the disk.

23. Which of the following is *not* a true statement regarding NetWare LANalyzer for Windows?

    ○ a. It requires the use of a specialized LAN adapter card and can run with either ODI or non-ODI drivers.

    ○ b. Token Ring interfaces must provide operation in promiscuous mode.

    ○ c. It uses the Microsoft Windows environment to provide the user a simple GUI interface.

    ○ d. The LANalyzer provides speedometer-like gauges which represent real-time packet activity on the cable.

24. Which two of the following are potential environmental problems that the network administrator should actively prevent?

    ☐ a. Unsecured file server consoles

    ☐ b. Viruses

    ☐ c. Air pollution

    ☐ d. Wire-tapping

25. An environmental security plan should include all except which one of the following?

○ a. Monitoring and supporting system controls.

○ b. Evaluating network segments for the effect of a malfunction on the organization.

○ c. Implementing cost-effective controls.

○ d. Eliminating system redundancy of critical network components.

Answers

1. C

2. A, B, D

3. A

4. D

5. A

6. C

7. B

8. A

9. B

10. D

11. D

12. B

13. C

14. B

15. A

16. C

17. D

18. A, C
19. B
20. C
21. C
22. B
23. A
24. B, C
25. D

Optimizing the Network

This chapter focuses on helping you monitor your network and keep it working at its optimal capabilities. Discussions included in this chapter show you where to look at your network operations for baseline and peak load conditions. As a network administrator or support engineer, you will be required to understand what to do to assist your network in working smoothly, what tools to use, and what should be done in certain conditions. The features covered in this chapter include the following:

◆ Viewing file server performance with MONITOR

◆ Tuning the server with SET commands

◆ Using LANalyzer for Windows

◆ Using PATCHMAN for loading NetWare enhancements

◆ Understanding Packet Burst

◆ Using bridges and routers

◆ Creating a disaster recovery plan

When you are preparing to make decisions on tuning and optimizing your network, you must consider the effects of doing so and rank them according to priority. You must remember that each network is unique and it consists of more than just a file server—it has many other elements to consider, such as the following:

♦ **Environmental factors.** Is your network read- or write-intensive?

♦ **Communications.** Do you route traffic through 16- or 32-bit boards, or split traffic through multiple boards?

♦ **Computer devices.** How do you handle clients, printers, and routers? Do you need a faster CPU?

♦ **Server memory.** Do you have enough? The more RAM you have installed in the server, the better it can perform.

♦ **Users.** How do users perceive their capability of getting the job done?

All these network components can affect the total operations of your environment. You must also consider not only the technical operation needs, but the business needs of your customers. You must determine the nature of their businesses—do they need quick responses on queries or transactions, as in financial institutions, for example? Performance may be the issue rather than response time. In past research polls, customers have indicated that reliability and security of the network are much more important than the optimal tuning aspects of network performance in most cases.

As you put a project plan together to provide yourself a checklist for network changes, look at the big picture first. Make decisions about whether the adjustment will have a positive effect, when you should stop, and when you should reverse your change if it is causing problems. You need to look at each tunable component area of the operating system and select the most effective order for parameter adjustments.

It is important that you do one adjustment at a time and test the effect of this change. Do not expect immediate results; NetWare is a dynamic operating system and it must adjust itself accordingly. Do your homework about the possible effects of the change first—check with other production environments to see what they have done and if the change was effective. It is also important to understand that if you have downed the server for any reason after you have made any changes, and it was working optimally, it can take an unidentified amount of time after bringing the server back up for it to begin the finely tuned processing again.

Viewing File Server Performance with MONITOR

 Use MONITOR to verify performance bottlenecks in the server and suggest possible remedies.

In the NetWare 3.1x Advanced System Administrator course, you are taught an overview of server memory components and how they operate. This is more detail than can be covered in this book, so refer to table 13.1 for a chart of the features of v3.x memory pools. This will refresh your knowledge in relation to what is seen through the MONITOR utility.

Table 13.1
NetWare 3.1x Memory Pools

Memory Pool	Description	Returnable After Use?
File Cache Buffers	Used for caching reads and writes.	Location where other pools return memory.
Cache Non-Movable	Subpool used by NLMs. Causes fragmentation. Nonexpandable.	Returnable to File Cache Buffers, but not as contiguous blocks.
Cache Movable	Subpool owned by NetWare. Used for internal system tables that change size dynamically (ex: DET). Expandable, and has no fragmentation.	Returnable to File Cache Buffers in contiguous blocks.

continues

Table 13.1, Continued
NetWare 3.1x Memory Pools

Memory Pool	Description	Returnable After Use?
Permanent Memory	Used by functions such as communication buffers or directory server; is cache (for one-way allocation pool) for long-term memory needs.	Not returnable unless the server is downed.
Semi-Permanent Memory	Subpool used by LAN and disk drivers.	Returnable only to the Permanent Memory pool, until the server is downed.
Alloc Short Term Memory	Pool used for small short-term allocations such as Drive Mappings and Queue Manager Tables.	Not returnable to Permanent Memory or File Cache Buffers.

The MONITOR file server console utility is used to display detail status features of the network. To bring up the screen shown in figure 13.1, at the file server console prompt, type the following:

```
LOAD MONITOR
```

and press Enter.

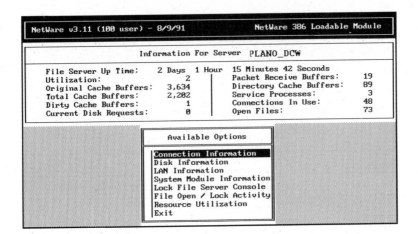

Figure 13.1
The MONITOR opening screen.

As you use MONITOR, you will be able to view details about the following:

◆ Overall activity and utilization of the network

◆ Memory resources that are being used

◆ Connection and open file activity

◆ Disk and LAN driver specifications

◆ Module and resource tag information

◆ Utilization of file server process loads

Note

The MONITOR utility will use a screen saver that resembles a snake traveling around the screen. The utilization of the network dictates the length of the snake around the screen—the higher the utilization, the longer the tail. If you do not want the snake to display, type the following parameter when loading MONITOR:

LOAD MONITOR NS

There are third-party utilities that can replace the snake screen saver. One example of an informational–style screen saver is made by Frye. The screen displays a real-time graph of server utilization with color-coded warnings of threshold exceptions. Threshold numbers will depend on the specific characteristics of all the components in your file server.

The initial screen that you see when you bring up MONITOR includes the Utilization percentage in the upper left column. This number shows what percentage of the file server's CPU is being used during the last second. This is an indication of a network board using CPU cycles or an NLM requesting processing time. You should use tools such as LANalyzer for Windows to keep a history of the CPU usage and compare this to the baseline utilization or normal workload activity of the network. If the utilization is consistently high, it could indicate that you may need to first do some performance tuning and then possibly a file server hardware upgrade (components first).

The Current Disk Requests number found in the bottom left column indicates the number of waiting disk requests for all drives in this server that have been queued by the operating system to be processed. If this number or if the Dirty Cache Buffers statistic is always high, you may want to consider upgrading your disk drive channel (host adapter).

The Dirty Cache Buffers statistic is a number, not a percentage. It is an indication of the number of buffers holding data that need to be written to disk. If this number is more than 70 percent of the Total Cache Buffers number, you need to increase the Maximum Concurrent Disk Cache Writes with a SET parameter at the file server console or in the AUTOEXEC.NCF file.

The Packet Receive Buffers number indicates the number of buffers that the NetWare operating system sets aside to handle client requests until the requests can be processed. The default value of 100 Minimum Packet Receive Buffers can be changed with the related SET parameter in the STARTUP.NCF file. The server will set aside this minimum amount when it is booted up. You also can set the Maximum Packet Receive Buffers to manage memory that affects service processes.

The Directory Cache Buffers number identifies the amount of buffers set aside to handle directory caching. The file server will continue to use these buffers as needed until this value reaches the maximum amount allowed. The increase in the number is determined by the amount of directory searches the file server is being requested to perform. If this number ever goes over 100, you need to increase Minimum Directory Cache Buffers and Maximum Directory Cache Buffers settings.

The Service Processes number is the amount of task handlers allotted for client requests. When this number is exceeded, the network operating system adds more task handlers to manage the requests. Once the memory is allotted for a service process, it is not returned unless the server is downed. This parameter can be changed for those servers with many users and heavy usage. If this number reaches 20, and the server has enough memory, increase the allotment by 5 (range is 5 to 40). If the cache buffers are around 20 percent (which is very low), do not use the Maximum Service Processes setting to alter the current setting. Only use this setting if you need to conserve memory until you are able to get more memory in the file server. Remember that when you change any SET parameters, allow the file server and the operating system enough time to adjust to the changes dynamically.

Other Available Options in MONITOR

The Connection Information selection found in the Available Options menu will show the active connections made to this file server. If you highlight an active connection, it will display the connection's open file records, the user, and the user's segment number and network interface card address. This Connection Information screen is primarily used to view who is using what files and to clear connections that have not been removed in a timely manner.

The disk information screen, as shown in figure 13.2, shows several details for consideration by a network administrator or support engineer. Most hard drives support this screen, but some drivers by a few manufacturers may not support this feature. You

should check this out from the vendor or Novell before purchasing this model. These details about the drives include the
following:

◆ **Hot Fix.** This is used with NetWare's read-after-write verification function to see if data in memory is the same data that
was written to the disk. If it does not match, Hot Fix will
redirect the block of data to the location the disk maintains
for recording the bad block addresses. If the disk is going
bad or the number of failures is high, you should consider
replacing your hard drive.

◆ **Partition Blocks.** This is used to indicate the block size in
this partition. The default size is 4KB blocks, but can be
changed to 8KB or 16KB blocks through the Volume Options
selection in the INSTALL.NLM. This change process is
destructive, so make sure you have a good backup before
changing the block size. If you change the disk block size,
you may need to alter the Cache Buffer Size in the
STARTUP.NCF file with the use of a SET command. It is
important to remember that the cache buffer size must be the
same as the smallest configured block size or the volume
will not mount.

◆ **Data and Redirection Blocks.** This number indicates the
available disk space minus the two percent (or hot fix space)
that the operating system reserves for the redirection blocks
used by the hot fix process. You may want to archive some
data or buy more disk space if you are running out.

◆ **Device Numbering.** This is the location that will show
device numbers (or codes) that can be used for troubleshooting error messages.

◆ **Locating Physical Drives in the Server.** The Drive Light
Status can be used to determine which device is attached to
that number. This can be documented for future reference.
To do this, select System Disk Drives, then the Normal Entry
option. Press Enter over the flashing light option. Watch the
LED lights on your drives in your file server to see which
one responds to this selection.

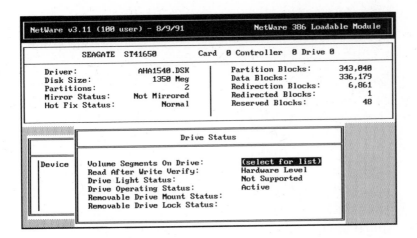

Figure 13.2

The MONITOR Disk Information screen.

The LAN Information selection shows details about each of the drivers loaded for the network interface cards included in the file server. The hooks for these details are pulled in with the NMAGENT.NLM that is loaded automatically during the file server boot up process. As shown in figure 13.3, there are many details you can use for troubleshooting or performance monitoring. In the General Statistics area of the screen, there may be some choices labeled Not Supported. This not supported choice was made by the vendor who developed this driver. Check the v3.1*x* System Administrator's Guide for specifics on NetWare-provided drivers.

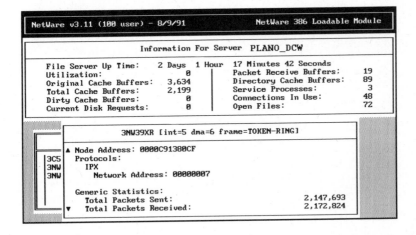

Figure 13.3

The MONITOR LAN Information screen.

In the LAN Information screen, there are several selections that can be proactively monitored for system performance. The following are the basic statistics to consider:

◆ **Total Packets Sent.** This statistic shows the number of packets being sent to the rest of the network through this NIC in the file server. Use this to monitor heavy traffic loads or if the NIC is communicating at all.

◆ **Total Packets Received.** This shows the number of packets the file server has received through this NIC in the file server. These requests include counts from other file server NICs (internal routers) and from clients that need services from other servers on other segments or on the backbone. You may wish to add another NIC of this type to lighten the traffic load on this NIC.

◆ **No ECB Available Count.** ECBs (Event Control Blocks) are the NetWare operating system's way of controlling the number of requests to which a server can respond. If the server runs out of Packet Receive Buffers to store requests, increments are made to this count. The file server will increment the available receive buffers to support incoming requests.

Monitor this statistic and if it starts to reach the default ceiling of 200, increment the Maximum Packet Receive Buffers setting by 10 until you believe the optimal performance for your network is reached. This is done by typing the following at the file server console or including it in the AUTOEXEC.NCF file:

```
SET MAXIMUM PACKET RECEIVE BUFFERS = nnn
```

where *nnn* is equal to the number of buffers required.

If you are using EISA or Microchannel Bus-Mastering cards, you may need to add 5 buffers for every one of these cards installed in the file server. If you are receiving error messages that say No ECB available count, increase the number of buffers to add 10 instead of 5 for each bus-master board.

◆ **Send or Receive Packet Too Big Count/Send or Receive Packet Too Small Count.** If there are any NICs that are malfunctioning on the network, they could be causing undersize and/or oversize packets. This is determined by viewing the Send or Receive Packet Too Big/Too Small Counts statistics.

If the SEND entry is being incremented, you should check the NIC in the server that is using this statistical driver. You may need to replace this card with a known working NIC and test to see if the problem fades away. If not, check NetWire or the NSEPRO for any enhancements to this driver version.

If the RECEIVE entry is being incremented, your trouble-shooting will depend on how the NIC is being used. If the NIC is attached to a backbone, you may need to use a proto-col analyzer, such as Frye's NetWare Management package or Thomas-Conrad's TXD software monitor, to trace the offender. If the file server NIC is attached directly to a segment with clients, the problem possibly is occurring from one of the client stations.

◆ **Receive Packet Overflow Count.** This statistic is responsible for tracking packets that are too large for the cache buffer, causing it to overflow. There possibly could be an applica-tion that is not negotiating the proper packet size with the server before sending the packets of data over the network. Check your client NET.CFG file for packet size settings, and if the server is setting the packet size limit, compare the two for any discrepancies. You also should check the application that could be causing the errors for improper coding of packet size requirements.

◆ **Checksum errors.** The NetWare IPX packet structure con-tains a checksum field that is used to verify that the IPX packets are conforming to the original XEROX header definition requirements. This entry will increase when the required calculated checksum for the packet does not match the checksum byte. If this entry continually increases, look for potential data or transmission problems.

637

The System Module Information selection in the MONITOR utility displays all the resource module information being used by the file server. This section shows the amount of memory and all the types of resource tags each module uses when it has been loaded into memory. If you suspect performance problems that could be related to the use of specific NLMs that are tying up needed memory or resources, unload them, allowing for your server to reallocate the memory dynamically (refer to table 13.1). You may want to reload only those NLMs that are critical to your operating environment. Check with the vendor of those NLMs to see if there is a history of problems; you might want to acquire the latest versions through the vendor's electronic bulletin board system or from NetWire.

The Lock File Server Console selection is used to lock the file server keyboard. This should be done by the network administrator so that no one can access any functions through the file server console. If you do not prevent access without monitoring this server constantly, untrained or destructive users could load unwanted NLMs (viruses, data tapping files, and so forth) or unload necessary NLMs that could be doing backups or UPS monitoring. Knowledgeable LAN people also could access the file server console through RCONSOLE if it is not protected properly.

To lock the keyboard, type in a password you can remember (see fig. 13.4). If you forget the password, the NetWare SUPERVISOR ID must be used to release the lock. The only other way to get around this is to power off the server; in that instance, someone will notice that there was unnecessary tampering going on. You also should view MONITOR for uptime or go through SYSCON for messages in the System Error Log to see if the server has been shut down at any time.

The File Open/Lock Activity selection enables you to display the number of connections that fit the following descriptions:

◆ They are using a particular file.

◆ They are open for a read or write operation.

◆ They show a count for the number of times a deny to read or write to this file has occurred.

- ◆ They show the status of the file if it is locked (no other access allowed) or if it is not locked.

- ◆ They indicate which connection numbers are using this file.

- ◆ They indicate the task number assigned by the client shell.

- ◆ They indicate the record lock status of this file.

You also can view which volumes are currently mounted on your server.

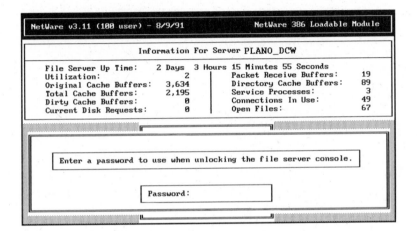

Figure 13.4

The MONITOR file server keyboard lock screen.

If you need access to an application that has been limited to connection use (meter license), and you need access to this application, view, through File Open/Lock Activity on this file, the Conn numbers attached. Then return to Connection Information and find out who is logged in to this connection number. Call or visit that person to see if that user's file has been saved recently (or do it yourself if the user is not there). After you make an extended effort to log that person out correctly, then clear the connection to release the lock status on the file you need.

The Resource Utilization selection enables you to view statistics for memory usage in your file server. As you select this option, the view at the top of the screen will change, as shown in figure 13.5.

Figure 13.5

The MONITOR Resource Utilization screen.

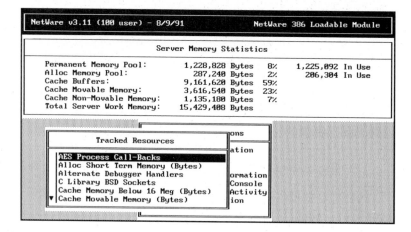

This screen displays the type of memory pools and buffers that can be monitored for determining what areas of memory are being used. The Bytes column represents how many bytes of memory are reserved for this particular memory or buffer. The Percentage column indicates the amount of available memory being used for this particular memory or buffer.

The In Use column indicates how many of the available bytes are being used by this particular memory pool. Seeing this information can assist you in deciding when to add more memory to your file server. You should refer to table 13.1 for detailed memory pool use information. The following list is what is referenced through Resource Utilization:

◆ Permanent Memory Pool includes the statistics for both permanent and semipermanent memory.

◆ Alloc Memory Pool allocates memory for temporary or short term use. This area also supports server advertising, user connection information, and drive mappings.

- Cache Buffers lists all the memory available for data caching. When the percentage reaches around 50 percent, you should start planning to buy more memory and unload any unnecessary modules. If the percentage is around 20 percent, you need to add more memory to your file server immediately.

- The Cache Movable Memory lists the memory buffers, which are rotating free blocks found in a certain range of memory. The NetWare operating system can move these around to improve memory usage. An example of what is found in this area is the function of hash tables.

- Cache Non-Movable Memory displays the amount of memory buffers that are allocated to a program temporarily.

- Total Server Work Memory displays the total amount of working memory for the server to use, minus what was needed for ROM BIOS, DOS, and the SERVER.EXE file booted from the CPU.

The first item to monitor from Resource Utilization for system performance is Alloc Memory Pool. The SET parameter Maximum Alloc Short Term Memory defines the size of this memory pool. The growth in this area could indicate problems with loadable modules that are not releasing memory when they are finished with it. You should check with the vendor, NetWire, or the NSEPRO for any updates about the suspected problem NLMs. Check the resource tags of the System Module Information selection to track the NLMs' growth patterns. You may choose to unload the NLMs that you suspect are causing problems.

The second item to monitor in Resource Utilization is the percentage value for Cache Buffers. If this number drops to around 20 percent, add more memory to your server immediately. Until you get more memory you can increase your cache buffer count temporarily by performing the following steps:

1. Unload any NLMs that are not needed for current operations (SBACKUP, INSTALL, TRACK ON, and so forth).

2. Use the REMOVE DOS command at the file server console prompt to release at least one-tenth of a megabyte of memory from the server being used by DOS.

3. Bring down the server and reboot it to recover unused blocks in the Permanent and Alloc Memory pools.

 Novell will state that the NetWare Operating System is tuned to the optimal defaults right out of the package. They do not encourage that you use any SET parameters to make any adjustments unless you have done enough investigation, performance monitoring, and baseline history research.

Processor Utilization through MONITOR

MONITOR has an additional selection called Processor Utilization that is not brought up at the default load statement entry. This parameter is added with the following entry at the file server console:

```
LOAD MONITOR P
```

The Available Options menu has the added selection that will display CPU utilization. If there is heavy activity placed on the CPU, the process load can be a critical factor in the performance capabilities of the file server. You can mark the processes you want to view by highlighting each one and tagging it with the F5 key, or you can view all the processes by pressing F3 (see fig. 13.6).

The processes and interrupts, the time (milliseconds), count (number of times the process ran during the time sample), and the load percentage (time divided by count) are the types of details found in the Processor Utilization selection of MONITOR. Some of these processes, such as the Polling Process, will always display a high percentage. If any other NLM-type process reaches a load of 60 percent, you need to monitor and possibly unload this potential problem. Do not leave MONITOR loaded with the P option for a long period of time because it takes a lot of server overhead to maintain the detail information screen.

```
NetWare v3.11 (100 user) - 8/9/91          NetWare 386 Loadable Module

                    Name            Time    Count    Load
    Fi
    Ut            0 Process        1,721      18    0.16 %      19
    Or  ADISK  Process                 0       0    0.00 %      89
    To  AES No Sleep Process       2,917      14    0.27 %       3
    Di  AES Sleep Process              0       0    0.00 %      48
    Cu  Auto Remove Right Process  3,145     502    0.29 %      70
        Cache Update Process         239       5    0.02 %
        Communication Ctr Process 21,293   3,618    1.98 %
        Console Command Process        0       0    0.00 %
        Directory Cache Process       61       4    0.00 %
        FAT Update Process           145       9    0.01 %
        Gated Process                  0       0    0.00 %
        HOTFIX Process                 0       0    0.00 %
        Monitor Main Process           0       0    0.00 %
        Polling Process          998,006   3,948   93.18 %
        REMIRR Process                 0       0    0.00 %
        Remote Process             6,496     107    0.60 %
     ▼  RSPX Process                   0       0    0.00 %
```

Figure 13.6

The MONITOR Processor Utilization screen.

Tuning the Server with SET Commands

Tune the server using appropriate SET commands.

As a network administrator or support engineer, you have the responsibility of balancing all of the issues in maintaining an optimally tuned network. You have to make decisions that make good business sense as well as include the issues of performance, reliability, and security.

NetWare has the capability of dynamically tuning itself over a period of time, using the default settings from the core package. There are four areas that the autotuning process will handle:

◆ Cache block sizing

◆ Physical Packet Receive Buffers

643

◆ Service processes

◆ Directory caching

It is difficult to measure the impact of changing any network parameters without the proper tools. Manual tuning can be unreliable without proven tests against which to measure the changes. You must do manual tuning sparingly unless you have your old configurations documented (so that you can put them back the way they were if your changes do not work).

Using benchmark data is not the best way to make decisions about performance tuning. As qualified LAN people, we all know that sometimes vendors have a tendency to stack their tests to their advantage. Each of our networks is unique in the components they contain. Tests usually are unrealistic, focusing on a particular component's performance rather than working with all the devices that represent a production environment.

When altering NetWare SET parameters, you should have a thorough understanding of their functions and impact on the overall network before making any changes. The SET parameters shown in figure 13.7 are never changed unless an NLM has been loaded that requires its modification for its service. You should base your performance tuning decisions on the actual workload of the file server.

Figure 13.7

SET parameters entry screen on the file server console.

```
:set
Setable configuration parameter categories
    1. Communications
    2. Memory
    3. File caching
    4. Directory caching
    5. File system
    6. Locks
    7. Transaction tracking
    8. Disk
    9. Miscellaneous
Which category do you want to view:
```

Tuning the v3.*x* File Server

There are several parameters that the SET command can affect in adjusting memory and performance processes in the file server. These parameter settings are in the following categories:

◆ Memory

◆ Communications subsystem

◆ File and directory caching

◆ The system processor

Memory

NetWare is a dynamically oriented operating system and will use memory for caching files extensively. As a network administrator or support engineer, you must have a complete understanding of the memory processes of the file server before you consider any fine-tuning adjustments. The items listed below are important memory parameter considerations:

◆ The more RAM in the file server, the more effectively your operating system can allocate the basic functional needs dynamically. As the use of the server increases, values will increment based on NetWare's "wait and see" algorithm for each process. This is done to make sure the system is not increasing its numbers based on temporary spikes in memory demand.

◆ The MONITOR utility is an important tool for observing memory allocations for a given number of resource tags. An NLM may have a resource tag in several different memory pools. The combination of these allocations has an effect on the total amount of memory that the server allocates. Check on these resource tags for potentially bad NLMs that are taking too much memory from several different areas. These NLMs can cause performance degradation or server crashes.

645

◆ Fragmentation of memory can occur in the Cache Non-Movable pool when NLMs are loaded and unloaded frequently. Volumes mounting or dismounting frequently also can cause fragmentation. There may not be a contiguous block of RAM to load a needed NLM such as MONITOR, even though the File Cache Buffer percentage seems sufficient. The only way to reorganize all the fragmented blocks is to down the server and bring it back up again. It would not hurt to down your file server periodically in order for the operating system to "clean itself up" when the server is powered back on.

The following are two important memory SET parameters:

◆ **MAXIMUM ALLOC SHORT TERM MEMORY.** This parameter controls how much memory the operating system can allocate to the Alloc Short Term memory pool. The file server will display warnings when operating system functions cannot be completed because this memory pool has reached its limits.

This parameter can be incremented in 1MB increments, to a maximum of 32MB. The default value is 8,388,608 (8MB). The range of values is 50,000 to 33,554,432 (32MB).

◆ **CACHE BUFFER SIZE.** Performance can be enhanced by increasing this parameter if block allocation sizes are more than 4,096 (4KB) on all volumes. This parameter is set in STARTUP.NCF, having additional possible values of 8192 (8KB) and 16,384 (16KB) (defaults at 4KB). Having a Cache Buffer Size that is larger than the block allocation size will decrease performance and will waste memory space. The file server will not mount any volumes that have a block allocation size smaller than the cache block size.

Remember, setting block sizes too large can waste disk space. When a block allocation size is set at 8KB and the file is 3KB in size, you lose 5KB of space. If you leave the default block size at 4KB, the file only loses 1KB of disk space. You need to evaluate your overall file space needs before you set the block size. If you have to change this setting, make sure you have a good backup beforehand. This change process is done through the INSTALL.NLM and is destructive to the volume.

The Communications Subsystem

Tuning the communication subsystem involves all of the components involved with the LAN's I/O channel performance. The factors that affect performance include the following:

◆ Network Interface Cards (NICs)

◆ Packet size

◆ Communication buffers

◆ SAP traffic

◆ The Packet Burst protocol

The parameters and important performance considerations for the communications subsystem include the following:

◆ When the client attaches to the file server, the packet size between it and the file server is negotiated at this time. The size of the packet is a process that is related to the type of the network interface card (NIC). It is better to use the largest allowable packet size, except when the file server's NIC will not allow the larger packet or the packet has to cross a router that does not understand the larger size. You can use a set parameter in the STARTUP.NCF file to increase the default packet size of 1,514 bytes. The proper syntax for this statement is the following:

```
SET MAXIMUM PHYSICAL RECEIVE PACKET SIZE= value
```

You must use the equal sign between the statement and the value. If your driver size is unknown, the following is a list of suggested (not maximum) packet sizes:

ARCnet	4,202
Ethernet	1,514
Token Ring (4 Mbps)	1,202
Token Ring (16 Mbps)	4,202

Newer ARCnet cards can handle packet sizes of 4,202, but older base ARCnet packet sizes are limited to 618. Older Token Ring 4 Mbps NICs will not always allow a packet size of 4,202, but it never hurts to try.

◆ NetWare uses a default packet size of 512 bytes when there are routers to be crossed. Because the NetWare operating system cannot anticipate what type of NIC will be on the other side of the router, you can use an NLM called Packet Burst to override this limitation. An earlier version of this Packet Burst NLM was called the Large Internet Packet Exchange (LIPX). The network administrator or the support engineer has the responsibility of determining if all the routers can pass the negotiated packet size between the transmitting nodes. NetWare v3.12 will provide this feature as a default.

◆ The Service Advertising Protocol (SAP) that advertises the services of gateways, print servers, and file servers can affect the efficiency of the communication subsystem. When clients initially attach to the network, they use SAP communication to find the nearest server. Routers will broadcast SAP traffic to exchange the different server's information—this is not the same as the Routing Information Protocol (RIP). SAP traffic can be limiting to large multiple server networks that include routers. The NetWare Service Advertising Restrictor (NSAR) that is bundled with NetWare's Multi-Protocol Router, can be used to mask or filter SAP packets, minimizing the SAP broadcast traffic on a network. The main module of the NSAR, RESTRICT.NLM, enables the network administrator or support engineer to view the list of services to be advertised. Availability of certain entries can then be restricted on particular segments to reduce the traffic flow.

The following SET commands also can be used to tune the communications subsystem:

◆ **MINIMUM PACKET RECEIVE BUFFERS.** The default setting is 10 and the maximum value allowed is 1,000. This parameter must be set in the STARTUP.NCF file. This command will establish the optimal performance level in buffering packets for this file server. It is used to avoid potential system performance degradation until the server boot up process is complete. Performance may degrade if processes must wait for allocation of Packet Receive Buffers. If performance characteristically suffers while Packet Receive Buffers are allocated dynamically soon after the server is booted, this parameter can be increased to force NetWare to allocate additional Packet Receive Buffers after the server is booted.

◆ **MAXIMUM PACKET RECEIVE BUFFERS.** The default setting is 100 and the range is 50 to 2000. Changes are established at the file server console command line or in the AUTOEXEC.NCF file. This is used to avoid excessive use of communication buffers during server usage peaks.

◆ **NEW PACKET RECEIVE BUFFER WAIT TIME.** The default setting is 0.1 seconds with a maximum allowed of 20 seconds. Changes are established at the file server console command or in the AUTOEXEC.NCF file. You may want to use this command to control the amount of time the operating system will wait before spawning a new buffer.

File and Directory Caching

As part of the research you do in deciding whether your network needs tuning, you must determine whether your environment is read- or write-intensive. You can fine-tune these networks with the resources that you have, but it is best to have a lot of memory available for the operating system to allocate it dynamically as it is needed. The amount of File Cache Buffers that you should have available for your server should be at least 40–60 percent of total server memory. If you are working with image data files, available

649

File Cache Buffers should be more than the 60 percent of the total server memory amount.

The following are recommended settings for file caching parameters:

◆ **MAXIMUM CONCURRENT DISK CACHE WRITES.**
Setting this parameter higher will favor write-intensive environments. Decreasing this parameter will help read-intensive environments. The default value is 50, the range settings are from 10 to 100. This parameter will determine how many write requests are queued for the disk I/O control. The amount queued is displayed in MONITOR with the Dirty Cache Buffers numbers.

◆ **CACHE BUFFER SIZE.** The default value is 4,096 (4KB) with 8,192 (8KB) and 16,384 (16KB) settings available. The Cache Buffer Size and the Volume Block Size must be identical in order for the operating system to run in an optimal mode. Certain applications require larger block sizes and these should be kept on a separate volume. If the file server has mixed block sizes with these volumes, the Cache Buffer Size must be configured for the smallest volume block size or the volume will not mount.

◆ **TURBO FAT REUSE WAIT TIME.** The default setting is 5 minutes and 29.6 seconds. The range is 0.3 seconds to 1 hour, 5 minutes and 54.6 seconds. When the operating system needs to index and access files that exceed 64 FAT entries, NetWare will create a turbo FAT index for each of these large files. Memory in the file server will be flushed if these large files have not been used in the allotted wait time. To keep the performance level up on accessing these large files, the interval wait time can be increased to keep these files in server RAM a bit longer.

◆ **MINIMUM FILE CACHE BUFFERS.** The default setting is 20, with a range of 20 to 1,000 available. This is set to maintain a minimum amount of file cache buffers in RAM that the other memory pools cannot borrow from. A setting that is too high will reduce the number of NLMs that can be loaded on the file server at one time.

◆ **IMMEDIATE PURGE OF DELETED FILES.** The default value is OFF. The file server will perform a number of tasks that will keep a deleted file in the hidden directory on the volume from which it was deleted. This hidden directory on the volume is called DELETED.SAV. To improve security and increase performance, turn this setting to ON. The drawback to this is that you will have no immediate access to deleted files unless they have been backed up on a regular basis.

The following are recommended settings for directory caching parameters:

◆ **Name Space Support.** If you will be using MACs, OS/2, or NFS machines, you need to add this to each volume where the files for the applications will reside. You should do this setup at volume creation so that the directory entry tables will provide sequentially consistent forks to the file locations. You also should create separate volumes for the different name space support styles and use these volumes for only these types of files.

◆ **MAXIMUM DIRECTORY CACHE BUFFERS.** The default setting is 500 with the range of values from 20 to 4,000. This parameter is used to control the number of directory cache buffers allocated by the server. If directory searches seem sluggish, increase this setting. If you determine too much memory is being allocated for your current operating system, reduce this value.

◆ **MINIMUM DIRECTORY CACHE BUFFERS.** The default setting is 20 with the range of values from 10 to 2,000. This parameter needs to be high enough that directory searches can be done quickly, but not high enough to degrade system performance.

The System Processor

There are many components that affect the tuning process in a network environment. If you have checked out all the software performance factors and they seem to be optimally set, as a last resort, check the processor in the file server CPU. A more powerful CPU may or may not be the answer. Before you make an investment, try to rent, lease, or borrow a different server to see if this is the real problem.

Remember that the MONITOR utility will use the Utilization statistic to check on CPU cycles. Also, use the Processor Utilization selection in the Available Options menu as a tool for checking on loads to the server. As an example, check the NIC card in the server and see if it is causing an interrupt to put unacceptable demands on the server processing load.

Tuning the v4.*x* File Server

The v4.*x* operating system is different from any previous operating system made by NetWare. The enhancements made with this product have provided a performance improvement over earlier NetWare versions. The areas of enhancement include the following:

◆ **Optimized Code Paths.** These include directory searches, reads, writes, opens, and closes to files. NetWare 4.*x* has a slightly higher utilization of the CPU because of the background tasks it performs. More time is spent on background processes during light workloads. The improvements in the core code paths are apparent in heavier workloads—the utilization overhead is decreased with the change in priority of operating system tasks.

◆ **Disk Block Default Size.** The new default disk block sizes are based on volume size, not the performance criteria as set in v3.1*x*. The recommended default block size for all volumes is 64KB. The 64KB block allows the disk channel to be accessed by network users more efficiently for read and write requests. It also allows a more efficient access to mass storage devices such as CD-ROM and magneto-optical drives.

The newer defaults are listed below:

Volume Size	Default
Less than 32MB	4KB
32 to 149MB	8KB
150 to 499MB	16KB
500 to 1,999MB	32KB
2,000MB and up	64KB

◆ **Block Suballocation.** Unlike v3.1*x*, this feature will allow multiple file endings to share the same block. The unit of suballocation within a block is a single sector, which can contain 512 bytes. The benefit is that you do not have as much wasted disk space as in v3.1*x*, but the overhead for the operating system to manage this process is increased.

◆ **Read-Ahead.** As each file open request is made, NetWare 4.*x* will begin to track file access patterns. If it is determined that the file is being accessed sequentially, data will be moved into cache in a staged mode. Read-ahead will start when the data being accessed has reached the midpoint of the block. If the file is being accessed in a random mode, read-ahead is not started because of the increase in overhead. Read-ahead requests are placed in queue in a lower priority than regular reads and writes. Larger disk block allocations allow these types of read tasks to be accomplished in a single rotation of the disk, which improves performance in accessing data more quickly.

◆ **Prioritization of Disk Requests.** This is used to balance the requests to the operating system for reads and writes, rather than having one dominate the other. The disk elevator that loads these requests does not use the normal first-in, first-out (FIFO) build sequence. There are four bins that provide a tier of priority in what the disk elevator can seek. These bins include the following:

Critical Events (TTS Log file writes)

Read Requests

Write Requests

Read-Ahead Requests

The critical events are guaranteed events and always are processed with a greater priority than the other bins. Reads are foreground tasks, writes are background tasks, and read-ahead requests use a priority level that does not interfere with any other events. The priority level is calculated by taking a percentage of current requests from each bin and loading them into the disk elevator. The higher the priority, the more requests get placed in the elevator.

File and Directory Caching SET Parameters

As with NetWare 3.1x, it is best to have a lot of memory available for caching in the file server. In NetWare 4.x, many types of processes that the operating system must manage are taking place at the same time. Depending on whether your environment is read- or write-intensive, use the following SET parameters to prevent bottlenecks in file and directory access:

◆ **MAXIMUM CONCURRENT DISK CACHE WRITES.** The default is 50, with a range of 10 to 4,000. This is beneficial to large disk arrays that can handle many disk requests. The default number possibly could be reducing the performance on these types of systems.

◆ **DIRTY DISK CACHE DELAY TIME.** The default is 3.3 seconds, with a range of 0.1 to 10 seconds. This can be used for file servers that have file cache to spare. Your workload may include a high number of sequential writes, and you could improve your performance and disk space issues. By delaying the write long enough to have two write requests satisfied with one write request, it would improve the probability of impacting one block to complete this request.

The following are recommended settings for directory caching parameters:

- **MAXIMUM CONCURRENT DIRECTORY CACHE WRITES.** The default is 10, with a range of 5 to 50. This is recommended for file servers that have a large directory cache that is frequently accessing large numbers of small files, and your disk channel has a high throughput rate. A directory cache write is created every time a directory modification, addition, or deletion is processed by the server through the disk channel.

- **DIRECTORY CACHE BUFFER NONREFERENCED DELAY.** The default is 5.5 seconds, with a range of 1 to 300 seconds. Changing this setting provides no benefit to performance if the directory cache is tuned to the user's workload environment. This parameter is the amount of time the system will wait before the directory cache buffer is a candidate for release from memory.

- **DIRTY DIRECTORY CACHE DELAY TIME.** The default is 0.5 seconds, with a range of 0 to 10 seconds. If your file server has a large directory cache, your performance could benefit by increasing this delay time.

File System Parameters

In NetWare 4.x, you can link multiple servers together with the appropriate commands and create one large virtual server. The accessibility of these disks on these servers can create many files, requiring the operating system to manage the reliability of finding this data. The file system can be set to improve the storage and reliability of data by using the following SET parameters:

- **IMMEDIATE PURGE OF DELETED FILES.** The default is OFF. Excess disk space is used to store deleted files that can be recovered immediately or at a later period. The performance tradeoff is that the system has to use overhead to manage this function of tracking the deleted files. Novell recommends that this be left at the default.

♦ **ENABLE DISK READ AFTER WRITE VERIFY.** The default is ON. You can view through MONITOR's Disk Information for the current driver setting for read-after-write verification. This setting provides a global variable to the disk driver that is ignored most of the time. Reliability is more important than performance, so leave this turned ON.

NCP Packet Signature Parameters

The proper transmission of packets and the level of security involved in this process is an important function of NetWare. The communication between the server and the client can be monitored by the network operating system and the client's shell. Upon login, a packet signature is established to determine to what level data passing is allowed. The accuracy of these packets is included in this process. Use the following SET parameters to determine the levels of packet management for NetWare 4.*x*:

♦ **NCP PACKET SIGNATURE OPTION.** The default is 1, with options 0, 2, and 3 also available. Packet signing is recommended for networks requiring a high level of security. This parameter sets a level of this security feature for enforcement, in conjunction with the client setting in the NET.CFG file called SIGNATURE LEVEL=. The option requires a signature with each NCP packet sent between the file server and the client. Refer to your client installation guide for details on the setup options and the explanation of what each level does. Performance issues are significant in production environments when it is related to normal operations. The Login process has a minimal performance effect because it is done infrequently. You can get more details on performance recommendations in the December 1992 *NetWare Application Notes* in an article titled "NCP Packet Performance Considerations" (which can be found on your NSEPRO).

♦ **ENABLE IPX CHECKSUMS.** The default is 1, with options 0 and 2 also available. This is not supported by the Ethernet 802.3 frame type. A checksum provides an error detection method that calculates the total number of bits that encompass the data being sent between one computer and another. The end that receives the data transmission will repeat this checksum process and compare it to the original value for accuracy. This feature is available for third-party developers to capture with IPX APIs so that they can monitor data corruption during transmissions. Novell does not recommend the use of this setting without justification because of the overhead in performance it will demand from the operating system.

Using LANalyzer for Windows

Use protocol analyzer to diagnose performance problems and help alleviate overloaded networks or servers.

As a network administrator or support engineer, you should be aware of as many tools as possible that can help you monitor your network. A protocol analyzer can help you monitor how your network is currently operating. This tool provides information about variable trends such as a Cyclical Redundancy Check (CRC). The CRC can measure the integrity of a transmitted block of data over a time period. The protocol analyzer can monitor network traffic on a packet-by-packet basis, decode packet samples, and provide reports in a graph format. A protocol analyzer is a good tool to monitor network performance, troubleshoot network errors, assist in optimizing the network, and provide information for growth plans.

Novell uses the term *network analyzer* to refer to a protocol analyzer.

Protocol analyzers can be software only, or have a hardware and software combination. They can vary in price and functionality. High-end analyzers are faster, can decode improperly framed packets, can transmit traffic and receive data at the same time for testing purposes, and have more decodes for use.

The discussion in this chapter is restricted to the software tool provided by Novell called LANalyzer for Windows. Novell used to support a hardware-based tool called LANalyzer for Ethernet or LANalyzer for Token Ring. The license to the hardware-based product was sold to Network Communications Corporation and is available only from that company.

Steps for Working with Packet Decodes

Decoding packets is sometimes an overused feature in a protocol analyzer. Resources from within the analyzer, such as alarms and trends analysis, can provide the information needed to solve more than 90 percent of the problems. The information in these steps can be used with any protocol analyzer. Use the following steps for preparation in decoding packets on a network:

1. Make sure that the tool you are going to use is configured properly and is functioning correctly.

2. Look at performance data, such as bandwidth utilization and transmission errors, before you capture specific packets. The data that you view may give you enough details on developing strategies for solving the problem.

3. Set the definition in the analyzer for what type of packets you want to capture (Ethernet or Token Ring) and where from (x to y).

4. Start the initial capture routine.

5. Define how you want the analyzer to display the data being captured. Do you want to see raw hex data, the decoded version of the data, or both types? Options for this information vary among types of protocol analyzers.

6. Check the data for any inconsistencies or errors.

7. View the data from the packet and narrow to the area or field from which the potential problem could be coming. Develop a potential solution or hypothesis, then implement this solution. After this change has been made, take additional measurements to see if your fix worked.

Using the LANalyzer for Windows Tool

The LANalyzer for Windows (LZFW) is a software tool that is maintained by some highly technical Novell engineers who understand very detailed levels of data communication functions. Read the documentation carefully before you install the product for setup requirements. The screen shown in figure 13.8 is the main display entry point. This screen is also called the *dashboard*.

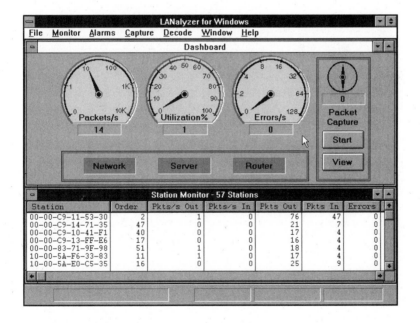

Figure 13.8

The LZFW dashboard screen.

The LZFW does not require that you be highly technical to use this product successfully. It will aid you as a network administrator or support engineer in gathering data, sorting the information, and providing reports on how your network is functioning.

Ways to Use LZFW

You can monitor real-time activity by using the gauges on the dashboard or information from the detail windows or alarm indicators. The ring monitor screen displays information specific to the Token Ring protocol. The station monitor section displays node information on errors and the traffic each generates. There are separate screens for information on routers and servers on the network.

You can plan for growth in your network by identifying the trends, diagnosing problems as they occur, and understanding what are usual measurements for your environment. Trend graphs can be used to view a period of activity over time (see fig. 13.9). There are graphic displays available for percentage of utilization, packets, and kilobytes transmitted.

Figure 13.9

A LZFW Trend Graph example.

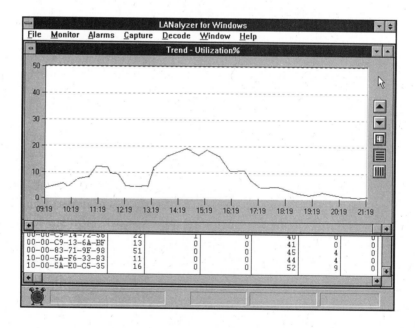

There are many types of reports that can be printed for documentation history. These reports also can be used to present to the vendor for support, to your management or peers, and to the customer for justification reasons. The types of reports that can be generated include alarm logs, station monitor data, ring monitor data, trend graphs, and detail graphs.

LZFW displays alarm indicators in the bottom left corner of the screen to indicate that there is some unusual activity occurring on your network (see fig. 13.10). When you double-click on this alarm indicator, the LZFW window displays information about the network activity that caused the alarm to go off. A NetWare Expert icon appears when the alarm indicator occurs. This enables you to get more details about the causes of the alarm and some possible solutions to these problems.

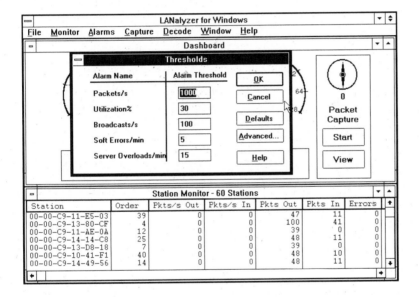

Figure 13.10

LZFW alarm threshold defaults.

Using the LZFW and the OSI Model

The following list of problems is used to diagnose trouble that can be found at the Network Layer and above on Ethernet and Token Ring networks:

◆ Address conflicts and invalid addresses

◆ Routing inefficiencies and configuration problems

The following list of problems is used to diagnose trouble that can be found for Ethernet and Token Ring networks at the Data Link Layer:

- ◆ Faulty LAN drivers
- ◆ Different Data-Link protocols used by the file server and the clients

The following list of problems is used to diagnose trouble that can be found for Token Ring networks at the Physical Layer:

- ◆ Crosstalk on unshielded twisted-pair cabling
- ◆ Defective network interface card
- ◆ Broken twisted-pair cable (shielded or unshielded)

The following list of problems is used to diagnose trouble that can be found for Ethernet networks at the Physical Layer:

- ◆ Defective transceivers, repeaters, or NICs
- ◆ Segment not properly terminated or grounded
- ◆ Crosstalk on unshielded twisted-pair cabling
- ◆ Bad connections to the hub
- ◆ Defective 10BASE-T hubs
- ◆ The spacing of taps on thick ethernet not following requirements

Using LZFW to Baseline Network Performance

When you *baseline*, you are taking a measurement of the performance of your network over a period of time. You can take this detailed information and insert it into reports such as trend graphs to keep as reference for network history documentation. Alarm thresholds can be set based on the information from your baseline reports. When a change in the network environment occurs, either higher or lower than the baseline, it is called an exception to normal performance.

The LZFW can capture data for a period of six months, and you should use at least a one-month period of data to represent the baseline of your network. If you need to keep data for longer than six months, develop some spreadsheets with macros to help you calculate the differences. You may want to be careful about trying to print all the reports from a long period of time because they can be rather lengthy. (Save a tree, do not waste paper!)

As part of your baseline information, you want to track data on routers on your network, your most active users, and activity from your servers. This information can be used to help establish your basic network load balance for planning of future growth.

 Note   To make a list of all your local servers and routers, use the Route and Server monitor screens in LZFW to gather the details.

To determine which stations are the most active, use the packets-per-second and the kilobytes-per-second measurements.

Setting Alarm Thresholds

The setting of thresholds needs to be based on your devices and the functionality of your entire network. Larger networks may require higher threshold settings than what usually are recognized as standard defaults. In the Alarm-Threshold selections in LZFW, Novell provides some defaults that are referenced from their experiences with standard networks. These defaults are seen in figure 13.10.

Macintosh clients that use the AppleTalk protocol or System 7 identify themselves as servers on a NetWare network. If they log out or power off, they potentially can send an alarm condition that a server has gone down. If the Advanced Alarms are enabled, there is no threshold tolerance for when they occur. You should view these notices immediately when they happen.

Alarm Indicators

An unusual network activity will activate a network alarm when the threshold has been exceeded. The LZFW package will respond to these alarms in the following ways:

◆ An alarm clock will appear in the lower left corner of the Station Monitor display.

◆ The network alarm indicator on the main dashboard will turn to red.

◆ A ticker-tape message will begin to display in the bottom left corner of the window.

◆ If you have enabled the sound for the alarm, it will begin to beep. This is a benefit when you have LZFW running in the background behind your other open Windows applications.

Dealing with Network Alarms

The NetWare Expert is an artificial intelligence type database that contains information on the errors occurring and the possible solutions for these types of errors. You do not have to be knowledgeable at a technically conceptual level to work with this information. The following are some examples of what the NetWare Expert can handle in dealing with Ethernet issues:

◆ Oversize or undersize packet errors

◆ Errors occurring because the threshold for error rates, packets per second, fragment error rate, percentage of utilization, CRC error rate, or broadcast rates have been exceeded

◆ Jabber errors

Note To work the NetWare Expert, use the following steps:

1. Read the error message.

2. Open the error log.

3. Ask the NetWare Expert for help with the problems and their solutions.

Typical Ethernet Errors Reported by LZFW

Ethernet uses a collision-oriented protocol in its communication process (see Chapter 6, "Working with Network Interface Card Configurations," the CSMA/CD example). There are several potential areas to attack when troubleshooting Ethernet because it is such an active protocol.

LZFW was originally developed to monitor Ethernet traffic, and it is used as the primary example for troubleshooting in the NetWare Service and Support course. The following items are recommended details to be aware of when using LZFW to monitor Ethernet networks:

◆ **CRC/Alignment Error.** This is indicated when a packet does not divide evenly by the number of bits in a byte (8) or when the packet has an incorrect Frame Check Sequence (FCS). If the packet seems to be of normal length, cable problems usually are the cause of this error. Use a tool such as a TDR to scan the cable and check the routing and all connection points. Look for crosstalk or noise directed to the cable also. If these steps do not solve the problem, replace the transceiver or the NIC.

◆ **Fragment Error.** Packets with less than 64 bytes and an incorrect FCS usually are indicated with this type of error. Ethernet is a collision-oriented topology and it will have some errors that are usual because of this medium. If the network load is high, and the fragment errors are more than five percent of the total number of packets, you may need to consider including bridges or routers in your network. If this error occurs when the network traffic is low, you may need to isolate a faulty transceiver or network board and have it replaced.

◆ **Less Common Errors.** The following are less common errors:

 ◆ Jabber errors are packets with a faulty FCS and more than 1,518 bytes.

 ◆ Undersized packets are packets with a faulty FCS and less than 64 bytes. The Asynchronous Transfer Mode (ATM) is a newer technology that competes with FDDI for use on high-speed WAN links and uses a 53-byte packet size. LZFW may report the ATM packets as undersized.

 ◆ Oversize packets are packets with a good FCS but they are longer than 1,518 bytes.

Diagnosing Overloaded Networks

When the bandwidth utilization on the cable media seems to have a slow response, there could be too many devices trying to transmit their kilobytes of data on this system. If you set your alarm thresholds properly, an overloaded network is easy to find. The users will tell you first when the network is running slowly. Another indicator of network saturation can be found in LZFW by the higher number fragments and utilization percentage. The symptoms of this type of overloaded network can include the following:

◆ Clients send duplicate requests.

◆ You get an error message of `Error receiving/sending on network (file server name)`.

◆ Response time for loading or opening applications seems to be slow.

There also can be several types of causes for network overload to occur:

◆ Unusually large file transfer (CAD drawings) cross the network.

◆ The number of devices on the network have increased since the original design.

◆ The number of applications that are being launched from the file server has grown.

At the time the NetWare client transmits packets of data on the network, the IPX Retry Count is set to 0 and the IPX Receive Timer Counter starts to increment its counter. The client will do the following if the file server does not respond within the Receive Timeout maximum:

◆ Reset the Receive Timeout counter to 0.

◆ Increment the Retry Count by 1.

◆ Retransmit (could see an NCP message Type 9999).

The maximum number of retries is 20, and if the client does not receive any response after 20 attempts, the message `Error receiving on network (file server name)` is displayed on the client's screen. This error message indicates that the file server cannot access a cable system within the allotted time period because of the heavy utilization or bandwidth overload. This is NetWare's control mechanism in managing congestion on the network.

The possible solution to alleviating bandwidth overload is to include bridges or routers in your network. If you split up the cable segment, you need to make sure you balance your heavy users and large applications across all the segments. You also may want to reschedule workloads to spread out the heavy usage. After you have reconfigured your network, use LZFW to monitor the adjustments.

The following steps can be used in LZFW to analyze high-bandwidth utilization:

1. Open the network Alarms Log and read the messages.

2. Open the Detail-Utilization screen to determine whether the high amount of activity is only temporary.

3. Sort the most active clients to the top through the Station Monitor screen, based on the kilobytes-out column.

4. Define a filter to capture the traffic for a few of the active clients.

5. Monitor the activity of these busy clients and ask the users of those stations what it is they are doing at the moment.

6. If the high amount of activity seems to be temporary, monitor the most active client with the Trend-Utilization% window to verify that the problem is not recurring.

 A client must transmit at least one good packet to be entered into the LZFW Station Monitor screen. If the client is sending nothing but a bad stream of packets, it will never get listed. When this is happening, replace the NIC drivers at the client to start the troubleshooting process.

Diagnosing Overloaded Servers

If you suspect that your file server is being overloaded, there are many questions you must ask yourself to determine who or what is causing the problem. A bad NLM could be using up the resources—confirm this with the LOAD MONITOR -P option at the file server console.

NetWare file servers will use the request/reply portion of NCP calls to answer requests to the server. Use LZFW Station Monitor to sort out the clients (from the Packets Out column) that are using the most NCP requests of the server. A possible alleviation of this overload response request could be moving this user to another server or checking the shell versions being used at the client. The shells or VLMs being used may be slightly outdated and need to be upgraded.

Other solutions that can be used as a last resort for alleviating server overload include the following:

◆ Upgrade the hard drive and or memory.

◆ Upgrade the CPU processor chip (33Mhz to 66Mhz).

◆ Try out a new server. (Remember: rent, lease, or borrow first!)

Steps to Analyze Excessive Broadcasts with LZFW

Router configuration errors are a common cause of excessive broadcasts. Use the following steps in LZFW to analyze this problem:

1. Solve any other alarm problems first to make sure they are not causing the problem.

2. Define a capture filter to find out which clients are transmitting the most broadcasts. This capture filter should include information about the broadcast address of the destination client. Apply this filter to the Station Monitor and sort the monitor window by the Packets Out column.

3. Monitor the Packet Capture Buffer through a display filter that shows the most active broadcasting client as the source.

4. Analyze the decode data as a resource when working with your hardware vendors to alleviate this problem.

A corrupted shell can send repetitive Get Nearest Server packets to the file server. This message is viewed with the use of the TRACK ON console command on the file server. This problem can be corrected by first trying to replace the NetWare shell or VLMs at the problem client. If this does not work, replace the network interface card in the client.

Steps to Analyze Excessive Packets with LZFW

There could be an alarm indicating excessive packets, but the network seems to be running normally and there are no excessive broadcasts. Use the following steps to analyze this problem:

1. View the Network Alarm Log for messages.

2. Monitor the Detail-Packet-per-second window to determine whether the error condition is continuous or temporary.

3. Observe the Trend-Utilization% screen and compare it to your baseline data.

4. If the utilization seems normal, you may be sending a lot of small packets. This can be monitored by capturing a sample of packets going across your network. If the packets captured are of different sizes and the network performance is not being affected, you may want to raise the alarm threshold to alleviate any false alarm conditions.

The network performance could be improved by upgrading the drivers for the NIC. You may need to upgrade the NIC itself. You also could increase the packet size of the NICs that have configurable drivers.

Using PATCHMAN for Loading NetWare Enhancements

 Install performance-enhancing patches using PATCHMAN.

After your network performance analysis is complete, you might decide that, as part of your solution, you need to add a patch to an NLM running on your file server. You have checked NetWire or the NSEPRO and have found what you need to apply this fix. The utility you need to apply these patches is called PATCHMAN.NLM. You must use version 3.11 (v3.10 does not work), and it can be found as part of a compressed file called UPD311.EXE. Do not load any patches unless you are sure you will need them.

Note The PATCHMAN module is for use with NetWare 3.11 only. The release of NetWare 3.12 included all the necessary enhancements made to any NLMs in v3.11.

There are three types of patches available for the NetWare operating system:

◆ **STATIC.** The effects of this patch are permanent once it is applied. The static patch is a DOS executable that modifies the SERVER.EXE file. Do not apply the patch to the original SERVER.EXE file on the original master disk. Before you apply the patch to your boot up disk (hard or floppy drive), make a copy of the SERVER.EXE from the boot disk and keep it in another location.

◆ **SEMI-STATIC.** These patches can be loaded while the server is running, but you cannot unload these patches to reverse the effects while the server is still running. To remove the effects of these patches, you must down the server, then bring it back up without reloading the fixes.

◆ **DYNAMIC.** These patches are actual NLM files that can be loaded and unloaded while the server is running. You can unload this type of patch to reverse the effects to the operating system.

The semi-static and dynamic patches do not modify the operating system on the boot disk, they only modify what is loaded in memory on the file server. Therefore, these two types of patches must be loaded each time the server is brought up in order for them to take effect. If you want these patches to be loaded automatically each time the server is brought up, place them in the AUTOEXEC.NCF file with a LOAD command.

671

PATCHMAN.NLM is a *patch manager* and needs to be loaded only once before you load any semi-static or dynamic patches. If you try to load any patches without loading PATCHMAN, the patches will search the SYS:SYSTEM directory for the PATCHMAN.NLM and load it automatically. If you need to unload PATCHMAN, you must unload all the patch files before you can do so.

To view the types of patches that are loaded on your file server, type **PATCHES** at your file server console command line. Each will be displayed and grouped according to type, whether it is a dynamic, semi-static, or a static patch. If you type the console command **MODULES**, it will not show which semi-static or static patches are loaded. It will show only the dynamic ones.

The following list shows the proper order in which you would load semi-static and dynamic patches:

1. Copy the PATCHMAN.NLM into the SYS:SYSTEM directory on the file server.

2. Rename any older patches that you are replacing with an OLD extension so that you do not overwrite any existing files. You may need to recover your old ones if there are problems with the new ones.

3. Copy the needed patches to the SYS:SYSTEM directory.

4. Edit the AUTOEXEC.NCF file to include the PATCHMAN.NLM and load the new patches.

Test these changes for a period of time to determine if they have the proper effect required for your network. If they are causing performance degradation, unload the dynamic patches immediately or down the file server. If you have loaded them in the AUTOEXEC.NCF, remember to start the server with the SERVER -NA parameter setting.

Understanding Packet Burst

Describe the implications of using Burst Mode in optimizing the handling of large files.

To optimize a network that is using files that require large blocks of data for read and write transmissions, use the NetWare 3.12 operating system, which includes the Packet Burst protocol as a default (see fig. 13.11). The clients attaching to these packages require the use of the VLM.EXE file to be able to take advantage of this function.

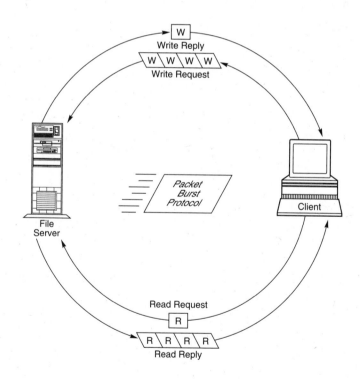

Figure 13.11

The functionality of the Packet Burst protocol.

673

Packet Burst, also known as burst mode, is a protocol that can speed up the transmission of multiple-packet NetWare Core Protocol (NCP) read and writes. The NCP is a procedure used by the NetWare operating system to receive and respond to client requests. NCPs handle requests for printing, clearing a connection, or manipulating files and directories. Responding to all these requests over a wide area network (WAN) can cause a significant degradation in network performance. Packet Burst sends a series of packets (burst), removing the requirement for sequencing and acknowledging each packet. A client can send a read or write request for blocks of data up to 64KB in size. This can reduce the amount of traffic on the network.

Packet Burst has the capability of monitoring its processes for dropped packets, retransmitting only those packets it handled that have been dropped. The client and the file server negotiate with each other to see if they both use Packet Burst. If they do (almost like a sliding-window used by NCP), they then determine what the maximum Packet Burst transmission size can be between them. There are separate parameters used for setting the size of the read and write windows. The default write window is 10 packets and the read window is 16 packets.

SDLC uses a true sliding-window implementation. The following two features differentiate Packet Burst from SDLC:

♦ The response for a lost packet is retransmitted from the lost packet to the end of the transmission for SDLC. Packet Burst will have error recovery procedures that will retransmit only lost packets.

♦ SDLC does not have a fixed maximum window size and the timing for communications between the client and file server is different. As the client and the file server detects changes on the network, the window size will adjust automatically. The packet size for Ethernet has changed from 1,024 to 1,500 bytes to handle the timing changes with use of VLMs.

Large Internet Packet Basics

The Large Internet Packet (LIP) can be used to enhance network performance by working with routers to increase the speed of data transmission. As with Packet Burst, LIP is included with the NetWare 3.12 client software and as part of the operating system.

In previous versions of NetWare, if a file server found a router between itself and a client, the maximum packet size was set at 576 bytes (512 for data, 64 for header info). LIP allows the negotiation of the packet size to be a larger amount when the communication occurs through a router between a client and a file server. The maximum packet size that LIP allows is 4,202 bytes, with this dependent on the allowable maximum physical packet size on the file server. LIP will not be effective for some routers that have hard-code maximum packet sizes. Routers such as Cisco, 3COM, Wellfleet, and NetWare's Multi-Protocol Router will function with LIP.

You can disable LIP at the file server with the following SET parameter:

```
SET ALLOW LIP = OFF
```

Using Bridges, Hubs, and Routers

 Compare the functionality of bridges and routers.

Your network may contain other devices besides a file server, a printer, and a few clients that affect the overall performance of your environment. The growth in technology has afforded the development of enterprise-type networks. The devices that can provide the wide area network connectivity include bridges, hubs, and routers. These devices usually are assigned a physical address that is designated by the manufacturer to identify this particular device. The type of addresses that can be assigned by the vendor are Media Access Control (MAC) addresses. A network administrator can use logical addresses through a software management package to identify or group devices.

Bridges

A *bridge* is a type of device that can connect two LAN segments at the Data Link Layer of the OSI model. Bridges operate with the source and destination addresses of the nodes involved in the transmission of data. Bridges are selective about the traffic they allow to cross, basing this on the addresses of the transmitting devices. Bridges logically connect two physically separate segments. These types of devices can be used to divide a busy network segment. Bridges can be a separate box, work in tandem with another remote bridge, or work as a PC with the software and hardware together. There are two types of bridges found in a network:

◆ **Transparent.** This type of bridge uses its own intelligence to store address information in internal tables, determining whether to forward a frame to the next segment between source and destination devices.

◆ **Source-Routing.** This type of bridge is not as intelligent as the transparent bridges. Source routing is primarily found on IBM-type networks. They require that the entire route be transmitted by the source node, along with the packet that is being sent.

Bridges can be used across the internet to extend a connection to a remote branch site. The amount of nodes and the types of traffic dictate the use of a bridge or a router across the internet. A bridge is most effective for small remote branches performing queries, small file transfers, or minimum printing. Bridges are primarily used to extend local LAN segments or to break up traffic loads across a segment.

Hubs

A *hub* usually is located in a wiring closet or in a central location in the scheme of the network design. There are various types of hubs on the market. There are "intelligent" hubs that can sense problems on a segment and shut this segment down without affecting the rest of the network. They also can be remotely monitored for troubleshooting purposes. Another name for a hub is a multistation access unit (MAU or MSAU). Hubs can be associated with different types of Physical Layer media, such as 10BASE-T Ethernet, FDDI, and standard Ethernet. Hubs do not extend the maximum cable distances allowed based on that topology's rules.

Routers

A *router* is a network device that operates with the Physical, Data Link, and Network Layers of the OSI reference layer model. It uses algorithms to calculate the best path through the internetwork, using logical rather than physical addresses. Routers also can use the MAC layer addresses of the network cards assigned by the vendor for routing purposes. Routers do more processing than bridges, and at times can seem slower. A router can perform "on-the-fly" changes of path destinations between the transmitting and receiving nodes.

Routers are preferred devices that are used on the campuswide network or across the internet link. Use routers when you have a large remote branch or are doing large file transfers, querying large databases, or using multimedia-type applications on the campus network or internet link.

Additional Notes on Routers, Bridges, and Hubs

The following are additional considerations to remember about routers, bridges, and hubs:

◆ Routers from different vendors may not interconnect because of the lack of standards in this industry in the past.

◆ Routers can be as much as three times slower than bridges because the routers use logical addresses to choose the best path for frame transmission (speed may be an issue). There are routing bridges (brouters) that can be found that provide the benefits of both devices.

◆ Remember the 5-4-3 Ethernet rule (see Chapter 6)!

◆ Use a bridge or a router to divide a segment that has a load on the segment of 60–70 percent of capacity. A faster server does not always improve the performance degradation issues.

◆ There are certain source-routing bridges that require a smaller packet size in order to operate. This could increase transmission time.

◆ When bridges are placed on an internet, the information passing through the bridge—at best—will perform at 60 percent of its throughput capabilities. If multiple bridges are added or the bridge has a slow clock and processor, the throughput can be reduced even more. A bridge performs better on a segment where traffic needs to be isolated.

◆ Repeaters and hubs often function as repeating devices (no more than four in a series), and often are arranged in tree-type structures. The NICs will require that the SQE test must be turned off.

◆ When planning for bridges in your network, you must consider the performance difference with different link speeds. It will take a remote bridge longer to respond than the one on the local LAN. As an example, it could take an application with a 640KB size approximately 9.1 minutes to travel over a 9.6 Kbps link!

◆ If you are using IBM source-routing bridges with a NetWare server using Token Ring, you must load ROUTE.NLM. You also will need to load ROUTE.COM (loaded after IPX or

IPXODI) from the clients. This allows these bridges to forward IPX/SPX packets. Make sure the Token Ring LANs using source-routing have the latest version of the NetWare shell loaded.

◆ Routers and bridges must have sufficient speed to handle the applications they are expected to work with. A link speed of 9.6—19.2 Kbps should handle host access, e-mail, network management tools, and file transfer traffic. For database servers, a minimum link speed of 56 Kbps should be used. Remote program access and extensive data file transfers require a link speed of 1.544—2.048 Kbps.

Creating a Disaster Recovery Plan

Explain the role of third-party software products in creating the optimal disaster recovery plan.

An important function of a network administrator is to develop a disaster recovery plan. This plan should be included as part of your readily accessible network documentation. The following are recommended items to include in your disaster recovery plan:

◆ Location of copies of all original disks of applications and the operating system (in a locked, fireproof area)

◆ Listings of all CONFIG.SYS files, AUTOEXEC.BAT, INI, or other BAT files for all clients (if they are all set up the same, one copy of each will be sufficient)

Files found on the file server, such as NET$LOG.DAT, BAT built for accessing special programs, any MENU listings, and NCF files (screen prints of any other system settings will do if you do not have a third-party utility that could pull security or other details in a report format)

679

◆ Accessible history logs of adjustments, problem logs with solutions, and backup logs

◆ Addresses and phone numbers of vendors of all components in your network

◆ Escalation schedule and contact phone numbers for support

◆ Technical documentation, such as drawings of components in the file server and how they are set up (slots, IRQ, memory addresses, and so forth), floor plans, cable details, and installation booklets from component manufacturer

◆ A listing of the equipment that is available out on your network that could be used to rebuild your server temporarily

◆ Backup script information

◆ A listing of applications that would give the users access to enough to enable them to do their primary job function

◆ Details on printers and print server information

◆ Phone numbers and addresses of all your co-workers, customers, and managers so that you can check on them after an emergency (earthquake, hurricane, and so forth)

◆ A listing of the basic step order for rebuilding your network and the priority of each additional network device (besides the file server being first) to be added back in to the environment

◆ Details on what to do if a virus is found

All the documentation in the world will not matter if you do not maintain good backups. The backups must be current and done based on the cost of the data and the needs of the users to get to this data. A backup is not a good backup until you know you can restore it successfully. Remember, if your server crashes in the middle of the period between backups, the data modified in that prior period from the last backup will be lost. You should put a priority on the testing of your backups on a regular schedule (maybe at least once a month!). Use the following recommendations to test your backups:

◆ You should rotate tape usage, never overwriting your most recent tape.

◆ Make sure that you have enough tapes and backup unit capacity to recover the data effectively and efficiently.

◆ Make sure that your tape backup software has the capability of verify-after-backup by comparing files on the server to files on the tape. Leave this option turned on!

◆ View the backup and error logs regularly. Search the tapes to make sure the backed up files can be found.

◆ When you test your backups, periodically restore data to a test area on the server. Do not overwrite existing files.

◆ Use a reputable software and hardware vendor.

If you have lost data on the file server, test your backups first. If you cannot get your drive to accept these backups, consider involving professionals experienced with performing data recovery services.

Remember, hardware cannot be repaired by software! Utilities that re-create a volume or write to the hard disk reduce the options of using a data recovery service. Do not use a utility such as NetWare's VREPAIR if the data cannot be replaced by an attempt at restoring backups.

If you have ruled out hardware as the cause for the problem, VREPAIR or other software utilities can be used. The purpose of VREPAIR is to create a mountable volume. It can be run on a dismounted volume with corrupted data while the other volumes are running (as long as it is not the SYS: volume).

Choose VREPAIR in the following circumstances:

◆ Good backups are available.

◆ A power failure has caused a volume to become corrupt.

◆ The file server console displays a `mirroring mismatch` error when the server boots up.

◆ After you replace faulty hardware, data structure errors prevent a volume from mounting.

681

If you are running VREPAIR on a volume with NAME SPACES loaded, make sure that you have the NLM repair module that matches the name space loaded located in the same area where VREPAIR is found. Make sure you read the file server console carefully while you are performing this process.

There are third-party utilities such as Ontrack Data Recovery's NetUtils3 that can help you in disaster recovery. This tool will enable you to do the following:

♦ Rebuild the file structure from within the volume.

♦ Examine, modify, or save any sector on a server hard drive.

♦ Perform analysis on the server drive without restoring any data (the defective sectors will be recorded in Hot Fix so that NetWare does not attempt to restore data to those bad spots).

♦ Recover files from any volume with errors (you can recover any files which do not have current backups and files can be recovered to another "live" file server through a client connection, to a DOS partition, or to floppy disks).

Utilities available in NetUtils3 include the following:

♦ **NetScan3.** This tool is designed to examine and nondestructively repair NetWare structural errors that can occur on a volume. This tool also can examine a V3.1*x* volume for defective sectors and redirect defective blocks to valid blocks within that volume.

♦ **NetFile3.** This tool is a file recovery and file editor that lets you access a file in a NetWare volume. Files can be recovered from a corrupted volume and saved to a DOS partition on another device or to DOS-formatted disks. You could log into a client and copy the files to another server, repair the defective volume, then restore the files back to the original file server.

♦ **NetDisk3.** This tool is a sector editor that enables you to examine and modify the data in any sector on any device (optical or hard disk). It can access data from a file server device, even if NetWare and DOS are no longer able to recognize partitions on the device.

Check with Ontrack Data Recovery for future enhancements of this type of tool.

Review Questions

1. What two aspects in a LAN environment have research polls shown that users consider most important for an operational network?

   ☐ a. Speed

   ☐ b. Reliability

   ☐ c. Security

   ☐ d. Services

2. Which NetWare 3.1x Memory Pool is used for internal NetWare system tables that change size dynamically?

   ○ a. File Cache Buffers

   ○ b. Cache, Non-Movable

   ○ c. Cache, Movable

   ○ d. Permanent Memory

3. Which NetWare 3.1x Memory Pool is returned only when the server is down?

   ○ a. File Cache Buffers

   ○ b. Cache, Non-Movable

   ○ c. Cache, Movable

   ○ d. Permanent Memory

4. Which of the following does the length of the snake on the MONITOR utility's screen saver indicate?

   ○ a. Network utilization

   ○ b. Amount of time that screen saver has been active

○　c.　Workstations still active on the file server

○　d.　That the screen saver is still functioning

5.　The MONITOR utility reports file server utilization, which can indicate which *two* possibilities?

☐　a.　CPU cycles

☐　b.　Number of disk requests

☐　c.　Number of workstations logged in

☐　d.　NLM process requests

6.　If you highlight an active connection shown in MONITOR's Connection Information option, which of the following happens?

○　a.　Displays number of available service processes

○　b.　Provides user information such as NIC address

○　c.　Shows available Receive Buffers

○　d.　Indicates buffers to be written to memory

7.　Which of the following is not displayed by the Disk Information screen of MONITOR?

○　a.　Hot fix information

○　b.　Checksum errors

○　c.　Partition blocks

○　d.　Device numbering

8.　If you suspect that a file server NIC is malfunctioning, you can check which LAN Information statistic for an indication of the problem?

○　a.　Send Packet Size (too big/small) Count

○　b.　Receive Packet Overflow Count

○　c.　Checksum Errors

○　d.　Total Packets Received

9. Which of the following is not one of the items of information that the File Open/Lock Activity selection of MONITOR allows you to display?

○ a. Using a particular file

○ b. Open file for a read/write operation

○ c. List of files used in the past 60 minutes

○ d. File status

10. Hash tables are found in which Memory Pool?

○ a. Permanent Memory Pool

○ b. Cache Buffers Pool

○ c. Alloc Memory Pool

○ d. Cache Movable Memory Pool

11. The MONITOR selection that lets you see CPU utilization, and which is not brought up at the default load statement, can be brought up by typing

○ a. LOAD MONITOR C

○ b. LOAD MONITOR S

○ c. LOAD MONITOR P

○ d. LOAD MONITOR F

12. Which of the following is not one of the four areas that NetWare is capable of dynamically tuning over a period of time, using default settings from the core package?

○ a. Cache Block Sizing

○ b. Physical Packet Receive Buffers

○ c. Hot Fix Redirection Area

○ d. Service Processes

13. The result of setting block sizes too large is

   ○ a. Insufficient memory for the cache buffer

   ○ b. Wasted disk space

   ○ c. Memory fragmentation

   ○ d. Insufficient Memory Pool warnings

14. The client/file server packet size is negotiated

   ○ a. When the client attaches to the file server

   ○ b. When the file server sends its first packet

   ○ c. When the client sends its first packet

   ○ d. When the file server is first installed

15. The default packet size that NetWare uses when packets must cross the router is

   ○ a. 640 bytes

   ○ b. 320 bytes

   ○ c. 1,024 bytes

   ○ d. 512 bytes

16. Which parameter should be increased if you want to favor write-intensive environments?

   ○ a. Cache Buffer Size

   ○ b. Packet Receive Buffers

   ○ c. Maximum Concurrent Disk Cache Writes

   ○ d. Immediate Purge of Deleted Files

17. Which of the following is not one of the areas of performance enhancements found in the NetWare 4.x environment?

   ○ a. Optimized code paths

   ○ b. Disk block default size

○   c.   Turbo-FAT Reuse Wait Time

○   d.   Block suballocation

18. Which feature of NetWare 4.*x* enables multiple file endings to share the same block?

○   a.   Optimized code paths

○   b.   Disk block default size

○   c.   Turbo-FAT reuse wait time

○   d.   Block suballocation

19. If your network is reporting oversize or undersize packet errors, jabber errors, threshold errors, or other types of errors, which database can you use to find potential solutions for these errors?

○   a.   LZFW

○   b.   NetWare Expert

○   c.   MONITOR

○   d.   PATCHMAN

20. Which utility would you use to load corrections to an NLM?

○   a.   NSEPRO

○   b.   PATCHMAN

○   c.   MONITOR

○   d.   LZFW

21. Which *two* of the following patches do not modify the operating system on the boot disk?

☐   a.   Static

☐   b.   Semi-static

☐   c.   Dynamic

☐   d.   Transit

22. A protocol that speeds up the transmission of multiple-packet reads and writes is called

    ○   a.   NCP

    ○   b.   Large Internet Packet

    ○   c.   Packet Burst

    ○   d.   Source Routing

23. The type of device that can connect two LAN segments at the Data Link Layer of the OS model is called

    ○   a.   Bridge

    ○   b.   Router

    ○   c.   Hub

    ○   d.   MAU

24. One thing to consider when planning for bridges in your network is

    ○   a.   Different vendors may not be able to interconnect.

    ○   b.   You can use only 6 hubs in a series.

    ○   c.   Performance may differ with different link speeds.

    ○   d.   ROUTE.NLM always must be loaded.

25. Which of the following is *not* a time when VREPAIR should be used?

    ○   a.   A power failure has corrupted a volume.

    ○   b.   Faulty hardware has been recently replaced.

    ○   c.   A Mirror Mismatch error displays on boot up.

    ○   d.   No backups are available to restore.

Answers

1. B, C
2. C
3. D
4. A
5. A, D
6. B
7. B
8. A
9. C
10. D
11. C
12. C
13. B
14. A
15. D
16. C
17. C
18. D
19. B
20. B
21. B, C
22. C
23. A
24. C
25. D

PART 3

Installation and Configuration for NetWare

Installing NetWare 3.11

NetWare 3.0 introduced a dramatically new way to install, configure, and manage NetWare. Anyone who has ever performed a server installation for a version of NetWare 2.*x* is familiar with the difficulty that was encountered in accomplishing the initial installation. More significant, however, was the effort required to reconfigure the server, particularly to add or reconfigure hard drives and network cards. Such reconfigurations required that almost the entire installation process be repeated because the NetWare 2.*x* operating system software had to be custom-built for each configuration. This was a process called "generating the OS."

NetWare 3.0 introduced the concept of the NetWare Loadable Module, which makes it possible to add or modify virtually any software changes "on the fly." NLMs are the basic software building blocks for both NetWare 3.*x* and 4.*x* servers. Unless hardware changes require that the server be powered down, it is seldom necessary to stop the server to make configuration changes. NetWare 3.*x* is nimble, versatile, and far easier to manage than any version of NetWare 2.*x*.

This and the next two chapters as well as Appendix C, guide you through typical installations of the three versions of NetWare that are currently most prominent: versions 3.11, 3.12, and 4.01. As you study the examples, you will be given numerous suggestions and warnings of potential problems. The installation of NetWare 3.*x* and 4.*x* generally is trouble-free if the hardware selected is "standard," meaning that all necessary drivers are included with NetWare.

Generally, more basic hardware configurations may not offer the highest performance levels; this should be a consideration if you want increased performance. Note, however, that the more basic the file server configuration is, the less complex NetWare installation is.

The remainder of this chapter takes you through an example of a NetWare 3.11 installation. NetWare 3.11 installation involves the following steps:

1. Assembling the hardware for your server and recording all interrupt, I/O address, DMA, and base memory address settings

2. Booting the server with DOS and creating a bootable DOS partition on your hard disk (or creating a bootable floppy)

3. Copying necessary system files to your boot disk

4. Running the SERVER.EXE utility to load the NetWare operating system and define the server

5. Loading the required disk drivers

6. Using the INSTALL module to create and mount volumes

7. Copying the SYSTEM and PUBLIC files onto the server

8. Loading the LAN drivers and other necessary modules, binding protocols to the LAN drivers

9. Creating the server boot files

Assembling the Hardware

 Identify the required software and hardware necessary to install the NetWare 3.11 operating system.

Your first concern should be to select components that are certified and proven to work properly with NetWare; performance should be second. A high-performance system that is down much of the time is less productive than a reliable, lower-performance system. The following sections assume that you have a properly configured file server that can deliver the expected level of performance and reliability. Proper configuration of the server involves all aspects of the hardware, from the amount of installed RAM to the types of disk drives, the controllers, and the switch settings on the cards installed in the server.

Before you begin the installation process, make a list of all the I/O addresses, interrupts, memory addresses, and DMA channels used by your hardware. Start with your server's standard equipment, including the serial ports, parallel ports, video adapters, and all other known settings used by your system. You must know this information so that you can determine where you can install the required network hardware. Have a thorough picture of what's inside your server before you start adding NICs, disk drives, or other components.

Each network interface card and other required hardware should supply documentation that describes the supported settings. Using the supplied documentation and the list you created, you should be able to determine where each hardware card can reside. If documentation is not available for system components, you can use a utility such as CHECKIT PRO, described in Chapter 12, "Troubleshooting Concepts and Tools," to determine I/O addresses, interrupts, memory addresses, and DMA channels for the installed hardware on your server. Chapter 12 also describes the MicroHouse Technical Library and NSEPro, which are excellent research tools in this area.

Remember that the interrupts and addresses usually used by LPT and COM ports are available if those resources are disabled in your server. LPT and COM ports will be required to support printers that are attached to the server. A COM port may be required if you are configuring a modem for remotely managing the server.

Watch out for I/O and memory overlap. Although the documentation may not mention memory overlap, not all hardware devices operate true to the published specifications.

You may experience problems if two cards are installed at adjoining I/O addresses. Suppose that card A is installed at I/O 300h, and card B is installed at I/O 308h. These settings may appear to work properly, but card A needs 10 bytes of memory, which places it two bytes into card B's space. This type of problem is sometimes difficult to locate because the network may appear to function properly at first. Put all known information in the list you create.

When you install NetWare, you will need to know the make and model for each network card, as well as the settings for the card. You also need to know the type and settings for your hard drive controllers.

Few of the newest NICs are supported by drivers that shipped with NetWare 3.11. Unless you are using a classic card, such as the Novell NE1000 or NE2000, the 3Com 3C503 or 3C509, or the IBM Token Ring adapter, you need to obtain drivers from the disks shipped with the adapter, from NetWire, or from the vendor. Driver files for network interface cards end with the file name extension LAN.

NetWare 3.11 ships with a limited set of hard drive controller drivers, including the following:

♦ ISADISK for use with standard AT-class ISA controllers (ST506 MFM or RLL, and ESDI disks when other drivers are unavailable)

♦ DCB for Novell's DCB Disk Coprocessor Board (now distributed by other vendors)

♦ PS2ESDI for PS/2s with ESDI drives

♦ PS2MFM for IBM PS/2s with MFM drives

♦ PS2SCSI for IBM PS/2s with SCSI drives

As you can see, the technologies supported are extremely limited. If you are using a SCSI adapter, drivers will usually accompany the adapter or be available from the adapter vendor. An IDE driver is available from NetWire. Disk driver files end with the extension DSK.

Make sure that you carefully examine your list of hardware settings. If you find any potential conflicts, reconfigure one of the components, if possible. This is better than having to isolate the cause of transient network problems after the network is operational.

Test the equipment for proper DOS operation. Start by booting DOS from drive A to confirm that the computer is operating, and then check the amount of installed extended memory. The available memory should be displayed during the memory test when you cold-boot your PC. NetWare 3.11 requires a certain amount of extended memory to operate properly.

NetWare 3.11 requires 2MB of memory for the operating system, plus memory for each volume.

In addition to memory for NetWare, you must determine the approximate amount of memory required for the NetWare 3.11 volumes. Start by determining the block size that will be used. 4MB blocks are almost always most appropriate, and that size will be used in these examples. Once you have determined the block size, use the appropriate formula for each volume:

♦ For a DOS volume, the memory required =

$$\frac{\text{volume size (in MB)} \times .023}{\text{block size}}$$

♦ For a volume that will support Macintosh or Unix files, the memory required =

$$\frac{\text{volume size (in MB)} \times .032}{\text{block size}}$$

For example, to determine the memory required for a 650MB DOS volume that will not support additional name space, the calculation is as follows:

$$\frac{650 \times .023}{4} = \frac{14.95}{4} = 3.73$$

continues

697

Calculate the memory required for each volume on the server. Then add the 2MB required for the operating system. Round the sum up to at least the next highest megabyte. In the previous example, minimum memory in megabytes is 3.73 + 2, which is 5.73MB. The best memory configuration in this case must be at least 6MB, but 8MB makes more sense in many hardware configurations. Memory is much more economical in larger increments, and 4MB, 16MB, or even 32MB increments may make the most sense in the long run.

Do not be afraid of having more than the minimum amount of memory. One of the best ways to enhance NetWare's performance is to give it more memory with which to work.

Install the required memory before you proceed with NetWare installation.

A synopsis of hardware and software requirements:

Minimum Hardware Requirments:

◆   File Server

   The File Server needs to be a PC using 386 or better architecture.

◆   4MB memory, 8MB preferred

◆   Hard drive space sufficient to load all applications, plus space for data storage. NetWare needs 10MB of space.

◆   Network board for server and one network board for each workstation.

◆   Cabling and cable components to connect workstations.

Minimum Software Requirements:

◆ NetWare 3.11 disks.

◆ DOS 3.3 or newer.

◆ Additional third-party hardware drivers as required.

Creating the Boot Partition

 Describe the terms and files used with the NetWare 3.11 installation process.

Insert a bootable copy of DOS in your server's A drive and boot the server. You may use Microsoft MS-DOS, IBM PC DOS, or Novell's DR DOS 6.0 or Novell DOS 7.0.

Your next step is to create a DOS partition used to boot the server and start NetWare. If this is the first time you are installing DOS on your PC, most current DOS releases include an installation routine that automates the process. You cannot use fully automatic installation because this will allocate the entire hard drive for DOS and leave nothing for NetWare. However, you may be able to use a custom installation procedure within the installation program, such as the Custom Installation option in MS-DOS.

After you boot the system on DOS, you ordinarily create a C: bootable drive partition on the system disk. The DOS partition is created by using FDISK. If you are using MS-DOS, follow these steps:

1. Use FDISK option 3 to delete any existing partitions on the drive.

2. Use FDISK option 1 to create a primary partition on your first hard drive. For NetWare 3.11, the partition you create should be at least 3MB in size.

3. Use FDISK option 2 to make the primary partition the active partition.

 Creating a 5MB partition leaves room to upgrade to NetWare 4 without reconfiguring partitions. You also may want to allow space for diagnostic utilities and other programs that you may want to run under DOS.

After the DOS FDISK utility creates the partition, the partition must be formatted as a bootable drive with the command **FORMAT C: /S**. If the FDISK or the FORMAT command fails, a hardware problem is evident and must be solved before you proceed with the installation.

 In rare cases, you may find that the disk drive requires a low-level format. A low-level format is a level below the format created with the DOS FORMAT command, which creates a DOS Drive. Most disks are low-level formatted at the factory, but the low-level format information can be damaged.

If all your hard drives's hardware appears to be in working order, try using a utility to low-level format the drive. Many manufacturers ship a low-level format utility with their drives. Some modern BIOS utilities also have the capability to perform a low-level format.

If you don't want to create a DOS partition on your hard drive, you may create a bootable floppy from which to start your server. Do this by formatting the A: disk with the /S option. Be aware, however, that booting your server from a floppy disk adds considerable time to the process of bringing the network up from a cold start.

The *speed indicator* determines the relative speed difference between computers that run as 3.11 file servers. Table 14.1 offers some common examples.

Table 14.1
Common Speed Measurements

CPU	Rating	Clock Speed	Wait State	Novell Speed
386	16	MHz	1	121
386	25	MHz	0	242
386	33	MHz	0	342
486	33	MHz	0	914
486	66	MHz	0	1830

Following the speed display, you are prompted to enter a file server name. Type in a name (2 to 47 characters long with no periods or spaces) and press Enter.

Next, you are prompted for the internal network number. In Chapter 8 you read about the requirement for a unique internal network number for each NetWare 3.x and 4.x server. Type any hexadecimal number (one to eight digits in length) and press Enter. Note that this number must be different from all other internal or external network numbers of connected networks or servers.

 Novell NetWare 386 uses an internal network structure that enables NLMs to communicate. This internal network requires that the "NET" numbers for segment address and "NET" numbers for file server address be different.

After the SERVER command loads, a header or banner appears that displays the NetWare version and user count. The user count confirms the number of user connections that this particular version allows.

Provide information requested by the NetWare 3.11 installation.

The SERVER command can be entered with command-line parameters. Use the following parameters to troubleshoot suspected problems with file server boot files or to change buffer size:

◆ **-NA** prevents AUTOEXEC.NCF file execution

◆ **-NS** prevents STARTUP.NCF file execution

◆ **-C** enables you to modify the cache buffer size from the default of 4KB per block

After the banner is displayed, you should see a colon (:) prompt, which is the normal prompt for the NetWare console. You can load the appropriate disk driver and continue to create a Novell volume.

Collect the following pieces of information before beginning the installation:

◆ What you will call the server

◆ Your choice for the internal IPX number

◆ The disk driver needed (file name convention for disk drivers is *.DSK)

◆ Hard disk controller settings

◆ The LAN driver (network board driver) needed (file name convention for LAN drivers is *.LAN)

◆ Network board settings

Loading Disk Drivers

Next you must load a disk drive to enable NetWare to communicate with your hard drive. Novell supplies the following five standard driver files:

- ◆ **ISADISK** is used with most MFM and ESDI drives in servers equipped with the ISA bus.

- ◆ **DCB** is used with the original Novell disk coprocessor board or any DCB-compatible, such as the Adaptec 4000 series disk controllers.

- ◆ **PS2ESDI** is used for ESDI drives in servers equipped with the MicroChannel Architecture bus.

- ◆ **PS2MFM** is used for MFM drives in MicroChannel PCs.

- ◆ **PS2SCSI** is used for drive systems using IBM SCSI controllers in MicroChannel PCs.

An IDE driver is available from NetWire. Other disk drivers are supplied by the controller manufacturer or distributor. Note that Novell must certify any drivers. The reliability of the disk driver is critical to the operation of your file structure. The files for disk drivers all have a DSK file name extension.

Note Currently, Compaq is the only AT-type ESDI controller certified to allow duplexing with the standard ISADISK driver.

A few cases have been reported in which the new 3.11 ISADISK driver failed to operate properly. Novell says that the driver was optimized for higher performance, and therefore may not operate with some less compatible controllers. The solution is to use the ISADISK driver from the earlier NetWare 3.10.

Next, you load the disk driver required for your system. This may be a driver provided by Novell with NetWare 3.11, or it may be one provided by the vendor of your disk controller card; you should have copied this driver to the boot disk.

The following example illustrates the procedure you follow to load the driver name. Suppose that you want to load a custom driver written by Procomp for its SCSI disk coprocessor controller. After SERVER is started, load the driver by name as follows:

```
LOAD DRA
```

After the disk driver is loaded, you will be prompted for any necessary hardware configuration information. Most drivers will suggest the default values for the hardware being installed, allowing you to change values as required. In this case, you are asked for the PORT number and the INTERRUPT number, which you must determine from your own hardware settings and documentation. For this example, a port of 340h and an interrupt of B or 11 are used.

Duplexing Versus Mirroring

If you intend to implement disk duplexing, you need to install a second disk controller card. To activate this card, load the disk driver a second time by following the preceding instructions. Each card must be configured with different ports and interrupts, and you enter the second card's parameters the second time you load the disk driver.

The second driver is not really loaded twice. The second LOAD command simply tells the system to use the driver twice, which is defined as *re-entrantly* loading the driver.

Duplexing with a second disk channel improves disk read performance because the system can read from each disk concurrently. Mirroring uses only a single controller and provides no added read performance or disk write performance loss. Both options provide a redundant disk drive for data protection, but with a cost-versus-performance trade-off. Only duplexing provides data protection in case of a disk-channel failure.

Creating Partitions and Volumes

You now are ready to load the installation program and start the actual installation process. To load the INSTALL program from the DOS drive C, type the following and press Enter:

```
LOAD INSTALL
```

You should see the main Installation Options screen (see fig.14.1).

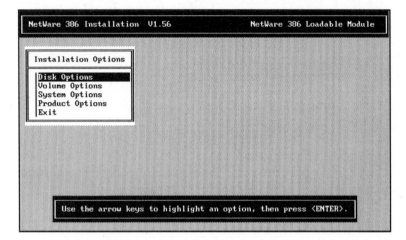

Figure 14.1

The Installation Options menu.

Novell makes it easy to walk through the installation process, beginning with Disk Options and continuing with Volume Options, System Options, and Product Options.

Disk Options

After INSTALL's main screen appears, select Disk Options by highlighting it on the Installation Options menu and pressing Enter. You see a screen such as the one in figure 14.2.

Figure 14.2

The Available Disk
Options menu.

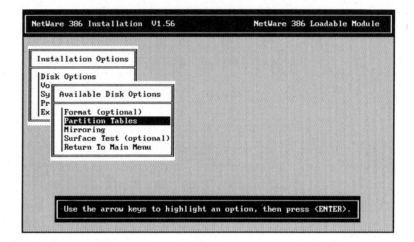

 Note

The Available Disk Options menu includes the
following options:

◆   Format

◆   Surface Test

◆   Mirroring

◆   Partition Tables

◆   Return To Main Menu

To create a NetWare volume, select the Partition Tables option by
highlighting the option and pressing Enter. You should see a list
of the drives attached to the controller. Figure 14.3 shows two
devices attached to a SCSI controller.

 Warning

If no drives or the wrong drive type appear in this
window, do not proceed! If the Available Disk
Drives window is empty, check all connections to
the drive and confirm the driver software options
you are loading. If the wrong drive type appears in
the window, do not proceed with the install process. You could write to the disk incorrectly. Back
up by pressing Esc, follow the instructions at the
bottom of the screen, and then confirm all hardware and software steps performed previously.

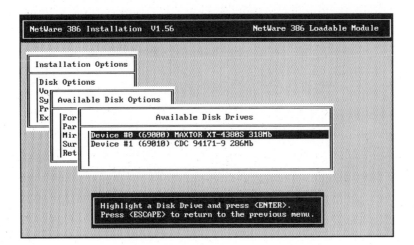

Figure 14.3

The Available Disk Drives window.

If the disk drive or drives shown are correct, select the first device and press Enter. You should see the Partition Type screen that contains the options to create and modify the partitions.

Before you create a partition, you have the option of changing the size of the hot fix area assigned to the partition. See Chapter 13 for more information about NetWare's hot fix feature.

The Change Hot Fix option, located in the Partition Options menu, enables you to modify the size of the Hot Fix Redirection Area. Novell suggests that you do not make the Hot Fix Area any smaller than the default.

 You also can use the Change Hot Fix option to match drives of different physical sizes, making them appear to be the same size, when mirroring or duplexing is desired.

To create the partition, select the Create NetWare Partition option. The Partition Information screen you see next displays the following information:

♦ Partition size

♦ Data area

♦ Redirection area

709

The Partition Size and Redirection Area fields accept entries. The Data Area simply displays the available data area size after hot fix is deducted from the partition.

You are allowed only one NetWare partition on each disk. With the exception of the disk that is used to boot DOS, all free space on each disk is ordinarily used to create the NetWare partition. The size of the partition is shown in the Partition Size field. You can change the partition size at this time if desired. You also can change the hot fix size on this screen by changing the value in the Redirection Area field. To accept the entries and create the partition, press Escape; then select Yes at the `Create partition?` prompt to complete the process.

Figure 14.4 shows the Partition Type screen after the NetWare partition is created. When you first enter this option, you see only the DOS partition you created with the DOS FDISK utility. If the DOS partition does not appear correctly on this screen, do not proceed until the problem is solved.

Figure 14.4

The Partition Options menu.

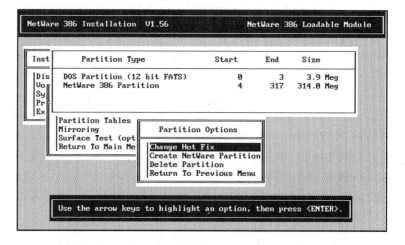

After you create the Novell partition, return to the Installation Options menu. (Each time you press Esc, you back up one menu level.) Select Volume Options and press Enter.

To create a new volume, press Insert in the Volumes screen. This is necessary during initial server installation because no volumes have been created at this point. This will bring up the Volume Information screen.

Volume Options

The Volume Information screen (see fig. 14.5) enables you to choose the volume configuration.

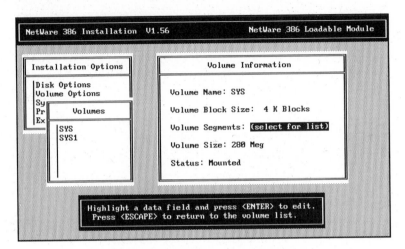

Figure 14.5

The Volume Information window.

The first NetWare volume must have the name SYS:, but the following volume names can be of your choice. To create this first volume using the entire disk space (as in fig. 14.5), press Esc to return to the volume list. Any volume option modifications must be completed at this time. To make changes later, you must delete the volume, which causes you to lose all data on that volume.

The following actions are available when creating a volume:

◆ You can enter a new name in the Volume Name field.

◆ You can change the block size by pressing Enter in the Volume Block Size field and selecting a new block size from the list provided. 4KB blocks are generally the best compromise, however. Small block sizes need more memory. (See the memory calculation formulas earlier in this chapter.) Large block sizes use disk space less efficiently when small files are present.

◆ If the server has only one available partition, you are shown the Initial Segment Size, which allocates all available partition space to the volume being created. If you want to reduce the size of the volume, enter a new Initial Segment

711

Size in blocks. The formula for calculating blocks is shown in the following note.

◆ If the server has more than one partition, you can specify which partition is to be used by this volume. Select a segment by pressing Enter in the Volume Segments field. You see a list of available volume segments from which to choose.

If you want to create a volume that does not use the entire partition space, you can calculate the segment size by multiplying the desired size of the volume (in megabytes) by 1,024, and then dividing by block size. The sum is the number of blocks equal to the desired segment size. For example, if you want to create a 50MB volume on a 100MB drive, and the volume block size is the default value of 4KB, the number of blocks in the segment is as follows:

$(50 \times 1,024)/4 = 12,800$ blocks

Therefore, 12,800 blocks equals a 50MB volume. This information is entered into the Initial Segment Size field.

To examine the information for an existing volume, highlight a volume name on the Volumes menu and press Enter. With existing volumes, you cannot modify the block size. However, you can change the following information:

◆ You can rename the volume. However, you must never rename the SYS: volume.

◆ You can add volume segments to expand the size of the volume. These segments can be taken from the same partition as the original volume or from a partition on a separate drive. Volumes that consist of segments from several drive partitions are called *spanned volumes*.

◆ You can mount or unmount the volume. You might need to unmount a volume to delete it or to run VREPAIR as described in Chapters 12 and 13.

Volume spanning is a feature of NetWare 3.11 that enables multiple drive partitions to be linked logically into a single volume. This feature increases performance because the drives operate in a parallel manner, enabling them to access more data with less mechanical movement. To create a spanned volume, add volume segments to obtain the desired size.

Volume spanning provides very high performance, but not without cost. The rule of thumb is that your disk access time is divided by the number of drives. Note, however, that the possibility of failure is multiplied by the same number.

Novell suggests that you implement duplexing whenever a volume is spanned. This technique also adds to performance by allowing the same split reads available with normal duplexing.

The individual block size of a volume can be modified from the 4KB default. You can select sizes of 4KB, 8KB, 16KB, 32KB, or 64KB. Unless you have a special application that can benefit from a large block size, use the default. A larger block degrades the performance of most applications. This feature is intended for very large database systems with large data blocks. Note that any calculations made with formulas listed earlier must be revised if block size is changed.

After you enter the specifications for your volume, press Escape and answer Yes to the Create volume? prompt.

The volume is then created, but not mounted, meaning that it is unavailable for use. You must highlight the new volume in the Volumes display, move to the Status field, and change the status to Mounted to enable the volume.

Copying the System and Public Files

After you create the NetWare volume or volumes, go to the System Options menu to complete the initial installation. Press Esc to back up to the Installation Options menu, highlight System Options, and then press Enter. The System Options menu (see fig. 14.6) enables you to load the remaining software and create the files required to boot automatically as a file server.

You must first copy all System and Public utilities. Select the Copy System and Public Files option by highlighting that choice on the Available System Options menu. Then press Enter and follow the prompts. If you did not mount the SYS: volume, you are prompted to do so now. After mounting volume SYS:, a window appears, and you are asked to insert the System-2 disk and press Esc. You will be prompted to insert additional disks until all files are copied. Continue this process until finished.

Figure 14.6

The Available System Options menu.

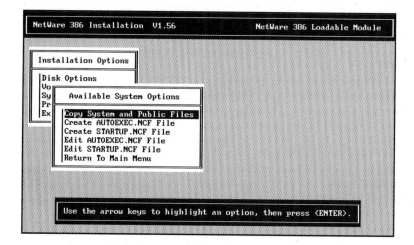

Loading LAN Drivers

The next step in the installation process is loading the LAN or network interface drivers. This explanation assumes that you have installed and tested the network cabling.

Two steps are required to fully activate a network card:

1. Load the network driver for the card.

2. Bind at least one protocol to the card driver.

 LAN drivers for NetWare 3.11 are NLMs that must be loaded to make the network function as a network. These modules drive the LAN cards in the server, enabling communication between the server and the nodes of the network. LAN drivers all have the file name extension LAN.

Loading a Network Driver

Next, you must load a network driver—in this example the NE2000 driver included with NetWare (see fig. 14.7). This driver was copied to the SYS: volume during installation and does not have to be loaded from the C drive. Enter the following command from the console prompt to load the driver:

    LOAD NE2000

```
:load ne2000
Loading module NE2000.LAN
   NetWare NE2000   v3.11 (910131)
   Version 3.11    January 31, 1991
Supported I/O port values are 300, 320, 360
I/O port: 300
Supported interrupt number values are 3, 4, 5
Interrupt number: 3
:
```

Figure 14.7

Loading the NE2000 driver.

As shown in figure 14.7, you are prompted for port and interrupt option settings. This particular NIC is configured to use port 300h and interrupt 3. (Your settings depend on your particular hardware configuration.) Because both drivers are loaded with no command-line parameters, use the default FRAME type. Use the BIND command (see fig. 14.8) to bind the proper protocol to the driver, which is IPX in this case.

715

Figure 14.8

Binding the IPX
protocol to the driver.

```
:bind ipx to ne2000
Network number: 5
IPX LAN protocol bound to NetWare NE2000   v3.11 (910131)
:
```

 If the LOAD command fails, check all the hardware switch and jumper settings. Improper settings and conflicts with other devices are the most common problems.

Check that you do not have a switch setting reversed. It is quite common to have the "on" and "off" or "1" and "0" settings in a mirror image.

Next, you must bind a protocol to the LAN driver. To support the IPX protocol, enter the following command:

```
BIND IPX TO NE2000
```

As shown in figure 14.8, you are asked for the network number to which the card is attached. See Chapter 8, "Addressing Your Network," for more about network addresses. The NE2000 is now active and in communication with the network.

 The default Ethernet frame type for NetWare 3.11 is Ethernet_802.3.

Adding a Second Network Card

Suppose that you have a system that is a little more complicated than the average setup. This system has both a Standard Microsystems 16-bit ARCnet interface and a Novell NE2000 16-bit Ethernet interface. To load a second type of network card, the procedure is the same as for the first.

The ARCnet driver used in this example is not included with NetWare 3.11, but was previously copied to the DOS C: partition.

Use the LOAD command to install the ARCnet driver by entering **LOAD C:\PC500386**. PC500386 is simply the file name of the driver, and for now it is located on drive C. After you load the driver, you are prompted for the hardware settings of PORT and INTERRUPT, which you must determine from your own hardware settings and documentation. In this example, use a port of 2E0h and int 9.

Use the BIND command to bind the proper protocol to the LAN driver. In most cases, you will be binding the IPX protocol. Type **BIND IPX TO PC500386** and press Enter. You are prompted for a Network number, which is the network number assigned to the cable segment to which you are connected. For this example, use three (3).

You are now connected to both the Ethernet network using the NE2000 card and the ARCnet network.

Miscellaneous problems have been encountered with the installation of 8-bit network interface cards in NetWare file servers. Novell suggests that you use no fewer than 16-bit cards in the file server to prevent problems. Do not be tempted to install a high-performance file server system such as NetWare 3.11 and attempt to use a low-cost workstation interface card.

Binding Additional Frame Types

The following example illustrates how you can load a second frame type so that one network card operates as two cards. This example uses a second Ethernet frame type to communicate with a TCP/IP system. Now you can load a different frame type to support the IP packet protocol to enable the routing of TCP/IP packets. Follow the preceding method, and load the NE2000 driver a second time (see fig. 14.9).

Figure 14.9

Loading the
Ethernet II
frame type.

```
:load ne2000
Loading module NE2000.LAN
Do you want to add another frame type for a previously loaded board? y
Supported frame types for NE2000 using I/O Port 300h to 31Fh, Interrupt 3h are:
    1. ETHERNET_II
    2. ETHERNET_802.2
    3. ETHERNET_SNAP
Select new frame type: 1
    Previously loaded module was used re-entrantly
:
```

You can choose to add another frame type. When asked if you
want to add another frame type for a previously loaded board,
type **Yes** or **Y** and press Enter to obtain the list of supported
frames. For the purpose of this example, select the Ethernet II
frame, and the previous driver is used re-entrantly.

Adding TCP/IP Support

The Ethernet/II frame type is required to connect to a TCP/IP
network. To enable the server to support TCP/IP, the TCP/IP
support NLM is required. This NLM is loaded simply by using the
LOAD command, as in figure 14.10.

Figure 14.10

Loading the TCP/IP
support NLM.

```
:load tcpip
Loading module TCPIP.NLM
    TCP/IP  v1.00 (910219)
:
```

Binding Additional Protocols

Now you are ready to bind the IP protocol to the driver as you did
when binding IPX. The command is **BIND IP TO NE2000**. A list
of NE2000 boards and frame types available for use is displayed.
Select the required card. In this case, select the Ethernet II frame or
board 2. Type **2** and press Enter.

You then are prompted for the IP address, which is nothing like
the native MAC addressing Novell uses. In the TCP or IP environment, each portion of the address has a particular meaning. Each
portion must be assigned to prevent problems because TCP
networks are generally quite large, and each node must have a
unique address while conforming to the numbering conventions

of the network. In a large network, two nodes with the same IP address are difficult to trace. Figure 14.11 displays a screen print of this information.

```
:bind ip to ne2000
Several boards are using the NE2000 LAN driver
    1. NetWare NE2000  v3.11 (910131) using I/O Port 300h to 31Fh, Interrupt 3h
 Frame type: ETHERNET_802.3
    2. NetWare NE2000  v3.11 (910131) using I/O Port 300h to 31Fh, Interrupt 3h
 Frame type: ETHERNET_II
Select board to bind: 2
IP address: 192.68.205.1
IP: Bound to board 3.  IP address 192.68.205.1, net mask FF.FF.FF.0
IP LAN protocol bound to NetWare NE2000  v3.11 (910131)
:
```

Figure 14.11

Binding IP to NE2000.

Creating the Startup Command Files

Provide installation specifications for the NetWare 3.11 server, and enter the information in the appropriate configuration file with the correct format.

One step remains to complete installation. You must create the STARTUP.NCF and AUTOEXEC.NCF files that load your drivers and perform other startup functions when the server is booted.

Creating STARTUP.NCF

To return to the INSTALL utility, press Alt+Esc. If you have been following the steps in this chapter, INSTALL's System Options menu will still be displayed. If not, display it at this time.

Next select the Create STARTUP.NCF File option. This option enables you to create the file needed to load the disk driver automatically and set particular operating environment features as seen in figure 14.12.

719

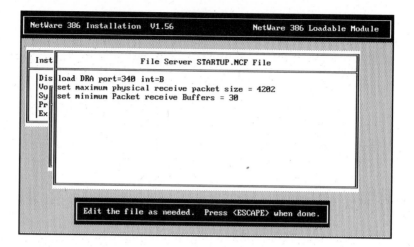

The STARTUP.NCF file contains the commands to load the disk
driver and the special SET commands. You can set the maximum
and minimum packet size. Figure 14.12 shows that the maximum
size for any transmitted packet on the network is 4,202 bytes, and
the minimum number of receive buffers on the server is 30. The
packet size allows proper operation of the ARCnet TURBO-II
standard, and the buffers of 30 help in heavy traffic situations. To
leave the editing screen for the STARTUP.NCF file, press Esc and
answer Yes to save the file. Press Esc until you return to the
Installation Options menu.

Next select Create the AUTOEXEC.NCF File. After you select this
option, the system should remember all the commands you
entered and automatically insert them into the AUTOEXEC.NCF
file (see fig. 14.13).

Check the file for accuracy. Notice that the PC500386 driver
loaded from drive C is not entered properly because INSTALL
assumes all LAN and disk drivers are loaded from SYS:. This
problem is simple to solve. Place **C:** before the driver, or place a
copy of the driver in the SYS:SYSTEM directory so that your
backup device also protects this file.

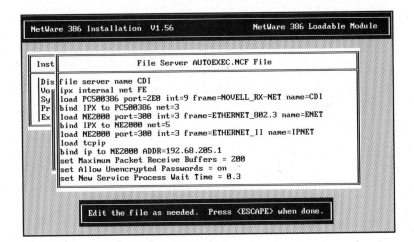

Figure 14.13

Creating the
AUTOEXEC.NCF file.

Study Note

Notice the parameter "name" in the AUTOEXEC.NCF file. This parameter is useful because it enables you to name the individual drivers and BIND to the name.

Although the earlier examples do not illustrate this technique, it is a simple matter to replace the LAN driver name with the assigned name, such as BIND IPX TO CDI NET=3.

Product Options

An optional step is to install software options, such as the Macintosh NLM. To install an option, select Product Options from the Installation Options menu and press Enter. Any products currently installed will be displayed. Figure 14.14 shows only one currently installed product, NetWare for Macintosh. To install a new product, press Ins. Insert the option disk in a floppy disk drive. Then enter the drive letter of the disk drive after the prompt Enter drive and/or path to new product source media. Follow any instructions that may be presented.

Figure 14.14

The Currently Installed Products list.

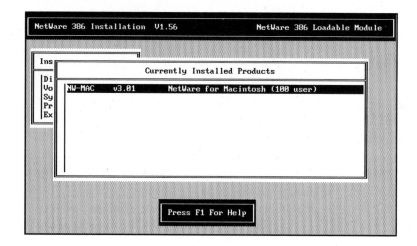

Flow chart for order of 3.11 installation:

Configure a DOS partition on the server

(FDISK and FORMAT)

Create a SERVER.311 directory

Copy Boot Files to server

SERVER.EXE

LOAD <Disk Driver>

LOAD INSTALL

(Create NetWare partitions and volumes)

MOUNT SYS

Install public and system files

LOAD <LAN Driver>

BIND <protocols> to <LAN Drivers>

Create STARTUP.NCF

Create AUTOEXEC.NCF

Reboot and Test

Modifying the 3.11 Operating System

LAN configurations change frequently. You need to know how to update your hardware and what changes need to be made to the NetWare software when your server configuration changes.

This section teaches you how to spot possible configuration problems with your server. These problems can require file server expansion. Common solutions to configuration problems include adding memory, splitting the network into multiple LAN cards, or adding one or more new disk channels.

Adding Memory

Many people overlook the importance of system memory. NetWare 3.11 is a high-level multitasking system that requires many times more memory than the average workstation. Most 3.11 file servers should not have fewer than 8MB of memory, and should have much more memory if large disk volumes are being used.

As a rule of thumb, the total number of cache buffers listed on the main MONITOR screen should be between 800 and 1,000. The amount of Cache Buffers listed under Resource Utilization should not be fewer than 20 percent.

If either of these statistics varies outside these ranges, Novell suggests that you add memory in increments of 1MB until the problem is solved.

Additional LAN Cards

As a rule of thumb, all numbers listed under the LAN driver statistics in the MONITOR utility, with the exception of Total Packets sent and received, should be as low as possible, if not zero. Different LAN cards display various statistics, but a high level of error and retries generally represents a defective card or a high level of traffic. The simplest solution to a traffic problem is to install another LAN card to handle some of the traffic load.

Identifying a network performance problem can require special equipment and a high level of traffic pattern knowledge for a particular topology. If you think you are experiencing problems due to statistics found in the monitor program, ask your vendor for suggestions.

Disk Channels

Disk Channel performance is difficult to analyze. A particular disk controller has a limit on the number of reads and writes it can perform in any given second, but most network file server loads are not consistent. Word processors, spreadsheets, and database applications present a different load to the disk controller. This inconsistency is compounded by the number of users and the work loads created in the office environment.

If the actual disk-access time appears to be slow, the system administrator can watch a few key MONITOR statistics. Two in particular, Dirty Cache Buffers and Current Disk Requests, can inform you of the file server's capability to handle the current load.

Current Disk Requests shows the number of disk requests in the queue waiting to be serviced; Dirty Cache Buffers is the number of file blocks in memory waiting to be written to disk. If these numbers are high, the disk system may be overworked; or, the file server may be too slow to process the request in memory. An overworked disk channel requires that you install another disk channel to assist with the load. But before you invest in additional hardware, talk to a reputable vender for a solution.

Review Questions

1. Which formula would you use to determine the amount of memory required on a DOS volume?

   ○ a. (Volume Size in MB × .023) divided by block size.

   ○ b. (Volume Size in MB × .032) divided by block size.

   ○ c. (Volume Size in MB × .23) divided by block size.

   ○ d. (Volume Size in MB × .32) divided by block size.

2. Which statement about v3.11 is most true?

   ○ a. You must always low-level format new drives.

   ○ b. You should create a DOS partition on the file server to store files the server may need if SYS: is not available.

   ○ c. Cache memory can be left enabled if v2.2 was installed prior to this installation.

   ○ d. You must make disk copies of all the NetWare disks prior to installation.

3. Which is true about an internal NET number?

   ○ a. It *must* be unique.

   ○ b. It is used by NLMs for internal communications.

   ○ c. Both a and b

   ○ d. Neither a nor b

4. Which parameter syntax would you use to prevent both the AUTOEXEC.NCF and the STARTUP.NCF scripts from loading?

   ○ a. SERVER -C

   ○ b. SERVER -NA,NS

   ○ c. SERVER -NA -NS

   ○ d. SERVER -NAS

725

5. Which statement about mirroring versus duplexing is false?

  ○ a. Duplexing occurs on a single controller.

  ○ b. Mirroring duplicates data over multiple drives.

  ○ c. Duplexing requires you to load the driver twice.

  ○ d. Mirroring does not add read performance.

6. Which option does not appear on the Available Disk Options menu?

  ○ a. Format

  ○ b. Mirroring

  ○ c. Partition Tables

  ○ d. VREPAIR

7. Which statement about v3.11 installation is false?

  ○ a. Partitioning and Mirroring both appear under the Available Disk Options menu.

  ○ b. Low Leveling the drive is done from the Available Disk Options menu.

  ○ c. Creating a NetWare partition is found under the Partition Table option in Available Disk options.

  ○ d. Choosing the disk driver to use in AUTOEXEC.NCF is done in the Available Disk Options menu.

8. Which statement about v3.11 volume creation is false?

  ○ a. Naming volumes is done under Volume Options.

  ○ b. Your first volume should be called VOL1:.

  ○ c. Block size is chosen when creating a volume.

  ○ d. The default block size is 4KB.

9. When assembling the hardware, it is a good idea to test the equipment using DOS before installing NetWare.

   ○ A. True

   ○ B. False

10. A low-level format is:

    ○ a. Not recommended on old drives.

    ○ b. Below the DOS format.

    ○ c. Above the DOS format.

    ○ d. Not normally done at the factory.

11. Which floppies should be copied to the DOS partition after you create a bootable drive on the server?

    ☐ a. NLMS-1

    ☐ b. Utils-1

    ☐ c. System-1

    ☐ d. System-2

12. To create a volume, you must choose _____ Options from the _____ utility.

13. If no drives appear in the Available Disk Drives window in the Install utility:

    ○ a. Continue on, this is normal.

    ○ b. Continue on, a window will appear prompting you to mount the drives.

    ○ c. Press Ins to add drives.

    ○ d. Stop the procedure and check to find why the drives are not showing up.

14. The first NetWare volume must have the name _____.

15. All LAN cards must be loaded and bound at the time of installation for them to be recognized.

○   a.   True

○   b.   False

Answers

1. A

2. B

3. C

4. C

5. A

6. D

7. D

8. B

9. A

10. B

11. C, D

12. Volume, Install

13. D

14. SYS:

15. B

Installing NetWare 3.12

15
CHAPTER

NetWare 3.12 is similar to NetWare 3.11. Version 3.12 incorporates a few new features and changes, but the primary improvement in NetWare 3.12 is that it incorporates the most important patches that have been released for NetWare 3.11 since its introduction. Installation of NetWare 3.11 should be followed by installation of all the patches that are applicable to the network being serviced. This step is largely unnecessary with NetWare 3.12.

NetWare 3.12 has some original features that reflect NetWare's evolution. Here are the new features that affect installation:

◆ The default Ethernet frame type is now Ethernet 802.2, not Ethernet 802.3 as it was for version 3.11 and earlier. If your Ethernet clients will not be running the new DOS VLM requester that ships with NetWare 3.12, they will still be set up for Ethernet 802.3 frames, and you need to make changes to the frame type either at the server or at the workstation. The best strategy, however, is to upgrade your workstations to use the VLM requester.

◆ Although NetWare 3.12 remains available on floppy disks, a CD-ROM version is now available. This is definitely more convenient, and it is the only way to get the ElectroText on-line documentation, which, at 30MB, would be too cumbersome to ship or install from floppies.

◆ Version 3.12 installation has some new menu-driven procedures.

◆ Version 3.12 includes files for a wide variety of LAN card and disk drivers. Until new generations of devices appear, you will be less likely to need drivers that are not shipped with NetWare.

 Describe the differences between a NetWare 3.11 installation and a NetWare 3.12 installation.

Preparing Server Hardware

NetWare 3.12 installs on the same server hardware as NetWare 3.1x, and the server hardware discussion in Chapter 14 applies to NetWare 3.12 as well.

NetWare 3.12 includes large numbers of drivers for network cards and disk drives—far more than were provided with NetWare 3.11. Chances are excellent that your hardware will be supported by driver files that shipped with your copy of NetWare 3.12. However, if your hardware is not supported, most vendors provide appropriate drivers.

Your first concern should be to select components that are certified and proven to work properly with NetWare; performance should be second. A high-performance system that is down much of the time is less productive than a reliable, lower-performance system. The following sections assume that you have a properly configured file server that can deliver the expected level of performance and reliability. Proper configuration of the server involves all aspects of the hardware, from the amount of installed RAM to the types of disk drives, the controllers, and the switch settings on the cards installed in the server.

Before you begin the installation process, make a list of all the I/O addresses, interrupts, memory addresses, and DMA channels used by your hardware. Start with your server's standard equipment, including the serial ports, parallel ports, video adapters, and all other known settings used by your system. You must know this information so that you can determine where you can install the required network hardware. Have a thorough picture of what's inside your server before you start adding NICs, disk drives, or other components.

Each network interface card and other required hardware should supply documentation that describes the supported settings. Using the supplied documentation and the list you created, you should be able to determine where each hardware card can reside. If documentation is not available for system components, you can use a utility such as CHECKIT PRO (described in Chapter 12, "Troubleshooting Concepts and Tools") to determine I/O addresses, interrupts, memory addresses, and DMA channels for the installed hardware on your server. Chapter 12 also describes the MicroHouse Technical Library and NSEPro, which are excellent research tools in this area.

Remember that the interrupts and addresses usually used by LPT and COM ports are available if those resources are disabled in your server. LPT and COM ports will be required to support printers that are attached to the server. A COM port may be required if you are configuring a modem for remotely managing the server.

Watch out for I/O and memory overlap. Although the documentation may not mention memory overlap, not all hardware devices operate true to the published specifications.

You may experience problems if two cards are installed at adjoining I/O addresses. Suppose that card A is installed at I/O 300h and card B is installed at I/O 308h. These settings may appear to work properly, but card A needs 10 bytes of memory, which places it 2 bytes into card B's space. This type of problem is sometimes difficult to locate because the network may appear to function properly at first. Put all known information in the list you create.

When you install NetWare, you will need to know the make and model for each network card, as well as the settings for the card. You will also need to know the type and settings for your hard drive controllers.

Few of the newest NICs are supported by drivers that shipped with NetWare 3.11. Unless you are using a classic card such as the Novell NE1000 or NE2000, the 3Com 3C503 or 3C509, or the IBM Token Ring adapter, you need to obtain drivers from the disks shipped with the adapter from NetWire or the vendor. Driver files for network interface cards end with the file name extension .LAN.

NetWare 3.12 ships with a basic set of hard drive controller drivers for "generic" disk controllers, including the following:

- **ISADISK** for use with standard AT-class ISA controllers (ST506 MFM or RLL, and ESDI disks when other drivers are unavailable)

- **IDE** for use with IDE disk drives

- **DCB** for Novell's DCB Disk Coprocessor Board (now distributed by other vendors)

- **PS2ESDI** for PS/2s with ESDI drives

- **PS2MFM** for IBM PS/2s with MFM drives

- **PS2SCSI** for IBM PS/2s with SCSI drives

Also included are disk drivers for a wide variety of SCSI controllers. SCSI hard drives are probably the best choice for use in a NetWare server, and the inclusion of drives for many SCSI controller models is a welcome addition to NetWare 3.12.

Make sure that you carefully examine your list of hardware settings. If you find any potential conflicts, reconfigure one of the components, if possible. This is better than having to isolate the cause of transient network problems after the network is operational.

Test the equipment for proper DOS operation. Start by booting DOS from drive A to confirm that the computer is operating, and then check the amount of installed extended memory. The available memory should be displayed during the memory test when you cold boot your PC. NetWare 3.11 requires a certain amount of extended memory to operate properly.

NetWare 3.12 requires 2MB of memory for the operating system plus memory for each volume.

In addition to memory for NetWare, you must determine the approximate amount of memory required for the NetWare 3.12 volumes. Start by determining the block size that will be used. 4MB blocks are almost always most appropriate, and that size will be used in these examples. Once you have determined the block size, use the appropriate formula for each volume:

♦ For a DOS volume, the memory required =

$$\frac{\text{volume size (in MB) X .023}}{\text{block size}}$$

♦ For a volume that will support Macintosh or Unix files, the memory required =

$$\frac{\text{volume size (in MB) X .032}}{\text{block size}}$$

For example, to determine the memory required for a 650MB DOS volume that will not support additional name space, the calculation is as follows:

$$\frac{650 \times .023}{4} = \frac{14.95}{4} = 3.73$$

Calculate the memory required for each volume on the server. Then add the 2MB required for the operating system. Round the sum up to at least the next highest megabyte. In this example, minimum memory in megabytes is 3.73 + 2, which is 5.73MB. The best memory configuration in this case must be at least 6MB, but 8MB makes more sense in many hardware configurations. Memory is much more economical in larger increments and 4MB, 16MB, or even 32MB increments may make the most sense in the long run.

Do not be afraid of having more than the minimum amount of memory. One of the best ways to enhance NetWare's performance is to give it more memory to work with.

Install the required memory before you proceed with NetWare installation.

Configuring a CD-ROM Drive for Installation

This example demonstrates the installation of NetWare 3.12 from a CD-ROM. In addition to the basic hardware setup discussed earlier, you need to configure a SCSI controller card and a CD-ROM drive in your server.

If you are using a SCSI disk subsystem, you need to have a separate SCSI controller for your CD-ROM drive. NetWare installation accesses the CD-ROM drive by way of DOS and the CD-ROM drivers that are installed by DOS. However, NetWare uses its own SCSI drivers to support a SCSI disk subsystem. If you try a CD-ROM installation using a single SCSI controller, your system will hang when you load the NetWare SCSI card drivers.

This happens because both the DOS SCSI/CD-ROM drivers and the NetWare server SCSI drivers are attempting to control the same SCSI card. If you will be leaving the CD-ROM reader attached to the server, you will want to retain the second SCSI card in the server so that use of the CD-ROM does not reduce performance of your hard drive subsystem. If the CD-ROM reader will be removed after installation, the second SCSI card can be removed as well.

As just mentioned, the installation program reads programs from the CD-ROM by using the SCSI and CD-ROM drivers installed for DOS. You need to add the required driver files to your boot drive, and to modify CONFIG.SYS and AUTOEXEC.BAT to run the drivers. Most SCSI cards include setup programs that install the drivers and configure the CONFIG.SYS and AUTOEXEC.BAT files.

The CONFIG.SYS file will usually run two drivers: one for the SCSI card and one for the CD-ROM. These drivers are specific for each brand of SCSI controller. The following are the lines that are required for an Adaptec 1542 SCSI adapter (the parameters will vary depending on the installation):

```
DEVICE=C:\ADAPTEC\ASPI4DOS.SYS /D
DEVICE=C:\ADAPTEC\ASPICD.SYS /D:ASPICD0
```

A DOS CD-ROM routine will also be required. Usually this means using the MSCDEX program that is licensed by Microsoft. Here is the AUTOEXEC.BAT command that runs MSCDEX:

```
C:\DOS\MSCDEX.EXE /D:ASPICD0 /M:12 /S
```

Before you can proceed with a CD-ROM installation, configure the CD-ROM hardware and install the required drivers and commands in your server's DOS partition. Consult the documentation for your SCSI card and CD-ROM drive for the proper commands and syntax to use. If your equipment includes an automatic setup program, it usually will simplify driver installation.

After the drivers are configured, boot the server and see if you can access your CD-ROM drive. If you can, you are ready to continue with installation.

Creating the DOS Boot Partition

Although you can obtain a full DOS license for your server, the DOS partition can be created using only the SYSTEM_1 disk that is included with NetWare 3.12. SYSTEM_1 is a bootable DR DOS disk, and contains the FORMAT and FDISK utilities in a \DOSTOOLS directory. An EDITOR program is also provided to enable you to configure CONFIG.SYS and AUTOEXEC.BAT files.

Whichever version of DOS you select, use FDISK to create a primary DOS partition on the first physical hard drive. The partition should be at least 5MB in size. A larger partition can accomodate tools such as CHECKIT PRO for diagnosing server hardware problems. After creating the DOS partition, make the partition active.

Reboot the server with a DOS disk or the SYSTEM_1 disk. Then use the FORMAT /S command to format the DOS partition and install the DOS boot system files on the drive.

Do not install any high-memory or extended-memory managers in the DOS partition. The NetWare server must control all upper memory in the server and will conflict with DOS memory managers.

Installing the CD-ROM Software

The example installation in this chapter installs NetWare 3.12 from a CD-ROM. This is the most efficient way to install NetWare and the only way if you want to install the ElectroText on-line documentation.

After creating the DOS boot partition, copy the required files for your CD-ROM controller and drive to the boot drive. Then create CONFIG.SYS and AUTOEXEC.BAT files that contain the necessary startup commands to initialize your CD-ROM controller and drive.

Many vendors of CD-ROM drives and adapters provide a setup disk that is usually the most efficient way to configure your CONFIG.SYS and AUTOEXEC.BAT files. The commands contain numerous parameters that must be configured correctly. Although virtually all drives use the Microsoft MSCDEX program, the drivers required for the controller board will be different for each brand. Consult the vendor documentation.

Provide the information requested by the NetWare 3.12 installation process.

NetWare 3.12 Server Installation

If you have configured your system properly, your CD-ROM drive will be available as a DOS drive, often as drive D:. Insert the NetWare 3.12 CD-ROM in the drive and change to the drive letter that accesses your CD-ROM drive.

List the major steps and the order of execution in the NetWare 3.12 server software installation.

Install a NetWare 3.12 server.

1. **Run the INSTALL program.**

   The directory you install from depends on the language you want NetWare to use in displays. NetWare 3.12 is shipped in versions with language support for English, French, German, Spanish, and Italian.

   For English, CD to the \NETWARE.40\ENGLISH directory. For other languages, substitute FRANCAIS, DEUTSCH, ESPANOL, or ITALIANO for ENGLISH.

   In the appropriate language directory, enter the command **INSTALL**. Soon, the installation utility screen in figure 15.1 will be displayed. This screen reminds you that this default Ethernet frame type is now Ethernet_802.2. Press a key to continue.

   The first menu screen you see enables you to choose to install NetWare 3.12 or upgrade over a previous installation (see fig. 15.2). As with all screens seen in the installation process, this screen shows a list of active keys at the bottom of the screen. You will find that several keys are used to move from one screen to the next, and these key lists will be extremely helpful. Also note that F1 will display help for this screen. A help option is available for each installation screen.

737

Figure 15.1

The INSTALL frame type warning.

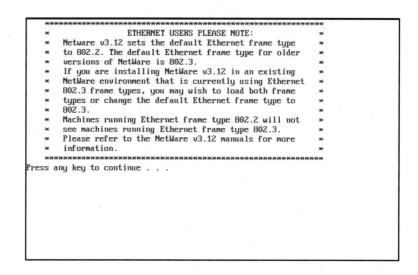

Figure 15.2

Selecting an Installation option.

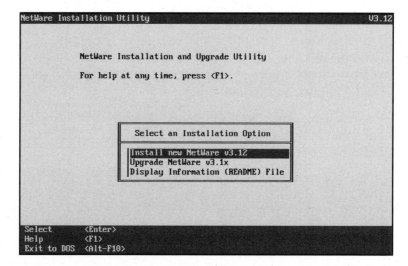

From the Installation option screen, select the option Install new NetWare 3.12 to proceed with the installation.

2. Verify the DOS partition.

The screen in figure 15.3 displays the existing disk partitions on C:. This screen can be used to reconfigure the DOS partition. However, you have already created a bootable DOS partition, and you should choose the option Retain current disk partitions.

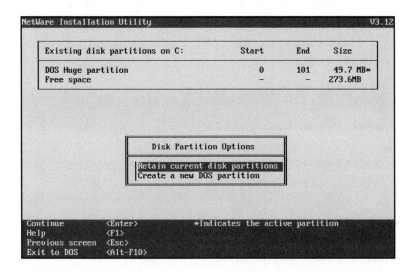

Figure 15.3

Configuring disk partitions in INSTALL.

Most screens in INSTALL enable you to back up to previous steps by pressing the Esc key. If you make a mistake, you can usually cancel the mistake by escaping to the previous step.

3. Name the server.

With your DOS position created, you are ready to proceed with the actual installation of server files. The screen in figure 15.4 instructs you to to enter a server name. This name should have been determined beforehand as part of your planning process.

Figure 15.4

Entering the server name.

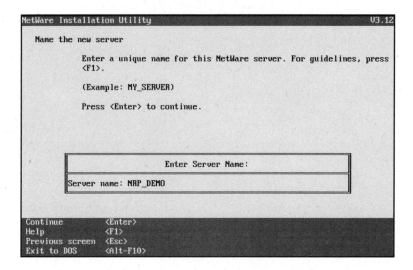

```
NetWare Installation Utility                                         V3.12

    Name the new server

            Enter a unique name for this NetWare server. For guidelines, press
            <F1>.

            (Example: MY_SERVER)

            Press <Enter> to continue.




              ┌────────────────────────────────────────────────────┐
              │                Enter Server Name:                    │
              ├────────────────────────────────────────────────────┤
              │Server name: NRP_DEMO                                 │
              └────────────────────────────────────────────────────┘


    Continue          <Enter>
    Help              <F1>
    Previous screen   <Esc>
    Exit to DOS       <Alt-F10>
```

With NetWare 3.*x* you can change server names fairly freely. When you install a server in NetWare 3.12, however, its name will appear several places in the NDS tree, and changing the name can be quite involved. For example, each volume on the server will be represented by a Volume object that incorporates the server name in its object name. Just as it was important to plan your Directory tree carefully, it is important to plan your server names carefully.

Type the server's name in the Server name: field and press Enter to continue.

4. **Specify an internal network number.**

   The next screen, shown in figure 15.5, requests an internal network number. The figure displays the randomly generated number that was provided by INSTALL. Ideally, you should be selecting a number based on a network management plan, and this number should have been determined as part of your network planning process. You can delete the number provided by INSTALL and enter one of your own. For this example installation, an internal network number of 2BAD was selected. This number will appear later when the AUTOEXEC.NCF file is created. Press Enter to accept the internal network number that is displayed.

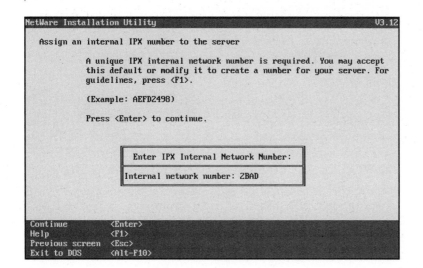

Figure 15.5

Entering the server internal network number.

5. **Specify the installation directory.**

    Next, you must specify the directory from which the server boot files are to be installed. As shown in figure 15.6, IN-STALL will select a default Source path that is directed at your CD-ROM drive. A directory named INSTALL has been selected in the subdirectory level below the language directory you chose to begin installation. There should be no need to change the Source path.

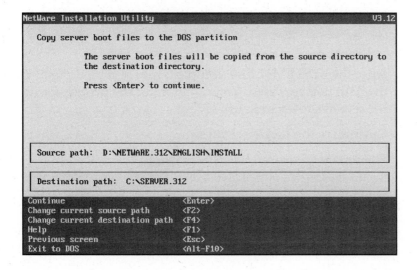

Figure 15.6

Selecting the boot file source and destination.

In most cases, you will want to copy the boot files into a directory on C:. The default subdirectory is named \NETWARE.312. Usually, you verify both defaults by pressing Enter.

INSTALL will proceed to copy the boot files, starting with the files on the SYSTEM_1 disk. You will have a SYSTEM_1 disk whether you are installing from floppies or CD-ROM. If the disk is not in the A: drive, as shown in figure 15.7, INSTALL asks you to Insert the disk labeled SYSTEM_1 in drive A or press <F2> to specify a different path. Insert the disk or specify a path and press Enter.

Figure 15.7

Loading files from the SYSTEM_1 disk.

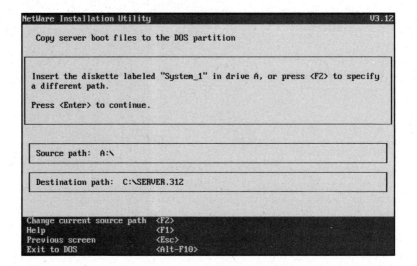

After the SYSTEM_1 disk is copied, files will be copied from the path you specified. You can monitor the progress with the screen shown in figure 15.7.

6. **Customize the locale settings.**

The screen in figure 15.8 enables you to customize three locale settings of your NetWare 3.12 installation. These values are derived from your current DOS configuration. The *Country Code* is a three-digit number that can be determined from your DOS manual. If you select this field and press Enter, a submenu is displayed from which you can select one of the alternative country codes (see fig. 15.9).

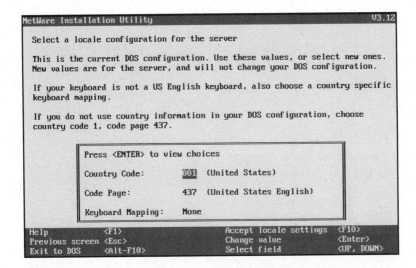

Figure 15.8

Options for customizing locale settings.

Figure 15.9

The menu of available country codes.

Code pages determine the character sets that can be displayed. Code page 437 is used for United States English. (Code page 437 is also known as the hardware code page because it corresponds to the display and keyboard defaults of IBM-compatible PCs.) NetWare 3.12 also supports the

Multilingual code page 850, which displays international characters. You can display a menu of code pages, shown in figure 15.10, by highlighting the Code Page field and pressing Enter.

Figure 15.10

The menu of available code pages.

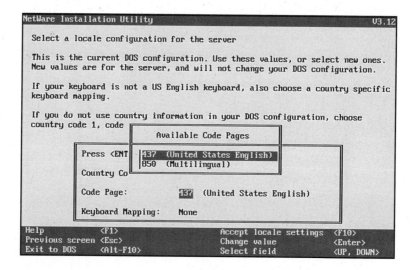

```
NetWare Installation Utility                                      V3.12

Select a locale configuration for the server

This is the current DOS configuration. Use these values, or select new ones.
New values are for the server, and will not change your DOS configuration.

If your keyboard is not a US English keyboard, also choose a country specific
keyboard mapping.

If you do not use country information in your DOS configuration, choose
country code 1, code ┌──────────────────────────────────┐
                     │       Available Code Pages       │
          Press <ENT │ 437  (United States English)     │
                     │ 850  (Multilingual)              │
          Country Co └──────────────────────────────────┘

          Code Page:             437   (United States English)

          Keyboard Mapping:      None

Help             <F1>                   Accept locale settings  <F10>
Previous screen  <Esc>                  Change value            <Enter>
Exit to DOS      <Alt-F10>              Select field            <UP, DOWN>
```

Alternative keyboard mappings enable you to customize the console keyboard for conventions of different countries. A menu of keyboard maps, shown in figure 15.11, can be displayed by highlighting the field and pressing Enter. After selecting the desired locale settings, press F10 to continue.

Note When using INSTALL, Enter is used to continue menu selection; F10 continues after filling in forms.

7. **Select the file format.**

NetWare 3.12 can support two file name formats, and you must select one from the screen in figure 15.12. The recommended format obeys DOS file name restrictions. The DOS file name format is case-insensitive and converts lowercase characters to uppercase for storage. DOS format does not permit the use of many characters from the extended character set.

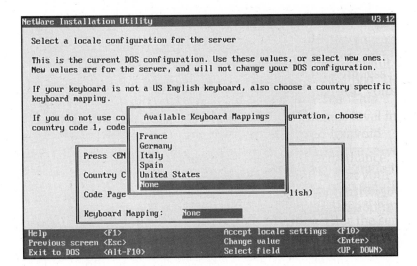

```
NetWare Installation Utility                                    V3.12
  Select a locale configuration for the server

  This is the current DOS configuration. Use these values, or select new ones.
  New values are for the server, and will not change your DOS configuration.

  If your keyboard is not a US English keyboard, also choose a country specific
  keyboard mapping.

  If you do not use co┌─────────────────────────┐guration, choose
  country code 1, code │  Available Keyboard Mappings │
                       ├─────────────────────────┤
                       │ France                  │
                       │ Germany                 │
          Press <EN    │ Italy                   │
                       │ Spain                   │
          Country C    │ United States           │
                       │ None                    │lish)
          Code Page └──────────────────────────┘
          Keyboard Mapping:    None

 Help           <F1>                  Accept locale settings  <F10>
 Previous screen <Esc>                Change value            <Enter>
 Exit to DOS    <Alt-F10>             Select field            <UP, DOWN>
```

Figure 15.11

The menu of available keyboard mappings.

```
NetWare Installation Utility                                    V3.12
  Select the filename format

     NetWare  -  allows extended lower case filenames (ü, é, ...)
     DOS      -  maps lower case characters to upper case in filenames

  You must use a shell (e.g. NETX.EXE) rather than a requester (e.g. VLM.EXE),
  to access lower case extended filenames.

  Press <F9> to view upper case mappings, <F1> for more information.

        ┌──────────────────────────────────────────────┐
        │ Select the format you desire and press <ENTER> │
        ├──────────────────────────────────────────────┤
        │ DOS Filename Format (recommended)            │
        │ NetWare Filename Format                      │
        └──────────────────────────────────────────────┘

 Help <F1>                                 Previous screen <Esc>
```

Figure 15.12

Selecting the file server file name format.

The NetWare file name format permits file names to contain upper- and lowercase characters as well as graphic and other extended characters. The NETX shell program supports the NetWare file name format. Even if you are not installing the VLM Requester on your network workstations, a time will certainly come when the Requester will be required for NetWare. Out of concern for future compatibility, you should select DOS file name format on this screen.

8. **Specify commands to be added to STARTUP.NCF.**

   Two files contain configuration information that is used when a NetWare server is started. A file named STARTUP.NCF is stored on the server boot drive and contains commands that are executed as the server is started. A file named AUTOEXEC.NCF is stored in the \SYSTEM directory and contains commands that are executed after the server is running, much as AUTOEXEC.BAT contains commands that are run after DOS is started.

   INSTALL now displays the screen in figure 15.13, giving you an option of entering commands that are to be added to the STARTUP.NCF file. You can easily add these commands in the future, and descriptions of the commands you might enter are beyond the scope of an installation tutorial. For this example, therefore, select the No response.

Figure 15.13

Choosing whether to enter startup commands.

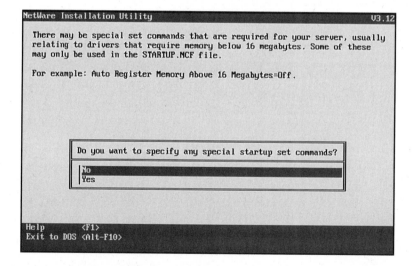

9. **Specify whether AUTOEXEC.BAT should start the server.**

   Ordinarily, you will want your server to start NetWare automatically when the server is rebooted. The screen in figure 15.14 gives you the option of having AUTOEXEC.BAT customized with the commands that will start SERVER.EXE whenever DOS is booted. Usually, you select Yes on this screen.

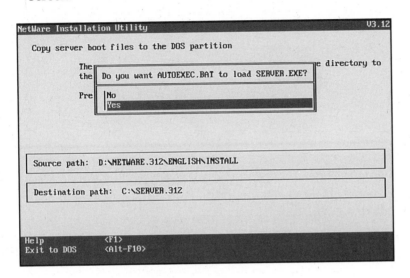

Figure 15.14

Choosing whether AUTOEXEC.BAT should be customized.

Running SERVER.EXE

At this point, INSTALL runs SERVER.EXE to start the server. You will see the message Loading... as this is taking place.

NetWare 386 calculates your file server performance speed by setting up a speed counter and watching the CPU time (ticks) as it increments the counter. After three CPU ticks, the counter is divided by 1,000, and the result is used as the speed indicator.

The speed indicator determines the relative speed difference between computers that run as NetWare file servers. Table 15.1 offers some common examples.

Table 15.1
Common Speed Measurements

CPU Rating	Clock Speed	Wait State	Novell Speed
386	16 MHz	1	121
386	25 MHz	0	242
386	33 MHz	0	342
486	33 MHz	0	914
486	66 MHz	0	1830

Following the speed display, you are prompted to enter a file server name. Type in a name (two to 47 characters long with no periods or spaces) and press Enter.

Next, you are prompted for the internal network number. In Chapter 8 you can read about the requirement for a unique internal network number for each NetWare 3.*x* and 4.*x* server. Type any hexadecimal number (one to eight digits in length) and press Enter. Note that this number must be different from all other internal or external network numbers of connected networks or servers.

Novell NetWare 386 uses an internal network structure that enables NLMs to communicate. This internal network requires that the "NET" numbers for segment address and "NET" numbers for file server address be different.

After the SERVER loads, a header or banner appears that displays the NetWare version and user count. The user count confirms the number of user connections that this particular version allows.

The SERVER command can be entered with command-line parameters. Use the following parameters to troubleshoot suspected problems with file server boot files or to change buffer size:

- **-NA** prevents AUTOEXEC.NCF file execution
- **-NS** prevents STARTUP.NCF file execution
- **-C** enables you to modify the cache buffer size from the default of 4KB per block

After the banner is displayed, you should see a colon (:) prompt, which is the normal prompt for the NetWare console. You can load the appropriate disk driver and continue to create a Novell volume.

Loading Disk Drivers

Next, you must load a disk drive to enable NetWare to communicate with your hard drive. The following drivers are used for generic types of hard drive:

- **ISADISK** is used with most MFM and ESDI drives in servers equipped with the ISA bus.

- **IDE** is used with the IDE hard drives currently shipped on most desktop PCs.

- **DCB** is used with the original Novell disk coprocessor board or any DCB-compatible, such as the Adaptec 4000 series disk controllers.

- **PS2ESDI** is used for ESDI drives in servers equipped with the Micro Channel Architecture bus.

- **PS2MFM** is used for MFM drives in Micro Channel PCs.

- **PS2SCSI** is used for drive systems using IBM SCSI controllers in Micro Channel PCs.

749

Note Currently, Compaq is the only AT-type ESDI controller certified to allow duplexing with the standard ISADISK driver.

Next, you load the disk driver required for your system. If you are using a generic type of disk drive, select a disk driver from the previous list. If you are using a SCSI disk controller, a driver may have shipped with NetWare. If not, you should copy the driver file to the NetWare DOS boot directory.

The server used to prepare this demonstration has IDE drives. Thus, the driver is loaded with the following command:

```
LOAD IDE
```

As shown in figure 15.15, after the disk driver is loaded, you will be prompted for any necessary hardware configuration information. Most drivers will suggest the default values for the hardware being installed, enabling you to change values as required. In this case, you are asked for the PORT number and the INTERRUPT number, which you must determine from your own hardware settings and documentation. For this example, a port of 1F0h and an interrupt of E or 14 are used.

Figure 15.15

Loading a disk driver.

```
NRP_DEMO:load ide
Loading module IDE.DSK
   NetWare IDE Device Driver
   Version 3.12    April 26, 1993
   Copyright 1993 Novell, Inc.  All rights reserved.
Supported I/O port values are 1F0, 170, 1E8, 168
I/O port: 1F0
Supported interrupt number values are E, B, F, C
Interrupt number: E
NRP_DEMO:
```

Duplexing Versus Mirroring

If you intend to implement disk duplexing (see Chapter 10, "Working with Storage Devices"), you need to install a second disk controller card. To activate this card, load the disk driver a second time by following the preceding instructions. Each card must be configured with different ports and interrupts, and you enter the second card's parameters the second time you load the disk driver.

The second driver is not really loaded twice. The second LOAD command simply tells the system to use the driver twice, which is defined as *re-entrantly* loading the driver.

Duplexing with a second disk channel improves disk read performance because the system can read from each disk concurrently. Mirroring uses only a single controller and provides no added read performance or disk write performance loss. Both options provide a redundant disk drive for data protection but with a cost-versus-performance trade-off. Only duplexing provides data protection in case of a disk-channel failure.

Creating Partitions and Volumes

You now are ready to load the installation program and start the actual installation process. To load the INSTALL program from the DOS drive C, type the following and press Enter:

```
LOAD INSTALL
```

You should see the main Installation Options screen (see fig. 15.16).

Novell makes it easy to walk through the installation process, beginning with Disk Options and continuing with Volume Options, System Options, and Product Options.

Figure 15.16

INSTALL's Installation Options screen.

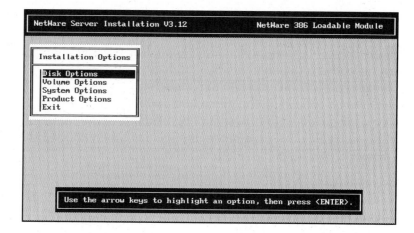

Disk Options

After INSTALL's main screen appears, select Disk Options by highlighting it on the Installation Options menu and pressing Enter. You see a screen like the one in figure 15.17.

Figure 15.17

The Available Disk Options menu.

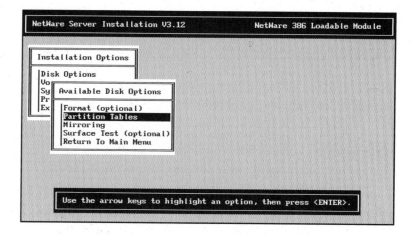

Note The Available Disk Options menu includes the following options:

- ◆ Format
- ◆ Surface Test
- ◆ Mirroring
- ◆ Partition Tables
- ◆ Return To Main Menu

To create a NetWare volume, select the Partition Tables option by highlighting the option and pressing Enter. That will bring up the Partition Options screen shown in figure 15.18. This screen displays information about the partitions that are on the hard drive. The DOS partition you created is shown as Other Partition Type.

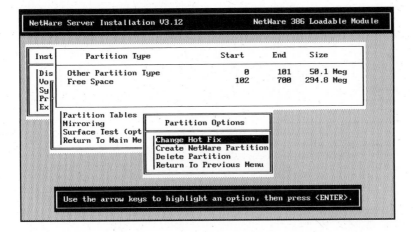

Figure 15.18

The Partition Options screen.

Before you create a NetWare partition, you have the option of changing the size of the hot fix area assigned to the partition. See Chapter 13 for a thorough discussion of NetWare's hot fix feature.

The Change Hot Fix option, located in the Partition Options menu, enables you to modify the size of the Hot Fix Redirection Area. Novell suggests that you do not make the Hot Fix Area any smaller than the default.

753

You also can use the Change Hot Fix option to match drives of different physical sizes, making them appear to be the same size, when mirroring or duplexing is desired.

To create the partition, select the Create NetWare Partition option. The Partition Information screen you see next displays the following information (see fig. 15.19):

♦ Partition size

♦ Data area

♦ Redirection area

Figure 15.19

Entering partition information.

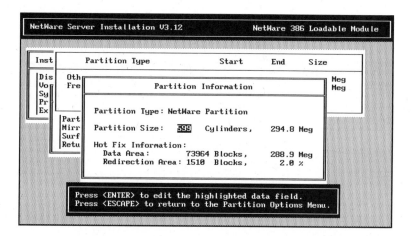

The Partition Size and Redirection Area fields accept entries. The Data Area simply displays the available data area size after hot fix is deducted from the partition.

You are allowed only one NetWare partition on each disk. With the exception of the disk that is used to boot DOS, all free space on each disk is ordinarily used to create the NetWare partition. The size of the partition is shown in the Partition Size field. You can change the partition size at this time if desired. You also can change the hot fix size on this screen by changing the value in the

Redirection Area field. To accept the entries and create the partition, press Escape; then select Yes at the `Create partition?` prompt to complete the process.

Figure 15.20 shows the Partition Type screen after the NetWare partition is created. When you first enter this option, you see only the DOS partition you created with the DOS FDISK utility. If the DOS partition does not appear correctly on this screen, do not proceed until the problem is solved.

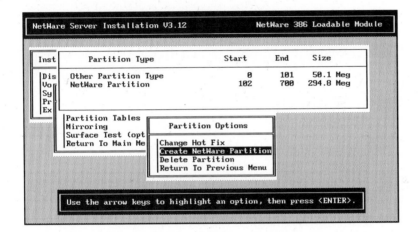

Figure 15.20

The partition list after creating a NetWare partition.

After you create the Novell partition, return to the Installation Options menu by pressing Esc. (Each time you press Esc, you back up one menu level.) Select Volume Options and press Enter. A Volumes list is displayed, which is currently empty (see fig. 15.21). Next you must create volumes within the NetWare partitions you have created. To create a new volume, press Insert in the Volumes screen.

To create a new volume, press Insert in the Volumes screen.

Figure 15.21

An empty Volumes
list.

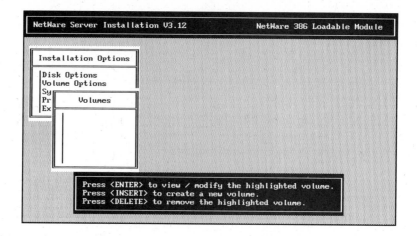

Volume Options

The New Volume Information screen enables you to choose the
volume configuration (see fig. 15.22).

Figure 15.22

Entering information
for the SYS volume.

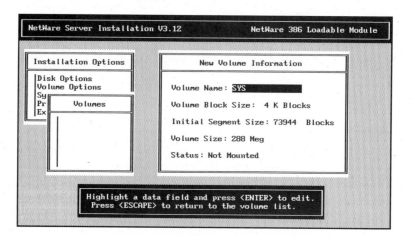

Unless you have a good reason for choosing another block size,
leave the Volume Block Size parameter at the 4KB Blocks default
value.

Selecting block sizes is more complicated than it might appear to be. Small block sizes use disk space more efficiently for the storage of small files but require more memory. Also, large files will be accessed less efficiently because data must be moved in units matching the volume block size.

Large block sizes require less memory and theoretically improve performance of large files because large blocks of data can be transferred.

File data is transferred via cache buffers, which have a default size of 4096 bytes, the same as the default volume block size. Performance is at its best when the size of the cache buffers matches the block size of the volume being serviced.

The size of the cache buffers is determined by the SET CACHE BUFFER SIZE= statement, and all cache buffers on the server have the same size.

The catch with changing volume sizes, therefore, is that it is not possible to match cache buffer size to volume block size if different volumes have different block sizes. If you adjust the cache and volume block size to optimize support for small files, performance with large files will suffer. Optimizing for large files can lower performance for small files. That's why the default 4KB volume block size is usually the best compromise.

Incidentally, this is not a problem with NetWare 4, which uses block suballocation to use disk space more efficiently.

The first NetWare volume must have the name SYS:, but subsequent volume names can be of your choice. Currently, all of the blocks in the partition are allocated to SYS. To create a smaller MB SYS volume, it is necessary to change the value in the Initial Segment Size field. Figure 15.23 shows the result of entering 25675 in the Initial Segment Size field. The volume size has been adjusted to 100MB and a 25675-block segment was assigned to SYS. The process of calculating this parameter is described below.

Figure 15.23

Mounting the SYS volume.

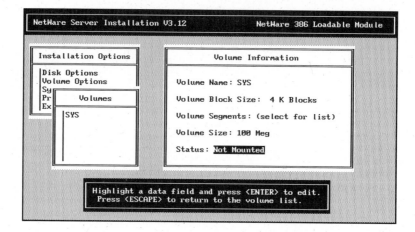

The following actions are available when creating a volume:

◆ You can enter a new name in the Volume Name field.

◆ You can change the block size by pressing Enter in the Volume Block Size field and selecting a new block size from the list provided. 4KB blocks are generally the best compromise, however. Small block sizes need more memory. (See the memory calculation formulas earlier in this chapter.) Large block sizes use disk space less efficiently when small files are present.

◆ If the server has only one available partition, you are shown the Initial Segment Size, which allocates all available partition space to the volume being created. If you want to reduce the size of the volume, enter a new Initial Segment Size in blocks. The formula for calculating blocks is shown in the following note.

◆ If the server has more than one partition, you can specify which partition is to be used by this volume. Select a segment by pressing Enter in the Volume Segments field. You see a list of available volume segments from which to choose.

Note If you want to create a volume that does not use the entire partition space, you can calculate the segment size by multiplying the desired size of the volume (in megabytes) by 1,024, and then dividing by block size. The sum is the number of blocks equal to the desired segment size. For example, if you want to create a 100MB volume and the volume block size is the default value of 4KB, the number of blocks in the segment are as follows:

(100 x 1,024)/4 = 25600 blocks

Therefore, 25600 blocks must be allocated to a 100MB volume. This information is entered into the Initial Segment Size field.

After a volume has been created, it must be mounted. This is done from the same screen that enables you to manage volumes that have already been created. From the Volumes screen, highlight the volume to be mounted or managed and press Enter. This will bring up the Volume Information screen for that volume, as shown in figure 15.23. With existing volumes, you cannot modify the block size. However, you can change the following information:

◆ You can rename the volume. However, you must never rename the SYS: volume.

◆ You can add volume segments to expand the size of the volume. These segments can be taken from the same partition as the original volume or from a partition on a separate drive. Volumes that consist of segments from several drive partitions are called spanned volumes.

◆ You can mount or unmount the volume. You might need to unmount a volume to delete it or to run VREPAIR as described in Chapter 12, "Troubleshooting Concepts and Tools."

Volume spanning is a feature of NetWare 3.12 that enables multiple drive partitions to be linked logically into a single volume.

This feature increases performance because the drives operate in a parallel manner, enabling them to access more data with less mechanical movement. To create a spanned volume, add volume segments to obtain the desired size.

 Volume spanning provides very high performance but not without cost. The rule of thumb is that your disk access time is divided by the number of drives. Note, however, that the possibility of failure is multiplied by the same number.

A volume can consist of up to 32 segments from one or more hard drives. New segments can be added to volumes even when the volumes are mounted, enabling administrators to increase volume size "on the fly." Once a segment is assigned to a volume, it cannot be unassigned.

Novell suggests that you implement duplexing whenever a volume is spanned. This technique also adds to performance by allowing the same split reads available with normal duplexing.

The individual block size of a volume can be modified from the 4KB default. You can select sizes of 4KB, 8KB, 16KB, 32KB, or 64KB. Unless you have a special application that can benefit from a large block size, use the default. A larger block degrades the performance of most applications. This feature is intended for very large database systems with large data blocks. Note that any calculations made with formulas listed earlier must be revised if block size is changed.

At this point, the volume is created but not mounted, meaning that it is unavailable for use. You must highlight the new volume in the Volumes display, move to the Status field, and change the status to Mounted to enable the volume.

After you press Esc and return to the Volumes list, you can press Insert to create additional volumes from the remaining partition space.

Copying the System and Public Files

After you create the NetWare volume or volumes, go to the System Options menu to complete the initial installation. Press Esc to back up to the Installation Options menu, highlight System Options, and then press Enter. One of the options on the System Options menu enables you to load the remaining software and create the files required to boot automatically as a file server (see fig. 15.24).

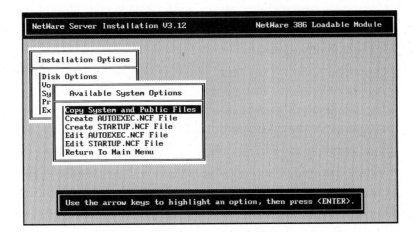

Figure 15.24

The Available System Options menu.

You must first copy all System and Public utilities. Select the Copy System and Public Files option by highlighting that choice on the Available System Options menu. Then press Enter. You will be presented with the screen in figure 15.25.

Figure 15.25

Specifying the source drive for copying files.

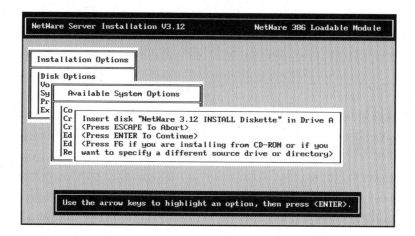

Because this example is installing from a CD-ROM, you must press F6 to enter a drive and directory path for your CD-ROM. After pressing F6, you will see the screen shown in figure 15.26, which enables you to specify the location of files to be copied. The drive letter will be the letter DOS assigned to your CD-ROM drive. The directory will be \NETWARE.312\ENGLISH (or a directory for another supported language version). Type the drive letter and directory, and press Enter.

Figure 15.26

Specifying the directory path for a CD-ROM.

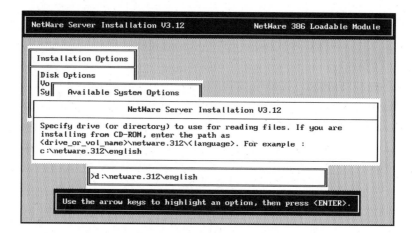

If you are installing from CD-ROM, just sit back while files are being copied. If you are copying from floppies, follow the prompts. If you did not mount the SYS: volume, you are prompted to do so now. After mounting volume SYS:, a window appears, and you are asked to insert the System_2 disk and press Esc. You will be prompted to insert additional disks until all files are copied. Continue this process until finished.

When all files are complete, you will see the message `File Upload Complete`. Press Enter to continue.

Loading LAN Drivers

The next step in the installation process is loading the LAN or network interface drivers. This explanation assumes that you have installed and tested the network cabling.

Two steps are required to fully activate a network card:

1. Load the network driver for the card.

2. Bind at least one protocol to the card driver.

 LAN drivers for NetWare 3.12 are NLMs that must be loaded to make the network function as a network. These modules drive the LAN cards in the server, enabling communication between the server and the nodes of the network. LAN drivers all have the file name extension LAN.

Loading a Network Driver

Next, you must load a network driver, in this example the 3C509 driver for a 3Com Etherlink III. This driver was included with NetWare 3.12 and was copied to the SYS: volume during installation. Therefore, it does not have to be loaded from the C drive.

Enter the following command from the console prompt to load the driver:

```
LOAD 3C509
```

This example installation was performed using an EISA server. As shown in figure 15.27, the driver prompted for a slot setting, in this case slot 4. In a later example, you will see installation of a non-EISA NIC that requires different settings. Because this Ethernet driver was loaded without a FRAME= parameter, the NetWare 3.12 default FRAME type of Ethernet_802.2.

Figure 15.27

Loading an NIC driver and binding the IPX protocol.

```
NRP_DEMO:load 3c509
Loading module 3C509.LAN
   3Com EtherLink III 3C509 Family
   Version 4.00e   January 7, 1993
   (C) Copyright 1992 3COM Corporation. All Rights Reserved.
Supported Slot values are 4
Slot: 4
NRP_DEMO:bind ipx to 3c509
Network number: B0FF0
IPX LAN protocol bound to 3Com EtherLink III 3C509 Family
3/11/94 6:15:23 pm:  0.0.0 Remote Console Connection Granted for
   000B0FF0:00608C85C72F
NRP_DEMO:
```

After the network driver is loaded, it must be bound to a protocol. The default NetWare protocol is named IPX, and the command is the following:

BIND IPX TO 3C509

After entering the BIND command, you will be asked to specify the network number for the network this card will connect to. In Chapter 8, "Addressing Your Network," you learn about network numbers. Essentially, each physical cabling system has a network number for each of the protocols it supports. The result of binding IPX is also shown in figure 15.27. The network card is now active and the server is able to exchange data with the network.

If the LOAD command fails, check all the hardware switch and jumper settings. Improper settings and conflicts with other devices are the most common problems.

Check that you do not have a switch setting reversed. It is quite common to have the "on" and "off" or "1" and "0" settings in a mirror image.

The default Ethernet frame time for NetWare 3.12 is Ethernet_802.2.

Adding a Second Network Card

Suppose that you have a system that is a little more complicated than the average setup. The 3C509 driver already loaded supports an Ethernet 10BASE-T network. This installation also has a Thin Ethernet network, and this example will also load an NE2000 card to support the coaxial network segment. To load a second type of network card, the procedure is the same as for the first. The NE2000 driver is also included with NetWare 3.12 and was installed for you.

Use the LOAD command to install the ARCnet driver by entering **LOAD NE2000**. As shown in figure 15.28, after you load this driver, you are prompted for the hardware settings of PORT and INTERRUPT, which you must determine from your own hardware settings and documentation. In this example, use a port of 360h and int 5.

Use the BIND command to bind the proper protocol to the LAN driver. In most cases, you will be binding the IPX protocol. Type **BIND IPX TO NE2000** and press Enter. You are prompted for a network number, which is the network number assigned to the cable segment to which you are connected. This example uses a network number of D00BE.

Figure 15.28

Loading an NE2000
NIC driver and binding
the IPX protocol.

```
NRP_DEMO:load ne2000
Loading module NE2000.LAN
   Novell NE2000
   Version 3.25    June 17, 1993
   Copyright 1993 Novell, Inc.  All rights reserved.
Supported I/O port values are 300, 320, 340, 360, 240, 280, 2C0
I/O port: 360
Supported interrupt number values are 2, 3, 4, 5, B, C, F
Interrupt number: 5
NRP_DEMO:bind ipx to ne2000
Network number: D00BE
IPX LAN protocol bound to Novell NE2000
NRP_DEMO:
```

You are now connected to both the Thin Ethernet network using
the NE2000 card and the 10BASE-T network using the 3C509.

 Miscellaneous problems have been encountered
with the installation of 8-bit network interface
cards in NetWare file servers. Novell suggests that
you use no fewer than 16-bit cards in the file server
to prevent problems. Do not be tempted to install a
high-performance file server system such as
NetWare 3.12 and attempt to use a low-cost workstation interface card.

Binding Additional Frame Types

The following example illustrates how you can load a second
frame type so that one network card operates as two cards. This
example uses a second Ethernet frame type to communicate with
a TCP/IP system. Now you can load a different frame type to
support the IP packet protocol to enable the routing of TCP/IP
packets. Follow the preceding method, and load the 3C509 driver
a second time (see fig. 15.29).

```
NRP_DEMO:load 3c509
Loading module 3C509.LAN
Do you want to add another frame type for a previously loaded board? y
Supported frame types for 3C509 using Slot 4, I/O Port 4000h to 400Fh, Interrupt
Ah are:
       1. ETHERNET_II
       2. ETHERNET_802.3
       3. ETHERNET_SNAP
Select new frame type: 2
   Previously loaded module was used re-entrantly
NRP_DEMO:
```

Figure 15.29

Adding a second frame type and protocol to a 3C509 card.

The frame type Ethernet_802.2 is already in use, and you will be prompted for another frame type. When asked if you want to add another frame type for a previously loaded board, type **Yes** or **Y** and press Enter to obtain the list of supported frames. For the purpose of this example, select the Ethernet_II frame, and the previous driver is used reentrantly.

Binding Additional Protocols

The Ethernet_II frame type is required to connect to a TCP/IP network. To enable the server to support TCP/IP, the TCP/IP support NLM is required. This NLM is loaded simply by using the LOAD command as in figure 15.30.

Now you are ready to bind the IP protocol to the driver as you did when binding IPX. The command is **BIND IP TO NE2000**. A list of NE2000 boards and frame types available for use is displayed. Select the required card. In this case, select the Ethernet II frame or board 2. Type **2** and press Enter.

Figure 15.30

Loading the TCP/IP support NLM.

```
NRP_DEMO:load tcpip
Loading module TCPIP.NLM
  TCP/IP for NetWare
  Version 2.02i    February 20, 1993
  Copyright 1992, Novell, Inc.  All rights reserved.
NRP_DEMO:
```

You then are prompted for the IP address, which is nothing like the native MAC addressing Novell uses. In the TCP or IP environment, each portion of the address has a particular meaning. Each portion must be assigned to prevent problems because TCP networks are generally quite large, and each node must have a unique address while conforming to the numbering conventions of the network. In a large network, two nodes with the same IP address are difficult to trace. Figure 15.31 displays a screen print of the previous process.

Figure 15.31

Binding IP as a second protocol on a card.

```
NRP_DEMO:bind ip to 3c509
Several boards are using the 3C509 LAN driver
    1. 3Com EtherLink III 3C509 Family using Slot 4, I/O Port 4000h to 400Fh, I
nterrupt Ah Frame type: ETHERNET_802.2
    2. 3Com EtherLink III 3C509 Family using Slot 4, I/O Port 4000h to 400Fh, I
nterrupt Ah Frame type: ETHERNET_II
Select board to bind: 2
IP address: 192.68.205.1
IP: Bound to board 2.  IP address 192.68.205.1, net mask FF.FF.FF.0
IP LAN protocol bound to 3Com EtherLink III 3C509 Family
NRP_DEMO:
```

You now have three combinations of boards and protocols loaded on the server, and it would be useful for you to examine a summary of the configuration information. Figure 15.32 shows the display produced by the CONFIG command. Examine this figure to identify the elements that were configured in this exercise.

```
3Com EtherLink III 3C509 Family
    Version 4.00e    January 7, 1993
        Hardware setting: Slot 4, I/O Port 4000h to 400Fh, Interrupt Ah
        Node address: 00608C83F61E
        Frame type: ETHERNET_802.2
        No board name defined
        LAN protocol: IPX network 000B0FF0

3Com EtherLink III 3C509 Family
    Version 4.00e    January 7, 1993
        Hardware setting: Slot 4, I/O Port 4000h to 400Fh, Interrupt Ah
        Node address: 00608C83F61E
        Frame type: ETHERNET_II
        No board name defined
        LAN protocol: ARP
        LAN protocol: IP  address 192.68.205.1  mask FF.FF.FF.0  interfaces 1

Novell NE2000
    Version 3.25    June 17, 1993
        Hardware setting: I/O Port 360h to 37Fh, Interrupt 5h
        Node address: 00001B3A0E0C
        Frame type: ETHERNET_802.3
        No board name defined
        LAN protocol: IPX network 0D00BD00
NRP_DEMO :
```

Figure 15.32

CONFIG displays the configurations of network cards.

Creating the Startup Command Files

One step remains to complete installation. You must create the STARTUP.NCF and AUTOEXEC.NCF files that load your drivers and perform other startup functions when the server is booted.

Creating STARTUP.NCF

To return to the INSTALL utility, press Alt+Esc. If you have been following the steps, INSTALL's System Options menu will still be displayed. If not, display it at this time.

Then select the Create STARTUP.NCF File option. This option enables you to create the file needed to load the disk driver automatically and set particular operating environment features. First, you must specify the directory path for STARTUP.NCF as seen in figure 15.33. Then a STARTUP.NCF file will be created and you will have the option of editing changes.

Figure 15.33

Specifying the path to STARTUP.NCF.

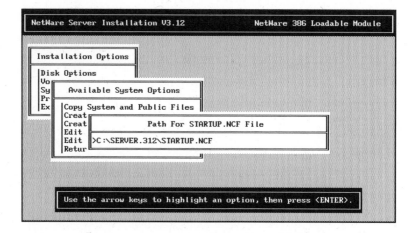

The STARTUP.NCF file editor is shown in figure 15.34. The STARTUP.NCF file contains the commands to load the disk driver and the special SET commands. The first line to LOAD IDE was created by INSTALL. The SET command lines in the example were edited manually as an example. To leave the editing screen for the STARTUP.NCF file, press Esc and answer Yes to save the file. Press Esc until you return to the Installation Options menu.

Figure 15.34

Editing STARTUP.NCF.

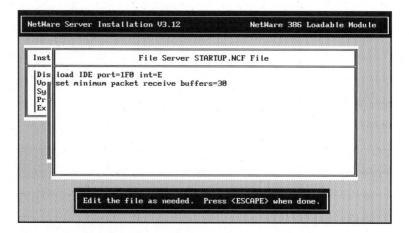

Next, select Create the AUTOEXEC.NCF File. After you select this option, the system will remember some of the commands you entered and automatically insert them into the AUTOEXEC.NCF file. The file that INSTALL creates is shown in figure 15.35.

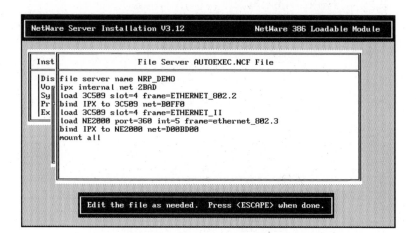

Figure 15.35

The AUTOEXEC.NCF file created by INSTALL.

It will be necessary for you to edit several changes, as shown in figure 15.36, into the file to ensure that the drivers and protocols are loaded and configured correctly. It is necessary to add NAME parameters to the various LOAD statements so that the driver for each frame type can be identified. Then the BIND statements are changed to bind to the drivers by name rather than by driver. It was also necessary to add the statement to LOAD TCPIP. After editing the file, press Esc and answer Yes to save it.

Notice the parameter "name" in the AUTOEXEC.NCF file. This parameter is useful because it enables you to name the individual drivers and BIND to the name.

Although the earlier examples do not illustrate this technique, it is a simple matter to replace the LAN driver name with the assigned name, such as BIND IPX TO CDI NET=3.

771

Figure 15.36

The AUTOEXEC.NCF
file after editing.

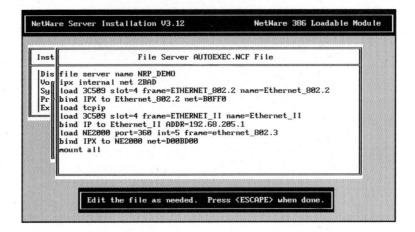

```
NetWare Server Installation V3.12          NetWare 386 Loadable Module

┌Inst┐┌──────────── File Server AUTOEXEC.NCF File ────────────┐
│Dis │file server name NRP_DEMO
│Vo  │ipx internal net 2BAD
│Sy  │load 3C509 slot=4 frame=ETHERNET_802.2 name=Ethernet_802.2
│Pr  │bind IPX to Ethernet_802.2 net=B0FF0
│Ex  │load tcpip
│    │load 3C509 slot=4 frame=ETHERNET_II name=Ethernet_II
│    │bind IP to Ethernet_II ADDR=192.68.205.1
│    │load NE2000 port=360 int=5 frame=ethernet_802.3
│    │bind IPX to NE2000 net=D00BD00
│    │mount all
│    └──────────────────────────────────────────────────────

     │ Edit the file as needed.  Press <ESCAPE> when done. │
```

The Available System Options menu has choices to
Create and to Edit the STARTUP and AUTOEXEC
files. Create generates a new file from the current
driver configuration of the server. Edit retains the
existing file and enables you to manually edit the
file.

Do not use Create if you have spent considerable
time customizing the startup files, since all of your
custom changes will be lost.

Product Options

An optional step is to install software options. To install an option,
select Product Options from the Installation Options menu and
press Enter. Any products currently installed will be displayed.
Immediately after installation, no products will be displayed. To
install a new product, press Ins.

You will be asked to Enter drive and/or path to new product source
media. If the option you are installing ships on a floppy disk,
simply enter **A:** or **B:**. If you are installing an option from the CD-
ROM, several choices are available. Here are the options along
with their directory paths:

Macintosh support	\NETWARE.312\ENGLISH \NW_MAC
Basic MHS and First Mail	\NETWARE.312\ENGLISH \BASICMHS
ElectroText online documents	\NETWARE.312\ENGLISH \DOC

Insert the option disk in a floppy disk drive, or install the CD_ROM in the drive. Then enter the drive letter and directory path of the disk drive. From there you will receive any necessary instructions. After the product is installed, it will appear in the Currently Installed Products list, as shown in figure 15.37.

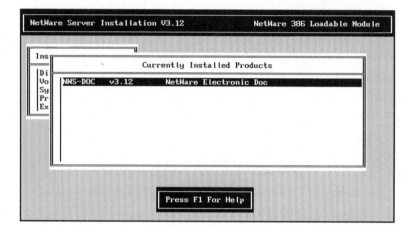

Modifying the 3.11 Operating System

LAN configurations change frequently. You need to know how to update your hardware and what changes need to be made to the NetWare software when your server configuration changes.

This section teaches you how to spot possible configuration problems with your server. These problems can require file server expansion. Common solutions to configuration problems include adding memory, splitting the network into multiple LAN cards, or adding one or more new disk channels.

Adding Memory

Many people overlook the importance of system memory. NetWare 3.11 is a high-level multitasking system that requires many times more memory than the average workstation. Most 3.11 file servers should not have fewer than 8MB of memory and should have much more memory if large disk volumes are being used.

As a rule of thumb, the total number of cache buffers listed on the main MONITOR screen should be between 800 and 1,000. The amount of Cache Buffers listed under Resource Utilization should not be fewer than 20 percent.

If either of these statistics varies outside these ranges, Novell suggests that you add memory in increments of 1MB until the problem is solved.

Additional LAN Cards

As a rule of thumb, all numbers listed under the LAN driver statistics in the MONITOR utility, with the exception of Total Packets sent and received, should be as low as possible, if not zero. Different LAN cards display various statistics, but a high level of error and retries generally represents a defective card or a high level of traffic. The simplest solution to a traffic problem is to install another LAN card to handle some of the traffic load.

 Identifying a network performance problem can require special equipment and a high level of traffic pattern knowledge for a particular topology. If you think you are experiencing problems due to statistics found in the monitor program, ask your vendor for suggestions.

Disk Channels

Disk Channel performance is difficult to analyze. A particular disk controller has a limit on the number of reads and writes it can perform in any given second, but most network file server loads are not consistent. Word processors, spreadsheets, and database applications present a different load to the disk controller. This inconsistency is compounded by the number of users and the work loads created in the office environment.

If the actual disk-access time appears to be slow, the system administrator can watch a few key MONITOR statistics. Two in particular, Dirty Cache Buffers and Current Disk Requests, can inform you of the file server's capability to handle the current load.

Current Disk Requests shows the number of disk requests in the queue waiting to be serviced; Dirty Cache Buffers is the number of file blocks in memory waiting to be written to disk. If these numbers are high, the disk system may be overworked, or the file server may be too slow to process the request in memory. An overworked disk channel requires that you install another disk channel to assist with the load. But before you invest in additional hardware, talk to a reputable vender for a solution.

Review Questions

1. Which formula would you use to determine the amount of memory required on a Macintosh volume?

    ○   a.   (Volume Size in MB x .023) divided by block size

    ○   b.   (Volume Size in MB x .032) divided by block size

    ○   c.   (Volume Size in MB x .23) divided by block size

    ○   d.   (Volume Size in MB x .32) divided by block size

2. Which statement about v3.12 is most true?

   ○ a. You must always low-level format new drives.

   ○ b. You should create a DOS partition on the file server to store files the server may need if SYS: is not available.

   ○ c. Cache memory can be left enabled if v2.2 is installed prior to this installation.

   ○ d. You must make disk copies of all the NetWare disks prior to installation.

3. Which is true about an internal NET number?

   ○ a. It *must* be unique.

   ○ b. It is used by NLMs for internal communications.

   ○ c. Both a and b.

   ○ d. Neither a nor b.

4. Which parameter syntax would you use to prevent both the AUTOEXEC.NCF and the STARTUP.NCF scripts from loading?

   ○ a. SERVER -C

   ○ b. SERVER -NA,NS

   ○ c. SERVER -NA -NS

   ○ d. SERVER -NAS

5. Which statement about mirroring versus duplexing is false?

   ○ a. Duplexing occurs on a single controller.

   ○ b. Mirroring duplicates data over multiple drives.

   ○ c. Duplexing requires you to load the driver twice.

   ○ d. Mirroring does not add read performance.

6. Which option does not appear on the Available Disk Options menu?

○ a. Format

○ b. Mirroring

○ c. Partition Tables

○ d. VREPAIR

7. Which statement about v3.12 installation is false?

○ a. Partitioning and Mirroring both appear under the Available Disk Options menu.

○ b. Low Leveling the drive is done from the Available Disk Options menu.

○ c. Creating a NetWare partition is found under the Partition Table option in Available Disk options.

○ d. Choosing the disk driver to use in AUTOEXEC.NCF is done in the Available Disk Options menu.

8. Which statement about v3.12 volume creation is false?

○ a. Naming volumes is done under Volume Options.

○ b. Your first volume should be called VOL1:.

○ c. Block size is chosen when creating a volume.

○ d. The default block size is 4KB.

9. What is the file name extension of a disk driver NetWare Loadable Module?

○ a. NLM

○ b. DRV

○ c. DSK

○ d. DIS

10. If you select Automatic volume configuration during installation, which of the following will occur?

   ○ a. Every disk drive will be automatically partitioned.

   ○ b. Disk device 0 will be partitioned and the entire partition will be assigned to SYS:.

   ○ c. A SYS: volume that is the minimum size required for NetWare will be created.

   ○ d. Volumes will be created on any partitions that have been created.

11. Which of the following is *not* true of Volumes?

   ○ a. Volumes can consist of segments on more than one hard drive.

   ○ b. Spanning volumes increases performance when reading files.

   ○ c. A hard drive partition can contain as many as twelve Volumes.

   ○ d. Spanned volumes should be duplexed for reliability.

12. The maximum number of segments that can be assigned to a volume is

   ○ a. 8

   ○ b. 16

   ○ c. 32

   ○ d. 48

13. Which of the following statements is true?

   ○ a. Segments can span up to eight disk drive partitions.

   ○ b. A disk drive can have only one NetWare partition.

   ○ c. Any volume can be renamed.

   ○ d. The block size of a volume can be changed after the volume is created.

14. NetWare 3.12 needs _____ of memory just for the operating system.

15. The primary DOS partition on a NetWare 3.12 server should be at least:

   ○ a. 3MB

   ○ b. 5MB

   ○ c. 10MB

   ○ d. 20MB

16. When installing from CD-ROM, the program that starts the installation process is:

   ○ a. INSTALL

   ○ b. SETUP

   ○ c. SERVER

   ○ d. ENGLISH

17. The default directory on the CD-ROM used to call the installation program on a typical U.S. installation is

   _____.

18. Which function key is used to change the current destination path?

   ○ a. F2

   ○ b. F3

   ○ c. F4

   ○ d. F5

19. The command used to start the file server on a NetWare 3.12 system is called _____.

20. The default Ethernet frame type on NetWare 3.12 is:

   O   a.   ETHERNET_802.2

   O ▸ b.   ETHERNET_802.3

   O   c.   ETHERNET_SNAP

   O   d.   ETHERNET_II

Answers

1. B

2. B

3. C

4. C

5. A

6. D

7. D

8. B

9. C

10. B

11. C

12. C

13. B

14. 2 megabytes

15. B

16. A

17. \NETWARE.312\ENGLISH

18. C

19. SERVER.EXE

20. A

Configuring the NetWare 3.1x Server

This chapter is a review of the areas of a NetWare 3.1x server that normally need to be configured after installation. These areas include:

- ◆ Configuring workstations
- ◆ Setting up system security
- ◆ Using menu and command line utilities
- ◆ Setting up network printing
- ◆ Viewing and tuning file server parameters

This chapter reutilizes some of the material in Chapter 13, "Optimizing the Network," in order to make it easier to study for this part of the CNE test.

Configuring Workstations

 Install the NetWare DOS Requester for MS Windows and DOS clients.

Because DOS cannot communicate directly with the network, the NetWare DOS Requester is provided with NetWare to let you connect DOS-based workstations to the network. The NetWare DOS Requester acts as a connections point between the workstation's local operating system and the network.

The NetWare DOS Requester consists of a series of files called *Virtual Loadable Modules* (VLMs). Typing VLM at the DOS prompt, or inserting it into a startup file, loads the NetWare DOS Requester.

In addition to loading the NetWare DOS Requester, a *communications protocol* (a set of rules that determine how the network and workstation will communicate) is needed for a workstation to communicate with the network. The communications protocol used with NetWare 3.12 is one that follows the *Open Data-Link Interface* (ODI) specification. To load the communications protocol, type **IPXODI** at the DOS prompt or insert the command into a startup file.

ODI is implemented through the *Link Support Layer* (LSL). The LSL takes incoming network information and sends it on to IPXODI so it can communicate with the PC. Load the LSL.COM file by typing **LSL** at the DOS prompt, or inserting the command into a startup file.

The final piece of communication software is the LAN driver. This is a file that activates and controls your PC's network board (NIC). You must load the LAN driver that matches the NIC installed in your PC. For example, if you have an NE2000 card installed in your PC, you would load the NE2000.COM file as your LAN driver.

Load the LAN driver by typing the name of the corresponding LAN driver file at the DOS prompt, or putting it into a startup file.

It is important to note that some LAN drivers support the ODI specification. These LAN drivers are known as *Multiple Link Interface Drivers* (MLIDs). MLIDs are required for NetWare 3.12 access.

All of these files are important to network communication. The order in which these files are loaded is important as well; some files cannot load if one or more of the other files has not first been loaded into memory.

 Modify the workstation configuration files with the appropriate information in the correct format.

After the NIC has been installed into the PC and the cabling has been attached, you can boot the PC using its local operating system. The connection software must then be loaded, in the following order:

1. LSL.COM

2. MLID (such as NE2000.COM)

3. IPXODI.COM

4. VLM.EXE

Once these files are loaded into the PC's workstation memory in the listed order, the PC can then communicate with the network. However, you as a user cannot access the network until you log in to the network.

 Log in to your NetWare 3.1x server.

The first step to logging in to the network is to change the default directory drive to the first available network drive. Most commonly, this is drive F:.

Once you have changed the default drive, type **Login** followed by a space, the name of the file server, a forward slash, and your assigned user identification name—also called the user login ID. An individual user login ID is assigned by the network administrator to each user on the network. Using separate IDs for different users helps to ensure the security of the network and to maintain the integrity of the network's data. Typing **Login** runs a file called LOGIN.EXE. This file is the software that completes the login process.

After you have entered your user ID, you are prompted to enter a password. The password can be anything you want; this helps to ensure that you are the network user that you claim to be. In addition, it also causes basic setup to occur specifically for you. For example, if you have a network login script set up for you, then logging in under your user login ID runs the login script.

As noted in the login instructions, you type in a file server name in order to log in to the network. Of course, before you can type in a file server name, a named file server must exist.

In DOS, you can name a storage device, whether it is a hard drive or a floppy disk. NetWare requires you to name storage device portions: the file server and its volumes. The next section discusses file server names and volumes.

Defining Security Levels

Set up network user accounts and apply account restrictions.

NetWare has seven different types of network users. You can combine many of these types with other types to fine-tune what a user can do on the system. The following list shows the different NetWare user types, ranging from the highest level to the lowest level:

◆ Supervisor

◆ Supervisor-equivalents

◆ FCONSOLE operators

◆ Workgroup managers

◆ PCONSOLE operators

◆ Account managers

◆ End users

Note The user Supervisor is an actual login account, while a Supervisor equivalent is a user account that can perform all the same functions as the Supervisor.

Workgroup managers have the power to create users and are, therefore, more authoritative than account managers.

Most users can be managed by a different type of user. By combining user types, you can create the Administrators and users to fully utilize your network. Figure 16.1 illustrates the hierarchy of network administration.

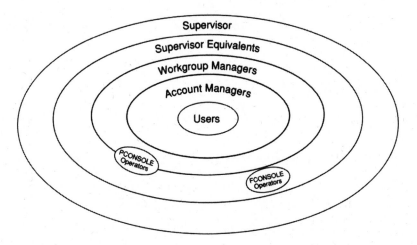

Figure 16.1

NetWare's subsets of the security divisions and their domains.

The Supervisor

The *Supervisor*, who has rights to every utility and file on the network, is the highest-level network user. Only one user named Supervisor is permitted on the network. This user is given all rights and privileges. The Supervisor can be viewed as having a "back door" into the network, meaning that he or she can get into the network in case of an emergency. Because of the Supervisor's high status, he or she is exempt from deletion by other users on the network. This capability does not, however, give the Supervisor full rights to all files on the network. If, for example, a file is marked as read-only, the Supervisor cannot delete the file until the attribute is changed to Read/Write.

The Supervisor password can be changed by the Supervisor or by the Supervisor equivalents (discussed in the following section). Many third-party network management programs that have system security still require the login ID of the Supervisor and do not function for the Supervisor-equivalent users.

The Supervisor-Equivalent

The *Supervisor-equivalent* user is a regular end user who has the same authority on the system as the Supervisor. Supervisor-equivalent users have the capability to create other Supervisor-equivalent users and can change the Supervisor account, including the password.

The FCONSOLE Operator

NetWare's FCONSOLE utility enables you to view certain information about the network. FCONSOLE operators have certain privileges depending on whether they also are Supervisor-equivalents.

FCONSOLE operators who have Supervisor equivalence can use all options available in FCONSOLE. FCONSOLE operators who do not have Supervisor equivalence, however, cannot clear connections or down the file server from FCONSOLE. Users who are not FCONSOLE operators or Supervisor-equivalents can use FCONSOLE, but are severely limited in the types of information they can see.

 Note Novell often refers to FCONSOLE operators as CONSOLE operators.

The Workgroup Manager

 Set up group accounts and user account management.

Workgroup managers can be users or a group of users. Workgroup managers can create, delete, and manage user accounts. They also can change passwords, account restrictions, and login scripts for users. Workgroup managers, however, can manage only those users and groups assigned to them or that they create. They cannot modify users or groups not in their list of managed users and groups.

The User Account Manager

 Set up login security including user account restrictions, time restrictions, station restrictions and intruder detection.

User account managers can be users or groups. User account managers can manage and delete accounts assigned to them. Unlike workgroup managers, user account managers cannot create users and groups.

787

The PCONSOLE Operator

NetWare has two types of PCONSOLE operators. One type, the *print queue operator*, manages and deletes print queues. The print queue operator cannot be assigned to a group. It must be assigned to individual users. The other type, the *print server operator*, manages and deletes print servers. The only type of user, however, that can create print servers and queues is the Supervisor.

Table 16.1 lists the functions that Administrators and end users can use on the network, and helps you visualize which types of users on the network can accomplish different management tasks.

Table 16.1
Security Domains

	Create/Delete Supervisor Equivalent	Create/Delete Workgroup Managers	Create Account Managers	Create/Delete Users	Inherits All Rights To Network	Create/Delete Print Queues and Servers	Manage Print Queues (by default)	Manage Print Servers (by default)	Use FCONSOLE (LIMITED) Access	Use FCONSOLE (UNLIMITED) Access
Supervisor	●	●	●	●	●	●	●	●		●
Supervisor Equivalent	●	●	●	●	●	●	●			●
Workgroup Manager			●	●					●	
User Account Manager			●						●	
Print Queue Operator							●			
Print Server Operator								●		
FCONSOLE Operator									●	

The End User

End users make up the majority of NetWare users. End users can perform only the functions given to them by the other six categories of users.

Exploring NetWare Security Levels

This section examines the various layers of NetWare security. In the process, you learn why NetWare can reliably provide the right level of protection for any company.

 Four levels of network security exist. The following list ranks these levels in order from lowest to highest:

- ◆ Login/Password
- ◆ Rights
- ◆ Attributes
- ◆ File server

Login/Password-Level Security

NetWare enables you to use passwords as a measure of security. At least a dozen parameters are available for this feature; each parameter can be set for individual users or as a default for all users.

NetWare offers a defense measure before the password ever comes into play. Suppose, for example, that you want to log in to a network. Because most small to mid-sized companies use first names for login names, you might assume that a login name is "Ann" and try to log in with that name. The system responds to this request by asking for a password. You try using common passwords, but the network denies access each time.

You can try different passwords continually, but NetWare never tells you whether a user named Ann is on that system. This feature is NetWare's first line of defense against *hackers* (unauthorized users). Instead of responding with a message that Ann is not a valid user name, NetWare simply asks you for a password.

User Account Restrictions

User Account restrictions permit the network Administrator to control how, when, and where a user accesses the network. User account restrictions are implemented by accessing the Supervisor Options menu of SYSCON. From this menu, network Administrators can initiate intruder detection, set time restrictions, and perform other network administrative (user Supervisor) tasks.

The first two items in the Supervisor Options menu affect only future users added to the system:

◆ Default Account Balance/Restrictions

◆ Default Time Restrictions

Default Account Balance/Restrictions and Default Time Restrictions have no effect on current users. As you add new users to the network, the parameters defined in these two options automatically are added to the new user's account.

When you create new user accounts on the network, you can set user account restrictions that are automatically implemented for each new user account. The account restrictions that you can set include:

◆ Whether or not the account has an expiration date

◆ The date the account expires

- Whether the user can have more than one network connection at a time

- The largest number of simultaneous network connections the user is allowed to have

- If a home directory for the user should be automatically created

- If the user is required to have a password

- What the minimum password length must be

- Whether or not the user is going to be required to change their password at specified intervals

- How many days are allowed between password changes

- Whether or not the user will be limited as to the number of times they can log in after their password has expired and has not been changed, also called *grace logins*

- How many grace logins the user is allowed

- Whether or not the user can reuse the same password or if they must supply a different password when changing their password

- If accounting is turned on, the maximum number of charges the user will be allowed on this server

- Whether or not the user will be allowed to use accounting credit

- If accounting is set on the server, what the lowest allowed balance will be on their account

Time Restrictions

This option is also part of the SYSCON utility. To access it, choose Default Time Restrictions from the Supervisor Options menu. When you choose this option, you can specify which days of the week, and which times of the day (in half-hour increments) the new users are allowed to log in to the network.

Station Restrictions

Station restrictions can be set for new users as well. They are set to define whether or not a new user is restricted in the number of network connections they can have; if so, the user must also specify the maximum number of allowed connections.

In addition to setting station restrictions for new user accounts, you can set them for existing users as well. This is also done using the SYSCON utility. However, instead of choosing Supervisor Options from the SYSCON Available Topics menu, you choose User Information from this same menu, then choose the user whose account you want to restrict. When the User Information menu appears, choose Account Restrictions and modify the user's account restrictions as needed.

Intruder Detection

Another security feature of NetWare is the capability of the network operating system to lockout a user account if the user attempts too many unsuccessful logins. This is known as intruder detection lockout. The Supervisor user (or a Supervisor-equivalent user) must set intruder detection lockout in order for it to work.

Intruder detection lockout is set using the SYSCON utility. To set intruder detection lockout, choose Supervisor Options from the Available Options menu. Then choose Intruder Detection/Lockout. You can now set the following intruder detection lockout specifications:

◆ Whether intruder detection is on or off

◆ The number of incorrect login attempts allowed, after which the user will be prevented from logging in to the network

◆ The length of time (in days, hours, and/or minutes) that the number of bad login attempts will be kept

◆ Whether or not the user is to be locked out after intruder detection has met its preset criteria that indicates an intruder is trying to access the network

◆ The length of time (in days, hours, and/or minutes) that the user is locked out if *Lock Account After Detection* is set to Yes

User Rights

Plan file system security using groups, users, directory rights, and Inherited Rights Masks and calculate effective rights.

The rights a user or group has in a directory or on a file are called *trustee rights*. Eight trustee rights exist in NetWare 3.1*x*. Trustee rights are the keys each user has for a directory or file.

NetWare 3.1*x* also has replaced the concept of 2.2's Maximum Rights Mask with the *Inherited Rights Mask (IRM)*. The IRM is a filter. Each directory has an IRM that allows all rights to flow through to subdirectories. The system Administrator can change the IRM to allow only certain rights to flow down to subsequent subdirectories. This change can be made by using the ALLOW command or the FILER menu utility, which are discussed later in this chapter.

You must remember the following rules when figuring the results of setting up an IRM:

1. IRMs only affect the rights that flow down from the directory above. If you are granted rights specifically through the GRANT command, FILER, or SYSCON, the IRM has no effect because these rights do not flow down.

2. *Effective rights* equal trustee rights when the user has been given the rights in a directory explicitly. In other words, when you give the user rights in a directory, those rights become her effective rights, and the IRM has no effect.

3. When the user has the Supervisory right, the IRM has no effect. The *Supervisory right*, described in the next section, gives the user all rights to all subdirectories under the directory in which it was granted.

4. Every directory has a full set of rights in its IRM by default. When you change a directory's IRM, you do not affect the IRMs of any of that directory's subdirectories.

5. IRMs cannot add rights back for the user; the IRM can state only what rights are not allowed to flow from a parent directory.

 Note NetWare security measures, from lowest to highest security, include the following:

◆ Login name

◆ Password

◆ Directory rights

◆ File rights

◆ Directory attributes

◆ File attributes

If a file is flagged Read Only and the directory or the file has the Erase right, the file cannot be deleted until the Read Only file attribute is changed to Read/Write.

Table 16.2 lists the rights common to both NetWare 2.2 and 3.1*x*.

Table 16.2
Rights Common to NetWare 2.2 and 3.1x

Right	Function
Read	Enables the user to see the contents of a file and to use the file.
Write	Enables the user to alter the contents of a file.
Create	Enables the user to make new files and directories.
Erase	Enables the user to delete existing files and directories.

Right	Function
File Scan	Enables the user to view files and subdirectories in a directory; without this right, you cannot see files.
Modify	Enables the user to change the attributes of a file; the user can change a file from Read/Write to Read-Only or from Nonshareable to Shareable.
Access Control	Enables the user to give any of the preceding rights to other users on the network.

Note In NetWare 2.2, you still can see subdirectories, even if you are denied rights; 3.1*x* hides subdirectories from the user.

In NetWare 3.1*x*, Modify also enables the user to change the attributes for directories; 2.2 does not enable you to set attributes for directories.

Version 3.1*x* has an eighth right, Supervisory, which gives all the other rights to the user or group. This right makes the user a *directory Supervisor*—someone who has control over what happens to a directory structure's branch. NetWare 2.2 only has seven rights.

The following rights are available to users:

◆ **Read.** When assigned to a directory, Read enables the user to see the contents of the files in the directory. The user can use or execute files in the directory.

When assigned to a file, Read enables the user to see the contents of a closed file and to use or execute the file, even if the directory does not allow the Read privilege.

◆ **Write.** When assigned to a directory, Write enables the user to alter the contents of files in the directory.

When assigned to a file, Write enables the user to alter the contents of the file even when the Write privilege is not given to the directory.

In either case, the file must be flagged Read/Write for the Write privilege to have any effect.

◆ **Create.** When assigned to a directory, Create enables the user to make new files and directories.

When assigned to a file, Create enables the user to salvage the file if it has been deleted.

◆ **Erase.** When assigned to a directory, Erase enables the user to delete existing files and directories.

When assigned to a file, Erase allows the file to be deleted even if the directory does not have the Erase right.

Files flagged as Read Only cannot be erased until they are flagged Read/Write.

◆ **File Scan.** When assigned to the directory, File Scan enables the user to view files and subdirectories in a directory. Without this right, you cannot see files.

NetWare 3.1x hides subdirectories from the user when he does not possess this right.

When assigned to a file, File Scan enables the user to view the file by using DIR. If the user does not have File Scan rights to other files, these files do not appear when the DIR command is issued.

 If you grant the File Scan right to a file, users can see subdirectories all the way back to the root directory. They cannot see any files in these directories, however, unless they have rights to them.

◆ **Modify.** When assigned to the directory, Modify enables the user to change the attributes and names of subdirectories.

When assigned to a file, Modify enables the user to change the attributes and the name of a file. This right enables the user to change a file from Read/Write to Read Only or from Nonshareable to Shareable.

◆ **Access Control.** When assigned to the directory, Access Control enables the user to give any of the preceding rights to other users on the network.

When assigned to a file, Access Control enables the user to give any of the preceding rights to another network user.

 Access Control does not enable you to assign the Supervisory right. You must be the Supervisor, a Supervisor equivalent, or a workgroup manager with the Supervisory right to the directory in which rights are assigned.

◆ **Supervisory.** When assigned to a directory, Supervisory gives all the other rights to the user or group. This right makes the user a *directory Supervisor*, someone who has control over what happens to a branch of the directory structure.

When assigned to a file, Supervisory enables the user to have all rights to that file.

Combining IRMs and Trustee Rights

Now that you understand what trustee rights can accomplish and how the IRM affects the outcome of flow-through, the next step is to take a look at combining trustee rights and IRMs.

The following example uses this directory structure:

```
        SYS:
        |       |
    APPS     DOCS
        |       |
    ACCT     JUNE
```

The following IRMs and rights have been assigned:

IRMs:

```
SYS:                    [SRWCEMFA]

SYS:APPS                [SR    F ]

SYS:APPS\ACCT           [SRWCEMFA]

SYS:DOCS                [SRWC  F ]

SYS:DOCS\JUNE           [SRWCE F ]
```

DAVE has the following rights:

```
SYS:APPS\ACCT           [ RWCE F ]

SYS:DOCS                [S       ]
```

BEV has the following rights:

```
SYS:                    [ R    F ]
SYS:DOCS                [ RWCEMFA]
```

PAULETTE has the following rights:

```
SYS:                    [S       ]
```

The following is a list of the rights of each user, based on the rules stated in the preceding section on IRMs.

DAVE

```
SYS:                    [       ]
                        Rule #1
SYS:APPS                [       ]
                        Rule #1
```

```
SYS:APPS\ACCT        [ RWCE F ]
                     Rule #2
SYS:DOCS             [SRWCEMFA]
                     Rule #3
SYS:DOCS\JUNE        [SRWCEMFA]
                     Rule #3
```

BEV

```
SYS:                 [ R    F ]
                     Rule #2
SYS:APPS             [ R    F ]
                     Rule #1
SYS:APPS\ACCT        [ R    F ]
                     Rule #5
SYS:DOCS             [ RWCEMFA]
                     Rule #2
SYS:DOCS\JUNE        [ RWCE F ]
                     Rule #1
```

PAULETTE

```
SYS:                 [SRWCEMFA]
                     Rule #3
SYS:APPS             [SRWCEMFA]
                     Rule #3
SYS:APPS\ACCT        [SRWCEMFA]
                     Rule #3
SYS:DOCS             [SRWCEMFA]
                     Rule #3
SYS:DOCS\JUNE        [SRWCEMFA]
                     Rule #3
```

Effective Rights

You can think of *directory rights* as locks that every directory has on your system. NetWare gives each directory a full set of locks by default.

Trustee rights act as keys that fit the directory locks. Each user can have his or her own set of unique keys. As an example, think of your own key ring. You have your own house key, car key, and so on. Chances are that no one has the same keys as you. Everyone has different locks that need to be opened. The same concept applies to networks. You have specific needs in directories. Some users have the same needs; others have different needs. Each user can have his or her own set of keys, or rights.

Effective rights are the trustee rights (keys) that actually match available directory rights (locks). If a lock exists and you do not have a key, you cannot perform the function. The only way you can use a right is to have matching locks and keys.

Trustee rights include all the rights you have been given individually combined with all the rights given to any groups to which you belong, as well as any you have been granted through security equivalency.

Effective rights are the trustee rights' results after they have been filtered by the *Maximum Rights Mask* (MRM) in NetWare 2.2 or the *Inherited Rights Mask* (IRM) in NetWare 3.1*x*.

NetWare automatically calculates your effective rights. You can view those effective rights by using SYSCON, FILER, or the command-line command RIGHTS. However, even though NetWare can calculate the effective rights for you, you still need to know how to manually calculate those rights.

Calculate effective rights by first looking at the directory for which you are calculating the rights. Any rights granted to you at that directory level are your effective rights for that directory. Rights granted at levels above that specific directory are subject to being filtered through the IRM. For example, if you are granted rights to the directory called TEST in the following example, your effective rights in directory TESTFILES will be R (Read) and W (Write) because the IRM at directory FILES filters out those rights you were granted at the directory called TEST (see fig. 16.2).

File Attributes

On the network, files are secured by the use of *attributes*, conditions placed on the files. These conditions help to control what can be done to the files and the ways in which the files can be used on the network. Many combinations of attributes are attached to files and directories. This section discusses NetWare attributes and how you can use them on your network.

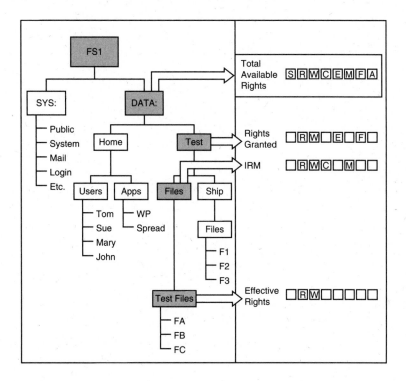

Figure 16.2

Effective Rights.

Archive Needed

NetWare uses the letter A to signify files that have been altered after the last backup. The Archive Needed attribute also is assigned to files that have been copied into another directory. Archive Needed looks for the DOS Archive Bit flag on a file.

Execute Only

Execute Only is designated with the letter X. After this attribute is placed on a file, it cannot be taken off. This attribute only affects files ending in COM or EXE, and is the only attribute that you cannot reverse.

Note Only users with Supervisor privileges can assign the Execute Only attribute.

Execute Only hinders application piracy by preventing files from being copied or downloaded.

Make sure that you have a copy of a file before you attach the Execute Only flag, because this attribute also prevents files from being backed up. In addition, many programs cannot operate when flagged with Execute Only.

Hidden File

The Hidden File attribute uses the letter H. Files hidden with this attribute do not show up when you use the DOS DIR command. If a user has the File Scan right, files hidden with this attribute appear after using NDIR.

Read Audit and Write Audit

NetWare still is in the process of perfecting a built-in audit trail on files. Currently, you can flag files with Ra for Read Audit and Wa for Write Audit, but they have no effect.

Read Only and Read/Write

You cannot write to, delete, or rename a read-only file. The Read Only attribute enables users to read and use files. Program files are most often flagged with Ro for read-only.

A Read/Write file attribute enables users to read from the file and write back to the file. This attribute is designated with Rw and is the default on newly created files. Flagging a file with Read Only deletes the Read/Write attribute. Data files are usually flagged with Read/Write.

When Read Only is used in NetWare 3.1*x*, the attributes of Delete Inhibit and Rename Inhibit also are included.

Shareable and Nonshareable

NetWare uses the letter S to designate shareable files. This attribute enables several users to access a single file at the same time. This flag is used most often with read-only files and database files.

Nonshareable, or Normal, is the system default. If you flag a file with N, you set the attributes as Nonshareable Read/Write. Nonshareable files normally are assigned to program files that are single-user applications. This attribute ensures that only one person can use the file at any one time.

System File

System files, flagged with Sy, are not listed after you use the DOS DIR command. These files cannot be deleted or copied. If you have the File Scan right, you can see these files by using the NDIR command.

Transactional

Files marked with T can be tracked using the *Transaction Tracking System* (TTS). TTS is a method the file server uses to track the integrity of database files during database file updates. All database files that need to be tracked while being modified must have this attribute.

Copy Inhibit

Marked as a C, Copy Inhibit prevents files from being copied to another directory. This attribute is used only with Macintosh files.

Delete Inhibit

The Delete Inhibit attribute is one half of the Read Only file designation. Rename Inhibit represents the other half of Read Only. The

Delete Inhibit flag, marked as a D, prevents files from being deleted.

Rename Inhibit

Along with Delete Inhibit, Rename Inhibit is the second Read Only attribute. Marked as an R, Rename Inhibit prevents users from renaming files.

Purge

Purge uses the letter P to show files considered purged when deleted. If you mark a file with the P flag, you ensure that it cannot be restored after it is deleted.

Using Directory Attributes

You also can use attributes on directories. The attributes discussed in the following sections can be used on directories in NetWare.

Hidden Directory

The Hidden Directory attribute uses the letter H. Directories hidden with this attribute do not show up when you use the DOS DIR command. If a user has the File Scan right, files hidden with this attribute appear.

System Directory

System directories, designated with Sy, are hidden from the DOS DIR command. These directories cannot be deleted or copied. If a user has the File Scan right, these directories appear when using the NDIR utility.

Purge Directory

This attribute uses the letter P to show directories in which all files are considered purged when deleted. This flag ensures that after the directory is deleted, any files in the directory cannot be restored.

Using Command-Line Security Utilities

This section discusses the command-line utilities available in NetWare that Administrators and managers can use to implement security by manipulating user accounts. Command-line utilities are used from the DOS prompt.

The RIGHTS Command

 Implement a file system security plan using command line and menu utilities.

The RIGHTS command shows the user which rights they have in any given directory. If you seem to have more rights in one directory than you were granted originally, then rights have flowed down from a higher directory. This event is referred to as flow-through. *Flow-through* automatically occurs to all subdirectories beneath the directory in which rights have been granted.

The following syntax is used for the RIGHTS command:

```
RIGHTS path
```

In the example shown in figure 16.3, the RIGHTS command is entered from the O prompt to see the available rights in that directory.

805

Figure 16.3

The RIGHTS command lists and explains each available right.

```
O:\OFFICE>rights
B386\SYS:OFFICE
Your Effective Rights for this directory are [SRWCEMFA]
      You have Supervisor Rights to Directory.     (S)
  *  May Read from File.                            (R)
  *  May Write to File.                             (W)
     May Create Subdirectories and Files.           (C)
     May Erase Directory.                           (E)
     May Modify Directory.                          (M)
     May Scan for Files.                            (F)
     May Change Access Control.                     (A)

*  Has no effect on directory.

     Entries in Directory May Inherit [SRWCEMFA] rights.
     You have ALL RIGHTS to Directory Entry.

O:\OFFICE>
```

The TLIST Command

The TLIST command displays the users who have been given explicit rights in a specific directory. Flow-through does not occur in TLIST. The TLIST command is typed in the following manner:

    TLIST path

In figure 16.4, the TLIST command shows that the user DBATEMAN and the group TECHS have all rights except Supervisory.

Figure 16.4

TLIST displays the rights granted to users and groups.

```
O:\OFFICE>tlist

B386\SYS:OFFICE
User trustees:
  DBATEMAN                                    [ RWCEMFA]
  ----
Group trustees:
  TECHS                                       [ RWCEMFA]

O:\OFFICE>
```

The GRANT Command

The GRANT command grants rights to users or groups. You also can use menu items in the User Information menu in SYSCON to grant rights. Any information changed by using the GRANT command is permanent and appears in the user's trustee information screens in SYSCON. The GRANT command is typed in the following manner:

    GRANT rightslist [FOR path] TO [USER¦GROUP] name

In figure 16.5, for example, the user DBATEMAN requests Read and File Scan rights in the SYS:SERVICE directory. The Supervisor uses the GRANT command and a shortcut to give him the rights. Instead of spelling out the full path name, the system needs only the drive letter that points to the proper path. The TLIST command is used after GRANT to verify that the rights are granted.

```
O:\SERVICE>grant r f for o: to dbateman

B386/SYS:SERVICE
SERVICE                               Rights set to [ R     F ]


O:\SERVICE>tlist

B386\SYS:SERVICE
User trustees:
     BACKUP                                      [ R     F ]
     DBATEMAN                                    [ R     F ]
     -------
Group trustees:
     ACCOUNTING                                  [ RWCEMFA]

O:\SERVICE>
```

Figure 16.5

The GRANT command gives rights to a user for a specific directory.

The REVOKE Command

The REVOKE command takes away rights from a user in either directories or files. REVOKE uses the following syntax:

REVOKE *rightslist* [FOR *path*] FROM [USER¦GROUP] *name*

Figure 16.6, for example, shows that the user DBATEMAN has more rights than necessary in the SYS:PUBLIC directory. The excess rights are removed by using the REVOKE command; the TLIST command is used to verify the process.

```
O:\PUBLIC>revoke c e m a for o: from dbateman
B386/SYS:PUBLIC
Trustee's access rights set to [ RW    F ]

Rights for 1 directories were changed for DBATEMAN.


O:\PUBLIC>tlist

B386\SYS:PUBLIC
User trustees:
   DBATEMAN                              [ RW    F ]
   -------
Group trustees:
   EVERYONE                              [ R     F ] Minimum rights ...

O:\PUBLIC>
```

Figure 16.6

The REVOKE command is used to deny rights from a user for a specific directory.

The REMOVE Command

The REMOVE command removes the user from the trustee list. REMOVE uses the following syntax:

```
REMOVE [USER¦GROUP] name [FROM path]
```

In figure 16.7, the user DBATEMAN is removed from the O directory by using the REMOVE command. The TLIST command then confirms the results.

Figure 16.7

The REMOVE command is used to remove a user from a trustee list.

```
O:\PUBLIC>remove dbateman from o:
B386/SYS:PUBLIC
User "DBATEMAN" no longer a trustee to the specified directory.

Trustee "DBATEMAN" removed from 1 directories.

O:\PUBLIC>tlist

B386\SYS:PUBLIC
No user trustees.
Group trustees:
   EVERYONE                                 [ R    F ] Minimum rights ...

O:\PUBLIC>
```

Making Trustee Assignments

Trustees can be either users or groups. A trustee may be assigned to directories or to files. Once a user or group becomes a trustee, access rights are assigned for the directories or files to which they were assigned as a trustee.

There is more than one way to receive rights. Rights can be granted to a user directly or might be given to a user from a direct trustee assignment. Rights also can be passed along to a user because of their membership in a group that has been given trustee rights to directories or files. In addition, a user can gain rights through a security equivalence.

Users with Supervisor or Supervisor-equivalent rights can grant rights to other users. When implementing and managing file system security needs to be easy, the best method to use when granting rights is to assign the trustee rights to a group; those users who should be given trustee rights are thus put into that group.

The previous section discussed command-line commands that can be used to give rights to a user or a group. Both SYSCON and FILER—NetWare menu utilities—can also be used to assign or delete trustees.

To make a user a trustee of a directory or file, run SYSCON. Choose User Information from the Available Topics menu, then choose the user to be made a trustee. Next, choose either Trustee Directory Assignments or Trustee File Assignments from the User Information menu.

If you select the Trustee Directory Assignments option in the User Information menu, you can grant rights to the user you chose as a trustee. To add rights, press Ins and enter the full path name, or press Ins again to select the path. Grant rights by pressing Ins and choosing the rights that you want to grant.

You can also modify the rights assignments on any directory by completing the following steps:

1. Press Enter on the directory whose trustee rights you want to change.

2. When the list of trustee rights granted appears, press Ins to see the list of trustee rights that have not been granted.

3. Press F5 to mark each right that you want to grant to the user, then press Enter. (To delete marked rights, press Del rather than Enter.)

Press Esc to return to the new rights. The list then is updated in the Trustee Directory Assignments window. Figure 16.8 shows the screens for modifying trustee directory rights.

Trustees can also be assigned using the FILER program. To grant a trustee assignment using this method, type **FILER** at the DOS prompt to open the FILER utility. Change to the directory that is to have a trustee assignment. Then return to the Available Topics Menu and choose Current Directory Information. When the Directory Information screen opens, choose Trustees. From the Trustee Name screen, press Ins to see a list of available users and groups. Choose the user or group to whom you want to grant trustee rights for this directory. You can then modify that user or group's rights by choosing the user or group name from the Trustee Name list, then pressing Ins and choosing the rights to be granted. Both File Scan and Read From File rights are granted automatically.

Figure 16.8

Screens for Granting Trustee Rights Using SYSCON.

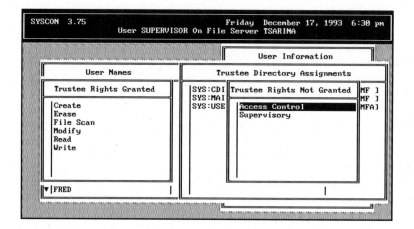

Setting Up Network Printing

 Set up a printing environment by creating and configuring a print queue, printer, and print server.

Novell's NetWare printing environment consists of three primary components:

- ◆ Print queues
- ◆ Print servers
- ◆ Printers

The next three sections of this chapter discuss each of these components.

Examining and Defining Queues Using PCONSOLE

The PCONSOLE menu utility enables System Supervisors to create and define queues and print servers. Queue operators and print server operators can manage queues and print servers from this menu, while users can place jobs into queues and manage their own print jobs from this menu.

The first PCONSOLE menu, the Available Options menu (see fig. 16.9), enables you to select from the following three options: Change Current File Server, Print Queue Information, and Print Server Information.

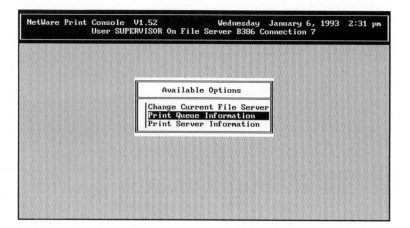

Figure 16.9

PCONSOLE'S main menu.

Perform basic network printing maintenance tasks, such as viewing and modifying printing information in PCONSOLE.

After you select the Print Queue Information option, a list of print queues appears on-screen (see fig 16.10). If you are a Supervisor-equivalent, you can create a new queue in this option by pressing Ins and entering the new queue.

Figure 16.10

PCONSOLE'S print queue information.

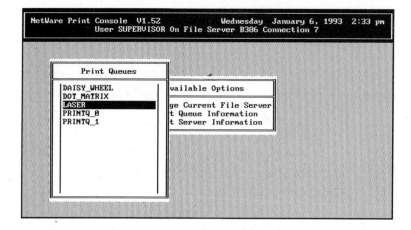

After highlighting a queue and pressing Enter, the Print Queue Information menu appears (see fig. 16.11). This menu has seven options, which are described in the following sections.

Figure 16.11

PCONSOLE'S specific queue information.

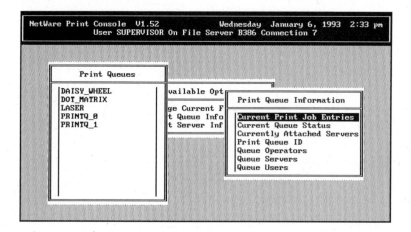

Current Print Job Entries

The Current Print Job Entries option in the Print Queue Information menu shows you all the jobs in a queue. Once you understand the information it provides, you can then access the options to manage print jobs.

The information is arranged in six columns, as illustrated in figure 16.12. The first column, Seq, which stands for *Sequence*, shows the order in which the jobs will be printed. The second column, Banner Name, is the name of the user sending the print job. Description, the third column, lists the file names. If the job is sent through a DOS command, such as PRINT, or a print screen, or is directed to a print device, this column shows the logical port from which the job was captured, and the word CATCH, as shown in the third job in figure 16.12. The Form column shows the form that has been mounted for this queue.

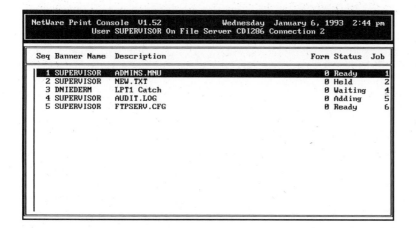

Figure 16.12

An example of PCONSOLE'S active jobs.

The fifth column, Status, displays one of five possible conditions: Active, Held, Adding, Waiting, and Ready.

The Active condition designates the job currently printing. No parameters can be changed for this job.

The only thing you can do to a job marked Active is delete it. Place the highlight bar on the desired print job and press Del. You also can use F5 to mark several jobs, then press Del. You are asked for confirmation if you attempt to delete the active job. The active job's deletion does not stop the printer. Before you can delete the active job and clear the job from the printer buffer, however, you must abort the job from the print server. Refer to the section on print servers later in this chapter.

Any jobs marked with the Held condition are not printed until the hold flag is removed. Two different hold flags can be placed on a job that has been queued to print. A User Hold can be placed on the file by pressing Enter on the job and changing the User Hold to Yes. The job owner and the queue operators can place and remove this flag. The Operator Hold flag can be placed or removed only by the queue operator. To set this flag, select job to be held by pressing Enter, and set the Operator Hold to Yes.

The Adding condition designates a job that is in the process of being sent by a user. If the user has exited an application and the job still says ADDING, the user should type **ENDCAP**, which forces the job into the Ready mode.

The Waiting condition is shown when a print job has been told to wait until a specific date and time before printing. To set deferred printing, press Enter on the queued job and set Deferred Printing to Yes. You can define the Target Date and Time for that file to be printed.

The Ready condition is put on any job available for printing.

The sixth column, Job, keeps track of the number of print jobs that have gone through the queue since it was created.

Note All 3.*1x* copies of NetWare currently do not show a valid number in the Job field.

Highlight any queued job and press Enter to display additional information about print jobs. Figure 16.13, for example, shows the information you can obtain and the parameters you can set for each queued job after pressing Enter.

```
NetWare Print Console  V1.52          Wednesday  January 6, 1993  2:45 pm
                  User SUPERVISOR On File Server CDI286 Connection 2

                         Print Queue Entry Information

Print job:          4              File size:        2052
Client:             SUPERVISOR[2]
Description:        LPT1 Catch
Status:             Waiting for Target Execution Date and Time

User Hold:          No             Job Entry Date:   January 6, 1993
Operator Hold:      No             Job Entry Time:   2:42:36 pm
Service Sequence:   3

Number of copies:   1              Form:             LETTERHEAD
File contents:      Byte stream    Print banner:     No
Tab size:                          Name:
Suppress form feed: No             Banner name:
Notify when done:   No
                                   Defer printing:   Yes
Target server:      (Any Server)   Target date:      January 7, 1993
                                   Target time:      2:00:00 am
```

Figure 16.13

Job entry information in PCONSOLE.

Table 16.3 explains what some of the terms stand for in the Print Queue Entry Information screen.

Table 16.3
Print Queue Entry Information

Item	Description
Print Job	Specifies the job number in the queue.
File Size	Specifies the size of the print job.
Client	Specifies who sent the print job.
Description	Specifies the name of the job.
Status	Denotes the condition of the job.

continues

815

Table 16.3, Continued
Print Queue Entry Information

Item	Description
User Hold	Denotes the print jobs that are placed or removed by the job owner or queue operator. Held jobs are not printed.
Operator Hold	Denotes the print jobs that are placed or removed by the queue operator. Held jobs are not printed.
Service Sequence	Specifies the order in which the job is to be printed.
Job Entry Date	Shows the date that the queue received the print job. This field cannot be altered.
Job Entry Time	Shows the time that the queue received the print job. This field cannot be altered.
Number of Copies	Specifies the number of copies of the file to be printed. This number can be set from 1 to 65,000.
File Contents	Specifies text or byte stream print jobs. Text converts indents to spaces. Byte stream enables the application to determine the printer codes.
Tab Size	Specifies the number of spaces to convert indents if File contents line is set to Text.
Suppress Form Feed	Sets the form feed to On or Off.
Notify When Done	Turns on or off notification of job completion.

Item	Description
Form	Sets the form number to use for the print job.
Print Banner	Sets the banner to On or Off.
Name	Displays the name printed on the banner. The sender's login name is the default.
Banner Name	Displays the file name by default.
Target Server	Displays the print servers that can service the current print job.
Defer Printing	Enables you to defer printing. Set to Yes or No.
Target Date & Time	Enables you to set the time and day. Default is set to the following day at 2:00 am.

You can add jobs at the Current Print Job Entries screen. Press Ins to bring up the current directory. Change to the directory that contains the file to be printed and press Enter. The next screen is a list of all files in the directory (see fig 16.14).

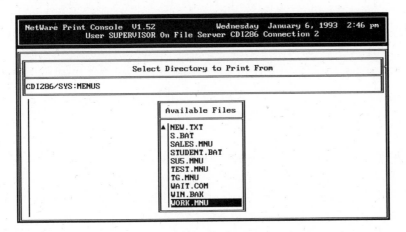

Figure 16.14

Selecting a file to print in PCONSOLE.

After you highlight the file in this list to be printed, press Enter. If you want to print several files, use F5 to mark each file, and then press Enter.

The Print Job Configurations screen displays the list of printer configurations that you can use (see fig. 16.15). Highlight the desired configuration and press Enter.

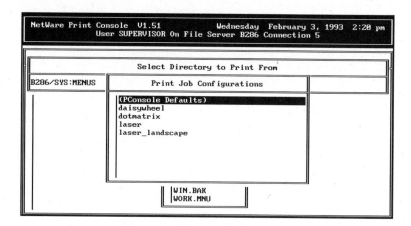

```
NetWare Print Console  V1.51              Wednesday  February 3, 1993  2:20 pm
                 User SUPERVISOR On File Server B286 Connection 5


                        Select Directory to Print From
   ┌──────────────┐    ┌───────────────────────────────────┐
   │B286/SYS:MENUS│    │      Print Job Configurations      │
   └──────────────┘    ├───────────────────────────────────┤
                       │(PConsole Defaults)                │
                       │daisywheel                         │
                       │dotmatrix                          │
                       │laser                              │
                       │laser_landscape                    │
                       │                                   │
                       │                                   │
                       │                                   │
                       │  ┌──────────┐                     │
                       │  │WIN.BAK   │                     │
                       │  │WORK.MNU  │                     │
                       │  └──────────┘                     │
                       └───────────────────────────────────┘
```

PCONSOLE then displays configuration options. It uses options set in PRINTCON but enables you to modify any fields. After changing any necessary fields, press Esc and save the job. This job now appears in the queue to be printed.

Current Queue Status

The Current Queue Status option of the Print Queue Information menu has the following five items (see fig. 16.16):

◆ **Number of entries in queue.** Displays the number of print jobs currently in a queue.

◆ **Number of servers attached.** Displays the number of file servers that have this queue defined.

◆ **Users can place entries in queue.** Enables users to place jobs (Yes) or not place jobs (No) in this queue.

◆ **Servers can service entries in queue.** Enables you to have jobs printed (Yes) or not printed (No) in this queue.

◆ **New servers can attach to queue.** Enables users on other file servers to use this queue (Yes) or denies users on other file servers access to this queue (No).

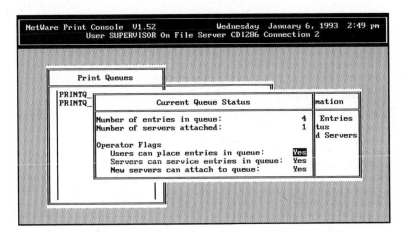

Figure 16.16
PCONSOLE'S Current Queue Status option.

Currently Attached Servers

The Currently Attached Servers option of the Print Queue Information menu shows a list of all servers using this queue. This option can be used to see which file servers currently are putting jobs into the queue.

 All PCONSOLE screens are viewed in *real time*. As jobs are added and deleted, servers attached, or print servers activated, you see the screens change.

Print Queue ID

The Print Queue ID option of the Print Queue Information menu indicates the name of the hexadecimally named subdirectory under SYS:SYSTEM with the QDR extension. Jobs printed to this queue are held in the subdirectory until printed.

Queue Operators

The Queue Operators option of the Print Queue Information menu lists all users who can manage the selected queue. *Queue operators* manage the queue and all jobs going through the queue. Supervisor equivalent users automatically are queue operators. Queue operators can rearrange the order in which jobs print. They also can mark print jobs as Held so that they do not print. To add users or groups to this list, press Ins and select the users or groups that you want to manage this queue. Press Enter to accept your choices.

Queue Servers

The Queue Servers option of the Print Queue Information menu lists all the print servers that can service the selected queue. To add servers to this list, press Ins and select the desired servers. Press Enter to accept your choices. After a printer is defined and attached to the selected queue, the print server for which the printer was configured appears on this list.

Queue Users

The Queue Users option of the Print Queue Information menu lists all the users and groups that can add jobs to this queue.

 The group labeled EVERYONE automatically becomes a queue user.

To modify this list, delete the group EVERYONE. You then can add users or groups to this list by pressing Ins and choosing the users or groups that can use this queue. Press Enter to accept your choices.

Installing Print Servers

 Note Print servers can be file servers or dedicated PCs. PSERVER.VAP files are used on a router or 2.2 server; PSERVER.NLM files are used on a 3.1x server; and PSERVER.EXE files are loaded onto a PC designated as a dedicated print server.

A NetWare print server can manage up to 16 printers. Up to five of those printers can be attached to the print server, and the rest can be remote printers. A *remote printer* is any printer hooked up to a workstation that is attached to the network and can share its printer with other network users.

The following procedure shows how to set up a basic print server that has two printers—one local and one remote. This setup can be modified to fit your networking needs.

1. Type **PCONSOLE**.

2. Select the Print Queue Information option from the Available Options menu.

3. Press Ins and add the new queue name, then press Enter. Repeat this step for every queue.

One Printer Servicing Multiple Queues

Figure 16.17 shows an example of one printer serviced by three queues. Determining whether one printer servicing multiple queues, or multiple queues servicing one printer is best for your network's organization is one of the decisions that must be made as part of advanced setup.

Figure 16.17

One printer serviced by multiple queues.

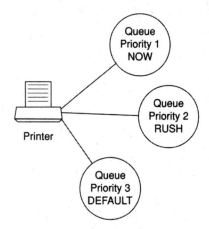

Other advances printing setup and management design considerations include such tasks as:

◆ Rearranging print queue users into workgroups

◆ Setting priorities for print queues

◆ Adding or renaming print queues as needed

◆ Assigning individual users to be print queue operators

◆ Adding or removing print servers

Each queue shown in this example (figure 16.17) is set at a different priority. The DEFAULT queue is set at priority 3, RUSH is set at priority 2, and NOW is set at priority 1. By setting up system defaults, users print to the DEFAULT queue. If a rush job comes in, it goes to the RUSH queue. In the event of a super-high priority job coming in while jobs are in the RUSH queue, the print job is sent to the NOW queue. Jobs currently printing are allowed to finish before priority queues are serviced.

One Queue Using Identical Printers

In the example shown in figure 16.18, one queue is used to service three printers. This setup requires identical printers. When a job enters the queue, the queue polls the printers to find the next available one and sends the job there. Jobs are processed quickly using this arrangement.

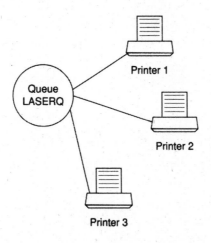

Figure 16.18

One printer queue servicing multiple printers.

1. Press Esc to return to the Available Options menu.

2. Select the Print Server Information option.

3. Press Ins to add the new print server name, type the new print server name, and press Enter (see fig. 16.19).

4. Select the Print Server Configuration option (see fig. 16.20).

5. Select the Printer Configuration option in the Print Server Configuration Menu (see fig. 16.21).

Figure 16.19

PCONSOLE'S Print Server Information option.

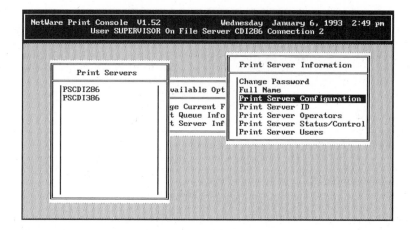

Figure 16.20

PCONSOLE'S Print Server Configuration Menu.

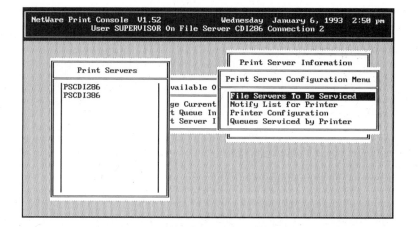

Figure 16.21

Choosing configured printers in PCONSOLE.

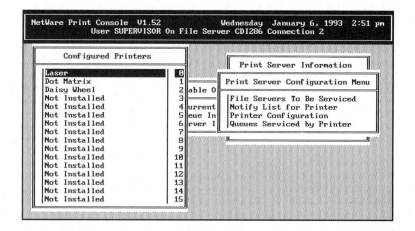

You now need to set up printers for local or remote ports. Select a printer number that you want to configure and press Enter. Add a logical name for the printer and press Enter. Next, press Enter on the Type field. This action displays the Printer types screen. The first seven options in this screen enable you to hook up a printer to the print server (see fig. 16.22). The next eight remote options in this screen are for remote printers.

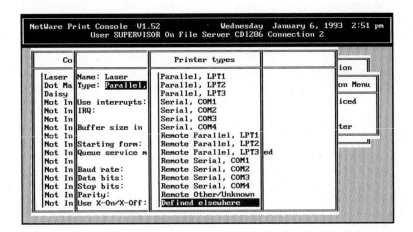

Figure 16.22

Selecting printer types in PCONSOLE.

Remote Other/Unknown has two functions in NetWare:

1. Enables printer setup for a workstation without definition of the printer port from PCONSOLE.

2. Enables you to attach printing devices that connect directly to the LAN, bypassing a workstation.

The last option on the Printer types screen, Defined elsewhere, assumes that another print server has this option defined.

When you select a printer type, NetWare displays several screens to modify the printer setup (see fig. 16.23). These screens present all the hardware configuration options for the printer; defaults usually work fine. If your printer requires special consideration, however, use these screens to customize the printer. When you are finished defining the printer options, press Esc. Then select Yes from the Save Changes menu and press Esc.

Figure 16.23

PCONSOLE'S Printer
Configuration menu.

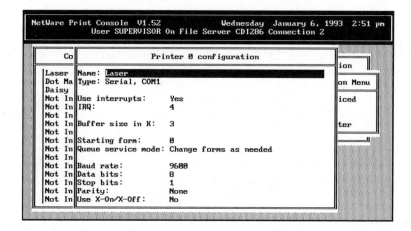

In the Print Server Configuration menu, select the Queues Serviced by Printer option. Next, select the defined printer name in the Defined Printers screen (see fig. 16.24).

Figure 16.24

Choosing a defined
printer.

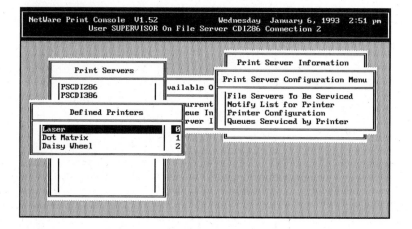

Press Ins to add a queue for each printer configured. Priority 1 is the highest queue priority that you can define, as shown in figure 16.25. Press Esc twice when finished.

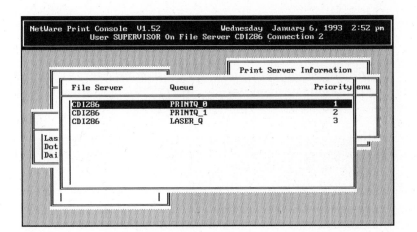

Figure 16.25

Adding a queue to a printer.

Note Queue priority enables a queue with higher priority to print all queued jobs before it looks to see if lower-priority queues have jobs waiting.

Next, select the Notify List for Printer option on the Print Server Configuration menu. Then press Ins to add users or groups who should be notified if problems arise, such as if the printer is offline or out of paper. At the top of the list of potential users and groups, the option labeled (Job Owner) (Unknown Type) appears (see fig. 16.26). This option reports any messages back to the job originator.

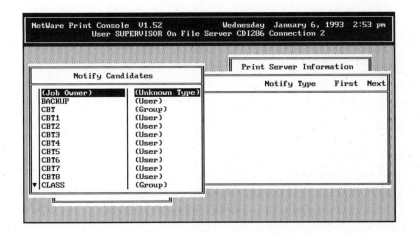

Figure 16.26

The Notify Candidates screen for printer problems.

After you select users or groups to be notified, the system prompts you for information about when they are to be notified and how often. By default, the persons in the notify list are first told of printer problems in 30 seconds and again every 60 seconds until the problem is solved (see fig. 16.27). Press Esc three times when you are finished making your selections.

Figure 16.27

The list of users to be notified in case of a printer problem.

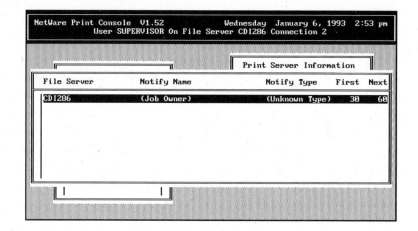

NetWare Print Console V1.52   Wednesday January 6, 1993 2:53 pm
              User SUPERVISOR On File Server CDI286 Connection 2

Print Server Information

File Server	Notify Name	Notify Type	First	Next
CDI286	(Job Owner)	(Unknown Type)	30	60

 Note

The default Queue Operator is the group EVERY-ONE.

The default Print Server Operator is the user SU-PERVISOR.

Select the Print Server Operators option in the Print Server Information menu. Then press Ins to add any users or groups that need to support the print server. After you make your selections, press Alt+F10 to return to DOS.

At the file server, type the following to launch the print server. You should spool printer 0:

    S *nn* TO *queuename*

Note The S nn TO queuename command enables the
Administrator to accomplish the following:

◆ **Create a path for a default queue.** This procedure
helps when a user issues a CAPTURE or NPRINT
statement without any flags. If a default queue is
not chosen with the spool statement, the user
receives an error message.

◆ **Route jobs from applications that print to printer
numbers.** Many older applications are hard-coded
to print to printer numbers. NetWare no longer
enables the user to specify a printer number. To
ensure that the file prints, a spool statement also
enables Administrators to designate to which
queue a job goes if the application sends it to a
printer number.

◆ **Print on a 2.2 system.** NetWare 2.0a uses the
SPOOL statement rather than the CAPTURE
statement. This option enables 2.0a system users to
print on both 2.0a and 2.2 operating systems.

At the workstation designated as the dedicated print server, log in
as a user who has Read and File Scan rights to the SYS:PUBLIC
directory. Type the following command to launch the print server:

```
PSERVER printservername
```

Any workstation used as a print server must have the number of
its *sequenced packet exchange* (SPX) connections increased. Create a
text file called NET.CFG. Older versions of NetWare had you
create a SHELL.CFG file, which also can be used. Place the line
SPX=60 in this file. This file needs to be in the directory from
which IPX.COM is called when attaching to the file server (see fig.
16.28).

829

Figure 16.28

The SHELL.CFG file and its contents.

```
A:\SHELLS>dir

 Volume in drive A is SYS
 Directory of   A:\SHELLS

SHELL     CFG         8  11-08-91   6:32p
TEMP      FIL         7   7-31-91   6:42p
IPX       COM     29919  10-10-91   6:38p
AUTOEXEC  BAT        13   8-01-91   9:35a
NET3      COM     49198   2-06-91   4:44p
NET4      COM     49625   2-06-91   4:39p
NETBIOS   EXE     21506  11-15-90   3:48p
        7 File(s)  60473344 bytes free

A:\SHELLS>type shell.cfg
SPX=60

A:\SHELLS>
```

No matter where the print server is activated—at a dedicated print server or at the file server—the print server screen looks the same. Figure 16.29 provides an example of a typical print server screen. When you press the spacebar, you can see the next group of printers—8 through 15.

Figure 16.29

An example of the print server information screen.

```
            Novell NetWare Print Server V1.21
                 Server PSCDI386 Running

0: Laser                      4: Not installed
   Printing
   Job #: 7, 080991.RPT
   Queue: CDI286/LASER

1: Dot Matrix                 5: Not installed
   Not connected

2: Daisy Wheel                6: Not installed
   Not connected

3: Not installed              7: Not installed
```

The final step in installing a print server to host a remote printer is to type **RPRINTER** at each of the Remote Stations. A list of print servers then appears (see fig 16.30). After choosing the print server, all available remote printer setups appear (see fig 16.31). Select the workstation that you want, and NetWare displays a message telling you that a successful installation has occurred (see fig. 16.32).

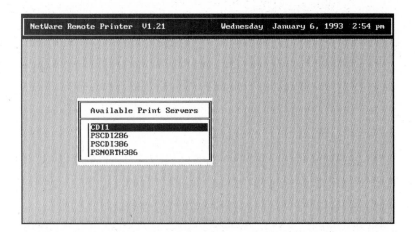

Figure 16.30
RPRINTER's main menu selections.

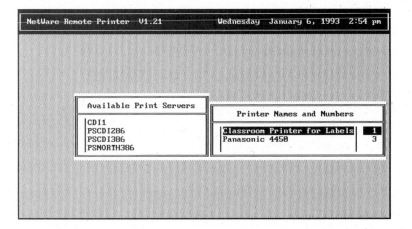

Figure 16.31
RPRINTER's remote printer choices.

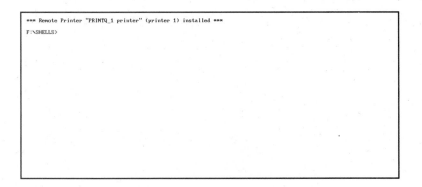

Figure 16.32
RPRINTER's installation confirmation.

831

RPRINTER

The RPRINTER command has several options. The full syntax line for this command is as follows:

```
RPRINTER printservername printernumber flag
```

By placing the print server name and printer number in the command line, you can avoid using the menu.

The -R flag removes the RPRINTER from the workstation's memory.

The -S flag displays the status of the RPRINTER.

After the print server is installed, workstations can send jobs to network printers by indicating the queue name attached to those printers. The next section describes this process.

Controlling the Print Server

After you get the print server up and running, a new option appears in the Print Server Information menu (see fig. 16.33). This option, Print Server Status/Control, enables a print server operator to manage the print server (see fig. 16.34).

Figure 16.33

The Print Server Information menu.

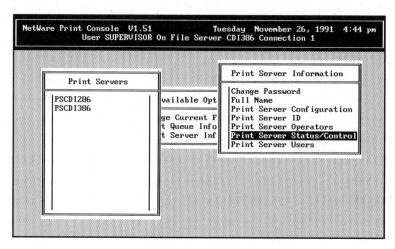

Under Printer Status, a print server operator can view information about the job currently being serviced. Figure 16.35 shows a job that has just entered the queue.

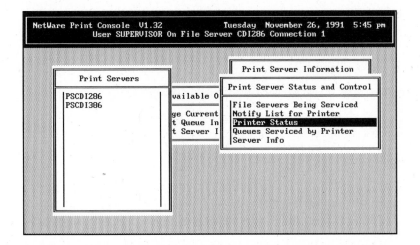

Figure 16.34

The Print Server Status and Control menu.

```
NetWare Print Console  V1.32        Tuesday  November 26, 1991  5:45 pm
                 User SUPERVISOR On File Server CDI286 Connection 1

                                        ┌─ Print Server Information ──┐
         ┌──── Print Servers ────┐      │ Print Server Status and Control │
         │ PSCDI286              │ vailable 0
         │ PSCDI386              │       │ File Servers Being Serviced │
         │                       │ ge Current│ Notify List for Printer │
         │                       │ t Queue In│ Printer Status          │
         │                       │ t Server I│ Queues Serviced by Printer │
         │                       │           │ Server Info             │
```

Figure 16.35

An example of a print job status.

```
NetWare Print Console  V1.51        Thursday  September 26, 1991  9:22 pm
                 User SUPERVISOR On File Server CDI286 Connection 4

                         ┌──────── Status of Laser ────────┐

         Status:            Printing job              │ Printer Control │

         Service mode:      Change forms as needed
         Mounted form:      0

         File server:       CDI286
         Queue:             LASER
         Job number:        9
         Description:       090691.RPT
         Form:              0

         Copies requested:           1       Finished:        0
         Size of 1 copy:          2022       Finished:        0
         Percent completed:       0.00
```

The status line shows that this job is being sent to the printer. The following service modes are available:

◆ **Change forms as needed.** Prompts the user to change forms each time a different form is encountered.

◆ **Minimize form changes across queues.** Specifies that the printer prints all jobs with the same form number before proceeding to the next highest form number. This procedure is done for all queues, regardless of queue priorities.

◆ **Minimize form changes within queue.** Specifies that the printer prints all jobs within a high-priority queue that share similar form numbers before servicing lower-priority queues.

◆ **Service only currently mounted form.** Prints only the jobs that have the current form number.

When the printer status screen appears, the Printer Control field is highlighted. Press Enter to display the next options menu (see fig. 16.36). The following options enable you to modify the print job currently printing. These options are not available from the Print Queue options, which enable you to modify only those print jobs not currently printing.

Figure 16.36

The Printer Control menu.

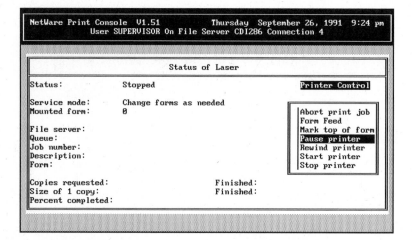

```
NetWare Print Console  V1.51                Thursday  September 26, 1991  9:24 pm
                    User SUPERVISOR On File Server CDI286 Connection 4

                                Status of Laser

Status:              Stopped                            Printer Control

Service mode:        Change forms as needed
Mounted form:        0                               Abort print job
                                                     Form Feed
File server:                                         Mark top of form
Queue:                                               Pause printer
Job number:                                          Rewind printer
Description:                                         Start printer
Form:                                                Stop printer

Copies requested:                    Finished:
Size of 1 copy:                      Finished:
Percent completed:
```

◆ **Abort print job.** Enables the printer to abandon the current job. The job then is deleted from the queue. This method is the best way to stop a print job, because it clears the job from the print buffer.

◆ **Form feed.** Specifies that the printer advance to the top of the next page.

◆ **Mark top of form.** Prints a row of asterisks (*) across the top of the page to check form alignment.

◆ **Pause printer.** Temporarily pauses the printer. To restart the printer, select the Start Printer option.

◆ **Rewind printer.** Enables the printer to rewind a specific number of bytes or advance a specific number of bytes. This line also enables you to specify which copy to print if multiple copies are specified at the time of printing.

◆ **Start printer.** Starts the printer if stopped or paused.

◆ **Stop printer.** Stops the printer and returns the print job to the queue. Printing is stopped until the printer is started again by using the Start Printer option.

You now can select the Server Info item of the Print Server Status and Control menu.

You can make both permanent and temporary changes to print queues or printers using PCONSOLE.

Permanent changes are made using the regular PCONSOLE menus. To make a change permanent using this method, you must first bring the print server down and then reload it.

Temporary changes do not require that the print server be first downed to take affect. Temporary changes are made in the Print Server Status and Control screen of the PCONSOLE utility.

After selecting the Server Info item of the Print Server Status and Control menu, the Print Server Info/Status screen (see fig. 16.37) displays the following information about the print server:

◆ **Print server version.** Specifies that the print server version is 1.2.1.

◆ **Print server type.** Specifies that the print server is running on a dedicated DOS machine rather than on the file server.

◆ **Number of printers.** Specifies that the print server is hosting three printers.

◆ **Queue service modes.** Denotes the number of service modes available.

◆ **Current server status.** Specifies that the print server is currently running.

Figure 16.37

An example of the Print Server Info/ Status screen.

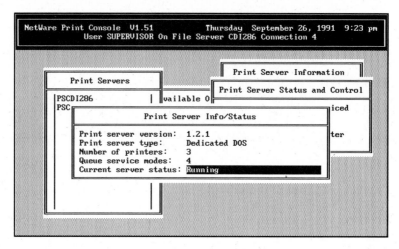

When you select the Current server status option, a screen appears (see fig. 16.38) that enables the server operator to do the following three things:

♦ Down the print server immediately.

♦ Down the print server after the last job is printed.

♦ Enable the server to continue running.

Figure 16.38

The Print Server Info/ Status menu.

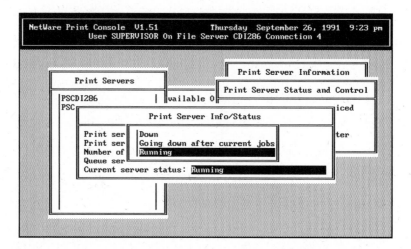

Viewing and Tuning the File Server

When you are preparing to make decisions on tuning and optimizing your network, you must consider the effects of doing so and rank them according to priority. You must remember that each network is unique and it consists of more than just a file server—it has many other elements to consider, such as the following:

◆ **Environmental factors.** Is your network read- or write-intensive?

◆ **Communications.** Do you route traffic through 16- or 32-bit boards, or split traffic through multiple boards?

◆ **Computer devices.** How do you handle clients, printers, and routers? Do you need a faster CPU?

◆ **Server Memory.** Do you have enough? The more RAM you have installed in the server, the better it can perform.

◆ **Users.** How do users perceive their capability of getting the job done?

All these network components can affect the total operations of your environment. You must also consider not only technical operation needs, but the business needs of your customers. You must determine the nature of their businesses—do they need quick responses on queries or transactions, as in financial institutions, for example? Performance may be the issue rather than response time. In past research polls, customers have indicated that reliability and security of the network are much more important than the optimal tuning aspects of network performance in most cases.

As you put a project plan together to provide yourself a checklist for network changes, look at the big picture first. Make decisions about whether the adjustment will have a positive effect, when you should stop, and when you should reverse your change if it is causing problems. You need to look at each tunable component area of the operating system and select the most effective order for parameter adjustments.

It is important that you do one adjustment at a time and test the effect of this change. Do not expect immediate results; NetWare is a dynamic operating system and it must adjust itself accordingly. Do your homework about the possible effects of the change first—check with other production environments to see what they have done and if the change was effective. It is also important to understand that if you have downed the server for any reason after you have made any changes, and it was working optimally, it can take an unidentified amount of time after bringing the server back up for it to begin the finely tuned processing again.

Viewing File Server Performance with MONITOR

Use MONITOR to verify performance bottlenecks in the server and suggest possible remedies.

In the NetWare 3.1x Advanced System Administrator course, you are taught an overview of server memory components and how they operate. This is more detail than can be covered in this book, so refer to table 16.4 for a chart of the features of v3.x memory pools. This will refresh your knowledge in relation to what is seen through the MONITOR utility.

Table 16.4
NetWare 3.1x Memory Pools

Memory Pool	Description	Returnable After Use?
File Cache Buffers	Used for caching reads and writes.	Location where other pools return memory.
Cache Non-Movable	Subpool used by NLMs. Causes fragmentation. Nonexpandable.	Returnable to File Cache Buffers, but not as contiguous blocks.
Cache Movable	Subpool owned by NetWare. Used for internal system tables that change size dynamically (ex: DET). Expandable, and has no fragmentation.	Returnable to File Cache Buffers in contiguous blocks.

Memory Pool	Description	Returnable After Use?
Permanent Memory	Used by functions such as communication buffers or directory server is cache for one-way allocation pool for long-term memory needs.	Not returnable unless the server is downed.
Semi-Permanent Memory	Subpool used by LAN and disk drivers.	Returnable only to the Permanent Memory pool, until the server is downed.
Alloc Short Term Memory	Pool used for small short-term allocations such as Drive Mappings and Queue Manager Tables.	Not returnable to Permanent Memory or File Cache Buffers.

The MONITOR file server console utility is used to display detail status features of the network. To bring up the screen shown in figure 16.39, at the file server console prompt, type the following:

```
LOAD MONITOR
```

and press Enter.

As you use MONITOR, you will be able to view details about the following:

- ◆ Overall activity and utilization of the network
- ◆ Memory resources that are being used
- ◆ Connection and open file activity
- ◆ Disk and LAN driver specifications

839

◆ Module and resource tag information

◆ Utilization of file server process loads

Figure 16.39

The MONITOR opening screen.

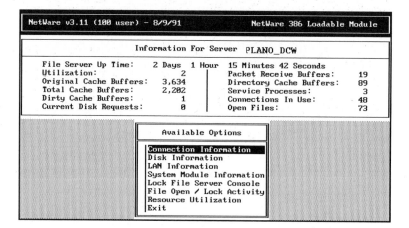

Note The MONITOR utility will use a screen saver that resembles a snake traveling around the screen. The utilization of the network dictates the length of the snake around the screen—the higher the utilization, the longer the tail. If you do not want the snake to display, type the following parameter when loading MONITOR:

LOAD MONITOR NS

There are third-party utilities that can replace the snake screen saver. One example of an informational style screen saver is made by FRYE. The screen displays a real-time graph of server utilization with color-coded warnings of threshold exceptions. Threshold numbers will depend on the specific characteristics of all the components in your file server.

The initial screen that you see when you bring up MONITOR includes the Utilization percentage in the upper left column. This number shows what percentage of the file server's CPU is being used during the last second. This is an indication of a network board using CPU cycles or an NLM requesting processing time. You should use tools such as LANalyzer for Windows to keep a history of the CPU usage and compare this to the baseline utilization or normal workload activity of the network. If the utilization is consistently high, it could indicate that you may need to first do some performance tuning and then possibly a file server hardware upgrade (components first).

The Current Disk Requests number found in the bottom left column indicates the number of waiting disk requests for all drives in this server that have been queued by the operating system to be processed. If this number or if the Dirty Cache Buffers statistic is always high, you may want to consider upgrading your disk drive channel (host adapter).

The Dirty Cache Buffers statistic is a number, not a percentage. It is an indication of the number of buffers holding data that need to be written to disk. If this number is over 70 percent of the Total Cache Buffers number, you need to increase the Maximum Concurrent Disk Cache Writes with a SET parameter at the file server console or in the AUTOEXEC.NCF file.

The Packet Receive Buffers number indicates the number of buffers that the NetWare operating system sets aside to handle client requests until the requests can be processed. The default value of 100 Minimum Packet Receive Buffers can be changed with the related SET parameter in the STARTUP.NCF file. The server will set aside this minimum amount when it is booted up. You also can set the Maximum Packet Receive Buffers to manage memory that affects service processes.

The Directory Cache Buffers number identifies the amount of buffers set aside to handle directory caching. The file server will continue to use these buffers as needed until this value reaches the maximum amount allowed. The increase in the number is determined by the amount of directory searches the file server is being requested to perform. If this number ever goes over 100, you need to increase Minimum Directory Cache Buffers and Maximum Directory Cache Buffers settings.

The Service Processes number is the amount of task handlers allotted for client requests. When this number is exceeded, the network operating system adds more task handlers to manage the requests. Once the memory is allotted for a service process, it is not returned unless the server is downed. This parameter can be changed for those servers with many users and heavy usage. If this number reaches 20, and the server has enough memory, increase the allotment by 5 (range is 5 to 40). If the cache buffers are around 20 percent (which is very low), do not use the Maximum Service Processes setting to alter the current setting. Only use this setting if you need to conserve memory until you are able to get more memory in the file server. Remember that when you change any SET parameters, allow the file server and the operating system enough time to adjust to the changes dynamically.

Other Available Options in MONITOR

The Connection Information selection found in the Available Options menu will show the active connections made to this file server. If you highlight an active connection, it will display the connection's open file records, the user, and the user's segment number and network interface card address. This Connection Information screen is primarily used to view who is using what files and to clear connections that have not been removed in a timely manner.

The disk information screen, as shown in figure 16.40, shows several details for consideration by a network administrator or support engineer. Most hard drives support this screen, but some drivers by a few manufacturers may not support this feature. You should check this out from the vendor or Novell before purchasing this model. These details about the drives include the following:

◆ **Hot Fix.** This is used with NetWare's read-after-write verification function to see if data in memory is the same data that was written to the disk. If it does not match, Hot Fix will redirect the block of data to the location the disk maintains for recording the bad block addresses. If the disk is going bad or the number of failures are high, you should consider replacing your hard drive.

◆ **Partition Blocks.** This is used to indicate the block size in this partition. The default size is 4KB blocks, but can be changed to 8KB or 16KB blocks through the Volume Options selection in the INSTALL.NLM. This change process is destructive, so make sure you have a good backup before changing the block size. If you change the disk block size, you may need to alter the Cache Buffer Size in the STARTUP.NCF file with the use of a SET command. It is important to remember that the cache buffer size must be the same as the smallest configured block size or the volume will not mount.

◆ **Data and Redirection Blocks.** This number indicates the available disk space minus the two percent (or hot fix space) that the operating system reserves for the redirection blocks used by the hot fix process. You may want to archive some data or buy more disk space if you are running out.

◆ **Device Numbering.** This is the location that will show device numbers (or codes) that can be used for troubleshooting error messages.

◆ **Locating Physical Drives in the Server.** The Drive Light Status can be used to determine which device is attached to that number. This can be documented for future reference. To do this, select System Disk Drives, then the Normal Entry option. Press Enter over the flashing light option. Watch the LED lights on your drives in your file server to see which one responds to this selection.

Figure 16.40

The MONITOR Disk
Information screen.

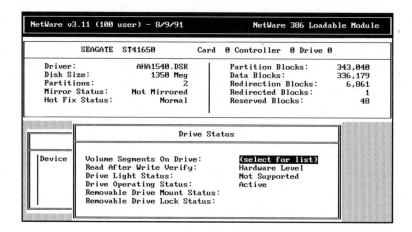

The LAN Information selection shows details about each of the
drivers loaded for the network interface cards included in the file
server. The hooks for these details are pulled in with the
NMAGENT.NLM that is loaded automatically during the file
server boot up process. As shown in figure 16.41, there are many
details you can use for troubleshooting or performance
monitoring. In the General Statistics area of the screen, there may
be some choices labeled Not Supported. This not supported choice
was made by the vendor who developed this driver. Check the
v3.1x System Administrator's Guide for specifics on NetWare-
provided drivers.

Figure 16.41

The MONITOR LAN
Information screen.

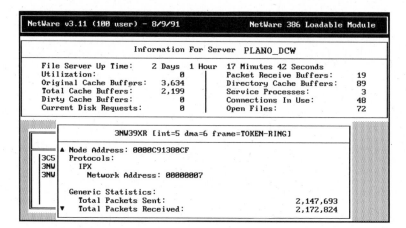

In the LAN Information screen, there are several selections that can be proactively monitored for system performance. The following are the basic statistics to consider:

◆ **Total Packets Sent.** This statistic shows the number of packets being sent to the rest of the network through this NIC in the file server. Use this to monitor heavy traffic loads or if the NIC is communicating at all.

◆ **Total Packets Received.** This shows the number of packets the file server has received through this NIC in the file server. These requests include counts from other file server NICs (internal routers) and from clients that need services from other servers on other segments or on the backbone. You may wish to add another NIC of this type to lighten the traffic load on this NIC.

◆ **No ECB Available Count.** ECBs (Event Control Blocks) are the NetWare operating system's way of controlling the number of requests to which a server can respond. If the server runs out of Packet Receive Buffers to store requests, increments are made to this count. The file server will increment the available receive buffers to support incoming requests.

Monitor this statistic and if it starts to reach the default ceiling of 200, increment the Maximum Packet Receive Buffers setting by 10 until you believe the optimal performance for your network is reached. This is done by typing the following at the file server console or including it in the AUTOEXEC.NCF file:

`SET MAXIMUM PACKET RECEIVE BUFFERS = nnn`

where *nnn* is equal to the number of buffers required.

If you are using EISA or Microchannel Bus-Mastering cards, you may need to add 5 buffers for every one of these cards installed in the file server. If you are receiving error messages that say **No ECB available count**, increase the number of buffers to add 10 instead of 5 for each bus-master board.

◆ **Send or Receive Packet Too Big Count/Send or Receive Packet Too Small Count.** If there are any NICs that are malfunctioning on the network, they could be causing undersize and/or oversize packets. This is determined by viewing the Send or Receive Packet Too Big/Too Small Counts statistics.

If the SEND entry is being incremented, you should check the NIC in the server that is using this statistical driver. You may need to replace this card with a known working NIC and test to see if the problem fades away. If not, check NetWire or the NSEPRO for any enhancements to this driver version.

If the RECEIVE entry is being incremented, your trouble-shooting will depend on how the NIC is being used. If the NIC is attached to a backbone, you may need to use a proto-col analyzer, such as Frye's NetWare Management package or Thomas-Conrad's TXD software monitor, to trace the offender. If the file server NIC is attached directly to a segment with clients, the problem possibly is occurring from one of the client stations.

◆ **Receive Packet Overflow Count.** This statistic is responsible for tracking packets that are too large for the cache buffer, causing it to overflow. There possibly could be an application that is not negotiating the proper packet size with the server before sending the packets of data over the network. Check your client NET.CFG file for packet size settings, and if the server is setting the packet size limit, compare the two for any discrepancies. You also should check the application that could be causing the errors for improper coding of packet size requirements.

◆ **Checksum errors.** The NetWare IPX packet structure contains a checksum field that is used to verify that the IPX packets are conforming to the original XEROX header definition requirements. This entry will increase when the required calculated checksum for the packet does not match the checksum byte. If this entry continually increases, look for potential data or transmission problems.

The System Module Information selection in the MONITOR utility displays all the resource module information being used by the file server. This section shows the amount of memory and all the types of resource tags each module uses when is has been loaded into memory. If you suspect performance problems that could be related to the use of specific NLMs that are tying up needed memory or resources, unload them, allowing for your server to reallocate the memory dynamically (refer to table 16.3). You may want to reload only those NLMs that are critical to your operating environment. Check with the vendor of those NLMs to see if there is a history of problems; you might want to acquire the latest versions through the vendor's electronic bulletin board system or from NetWire.

The Lock File Server Console selection is used to lock the file server keyboard. This should be done by the network administrator so that no one can access any functions through the file server console. If you do not prevent access without monitoring this server constantly, untrained or destructive users could load unwanted NLMs (viruses, data tapping files, and so forth) or unload necessary NLMs that could be doing backups or UPS monitoring. Knowledgeable LAN people also could access the file server console through RCONSOLE if it is not protected properly.

To lock the keyboard, type in a password you can remember (see fig. 16.42). If you forget the password, the NetWare SUPERVISOR ID must be used to release the lock. The only other way to get around this is to power off the server; in that instance, someone will notice that there was unnecessary tampering going on. You also should view MONITOR for uptime or go through SYSCON for messages in the System Error Log to see if the server has been shut down at any time.

The File Open/Lock Activity selection enables you to display the number of connections that fit the following descriptions:

- ◆ They are using a particular file
- ◆ They are open for a read or write operation

♦ They show a count for the number of times a deny to read or write to this file has occurred

♦ They show the status of the file if it is locked (no other access allowed) or if it is not locked

♦ They indicate which connection numbers are using this file

♦ They indicate the task number assigned by the client shell

♦ They indicate the record lock status of this file

Figure 16.42

The MONITOR file server keyboard lock screen.

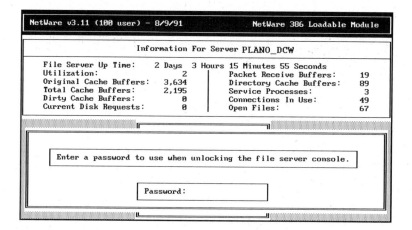

```
NetWare v3.11 (100 user) - 8/9/91          NetWare 386 Loadable Module

                      Information For Server PLANO_DCW
    File Server Up Time:    2 Days  3 Hours  15 Minutes 55 Seconds
    Utilization:              2           Packet Receive Buffers:    19
    Original Cache Buffers:  3,634        Directory Cache Buffers:   89
    Total Cache Buffers:     2,195        Service Processes:          3
    Dirty Cache Buffers:        0         Connections In Use:        49
    Current Disk Requests:      0         Open Files:                67


         Enter a password to use when unlocking the file server console.


               Password:
```

You also can view which volumes are currently mounted on your server.

Practical TIP

If you need access to an application that has been limited to connection use (meter license), and you need access to this application, view, through File Open/Lock Activity on this file, the Conn numbers attached. Then return to Connection Information and find out who is logged in to this connection number. Call or visit that person to see if that user's file has been saved recently (or do it yourself if the user is not there). After you make an extended effort to log that person out correctly, then clear the connection to release the lock status on the file you need.

The Resource Utilization selection enables you to view statistics for memory usage in your file server. As you select this option, the view at the top of the screen will change, as shown in figure 16.43.

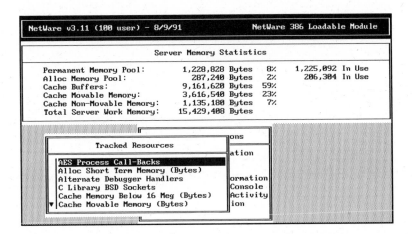

Figure 16.43
The MONITOR Resource Utilization screen.

This screen displays the type of memory pools and buffers that can be monitored for determining what areas of memory are being used. The Bytes column represents how many bytes of memory are reserved for this particular memory or buffer. The Percentage column indicates the amount of available memory being used for this particular memory or buffer.

The In Use column indicates how many of the available bytes are being used by this particular memory pool. Seeing this information can assist you in deciding when to add more memory to your file server. You should refer to table 16.3 for detailed memory pool use information. The following list is what is referenced through Resource Utilization:

◆ Permanent Memory Pool includes the statistics for both permanent and semipermanent memory.

◆ Alloc Memory Pool allocates memory for temporary or short term use. This area also supports server advertising, user connection information, and drive mappings.

- ◆ Cache Buffers lists all the memory available for data caching. When the percentage reaches around 50 percent, you should start planning to buy more memory and unload any unnecessary modules. If the percentage is around 20 percent, you need to add more memory to your file server immediately.

- ◆ The Cache Movable Memory lists the memory buffers, which are rotating free blocks found in a certain range of memory. The NetWare operating system can move these around to improve memory usage. An example of what is found in this area is the function of hash tables.

- ◆ Cache Non-Movable Memory displays the amount of memory buffers that are allocated to a program temporarily.

- ◆ Total Server Work Memory displays the total amount of working memory for the server to use, minus what was needed for ROM BIOS, DOS, and the SERVER.EXE file booted from the CPU.

The first item to monitor from Resource Utilization for system performance is Alloc Memory Pool. The SET parameter Maximum Alloc Short Term Memory defines the size of this memory pool. The growth in this area could indicate problems with loadable modules that are not releasing memory when they are finished with it. You should check with the vendor, NetWire, or the NSEPRO for any updates about the suspected problem NLMs. Check the resource tags of the System Module Information selection to track the NLMs' growth patterns. You may choose to unload the NLMs that you suspect are causing problems.

The second item to monitor in Resource Utilization is the percentage value for Cache Buffers. If this number drops to around 20 percent, add more memory to your server immediately. Until you get more memory you can increase your cache buffer count temporarily by performing the following steps:

1. Unload any NLMs that are not needed for current operations (SBACKUP, INSTALL, TRACK ON, and so forth).

2. Use the REMOVE DOS command at the file server console prompt to release at least one-tenth of a megabyte of memory from the server being used by DOS.

3. Bring down the server and reboot it to recover unused blocks in the Permanent and Alloc Memory pools.

Novell will state that the NetWare Operating System is tuned to the optimal defaults right out of the package. They do not encourage that you use any SET parameters to make any adjustments unless you have done enough investigation, performance monitoring, and baseline history research.

Processor Utilization through MONITOR

MONITOR has an additional selection called Processor Utilization that is not brought up at the default load statement entry. This parameter is added with the following entry at the file server console:

```
LOAD MONITOR P
```

The Available Options menu has the added selection that will display CPU utilization. If there is heavy activity placed on the CPU, the process load can be a critical factor in the performance capabilities of the file server. You can mark the processes you want to view by highlighting each one and tagging it with the F5 key, or you can view all the processes by pressing F3 (see fig. 16.44).

The processes and interrupts, the time (milliseconds), count (number of times the process ran during the time sample), and the load percentage (time divided by count) are the types of details found in the Processor Utilization selection of MONITOR. Some of these processes, such as the Polling Process, will always display a high percentage. If any other NLM-type process reaches a load of 60 percent, you need to monitor and possibly unload this potential problem. Do not leave MONITOR loaded with the P option for a long period of time because it takes a lot of server overhead to maintain the detail information screen.

Figure 16.44

The MONITOR Processor Utilization screen.

```
 NetWare v3.11 (100 user) - 8/9/91          NetWare 386 Loadable Module

              Name                  Time      Count    Load
    Fi
    Ut            0 Process         1,721        18    0.16 %    19
    Or  ADISK  Process                  0         0    0.00 %    89
    To  AES No Sleep Process        2,917        14    0.27 %     3
    Di  AES Sleep Process               0         0    0.00 %    48
    Cu  Auto Remove Right Process   3,145       502    0.29 %    70
        Cache Update Process          239         5    0.02 %
        Communication Ctr Process  21,293     3,618    1.98 %
        Console Command Process         0         0    0.00 %
        Directory Cache Process        61         4    0.00 %
        FAT Update Process            145         9    0.01 %
        Gated Process                   0         0    0.00 %
        HOTFIX Process                  0         0    0.00 %
        Monitor Main Process            0         0    0.00 %
        Polling Process           998,006     3,948   93.18 %
        REMIRR Process                  0         0    0.00 %
        Remote Process              6,496       107    0.60 %
    ▼   RSPX Process                    0         0    0.00 %
```

Tuning the Server with SET Commands

Tune the server using appropriate SET commands.

As a network administrator or support engineer, you have the responsibility of balancing all of the issues in maintaining an optimally tuned network. You have to make decisions that make good business sense as well as include the issues of performance, reliability, and security.

NetWare has the capability of dynamically tuning itself over a period of time, using the default settings from the core package. There are four areas that the autotuning process will handle:

◆ Cache block sizing

◆ Physical Packet Receive Buffers

◆ Service processes

◆ Directory caching

It is difficult to measure the impact of changing any network parameters without the proper tools. Manual tuning can be unreliable without proven tests against which to measure the changes. You must do manual tuning sparingly unless you have your old configurations documented (so that you can put them back the way they were if your changes do not work).

Using benchmark data is not the best way to make decisions about performance tuning. As qualified LAN people, we all know that sometimes vendors have a tendency to stack their tests to their advantage. Each of our networks are unique in the components they contain. Tests usually are unrealistic, focusing on a particular component's performance rather than working with all the devices that represent a production environment.

When altering NetWare SET parameters, you should have a thorough understanding of their functions and impact on the overall network before making any changes. The SET parameters shown in figure 16.45 are never changed unless an NLM has been loaded that requires its modification for its service. You should base your performance tuning decisions on the actual workload of the file server.

Figure 16.45

SET parameters entry screen on the file server console.

```
:set
Setable configuration parameter categories
    1. Communications
    2. Memory
    3. File caching
    4. Directory caching
    5. File system
    6. Locks
    7. Transaction tracking
    8. Disk
    9. Miscellaneous
Which category do you want to view:
```

Tuning the v3.*x* File Server

There are several parameters that the SET command can affect in adjusting memory and performance processes in the file server. These parameter settings are in the following categories:

◆ Memory

◆ Communications subsystem

◆ File and directory caching

◆ The system processor

Memory

NetWare is a dynamically oriented operating system and will use memory for caching files extensively. As a network administrator or support engineer, you must have a complete understanding of the memory processes of the file server before you consider any fine-tuning adjustments. The items that follow are important memory parameter considerations:

◆ The more RAM in the file server, the more effectively your operating system can allocate the basic functional needs dynamically. As the use of the server increases, values will increment based on NetWare's "wait and see" algorithm for each process. This is done to make sure the system is not increasing its numbers based on temporary spikes in memory demand.

◆ The MONITOR utility is an important tool for observing memory allocations for a given number of resource tags. An NLM may have a resource tag in several different memory pools. The combination of these allocations has an effect on the total amount of memory that the server allocates. Check on these resource tags for potentially bad NLMs that are taking too much memory from several different areas. These NLMs can cause performance degradation or server crashes.

◆ Fragmentation of memory can occur in the Cache Non-Movable pool when NLMs are loaded and unloaded frequently. Volumes mounting or dismounting frequently also can cause fragmentation. There may not be a contiguous block of RAM to load a needed NLM such as MONITOR, even though the File Cache Buffer percentage seems sufficient. The only way to reorganize all the fragmented blocks is to down the server and bring it back up again. It would not hurt to down your file server periodically in order for the operating system to "clean itself up" when the server is powered back on.

The following are two important memory SET parameters:

◆ **MAXIMUM ALLOC SHORT TERM MEMORY.** This parameter controls how much memory the operating system can allocate to the Alloc Short Term memory pool. The file server will display warnings when operating system functions cannot be completed because this memory pool has reached its limits.

This parameter can be incremented in 1MB increments, to a maximum of 32MB. The default value is 8,388,608 (8MB). The range of values is 50,000 to 33,554,432 (32MB).

◆ **CACHE BUFFER SIZE.** Performance can be enhanced by increasing this parameter if block allocation sizes are more than 4,096 (4KB) on all volumes. This parameter is set in STARTUP.NCF, having additional possible values of 8192 (8KB) and 16,384 (16KB) (defaults at 4KB). Having a Cache

Buffer Size that is larger than the block allocation size will decrease performance and will waste memory space. The file server will not mount any volumes that have a block allocation size smaller than the cache block size.

Remember, setting block sizes too large can waste disk space. When a block allocation size is set at 8KB and the file is 3KB in size, you lose 5KB of space. If you leave the default block size at 4KB, the file only loses 1KB of disk space. You need to evaluate your overall file space needs before you set the block size. If you have to change this setting, make sure you have a good backup beforehand. This change process is done through the INSTALL.NLM and is destructive to the volume.

The Communications Subsystem

Tuning the communication subsystem involves all of the components involved with the LAN's I/O channel performance. The factors that affect performance include the following:

◆ Network Interface Cards (NICs)

◆ Packet size

◆ Communication buffers

◆ SAP traffic

◆ The Packet Burst protocol

The parameters and important performance considerations for the communications subsystem include the following:

◆ When the client attaches to the file server, the packet size between it and the file server is negotiated at this time. The size of the packet is a process that is related to the type of the network interface card (NIC). It is better to use the largest allowable packet size, except when the file server's NIC will not allow the larger packet or the packet has to cross a router that does not understand the larger size. You can use a set parameter in the STARTUP.NCF file to increase the default packet size of 1,514 bytes. The proper syntax for this statement is the following:

```
SET MAXIMUM PHYSICAL RECEIVE PACKET SIZE= value
```

You must use the equal sign between the statement and the value. If your driver size is unknown, the following is a list of suggested (not maximum) packet sizes:

ARCnet	4,202
Ethernet	1,514
Token Ring (4 Mbps)	1,202
Token Ring (16 Mbps)	4,202

Newer ARCnet cards can handle packet sizes of 4,202, but older base ARCnet packet sizes are limited to 618. Older Token Ring 4 Mbps NICs will not always allow a packet size of 4,202, but it never hurts to try.

◆ NetWare uses a default packet size of 512 bytes when there are routers to be crossed. Because the NetWare operating system cannot anticipate what type of NIC will be on the other side of the router, you can use an NLM called Packet Burst to override this limitation. An earlier version of this Packet Burst NLM was called the Large Internet Packet Exchange (LIPX). The network administrator or the support engineer has the responsibility of determining if all the routers can pass the negotiated packet size between the transmitting nodes. NetWare v3.12 will provide this feature as a default.

◆ The Service Advertising Protocol (SAP) that advertises the services of gateways, print servers, and file servers can affect the efficiency of the communication subsystem. When clients initially attach to the network, they use SAP communication to find the nearest server. Routers will broadcast SAP traffic to exchange the different server's information—this is not the same as the Routing Information Protocol (RIP). SAP traffic can be limiting to large multiple server networks that include routers. The NetWare Service Advertising Restrictor (NSAR) that is bundled with NetWare's Multi-Protocol Router, can be used to mask or filter SAP packets, minimizing the SAP broadcast traffic on a network. The main module of the NSAR, RESTRICT.NLM, enables the network administrator or support engineer to view the list of services to be advertised. Availability of certain entries can then be restricted on particular segments to reduce the traffic flow.

The following SET commands also can be used to tune the communications subsystem:

♦ **MINIMUM PACKET RECEIVE BUFFERS.** The default setting is 10 and the maximum value allowed is 1,000. This parameter must be set in the STARTUP.NCF file. This command will establish the optimal performance level in buffering packets for this file server. It is used to avoid potential system performance degradation until the server boot up process is complete. Performance may degrade if processes must wait for allocation of Packet Receive Buffers. If performance characteristically suffers while Packet Receive Buffers are allocated dynamically soon after the server is booted, this parameter can be increased to force NetWare to allocate additional Packet Receive Buffers after the server is booted.

♦ **MAXIMUM PACKET RECEIVE BUFFERS.** The default setting is 100 and the range is 50 to 2000. Changes are established at the file server console command line or in the AUTOEXEC.NCF file. This is used to avoid excessive use of communication buffers during server usage peaks.

♦ **NEW PACKET RECEIVE BUFFER WAIT TIME.** The default setting is 0.1 seconds with a maximum allowed of 20 seconds. Changes are established at the file server console command or in the AUTOEXEC.NCF file. You may want to use this command to control the amount of time the operating system will wait before spawning a new buffer.

File and Directory Caching

As part of the research you do in deciding whether your network needs tuning, you must determine whether your environment is read- or write-intensive. You can fine-tune these networks with the resources that you have, but it is best to have a lot of memory available for the operating system to allocate it dynamically as it is needed. The amount of File Cache Buffers that you should have available for your server should be at least 40—60 percent of total server memory. If you are working with image data files, available File Cache Buffers should be more than the 60 percent of the total server memory amount.

The following are recommended settings for file caching parameters:

◆ **MAXIMUM CONCURRENT DISK CACHE WRITES.** Setting this parameter higher will favor write-intensive environments. Decreasing this parameter will help read-intensive environments. The default value is 50, the range settings are from 10 to 100. This parameter will determine how many write requests are queued for the disk I/O control. The amount queued is displayed in MONITOR with the Dirty Cache Buffers numbers.

◆ **CACHE BUFFER SIZE.** The default value is 4,096 (4KB) with 8,192 (8KB) and 16,384 (16KB) settings available. The Cache Buffer Size and the Volume Block Size must be identical in order for the operating system to run in an optimal mode. Certain applications require larger block sizes and these should be kept on a separate volume. If the file server has mixed block sizes with these volumes, the Cache Buffer Size must be configured for the smallest volume block size or the volume will not mount.

◆ **TURBO FAT REUSE WAIT TIME.** The default setting is 5 minutes and 29.6 seconds. The range is 0.3 seconds to 1 hour, 5 minutes and 54.6 seconds. When the operating system needs to index and access files that exceed 64 FAT entries, NetWare will create a turbo FAT index for each of these large files. Memory in the file server will be flushed if these large files have not been used in the allotted wait time. To keep the performance level up on accessing these large files, the interval wait time can be increased to keep these files in server RAM a bit longer.

◆ **MINIMUM FILE CACHE BUFFERS.** The default setting is 20, with a range of 20 to 1,000 available. This is set to maintain a minimum amount of file cache buffers in RAM that the other memory pools cannot borrow from. A setting that is too high will reduce the number of NLMs that can be loaded on the file server at one time.

◆ **IMMEDIATE PURGE OF DELETED FILES.** The default value is OFF. The file server will perform a number of tasks that will keep a deleted file in the hidden directory on the volume from which it was deleted. This hidden directory on the volume is called DELETED.SAV. To improve security and increase performance, turn this setting to ON. The drawback to this is that you will have no immediate access to deleted files unless they have been backed up on a regular basis.

The following are recommended settings for directory caching parameters:

◆ **Name Space Support.** If you will be using MACs, OS/2, or NFS machines, you need to add this to each volume where the files for the applications will reside. You should do this setup at volume creation so that the directory entry tables will provide sequentially consistent forks to the file locations. You also should create separate volumes for the different name space support styles and use these volumes for only these types of files.

◆ **MAXIMUM DIRECTORY CACHE BUFFERS.** The default setting is 500 with the range of values from 20 to 4,000. This parameter is used to control the number of directory cache buffers allocated by the server. If directory searches seem sluggish, increase this setting. If you determine too much memory is being allocated for your current operating system, reduce this value.

◆ **MINIMUM DIRECTORY CACHE BUFFERS.** The default setting is 20 with the range of values from 10 to 2,000. This parameter needs to be high enough that directory searches can be done quickly, but not high enough to degrade system performance.

The System Processor

There are many components that affect the tuning process in a network environment. If you have checked out all the software performance factors and they seem to be optimally set, as a last resort, check the processor in the file server CPU. A more powerful CPU may or may not be the answer. Before you make an investment, try to rent, lease, or borrow a different server to see if this is the real problem.

Remember that the MONITOR utility will use the Utilization statistic to check on CPU cycles. Also, use the Processor Utilization selection in the Available Options menu as a tool for checking on loads to the server. As an example, check the NIC card in the server and see if it is causing an interrupt to put unacceptable demands on the server processing load.

Tuning the v4.*x* File Server

The v4.*x* operating system is different from any previous operating system made by NetWare. The enhancements made with this product have provided a performance improvement over earlier NetWare versions. The areas of enhancement include the following:

◆ **Optimized Code Paths.** These include directory searches, reads, writes, opens, and closes to files. NetWare 4.x has a slightly higher utilization of the CPU because of the background tasks it performs. More time is spent on background processes during light workloads. The improvements in the core code paths is apparent in heavier workloads—the utilization overhead is decreased with the change in priority of operating system tasks.

◆ **Disk Block Default Size.** The new default disk block sizes are based on volume size, not the performance criteria as set in v3.1x. The recommended default block size for all volumes is 64KB. The 64KB block allows the disk channel to be accessed by network users more efficiently for read and write requests. It also allows a more efficient access to mass storage devices such as CD-ROM and magneto-optical drives.

The newer defaults are listed below:

Volume Size	Default
Less than 32MB	4KB
32 to 149MB	8KB
150 to 499MB	16KB
500 to 1,999MB	32KB
2,000MB and up	64KB

◆ **Block Suballocation.** Unlike v3.1x, this feature will allow multiple file endings to share the same block. The unit of suballocation within a block is a single sector, which can contain 512 bytes. The benefit is that you do not have as much wasted disk space as in v3.1x, but the overhead for the operating system to manage this process is increased.

◆ **Read-Ahead.** As each file open request is made, NetWare 4.x will begin to track file access patterns. If it is determined that the file is being accessed sequentially, data will be moved into cache in a staged mode. Read-ahead will start when the data being accessed has reached the midpoint of the block. If the file is being accessed in a random mode, read-ahead is not started because of the increase in overhead. Read-ahead requests are placed in queue in a lower priority than regular reads and writes. Larger disk block allocations allow these types of read tasks to be accomplished in a single rotation of the disk, which improves performance in accessing data more quickly.

◆ **Prioritization of Disk Requests.** This is used to balance the requests to the operating system for reads and writes, rather than having one dominate the other. The disk elevator that loads these requests does not use the normal first-in, first-out (FIFO) build sequence. There are four bins that provide a tier of priority in what the disk elevator can seek. These bins include the following:

> Critical Events (TTS Log file writes)
>
> Read Requests
>
> Write Requests
>
> Read-Ahead Requests

The critical events are guaranteed events and always are processed with a greater priority than the other bins. Reads are foreground tasks, writes are background tasks, and read-ahead requests use a priority level that does not interfere with any other events. The priority level is calculated by taking a percentage of current requests from each bin and loading them into the disk elevator. The higher the priority, the more requests get placed in the elevator.

File and Directory Caching SET Parameters

As with NetWare 3.1x, it is best to have a lot of memory available for caching in the file server. In NetWare 4.x, many types of processes that the operating system must manage are taking place at the same time. Depending on whether your environment is read- or write-intensive, use the following SET parameters to prevent bottlenecks in file and directory access:

◆ **MAXIMUM CONCURRENT DISK CACHE WRITES.** The default is 50, with a range of 10 to 4,000. This is beneficial to large disk arrays that can handle many disk requests. The default number possibly could be reducing the performance on these types of systems.

◆ **DIRTY DISK CACHE DELAY TIME.** The default is 3.3 seconds, with a range of 0.1 to 10 seconds. This can be used for file servers that have file cache to spare. Your workload may include a high number of sequential writes, and you could improve your performance and disk space issues. By delaying the write long enough to have two write requests satisfied with one write request, it would improve the probability of impacting one block to complete this request.

The following are recommended settings for directory caching parameters:

◆ **MAXIMUM CONCURRENT DIRECTORY CACHE WRITES.** The default is 10, with a range of 5 to 50. This is recommended for file servers that have a large directory cache that is frequently accessing large numbers of small files, and your disk channel has a high throughput rate. A directory cache write is created every time a directory modification, addition, or deletion is processed by the server through the disk channel.

◆ **DIRECTORY CACHE BUFFER NONREFERENCED DELAY.** The default is 5.5 seconds, with a range of 1 to 300 seconds. Changing this setting provides no benefit to performance if the directory cache is tuned to the user's workload environment. This parameter is the amount of time the system will wait before the directory cache buffer is a candidate for release from memory.

◆ **DIRTY DIRECTORY CACHE DELAY TIME.** The default is 0.5 seconds, with a range of 0 to 10 seconds. If your file server has a large directory cache, your performance could benefit by increasing this delay time.

File System Parameters

In NetWare 4.*x*, you can link multiple servers together with the appropriate commands and create one large virtual server. The accessibility of these disks on these servers can create many files, requiring the operating system to manage the reliability of finding this data. The file system can be set to improve the storage and reliability of data by using the following SET parameters:

◆ **IMMEDIATE PURGE OF DELETED FILES.** The default is OFF. Excess disk space is used to store deleted files that can be recovered immediately or at a later period. The performance tradeoff is that the system has to use overhead to manage this function of tracking the deleted files. Novell recommends that this be left at the default.

◆ **ENABLE DISK READ AFTER WRITE VERIFY.** The default is ON. You can view through MONITOR's Disk Information for the current driver setting for read-after-write verification. This setting provides a global variable to the disk driver that is ignored most of the time. Reliability is more important than performance, so leave this turned ON.

NCP Packet Signature Parameters

The proper transmission of packets and the level of security involved in this process is an important function of NetWare. The communication between the server and the client can be monitored by the network operating system and the client's shell. Upon login, a packet signature is established to determine to what level data passing is allowed. The accuracy of these packets is included in this process. Use the following SET parameters to determine the levels of packet management for NetWare 4.*x*:

◆ **NCP PACKET SIGNATURE OPTION.** The default is 1, with options 0, 2, and 3 also available. Packet signing is recommended for networks requiring a high level of security. This parameter sets a level of this security feature for

865

enforcement, in conjunction with the client setting in the NET.CFG file called SIGNATURE LEVEL=. The option requires a signature with each NCP packet sent between the file server and the client. Refer to your client installation guide for details on the setup options and the explanation of what each level does. Performance issues are significant in production environments when it is related to normal operations. The Login process has a minimal performance effect because it is done infrequently. You can get more details on performance recommendations in the December 1992 *NetWare Application Notes* in an article titled "NCP Packet Performance Considerations" (which can be found on your NSEPRO).

◆ **ENABLE IPX CHECKSUMS.** The default is 1, with options 0 and 2 also available. This is not supported by the Ethernet 802.3 frame type. A checksum provides an error detection method that calculates the total number of bits that encompass the data being sent between one computer and another. The end that receives the data transmission will repeat this checksum process and compare it to the original value for accuracy. This feature is available for third-party developers to capture with IPX APIs so that they can monitor data corruption during transmissions. Novell does not recommend the use of this setting without justification because of the overhead in performance it will demand from the operating system.

Summary

This chapter reviewed the following configuration information needed to complete a NetWare 3.1x installation:

◆ Planning NetWare security

◆ Using SYSCON and command line utilities to implement system, file, and user security

◆ Using PRINTCON to set up print servers and print queues

◆ Using Monitor and the Set parameters to tune the file server

Review Questions

1. The Novell product used to configure the workstation to allow it to log into the network is called the _____ _____.

2. The workstation files are made up of which of the following files?

☐ a. VLMs

☐ b. NLMs

☐ c. NET.CFG

☐ d. AUTOEXEC.NCF

3. The workstation's network interface driver is referred to as a _____.

4. Which utilities give you statistical information about the volumes?

○ a. LISTDIR, VOLINFO, CHKDSK

○ b. VOLINFO, CHKVOL, VOLDIR

○ c. VOLINFO, CHKDIR, CHKINFO

○ d. VOLINFO, CHKVOL, CHKDIR

5. Which of the following is not a valid option?

○ a. LISTDIR /T

○ b. NDIR SYS:*.dat /OW=SUPERVISOR /SUB

○ c. LISTDIR /O

○ d. NDIR \may.?? /FO /AC NOT BEF 2/5/92

6. Can an account manager delete a user?

○ a. Yes

○ b. No

○ c. Only if he/she manages that user

○ d. Only if he/she created that user

7. Which of the following cannot be assigned to a group of users?

○ a. Workgroup manager

○ b. Account manager

○ c. Print queue operator

○ d. Supervisor-equivalent

8. Who can create a workgroup manager?

○ a. Supervisor only

○ b. Supervisor and Supervisor-equivalents

○ c. Supervisor, Supervisor-equivalents, and account managers

○ d. Account managers

9. Which of the following is not a type of NetWare operator?

○ a. Print queue operator

○ b. Print server operator

○ c. Console operator

○ d. Account operator

10. Which user is most commonly found on an average network?

  ○ a. The end user

  ○ b. The Supervisor equivalent

  ○ c. The print server operator

  ○ d. The FCONSOLE operator

11. Which is not a level of NetWare security?

  ○ a. Login/Password

  ○ b. File server

  ○ c. Menus

  ○ d. Attributes

12. Which is the correct order of NetWare security from highest to lowest?

  ○ a. File server, rights, attributes, password

  ○ b. File server, attributes, rights, password

  ○ c. Attributes, rights, password, file server

  ○ d. Password, attributes, rights, file server

13. Which rights are necessary to use an executable file?

  ○ a. Read, Write, and File Scan

  ○ b. Read and File Scan

  ○ c. Read

  ○ d. Read and Access Control

14. The _____ right(s) enable(s) you to assign the Shareable attribute to a file?

15. Effective rights include:

    ○ a. All the rights you have, plus the rights of any groups to which you belong.

    ○ b. All of the rights assigned to your user account.

    ○ c. The rights assigned to the Supervisor.

    ○ d. All of your rights, minus the rights of any group to which you belong.

16. The _____attribute enables you to change the contents of a file.

17. Which of the following is not a feature of NetWare 3.1x Security?

    ○ a. Trustee rights

    ○ b. File rights

    ○ c. Directory attributes

    ○ d. Maximum Rights Mask

18. Which statement about rights is incorrect?

    ○ a. The C right enables you to create files and directories.

    ○ b. The C right enables you to salvage a file.

    ○ c. The M right enables you to rename a directory.

    ○ d. The A right enables you to change a file from Ro to Rw.

19. Which of the following is the only attribute that cannot be revoked after it is granted?

    ○ a. X

    ○ b. H

    ○ c. E

    ○ d. SY

20. Which statement about attributes is false?

    ○   a.   The A attribute is assigned to files that are new or have just been copied to a new directory.

    ○   b.   Ra and Wa are not currently being used.

    ○   c.   Workgroup managers can assign the X attribute if they have the S right.

    ○   d.   C is used only with Macintosh.

21. To make sure that files are removed from the file server's memory when they are deleted, place this flag on the file or directory.

    ○   a.   P

    ○   b.   C

    ○   c.   M

    ○   d.   X

22. Which command-line utility shows the effective rights of a user?

    ○   a.   RIGHTS

    ○   b.   TLIST

    ○   c.   GRANT

    ○   d.   ERIGHTS

23. Which statement takes the Access Control and Modify rights away from the user JOE for the file called DATA.FIL?

    ○   a.   REMOVE JOE FROM DATA.FIL

    ○   b.   REVOKE A M FOR JOE FROM DATA.FIL

    ○   c.   REMOVE A M FOR DATA.FIL FROM JOE

    ○   d.   REVOKE A M FOR DATA.FIL FROM JOE

871

24. Which of the following does NOT display the proper command syntax:

   - ○ a. RIGHTS path
   - ○ b. GRANT path
   - ○ c. TLIST path
   - ○ d. None of the above

25. The TLIST command:

   - ○ a. Displays users with explicit rights in a given directory
   - ○ b. Transfers rights to a user or group
   - ○ c. Cannot be used to view a user's rights
   - ○ d. None of the above

26. Which of the following commands requires that the list of rights be included?

   - ○ a. RIGHTS
   - ○ b. TLIST
   - ○ c. REMOVE
   - ○ d. GRANT

27. To take rights away from a user, issue the following command:

   - ○ a. REMOVE [user] *name* [FROM *path*]
   - ○ b. REMOVE [rights]
   - ○ c. REVOKE [username] [*rightslist*]
   - ○ d. REVOKE *rightslist* [FOR *path*] FROM [user] *name*

28. Which of the following statements is true?

   ○ a. The REVOKE command can be used to take away a list of specific rights from either a user or a group.

   ○ b. TLIST cannot display the new rights for a user until you exit SYSCON and restart this command-line utility.

   ○ c. If you seem to have more rights in a directory than you were originally granted, rights have flowed down from another directory.

   ○ d. None of the above statements are true.

29. Regarding the statement "REMOVE or REVOKE can be used interchangeably":

   ○ a. This is a true statement.

   ○ b. This statement is only true for users, not groups.

   ○ c. Both commands have a net effect of changing the user's rights to a given directory.

   ○ d. Both commands are menu-based utilities that allow the Supervisor to change a user or group rights.

30. Which of the following statements about trustees is false?

   ○ a. Trustees can be either users or groups.

   ○ b. Users with Supervisor or equivalent rights can make trustee assignments.

   ○ c. SYSCON and FILER can be use to make a trustee assignment and apply rights.

   ○ d. None of the above statements about trustees are false.

31. Rights can be given using all except:

   ○ a. FILER

   ○ b. TLIST

   ○ c. SYSCON

   ○ d. GRANT

32. One of the best ways to simplify system security is to:

    ○ a. Give Supervisor equivalency to all users and groups

    ○ b. Give all rights except Supervisor and Access Control to groups

    ○ c. Assign trustee rights to groups, then put the appropriate users into those groups

    ○ d. There is no best method for granting rights in order to simplify the process

33. Which is NOT a way that a user can receive rights?

    ○ a. Granting rights directly to the user

    ○ b. Making the user a Supervisor equivalent

    ○ c. Putting the user into a group that has no rights

    ○ d. Granting rights to a group to which the user belongs

34. The proper key to use in order to mark multiple rights to be granted is:

    ○ a. F5

    ○ b. F1

    ○ c. F3

    ○ d. Ins

35. Which of the following programs activate printing when loaded on a workstation?

    ○ a. PSERVER.EXE

    ○ b. PSERVER.VAP

    ○ c. RPRINTER.EXE

    ○ d. PSERVER.NLM

36. Of the following, which TWO programs provide printing services from a file server?

    ☐ a. PSERVER.VAP

    ☐ b. PSERVER.EXE

    ☐ c. RPRINTER.EXE

    ☐ d. PSERVER.NLM

37. Which printing program is best for light production printing?

    ○ a. PSERVER.EXE

    ○ b. PSERVER.VAP

    ○ c. RPRINTER.EXE

    ○ d. PSERVER.NLM

38. The main difference between printing on a stand-alone computer and printing on a network computer is:

    ○ a. Hexadecimal names are used instead of English names for print jobs on the network.

    ○ b. A stand-alone computer sends the print job to a printer buffer, but the print job on the network goes to a queue on the file server.

    ○ c. File server queues must have a name the same as a printer or the print job cannot be stored in a print buffer.

    ○ d. You can send only one print job at a time to be printed on the network, but you can send several jobs simultaneously to a stand-alone printer.

39. The PSERVER.EXE program runs:

   O a. On the 2.2 file server

   O b. On the 3.1x file server

   O c. On a print server attached to the network

   O d. On the workstation

40. Who can modify the print server by default?

   O a. Supervisor

   O b. Supervisor-equivalent users

   O c. Print queue operators

   O d. The group EVERYONE

41. Who can modify a print queue by default?

   O a. Supervisor

   O b. Supervisor-equivalent users

   O c. Print queue operators

   O d. The group EVERYONE

42. Which of the following statements is most true regarding PCONSOLE?

   O a. Queue operators can manage print servers from this menu.

   O b. Only print queue managers can place jobs in queues using this utility.

   O c. Users can place jobs into queues, but cannot manage jobs from this menu.

   O d. Users and print server operators must have Supervisor-equivalent rights to add jobs to queues.

43. If you are the Supervisor or a Supervisor equivalent, you can insert a job into a print queue using the PCONSOLE menu utility from which Print Queue Information menu option?

    ○ a. Current Print Job Entries

    ○ b. Current Queue Status

    ○ c. Queue Operator

    ○ d. Queue Servers

44. Which of the following is not a PCONSOLE print job status condition?

    ○ a. Active

    ○ b. Adding

    ○ c. OnHold

    ○ d. Ready

45. Which of the following is the status for any job available for printing?

    ○ a. Active

    ○ b. Adding

    ○ c. OnHold

    ○ d. Ready

46. Which of the following PCONSOLE print job parameters can you use to print your documents after you leave the office?

    ○ a. Status

    ○ b. Target time

    ○ c. Job entry time

    ○ d. Suppress form feed

47. Which NetWare 3.1*x* Memory Pool is used for internal NetWare system tables that change size dynamically?

    ○ a. File Cache Buffers

    ○ b. Cache, Non-Movable

    ○ c. Cache, Movable

    ○ d. Permanent Memory

48. Which NetWare 3.1*x* Memory Pool is returned only when the server is down?

    ○ a. File Cache Buffers

    ○ b. Cache, Non-Movable

    ○ c. Cache, Movable

    ○ d. Permanent Memory

49. Which of the following does the length of the snake on the MONITOR utility's screen saver indicate?

    ○ a. Network utilization

    ○ b. Amount of time that screen saver has been active

    ○ c. Workstations still active on the file server

    ○ d. That the screen saver is still functioning

50. The MONITOR utility reports file server utilization, which can indicate which *two* possibilities?

    ☐ a. CPU cycles

    ☐ b. Number of disk requests

    ☐ c. Number of workstations logged in

    ☐ d. NLM process requests

51. If you highlight an active connection shown in MONITOR's Connection Information option, which of the following happens?

   ○ a. Displays number of available service processes

   ○ b. Provides user information such as NIC address

   ○ c. Shows available Receive Buffers

   ○ d. Indicates buffers to be written to memory

52. Which of the following is not displayed by the Disk Information screen of MONITOR?

   ○ a. Hot fix information

   ○ b. Checksum errors

   ○ c. Partition blocks

   ○ d. Device numbering

53. If you suspect that a file server NIC is malfunctioning, you can check which LAN Information statistic for an indication of the problem?

   ○ a. Send Packet Size (too big/small) Count

   ○ b. Receive Packet Overflow Count

   ○ c. Checksum Errors

   ○ d. Total Packets Received

54. Which of the following is not one of the items of information that the File Open/Lock Activity selection of MONITOR allows you to display?

   ○ a. Using a particular file

   ○ b. Open file for a read/write operation

   ○ c. List of files used in the past 60 minutes

   ○ d. File status

55. Hash tables are found in which Memory Pool?

   ○ a. Permanent Memory Pool

   ○ b. Cache Buffers Pool

   ○ c. Alloc Memory Pool

   ○ d. Cache Movable Memory Pool

56. The MONITOR selection that lets you see CPU utilization, and which is not brought up at the default load statement, can be brought up by typing:

   ○ a. LOAD MONITOR C

   ○ b. LOAD MONITOR S

   ○ c. LOAD MONITOR P

   ○ d. LOAD MONITOR F

57. Which of the following is not one of the four areas that NetWare is capable of dynamically tuning over a period of time, using default settings from the core package?

   ○ a. Cache Block Sizing

   ○ b. Physical Packet Receive Buffers

   ○ c. Hot Fix Redirection Area

   ○ d. Service Processes

58. The result of setting block sizes too large is

   ○ a. Insufficient memory for the cache buffer

   ○ b. Wasted disk space

   ○ c. Memory fragmentation

   ○ d. Insufficient Memory Pool warnings

59. The client/file server packet size is negotiated

   ○ a. When the client attaches to the file server

   ○ b. When the file server sends its first packet

   ○ c. When the client sends its first packet

   ○ d. When the file server is first installed

60. The default packet size that NetWare uses when packets must cross the router is

   ○ a. 640 bytes

   ○ b. 320 bytes

   ○ c. 1,024 bytes

   ○ d. 512 bytes

61. Which parameter should be increased if you want to favor write-intensive environments?

   ○ a. Cache Buffer Size

   ○ b. Packet Receive Buffers

   ○ c. Maximum Concurrent Disk Cache Writes

   ○ d. Immediate Purge of Deleted Files

62. Which of the following is not one of the areas of performance enhancements found in the NetWare 4.x environment?

   ○ a. Optimized code paths

   ○ b. Disk block default size

   ○ c. Turbo-Fat Reuse Wait Time

   ○ d. Block suballocation

63. Which feature of NetWare 4.*x* enables multiple file endings to share the same block?

   ○ a. Optimized code paths

   ○ b. Disk block default size

   ○ c. Turbo-Fat reuse wait time

   ○ d. Block suballocation

Answers

1. DOS Requester

2. A,C

3. MLID, Multiple Link Interface Driver.

4. C

5. D

6. C

7. C

8. B

9. D

10. A

11. C

12. B

13. B

14. File Scan and Modify

15. A

16. Read/Write

17. D

18. D

19. A
20. C
21. A
22. A
23. D
24. B
25. A
26. D
27. D
28. C
29. C
30. D
31. B
32. C
33. C
34. A
35. A
36. A,D
37. C
38. B
39. D
40. A
41. B
42. A
43. A
44. C

45. D

46. B

47. C

48. D

49. A

50. A,D

51. B

52. B

53. A

54. C

55. D

56. C

57. C

58. B

59. A

60. D

61. C

62. C

63. D

Upgrading

This chapter discusses the different procedures available to upgrade NetWare 2.*x* and 3.*x* to NetWare 3.*x* and 4.*x*. Each NetWare upgrade presents a new set of problems because most file servers have been tailored to meet the particular demands of each company. In this chapter, you are given the standard procedures to accomplish a NetWare upgrade.

General Information on Upgrading

The first step in preparing for an upgrade is to make sure that your hardware is compatible with the new version of the operating system to be installed. This is an important step when you upgrade any software package.

 Note If hardware settings must be changed because additional equipment is to be added or because the current settings are not supported, it is a good idea to make the changes while still running the older system and confirm proper operation. This enables you to solve any possible problems before you start the upgrade.

Before you start the upgrade process, list the hardware configuration currently being used. Whether you are using a standard ISA disk controller or a high performance SCSI adapter, you should know the configuration before starting the upgrade.

Much of the configuration information can be obtained from the file server by typing **CONFIG** at the console prompt. The CONFIG command lists the LAN adapters and their appropriate settings, including the current network address.

Information on NetWare 2.*x* disk controllers can be obtained from the FCONSOLE menu utility by selecting the disk channel option under the STATISTICS SUMMARY option.

You should also know the configuration of each LAN adapter currently being used. LAN adapters are commonly set to options other than the default. If your file server uses more than one LAN adapter, you must record all settings. Table 17.1 lists some common PC hardware configurations. Use this table to confirm that your system does not have conflicts that can cause problems.

Table 17.1
Common Hardware Configurations

Device	INT	I/O Decode (h)	MEM Decode	DMA
Com1	4	3F8-3FF		
Com2	3	2F8-2FF		
LPT1	7	378-37F		
LPT2 (cannot be used with XT controller)	5	278-27F		
If LPT3 exists,				
LPT1	7	3BC-3BE		
LPT2	5	378-37A		
LPT3		278-27A		

Device	INT	I/O Decode (h)	MEM Decode	DMA
XT controller	5	320-32F	C800:0000-3FFF	3
AT controller	14	1F0-1F8 170-177		
Floppy controller	6	1F0-1F8 3F0-3F7		2
Tape controller	5	280-28F		3
Novell disk coprocessor	11.10, 12, or 13	#1 340-347 #2 348-34F		
Novel SCSI adapter	2, 3, or 5	340-343 (enhanced only)	D000:0000-7FFF	1, 3, or none
EGA	2	3C0-3CF	A000:0000-1FFFE or B000:0000-7FFF or B800:0000-7FFF	0
Monochrome adapter		3B0-3BF	B000:0000-7FFF	0
Color graphics adapter		3D0-3DF	B800:0000-7FFF	0
Hercules monochrome (286A server)		3B4-3BF	B000:0000-7FFF B800:0000-7FFF	

Confirm with the individual manufacturers that every interface card supports the new operating system. In many cases, new driver software is required. Just because the LAN adapter driver worked in an earlier version of NetWare does not mean it will work on a newer version. Have everything ready before you start the upgrade, and things will go much smoother.

Any major operating system upgrade can destroy data. As a precaution, always make a complete backup of your system first.

 Describe suggested preparations to perform prior to an upgrade.

Upgrading NetWare 2.*x* to NetWare 3.11

This section covers methods for upgrading from NetWare 2.*x* to NetWare 3.11. The NetWare 3.11 product is a completely different system from NetWare 2.*x*. NetWare 3.11 is a true 32-bit operating system that uses NetWare Loadable Modules (NLMs) to add functionality. Upgrading to NetWare 3.11 can be done in two methods: *backup method* and *transfer method*. Both of these methods are discussed here. Then the newest method offered by Novell—called *Migrate*—also is discussed. The migration method is not included with NetWare 3.11 but is included with versions 3.12 and 4.01.

 Always make a complete backup of any system before upgrading.

Make sure that all users are logged out and run the BINDFIX utility on the original file server before you perform an upgrade. This ensures that any existing Bindery problems are solved before the upgrade is started.

Describe the utilities used for a NetWare 3.11 to
NetWare 3.12 server

Backup Method Upgrade

The backup method is required if you will be installing NetWare
3.11 on the same server that is currently being used for NetWare
2.x. As shown in figure 17.1, files are backed up from the NetWare
2.x server to a tape or DOS device. Then the server is upgraded to
NetWare 3.11 and files are restored.

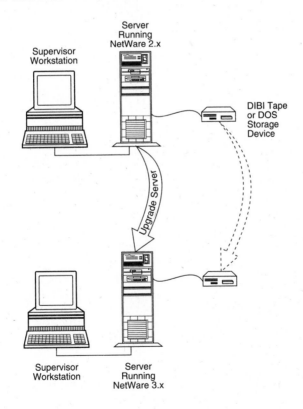

Figure 17.1

The backup method of
upgrading a server.

The backup method requires that you use the UPGRADE utility to perform a complete backup of all data, and then restore using the Novell UPGRADE utility. The problem with this method is that you must have the appropriate UPGRADE driver to allow your existing tape drive or other backup device to use the UPGRADE utility. Currently, Novell supplies drivers for a DOS device (C drive) or a WANGTEK tape drive. This method of upgrading is not very efficient and is not the preferred method.

Due to the changes in NetWare attribute information, a full backup from NetWare 2.x and restore to NetWare 3.11 will result in data corruption. Although it is possible to perform a DOS file-only backup without NetWare security information, this method is not considered a full system upgrade because all security and trustee information must be recreated manually.

To perform the backup method of upgrading your file server, you are required to execute the following steps:

1. Confirm all hardware and software drivers as discussed in the earlier upgrade procedure.

2. Install the appropriate driver file needed to operate your backup device. (DOS Drive and Wangtek Tape Drivers are supplied by Novell.)

3. Run the UPGRADE menu utility and back up all data and security information (bindery files).

4. Install NetWare 3.11, following the directions for a standard installation.

5. Rerun the UPGRADE menu utility and restore all data and security information.

Note All user passwords will be corrupt after the upgrade. This is normal; they will need to be reissued by using the SYSCON menu utility.

Transfer Method Upgrade

The transfer method assumes that you are upgrading both hardware and software. As shown in figure 17.2, this method provides a system of transferring all data and security across the network cable from the 2.*x* file server to the 3.11 file server. This method also assumes that you have already configured and installed the new 3.11 file server and that it is attached to the network cable. To confirm proper connectivity, you should be able to log in to both file servers.

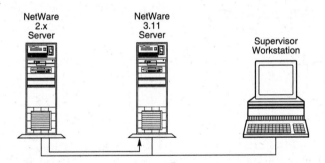

Figure 17.2

The transfer method of upgrading a server.

The operation screen of the UPGRADE menu utility looks similar to the backup method. The transfer method requires that you execute the following steps:

1. Install the new NetWare 3.11 file server.

2. Connect the file servers to the network cable.

3. Run the UPGRADE utility and select the transfer method.

At this time, the UPGRADE program begins by converting the security information and copies or transfers all data and information over to the new file server.

When running UPGRADE, you must be logged in to the 2.*x* file server as user SUPERVISOR, and all other workstations must be disconnected or turned off.

Upgrading NetWare 3.*x* to NetWare 3.11

This section briefly discusses the procedure used to upgrade the earlier NetWare 3.0 and 3.10 systems to 3.11. This upgrade is the simplest to perform, but you should be aware of a few issues.

As always, create a list of the current hardware and document the configuration and hardware settings. In most cases, this upgrade does not need this information, but the few minutes it takes to record this information can save you hours if a problem occurs.

Remember always to make a full backup. This is considered an upgrade, and data loss is possible. Perform the following steps:

1. Update the file server boot files by copying the disks SYSTEM-1 and SYSTEM-2 to the boot or C: partition.

2. Execute the SERVER command with the command to prevent the AUTOEXEC.NCF from running by typing **SERVER -NA**.

3. Load the INSTALL utility, select System Information, and transfer all system and public files.

4. Down the file server and reboot.

 If your file server is currently operating with a Novell DCB and NetWare 3.0, you must re–create the partition information. To perform the upgrade in this case, you need to perform a full backup and then restore after installing the newer NetWare 3.11.

Before you upgrade:

- ◆ Back up all files on your file server.

- ◆ You will need 6MB of memory in the file server. 8MB is preferred.

- ◆ Make sure that you have at least 25MB of disk drive space available on the file server.

- ◆ Make certain that no users are logged into the network. Use DISABLE LOGIN at the file server if necessary.

Installing and Upgrading NetWare 3.11 from a Master Server

Upgrade a NetWare 3.11 server to a NetWare 3.12 server.

NetWare's INSTALL NLM has a special option that enables you to install or upgrade from a master set of files on another server. This is a convenient way to upgrade or install large numbers of servers on the same network.

First, you must create a special directory structure on the master server that all other machines can utilize in installation or upgrading. The following step-by-step instructions walk you through the procedure necessary to create and use the directory structure.

To use INSTALL -J to create a v3.11 file server, follow these steps:

1. At your master server with approximately 20MB free, create a directory tree something like SYS:NETWARE\V3.11.

893

2. Make the following subdirectories under the
   SYS:NETWARE\V3.11 directory:

   ◆ SYSTEM-1

   ◆ SYSTEM-2

   ◆ SYSTEM-3

   ◆ UPGRADE

   ◆ DOSUTIL-.1

   ◆ DOSUTIL-.2

   ◆ DOSUTIL-.3

   ◆ DOSUTIL-.4

   ◆ BACKUP-1

   ◆ BACKUP-2

   ◆ LAN_DRV_.001

   ◆ PRINT-1

   ◆ PRINT-2

   ◆ HELP-1

   ◆ HELP-2

   ◆ HELP-3

   ◆ BTRIEVE

3. Use the XCOPY command to copy each Novell red disk into
   the appropriate directory, for example: **XCOPY A:*.***
   \NETWARE\V3.11\SYSTEM-1*.* /S, changing "SYS-
   TEM-1" for the appropriate disk.

4. When you are finished, delete SERVER.EXE from SYSTEM-1
   for security reasons.

5. Keep updates in the appropriate directories. To load other
   applications such as DOS, add new directories and change
   the DOS file in SYSTEM-2\FILEDATA.DAT.

Follow these steps to build a new v3.11 file server:

1. Use FDISK, along with FORMAT C: /S, to create the 5MB DOS boot partition.

2. Copy the SYSTEM-1 and SYSTEM-2 disks to drive C.

3. Run SERVER and enter the name and Internal IPX Number.

4. LOAD the disk driver.

5. LOAD INSTALL and create the required partitions and volumes.

6. DOWN the server.

7. Boot the server as a workstation using a DOS floppy and log in to your master server.

8. Enter the command **MAP ROOT F:=SYS:NETWARE\V3.11.**

9. Change to drive C.

10. Run SERVER. Enter **SERVER -NA -NS** if STARTUP.NCF and/or AUTOEXEC.NCF already exist. You are prompted for a server name and an internal IPX number.

11. LOAD the disk driver.

12. LOAD INSTALL -J.

13. Select System Options.

14. Select Copy System and Public Files.

15. At the Volume SYS needs to be mounted... message, press Esc to continue.

16. At the Mount Volume SYS window, choose YES.

17. When prompted to insert disk, press F6.

18. NetWare prompts you for a path. Delete the A:\, type **F:,** and then press Enter.

19. At the Is the drive a floppy? message window, answer NO.

    All v3.11 files download from the master server.

895

20. Issue the **DOWN** command to down the new server, and then type **EXIT** to return to drive C.

21. Log out, reboot the new file server, and then finish up the install (LOAD, BIND, and so forth).

 After you are famliar with the sequence, perform step 1 (FDISK, and so on) and copy only SERVER.EXE from the red Novell disks. Then jump down to step 7 (log in to master server) and manually copy the SYSTEM-1 and SYSTEM-2 directory files from the master server to your drive C. This gives you the latest updates. Next, load the disk driver and install -J, and then do the partitioning and volume creation. Finally, continue with step 13 (select System Options) to the end.

Performing In-Place Upgrades

In some cases, the in-place upgrade method can upgrade a NetWare version directly on the server. Here are the cases in which in-place upgrades can be performed:

- ◆ Upgrading NetWare 2.1x to 3.12
- ◆ Upgrading from NetWare 3.01 or 3.11 to 3.12
- ◆ Upgrading NetWare 3.1x to 4.x

In-place upgrades cannot be used for the following:

- ◆ Upgrading from NetWare 2.0a
- ◆ Upgrading from NetWare 3.0
- ◆ Upgrading directly from NetWare 2.x to 4.x. First you must upgrade to 3.11 or 3.12. Then you can upgrade to 4.x.

Because in-place upgrades overwrite the same server, the risk of data loss is very real. Server backups must be performed prior to the upgrade.

When upgrading bindery servers to NetWare 4.*x*, the user bindery information is installed in the context of the server that is being upgraded.

Performing an In-Place Upgrade from NetWare 2.*x* to 3.12

An in-place upgrade utility is available that can convert a NetWare 2.*x* server to NetWare 3.12. The key to the conversion is the 2XUPGRDE NLM that converts the file storage system. The procedure is quite involved and cannot be summarized here. Consult the NetWare 3.12 Installation and Upgrade manual for detailed procedures.

Performing an In-Place Upgrade from NetWare 3.1*x* to 3.12 or 4.*x*

Upgrading from NetWare 3.1 or 3.11 to NetWare 3.12 or 4.*x* is easily performed using a variation of the installation procedures described in Chapters 15 and 16. The Installation Options menu has a choice to Upgrade NetWare 3.1*x* to 3.12. A similar choice is available in NetWare 4.*x* installation.

Be sure to back up the NetWare files in your DOS boot directory. Even if you make an archive backup of the server files, the backup will not include the DOS partition, which must be backed up separately.

 Describe the procedures and results of the NetWare 3.11 to NetWare 3.12 upgrade.

The upgrade procedure differs little from a new installation. Here are some differences:

◆ You must specify a directory for the server files on the DOS directory. In most installations, NetWare 3.11 startup files were installed in the root directory of the DOS boot drive. The preferred procedure with NetWare 3.12 is to create a directory, usually named \SERVER.312 (or \SERVER.401 for NetWare 4.01), and copy the NetWare startup files to that directory.

◆ You will be asked for the path to your existing SERVER.EXE file. This enables INSTALL to locate your STARTUP.NCF file.

◆ You have a choice of invoking your existing STARTUP.NCF file when INSTALL runs SERVER.EXE. If you choose to use the existing STARTUP.NCF, the file will be copied into the directory you specified as the location for SERVER.EXE.

◆ Invoking the old STARTUP.NCF should be done with caution because it may result in starting old versions of disk drivers that are incompatible with the NetWare version to which you are upgrading. Incompatible drivers may work for awhile and fail unexpectably.

◆ If you are upgrading to NetWare 3.12, don't choose to create new STARTUP.NCF or AUTOEXEC.NCF files or you will lose your settings from your previous installations.

◆ You will want to have the NetWare 4.x upgrade procedure create an AUTOEXEC.NCF file that contains time server information and other NetWare 4-specific commands. Be sure to review LAN drivers and other information to ensure that the new commands are correctly entered.

◆ Examine the AUTOEXEC.NCF file for required changes. Remember that the default Ethernet protocol changes to Ethernet_802.2 for NetWare 3.12 and 4.x. If your workstations are still configured for Ethernet_802.3 frames, you may want to enable both frame types on the server so that all workstations are supported while you upgrade their client software.

When the upgrade of the file server is finished there are still several steps required to finish the upgrade and verify that the upgrade was successful.

   ◆   Update the workstation files.

   ◆   Test all applications to make sure that they still function properly.

   ◆   Print from the applications to ensure that the queues still function.

Exploring the Novell Migrate Utility

The MIGRATE utility is the most current tool for upgrading NetWare servers and is required for upgrading to NetWare 4.01. MIGRATE makes it possible to move bindery-based information on NetWare 3.1x servers into the NetWare 4.01 NDS environment.

MIGRATE can be used to upgrade all 2.x servers to NetWare 3.x.

MIGRATE can be used to upgrade all 2.x and 3.x servers to NetWare 4.x.

MIGRATE is included with NetWare 3.12 and 4.01. It is also available from NetWire.

The MIGRATE utility provides for two methods of upgrading:

   ◆   *Across-the-wire* upgrading upgrades between two running servers, using a workstation to copy files. This procedure is depicted in figure 17.3. With across-the-wire upgrades, MIGRATE moves both data files and bindery information to the new server.

899

Figure 17.3

Across-the-wire migration.

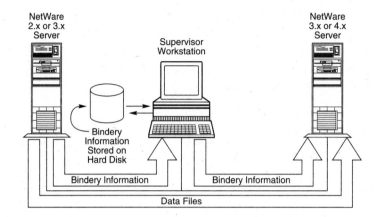

◆ A *same-server* migration enables you to upgrade the operating system on the same server hardware. With a same-server migration, MIGRATE copies only the bindery information to the upgraded servers. Application and data files must be copied using a separate tape backup procedure. The process is illustrated in figure 17.4.

Figure 17.4

Same-server migration.

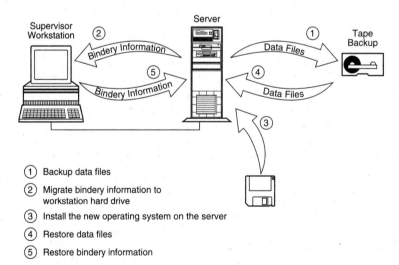

① Backup data files

② Migrate bindery information to workstation hard drive

③ Install the new operating system on the server

④ Restore data files

⑤ Restore bindery information

Both methods preserve accounting methods, login scripts, print server and queue definitions, user accounts, and other system-level information. The primary differences arise because a same-server migration does not copy application or data files or the information associated with those files.

Novell's Migrate utility is currently aimed at assisting with NetWare 4.0 upgrades but also offers some interesting options for NetWare 3.12 systems.

Performing Across-the-Wire Migration to NetWare 3.12 and 4.01

Although an across-the-wire migration requires two servers, it is the preferable approach for the following reasons:

◆ Application and data files are copied to the new server. If necessary, attributes for these files are converted to the conventions of the new server.

◆ Files on the new server will not be overwritten by files on the old server having the same file name. This ensures that obsolete files will not be accidentally copied. You cannot have the problem of overwriting files that can happen with tape backups.

◆ System files from the old server are not migrated.

◆ All trustee rights to directories and files are migrated.

Here are the steps required to perform an across-the-wire upgrade:

1. Log all users off the old server and keep them off during the migration process.

2. Run BINDFIX on the old server to remove old user accounts and directories.

3. Use SALVAGE to restore any deleted files that are to be migrated.

4. Back up the source server using your choice of backup utilities. Then delete any files you do not want to have copied.

5. Install and configure NetWare 3.12 or NetWare 4.01 on the new server, as described in Chapters 15 or Appendix C. The new server must have a different name from the old server being upgraded because two servers cannot have the same name.

6. Create a directory named MIGRATE on a workstation hard drive.

7. Copy the utilities from the Migration disk to the MIGRATE directory. If you are installing NetWare from a CD-ROM, copy all of the files from the following directory on the CD-ROM to the MIGRATE directory:

   NetWare 3.12:
   \CLIENT_____\MIGRATE\ENGLISH

   NetWare 4.01:
   \CLIENT\UPGRADE_____\MIGRATE\ENGLISH

   The _____ consists of 8 underscore characters. Substitute the appropriate language for **ENGLISH** if you are using a different language version.

8. Log in or attach as a supervisor to both the source and destination servers.

9. Switch to the directory containing the migration utilities that you copied in step 4.

10. Enter the command **MIGRATE**.

11. First you will see the screen in figure 17.5. If you choose a **Standard Migration**, all of the resources including data files will be transferred across the wire to the destination server. This example will use the **Custom migration** option.

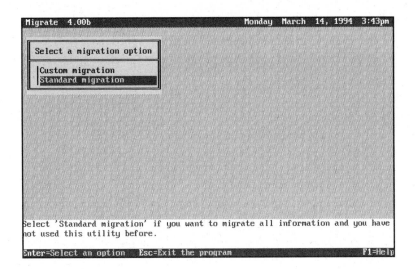

Figure 17.5

Selecting a migration
option.

12. Custom migration gives you the option of performing an
    across-the-wire or a same-server migration, which you select
    in the menu of figure 17.6.

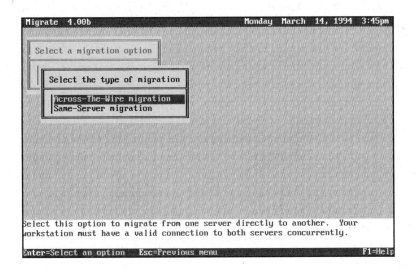

Figure 17.6

Selecting a migration
type.

13. Next, the menu in figure 17.7 requests you to select the
    source LAN type. Notice that IBM LAN Server and PCLP
    servers are available as migration sources.

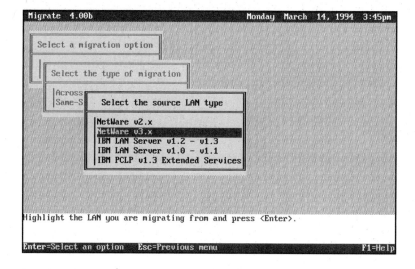

Figure 17.7

Selecting the source LAN type.

14. Next, from the menu in figure 17.8, specify the destination LAN type.

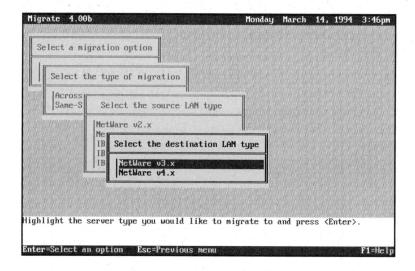

Figure 17.8

Selecting the destination LAN type.

15. Now you must specify the migration source and destination server and volumes. Figure 17.9 shows the form you must complete.

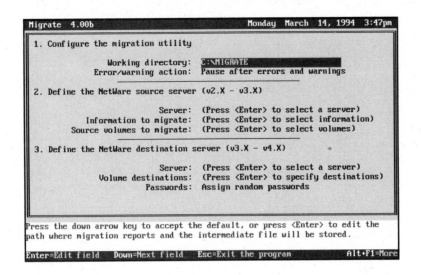

Figure 17.9

Entering source and destination server information.

The Error/warning action field enables you to specify whether MIGRATE should halt and display error messages. Because error messages are logged in a file, you can safely change this field to **Do not pause after errors or warnings**.

You can press Enter in each source and destination field to obtain a list of available servers or volumes.

If you press Enter in the Information to migrate field, the menu of figure 17.10 enables you to specify which types of data will be migrated to the new server. Data files can be migrated only in an across-the-wire procedure, but all other data types may be migrated in across-the-wire or same-server migrations.

Two choices are available for passwords on the destination server:

◆ **Assign random passwords** creates a new randomly generated password for each user. A NEW.PWD file containing all new passwords is created.

◆ **Assign no passwords** leaves user accounts without passwords so that they may specify a password when they first log into the new server. This is a less secure option.

When all information is complete, the available key list at the bottom of the screen permits you to press F10 to continue.

Figure 17.10

Selecting information to be migrated.

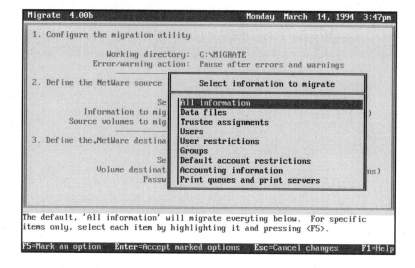

16. Now you must choose an option from the menu in figure 17.11. Choose Start migration to continue.

Figure 17.11

Selecting a migration action.

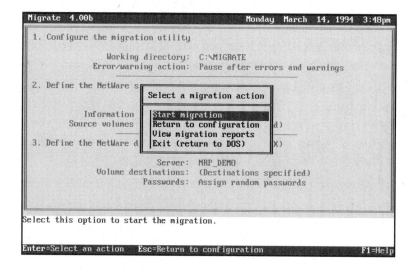

17. A scrolling display, shown in figure 17.12, will update you on the progress of the migration. If you instructed MIGRATE to Pause after errors, error messages like the one in

the figure will be presented. Notice that migration messages are being logged to a file named MIG001.RPT. You can examine this file later.

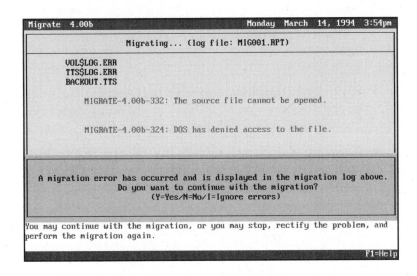

Figure 17.12

Monitoring the migration process.

18. After migration is complete, you will return to the menu in figure 19.11. There you can choose View migration reports to examine the migration log.

19. Troubleshoot the new server as required. Here are some of the things to be examined:

   ◆ If you chose random password generation, the file NEW.PWD contains a list of user ids with their new passwords. You will need to distribute this information to users.

   ◆ If the server name has been changed, you will need to update all server name references, such as drive mappings, in the login scripts.

   ◆ Any changes to directory paths must also be entered into login scripts.

   ◆ If you upgraded from NetWare 3.x to 4.x, you will need to recreate new system login scripts. NetWare 4.x system login scripts are associated with container

907

objects (primarily Organizations and Organization Units) not with the server. You must create a login script for each container object that provides a user login context.

♦ Test all applications on the new server. Upgrade any applications that require new versions to work with the operating system in your new server.

♦ If any directories were merged between the old server and the new, examine the files in the merged directories to ensure that they belong together.

♦ Examine print server definitions. Be sure that printers that are physically attached to the server conform to the hardware configuration of the print server.

Performing Same-Server Migration

The steps required to perform a same-server migration are the following:

1. Use a NetWare-certified backup method to back up all data and application files that you want to migrate to the new server. A same-server migration will not migrate these files.

2. Use MIGRATE to copy server definition information to the hard drive of a workstation. Information related to data and application file attributes, trustee rights, and so forth are not copied in this step.

3. Install the new operating system on the server.

4. Use MIGRATE to copy server definition from the workstation hard drive to the upgraded server.

5. Restore the files that were backed up in step 1.

6. Use system administration tools to redefine trustee rights and file and directory attributes. Be aware that definitions of some rights and attributes have changed between versions of NetWare, particularly between NetWare 2.15 and later versions, such as 2.2, 3.x, and 4.x.

7. If you upgraded from NetWare 3.0*x* to 4.*x*, bindery information from the old server was installed in the context in which the upgraded server was installed. Review this information as required.

Review Questions

1. What is the most important first step in upgrading?

   ○ a. Making certain that the new operating system is compatible with the hardware you are using

   ○ b. Running BINDFIX

   ○ c. Preparing the hard disk

   ○ d. Making sure that all users are logged off the network

2. Use the -U option with INSTALL when:

   ○ a. You are performing the upgrade on a machine that is not the file server.

   ○ b. You want to Undo a previous configuration.

   ○ c. You want to go straight to the Upgrade menu option.

   ○ d. This is not a valid option.

3. Before upgrading, you should:

   ○ a. Run MIGRATE

   ○ b. Run VREPAIR

   ○ c. Run BINDFIX

   ○ d. Run BINDREST

4. Why do you document your settings before upgrading?

   ○ a. Novell says to do this.

   ○ b. So that when you are asked questions during the installation, you know what settings worked previously.

   ○   c. To have a permanent record of the settings in case you need to regenerate the system.

   ○   d. They are needed for registering products.

   ○   e. b and c.

5. ZTEST does not:

   ○   a. Destroy all data on the disk.

   ○   b. Test the entire disk.

   ○   c. Check track zero.

   ○   d. a and b.

   ○   e. b and c.

6. Which is not a valid method of upgrading a v3.x server?

   ○   a. MIGRATE

   ○   b. UPGRADE

   ○   c. INSTALL -J

   ○   d. INSTALL at the DOS prompt

7. What option enables you to run SERVER.EXE but not load the AUTOEXEC.NCF?

   ○   a. SERVER NA

   ○   b. LOAD INSTALL -NA

   ○   c. LOAD SERVER -NA

   ○   d. SERVER -NA

8. Which is not an important step when upgrading?

   ☐   a. Make disk copies of all working disks.

   ☐   b. Make sure that you have a current backup.

   ☐   c. Run BINDFIX to eliminate bindery problems.

   ☐   d. Document all current hardware settings.

9. Which statement about upgrading NetWare is false?

☐ a. Upgrading from v2.x to v3.x corrupts all passwords.

☐ b. The UPGRADE utility reads all configuration information from the v2.x system so you do not have to input an internal IPX address.

☐ c. When using the transfer method, you must be the only user logged in, and you must be logged in as SUPERVISOR.

☐ d. If you are using the transfer method, it is assumed that you are upgrading both hardware and software.

10. Which statement about using MIGRATE is false?

○ a. MIGRATE can convert all NetWare 2.x and 3.x servers to NetWare 4.x.

○ b. Same-server migration copies all information from the source server to the destination server.

○ c. Same-server migration converts file attributes to the format used by the new server.

○ d. Across-the-wire migration does not create a NetWare 4.x system login script.

Answers

1. A
2. C
3. D
4. A
5. B
6. D
7. B

8. A, B

9. A, B, C, D

10. C

PART 4

NetWare TCP/IP

Certification Note

Soon, NetWare systems engineers will find that a thorough understanding of TCP/IP is a career requirement. Those who demand the most thorough TCP/IP coverage should examine NRP's new CNE Training Guide: *NetWare TCP/IP and NFS* (ISBN 1-56205-409-0). Written by Karanjit Siyan, author of NRP's *NetWare: The Professional Reference*, this book provides exceptionally thorough coverage of two CNE electives: NetWare TCP/IP and NetWare NFS.

With NetWare TCP/IP and NFS you will receive a CD-ROM that includes a copy of Linux, a version of Unix that has been adapted for use on DOS PCs. Linux will enable you to gain hands-on experience with Unix and with TCP/IP networking.

Learning the History of TCP/IP and the Internet

As with all communications systems, the development of the TCP/IP protocol suite is an ongoing process. The suite is constantly evolving to suit the needs of business and research networks. In Chapter 5 you learned about the packet structure and the purpose of the fields in each packet. Chapter 9 also provided a brief overview of the TCP/IP protocol suite. This chapter takes you further into the protocols that use these packets.

Prior to the computer revolution that took hold in the 1960s, the main topic of networking was transmitting bits across a communication medium in an efficient and reliable way. In the mid '60s the focus switched to using a packet-switched communication medium while still maintaining reliability and efficiency. In the mid '70s emphasis was placed on network architecture and how communication services could be provided across interconnected networks. From this need, what we know as the TCP/IP protocol suite was born.

The official name of the technology described in this chapter is the TCP/IP Internet Protocol Suite. It is most commonly referred to as TCP/IP after the names of the two main standards. TCP/IP can be used to communicate across any set of interconnected networks.

In this section you will learn about:

- ◆ The history of the ARPANET
- ◆ The Internet
- ◆ Why TCP/IP became so popular
- ◆ The basic goals of TCP/IP
- ◆ Who were the principal players in developing the TCP/IP protocol suite

Learning the History of the ARPANET

The history of TCP/IP begins with the introduction of ARPANET. TCP/IP was introduced by the Advanced Research Project Agency (ARPA) in an effort to combine the islands of automation that characterized computer systems prior to 1973. In the late sixties, many U.S. universities and research centers began looking for a way to connect all of their computer systems using existing resources. The idea of a convenient mechanism through which they could exchange data became a priority.

Many other organizations in the corporate and industrial sectors needed to combine workstations, hosts, and servers into local networking communities. To have an internetwork of the many devices currently in place, the individual networks needed to be connected. The devices that would connect the internetworks would be called *gateways*. These gateways would need to have a common set of procedures to forward the data to and from each network. Decisions would have to be made via address information on where the information or data was destined.

It was decided that this project would require the use of the current knowledge and implementation of networks in general. A packet-switched network, as described in Chapter 1, was the specific implementation that was chosen. It was in accordance with these concepts that the Advanced Research Projects Agency (ARPA) formed ARPANET.

Note In 1972 ARPA, which is a U.S. government organization, began promoting primarily military interests and became known as the Defense Advanced Research Projects Agency (DARPA). The ARPANET became what we know of today as the DARPA Internet. The DARPA Internet and the ARPANET are part of the global TCP/IP Internet. You will learn more about the TCP/IP Internet in the next section.

The ARPANET network communicated through leased lines that were connected through special switching nodes. These nodes were called Internet Message Processors (IMPs). A host computer could connect to the network via an IMP.

The first proposal for the ARPANET, which was made in mid 1968, consisted of four IMPS, one each in the University of California in Los Angeles (UCLA) and in Santa Barbara (USCB), the University of Utah, and Stanford Research Institute (SRI). The contract was implemented by Bolt Beranek & Newman (BBN) in late 1968.

 Note BBN has had a significant impact on the development of the TCP/IP architecture.

ARPANET began to be regularly used in 1971. It became a success through the uniform implementation of three services that connected the computer networks:

◆ Remote Login

◆ File Transfer

◆ Electronic Mail

These services will be discussed in detail in Chapter 19.

The Original ARPANET Interface Protocol

Originally, 56Kbps leased lines were used for interconnection. The interface protocol used was called *1822,* which was the number assigned to the report that described it. The purpose of 1822 was to offer reliable delivery of a packet to a destination node. 1822 did not become an industry standard. This caused DARPA to replace the interface protocol with the CCITT X.25 standard that was briefly discussed in Chapter 6. X.25 is used to connect DTEs and DCEs over public packet-switched networks. It is suspected that X.25 may become the only standard for packet-switching in the future. Both 1822 and X.25 exist on the Internet today.

Introducing TCP/IP

By 1973 it was determined that the interconnection protocols that were currently used were inadequate. A project was undertaken to define the goals of the architecture to be used. In 1974, Vinton G. Cerf and Robert E. Kahn wrote *A Protocol for Packet Network Interconnections,* which described the architecture objectives:

- ◆ Standardized application protocols
- ◆ End-to-end acknowledgment of packets
- ◆ Connectivity throughout the network
- ◆ Independence between the underlying network technology and the host computer architecture

The last two goals represented a new utilization of current technology and were considered novel requests. Because users previously had chosen hardware technology based upon their communication needs, a great diversity in hardware solutions existed.

A new technology that would hide the details of network hardware would permit computers to communicate independently of their physical network connections. The results of this study became the fundamental protocols that make up the TCP/IP protocol suite. Because of the success of the TCP/IP standard protocols to allow substantially different communication media to transmit data, OSI has adopted TCP/IP as part of the OSI technology.

TCP/IP implementation met the goals as laid down by Cerf and Kahn through:

◆ Dynamic routing

◆ Packet-switching at computer nodes

◆ Connectionless Network Layer protocols

◆ Security built into the transport protocols

◆ A common set of application programs

The Defense Communications Agency (DCA) assumed responsibility for operating the network, which was still considered a research network, in 1975. The version of TCP/IP that is found on most UNIX computers was implemented in 1981. The full transition from the original Network Control Protocol to TCP/IP finally occurred in 1982.

The Department of Defense adopted the TCP/IP protocol suite as its standard, which led to other government departments also accepting the protocol. This created a large market for the technology. In 1984, the original ARPANET was split into two parts:

◆ ARPANET

◆ MILNET

The result was that ARPANET would be responsible for the interconnection of research sites. The interconnection of military sites was turned over to the MILNET.

Note

Why are TCP/IP and UNIX so frequently seen together?

The success of TCP/IP and UNIX is mostly due to the University of California in Berkeley. Berkeley took on an implementation of TCP/IP on the behalf of DARPA for use with its UNIX network. This system became known as 4.2BSD (Berkeley System Distribution) UNIX. The source code for 4.2BSD was made available as public domain software in 1983. Because research results and developments of U.S. universities belong to the American people, 4.2BSD is available for a nominal cost as long as the originator's copyright is recognized. Presently, almost all versions of TCP/IP for UNIX are based on the Berkeley code.

TCP/IP has been rapidly expanding in universities and research centers and has become the standard communications subsystem for all UNIX connectivity.

Later, AT&T's System V UNIX adopted TCP/IP. Novell now owns the AT&T System V UNIX.

Exploring TCP/IP and the Internet

TCP/IP is considered to be a successful industry standard. It is not a proprietary networking solution like DECnet or AppleTalk or even NetWare. Many vendors offer products that support TCP/IP. Almost any computer can be a TCP/IP host:

♦ DOS computers

♦ Mainframes

♦ Mini computers

♦ SUN workstations

♦ IBM, DEC, and Apple computers

TCP/IP has proven viable on very large scale networks. TCP/IP is the base technology for a large internetwork that connects the U.S. government, most major research institutions, and a great number of corporations. This internet is called the TCP/IP Internet. The TCP/IP Internet, which is normally referred to as just the Internet, spans the globe.

Although initially a U.S. creation, with members such as the *National Science Foundation (NSF), the Department of Defense (DoD), the National Aeronautics and Space Administration (NASA), the Department of Energy (DOE), the Health and Human Services Agency (HHS), and CypressNet at Purdue,* the Internet is accessible throughout the world to organizations and individuals who want to tap into Internet resources. All activity on the Internet takes place in *real-time,* meaning that your connection activities and all communications happen as you type. The only delays are those that occur due to the load of activity on the Internet at that time.

More about other Internet Participants...

NSFnet—National Science Foundation (NSF) on the Internet
NSFnet is a communications network for research and scientific centers. The backbone consists of 56Kbps lines between the NSF *supercomputer centers,* which consist of about 10 universities. The primary connection between the NFSnet backbone and the ARPANET is at Carnegie Mellon University.

CSNET—Computer Science Network
CSNET was created by NFS to offer low-cost connections to small schools and industry, either through X.25 connections or through a dialup connection to their minicomputers.

MERIT, Inc.
MERIT, Inc. is a computer network consortium of eight state-supported universities in Michigan, along with NSF. This consortium is designed to develop and manage an enhanced backbone

network for the NFSnet backbone. The consortium is necessary because ARPANET can no longer support the demand for Internet access. This project is being conducted in partnership with IBM and MCI.

Most of the traffic on the Internet consists of electronic mail and file transfer. The method used to transfer files is FTP (file transfer protocol), which is discussed in Chapter 19. The account name you log in with should be *anonymous* and your password should be your e-mail address. There are some other issues involving etiquette on the Internet. The general rule of thumb is to remember that heavy activity degrades the performance of the system. Many people use the Internet for business purposes. Therefore, if your interest in the Internet is personal, do your large downloads when the site you are communicating with is at off-business hours.

Currently, the Defense Information Systems Agency (DISA) has the primary responsibility for determining the official Department of Defense Network (DDN) protocols, policy guidelines, architecture, strategies, and procedures. The DDN Network Information Center (DDN-NIC) provides services to the users, administrators, and managers of the hosts that use the Internet.

Any development of new protocols and the continued maintenance of the existing protocols is governed by the Internet Architecture Board (IAB). New ideas for protocols are submitted to the IAB for recommendation.

Request for Comments (RFC)

As application protocols are proved to be useful and able to be implemented, the specifics are put into a document called a Request for Comments (RFC). RFCs bring the protocol to the attention of the Internet community. RFCs are numbered in sequence and there are more than 1,300 in existence.

The DDN-NIC provides a library of RFCs for the public to examine. RFCs can prove so useful that they become a *recommended* protocol. Many RFCs are research ideas that are not ready for implementation. Not all RFCs describe protocols: some provide documentation, insights, or ways to implement protocols. Some are light reading, such as RFC968, titled "'Twas the Night before Startup."

The DDN-NIC was moved from Menlo Park, California, where SRI International had provided user services. In late 1991, Government Systems, Inc. took over the responsibilities. The current NIC address is:

DDN Network Information Center
14200 Park Meadow Drive
Chantilly, VA 22021

Figure 18.1 shows a timeline of events that shaped the course of the TCP/IP Protocol Suite.

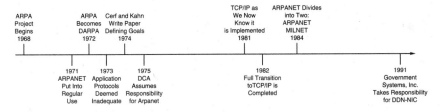

Figure 18.1

The TCP/IP protocol suite timeline.

Summary

The ease of combining TCP/IP networks together with an open-door policy that allowed commercial research networks and academic research facilities to connect to the ARPANET generated a new supernetwork called the Internet. Because of the need for convenient and reliable communications a set of protocols was needed. Out of this need came the TCP/IP protocol suite.

In this chapter you learned about:

- The reasons TCP/IP was needed
- How the Internet was formed
- The goals of the TCP/IP protocol suite

In addition to the goals of internetworking mentioned in the last section, TCP/IP provides many other convenient communication protocols:

- **The ability to discover physical addresses.**
  This is known as Address Resolution Protocol (ARP) and Reverse Address Resolution Protocol (RARP). ARP and RARP match up TCP/IP addresses and MAC addresses. In Chapter 19 you will learn more about these two protocols.

- **Directory Services for mapping user-defined host names to network addresses.**
  A hosts database file allows the system administrator to match TCP/IP addresses to common names that users will recognize. The hosts file will be discussed further late in Chapter 19.

- **Transparent access to remote files.**
  Telnet sessions allow the user to access the hosts as if they are hard-wired to the hosts. This ability is discussed in Chapter 19.

- **Network management for hosts, routers, and other network devices.**
  This is known as Simple Network Management Protocol (SNMP). SNMP allows centralized management of all SNMP nodes. SNMP will be discussed in depth in Chapter 21.

Review

Chapter 18 is a full introduction to the world of TCP/IP. The information presented was intended to give the CNE the background necessary to understand the next four chapters. There are no test objectives pertaining to the information in this chapter.

There is a world of knowledge contained in the RFCs that were mentioned in this chapter. It is worth the effort to read several of these documents prior to actually implementing a TCP/IP system. The following material includes the RFC numbers and names that should be of interest to you. These RFCs are included on the CD-ROM that comes with this book.

RFC768	User Datagram Protocol (UDP)
RFC783	The TFTP Protocol (Revision 2)
RFC791	Internet Protocol (IP)
RFC792	Internet Control Message Protocol (ICMP)
RFC793	Transmission Control Protocol (TCP)
RFC821	Simple Mail Transfer Protocol (SMTP)
RFC826	An Ethernet Address Resolution Protocol (ARP)
RFC827	Exterior Gateway Protocol (EGP)
RFC854	Telnet Protocol Specification
RFC950	Internet Standard Subnet Procedure
RFC959	File Transfer Protocol
RFC1014	XDR—External Data Representation Standard
RFC1050	RPC—Remote Procedure Call Protocol Specification
RFC1057	RPC—Version 2
RFC1066	Management Information Base for Network Management of TCP/IP-based internets (MIB)
RFC1098	A Simple Network Management Protocol (SNMP)
RFC1156	MIB—Replaces RFC1066
RFC1157	SNMP—Replaces RFC1098
RFC1234	Tunneling IPX Traffic Through IP Networks

These topics will also be covered in the next few chapters. The RFCs cover each topic in great detail and will help with implementation. The focus of the rest of this section is to provide you with a better understanding of how TCP/IP relates to the NetWare environment.

Investigating the TCP/IP Protocol Suite

This chapter deals with the layers and protocols that comprise the Department of Defense (DoD) networking model.

After reading this chapter you can:

◆ List the layers of the DoD model

◆ Identify the protocols used at each layer

◆ Create a hosts file

◆ Evaluate an IP Address

◆ Determine how subnet masks are used

As you learned in the last chapter, the Internet is a collection of cooperative, interconnected networks. Any communication system capable of transferring packets is considered to be a single network, independent of where it is located, how large or small it is, or what its throughput characteristics are. The Internet treats all networks equally, regardless of whether they belong to a single corporation or are a direct link between two computers. Figure 19.1 shows the typical cloud to represent the Internet. The "cloud" is an icon that is used to indicate that something undefined to the user is happening. The computers attached to the cloud use the mechanism inside of the cloud to communicate to other computers.

Figure 19.1

The Internet shown using the typical "cloud."

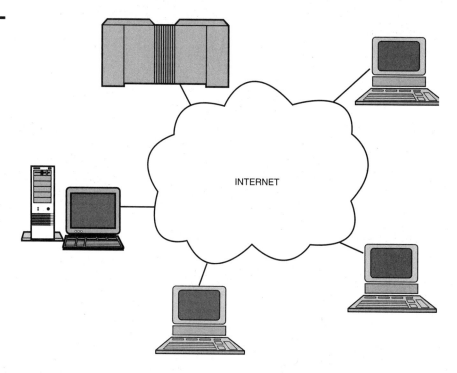

The cloud is more complex than it appears to the user. Figure 19.2 shows a representation of the types of configurations that make up the Internet. You can see gateways that connect smaller clouds. These clouds are physical networks that belong to organizations and are truly macrocosms in themselves. In figure 19.2, you see the same computers on the outside connecting to the cloud, but now you see that they attach to smaller clouds representing physical networks that are connected through gateways.

The next question is "How are these computers able to talk to each other despite the distance and diversity?" The answer is a common set of protocols, which enable all TCP/IP hosts to talk to each other. These protocols have specific formats and conventions that all TCP/IP hosts follow. The protocols that comprise the TCP/IP protocol suite function at specific layers of the network model. The model, called the DoD Model, is similar to the OSI Model.

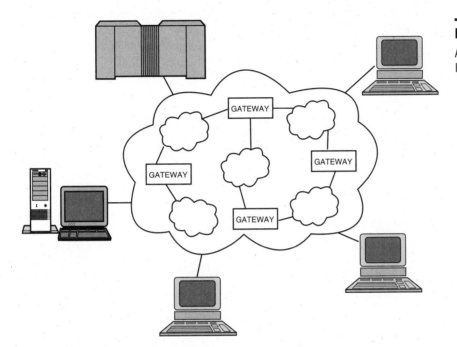

Figure 19.2

An internal view of the Internet "cloud."

Comparing the DoD Model to the OSI Model

Identify and describe the four layers of the TCP/IP protocol suite.

As you learned in Section 1, the OSI Model is an international effort to create standards for computer communications. But before an OSI Model existed, the Department of Defense (DoD)

929

Model was used. The DoD Model is made up of four layers that correspond somewhat to the later OSI Model. In fact, the DoD Model had a great influence on the creation of the OSI Model. The four layers are as follows:

♦ **Process/Application.** This layer is responsible for the user's interface with the network.

♦ **Host-to-Host.** This layer is responsible for creating and maintaining connections between communicating hosts.

♦ **Internet.** This layer is responsible for routing data between hosts.

♦ **Network.** This layer is responsible for the physical connection between hosts.

You should remember the memory technique for the order of the layers of the OSI Model from Chapter 3. They are repeated in the following table for comparison with the DoD model.

OSI	Layers	DoD	Layers
All	Application	Put All	Process/
People	Presentation	Application	
Seem	Session		
To	Transport	Hardware	Host-To-Host
Need	Network	Into	Internetwork
Data	Data–Link	Networking	Network
Processing	Physical		

Figure 19.3 shows the layers of the OSI Model and how they compare to the DoD Model. Although some implementations of protocols are exceptions to the comparison of the two models,

most of the functions of the Application, Presentation, and Session layers are performed in the DoD Process/Application layer. Similarly, the OSI Transport layer is most analogous to the DoD Host-to-Host layer, and the OSI Network layer is closely related to the DoD Internet layer. Finally, the OSI's Data Link and Physical layer's functions are handled at the DoD Network Access Layer.

DoD MODEL	OSI MODEL
PROCESS/ APPLICATION	APPLICATION
	PRESENTATION
	SESSION
HOST-TO-HOST	TRANSPORT
INTERNET	NETWORK
NETWORK ACCESS	DATA-LINK
	PHYSICAL

Figure 19.3

Comparison of DoD Model and OSI Model layers.

 Use the following chart as a simple guide to remember the layers of the OSI Model and their primary functions:

Layer	Name	Function	Description
7	Application	User Interface	Command interfaces with network.
6	Presentation	Data Translation	Data is converted to and from computer code.
5	Session	Dialogue Management	Sender and recipient connections are set up.

continues

931

Layer	Name	Function	Description
4	Transport	Reliability	Quality and reliability of data transmission is managed.
3	Network	Routing	Data is routed through network.
2	Data–Link	Packaging	Data is packaged and unpackaged for transmission.
1	Physical	Real connection	Bits and bytes are transferred from sender to recipient.

The following sections describe the most commonly used protocols and the layers at which they function.

 List and describe the most commonly used protocols contained within the TCP/IP protocol suite.

Exploring the DoD Layers

Figure 19.4 shows the four layers and several of the most popular protocols. These protocols are illustrated over the next several pages, starting with the protocols that comprise the Process Application layer.

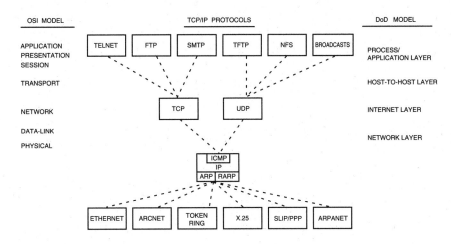

Figure 19.4

Popular DoD protocols and the layers in which they function.

The Process/Application Layer

The Process/Application layer has a set of standardized application protocols. For file transfer, File Transfer Protocol (FTP) and Trivial File Transfer Protocol (TFTP) are used. For terminal emulation, TELNET is used. The protocol for mail transfer is Simple Mail Transfer Protocol (SMTP).

FTP and TFTP

To explain the difference between the File Transfer Protocol (FTP) and Trivial File Transfer Protocol (TFTP), you first must understand how file and directory security on a UNIX system work.

When you obtain a long list of file information on a UNIX host by typing `ls -l`, you get a format that looks something like the following:

```
- rwx r-x --- 1 dniederm admin 258 Jun 03  17:10  example.file
```

The first 10 characters are your primary concern. The following information follows the first ten characters:

933

```
1                    How many links to this file
dniederm             The file owner
admin                The file group
258                  The size of the file
June 03 17:10        The time the file was last updated
example.file         The name of the file
```

Focusing on the first ten characters, you can group them into the following four sets:

File or Directory

The first character defines whether what you are looking at is a file (-), a directory (d), or a special file (l, s or c).

The next nine characters can be grouped into sets of three: Owner, Group and Other.

◆ The first character in each group designates whether you have Read privileges.

◆ The second character designates Write privileges.

◆ The third character designates executable privileges.

Owner

This set of privileges is what the owner of the file has for the file or directory. The owner is the person who created the file or the person to whom the administrator has given ownership.

In the example, the owner is dniederm and the rights are Read, Write, and Execute.

Group

This set of rights belongs to the group assigned to the file. Each user belongs to a default group. When a user creates a file or directory, the default group is attached to the entry. Any other user who belongs to this group has this set of rights to the file or directory.

In the example, the group is admin and the rights are Read and Execute.

Other

This set of rights is for users who are not owners and do not belong to the group.

In the example, if you are not dniederm and if you do not belong to the group admin, you have no rights to this file.

It is necessary to know UNIX security so that you are able to determine what rights you have when you use TFTP, as opposed to FTP.

FTP is designed to enable a user to transfer files to and from a remote TCP/IP host. When you enter the FTP program, you are able to get directory listings from your local file structure and from the remote structure. Files can be transferred as either ASCII or binary, depending on whether you want to transfer text or programs. This program does little more. To actually run a program, you need to use TELNET, which is described in the next section.

When you use FTP, you need an account login ID and a password. Because you have to give an actual user name, which has a default group, you are limited to the user and group rights.

TFTP does not support an account name or password, therefore the only rights you have are those granted to the Other field.

Another notable factor is that TFTP takes less overhead than FTP because FTP uses the Transmission Control Protocol (TCP), while TFTP uses User Datagram Protocol (UDP). TCP and UDP are discussed later in this chapter. A UDP packet is smaller than a TCP packet.

TELNET

TELNET provides access to a computer connected to the network. The connection is in the form of a terminal session that appears to users to be hard-wired directly to the host.

Novell has a product called LAN WorkPlace for DOS/Windows that supplies a DOS version of TELNET called TNVT220.EXE. TELNET and TNVT220 enable you to run applications from the TCP/IP hosts. The interface looks the same as it would if you were using the console on the host itself.

Several NetWare products give you an NLM called XCONSOLE. XCONSOLE is similar to RCONSOLE for a UNIX host. From the UNIX host, you add the NetWare file server to the xhost list with the xhost command. Then, you TELNET into the file server. For example, if your NetWare server name is MERLIN, you type LOAD XCONSOLE on MERLIN. At the UNIX host, you type the following:

```
% xhost + merlin
% telnet merlin
```

After a few questions about the type of monitor interface you are using, you see the same screen that the file server sees. This way is convenient for checking file server information from a UNIX host, as well as a good example of utilizing TELNET.

SMTP

SMTP is Simple Mail Transfer Protocol. It is the engine that delivers mail on the TCP/IP host. Novell has a similar product for the NetWare file servers called Message Handling Service (MHS). In both cases, the engines receive mail from the user interface and deliver the mail to the intended recipient. Standard user interfaces for UNIX are mail and mailx. MHS uses third party products for user interface. Novell also provides a gateway between SMTP and MHS.

Other protocols that function on this layer are the Network File System (NFS) and broadcasts.

NFS

Network File System (NFS), which lets your file server provide services as a distributed file system for TCP/IP hosts, functions at the Process/Application layer. NFS offers transparent access to a UNIX hosts file structure, similar to the access a NetWare file server offers to DOS clients.

Broadcasts

A *broadcast* is a packet delivery system that delivers a copy of a given packet to all attached hosts. When a broadcast message is sent, all attached nodes receive the message. This mechanism functions at the Process/Application layer.

The Host-To-Host Layer

The Host-To-Host layer is responsible for the following:

- ◆ The integrity of data transfer
- ◆ Setting up reliable, end-to-end communications
- ◆ Error-free delivery of data units
- ◆ Ensuring that the sequencing of data units is correct
- ◆ Ensuring no loss or duplication of data units

The two protocols that function at this layer follow:

- ◆ Transmission Control Protocol (TCP)
- ◆ User Datagram Protocol (UDP)

TCP

TCP provides a reliable connection between communicating hosts. TCP also sequences and acknowledges packets.

TCP is similar to SPX, which was described in Chapter 5.

TCP is like a polite telephone conversation. Recall a recent phone call made by you. When the recipient answered with "Hello," you probably responded with "Hi, this is ...". The conversation then continued, revolving around the topic that prompted the phone call.

Each time something was said it was prompted by what was said previously. If one of the parties asked the current time and the other responded that the sky was blue, the first party would realize that the question was misunderstood and the conversation would back up just a bit and attempt to resolve the misunderstanding.

This is the function of TCP. There is more overhead because of the tracking that must be done to ensure that the packet flow is flawless.

The upper layer protocols that use TCP are:

♦ FTP

♦ TELNET

♦ SMTP

UDP

The User Datagram Protocol is considered to be connectionless, and therefore is unreliable. UDP assumes that an upper layer protocol will take the responsibility for ensuring that packets are acknowledged.

UDP is like the postal system. If you forget about a utility bill and don't get it into the mail until the day before it is due, you won't immediately know if your account will be credited. When the statement arrives later the next month you will be able to determine if they received your check and take appropriate action if necessary. The point is that you need to wait for another mechanism to alert you to a potential problem.

The function of UDP is to deliver the data, but it does not check to make sure that the data was received.

UDP is similar to IPX, which was described in Chapter 5.

Upper layer protocols that use UDP include:

- TFTP
- NFS
- Broadcasts

The Internet Layer

The next layer down the model is the Internet Layer. The Internet layer is responsible for finding the "best" router. In some cases, *best* is the fastest route, in other networks *best* is the cheapest route. For example, it may be faster to use a T 1 link, but that would not be the cheapest link.

The Internet Layer is made up of the following four protocols:

- Internet Protocol (IP)
- Internet Control Message Protocol (ICMP)
- Address Resolution Protocol (ARP)
- Reverse Address Resolution Protocol (RARP)

Internet Protocol

The Internet Protocol (IP) is responsible primarily for the addressing of computers and the fragmentation of packets. IP provides datagram service between communicating hosts. IP also performs fragmentation and reassembly of datagrams.

 A datagram in TCP/IP is defined as the unit of data to be transmitted, a TCP or UDP header, and the IP header.

No mechanisms exist at this layer for end-to-end reliability or flow control. IP makes a "best attempt" effort to forward packets to the next destination.

IP relies on three other protocols to provide information about the network so that IP can send datagrams: ICMP, ARP, and RARP.

ICMP

The Internet Control Message Protocol (ICMP) is responsible for transporting error and diagnostic information for IP. Because errors occur occasionally on all networks, a mechanism is needed to let the TCP/IP hosts involved know which errors or conditions have been detected.

The following sections compile a list of functions that require an ICMP packet.

Echo Request and Echo Reply

ICMP reports back if a host is available for communications. The Application/Process layer utility that uses this ICMP packet is *ping*. Ping enables you to determine whether another host is functioning. If you want to know if the host MERLIN is available for a TELNET session, you can type

```
ping merlin
```

Using Novell's LAN WorkPlaces Ping command, if Merlin is available, the following message is returned:

```
Merlin is alive
```

If Merlin is off-line, the following message appears:

```
Host unavailable
```

ICMP provides this information.

Destination Unreachable

Destination unreachable is reported if:

1. The network, host, protocol, or port is not available.

2. The packet is too large and requires fragmentation, but the Don't Fragment (DF) bit has been set. Refer to Chapter 5 for more information.

3. A specific path provided by IP is not present.

Source Quench

If the receiving host's buffer is full or if it cannot keep up with the rate of the sending host, a Source Quench is reported by ICMP to the sending host.

Redirect

If ICMP finds a better path to the receiving host, ICMP sends the route address back to the sending host.

Time Exceeded for a Datagram

Packets on the Internet have a Time To Live (TTL). This means that packets that cannot find a destination are removed from the communication path after a specified time. When the removal occurs, ICMP reports to the sending host that the TTL has been exceeded.

Parameter Problem on Datagram

ICMP can report to the sending host when a packet must be discarded due to a bad entry in the IP Protocol header.

Time Stamp Request and Time Stamp Reply

ICMP can provide information on packet time stamps on request. The time stamps provide an understanding of how long the remote system spends buffering and processing a datagram.

Netstat is a utility, provided in UNIX and in LAN WorkPlace for DOS v4.0 from Novell, that can report statistical information about ICMP messages.

ARP

Address Resolution Protocol (ARP) translates a software address provided by IP into a hardware address that is used by the Network Access layer.

This protocol is necessary because an Ethernet hardware address is 48 bits long, while an IP address is only 32 bits long. No direct association in the two addresses is possible, so a mechanism is needed to convert the IP address to a physical address.

ARP functions as follows:

1. IP presents a datagram to the Network Access layer, which searches a temporary table for a physical address to match up with the IP address for the destination host. If an entry exists, the packet is sent to that physical address.

2. If no entry exists, an ARP broadcast is sent out on the network requesting the physical address of the intended host.

3. All computers on the network receive the ARP broadcast and determine whether the requested address is the same as its own. The host with the same IP address as was requested replies back to the originator with its physical address.

4. The originating host updates its table and sends the initial datagram to the recipient with the proper physical address.

RARP

Reverse Address Resolution Protocol (RARP) functions in the reverse order as ARP. RARP is used when a diskless workstation, which already knows its own hardware address, needs to acquire an IP address. RARP also sends a broadcast, but the recipient of the broadcast must be an RARP server. An RARP server provides IP addresses. Another version of this service is called BOOTP and is more efficient than RARP. BOOTP is provided in many UNIX systems and with Novell's LAN WorkGroup product.

Network Access Layer

The Network Access Layer describes the way the physical connection between connecting nodes should take place. Several connection types are supported. The most popular are listed in the following sections.

Connection Types

Several methods are used for connection between TCP/IP hosts. Several of the protocols have been explored in other chapters. Those chapters are listed here for reference.

Ethernet and 802.3

See Chapter 4 for detailed information on these protocols.

 Study table 4.5 for Ethernet and 802.3 specifications.

 The Ethernet hardware address is a six byte address. The first three bytes are assigned by the IEEE. Each vendor is assigned a number when it registers its boards with the IEEE. The last three bytes are assigned by the vendor, theoretically guaranteeing the uniqueness of hardware addresses.

When you use the userlist command with an /e option on a NetWare server, it displays the users currently logged in, as well as their MAC layer address. Novell Eagle boards all start with the number 00001b.

Token Bus (ARCnet) and 802.4

See Chapter 4 for detailed information on these protocols.

Token Ring and 802.5

See Chapter 4 for detailed information on these protocols.

 Study table 4.6 for Ethernet and 802.3 specifications.

X.25

X.25 is a CCITT standard protocol for transport layer services. X.25 carries packets along a virtual connection and delivers the packet to an end host that has agreed to use the X.25 protocol. The TCP/IP packets are transmitted along the path as if they were X.25 data.

SLIP

The Serial Line Interface Protocol (SLIP) transmits data byte by byte over a serial line. SLIP is typically used at speeds from 1200 bits per second to 19.2 kilobits per second, synchronous or asynchronous. SLIP provides no error checking.

PPP

The Point-to-Point Protocol (PPP) is used over either synchronous bit-oriented or asynchronous duplex circuits. PPP was designed so that it could transport data packets from multiple protocols, like DECNet, OSI, or IP.

Each layer in this section is responsible for helping the next layer resolve the source host and destination host by using addresses, as follows:

◆ The Process/Application layer provides a Host Name.

◆ The Host-to-Host layer consults a *hosts table* or DNS, to match up the name provided by the Process/Application Layer to an *IP Address.*

◆ The Internet layer invokes the ARP mechanism to match the *IP Address* to a physical address. This also is known as a *Media Access Control (MAC) Layer Address.*

◆ The Network Layer adds the hardware addresses into a MAC header. A Cyclical Redundancy Check (CRC) is added to the tail of the packet for error control.

The next section explains the addressing schemes of each layer in more detail.

Making IP Addressing Less Complex

It is frequently noted that the most complex part of the TCP/IP protocol suite is the addressing. Taking Ethernet as an example, the hardware address is 48 bits. An IP address is 32 bits. As a result, no direct connection can exist between the two numbers. This is why ARP is needed, so that the two numbers can be matched up in a cached table. The computer needs the hardware address and the TCP/IP protocol needs the IP address. IP addresses are discussed over the next few sections.

The user also needs some means to easily recognize the address of the intended host. It is not easy to remember a MAC address, for example 00-00-1b-2e-dc-12. Nor is it much easier to remember that the IP address is 192.68.205.5. To make it more practical, a *hosts table* can be created to match the IP address to an ASCII name that you can recognize.

Hosts Table

The hosts table is a text file that maps the commonly used host name to that host's IP address. On a UNIX host, this file resides in the /etc directory. On a NetWare server, the hosts file is kept in the SYS:ETC directory. The hosts file is the same format for both DOS systems and UNIX systems. The following is an example of a hosts table:

```
127.0.0.1          loopback lb localhost
192.68.205.5       bart # UNIX host
192.68.205.1       merlin backbone-router
192.68.208.1       C312 # Classroom C router
192.68.209.1       D40 # Classroom D router
192.68.207.7       dniederm ftp-host
26.2.0.74          wsmr-simtel20.army.mil simtel20
192.67.67.20       sri-nic.arpa nic.ddn.mil nic
```

The format for the hosts file follows:

```
<IP Address> <Host Name> <Alias> #<Comments>
```

IP Address

This address is assigned to the host. On a NetWare server, this assignment is made when you bind the protocol to the network board. On a workstation, the IP address is assigned in the net.cfg file. The next section talks more about this address.

Host Name

The host name is the primary name by which you reference that host. This name is arbitrary and is chosen by the system administrator. The host name for a NetWare server should be the same as the server name.

Alias

If the host name is not the name that all the users want to use, you can assign alias names to the host. A space is required between each name.

Comments

A pound sign (#) is used to start a comment. Anything on a single line past the # is considered to be a note and is ignored by any application using the file.

Because many TCP/IP programs use the hosts table, it takes longer for the application to search large tables for entries. The hosts table should contain only those hosts that you need to contact on a regular basis. To communicate with computers that are not in the hosts table, you need to reference that host by using its IP address.

Domains

An additional service that many UNIX systems, Novell's NetWare/IP and NFS Gateway products can provide, is called the Domain Name System (DNS). DNS allows a central service to provide the hosts table to all connected hosts via the network itself. This service reduces the need for duplicating the host's table across multiple file servers.

Another function of the DNS is to narrow down the exact location of a host through *domains*. A domain points to a host by giving it a specific Internet path. A full domain path might look like the following:

```
bart.backbone.comdata.edu.
```

Each part of the domain name indicates a location or host name. In the preceding example, `bart` is the host name, `backbone` is a subdomain within a company, `comdata` is a subdomain which is a company designation, and `edu` is a domain type. The syntax is:

```
<host name> <subdomain> <domain type>
```

Host Name

The host name is in the host's table.

Subdomain

The subdomain can be several layers deep. Subdomains are usually a company designation and divisions within that company.

Domain type

The domain type is a subdivision of the Internet that signifies the kind of organization to which you belong. In the U.S., these subdivisions include the following:

- ◆ MIL—for military installations
- ◆ COM—for corporations (COMmercial)
- ◆ EDU—for education and research facilities
- ◆ ARPA—for ARPAnet members

Foreign countries use a two letter designation instead of the U.S. subdivisions; for example, JP for Japan, DE for Germany (Deutschland), and so on. A complete listing of updated Internet country codes is featured in New Riders Publishing's *Riding the Internet Highway.*

At the end of the domain name is a period (.). This period stands for the root servers on the Internet, of which about a dozen exist. These names help Internet users determine with whom they are communicating and where they are located.

IP Addresses

Given an Internet address for a host, identify the class, network, and node address of the host.

Each TCP/IP host must have an IP address. If you anticipate ever connecting to the Internet, then you need to apply to the Internet for an address. The Internet provides you with a network number and you add on to that number for each host.

 Note You can assign your own numbers without the Internet, but getting an Internet-assigned number can help alleviate problems if you need to connect to the Internet at a later date.

IP addresses are stated in four byte dotted decimal notation:

xx.xx.xx.xx

The first, or left-most, byte is used to specify the address class.

Classes

Five classes, A through E, of IP addresses exist. The following chart lays some groundwork for understanding IP addresses. The first column states the class; the second column shows the number range for the first byte that defines the range. The third column contains a binary bit pattern that is the beginning of the range byte. This pattern is helpful if you forget to which class an address belongs. The class is important because part of the address is assigned to the network and part of it designates the host address. The last column shows which bytes are for the network (N) address and which bytes are for the host (H).

Class	Address Range	Left-most Bit Pattern	Network/Host Designation
A	0—127	0	N H H H
B	128—191	10	N N H H
C	192—223	110	N N N H
D	224—239	1110	Multicast addresses
E	240—255	1111	Internet experimentation

Classes D and E are not used for host addressing. The following three numbers also are not used in the first byte for addressing:

- **0.** This number was used for broadcast addresses in older systems and is reserved for special use.

  An address given to the host by a diagnostic application as 0.0.0.0 indicates that the address is referring to that host.

  An address given to a class C host as 0.0.0.5 indicates the host with an address of 5 on the current network. If the network address was 192.68.205, then the address is referring to host 192.68.205.5.

- **127.** 127 refers to a diagnostic function called *loopback*. If the first byte of an address is 127, then the command using the address, which is usually a diagnostic or statistical tool, reports information about the host issuing the command. In essence, 127 sends information back to itself. This is useful for testing if a station is communicating properly over the network.

  Although the last three bytes can be any number, you will see this number most commonly as 127.0.0.1.

- **255.** 255 is used for broadcast and multicast messages. A broadcast to all hosts is 255.255.255.255. A multicast to all hosts on the network 192.68.205 is sent as 192.68.205.255.

This method of addressing has a problem, however. The problem is that when the system designers came up with the addressing scheme, they originally anticipated hundreds of networks with thousands of nodes. They never dreamed that TCP/IP would be so widely accepted. Currently, several hundred thousand network numbers are assigned, with millions of nodes. So many addresses are assigned that they are expected to be exhausted within the next few years.

This problem becomes even more of a concern because of the availability of numbers. Take a look at the following chart to get a perspective on the numbers of network-host combinations that are available:

Theoretical Maximum		
Class	Number of networks	Number of hosts per network
A	127	16,777,216
B	16,384	65,534
C	2,097,152	254

A company applying for an Internet number is likely to get a class C address, because more of them exist to assign. Class A and B addresses are almost totally assigned. Class C addresses are getting close to running out, as well. If you get a class C address and you have more than 254 workstations that need IP addresses, you need to take additional steps to address all of your workstations. Applying for additional numbers may not be a viable solution. A common method for increasing the possible number of segments on your network is called *subnet masking*.

Subnet Masking

Subnetting allows you to break your network into smaller pieces. Each piece has a certain number of hosts that it can support. In essence, you are using a two-fold address: an actual IP address plus a subnet mask. All data packets are known by the combination of these two numbers, which ensures unique numbers on your network.

On a UNIX system, the ifconfig command sets up the mask for the host. On a NetWare server, the mask is set when you bind the protocol to the network board. On a NetWare workstation, the net.cfg file has a mask address that matches the address on the file server's network board to which the workstation is attached.

The subnet mask is utilized on a bit level. It is represented in the same four-byte, dotted decimal notation that an IP address uses. The address starts out by putting 255 in the Network Address portion of the IP address. A Class A address starts off as 255.0.0.0; a Class B address starts as 255.255.0.0; a Class C address starts as 255.255.255.0.

The first byte past the network portion of the address is the field that is used for subnet masking. Because a byte is just a collection of 1s and 0s, a 1 acts as a designator for the subnet address and a 0 is used to signify the host.

The following chart is a list of commonly used subnet masks for a class B network, their bit patterns, and the theoretical number of subnet possibilities and hosts per subnet.

Subnet Mask	Bit patterns	Subnets	Hosts
255.255.255.0	11111111.11111111.11111111.00000000	254	254
255.255.254.0	11111111.11111111.11111110.00000000	126	510
255.255.252.0	11111111.11111111.11111100.00000000	62	1,022
255.255.248.0	11111111.11111111.11111000.00000000	30	2,046
255.255.240.0	11111111.11111111.11110000.00000000	14	4,094
255.255.224.0	11111111.11111111.11100000.00000000	6	8,190
255.255.192.0	11111111.11111111.11000000.00000000	2	16,382

This list is not exhaustive, because the RFC admits you do not need to use contiguous bits for the mask. But for all intents and purposes, it is easiest to learn and administer contiguous bit subnet masks.

Also notice that fewer hosts and subnets exist than you might have calculated. The addresses of 0 and 255 in the subnetted byte are not allowed.

To get a better grasp of this concept, take a look at the following scenarios:

The company BD-RETREAT applies to the Internet for a class B address and receives the address 145.173.0.0. The last two bytes are assigned by the administrator of BD-RETREAT. BD-RETREAT has two cable segments on its network, which means that it must subnet the address.

The company assigns the number 145.173.45.1 to the first board in the file server. If it uses the system defaults, the number appears to the server as:

Network	Host
145.173	45.1

Because it needs to subnet, the company decides on an easy mask based on the bit patterns. The mask it chooses is 255.255.240.0, which lists the subnet byte (240—the first byte after the network portion of the IP address) pattern as 11110000. The 1s act as the subnet and the 0s are for the host.

Network	Subnet	Host
255.255	240	0

45 is represented in binary as 00101101. To figure out what the subnet number is, you use the bits pattern of the subnet number in the subnet mask. Class A addresses use the second octet, Class B addresses use the third octet, and Class C addresses use the fourth octet for the subnet position.

```
240 = 11110000
 45 = 00101101
```

The pattern then is:

	Subnet	Host
	1111	0000 (240) *from the top line*
	0010	1101 (45) *from the second line*
Decimal	32 +	13 = 45

As long as all nodes connected to the network board with the address of 145.173.45.1 have a bit pattern in the third byte that starts 0010, they are on the same subnet. After the bit pattern changes for the first four bits, then the subnet changes.

Because the server had two network boards, another address needed to be chosen. It is acceptable and easier to administrate if the same subnet mask is used on the second board. A new subnet number, however, must be chosen. This number should have a bit pattern in the third byte that is different than 0010. A bit pattern of 0100 was arbitrarily chosen. This choice makes the subnet number 64. The last 4 bits still remain, and just to make it easy, the pattern 1101 is chosen, which matches the host bit pattern of the previous address. The address assigned to the second board is 145.173.77.1.

	Subnet		Host	
	1111		0000 (240)	
	0100		1101 (77)	
Decimal	64	+	13	= 77

Figure 19.5 gives you a graphic depiction of what was assigned.

Figure 19.5

A subnetted network from the example.

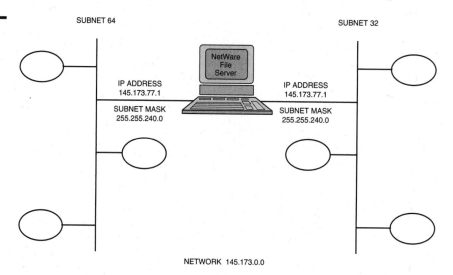

SUBNET 64

SUBNET 32

IP ADDRESS
145.173.77.1

SUBNET MASK
255.255.240.0

NetWare
File
Server

IP ADDRESS
145.173.77.1

SUBNET MASK
255.255.240.0

NETWORK 145.173.0.0

Summary

You have just finished the most complicated part of understanding TCP/IP: addressing the networks and hosts. Refer to the RFCs listed in Chapter 18 to further explore the mechanism that allows subnet masks to be transmitted over a TCP/IP network.

You also learned about the DoD model in this chapter. The DoD model is made up of the following four layers:

◆ Process/Application

◆ Host-To-Host

◆ Internet

◆ Network Access

Each of these layers is made up of protocols that allow the user to communicate over the network.

Each layer is responsible for assisting in helping the other layers resolve addresses. The three types of addresses follow:

◆ Host names

◆ IP addresses

◆ MAC or physical addresses

Host names are kept in a hosts table or on a DNS server, which is an ASCII text file kept in an etc directory, either on the root of a UNIX host or on the SYS: volume of a NetWare server. The hosts table is maintained by the system administrator.

The IP address can be assigned by the Internet or you can assign your own if you are not planning to attach to the Internet. Five classes of addresses exist, but only Class A, Class B, and Class C can be used for host addressing. Each class has a range of addresses that can be used. Part of the address represents the network and the rest of the address signifies the host.

Because only a finite number of addresses exists, you can use subnet masking to increase the number of available addresses.

Now that you understand the protocol in general, your next goal is to learn how TCP/IP is administered on a NetWare server.

In the next chapter, you learn about the following:

♦ Interfaces and frame types that are supported by TCP/IP and NetWare.

♦ Installing and configuring TCP/IP on a NetWare server.

♦ Maintaining the database files needed on the NetWare server.

Review Questions

1. Which TCP/IP protocol provides a connection oriented delivery service between hosts at the Transport layer of the OSI model?

    ○   a.   TCP

    ○   b.   UDP

    ○   c.   IP

    ○   d.   ICMP

2. Which statement concerning the UDP protocol is true?

    ○   a.   UDP converts data.

    ○   b.   UDP functions at the data-link layer.

    ○   c.   UDP provides a service similar to IPX.

    ○   d.   UDP provides a service similar to SPX.

3. The Internet Layer of the DoD model maps to the _____ Layer of the OSI model.

4. The Process/Application Layer of the DoD model maps to which three layers?

    ☐   a.   Application

    ☐   b.   Transport

    ☐   c.   Session

    ☐   d.   Presentation

5. What is the Network Portion of the IP address 162.45.77.210?

    ○   a.   162.45

    ○   b.   162.45.77

    ○   c.   45.77.210

    ○   d.   77.210

6. What is the Host Portion of the IP Address 192.68.205.5?

   ○ a. 192.68.205

   ○ b. 68.205.5

   ○ c. 205.5

   ○ d. 5

7. Which statement about address resolution is false?

   ○ a. ARP resolves software addresses to hardware addresses.

   ○ b. RARP requires an RARP server on the network.

   ○ c. ARP reads the hosts table.

   ○ d. ARP tables are kept in cache memory.

8. The address 223.251.102.66 is a class _____ address.

9. Which protocol(s) allow you to transfer files to and from a remote host?

   ☐ a. SMTP

   ☐ b. NFS

   ☐ c. FTP

   ☐ d. TFTP

10. Which layer(s) of the OSI model map to the DoD model's Network Access Layer?

    ☐ a. Data-Link

    ☐ b. Physical

    ☐ c. Network

    ☐ d. Transport

11. If the subnet mask of 255.255.224.0 is used, what is the bit pattern of the subnet byte?

    ○ a. 01110000

○   b.   11110000

○   c.   11100000

○   d.   11000000

12.   For a subnet mask for a class B address, in which byte can you start the subnetting?

○   a.   1st

○   b.   2nd

○   c.   3rd

○   d.   4th

13.   In a subnet mask, a _____ is used to define the subnet portion of the byte.

14.   Which IP address is located on the same subnet as 150.210.178.101 if the subnet mask is 255.255.248.0?

○   a.   150.210.171.62

○   b.   150.210.179.32

○   c.   150.210.167.112

○   d.   150.210.168.215

15.   What is the subnet number of the IP address 135.14.100.5 if the subnet mask is 255.255.224.0?

16.   Which address would not need a router to communicate with a host whose address is 162.160.136.101 if the subnet mask is 255.255.240.0?

○   a.   163.160.136.102

○   b.   162.160.144.44

○   c.   162.160.127.110

○   d.   162.160.135.210

17. Which address is used for diagnostics purposes, called loopback?

   ○ a. 127.0.0.1

   ○ b. 191.0.0.0

   ○ c. 255.255.255.0

   ○ d. 1.0.0.127

18. Which statement about cdc.classroomc.comdata.edu. is true?

   ○ a. cdc is the company name.

   ○ b. edu is the domain type.

   ○ c. comdata is the domain type.

   ○ d. edu is a root server.

19. Which statement about ftp is false?

   ○ a. ftp requires a login name and password.

   ○ b. ftp uses more overhead.

   ○ c. ftp is supported by UDP and SPX.

   ○ d. You cannot run an application with ftp.

20. Which protocol reports diagnostic information back to the host?

   ○ a. RIP

   ○ b. ICMP

   ○ c. ARP

   ○ d. IP

21. Fill in the following chart:

	OSI Model	*Protocols*	*DoD Model*
7			
6			
5			
4			
3			
2			
1			

Answers

1. A
2. C
3. Network

4. A, C, D

5. A

6. D

7. C

8. C

9. C, D

10. A, B

11. C

12. C

13. 1

14. B

Answer 14 Explanation

150.210.178.107 (IP address provided)

255.255.248.0   (Subnet Mask provided)

Step 1. - Find the octet that represents the subnet portion of the IP address.

The third position is the subnetted portion of the IP address in a Class B address. This means that 178 of the IP address and 248 of the Subnet Mask are the numbers we need to concentrate on.

Step 2. - Determine the bit pattern for the subnet mask.

The bit pattern for the Subnet Mask number 248 is 11111000.

The bit pattern for the IP Address 178 is 10110010

Step 3. - Determine which bits in the pattern discovered in step 2 represent the subnet number.

248 is **11111**000

178 is **10110**010

The 1s in the Subnet Mask are used to represent the bits that will be used for the subnet number. The 0s are used for the host portion of the address. The first five bits in the mask are 1s. The corresponding bits in the IP address are 10110.

Step 4. - Determine from the bit pattern determined in Step 3 what is the subnet number.

Remember that a bit is calculated as follows:

128	64	32	16	8	4	2	1
x	x	x	x	x	x	x	x

A 1 indicates that you use this number, a 0 ignores the number.

The bit pattern discovered in Step 3 showed that 10110 was the subnet number. The remaining three bits are of no concern in figuring the subnet number. This means that 10110xxx can represent the subnet number. This would give us the following pattern:

128	64	32	16	8	4	2	1
1	0	1	1	0	x	x	x

128+1+16=145. 145 is our subnet number.

Step 5. - Determine the bit patterns in the subnet portion of the IP addresses given in the answer choices.

Remembering from Step 1 that the third octet is the number you need to calculate, your answer choices are:

a. 171 whose bit pattern is 10101011

b. 179 whose bit pattern is 10110011

c. 167 whose bit pattern is 10100111

d. 168 whose bit pattern is 10101000

Step 6. - Match the bit pattern established by the Subnet Mask to the answer choices to determine which match the subnet number discovered in Step 4.

The Subnet Mask determined that the leftmost five bits would be used the calculate the subnet number.

The subnet number was calculated to be 145, which carries a bit pattern of 10110.

The only answer choice that matches the leftmost five bits isb.

The address 150.210.179.32 is located on the same subnet as 150.210.178.101.

15. 96

16. D

Answer 16 Explanation:

This question is asking essentially the same thing as question 14 but is phrased in a less direct manner. Expect this type of phrase manipulation on your test.

In this example, you can immediately disregard choice A, since the network portion of this address (163.160) does not match the intended IP address (162.160).

Using the same steps as shown in question 14, you can determine that the subnet number is 128, with the bit pattern of 1000. The only choice from the remaining numbers that has a matching bit pattern is d.

17. A

18. B

19. C

20. B

21.

OSI Model		Protocols	DoD Model
7	Application	FTP, TFTP SMTP, NFS	Process/ Application
6	Presentation	broadcasts	
5	Session		
4	Transport	TCP, UDP	Host-To-Host
3	Network	IP, ICMP ARP, RARP	Internet
2	Data-Link	ARCnet, Ethernet Token Ring, X.25	Network Access
1	Physical	SLIP, PPP	

Combining NetWare and TCP/IP

20

In Chapters 18 and 19, you learned about the TCP/IP Protocol Suite and how it is interpreted by the industry. In this chapter, you learn about using the TCP/IP transport on a NetWare network. The versions of NetWare that use the protocol in the method that will be discussed are v3.1 and v4.*x*.

In this chapter, you learn about the following:

♦ The products that Novell produces that rely upon the TCP/IP Protocol Suite

♦ The supported interfaces, their frame types, and what is needed to use them on a NetWare server

♦ The database file used by NetWare

♦ The NLMs that NetWare servers use

♦ The syntax for loading and binding the TCP/IP protocols

NetWare and TCP/IP offer a Local Area Network (LAN) the ability to "right-size" its environment. Right-sizing is a concept that allows a network to expand by requiring the different network systems to perform only the functions that they can do best. Suppose, for example, that a medium-sized company is relying on its NetWare server to run word processing, spreadsheet, and database applications, as well as a CAD/CAM engineering application.

After noticing some uncomfortable delays, the company does a study to find out what takes the most processing time. It discovers that the NetWare server spends most of its time crunching the numbers for the CAD/CAM program and that very little time is spent on the other applications. A different system that could help solve this dilemma is a UNIX host. The UNIX host on a multiprocessor platform can really help a processor-intensive application to deliver faster results, while the NetWare server excels when file-intensive programs are used.

In a well-integrated network, each computer system performs only the tasks to which it is best suited. The NetWare server provides expedient file access and security, and convenient backup for all systems. A multiprocessing system provides the number crunching ability for the network.

Introducing NetWare Products that Use TCP/IP

Novell has several products to help integrate the TCP/IP-based network with the NetWare servers and DOS workstations. The following are two different types of products for TCP/IP connectivity:

◆ **Server Solutions**

These applications are intended to go on a NetWare Server or to provide server functionality.

◆ **Client Solutions**

These applications are for the workstation and do not require a NetWare Server to function.

Server Solutions

The following is a list of programs that run on a NetWare file server and provide connections to TCP/IP hosts.

NFS

The Network File System (NFS) product that Novell offers provides the following features:

FTP Server

The NFS product includes NLMs that allow TCP/IP hosts to FTP onto your server to copy files to and from the server.

LPD Services

The Line Printer Daemon (LPD) services allow UNIX users to print on NetWare printers while using UNIX print commands. This service also allows NetWare users to print to UNIX printers using NetWare print commands.

XCONSOLE

XCONSOLE is an NLM for the NetWare server that allows a UNIX host to TELNET into the server. The end result is RCONSOLE on a UNIX host.

Lock and Status Daemons

UNIX is considered to use a stateless protocol, which means that the host does not need to be burdened with remembering what has happened in the past. Because NetWare is a stateful protocol, a NetWare server can remember past events by putting records of them in cache or as files on the hard drive. For a file to be locked, the server must remember that it had previously been opened. When a UNIX user wants to use files on a NetWare server, which can be done through the NFS product, then the NetWare server can provide file locking features to the UNIX user through the Lock Daemon.

The Status Daemon informs UNIX users that the server is ready to allow the locking of files. After a NetWare server recovers from a crash, the Status Daemon reports that files had previously been locked and waits a specified period of time for those locks to be reclaimed.

File Sharing

The most powerful part of the NFS product is allowing a NetWare directory structure to be exported for use on a UNIX network. The UNIX users attached to the UNIX host can CD into a directory and find files and directories that look just like normal UNIX files and directories which are actually on a NetWare File Server. File sharing is easier than using FTP to copy files and allows the NetWare server to easily back up the files. UNIX backups are notoriously difficult and unfriendly.

FLeX/IP

Not all "right-sized" systems need full-blown NFS, which can be a rather expensive item. A select portion of the NFS product, therefore, was put into the FLeX/IP product as follows:

- F for FTP Server
- L for LPD Services
- e to make it pronounceable
- X for XCONSOLE
- IP for the Internet Protocol that is needed to make it work

NFS Gateway

In the NFS product, you are able to mount NetWare drives on a UNIX box. In some instances, it is convenient to mount a UNIX directory structure on a NetWare server and access it as a volume name. The NFS Gateway product allows you to select a directory structure on UNIX and give it a volume name. When you change to that volume, you have access to the files and directories on the UNIX host.

The NFS gateway product also allows the file server to become a Domain Name Server, which provides all workstations with a common hosts file and domain name, as was discussed in Chapter 19.

LAN WorkGroup

LAN WorkGroup is a suite of products that allows the user to have access to TCP/IP Process/Application layer protocols.

BOOTP Server

This service allows the NetWare server to provide IP addresses to workstations. The BOOTP server matches a MAC address to an IP address. Each time a station requests an IP address, the BOOTP server checks the MAC address. If the station has been on before, it is given the same IP Address. If no match is found, then a new address is assigned, preventing the necessity of customizing each workstation.

LAN WorkPlace for DOS/Windows

These files are kept on the network and are used by workstations. LAN WorkPlace is a set of protocols for the user that includes Ping, FTP, TELNET, and many other convenient programs.

NetWare/IP

NetWare's native language is IPX/SPX. The NetWare/IP program allows the server to speak only TCP/IP. It provides the following three services:

DNS

Domain Name Services (DNS), to provide a common hosts table and domain names.

DSS

Domain SAP/RIP Server (DSS), to provide SAP and RIP information on a regular basis. DNS is a protocol that provides access to a
distributed database of domain-related information such as host
names.

NetWare performs SAP and RIP services every 30
to 60 seconds. This service is considered to be a
paranoid protocol or *ping-pong protocol*. Each
NetWare server takes up valuable process time and
cable bandwidth by constantly reporting who and
where it is.

TCP/IP is a *polite protocol*, meaning that it only
broadcasts when it needs to discover addresses.
NetWare/IP increases the time between SAPs and
RIPs, and the SAPs and RIPs are limited to only
specified servers.

NWIP

The NWIP servers function the same as the normal NetWare
servers, except that IPX is not bound to the network boards.

Novell has one final product for use with TCP/IP, but this product does not need to be run from a NetWare server.

UnixWare Application Server

The UnixWare Application Server is UNIX on an Intel-based
platform. It has all of the features and functions of any System V
Version 4 type of UNIX. In addition, it has one feature that no
other UNIX system will ever have: the ability to talk directly to a
NetWare server. By default, the UnixWare Application Server
talks IPX/SPX, but also has the ability to speak TCP/IP.

Client Solutions

Each of the products already listed provided services to the client. The next list is a set of products that Novell offers for the clients to make use of TCP/IP host services.

LAN WorkPlace for DOS/Windows

LAN WorkPlace contains all of the client's Process/Application layer protocols as LAN WorkGroup. LAN WorkPlace differs from LAN WorkGroup in the following ways:

◆ It does not need a NetWare file server. It can connect to a UNIX host without first connecting to a file server.

◆ LAN WorkPlace does not include BOOTP services.

Except for the reasons above, the client portion of LAN WorkGroup and LAN WorkPlace are identical.

TN3270 for LAN WorkPlace

If you have an IBM 3270 Mainframe that talks TCP/IP, the TN3270 for LAN WorkPlace product allows the workstation to emulate an IBM terminal while still utilizing many of the LAN WorkPlace features.

NFS Client

NFS Client allows the workstation to map a drive to a UNIX host. When you change to that drive, you see the UNIX host's files and directories.

DOS Client Kit

This product is new from Novell. It includes recent VLMs and other client programs. The TCPIP.EXE and IPTUNNEL.COM programs for the workstation are included in this package. In the past, you were required to purchase products like LAN

WorkPlace or Schneider and Koch's SK-IP/IPX Gateway to get the client protocol support programs.

UnixWare Personal Edition

The UnixWare Personal Edition is essentially the same product as the UnixWare Application Server, but some of the programs for network administration have been omitted. This version allows only two concurrent connections: one for the prompt interface and one for an X-Windows graphical interface.

Programming Solutions

Novell also has put together a package for the programmer who wants to create NetWare file server NLMs. Following are the two versions of these Novell C Network compilers:

♦ AT&T Streams Transport Layer Interface (TLI) Compiler

♦ 4.3 BSD UNIX Socket Compiler

The compilers allow the programmer to take UNIX programs written in C programming language and recompile them to run as NLMs.

Now you have an idea of the types of applications that use TCP/IP and NetWare. The next section discusses the different interfaces commonly used and the differences in how they are used between IPX/SPX and TCP/IP.

Exploring the Supported Interfaces

In this section, you learn about the frame types TCP/IP requires when you use Ethernet, Token Ring, and ARCnet. You also learn about how to have IPX/SPX and TCP/IP coexist on your NetWare LAN.

Ethernet

TCP/IP and Ethernet are the original combination. NetWare, however, uses the IEEE 802.3 specifications for Ethernet. TCP/IP uses an ETHERNET_II frame specification.

The default Ethernet frame type for v3.12 and v4.*x* is what NetWare calls the ETHERNET_802.2 frame. This frame type is the same as the IEEE specification for 802.3.

Prior versions of NetWare used the frame type of ETHERNET_802.3 for default. The ETHERNET_802.3 frame type did not make use of the LLC field that is defined in the standard IEEE 802.2, and was considered 802.3 RAW.

Before the IEEE set standards for the CSMA/CD protocols listed previously, the ETHERNET_II frame type was used. This frame type is the one that TCP/IP requires.

Only one small difference exists between the frame types, as you can see in the following figure. Figure 20.1 shows the three frame types for comparison.

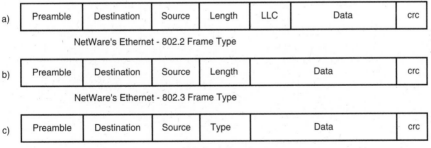

Figure 20.1

(a) Ethernet_802.2 frame type,
(b) Ethernet_802.3 frame type, and
(c) Ethernet_II frame types shown for comparison.

975

Because of the differences, you have two choices for allowing IPX/SPX and TCP/IP to coexist on a file server.

Loading the LAN Driver Twice

Using this method, you load the LAN driver twice on the file server. Each time you load the LAN driver, you need to specify a different frame type. When you bind IPX, you bind it to the network board with either the ETHERNET_802.3 or ETHERNET_802.2 frame type used. For binding IP, you use the same network board, but the ETHERNET_II frame type.

Later in this chapter, you learn about the syntax for loading the LAN driver.

This method is the easiest but not the cleanest. This method is more demanding of cable bandwidth because multiple frame types need to exist on the network. Expect a slight decrease in performance with this method.

Reconfigure All Network Devices to Use Only ETHERNET_II

ECONFIG is used to convert older NetWare utilities so that they can use the ETHERNET_II frame type instead of ETHERNET_802.3.

This method is more complicated and time consuming, but it is more effective at allowing both TCP/IP and IPX/SPX on your network. This method requires the use of a program called ECONFIG. ECONFIG comes with NetWare v2.*x*. ECONFIG changes the frame type used by various NetWare devices to ETHERNET_II.

The workstation is a separate issue. To have multiple protocols supported at the workstation requires that you use ODI drivers. The TCPIP.EXE program needs to be run before the NETX.EXE or VLM.EXE for best functionality.

The NET.CFG file needs the following modifications if you are using LAN WorkPlace. Similar modifications are made with other programs.

Link Support

    Buffers 8 1500

    MemPool 4096

Protocol TCPIP

PATH SCRIPT	C:\NET\SCRIPT
PATH PROFILE	C:\NET\PROFILE
PATH LWP_CFG	C:\NET\HSTACC
PATH TCP_CFG	C:\NET\TCP
ip_address	192.68.205.25

These statements tell the system how much memory to allocate for TCP/IP, where the LAN WorkPlace configuration files can be found, and what the IP Address is for the workstation.

This information is necessary for the CNE, but you are not tested on it during the TCP/IP Transport test.

Each of the following devices needs to be reconfigured for ETHERNET_II packets.

The 3.x or 4.x File Server

Load the LAN driver once, but bind both IP and IPX to that board with the ETHERNET_II Frame type.

977

The 2.x File Server

Use the ECONFIG program to change either the compiled version of the server boot program, or to change the precompiled files that are used during the installation.

The compiled file is called NET$OS.EXE and is found in the SYS:SYSTEM directory on the file server. V2.x systems allowed only four network boards, labeled A through D. You need to use ECONFIG once for every configured board. If you had two boards in the server, Token Ring and Ethernet, then the board to be configured would be B. The syntax for the command would be the following:

```
ECONFIG NET$OS.EXE B:E
```

- ◆ **ECONFIG** is the command
- ◆ **NET$OS.EXE** is the configured server boot file
- ◆ **B** is the LAN Board to be reconfigured
- ◆ **:** is the delimiter
- ◆ **E** specifies the reconfiguration to ETHERNET_II

The same process can be done for the precompiled files, NET$OS.EX1 and NET$OS.EX2. The same syntax applies.

The benefit to performing this process on the compiled version is that you do not have to worry about changing the original files. The drawback is that if you need to recompile from the original files you may not remember that this process has been executed on the original and a second step would be needed.

The External Router

NetWare allows you to create an external router using the ROUTEGEN program. This program creates an executable file called ROUTER.EXE. The router, like the v2.x file server, is allowed four network boards. You need to use ECONFIG on the ROUTER.EXE file.

In the following example, you need to reconfigure the two network boards in the router. You type the following:

```
F:\ROUTER\>econfig router.exe a:e
```

The first board is configured. To configure the second board, type the following:

```
F:\ROUTER\>econfig router.exe b:e
```

The directory in the previous example is one that you would have created and placed the ECONFIG program and the ROUTER.EXE to be reconfigured. ECONFIG can be run from any directory.

Workstations Running IPX.COM

If you still have workstations running IPX.COM instead of the ODI drivers, then you need to reconfigure IPX.COM by typing the following:

```
ECONFIG IPX.COM SHELL:E
```

This step would be done from the directory in which IPX.COM is held.

Workstations Using ODI Drivers

Under the heading of Link Driver in the NET.CFG file, you need to add the following lines:

```
Frame      Ethernet_II
Protocol IPX 8137 Ethernet_II
```

 The following list shows the protocol numbers used by IPX with the associated frame types:

Frame Type	Protocol Number
Ethernet_II	8137
Ethernet_802.3	0
Ethernet_802.2	E0

Token Ring

The Token Ring network board needs to be added twice. No TCONFIG program exists, so Token Ring must be loaded twice, with each load using a different frame type.

The two frame types for Token Ring are:

For IPX   use   IBM_TOKEN-RING

For IP   use   TOKEN-RING_SNAP

The Token Ring LAN drivers typically are not as forgiving as the Ethernet drivers. If you load an Ethernet board a second time, the network asks you which frame you would like to use. If you load a Token Ring board a second time without using a different frame type on the load statement, you are informed that what you are trying to do cannot be accomplished. When you put the frame type as part of the statement, the system allows you to continue.

ARCnet

ARCnet is the simplest medium to use with TCP/IP. It has only one frame type. No extra parameters are needed to load ARCnet using both IP and IPX.

Several files need to be either loaded, modified, or moved on the NetWare server for TCP/IP to function properly.

Investigating NetWare TCP/IP Files and Directories

When you install NetWare, a directory called ETC (commonly pronounced "et-see") is created off of SYS: with several sub directories. One of those directories is called SAMPLES. In the

SAMPLES directory, you can find examples of the files that should appear in the ETC directory. Some of the files just need to be moved to ETC, while others need to be customized for your network.

Database Files

Identify database files and modules that make up your TCP/IP transport system.

SERVICES, PROTOCOL, HOSTS, NETWORKS, and GATEWAYS are called DATABASE files, but they are simply ASCII text files that you can modify with any text editor.

The following files need to be located in the SYS:ETC directory:

HOSTS

The HOSTS file is the same as the one talked about in Chapter 19. The HOSTS file needs to be modified to include your TCP/IP host names and file server names. The following example comes from the SYS:ETC\SAMPLES directory:

```
#
# SYS:ETC\HOSTS
#
#   Mappings of host names and host aliases to IP address.
#
127.0.0.1   loopback lb localhost   # normal loopback address
#
# examples from Novell network
#
130.57.4.2      ta tahiti ta.novell.com loghost
130.57.6.40     osd-frog frog
130.57.6.144    sj-in5 in5
```

```
192.67.172.71   sj-in1 in1
#
# interesting addresses on the Internet
#
192.67.67.20    sri-nic.arpa nic.ddn.mil nic
26.2.0.74       wsmr-simtel20.army.mil simtel20
```

The numbers normally are entered as decimal numbers. If you need to enter hexadecimal numbers, you must preface each number with 0x or 0X.

0x72.0x12.0xAB.0x1F would be the same as 114.18.171.31.

NETWORKS

The NETWORKS file names the network portion of an IP address and allows comments. The following example comes from the SYS:ETC\SAMPLES\NETWORKS file:

```
#
# SYS:ETC\NETWORKS
#
#    Network numbers
#
loopback   127          # fictitious internal loopback network
novellnet 130.57     # Novell's network number

#
# Internet networks
#
arpanet   10    arpa   # historical network
milnet    26    # not so historical military net
ucb-ether    46    # Go bears!
```

SERVICES

The SERVICES file lists the TCP/IP service name, the port and the transport protocol (UDP or TCP) the service uses, and any alias the service has. The following is the SYS:ETC\SAMPLES\SERVICES file:

```
#
# SYS:ETC\SERVICES
#
#   Network service mappings.  Maps service names to transport
#   protocol and transport protocol ports.
#
echo        7/udp
echo        7/tcp
discard     9/udp       sink null
discard     9/tcp       sink null
systat      11/tcp
daytime     13/udp
daytime     13/tcp
netstat     15/tcp
ftp-data    20/tcp
ftp         21/tcp
telnet      23/tcp
smtp        25/tcp      mail
time        37/tcp      timserver
time        37/udp      timserver
name        42/udp      nameserver
whois       43/tcp      nickname  # usually to sri-nic
domain      53/udp
domain      53/tcp
hostnames   101/tcp     hostname  # usually to sri-nic
sunrpc      111/udp
sunrpc      111/tcp
#
#
# Host specific functions
#
tftp        69/udp
rje         77/tcp
finger      79/tcp
link        87/tcp      ttylink
supdup      95/tcp
iso-tsap    102/tcp
x400        103/tcp     # ISO Mail
x400-snd    104/tcp
csnet-ns    105/tcp
pop-2       109/tcp     # Post Office
uucp-path   117/tcp
nntp        119/tcp     usenet# Network News Transfer
ntp         123/tcp     # Network Time Protocol
```

```
NeWS        144/tcp    news  # Window System
#
# UNIX specific services
#
# these are NOT officially assigned
#
exec        512/tcp
login       513/tcp
shell       514/tcp    cmd    # no passwords used
printer     515/tcp    spooler   # experimental
courier     530/tcp    rpc   # experimental
biff        512/udp    comsat
who         513/udp    whod
syslog      514/udp
talk        517/udp
route       520/udp    router routed
new-rwho    550/udp    new-who    # experimental
rmonitor    560/udp    rmonitord   # experimental
monitor     561/udp    # experimental
ingreslock 1524/tcp
snmp        161/udp    # Simple Network Mgmt Protocol
snmp-trap   162/udp    snmptrap   # SNMP trap (event) messages
```

PROTOCOL

The PROTOCOL file lists the protocol name, a value for the lower level TCP/IP protocols, any alias the protocol has, and any applicable comments about the protocol.

The numbers are used in the IP header of the packet, telling IP which protocol gets the data next. The following is the SYS:ETC\SAMPLES\PROTOCOL file:

```
#
# SYS:ETC\PROTOCOL
#
#   Internet (IP) protocols
#
ip      0    IP    # internet protocol, pseudo protocol number
icmp    1    ICMP  # internet control message protocol
igmp    2    IGMP  # internet group multicast protocol
ggp     3    GGP   # gateway-gateway protocol
tcp     6    TCP   # transmission control protocol
pup     12   PUP   # PARC universal packet protocol
udp     17   UDP   # user datagram protocol
```

GATEWAYS

The GATEWAYS file is used only when a static route must be created. When you use the IPCONFIG program on the server, it automatically creates this file. The IPCONFIG program, the GATEWAYS file and the format are discussed more in depth in Chapter 22 along with static routing.

File Server Files

 List and describe the features of Novell's NetWare TCP/IP NLMs.

Six NLMS are used with NetWare TCP/IP.

TCPIP.NLM

The TCPIP.NLM provides the TCP/IP protocol service to NetWare. Several parameters are used with this NLM that are discussed in the next section.

SNMP.NLM

Simple Network Management Protocol (SNMP) support is provided with NetWare TCP/IP. NetWare SNMP allows you to monitor and manage other NetWare SNMP servers from a single server. You learn more about this function in Chapter 21.

SNMPLOG.NLM

The SNMPLOG NLM provides SNMP with a mechanism to report significant events on the network and write the information into a file. Chapter 21 provides more information about this function.

985

TCPCON.NLM

TCPCON is the console utility that allows you to view and manage SNMP agents. TCPCON is explored in depth in Chapter 21.

IPCONFIG.NLM

The IPCONFIG NLM enables you to create static routes. A static route is a route that must be used to talk to computers on cable segments other than the one on which you are. More about this NLM is found in Chapter 22.

IPTUNNEL.LAN

The IPTUNNEL NLM is a LAN driver. Chapter 22 talks more about IPTUNNELing, which places an IPX packet inside of an IP packet. IPTUNNEL is used when the cable segment cannot or will not allow multiple packet types.

Preparing Your File Server for TCP/IP

To use TCP/IP on your file server, you must make sure that the server can handle the new packet information and load.

Configuring the File Server

Configure a NetWare server for TCP/IP.

Two set statements need to be addressed at the file server. One needs to be set in the STARTUP.NCF file and the other in the AUTOEXEC.NCF file.

STARTUP.NCF

The following statement should be added to each file server's STARTUP.NCF file:

```
SET MAXIMUM PHYSICAL RECEIVE PACKET SIZE=####
```

is a number that determines the maximum size of packets that can be transmitted on any of the server's networks.

If you use Token Ring or Ethernet boards, the default is acceptable. The default is 1514. This number should be increased to 2048 if you use ARCnet and do not use Token Ring or Ethernet.

 The largest packet that can be transmitted over an IEEE 802.3 or Ethernet network is 1514 bytes. Any Ethernet packet includes the MAC address:

Destination =	6 Bytes
Source =	6 Bytes
Type =	2 Bytes
Data =	46 to 1500 Bytes
for a total of	1514.

The preamble and CRC are not counted in the packet size.

AUTOEXEC.NCF

The following statement should be added to each file server's AUTOEXEC.NCF file:

```
SET MAXIMUM PACKET RECEIVE BUFFERS=###
```

is a number that determines the maximum number of packet receive buffers that the OS can allocate.

Before increasing this parameter, use MONITOR to view the server's current use of packet receive buffers and service processes. If the number is at its maximum, increase this value in increments of 10 until you have one packet receive buffer per workstation. If you have EISA or microchannel bus master boards in your server, increase the number to at least 20 buffers per board.

The default value is 100.

 Identify console commands used to load and unload Novell's TCP/IP NLMs.

Three steps need to be completed on the file server in order for TCP/IP to be used:

1. Load the network board with the appropriate frame type

2. Load TCPIP

3. Bind IP to the network board

Each step has a set of parameters specifically for TCP/IP.

Loading the Network Interface

When loading the network board, you need to specify the proper frame type as mentioned in the last section.

In the following example, an Ethernet board is loaded. The board is configured for an interrupt of 5, with an I/O port of 320. The frame type is Ethernet_II.

```
:LOAD NE2000 INT=5 PORT=320 FRAME=ETHERNET_II NAME=E_II
```

 A name can be given to the board. When IP is bound, it is bound to the board name. This factor is important when you have loaded the same network board out multiple times. If you do not name the boards, some of the modules do not load when the file server is rebooted because the system waits until the frame type is chosen.

Loading TCP/IP

The TCP/IP NLM autoloads the following NLMs:

SNMP.NLM

STREAMS.NLM

CLIB.NLM

The TCP/IP NLM has three parameters:

Parameter	Options	Default
Forward	Yes No	No
RIP	Yes No	Yes
Trap	IP Address	127.0.0.1

Forward

This option enables the server to route IP packets to other cable segments. The default is No forwarding, which means that packets intended for hosts on other segments are discarded.

RIP

RIP is the Routing Information Protocol. NetWare servers use the RIP protocol to communicate all routing information that each server finds. The default is that RIP is enabled. It is suggested that this option remain enabled.

Trap

A trap is a special event that is reported to SNMP. Traps are discussed in Chapter 21. When an event is trapped, it is sent back to the host generating the trap, or loopback (127.0.0.1). If you manage multiple servers, it is more advantageous to monitor all trapped events from one server. When you load TCP/IP, you can send all trapped events to a specific server address.

In the following example, TCP/IP has been loaded so that IP packets can be routed and all trapped events are sent to the server with the address of 192.68.209.1:

```
:LOAD TCPIP FORWARD=YES TRAP=192.68.209.1
```

Binding TCP/IP

Eight parameters are available when binding the protocol IP to the network board.

Parameter	Options	Default
ADDR	IP Address	none
MASK	IP Mask	Class Default
ARP	Yes No	Yes
POISON	Yes No	No
DEFROUTE	Yes No	No
GATE	IP Address	None
COST	Number	1
BCAST	Broadcast Address	255.255.255.255

ADDR

ADDR represents the IP address that you assign to this network board. This parameter is the only one that is required. If you do not specify this parameter when you bind IP to the network board, the system waits and prompts you for the information before continuing.

MASK

MASK allows you to specify the subnet mask number to use over this interface. If you do not specify a mask, then the system assumes the standard subnet mask for the class address you are using.

Class A—255.0.0.0

Class B—255.255.0.0

Class C—255.255.255.0

ARP

The ARP option allows you to turn ARP off, which normally is not recommended. IPX/SPX expects to use RIP and TCP/IP expects to use ARP.

POISON

When hosts request routing information, the following happens: Host A requests routing information from host B; host A also provides host B with routing information that host A knows about, thereby updating both hosts' routing tables. Two methods are employed for exchanging routing information between two hosts. The first, called *Split Horizon,* is used by NetWare and many other current networking products.

Split Horizon states that host A does not give host B routing information it knows was acquired by host B. Instead, only information that host B does not know about is exchanged.

The second and older method, *Poison Reverse*, says that host A tells host B everything it knows, but information that host A has that was previously provided by host B is reported back to host B with its metric set to infinity (16 on a NetWare network). When host B gets the information back with this high metric, host B assumes that host A needs that address updated.

The POISON option allows you to use Poison Reverse instead of Split Horizon in case you have a TCP/IP host that only provides Poison Reverse reporting.

DEFROUTE

This option allows the file server to advertise itself as the primary route, forcing all routing to go through that server.

GATE

This option is used in place of the DEFROUTE statement if another host is on the network through which all routing is supposed to occur. The GATE option allows you to specify the address of the default router.

COST

The COST parameter allows you to specify how accessible this network interface should be for routing purposes. Lowering the cost tells other hosts that this is a preferable route. A cost of 1 is the most accessible.

BCAST

The broadcast address normally is 255.255.255.255. Older systems used 0.0.0.0 for broadcasts. The BCAST option allows you to specify the broadcast address.

Reviewing Examples of Configuring Your File Server

To help make the setup more realistic, this section sets up a network and shows the steps necessary to configure the network to use TCP/IP and IPX/SPX.

Sample Scenario

BD-RETREAT has two file servers, one UNIX host, and 21 work-stations that need to access both the server and the UNIX host.

Figure 20.2 is a diagram of BD-RETREAT's network.

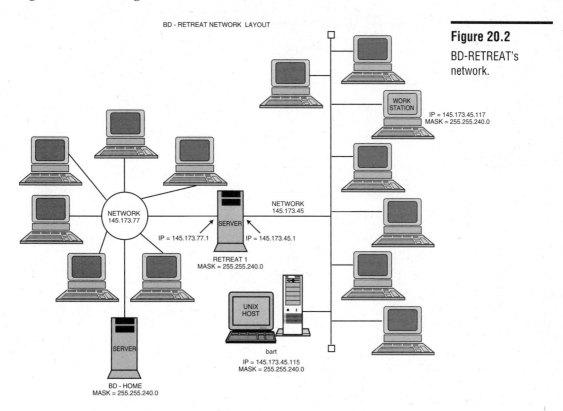

BD - RETREAT NETWORK LAYOUT

Figure 20.2
BD-RETREAT's network.

993

The file server acts as a router with two cable segments: Token Ring and Ethernet. The UNIX host, bart, is on the Ethernet segment. The server BD_HOME is on the Token Ring segment. The File Server RETREAT1 provides routing services.

Sample STARTUP.NCF

The STARTUP.NCF file needs only the extra line setting the maximum physical receive packet size. This file happens to be the same on both servers.

```
LOAD AHA1540 PORT=234 INT=A DMA=5 ABOVE16=Y
LOAD NFS
SET MAXIMUM PHYSICAL RECEIVE PACKET SIZE=2048
```

Sample AUTOEXEC.NCF

The AUTOEXEC.NCF file shown is what was already working in the file server RETREAT1. The areas in the file that are shaded are the items added for TCP/IP.

In this example, the network interface drivers are loaded out twice with Ethernet, instead of forcing all devices to speak only ETHERNET_II. The server also advertises itself as the default route.

```
File Server Name RETREAT1
IPX Internal Net FB431
set maximum packet receive buffers=300

LOAD NE2000 INT=5 PORT=320 FRAME=ETHERNET_802.3 NAME=IPX-802
LOAD NE2000 INT=5 PORT=320 FRAME=ETHERNET_II NAME=IP-E2
LOAD TOKEN INT=2 PORT=A20 FRAME=IBM_TOKEN-RING NAME=IPX-TR
LOAD TOKEN INT=2 PORT=A20 FRAME=TOKEN-RING_SNAP NAME=IP-TR

LOAD TCPIP FORWARD=YES

BIND IPX TO IPX-802 NET=1871
BIND IPX TO IPX-TR NET=CD1A
BIND IP TO IP-E2 ADDR=145.173.45.1 MASK=255.255.240.0 DEFROUTE=YES
BIND IP TO IP-TR ADDR=145.173.77.1 MASK=255.255.240.0
```

```
Mount all
Load remote;xyz
Load rspx
Load Monitor /p
```

The following AUTOEXEC.NCF file comes from the BD-HOME server. In this example, the server does not perform any routing functions. To make administration easier, all trapped events are sent to RETREAT1. Again, the shaded items indicate that which was added to the existing file to enable TCP/IP.

```
File Server Name BD-HOME
IPX Internal Net FB542
set maximum packet receive buffers=300

LOAD TOKEN INT=2 PORT=A20 FRAME=IBM_TOKEN-RING NAME=IPX-TR
LOAD TOKEN INT=2 PORT=A20 FRAME=TOKEN-RING_SNAP NAME=IP-TR

LOAD TCPIP TRAP=145.173.77.1

BIND IPX TO IPX-TR NET=CD1A
BIND IP TO IP-TR ADDR=145.173.77.100 MASK=255.255.240.0

Mount all
Load remote;xyz
Load rspx
Load Monitor /p
```

Hosts Table

The following hosts table is copied to all servers and workstations. Workstations use LAN WorkPlace. The file also needs to be placed on the UNIX host via FTP.

```
145.173.77.100          BD-HOME
145.173.77.1            RETREAT1 RETREAT1-TR
145.173.45.1            RETREAT1-ETHERNET
145.173.45.115          bart
```

Workstations

The workstations, as mentioned previously, use LAN WorkPlace client software. The modifications that follow the next sections are made to the workstation files; bold areas indicate that which was added to existing files.

NET.CFG

The NET.CFG file needs to be configured to support TCP/IP. This workstation is connected to the Ethernet segment.

Three sections are used by TCP/IP:

Link Driver

In this section, you want to add the Ethernet_II frame type and you want to tell the system which frame type to use with IPX.

Link Support

The Link Support header defines the number and size of the receive buffers. If you make heavy use of multiple TCP connections, this number should be increased from the default of 8 1500.

The Link Support option also allows for an adjusted memory pool statement. TCP data is copied into this pool before being sent onto the network. This pool should be increased if the receiving node can handle larger amounts of data in its memory buffers.

Protocol TCPIP

The Protocol TCPIP heading allows you to specify the location of the configuration files required by LAN WorkPlace. You also are able to set the workstation's IP address, the router it should use, and the subnet mask it should use.

Additional information about configuring the workstation for TCP/IP can be found in the Novell red manual *TCP/IP Transport for DOS Configuration Guide.*

```
Link Support
    Buffers 8 1500
    MemPool 4096

Link Driver NE2000
    Port 360
    Int 5
    Frame ETHERNET_802.3
    Frame Ethernet_II
    Protocol IPX 0 ETHERNET_802.3

NetWare DOS Requester
    show dots = on
    PB BUFFERS=5
    get local target stacks = 5
    PREFERRED SERVER=BD-HOME
    FIRST NETWORK DRIVE=F
    CACHE BUFFERS=20
    max tasks = 50

Protocol IPXODI
    SPX CONNECTIONS = 30
    SPX ABORT TIMEOUT = 1080
    SPX VERIFY TIMEOUT = 108
    SPX LISTEN TIMEOUT = 216

Protocol TCPIP
    PATH SCRIPT      C:\NET\SCRIPT
    PATH PROFILE     C:\NET\PROFILE
    PATH LWP_CFG     C:\NET\HSTACC
    PATH TCP_CFG     C:\NET\TCP
    ip_router        145.173.45.117
    ip_address       145.173.45.1
    ip_netmask       255.255.240.0
```

Startup Batch File

In the file that you use to load your ODI drivers, you should add a line that loads TCPIP.EXE. The following file, called STARTNET.BAT, is used on the BD-RETREAT network for the workstations:

```
SET NWLANGUAGE=ENGLISH
SET TZ=EST5EDT
```

```
LH C:\NWCLIENT\LSL
:DRIVER1
LH C:\NWCLIENT\NE2000.COM
LH C:\NWCLIENT\IPXODI
LH C:\NET\BIN\TCPIP.EXE
LH C:\NWCLIENT\VLM
```

Summary

This chapter began with an introduction to several products that Novell offers that use the TCP/IP Protocol Suite. Half of these products are for use on the file server, while the other half are intended for the workstation to connect to TCP/IP hosts.

The second section in this chapter taught you about the issues to be aware of when using Ethernet, Token Ring, and ARCnet. Ethernet offers two options: loading the LAN driver twice with different frame types, or using the ECONFIG utility to allow all NetWare devices to use the ETHERNET_II frame type. Token Ring requires that you load the LAN driver out twice. The Token Ring TCP/IP frame type is TOKEN-RING_SNAP. ARCnet has only one frame type.

You also learned about configuring your NetWare server to use the TCP/IP transport protocol. You discovered that several areas need to be set up by the administrator.

♦ The AUTOEXEC.NCF and STARTUP.NCF needed SET parameters to define the buffers needed for packets to be stored when routing.

♦ The database files needed to be customized to your environment. These files include the following:

> SERVICES
>
> PROTOCOLS
>
> GATEWAYS
>
> HOSTS
>
> NETWORKS

♦ The workstation's NET.CFG file needs to be modified to include memory buffer configuration, protocol definitions, IP address, router, and subnet mask.

You also learned about the six NLMs used by TCP/IP:

♦ TCPIP.NLM

♦ SNMP.NLM

♦ SNMPLOG.NLM

♦ IPCONFIG.NLM

♦ TCPCON.NLM

♦ IPTUNNEL.LAN

Finally, you learned about the three steps needed to be performed at the file server to load and bind IP. Each step has a list of special parameters defined in this chapter.

The three steps are as follows:

♦ Load the LAN driver

♦ Load TCP/IP

♦ Bind IP to the LAN driver

Now that you are familiar with the steps that are taken for the file server to use TCP/IP, you need to learn about managing the running system. The next chapter deals with the following:

♦ Managing TCP/IP through the TCPCON utility

♦ Learning about Community Names

♦ Viewing TCP/IP protocol statistics

Review Questions

1. Which statement about TCP/IP is false?

   ○ a. TCP/IP uses less bandwidth than IPX/SPX.

   ○ b. TCP/IP is older and more mature than IPX/SPX.

○   c.   TCP/IP is easier to administrate than IPX/SPX.

○   d.   TCP/IP is supported on most UNIX systems.

2.   Which compiler is used for BSD UNIX APIs?

○   a.   Streams

○   b.   ODI

○   c.   TLI

○   d.   Sockets

3.   Which frame type is normally used with Ethernet TCP/IP systems?

○   a.   ETHERNET_II

○   b.   ETHERNET_802.2

○   c.   ETHERNET_802.3

○   d.   ETHERNET_SNAP

4.   The _____ frame type is normally used with Token Ring TCP/IP systems.

5.   Which field is unique to Ethernet_II?

○   a.   Length

○   b.   Type

○   c.   LLC

○   d.   CRC

6.   Which lines need to be added to the AUTOEXEC.NCF file to load Token Ring for use with IPX/SPX and TCP/IP?

☐   a.   Load the LAN driver twice.

☐   b.   Load TCPIP.

☐   c.   Load TCPIP forward=yes.

☐   d.   Bind IP to the TOKEN-RING_SNAP frame type.

7. Which command(s) would you use to tell your 3.x server to use the ETHERNET_II frame type?

☐　a.　IFCONFIG

☐　b.　ECONFIG

☐　c.　Load NE2000 INT=5 PORT=320
　　　FRAME=ETHERNET_II NAME=IP-E2

☐　d.　Bind IP to IP_E2

8. Which file does not require ECONFIG to run on it to use the ETHERNET_II frame type?

○　a.　SERVER.EXE

○　b.　NET$OS.EXE

○　c.　NET$OS.EX1

○　d.　NET$OS.EX2

9. In the statement ECONFIG ROUTER.EXE C:E, what does C:E represent?

○　a.　Find the ECONFIG program on the C: drive.

○　b.　Change Lan card C to use the ETHERNET_II frame type.

○　c.　Find the ROUTER.EXE program on the C: drive.

○　d.　Change to Ethernet_II.

10. The protocol number for ETHERNET_II frame type is:

○　a.　0

○　b.　127

○　c.　213

○　d.　8137

11. The hosts, protocol, services, networks, and gateways files are referred to as _____ files.

12. Which is the correct syntax for adding a hexadecimal number to the hosts file?

    ○ a. 0x64.c1.f4.12   cdi

    ○ b. 0x64.0xc1.0xf4.0x12   cdi

    ○ c. Hx64.Hxc1.Hxf4.Hx12   cdi

    ○ d. X64.Xc1.Xf4.X12   cdi

13. The following line would come from which database file?

    ```
    netstat 15/tcp
    ```

    ○ a. SERVICES

    ○ b. NETWORKS

    ○ c. HOSTS

    ○ d. PROTOCOLS

14. The following line would come from which database file?

    ```
    IPNET   192.68.205     #CDI Backbone
    ```

    ○ a. SERVICES

    ○ b. NETWORKS

    ○ c. HOSTS

    ○ d. PROTOCOLS

15. In the following file, why does arpanet list its network number as just 10, while novellnet lists its number as 130.57?

    ```
    #
    # SYS:ETC\NETWORKS
    #
    #    Network numbers
    #
    loopback    127      # fictitious internal loopback network
    novellnet   130.57      # Novell's network number
    ```

```
#
# Internet networks
#
arpanet      10    arpa   # historical network
```

- ○ a. Novellnet has a subnet that needed defining.

- ○ b. Arpanet belongs to the Internet.

- ○ c. Arpanet's address is a class A, while Novellnet's address is a class B.

- ○ d. There is a mistake in the file.

16. The NLM that provides the transport protocol service for TCP/IP is:

- ○ a. SNMP.NLM

- ○ b. TCPIP.NLM

- ○ c. TCPCON.NLM

- ○ d. IPTUNNEL.NLM

17. Which statement should be added to the STARTUP.NCF file if you are using ARCnet?

- ○ a. SET MINIMUM PACKET RECEIVE BUFFERS = 400

- ○ b. SET MINIMUM PACKET RECEIVE SIZE = 2048

- ○ c. SET MAXIMUM PACKET RECEIVE SIZE = 2048

- ○ d. SET MAXIMUM PACKET RECEIVE BUFFERS = 400

18. Which step is not needed to load and bind IP on your file server?

- ○ a. Load NE2000 PORT=320 INT=5 FRAME=ETHERNET_II NAME=E2

- ○ b. Load SNMP

- ○ c. Load TCPIP

- ○ d. Bind IP to E2 ADDR=192.68.205.5

1003

19. Which TCP/IP default parameter is not correct?

  ○   a.   Forward=No

  ○   b.   RIP=Yes

  ○   c.   Trap=loopback

  ○   d.   ARP=Yes

20. Which NLM is not automatically loaded when TCP/IP is loaded?

  ○   a.   SNMP.NLM

  ○   b.   STREAMS.NLM

  ○   c.   SNMPLOG.NLM

  ○   d.   CLIB.NLM

21. Which parameter is not a valid default when binding IP for a class B address?

  ○   a.   MASK=255.255.0.0

  ○   b.   DEFROUTE=No

  ○   c.   COST=1

  ○   d.   BCAST=0.0.0.0

22. The alternative to using Split Horizon to exchange routing information between hosts is called _____.

Answers

1. C

2. D

3. A

4. TOKEN-RING_SNAP

5. B

6. A, B, D

7. C, D

8. A

9. B

10. D

11. DATABASE

12. B

13. A

14. B

15. C

16. B

17. C

18. B

19. D

20. C

21. D

22. POISON REVERSE

Managing TCP/IP

In the last chapter, you learned about setting up a file server to support the TCP/IP protocols. In this chapter, you discover how to monitor and manage a NetWare TCP/IP network.

In Chapter 21, you explore the following:

◆ Simple Network Management Protocol (SNMP)

◆ SNMP Managers and SNMP Agents

◆ Community names

◆ The console menu utility for monitoring and managing SNMP File Server Agent—TCPCON

◆ Simple TCP/IP troubleshooting

As the Internet grew, it became necessary to devise a way to allow centralized management of networks. System administrators needed an automated tool that could monitor the network, allowing changes to the host and problem diagnostics. SNMP evolved into that much-needed mechanism.

Discovering Simple Network Management Protocol (SNMP)

SNMP is the current standard protocol that provides TCP/IP network monitoring and diagnostics. SNMP consists of three basic modules.

◆ The Protocol for managing the information—Simple Network Management Protocol (SNMP)

◆ The Definition of the structure of the information—Structure of Management Information (SMI)

◆ The Container for the database—Management Information Base (MIB)

The Protocol, SNMP

SNMP attempts to minimize the quantity and complexity of management functions. The protocol is independent of the architecture of the hosts.

SNMP defines two sides of management, as follows:

Managers

Managers request information from an Agent's MIB. Managers request that changes be made to Agents based on information contained within the Agent's MIB.

Agents

Agents respond to a Manager's request by providing information or by making changes to themselves based on the Manager's requests. Agents hold information in an MIB.

 SNMP uses ASN.1 to enable SNMP to send information about any arbitrary data type, providing needed flexibility. More information about ASN.1 is found in Chapter 5.

The number of functions has been limited so that complexity is limited. This limitation allows more flexibility in the long run. The SNMP protocol consists of only five functions.

Labels in SNMP protocols are made up of compound words that are frequently truncated. Each new word is capitalized, but the whole label is stated as a single word. For example, icmpInMsgs stands for Incoming ICMP Messages.

GetRequest

When a Manager wants to get information from an Agent's MIB, it issues a function called a GetRequest.

GetNextRequest

When a Manager wants to get multiple pieces of information, such as from a table or array, the Manager issues a GetNextRequest function until the entire table or array has been satisfied.

GetResponse

Agents issue GetResponse functions to satisfy GetRequest or GetNextRequest inquiries. A GetResponse with an error can also be returned in response to a Set-Request when the instance does not exist or the given value is bad.

Trap

A *Trap* is a special event noted by the Agent and reported to the Manager. An example of a Trap is when the IP protocol is bound to a network board. The Agent in this case reports a *link up* trap.

Following are the six different types of Traps:

Cold Boot

A Cold Boot signifies that the Agent is reinitializing itself and that a change to the Agent's configuration is anticipated.

Warm Boot

A Warm Boot happens when the Agent reinitializes, but no change to the configuration is expected.

Link Up

A Link Up state occurs when the communications link is brought on-line.

Link Down

A Link Down signifies that the communications link has been broken.

Authentication Failure

When a Manager attempts to contact an Agent, the Manager sends a catchword, also known as a community name, along with its request to view or modify the Agent's MIB. The Agent is set up to accept two catchwords. One catchword enables read-only access to its MIB; the other enables read-write privileges. The Manager can provide only one catchword. If it matches a catchword on the Agent, access is given based on which word is provided. If the word does not match, then an Authentication Failure Trap is generated.

Enterprise Specific

Since SNMP was designed to allow ignorance of the host's architecture, it also allowed for vendors providing specialized equipment to report significant events through the SNMP mechanism. When a vendor creates an intelligent device on the network, such as an intelligent hub, events generated at that hub can be reported as Enterprise Specific Traps.

Loss of EGP Neighbor

On the Internet, an Exterior Gateway Protocol (EGP) neighbor is a device that connects networks to the Internet. When a Loss of EGP Neighbor Trap is generated, it means that a gateway to the Internet is down.

SetRequest

The SetRequest function is probably the most powerful of the five functions. SetRequest is used by the Manager to change a parameter in the Agent's MIB. All changes made to the MIB from the Manager are done through the SetRequest function.

Structure of Management Information—SMI

Just as the OSI layer defines the characteristics of network communications, the SMI describes the basic types of information that are provided in an Agent's MIB.

In other words, SMI sets the parameters for what types of information can be manipulated by SNMP.

The following is a host list of the basic types of information SNMP is able to monitor:

- ◆ TimeTick
- ◆ Counter
- ◆ Gauge
- ◆ ipAddress

SMI also defines the values for items held in the MIB. For example, *ipAddress* is defined as a 4-octet string and *Counter* as an integer in the range of 0 to 2^{32}-1.

Management Information Base—MIB

The MIB is a virtual information store, containing manageable objects. The manageable objects are divided into eight groups.

System

This group includes the full name of the Agent, version information about the Agent's hardware type, operating system and networking software, and how long the system has been up.

Interfaces

This group contains information on the network interface boards in the Agent. It includes diagnostic statistics on packets going to and from the Agent.

Address Translation

This group contains information about the ARP table entries used to map the IP address to the hardware address.

IP

The IP group contains statistical information about the IP protocol datagram successes and errors, discards, fragmentation, routing and subnet address information.

ICMP

The ICMP group contains statistical information about the ICMP protocol including ICMP input and output statistics.

TCP

The TCP group contains statistical information about the TCP protocol including information about current TCP connections.

UDP

The UDP group contains statistical information about the UDP protocol including information on incoming datagrams, ports not available when needed, incoming errors, and outgoing datagrams.

EGP

The EGP group contains statistical information about the EGP connection and EGP tables.

A proposal to revise the structure of the MIB was introduced as MIB-II in 1991. MIB-II includes the following:

◆ Additional manageable objects

◆ Clarification to improve readability of the MIB

◆ Better support for multi-protocol objects

◆ Upward compatibility with the SMI, MIB, and SNMP

Using SNMP on a NetWare Network

In the previous section, you learned about the SNMP protocol and all of its components on a general level. In this section, you learn about how SNMP is implemented on a NetWare network.

 Note Remember that this chapter deals primarily with the TCP/IP programs that come with the NetWare operating system. References to other products are added to give you a better perspective on how client software fits in with the server software.

Agents

On a NetWare TCP/IP network, an Agent is any file server running the SNMP.NLM. Other programs, such as Novell's LAN WorkPlace for DOS/Windows, allow workstations to become Agents.

Managers

On a NetWare TCP/IP network, the Manager is any file server that runs TCPCON.NLM. LAN WorkPlace for DOS/Windows provides a LWPCON.EXE for the workstation to perform Manager functions. The next section walks you through all of the TCPCON.NLM screens.

Traps

NetWare supports all of the Traps mentioned in the last section, with the exception of Loss of EGP Neighbor.

Community Names

Managers need to submit community names when they request information from an Agent. Later in this chapter, you learn how to load TCPCON.NLM with a community name. First, you need to set up the community names that the Agent accepts. At the NetWare file server, you need to use the community name variables when you load SNMP. Community names can be either *read-only* or *read-write*.

Loading SNMP on the File Server

This section describes the variables used when loading SNMP. The following three options can be used when loading SNMP on the file server:

- ◆ MonitorCommunity
- ◆ ControlCommunity
- ◆ TrapCommunity

Explaining the Community Names

The CONTROL and MONITOR community names define what type of access the Manager has to the Agent.

- ◆ CONTROLCOMMUNITY gives READ and WRITE access
- ◆ MONITORCOMMUNITY gives READ ONLY access

Community names are ASCII words that can be up to 32 characters long. These names are case–sensitive. The following characters are NOT valid in the community name:

- ◆ space
- ◆ tab
- ◆ [
- ◆ =
- ◆ :
- ◆ ;
- ◆ #

Syntax

```
LOAD SNMP <options>
```

CONTROLCOMMUNITY

Disables all **read/write** community names.

CONTROLCOMMUNITY=

Enables all **read/write** community names.

CONTROLCOMMUNITY=<ascii word>

Sets the **read/write** community name to the ASCII word specified.

MONITORCOMMUNITY

Disables all **read-only** community names.

MONITORCOMMUNITY=

Enables all **read-only** community names.

MONITORCOMMUNITY=<ascii word>

Sets the **read-only** community name to the ASCII word specified.

ControlCommunity can be stated as:

    CONTROLCOMMUNITY

    CONTROL

    CON

    C

MonitorCommunity can be stated as:

    MONITORCOMMUNITY

    MONITOR

    MON

    M

TRAPCOMMUNITY=<ASCII word>

Sends the ASCII word with trapped messages to the destination host.

1016

The Manager is supposed to be able to monitor all of the Agent's MIB information. Trap events are held in a file, not in the MIB. When TCPCON is loaded on a NetWare server it is able to see only its own trap messages.

Since it would be more convenient to monitor all trapped messages from all Agents from one server, you can use the TRAP= option when loading TCP/IP to tell the Agent where trapped events should be sent. In the previous chapter, you learned that you could route trapped events to a specific host IP address.

The TRAPCOMMUNITY option is used to send a community name to the host to which the Traps are routed. The SNMP protocol on NetWare allows a MONITORCOMMUNITY name to add trap messages.

Community Name Defaults:

> CONTROLCOMMUNITY is disabled
>
> MONITORCOMMUNITY is public
>
> TRAPCOMMUNITY is public

COMMUNITY NAMES ARE CASE SENSITIVE!

Examples

LOAD SNMP MON=VIEW CON=CHANGE

In this example, any manager submitting a community name of VIEW is able to see, but not change, the Agent's MIB. Any manager submitting a community name of CHANGE is able to see AND change the Agent's MIB.

LOAD SNMP MON= CON TRAPCOMMUNITY=VIEW

In this example, any community name submitted to this Agent is able to view the Agent's MIB.   NO community name is allowed to change the MIB, however. Finally, when this Agent sends trapped events to a different host, the community name of VIEW is sent along with the information. It is assumed that the destination Agent is set up with a community name of VIEW.

LOAD SNMP

In this example, Managers submitting the community name of public are able to see the Agent's MIB. No one has the ability to change the MIB.

Loading the SNMP Log

The SNMP Agent always knows about trapped events, but unless the SNMPLOG.NLM is actually loaded, the trapped messages are ignored.

The SNMPLOG.NLM must be loaded for trapped messages to be written to the binary file, SNMP$LOG.BIN

No parameters for loading SNMPLOG exist. SNMPLOG needs to be loaded AFTER SNMP has been loaded.

TCPCON

Load the TCPCON module to display the network statistics for a host on your network.

The following section shows you the TCPCON.NLM screens. TCPCON is the NetWare Manager program. Through TCPCON, you can access an Agent's MIB.

If a single server runs both the SNMP.NLM and the TCPCON.NLM, then that server is both an Agent and Manager.

Key List

Key	Function
F1	Help.
Up Arrow	Cursor moves up the list to highlight an item.
Down Arrow	Cursor moves down an item to highlight an item.
INS	Adds an item to the table.
DEL	Removes an item from the table.
TAB	Toggles display in some menus from the Host Name to the IP Address. TAB requires that entries are made in the host table on the server you are viewing.
ENTER	Chooses or Modifies a highlighted item.

Syntax

```
LOAD TCPCON <options>
```

Target (IP address or Host name)

The Target IP address or host name indicates which Agent you want to view.

If you do not specify a target, then the default agent is the loopback. In other words, if you do not set the target, you look at your own MIB.

COMMUNITY=<ASCII word>

The COMMUNITY= parameter allows you to set the community name that you, as the Manager, present to the Agent.

The default is public.

Poll=<integer>

This option indicates the time in seconds that the SNMP request message poll rate asks the Agent to update its statistical information to the Manager.

Range: 0 to 900 seconds

The default is every 1 second.

Retry=<integer>

This option indicates the number of consecutive unanswered requests that must occur before the HOST UNAVAILABLE error is displayed.

Range: 1 to 100 tries

The default is 3 tries.

Sort=<yes or no>

The Sort option provides an alphabetical listing of the host table entries. Setting this option to no displays the host entries in the order in which they are entered into the hosts table.

The default is yes to sort.

From this option box, you can either type the name of the host you want to change to if it is in the hosts table, or you can type in the IP address of the host. Another option is to press the Insert key. This brings up the hosts table. Using your arrow keys to highlight the desired host, press enter to view that host's MIB. Figure 21.3 shows you what the hosts table looks like when you press Insert. The information displayed is for the host you changed to until you change hosts again or exit TCPCON.

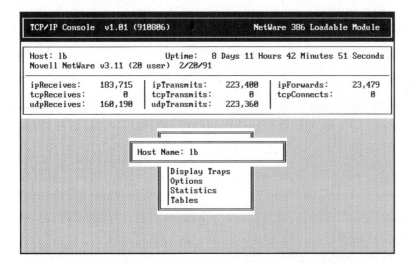

Figure 21.2

TCPCON allows you to specify the Agent's MIB to view.

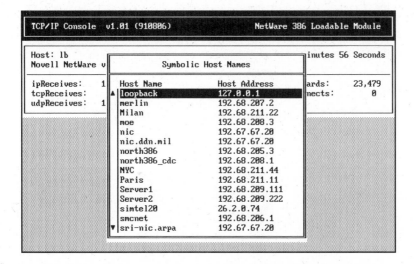

Figure 21.3

Viewing the hosts table from TCPCON.

Displaying Traps

When you change hosts, all screens will reflect the information obtained from that host's MIB, with the exception of Trapped Messages.

The trapped messages that are shown in figure 21.4 came from several Agents. The server is called b386. Trap messages came from the servers Detroit and Flint. b386 reported two different enterprise specific traps. More information about those traps can be found from the third party vendor producing the trap messages. Detroit and Flint reported that their interfaces were bound, generating Link Up messages from their network interfaces.

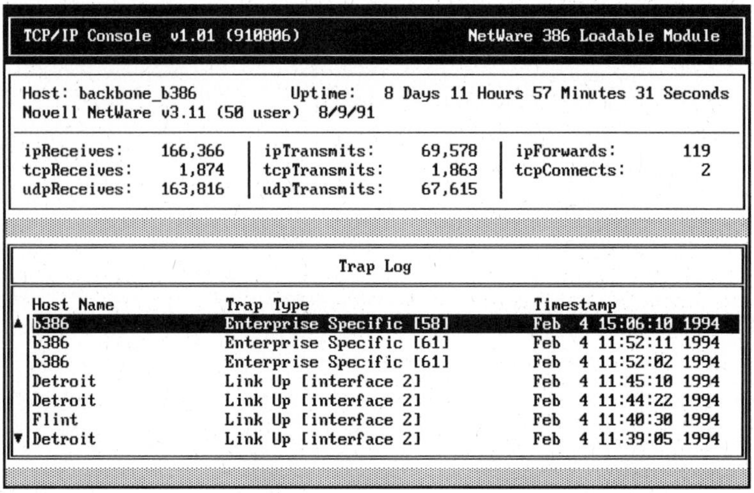

Figure 21.4

Trapped Message seen on the server b386.

```
┌──────────────────────────────────────────────────────────────────────┐
│ TCP/IP Console  v1.01 (910806)            NetWare 386 Loadable Module  │
├──────────────────────────────────────────────────────────────────────┤
│ Host: backbone_b386           Uptime:   8 Days 11 Hours 57 Minutes 31 Seconds │
│ Novell NetWare v3.11 (50 user)  8/9/91                                 │
│                                                                        │
│ ipReceives:    166,366 │ ipTransmits:   69,578 │ ipForwards:     119   │
│ tcpReceives:     1,874 │ tcpTransmits:   1,863 │ tcpConnects:      2   │
│ udpReceives:   163,816 │ udpTransmits:  67,615 │                       │
├──────────────────────────────────────────────────────────────────────┤
│                                                                        │
│                              Trap Log                                  │
├──────────────────────────────────────────────────────────────────────┤
│   Host Name       Trap Type                      Timestamp            │
│ ▲│b386            Enterprise Specific [58]        Feb  4 15:06:10 1994  │
│   b386            Enterprise Specific [61]        Feb  4 11:52:11 1994  │
│   b386            Enterprise Specific [61]        Feb  4 11:52:02 1994  │
│   Detroit         Link Up [interface 2]           Feb  4 11:45:10 1994  │
│   Detroit         Link Up [interface 2]           Feb  4 11:44:22 1994  │
│   Flint           Link Up [interface 2]           Feb  4 11:40:30 1994  │
│ ▼│Detroit         Link Up [interface 2]           Feb  4 11:39:05 1994  │
│                                                                        │
└──────────────────────────────────────────────────────────────────────┘
```

Using the Tab key helps to make this screen a little easier for diagnostics. The Tab key takes the host names away and shows you their IP addresses instead. Figure 21.5 is the same screen as figure 21.4, except that the Tab key has been pressed, which can be helpful when you question who it was who sent the event. The IP address is sent with the Trap. When you see the host name, you see only what the local host table can translate. In figure 21.6, you are looking at the server A312. In the Host Name column, you see host names, except for 192.68.209.1. You do not see a host name because the address is not in the host table. Sometimes, with multiple host tables, mistakes in names are made. Seeing the IP address is a good way to track the source of the message.

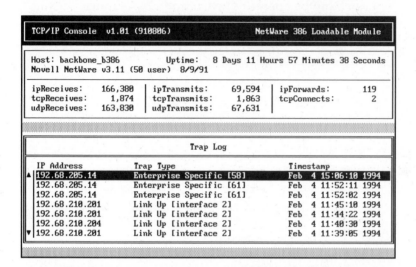

Figure 21.5

Using the TAB key to view IP addresses in TCPCON.

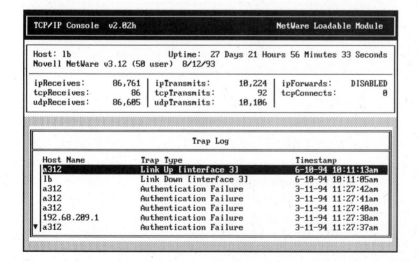

Figure 21.6

Viewing the Trap Messages in TCPCON when an address is not in the hosts table.

Options

The next option from the main menu is Options, which are the same as those that came from the LOAD TCPCON statement discussed earlier in this section. After TCPCON has been loaded, these options can be altered. The Community Name is the one provided by the Manager to the Agent. As you change hosts, you may also need to change the community name.

Figure 21.7 shows the default option screen.

Figure 21.7

Default TCPCON Options.

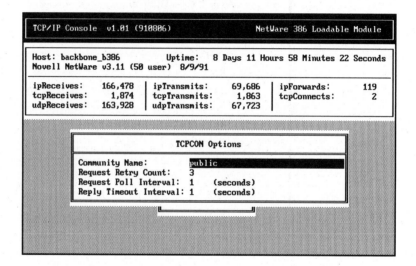

```
┌─────────────────────────────────────────────────────────────────────────┐
│ TCP/IP Console  v1.01 (910806)              NetWare 386 Loadable Module  │
├─────────────────────────────────────────────────────────────────────────┤
│ Host: backbone_b386          Uptime:   8 Days 11 Hours 58 Minutes 22 Seconds │
│ Novell NetWare v3.11 (50 user)  8/9/91                                    │
│                                                                          │
│ ipReceives:     166,478 │ ipTransmits:      69,686 │ ipForwards:    119  │
│ tcpReceives:      1,874 │ tcpTransmits:      1,863 │ tcpConnects:     2  │
│ udpReceives:    163,928 │ udpTransmits:     67,723 │                     │
├─────────────────────────────────────────────────────────────────────────┤
│                                                                          │
│              ┌────────────────────────────────────────────┐             │
│              │              TCPCON Options                │             │
│              ├────────────────────────────────────────────┤             │
│              │ Community Name:       public               │             │
│              │ Request Retry Count:  3                     │             │
│              │ Request Poll Interval: 1    (seconds)       │             │
│              │ Reply Timeout Interval: 1   (seconds)       │             │
│              └────────────────────────────────────────────┘             │
│                                                                          │
└─────────────────────────────────────────────────────────────────────────┘
```

Statistics

The third option off the main menu is Statistics. Statistics are recorded in the following four areas: ICMP, IP, TCP and UDP. All related statistics are grouped into these areas and are displayed separately for your convenience, as shown in figure 21.8.

All of the statistics shown in the following four groups are defined in the RFC 1156. NetWare attempts a simple explanation for each statistic.

To see the explanation for an item, press F1 when you first get into the screen. Figure 21.9 shows the ICMP statistics help screen.

To see an explanation for a specific item in the table, you must move your cursor to the item and press enter. The cursor blinks where the number is shown. Pressing F1 at this time shows the definition for that specific item. Figure 21.10 shows that the item icmpInMsgs was highlighted when F1 was pressed.

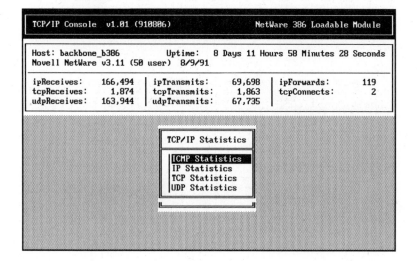

Figure 21.8

TCP/IP statistics groupings.

ICMP Statistics

Figure 21.11 shows the ICMP statistics screen. In the left-hand column, you see all of the ICMP Incoming datagram statistics. In the right-hand column, you see all of the ICMP Outbound statistics. This screen is not editable.

Figure 21.9

The ICMP Statistics Help screen.

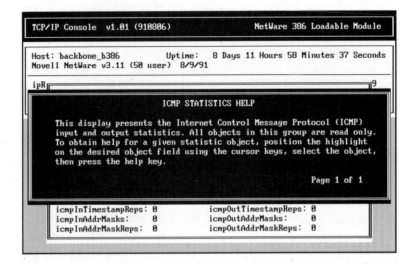

```
TCP/IP Console  v1.01 (910806)              NetWare 386 Loadable Module

Host: backbone_b386          Uptime:   8 Days 11 Hours 58 Minutes 37 Seconds
Novell NetWare v3.11 (50 user)  8/9/91

ipR                                                                      9
┌──────────────────────────────────────────────────────────────────────┐
│                    ICMP STATISTICS HELP                                │
│                                                                        │
│     This display presents the Internet Control Message Protocol (ICMP) │
│     input and output statistics. All objects in this group are read only.│
│     To obtain help for a given statistic object, position the highlight│
│     on the desired object field using the cursor keys, select the object,│
│     then press the help key.                                           │
│                                                                        │
│                                                     Page 1 of 1        │
└──────────────────────────────────────────────────────────────────────┘
      icmpInTimestampReps: 0          icmpOutTimestampReps: 0
      icmpInAddrMasks:     0          icmpOutAddrMasks:     0
      icmpInAddrMaskReps:  0          icmpOutAddrMaskReps:  0
```

Figure 21.10

The icmpInMsgs Help screen.

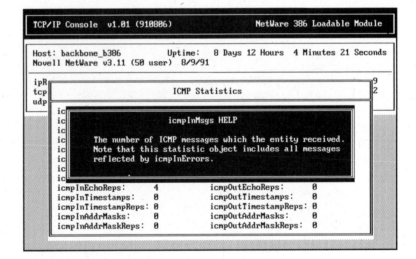

```
TCP/IP Console  v1.01 (910806)              NetWare 386 Loadable Module

Host: backbone_b386          Uptime:   8 Days 12 Hours  4 Minutes 21 Seconds
Novell NetWare v3.11 (50 user)  8/9/91

ipR                                                                      9
tcp                        ICMP Statistics                               2
udp
   ic┌────────────────────────────────────────────────────┐
   ic│                  icmpInMsgs HELP                   │
   ic│                                                    │
   ic│    The number of ICMP messages which the entity received.│
   ic│    Note that this statistic object includes all messages│
   ic│    reflected by icmpInErrors.                      │
   ic│                                                    │
   ic└────────────────────────────────────────────────────┘
   icmpInEchoReps:     4          icmpOutEchoReps:       0
   icmpInTimestamps:   0          icmpOutTimestamps:     0
   icmpInTimestampReps: 0         icmpOutTimestampReps: 0
   icmpInAddrMasks:    0          icmpOutAddrMasks:      0
   icmpInAddrMaskReps: 0          icmpOutAddrMaskReps:   0
```

IP Statistics

Study Note

When you take a look at figure 21.12, notice the punctuation marks after the first two items in the left-hand column. Can you see a difference between those items and the rest of the items in this table?

MIB items that can be changed in the Statistics Menus and the Tables Menus are designated by a colon, then a period (:.). Items that are read-only are designated with only a colon (:).

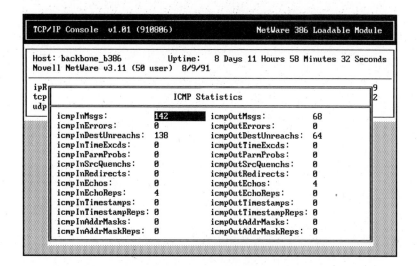

Figure 21.11

The ICMP Statistics table.

Figure 21.12 shows the IP Statistics table. The first two items in this table can be modified. Pressing Enter while highlighting ipForwarding brings up the menu shown in figure 21.13. The options you can choose are gateway and host. When TCPIP was loaded with forward=yes, then this item is set up as a gateway for forwarding IP datagrams. If your Agent was set up with a Control Community name and the Manager supplies that name, you can change this field. If host shows in this field and you want to forward IP datagrams, you can change the ipForwarding option to gateway.

When you press enter on the change, you then need to press ESC to save the changes. Figure 21.14 shows that the ESC key has been pressed and that a change is requested. If the Agent did not have a Control community name set up, or if the Manager did not provide the Control community name, then an error appears, as

1029

shown in figure 21.15. Although the error is slightly cryptic, it means that the host was not able to honor the request. This is known as an Authentication Failure.

Figure 21.12

The IP Statistics table.

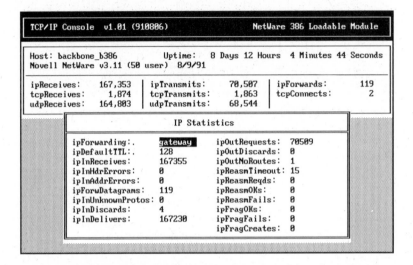

Figure 21.13

Changing ipForwarding from a gateway to a host.

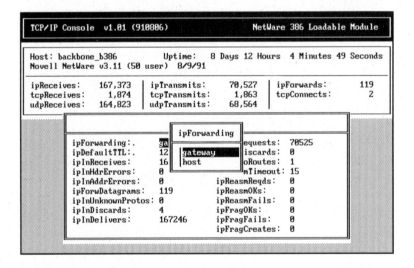

The other option that can be changed is the TTL, or Time To Live. If the transport layer does not supply a TTL value, then the IP can provide a TTL value. See Chapter 5 for more information on TTL.

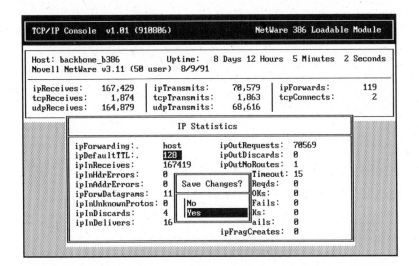

Figure 21.14

Saving changes to the MIB.

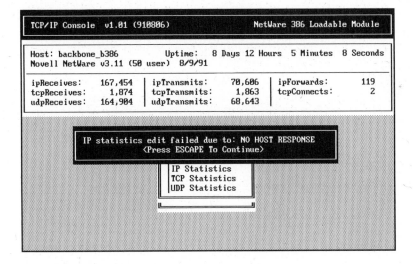

Figure 21.15

Error Message generated when you are not authorized to change the MIB.

TCP Statistics

The TCP Statistics table, shown in figure 21.16, shows TCP input and output statistics. The tcpRtoAlgorithm is the Van Jacobson algorithm, which is used to determine the Timeout value used for retransmitting unacknowledged datagrams.

1031

Figure 21.16

The TCP Statistics table.

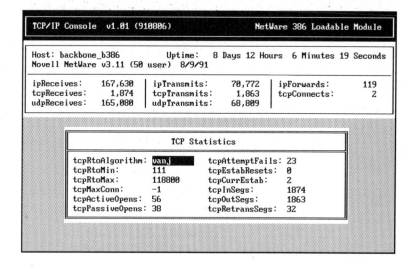

UDP Statistics

The smallest table, UDP Statistics, is shown in figure 21.17. This table shows the number of Incoming and Outbound UDP datagrams recorded on this host. It also shows the number of datagrams that could not find an application at the destination port. The udpInErrors is the number of datagrams that could not be delivered.

Figure 21.17

The UDP Statistics table.

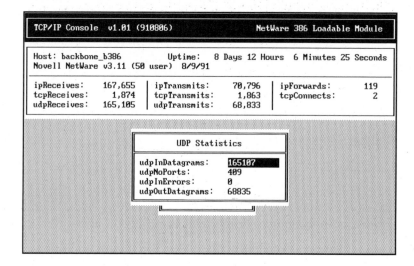

The best way in which to handle these statistics is to periodically get into RCONSOLE and take screen prints of these tables. Compare them monthly and see if anything changes. Anything listed as an error should be monitored to keep the errors at a minimum.

Load the TCPCON module to display and modify a system's TCP/IP tables.

Tables

The last item from the main menu is Tables. Figure 21.18 shows that you can view and change five tables from this menu.

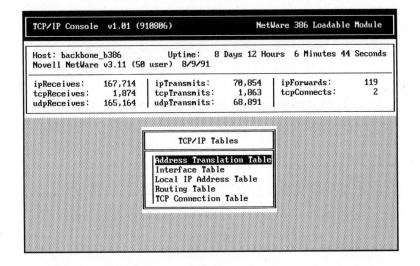

```
TCP/IP Console  v1.01 (910806)          NetWare 386 Loadable Module

Host: backbone_b386         Uptime:   8 Days 12 Hours  6 Minutes 44 Seconds
Novell NetWare v3.11 (50 user)  8/9/91

ipReceives:    167,714   ipTransmits:    70,854   ipForwards:    119
tcpReceives:     1,874   tcpTransmits:    1,863   tcpConnects:     2
udpReceives:   165,164   udpTransmits:   68,891

                       TCP/IP Tables

                 Address Translation Table
                 Interface Table
                 Local IP Address Table
                 Routing Table
                 TCP Connection Table
```

Address Translation Table

This table is the ARP table. The Address Translation Table is a dynamic table that shows the Host Names or IP Addresses if you press TAB, the hardware address (known as the MAC Address) that was discovered using ARP, and the network interface

1033

through which the address was found. Figure 21.19 shows that on the lb server, the ARP table must find the MAC addresses for the backbone host, the backbone_c386 host, and the host bart. Each of the addresses are found by going to the third interface board. Interface boards are discussed in the next section. Figure 21.20 shows the same table as figure 21.19, after the TAB key is pressed.

Figure 21.19

The ARP Table for lb displayed with host names.

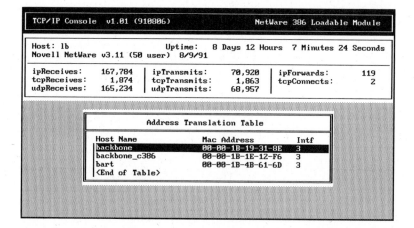

Figure 21.20

The ARP table for lb displayed with IP addresses.

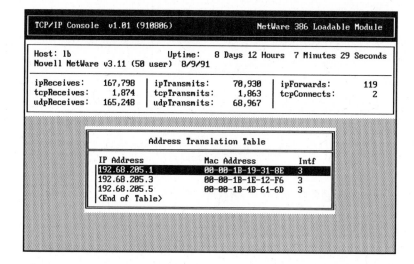

After about 5 to 10 minutes, any path that has not been used again is purged from this table to limit the size of the ARP table. It also serves to make sure that if a new device is swapped in with the same IP–Address, but a different MAC address, the old MAC address will time out. If the address is needed again, another ARP broadcast discovers the MAC address.

Interface Table

The next item, the Interface Table, shows all of the network boards in the Agent. Figure 21.21 shows the four interfaces listed in the North386 server. Each interface is listed as a Novell NE2000 Ethernet board. Notice that the second column where MAC Addresses are shown contains only two different addresses. This figure shows how the table looks when you have multiple protocols bound to a board.

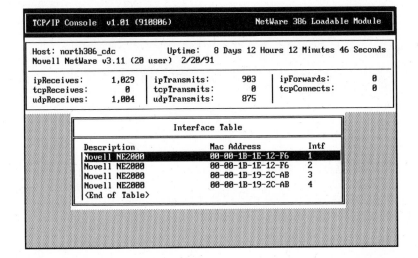

Figure 21.21

The Interface Table for the Agent.

To learn more about the interface, you can highlight it with your arrow keys, then press enter. Figure 21.22 shows the information for the first interface. Notice the third line. This line indicates the protocol bound to this board, which happens to be IPX using the 802.3 frame type.

Also notice the highlighted item in figure 21.22. The ifAdminStatus has a :. after the label, indicating the item can be changed if you have used the control community name. This item allows you to disable the interface for administration.

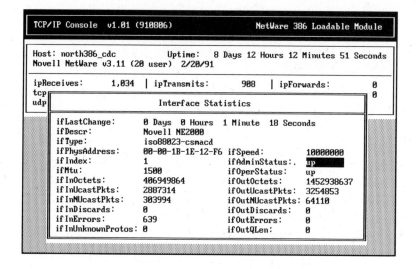

Figure 21.23 shows the second interface board. Notice that the ifPhysAddress is the same as in figure 21.22. The item above, ifType, shows Ethernet-csmacd, which indicates that the IP protocol was bound with the Ethernet_II frame type.

Local IP Address Table

The third menu option shows the IP addresses, subnet masks, and broadcast addresses used in the Agent.

Figure 21.24 shows that two addresses are assigned, one to interface number 2 and one to interface number 4. It also shows that they use all 1s for the broadcast, which is default. Both addresses also use the same subnet mask of 255.255.255.0.

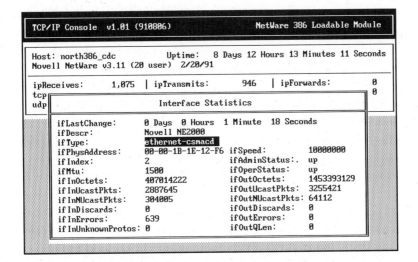

Figure 21.23

Viewing the IP protocol bound to the Interface using the Ethernet_II frame type.

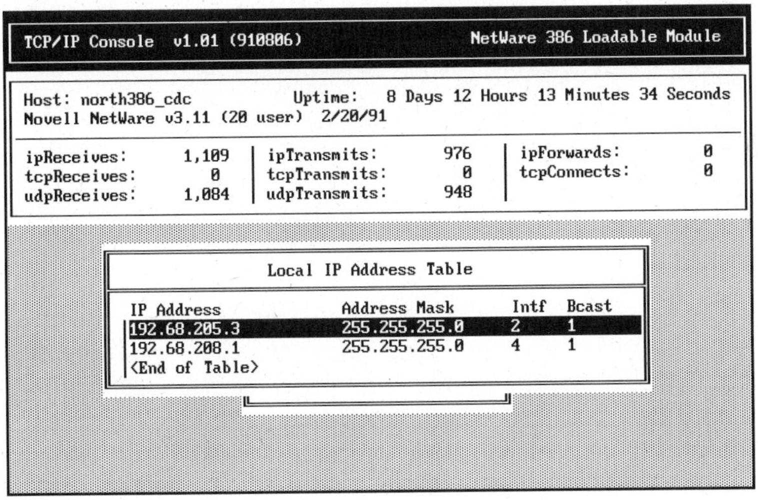

Figure 21.24

Local IP address Table for North386.

Routing Table

The next option shows the routing table, which is a listing of the routes that must be taken to get to a remote node. Figure 21.25 shows the routing table.

Figure 21.25

The Routing Table.

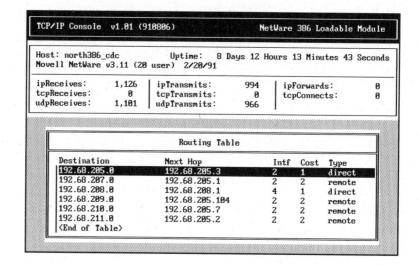

```
TCP/IP Console  v1.01 (910806)                  NetWare 386 Loadable Module

Host: north386_cdc            Uptime:   8 Days 12 Hours 13 Minutes 43 Seconds
Novell NetWare v3.11 (20 user) 2/20/91

ipReceives:     1,126  ipTransmits:     994  ipForwards:       0
tcpReceives:        0  tcpTransmits:      0  tcpConnects:      0
udpReceives:    1,101  udpTransmits:    966


                              Routing Table

        Destination         Next Hop          Intf  Cost  Type
        192.68.205.0        192.68.205.3       2    1     direct
        192.68.207.0        192.68.205.1       2    2     remote
        192.68.208.0        192.68.208.1       4    1     direct
        192.68.209.0        192.68.205.104     2    2     remote
        192.68.210.0        192.68.205.7       2    2     remote
        192.68.211.0        192.68.205.2       2    2     remote
        <End of Table>
```

♦ The first column, Destination, shows the network portion of the IP address.

♦ The second column, Next Hop, indicates the entire IP address of the host that you need to contact to route to the Destination in the first column.

♦ The third column, Intf, is the interface number that can be used to reach the Next Hop.

♦ The fourth column, Cost, is the expense associated with using a particular route. The lower the Cost, the more desirable it is to use that path. Conversely, higher Cost routes indicate paths that should not be taken unless lower cost routes have been tried and found unavailable.

♦ The fifth column, Type, specifies that the route is either Direct, meaning that the path is attached to the router, or Remote, meaning that the destination network is not directly connected to the router.

Using the first two lines of figure 21.25 as an example, the routes could be described as follows:

"To get to any destination network whose network IP address is 192.68.205.anything, you must first contact the host with the IP address of 192.68.205.3. 192.68.205.3 can be reached through interface number 2 at a cost of 1, highly desirable, and is located directly on this host.

To get to any destination network whose network IP address is 192.68.207.anything, you must first contact the host with the IP address of 192.68.205.1. 192.68.205.1 has a cost of 2, which is less desirable than 1, and is shown as remote, which means that it is not on this host. If it is not on this host, then the system looks at the network portion of the IP address, which is 192.68.205.

From the previous paragraph, you saw that to get to any network IP address of 192.68.205, you first had to go to 192.68.205.3. In order to communicate with a host on the network 192.68.207, you first had to route to 192.68.205.3. 192.68.205.3 routes the packet to 192.68.205.1, who knows where the network 192.68.207 is located and delivers the packet."

In the next chapter, you learn how to add routes to this table.

TCP Connection Table

The TCP Connection Table is the last table you explore. This table displays an entry for each TCP connection on the host. In figure 21.26, you can see two current tcpConnects at the top (third column, middle of screen). To see what is happening on those two connections, you can look at the TCP Connection table.

◆ The first Column is the Local Host. In figure 21.26, the local host is A312. The second column shows the port number that is being used locally. The port number comes from the PROTOCOLS database file discussed in Chapter 20.

◆ The third column shows the remote host. In the example, the remote host is bart. The fourth column shows the port being used by the remote host.

◆ The last column shows the state of the connection. Established means that it is currently active. Listen means no connection to the port or protocol exists.

Figure 21.26

The TCP Connection Table.

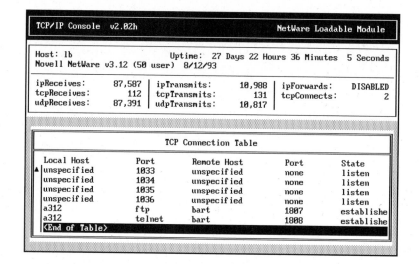

```
TCP/IP Console  v2.02h                          NetWare Loadable Module

Host: lb                         Uptime:  27 Days 22 Hours 36 Minutes  5 Seconds
Novell NetWare v3.12 (50 user)  8/12/93

ipReceives:      87,587  | ipTransmits:    10,988  | ipForwards:    DISABLED
tcpReceives:        112  | tcpTransmits:      131  | tcpConnects:          2
udpReceives:     87,391  | udpTransmits:   10,817  |


                            TCP Connection Table

   Local Host         Port        Remote Host         Port      State
 ▲ unspecified        1033        unspecified         none      listen
   unspecified        1034        unspecified         none      listen
   unspecified        1035        unspecified         none      listen
   unspecified        1036        unspecified         none      listen
   a312               ftp         bart                1807      establishe
   a312               telnet      bart                1808      establishe
   <End of Table>
```

Summary

In this chapter, you learned about managing the TCP/IP network through the following:

- ♦ Loading the SNMP.NLM and the SNMPLOG.NLM.

  The SNMP.NLM gets automatically loaded when you load TCPIP.NLM. SNMPLOG.NLM needs to be manually loaded. SNMPLOG.NLM writes to a binary file, SYS:ETC\SNMP$LOG.BIN.

- ♦ Monitoring Trap Events.

  Trap Events are reported by an Agent (running SNMP and SNMPLOG) to a Manager (running TCPCON). Following are the seven different types of trapped messages:

  Link Up

  Link Down

  Authentication Failure

Loss of EGP Neighbor

Cold Start (Cold Boot)

Warm Start (Warm Boot)

Enterprise Specific

◆ Viewing MIB Information.

All Agents have an MIB, which contains information and statistics regarding the host's use of the TCP/IP protocols.

◆ Setting and using Community names.

The following are the three different Community names: CONTROLCOMMUNITY, MONITORCOMMUNITY and TRAPCOMMUNITY. The CONTROLCOMMUNITY allows the Manager read and write access to the Agent's MIB. The MONITORCOMMUNITY allows the Manager read–only access to the Agent's MIB. The TRAPCOMMUNITY is the community name that is sent with Trap messages when Trap events are sent to a different host.

◆ Monitoring the Agent's MIB through TCPCON.

This allows you to view and monitor the following areas:

Trap Events

Setting Options

Changing Hosts

ICMP, IP, UDP, and TCP statistics

Address Resolution Table (ARP Table)

Interface Table

Local IP Address Table

Routing Table

TCP Connection Table

In the next chapter, you learn about the following:

◆ Routing Protocols

◆ Configuring your NetWare server to route IP packets

◆ IPTunneling

Review Questions

1. Which protocol is used to centrally manage the TCP/IP hosts?

   ○ a. TCPCON

   ○ b. TCPIP

   ○ c. SNMP

   ○ d. SNMPLOG

2. Each Agent has a _____ which contains information and statistics about its TCP/IP configuration.

3. Which statement about SNMP is false?

   ○ a. SNMP is a relatively uncomplicated protocol for managing TCP/IP hosts.

   ○ b. SNMP is made up of five functions.

   ○ c. NMP is a required portion of TCP/IP.

   ○ d. SNMP is included for both the file server and the workstation by Novell.

4. Which is not a valid Trap event?

   ○ a. Cold Boot

   ○ b. Router Down

   ○ c. Authentication Failure

   ○ d. Link Up

5. The _____ Trap is for third party vendors who can supply Trap messages regarding their equipment.

6. An Agent on NetWare must run:

   ○ a. SNMP

   ○ b. SNMPLOG

   ○ c. TCPCON

   ○ d. A and B

   ○ e. A, B, and C

7. How does an SNMP Agent decide on what it will let a Manager do to its MIB?

   ○ a. The Manager provides a password to the Agent.

   ○ b. A Trap is sent to the Agent requesting access.

   ○ c. The Agent matches the Community name given by the Manager to the Community name established when loading the Agent.

   ○ d. The IP address must appear in the hosts table.

8. The following commands were loaded at the file server:

```
LOAD SNMP CONTROL=TEST
LOAD TCPCON COMMUNITY=TEST
```

What is the Manager able to do to the Agent's MIB?

   ○ a. View Only

   ○ b. View and Change

   ○ c. Nothing

9. The following commands were loaded at the file server:

```
LOAD SNMP CONTROL=TEST
LOAD TCPCON COMMUNITY=public
```

What is the Manager able to do to the Agent's MIB?

   ○ a. View Only

   ○ b. View and Change

   ○ c. Nothing

10. The following commands were loaded at the file server:

```
LOAD SNMP MONITOR=VIEW
LOAD TCPCON COMMUNITY=TEST
```

What is the Manager able to do to the Agent's MIB?

○ a. View Only

○ b. View and Change

○ c. Nothing

11. The following commands were loaded at the file server:

```
LOAD SNMP MONITOR=VIEW
LOAD TCPCON COMMUNITY=public
```

What is the Manager able to do to the Agent's MIB?

○ a. View Only

○ b. View and Change

○ c. Nothing

12. The following commands were loaded at the file server:

```
LOAD SNMP MONITOR= CONTROL=TEST
LOAD TCPCON COMMUNITY=TEST
```

What is the Manager able to do to the Agent's MIB?

○ a. View Only

○ b. View and Change

○ c. Nothing

13. The following commands were loaded at the file server:

```
LOAD SNMP MONITOR= CONTROL=TEST
LOAD TCPCON COMMUNITY=public
```

What is the Manager able to do to the Agent's MIB?

○ a. View Only

○ b. View and Change

○ c. Nothing

14. The following commands were loaded at the file server:

    ```
    LOAD SNMP CONTROL
    LOAD TCPCON COMMUNITY=TEST
    ```

    What is the Manager able to do to the Agent's MIB?

    ○ a. View Only

    ○ b. View and Change

    ○ c. Nothing

15. The following commands were loaded at the file server:

    ```
    LOAD SNMP CONTROL
    LOAD TCPCON COMMUNITY=public
    ```

    What is the Manager able to do to the Agent's MIB?

    ○ a. View Only

    ○ b. View and Change

    ○ c. Nothing

16. Which statement about Community names is not false?

    ○ a. SNMP uses Community names for Domain Naming

    ○ b. SNMP and TCPCON both use Community Names

    ○ c. The default for all Community names is public

    ○ d. The default for all Community names is PUBLIC

17. In TCPCON, what tells you that you can modify an entry?

    ○ a. A colon and a period after the entry (:.)

    ○ b. A colon alone (:)

    ○ c. A double line border around the menu

    ○ d. The item can be highlighted

18. The following command was issued at the file server:

    ```
    LOAD TCPCON CDI
    ```

Which statement below is true?

- ○ a. The Community name you are providing is CDI
- ○ b. You are loading the Agent
- ○ c. The first host you will see information for will be the host CDI
- ○ d. This is an invalid statement

19. Which item does not appear on the TCPCON main menu screen?

- ○ a. Available Actions Menu
- ○ b. Uptime
- ○ c. ipForwards
- ○ d. icmpReceives

20. Which statistics screen has items that you can modify?

- ○ a. ICMP
- ○ b. IP
- ○ c. TCP
- ○ d. UDP

21. Which Table shows you ARP information?

- ○ a. Address Translation Table
- ○ b. Interface Table
- ○ c. Local IP Address Table
- ○ d. Routing Table

22. Which Table shows you the MAC Address?

- ○ a. Address Translation Table
- ○ b. Routing Table
- ○ c. Interface Table
- ○ d. A and C

1047

23. Which item label is used to indicate the network board at the host?

    ○ a. lb

    ○ b. Intf

    ○ c. Port

    ○ d. Type

24. The _____ error would appear on the main TCPCON screen under tcpConnects if you could not contact a host.

25. What condition should occur to see a Link Down Trap message?

    ○ a. The file server crashes

    ○ b. The network board is unloaded

    ○ c. The protocol IPX is unbound from the network board

    ○ d. The protocol IP is unbound from the network board

26. What condition should occur to see an Authentication Failure?

    ○ a. The Manager contacts a host that is currently down

    ○ b. The Agent receives a Monitor Community name when it was expecting a Control Community name

    ○ c. The Agent is not in the Manager's host table

    ○ d. The Manager provides an invalid Community name to the Agent

Answers

1. C

2. MIB - Management Information Base

3. D

4. B

5. Enterprise Specific

6. A

7. C

8. B—View and Change because the Agent set Control to TEST and the Manager provided the community name of TEST which matched Control.

9. A—View Only because the Agent set Control to TEST and the default for Monitor is public. The Manager provided the community name of public which matches the Monitor default.

10. C—Nothing because the Agent set Monitor to View and the Control is disabled. The Manager provided the community name of TEST, which doesn't match with VIEW.

11. C—Nothing because the Agent set Monitor to View and the Control is disabled. The Manager provided the community name of public, which doesn't match with VIEW.

12. B—View and Change because the Agent set Control to TEST and allowed any ASCII word to work for Monitor. The Manager provided the community name of TEST, which matched the Control name.

13. A—View Only because the Agent set Control to TEST and allowed any ASCII word to work for Monitor. The Manager provided the community name of public and since any ASCII word would work for the Monitor name, the MIB could be viewed.

14. C—Nothing because the Control was disabled by the Agent and the default for Monitor is public. The Manager provided the name of TEST, which didn't match the Monitor name.

15. A—View Only because the Agent disabled all Control but left the Monitor default of public. The Manager provided the community name of public.

16. B

17. A

18. C

19. D

20. B

21. A

22. D

23. B

24. HOST UNAVAILABLE

25. D

26. D

Routing IP Over NetWare

22 CHAPTER

In the last chapter, you learned about managing a NetWare TCP/IP network. Although you were introduced to the TCPCON utility and each of its menu entries, you received minimal information about IP routing.

This chapter deals exclusively with routing IP packets over the network. IP routing occurs when the destination TCP/IP host is not on the same cable segment as the TCP/IP host that starts the communication.

In this chapter, you learn the following:

- ◆ Internetworking terms and devices
- ◆ Setting up your NetWare server to allow IP Packets to cross the router
- ◆ Creating an IPTUNNEL network

This chapter begins with a description of some internetworking terms as they are used in the TCP/IP world.

Defining Internetworking Terms

Part 1, specifically Chapter 5, of this book explained the function of the following devices in detail. This section should serve as a quick review.

Internetworking Devices

The function of the following devices is easiest to remember in terms of how they relate to the OSI layer.

Figure 22.1 shows the internetworking devices and the OSI layers at which they function.

Figure 22.1

OSI Layers and Internetworking Devices.

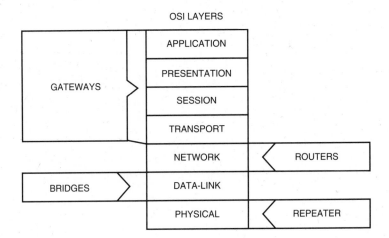

Repeaters

What it is:

A *repeater* is an electronic device that receives an electric signal from the cable and sends it again onto another cable segment.

How it works:

A repeater is the simplest of the internetworking devices because it does not need to understand what it receives. Signals simply are received and retransmitted only on similar topologies.

When to use it:

A repeater is used when the distance that a signal has to travel is more than the suggested length of cable for a particular topology.

Because signals fade or attenuate, a repeater is used to boost the signal and send it further.

Graphical representation:

Figure 22.2 depicts the use of a repeater. The signal comes into the repeater nearly faded, but it is put back onto the next cable segment stronger and able to travel further.

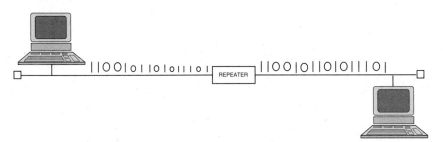

Figure 22.2

Using a repeater on a network segment.

Bridges

What it is:

A *bridge* connects similar topology segments on a network and supports all transport protocols.

How it works:

Bridges can filter network segments. A bridge contains a table of hardware addresses of hosts with which it communicates. These addresses are matched to a network board interface within the bridge. Bridges listen to all traffic. After receiving a packet, the bridge looks for the hardware address for the destination. Then, the table is read to find out which interface inside the bridge can talk to that destination. The packet then passes to the appropriate interface.

The key here is that shared media can get saturated. Splitting into a few segments and only passing traffic that needs to reduces the amount of traffic that has to be on each segment, while preserving the illusion of all nodes being on the same segment.

When to use it:

A bridge can be used when you need to have more workstations on the network than the cable segment allows. Bridges also are useful when traffic on the network benefits from being split into multiple segments, allowing the load to be balanced on multiple segments.

Graphical representation:

Figure 22.3 shows two cable segments connected by a bridge. A student machine, SU1 on cable segment CDC, wants to communicate with SUPERVISOR on cable segment BAC. SU1 sends the packet and the bridge receives it. The MAC address is read from the packet and compared with the bridge's table of addresses. The packet came in on segment CDC through interface C. The table shows that the destination can be reached through interface A. The packet is then passed to the appropriate interface board and sent to its final destination, SUPERVISOR.

Figure 22.3

Using a bridge to route traffic.

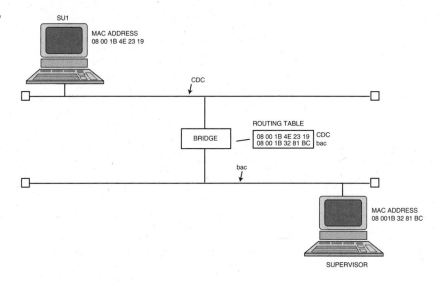

Routers

What it is:

A router connects LANs with segments that are different topologies. It connects different networks.

How it works:

Hosts contain tables that indicate which routers they can use. Routers receive packets sent by a host. The incoming packets are interpreted for destination information, both hardware and software addresses. The router consults its table for destinations or other routers that can reach the destination. The router rebuilds the packet using a frame type that is understood by the destination's topology.

Routers can be configured to accept multiple protocols and accept only packets using protocols for which they have been configured.

When to use it:

Routers are used when you have multiple networks that must be connected and the topologies used are not identical.

Graphical representation:

Figure 22.4 shows SU1 on network segment CDC wants to send a message to SU8 on network segment CD0. CDC is an Ethernet segment, while CD0 is Token Ring. The router receives the packet as Ethernet. The addresses are read and compared to a table. The destination is found and the packet is converted to Token Ring and sent to SU8.

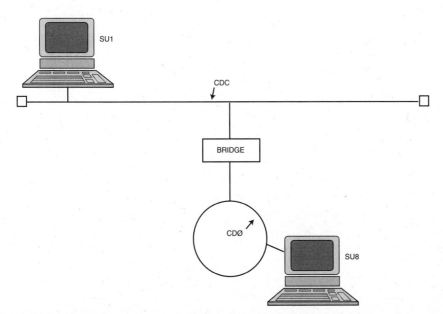

Figure 22.4

Using a router to connect networks.

Another device that you may see is called a brouter. Brouters perform the same functions as bridges and routers. A NetWare file server can connect similar topologies, such as Ethernet to Ethernet, or dissimilar topologies, such as Ethernet to Token Ring. A NetWare server is a Brouter.

Gateways

What it is:

A gateway connects significantly different networks. A NetWare server connected to an IBM mainframe is one example. Communications take place through the use of a gateway that converts packets from one protocol into another.

Another way that the term gateway is used is to describe a machine that has a specialized function. A mail gateway is one example. A mail gateway in TCP/IP can take messages from a UNIX SMTP system and send them to a NetWare MHS system for delivery. The term gateway is also often used to mean "router" in the TCP/IP world.

How it works:

A gateway must strip the incoming packet of all headers and resend only the data and addressing information from the sender in a format that can be understood by the destination host.

When to use it:

A gateway is used when a LAN needs to communicate with a system using a different protocol, or when a specialized service between two protocols is needed.

Graphical representation:

Figure 22.5 shows SU1 on cable segment CDC wanting to send a mail message to root on cable segment BAC. The user, root, is a UNIX user, while SU1 is a NetWare user. The gateway receives the MHS mail message and converts it to an SMTP mail message for delivery.

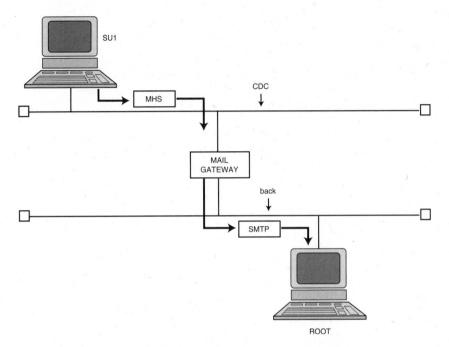

Figure 22.5
A mail gateway.

Repeaters are fast because packet interpretation is not needed. No network filtering takes place and, therefore, repeaters are not considered "intelligent."

Bridges are the fastest of the intelligent devices because the incoming packet needs interpretation for the MAC address information only. In a sense, bridges extend multiple segments of a single LAN.

Routers are slower than bridges because they need to interpret a deeper portion of the packet for address information. It is necessary to regenerate the packet with a frame format appropriate for the next topology. A router assumes that no protocol change has been made.

Gateways are the slowest of the devices because the entire packet must be rebuilt to accommodate the frame information of a different protocol.

1057

Routing Methods

The two protocols used to route using NetWare, IPX/SPX and TCP/IP, are ARP and RIP. This section describes these routing protocols.

Address Resolution Protocol—ARP

ARP is the preferred method to route using TCP/IP. When one host wants to communicate with a second host, the first host checks its ARP table to see if it has the second host's IP address and MAC Address. If the address of the destination host does not exist, then an ARP broadcast is sent requesting the MAC address to the IP address that is being broadcast. When the destination hears the broadcast, it responds with its MAC address. The information then is updated in the first host's ARP table for future use.

Routing Information Protocol—RIP

RIP is a protocol that updates the system every 30 seconds. The information sent by each routing host to all other routing hosts includes routes known and hops to get to the destination route. *Hops* are the number of routers that must be passed through to get to the destination. A hop of 2 means that two routers must be contacted to reach the destination.

When a router connects to the network, it requests hop information from all connected routers through a broadcast. This information allows the router to build a pathway to any destination and to determine the shortest route to each destination.

Routing IP Over NetWare

Now that you have had a refresher on the terms used to describe the different internetworking devices, the next topic is the routing of IP packets on a NetWare network.

Routing Tables

A file server's IP routing table can be seen through TCPCON, as you read in Chapter 21. The following is an example of a host's routing table:

Destination	Next Hop	Intf	Cost	Type
145.56.0.0	145.56.200.1	1	1	direct
192.68.205.0	145.56.200.8	1	3	remote
0.0.0.0	145.56.100.11	1	2	remote

The routing table is used to map out the network. As each new route is discovered, entries are added to this table. Entries are made to describe any host located on the network address (Destination), the router address that is needed to get you to hosts on the destination (Next Hop), the interface in the current machine that gets you to the next hop (Intf), how many routers you must pass through to get to the destination address (Cost), and whether the destination is connected to the current machine (Type).

Study Note

A destination of 0.0.0.0 indicates the default router.

A default router is used when a host tries to communicate to a destination IP address that is not known. The packet is sent to the default router in hopes that the router knows how to communication with the destination host. ICMP is relied upon to return the hardware address of the destination.

Adding Routes to the Routing Table

List and describe the routing protocols supported by your NetWare TCP/IP server.

A NetWare server can have the routing table updated in the following four ways: RIP, TCPCON, ICMP, or IPCONFIG.

RIP

Because RIP traffic is updated every 30 seconds, new routes and defunct routes are easily detected and added to the table.

TCPCON

You can add routes manually through TCPCON when you press insert from the Routing Table option. The screen you see is similar to figure 22.6.

Figure 22.6

Manually creating a route from TCPCON.

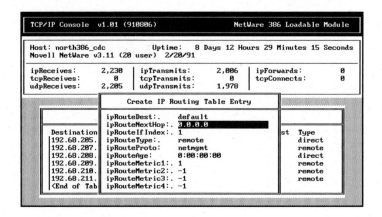

ipRouteDest

This entry is the destination of the route you want to add in dotted decimal notation.

ipRouteNextHop

This entry is the IP address of the next hop that must be reached to get to the destination.

ipRouteIfIndex

This entry is the interface in the current machine through which the next hop can be reached.

ipRouteType

This entry indicates whether the route is directly connected to the current machine (direct) or located on a different segment (remote).

ipRouteProto

This entry indicates the way in which the route was entered.

NETMGMT means that it was entered manually through TCPCON.

LOCAL means that the entry was added through IPCONFIG.

ICMP means that ICMP updated the route.

RIP means that the RIP mechanism added the route.

ipRouteAge

This entry is the amount of time that has passed since this route was last updated. You cannot modify this field.

ipRouteMetric

This entry is the same as a hop count. The metric usually indicates how many routers must be passed through to reach the destination.

ICMP

The Internet Control Message Protocol was introduced in Chapter 18. ICMP can update the route under the following circumstances:

- ◆ A destination is unreachable
- ◆ A closer route is discovered
- ◆ A host needs verification of its network address

ICMP can also update router information by informing routers of problems such as the following:

- ◆ A packet's Time-To-Live (TTL) has expired
- ◆ A router's buffer is full
- ◆ A router cannot keep up with traffic
- ◆ Problems in the IP header

IPCONFIG

Most of the routing information on a NetWare TCP/IP network comes from RIP. The need occasionally arises for a static route to be created. A static route is used when RIP is not an option or has been disabled.

To use IPCONFIG, you must create a GATEWAYS file in the SYS:ETC directory using the following options. Then, you type `LOAD IPCONFIG at the file server.`

Net

This entry is either the network name as it appears in the SYS:ETC\NETWORKS table, or the network portion of the IP address of the destination network.

Host

This entry is either the host name as it appears in the SYS:ETC\HOSTS table, or the IP address of the destination host.

You use either Net or Host but not both. Net allows you to contact any host on that network, while Host sets up a path to that host only.

Gateway

This entry is either the host name as it appears in the SYS:ETC\HOSTS table, or the IP address of the router that is used to get to the destination network or host.

Metric

The *metric* is a number in the range of 1 to 16. The lower the metric, the more desirable the route. Routes with low metrics indicate that the route is preferred over routes with high metrics. A route that requires three hops may be assigned a lower metric than a route that only requires one hop, but the hop is over a T-1 line which is more expensive.

 A metric of 16 indicates that the route is unreachable.

Active/Passive

This entry indicates whether the router can communicate routing information. An Active route assumes that the router is capable of updating its routing information. If the router does not confirm that the route is valid, then it is removed from the routing table.

A Passive route keeps the entry in the table for as long as the server is running or until you physically remove the Route.

An example of a gateways file that establishes a permanent entry for communication to any host on the network 140.200.0.0 using the router 192.68.205.4 at a cost of 1 is as follows:

```
NET 140.200.0.0 GATEWAY 192.68.205.4 COST 1 PASSIVE
```

Following a Routed Packet

Figure 22.7 shows two LAN segments connected through a router. The user, Brian, is connected to the network 192.68.207.0. Brian needs to get a file from UNIX host bart, which is located at 192.68.205.5. Brian issues the command ftp bart (#1). The host BRIAN looks at the hosts table (#2) to determine the IP address of the host bart. Because bart is not located on the same network as the host BRIAN, the routing table is consulted to find a router to get to the destination network (#3). It is discovered that, to talk to any host on the network 192.68.205.0, the router 192.68.207.1, called Router_A in the hosts table, can get to the destination bart.

A packet is built using the known information and is sent to the router. The MAC Header contains the immediate destination and the issuing source. In this case, BRIAN is the issuing source and the immediate destination is Router_A. The IP Header contains the ultimate destination and the original source. The packet came from BRIAN (original source) and is going to bart (ultimate destination).

The router strips off the MAC header that got the packet to its destination and reads the IP header. The MAC header is rebuilt (#5) with a new issuing source and a new immediate destination. The new issuing source is Router_B, which received the information internally from Router_A. The new immediate destination is bart, which is the next, and last, stop.

bart repeats the same procedure, but in reverse, when it responds to Brian's request for an FTP session.

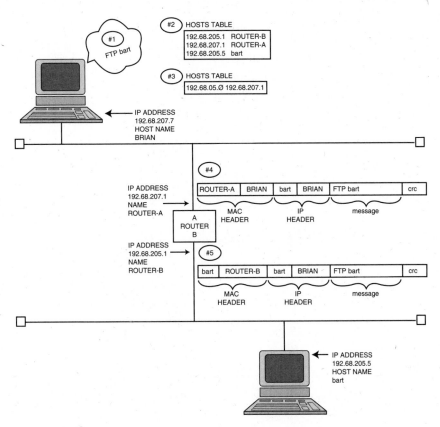

Figure 22.7

Following a routed packet.

Using IPTUNNEL on NetWare Servers

Configure your NetWare TCP/IP server to route
IPX packets over a TCP/IP internetwork.

Consider the following scenario: BD-Retreat had a large IP
network in place before NetWare was introduced within the
company. The implementation of NetWare in the company
necessitated that three file servers be connected to the existing IP

network. Each server has an Ethernet IPX/SPX network attached with approximately 30 workstations per network. Users on the NetWare servers need to talk to the TCP/IP nodes on the IP network, but rarely need to talk to IPX/SPX clients on the other two NetWare servers. This scenario is depicted in figure 22.8.

Figure 22.8

The BD-Retreat IP network with NetWare file servers.

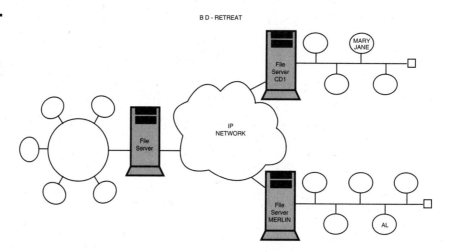

Management and the IP network administrators have decided that for performance and administration, only IP packet traffic is allowed on the IP network.

The BD-Retreat network is a prime candidate for IPTUNNEL. IPTUNNEL takes IPX packets and encapsulates them inside of an IP packet. If Jane, who is attached to file server CDI, wants to send an e-mail message to Al, who logs into the server Merlin, the message reaches CDI as an IPX packet. CDI takes the packet, puts it as the data portion of an IP packet and sends it across the IP network to the file server, Merlin. Merlin takes the IP packet, strips off the IP portion and passes the IPX packet within to Al.

Figure 22.9 shows the packet as it is tunneled through the LAN.

The previous example explains IPTUNNELing between file servers. A workstation attached to the IP network can also encapsulate an IPX packet intended for one of the NetWare file servers.

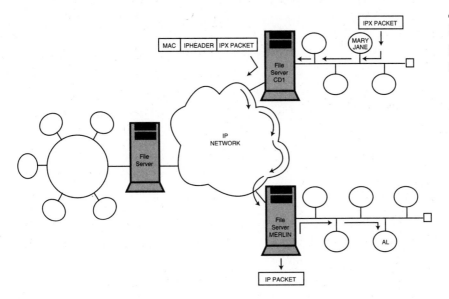

Figure 22.9

Encapsulating an IPX packet.

Requirements

To IPTUNNEL between file servers, you can use the IPTUNNEL.LAN driver that comes with NetWare v3.*x* and above.

An alternative to Novell's product is Schneider and Koch's SK-IPX/IP gateway.

Parameters

At the file server, you need to load the IPTUNNEL driver for each file server that communicates using IPTUNNEL. Then, you need to bind IPX to the IPTUNNEL LAN driver with a network number, creating a logical IPTUNNEL network.

The following parameters are used when loading IPTUNNEL.LAN:

Peer=<*Remote IP address*>

Each file server with which you want to communicate using IPTUNNEL is considered a Peer. You need to repeat the statement LOAD IPTUNNEL PEER=*x.x.x.x*, replacing *x.x.x.x* with the IP addresses of remote servers.

You need to limit the number of Peer file servers using IPTUNNEL. When data is transmitted via IPTUNNEL, each file server in the peer list receives the data. The more servers you have using IPTUNNEL, the more traffic you create. A practical limit is 10.

IPTUNNEL is great for infrequent traffic between users. If communications between remote users seems to be high, then you might want to consider relocating users or implementing NetWare/IP.

CHKSUM={ *YES/NO*}

The default for IPTUNNEL is checksum enabled. If you have other means for error checking, this option can be disabled.

Local={*local IP address*}

If you have more IP bound to more than one network board in the file server, Local allows you to specify which interface to use for IPTUNNELing. By default, IPTUNNEL uses the first board that was bound.

Port={*udp port #*}

This option allows you to tell the system which port number should be used with IPTUNNEL. This option is necessary when you are using a product other than NetWare.

◆ NetWare uses 213, which is the officially-assigned port for IPX.

◆ Schneider & Koch uses 59139.

SHOW=YES

The Show option displays the current IPTUNNEL Peers, Port, and Local IP address.

Binding the Protocol

After IPTUNNEL has been loaded, IPX needs to be bound to the driver. Then, a virtual LAN Address needs to be assigned. The address must be in the range of 1 to FFFFFFFE and must be a unique address on the LAN.

The syntax for binding IPX is the following:

```
BIND IPX TO IPTUNNEL NET=xxx
```

Where *xxx* is the network address assigned to IPTUNNELing.

Each server using IPTUNNEL shares the same NET address.

Examples

Figure 22.10 shows IPTUNNEL being loaded three times, each with a different peer. Look at figure 22.11 to get an idea of the layout of the IPTUNNEL.LAN.

Figure 22.10

Loading the
IPTUNNEL.LAN driver.

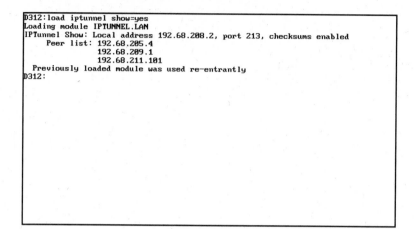

```
D312:load iptunnel show=yes
Loading module IPTUNNEL.LAN
IPTunnel Show: Local address 192.68.208.2, port 213, checksums enabled
     Peer list: 192.68.205.4
                192.68.209.1
                192.68.211.101
  Previously loaded module was used re-entrantly
D312:
```

Figure 22.11

Top view of the
IPTUNNEL network.

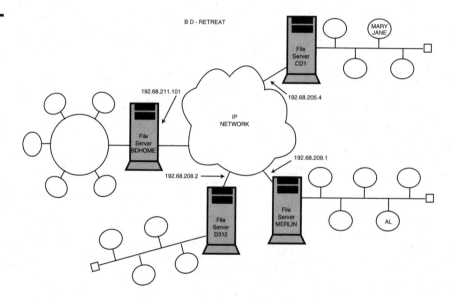

Using the LOAD IPTUNNEL SHOW=YES command, figure 22.12 shows the results from the previous LOAD IPTUNNEL commands.

After verifying the configuration, the next step, as seen in figure 22.13, shows the Bind statement that links IPX with the IPTUNNEL.LAN driver.

```
Novell NE2000
  Version 3.26    October 8, 1993
    Hardware setting: I/O Port 320h to 33Fh, Interrupt 5h
    Node address: 00001B4B5B9F
    Frame type: ETHERNET_802.2
    Board name: 802
    LAN protocol: IPX network 00CDC802

Novell NE2000
  Version 3.26    October 8, 1993
    Hardware setting: I/O Port 320h to 33Fh, Interrupt 5h
    Node address: 00001B4B5B9F
    Frame type: ETHERNET_802.3
    Board name: 803
    LAN protocol: IPX network 00000CDC

IP Tunnel for IPX
  Version 2.02i    February 20, 1993
    Hardware setting: I/O Port D5h
    Node address: 0000C044D002
    Frame type: IP
    No board name defined
    LAN protocol: IPX network 0DEB1871
D312:
```

Figure 22.12

Results from the
LOAD IPTUNNEL
SHOW=YES
command.

```
Novell NE2000
  Version 3.26    October 8, 1993
    Hardware setting: I/O Port 320h to 33Fh, Interrupt 5h
    Node address: 00001B4B5B9F
    Frame type: ETHERNET_II
    Board name: IPIP
    LAN protocol: ARP
    LAN protocol: IP  address 192.68.208.2  mask FF.FF.FF.0  interfaces 1

Novell NE2000
  Version 3.26    October 8, 1993
    Hardware setting: I/O Port 320h to 33Fh, Interrupt 5h
    Node address: 00001B4B5B9F
    Frame type: ETHERNET_802.3
    Board name: 803
    LAN protocol: IPX network 00000CDC

IP Tunnel for IPX
  Version 2.02i    February 20, 1993
    Hardware setting: I/O Port D5h
    Node address: 0000C044D002
    Frame type: IP
    No board name defined
    LAN protocol: IPX network 0DEB1871
D312:
```

Figure 22.13

Binding IPX to
IPTUNNEL.

To verify that the server D312 has been set up properly, the
CONFIG command was typed at the file server prompt. The
results, displayed in figure 22.14, show that the NE2000 driver
was loaded twice, once for Ethernet _II (IP) and once for
Ethernet_802.3 (IPX). The last section in the graphic shows the
configuration for IPTUNNELing.

Figure 22.14

Using CONFIG to verify configuration information.

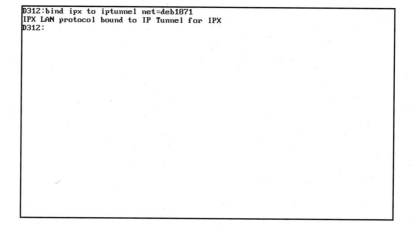

```
D312:bind ipx to iptunnel net=deb1871
IPX LAN protocol bound to IP Tunnel for IPX
D312:
```

The example was set up for only one of the file servers. Each of the remaining file servers would be set up identically, with the exception of who was in their peer lists.

Using IPTUNNEL at the Workstation

Workstations, just like file servers, can be set up to tunnel IPX packets. Two steps are necessary to set up the workstation. The first step is to modify the NET.CFG file. The second step is to add the IPTUNNEL.EXE to the startup file.

Requirements

To IPTUNNEL between a workstation on the IP network and a NetWare server, you need one of the following products:

◆ IPTUNNEL.EXE from either LAN WorkPlace, LAN WorkGroup or the DOS/Windows Client Kit

◆ Schneider & Koch's SK-IPX/IP Gateway Client

Updating NET.CFG

The following two headings must be added to the NET.CFG file on the workstation: Protocol IPX and Link Driver IPTUNNEL.

Protocol IPX

Under Protocol IPX you need to Bind IPTUNNEL. Newer workstation shell files require that you bind to the logical network board number. IPTUNNEL is the last logical board type loaded. The number assigned is the number of frame type loaded plus one.

Link Driver IPTUNNEL

Three parameters are under the heading IPTUNNEL.

gateway={*ipaddress*}

Because a workstation is not a peer for a file server, the workstation refers to servers that are able to tunnel as *gateways*. A separate gateway statement for each file server to which the workstation may want to tunnel packets must be listed here. The workstation does not see other servers not listed as gateways.

port={*udp port number*}

The port for IPX and NetWare is 213. If you are using the Schneider and Koch product, this port should be changed to 59139.

checksum={*yes/no*}

This option normally is enabled, but you can disable it by stating CHECKSUM=NO.

Both Checksum and Port are optional.

Example

Following is an example of a NET.CFG file for the network discussed previously:

```
Link Support
   Buffers 8        1568
   MemPool 4096
Protocol TCPIP
   BIND NE2000
   ip_address      192.68.208.100
   ip_router       192.68.208.1
   ip_netmask      255.255.255.0
Link Driver NE2000
   INT 5
   PORT    320
   Frame Ethernet_II
Protocol IPX
   Bind IPTUNNEL
(or BIND 2)
Link Driver IPTUNNEL
   gateway 192.68.208.1
   gateway 192.68.205.1
   gateway 192.68.209.1
```

Loading the Startup Files

Finally, the last step is to load IPTUNNEL.EXE.

A normal sequence of loading the workstation files would be the following:

LSL

NE2000 (or whatever your MLID is)

TCPIP

IPTUNNEL

IPXODI

VLM (or NETX)

Summary

In this chapter, you learned about the various internetworking devices that can be used to expand your TCP/IP network.

You also learned about adding and viewing routes through TCPCON and through protocols such as RIP and ICMP.

This chapter explained how to add a static route by creating a SYS:ETC\GATEWAYS file and then running IPCONFIG at the file server.

Finally, you learned how to set up IPTUNNELing at the file server by loading IPTUNNEL.LAN and binding IPX to IPTUNNEL. On a workstation, you learned that you must modify the NET.CFG and load the IPTUNNEL.EXE file in order to tunnel.

In the next chapter on TCP/IP Transport, you learn some simple UNIX commands that allow you to perform many of the tasks you need when connecting UNIX and NetWare.

Review Questions

1. At which OSI Layer does a router function?

   ○ a. Physical

   ○ b. Data-Link

   ○ c. Network

   ○ d. Transport

2. At which OSI Layer does a bridge function?

   ○ a. Data-Link

   ○ b. Network

   ○ c. Transport

   ○ d. Session

3. At which OSI Layer does a gateway function?

  ○ a. Data-Link

  ○ b. Network

  ○ c. Transport

  ○ d. Potentially all 7

4. Which intelligent device is fastest?

  ○ a. Router

  ○ b. Bridge

  ○ c. Repeater

  ○ d. Gateway

5. Which routing method does NetWare use with IPX/SPX?

  ○ a. ARP

  ○ b. RARP

  ○ c. ICMP

  ○ d. RIP

6. Which field in the routing table would indicate how many routers must be crossed to reach the destination network?

  ○ a. Destination

  ○ b. Next Hop

  ○ c. Intf

  ○ d. Cost

7. The address in the routing table that refers to the default router is _____.

8. Which of the following allows the administrator to manually add routes?

  ☐ a. TCPCON

  ☐ b. RIP

☐ c. ICMP

☐ d. IPCONFIG

9. What is the path AND name of the file that is used with IPCONFIG.NLM?

○ a. SYS:ETC\GATEWAYS

○ b. SYS:ETC\GATEWAYS.CFG

○ c. SYS:ETC\GATEWAY

○ d. SYS:ETC\IPCONFIG.CFG

10. Which parameter keeps the static route in the table when using IPCONFIG?

○ a. ACTIVE

○ b. PASSIVE

○ c. COST

○ d. KEEP

11. IPTUNNELing encapsulates a(n) _____ packet inside of an _____ packet.

12. Which statement about IPTUNNEL is true?

○ a. IPTUNNEL drivers are included for both the file server and workstation when you acquire the NetWare operating system.

○ b. IPTUNNEL is best used when only a few file servers need to pass IPX packets across an IP network.

○ c. The file server utility for tunneling is IPTUNNEL.NLM.

○ d. Each server must have its own unique IPTUNNEL address.

13. When using IPTUNNEL, file servers have _____, and workstations talk to _____.

    ○ a. gateways, peers

    ○ b. gateways, routers

    ○ c. peers, gateways

    ○ d. peers, hosts

14. Which two items need to appear in the NET.CFG file for the workstation to support IPTUNNEL?

    ☐ a. Protocol IPTUNNEL

    ☐ b. Protocol IPX

    ☐ c. Link Driver IPTUNNEL

    ☐ d. Link Driver IPX

15. The IPTUNNEL driver must be loaded after TCP/IP on both the file server and the workstation.

    ○ a. True

    ○ b. False

16. Which number indicates that a destination is unreachable?

    ○ a. 8

    ○ b. 16

    ○ c. 32

    ○ d. 64

17. When a TCP/IP packet is sent to a router, which addresses appear in the IP header?

    ☐ a. IP Address of the final destination

    ☐ b. IP Address of the router

    ☐ c. IP Address of the sender

    ☐ d. MAC Address of the router

18. Which item in the NET.CFG is optional?

- ○ a. Bind 2
- ○ b. gateway=192.68.205.5
- ○ c. port=213
- ○ d. Protocol IPX

Answers

1. C

2. A

3. D

4. B

5. D

6. D

7. 0.0.0.0

8. A, D

9. A

10. B

11. IPX, IP

12. B

13. C

14. B, C

15. A

16. B

17. A, C

18. C

Using Simple UNIX Commands

In Chapter 19, you learned about the DoD Model for networking and the protocols that are used on the four layers.

In this chapter, you round out your knowledge of the ways in which two Process/Application protocols are implemented. The chapter explores FTP and TELNET, teaching you the following:

◆ The most common FTP commands and how to use them

◆ The most common TELNET commands and their syntax

Learning FTP

File Transfer Protocol (FTP) is a utility designed to move files to and from a remote host.

FTP is limited in its functionality because its main purpose is to transfer files. FTP can accomplish the following tasks:

◆ *Put* files onto a remote host

◆ *Get* files from a remote host

◆ Create a directory on the remote host

◆ Change directories on both local and remote hosts

◆ List directory contents on both local and remote hosts, using DOS or UNIX directory commands

♦ Rename files on the remote host

♦ Change the transfer type to and from ASCII and BINARY

Most of the FTP tasks are listed here. FTP can differ slightly from version to version, so only the most common tasks are listed. FTP commands are used in lowercase.

The following set of FTP commands is used to open and close sessions.

open {*host name* or *IP address*}

To open an FTP session, you have two choices. The first is to type in the name or IP address of the host when you start FTP. If you want to start an FTP session with the host bart, for example, you type `ftp bart`, as shown in figure 23.1.

Figure 23.1

Starting an FTP session.

```
C:\NTGNT>cd\

C:\>ftp bart
FTP - Copyright (c) 1992, Novell, Inc.

220 bart FTP server (UNIX(r) System V Release 4.2) ready.
Remote User Name:dniederm
Remote Password:
ftp>
```

Your second choice is to use the *open* command. At the prompt, if you type FTP without any parameter you are put into an FTP shell. To open a session with the host bart, you type `open bart`.

close

Using the previous command, open, you are able to establish an FTP session with a host. When you are finished with that session and want to remain in the FTP shell, you type close. You can then start a new session with the open command.

bye

When you are finished using FTP and want to exit back to the operating system prompt, you type bye. Quit also works with many versions of FTP to end a session.

The next set of commands is used to move around the directory structure of the local and remote hosts from within the FTP session.

cd {*directory*}

The cd (change directory) command enables you to set the current directory to a specific location on the *remote* host.

lcd

The lcd (local change directory) command enables you to set the current directory to a specific location on the *local* host.

mkdir

The mkdir (make directory) command enables you to create a directory on the *remote* host.

dir

The dir (directory) command enables you to display the contents of a directory on the *remote* host in a UNIX long format.

ldir

The ldir (local directory) command enables you to display the contents of a directory on the *local* host in a DOS format.

Figure 23.2 shows the differences between dir and ldir in an FTP session.

Figure 23.2

Dir and ldir from an FTP session showing remote and local files.

```
C:\QUOTES>ftp 192.68.205.5
FTP - Copyright (c) 1992, Novell, Inc.

220 bart FTP server (UNIX(r) System V Release 4.2) ready.
Remote User Name:dniederm
Remote Password:
ftp> cd temp
ftp> dir
total 0
-rw-r--r--    1 dniederm other          0 Jun 28 10:53 94.information
-rw-r--r--    1 dniederm other          0 Jun 28 10:53 94.quote
-rw-r--r--    1 dniederm other          0 Jun 28 10:53 94.template
-rw-r--r--    1 dniederm other          0 Jun 28 10:53 january.document
ftp> ldir
cdi.qte            3    6-28-94   11:26   A
data.doc           6    6-28-94   11:30   A
template.doc      30    6-28-94   11:31   A
  3 File(s)
ftp>
```

ls

The ls (list) command enables you to display the contents of a directory on the *remote* host in a UNIX format.

lls

The lls (local list) command enables you to display the contents of a directory on the *local* host in a DOS format.

Figure 23.3 shows the differences between using ls and lls.

```
C:\QUOTES>ftp 192.68.205.5
FTP - Copyright (c) 1992, Novell, Inc.

220 bart FTP server (UNIX(r) System V Release 4.2) ready.
Remote User Name:dniederm
Remote Password:
ftp> cd temp
ftp> ls
.
..
94.information
94.quote
94.template
january.document
ftp> lls
cdi.qte
data.doc
template.doc
ftp>
```

Figure 23.3

Using ls and lls to see remote and local files.

The last set of commands describes how you can manipulate files on the local and remote hosts from within the FTP session.

ascii

This is the default FTP mode. When the files that need to be transferred are text files, you need to use the ASCII mode (although you can transfer ASCII files in binary mode). This mode is the fastest mode of transfer. To set the mode to ASCII, type `ascii` at the FTP prompt.

binary

When the files that need to be transferred are executable files, the proper mode for transfer is binary. Executable files transferred in ascii mode do not run. To set the mode to binary, type `binary` at the FTP prompt.

get {*remote file*} {*local file*}

The get command enables you to take a file from the *remote* host and place it onto the *local* host.

1085

As shown in figure 23.4, to get a UNIX file called january.document from the remote host and place it onto the local DOS host under the name of jan.doc you type:

```
get january.document jan.doc
```

```
C:\QUOTES>ftp 192.68.205.5
FTP - Copyright (c) 1992, Novell, Inc.

220 bart FTP server (UNIX(r) System V Release 4.2) ready.
Remote User Name:dniederm
Remote Password:
ftp> cd temp
ftp> get january.document jan.doc
ftp> lls
cdi.qte
data.doc
template.doc
jan.doc
ftp>
```

mget {*file names*}

The mget (multiple get) command enables you to move multiple files from the *remote* host to the *local* host using wild cards or multiple arguments.

When using mput or mget to move multiple files, the following options are asked after the first file to be transferred.

◆ n—do not transfer

◆ a—do all (this will disable the option menu)

◆ q—quit—do not do any more

◆ y—yes, do this one

As shown in figure 23.5, to get all documents that begin with 94 from the current directory on the remote host you type:

```
mget 94*
```

```
C:\QUOTES>ftp 192.68.205.5
FTP - Copyright (c) 1992, Novell, Inc.

220 bart FTP server (UNIX(r) System V Release 4.2) ready.
Remote User Name:dniederm
Remote Password:
ftp> cd temp
ftp> mget *.94
mget info.94 ?(n==don't,a==do all,q==do no more,y==do)? a
ftp> lls
cdi.qte
data.doc
template.doc
jan.doc
info.94
quote.94
template.94
ftp>
```

Figure 23.5

Using the mget command and the ls command to view the results.

put {*local file*} {*remote file*}

The put command enables you to take a file from the *local* host and place it onto the *remote* host.

As shown in figure 23.6, to take a DOS file called DATA.DOC and put it onto the remote UNIX host under the name of data.doc.dos you type the following at the FTP prompt:

```
put data.doc data.doc.dos
```

```
C:\QUOTES>ftp 192.68.205.5
FTP - Copyright (c) 1992, Novell, Inc.

220 bart FTP server (UNIX(r) System V Release 4.2) ready.
Remote User Name:dniederm
Remote Password:
ftp> cd temp
ftp> put data.doc data.doc.dos
6 bytes transmitted in 1 seconds (6 bytes/s)
ftp> ls
.
..
quote.94
template.94
data.doc.dos
info.94
january.document
ftp>
```

Figure 23.6

Use the put command and the ls command to view the results.

1087

mput

The mput (multiple put) command enables you to move multiple files from the *local* host to the *remote* host using wild cards or multiple arguments.

As shown in figure 23.7, to move the files cdi.qte and template.doc, you type the following:

```
mput cdi.qte template.doc
```

Figure 23.7

Using the mput command and the ls command to view the results.

```
C:\QUOTES>ftp 192.68.205.5
FTP - Copyright (c) 1992, Novell, Inc.

220 bart FTP server (UNIX(r) System V Release 4.2) ready.
Remote User Name:dniederm
Remote Password:
ftp> cd temp
ftp> mput cdi.qte template.doc
mput cdi.qte ?(n==don't,a==do all,q==do no more,y==do)? y
3 bytes transmitted in 1 seconds (3 bytes/s)
mput template.doc ?(n==don't,a==do all,q==do no more,y==do)? y
30 bytes transmitted in 1 seconds (30 bytes/s)
ftp> ls
.
..
quote.94
template.94
data.doc.dos
info.94
january.document
cdi.qte
template.doc
ftp>
```

delete {*filename*}

The delete command enables you to remove a single file from the *remote* host.

mdelete {*filenames*}

The mdelete command enables you to remove multiple files on the *remote host* using wild cards.

rename {*old filename*} {*new filename*}

The rename command enables you to change the name of a file on
the remote host.

Comparing UNIX Commands to DOS Commands

When you are using UNIX through terminal emulation, TELNET
or equivalent, you have access to normal UNIX commands. The
commands in the following list are the most popular commands
used in UNIX, and only the common parameters are discussed.
New Riders Publishing has many books on UNIX commands, in
case you need to gain more knowledge in using UNIX.

cat

Use the cat (catalog or concatenate) command to see the contents
of a file such as DOS TYPE or add to the file's contents, such as
DOS APPEND.

Syntax:

```
cat {filenames}
cat {filenames} > {new filename}
```

Example:

```
cat hosts
```

This command displays the contents of the hosts file.

DOS Equivalent: **APPEND, TYPE**

cd

Use the cd command to place yourself in a new directory.

The cd command by itself places you in your UNIX home directory.

Syntax:

```
cd {directory}
```

Example:

```
cd /etc
```

This command changes your directory to etc, which is off of the root (/).

DOS Equivalent: **CD *{directory}***

cp

Use the cp (copy) command to copy a file or a group of files from one directory to another.

Syntax:

```
cp {source file} {target file}
cp {files} {directory}
```

Examples:

```
cp hosts hosts.old
```

This command copies the contents of the host's file to a file in the same directory, called hosts.old.

```
cp *.94 /home/bchaffin
```

This command copies all of the files in the current directory that end in 94 to the directory /home/bchaffin.

DOS Equivalent: **COPY**

date

Use the date command to display the current date and time.

Syntax:

```
date
```

DOS Equivalent: **DATE, TIME**

grep

Use the grep command to search file contents for text strings.

Syntax:

```
grep {text} {files}
```

Example:

```
grep bart hosts
```

This command searches the file *hosts* for an entry called *bart*.

DOS Equivalent: **FIND**

ls

Use the ls (list) command to view the contents of a directory.

Syntax:

```
ls {options}
```

Options:

-l   The l is for a long descriptive listing.

-a   Shows hidden files.

Example:

```
ls -la
```

This command lists all files in the current directory, including hidden files. You also are shown information on file ownership, rights, size and date modified.

DOS Equivalent: **DIR**

man

Use the man command to see a text file that describes a UNIX command.

Syntax:

    man {command name}

Example:

    man grep

This command shows you a description of the grep command and all of its parameters.

DOS Equivalent: **HELP**

mkdir

Use the mkdir (make directory) command to create a new directory.

Syntax:

    mkdir {new directory name}

Examples:

    mkdir reports

This command makes a directory called reports directly underneath the current directory.

    mkdir /temporary

This command makes a directory called temporary off of the root.

DOS Equivalent: **MKDIR, MD**

mv

Use the mv (move) command to rename a file or to relocate a file.

Syntax:

```
mv {old file name} {new file name}
mv {file} {new location}
```

Examples:

```
mv jliy.quote july.quote
```

This command changes the file jliy.quote to a file called july.quote.

```
mv july.quote /temp
```

This command relocates the july.quote file to the directory temp.

DOS Equivalent: **RENAME**

pwd

Use pwd (print working directory) to find the name of the current directory.

Syntax:

```
pwd
```

DOS Equivalent: **CD**

rm

Use the rm (remove) command to delete a file or multiple files.

Syntax:

```
rm {filenames}
```

Examples:

```
rm *.94
```

This command removes all files with the extension 94 from the current directory.

DOS Equivalent: **DEL**

1093

rmdir

Use the rmdir (remove directory) command to delete an empty directory.

Syntax:

```
rmdir {directory}
```

Example:

```
rmdir temp
```

This command gets rid of the directory temp, which is expected to be located under the current directory.

DOS Equivalent: **RMDIR, RD**

 Quick chart of comparisons:

DOS COMMAND	UNIX COMMAND
APPEND	cat
CD	pwd
CD {directory}	cd
COPY	cp
DATE	date
DEL	rm
DIR	ls
FIND	grep

HELP	man
MD, MKDIR	mkdir
RD, RMDIR	rmdir
RENAME	mv
TIME	date
TYPE	cat

Summary

In this chapter, you learned:

◆ FTP commands are grouped into three types of commands: Session Control, Directory, and File.

◆ The reasons and syntax for using each of the FTP commands.

◆ There are TELNET commands and DOS commands that perform similar functions.

◆ The reasons and syntax for using popular TELNET commands.

You have now completed the last chapter in Part 4, "NetWare TCP/IP." Test the knowledge that you have acquired through this book by setting up a file server to accept the TCP/IP protocol as well as the IPX protocol, if possible. If you also have access to a UNIX system, exercise your knowledge by experimenting with FTP and TELNET. These extra measures help to solidify the book knowledge with real-life experiments.

Review Questions

1. Which of the following methods starts an FTP session?

   ☐   a.   C:\>ftp bart

   ☐   b.   C:\>open bart

   ☐   c.   ftp>open bart

   ☐   d.   ftp>ftp bart

2. Which FTP command does not end an FTP session?

   ○   a.   bye

   ○   b.   close

   ○   c.   quit

   ○   d.   end

3. Which FTP commands enables you to see local files?

   ○   a.   ldir, lcd

   ○   b.   lls, ldir

   ○   c.   ls, dir

   ○   d.   dir, lcd

4. Which statement about FTP commands is false?

   ○   a.   Rename only enables you to rename remote files.

   ○   b.   Mkdir enables you to create directories on local and
             remote hosts.

   ○   c.   Mdelete can only be used on the remote system.

   ○   d.   Delete can only be used on the remote system.

5. When transferring an executable file you should use the
   _____ mode.

6. Which FTP command would you use to transfer all files with the extension EXP from the local host to the remote host?

   ○ a. mput *.exp

   ○ b. mget *.exp

   ○ c. put *.exp

   ○ d. get *.exp

7. Which is the best FTP command to transfer the july.txt and aug.txt files from the remote host to the local host?

   ○ a. put july.txt aug.txt

   ○ b. mput july.txt aug.txt

   ○ c. mget july.txt aug.txt

   ○ d. mget *.txt

8. To transfer the file june.doc from the local system to the remote host, you must use the _____ command.

9. Which FTP command below changes the file name from test.june to test.july?

   ○ a. cp test.july test.june

   ○ b. mv test.june test.july

   ○ c. rename test.july test.june

   ○ d. rename test.june test.july

10. The default mode for FTP is:

   ○ a. ASCII

   ○ b. BINARY

   ○ c. TEXT

   ○ d. EXECUTABLE

11. Which TELNET command is equivalent to DOS APPEND?

- ○ a. type
- ○ b. append
- ○ c. cat
- ○ d. date

12. Which DOS command is equivalent to TELNET grep?

- ○ a. cat
- ○ b. find
- ○ c. type
- ○ d. dir

13. Which TELNET command is equivalent to DOS CD?

- ○ a. pwd
- ○ b. dir
- ○ c. lcd
- ○ d. ls

14. Which DOS command is equivalent to TELNET man?

- ○ a. FIND
- ○ b. HELP
- ○ c. DIR
- ○ d. EDIT

15. The _____ command in TELNET enables you to see the current time of the host.

16. Which TELNET command creates a directory under the current directory called quotes?

   ○ a. md \quotes

   ○ b. md quotes

   ○ c. mkdir /quotes

   ○ d. mkdir quotes

17. Which TELNET command quickly gets you to your home directory from any location?

   ○ a. cd home

   ○ b. home

   ○ c. cd

   ○ d. pwd

18. The _____ command enables you to see information on using a UNIX command.

19. Which TELNET command enables you to search all files with the extension 94 for the phrase "In 1994".

   ○ a. grep "In 1994" *.94

   ○ b. grep *.94 "In 1994"

   ○ c. find "In 1994" *.94

   ○ d. find *.94 "In 1994"

20. Which DOS commands use the same TELNET commands? Choose all that apply.

   ☐ a. TYPE

   ☐ b. MKDIR

   ☐ c. RMDIR

   ☐ d. CD

   ☐ e. RENAME

   ☐ f. DATE

1099

Answers

1. A,C

2. D

3. B

4. B

5. BINARY

6. A

7. C

8. put

9. D

10. A

11. C

12. B

13. A

14. B

15. DATE

16. D

17. C

18. man

19. A

20. B, C, D, F

NetWare and Networking Glossary

A
APPENDIX

A

Address. A unique value identifying a location of a node, network, or position in memory.

American National Standards Institute (ANSI). An organization responsible for the establishment of many standards for data communications and terminals. ANSI is responsible for the ASCII character set.

American Standard Code for Information Interchange (ASCII). A standard data communication code defined by ANSI. This code is used by most computer manufacturers to enable their devices to communicate with different brands of equipment.

Amplitude. A measure of the magnitude of a waveform.

Amplitude modulation. The technique of encoding analog or digital information by varying the amplitude of an analog waveform.

Analog data. Data that varies continually.

Analog signal. Representation of digital values by means of variations in waveform.

ANSI. *See* American National Standards Institute.

ASCII. *See* American Standard Code for Information Interchange.

Asynchronous. A data transmission mode in which synchronization is established for each character. Every character is preceded by a start bit and followed by one or more stop bits.

Attenuation. Loss in amplitude of a data signal.

B

Bandwidth. The capacity of a communication channel. In analog channels, bandwidth is the difference between the high and low frequencies that the channel can accommodate. In digital channels, bandwidth is the rate at which data can be transmitted.

Baseband. Form of transmission in which the entire bandwidth of a channel is devoted to one signal.

Baud. Signalling rate unit for analog communications. The measure of one baud is equal to one change of state per second.

Binary. A method of representing information in terms of two possible states. Binary numbering systems use digits with values of 1 and 0. Asynchronous communication uses "mark" and "space" states.

Binary Synchronous Communication (BSC). A Data-Link level communication protocol defined by IBM for use with synchronous channels.

Bisync. *See* Binary Synchronous Communications (BSC).

Bit-oriented protocol. Transmission of data by moving only one bit at a time.

Bits. A binary digit capable of having only two values, 0 and 1.

Bits/s. Bits per second. A measure of the bandwidth of a data communication channel. Can be abbreviated bps.

Block. A contiguous group of bits communicated as a unit.

Bottleneck. A point within communication where the data flow is at its weakest.

Bounded media. Any communication channel in which the signal is confined to a specific, physical path.

bps. *See* Bits/s.

Bridge. A device that functions at the Data-Link level to connect multiple networks into an internetwork. Bridges usually interconnect networks that are similar with regard to topologies and access methods.

Broadband. A transmission medium that has capabilties of carrying multiple signals simultaneously.

Buffer. Memory allocated for the temporary storage of incoming and outgoing data.

Bus. A configuration that allows multiple devices to communicate via a common channel.

Byte. A group of eight bits addressed as a unit. Memory in most microcomputers is organized in terms of bytes.

C

Carrier. Continuous frequency transmitted by a modem and capable of being modulated on the basis of the bits in a data stream.

Carrier-Sense Multiple Access/Collision Avoidance (CSMA/CA). A transmission method used on networks that allows only one carrier at a time on the line. Collision avoidance employs mechanisms that reduce the frequency with which collisions can occur.

Carrier-Sense Multiple Access/Collision Detection (CSMA/CD). A transmission method used on networks that allows only one carrier at a time on the line.

CCITT (Consultative Committee on International Telegraphy and Telephony). An organization setting international communications standards.

Channel. A means of transmission of data between devices on a computer system.

Character. A graphic symbol, such as a letter, a numeric digit, punctuation, or other special symbol.

Checksum. A calculated field computed by adding the bits of a block of characters for a result that can be used for error checking.

Chip. A silicon chip that houses electronic circuits for the purpose of passing electronic information and storing computer data.

Circuit. An electrical channel enabling two or more devices to communicate.

Circuit switching. A method of transmitting data whereby an unbroken circuit path is established between the communicating devices.

Clock. A timing device used in synchronization.

Coaxial cable. Cable consisting of a center conductor surrounded by a braided tubular conductor of uniform diameter. The two conductors are separated by a tubular polyethylene insulator and the cable is encased within a sheath.

Code. A system of rules and conventions according to which the signals representing data can be formed, transmitted, received, and processed.

Common carrier. A public access transmission facility that must be within public utility regulations.

Communications. Transfer of data between two devices.

Communications medium. A physical connection for communications that can consist of bounded or unbounded media.

Connectivity. Logical or physical connection between network workstations.

Consultative Committee on International Telegraphy and Telephony. *See* CCITT.

Control character. A character intended to initiate, modify, or stop a control function.

CPS (characters per second). Number of characters transmitted per second.

CPU (central processing unit). The device in which processing occurs within a computer system.

CRC (cyclic redundancy check). A means of ensuring the integrity of transmitted data. An algorithm is used to perform a calculation on the data as transmitted and received. If both calculations result in the same CRC value, the data is presumed to have been received correctly.

CSMA/CA. *See* Carrier-Sense Multiple Access/Collision Avoidance.

CMSA/CD. *See* Carrier-Sense Multiple Access/Collision Detection.

Cyclic redundancy check. *See* CRC.

D

Data Circuit-Terminating Equipment (DCE). Equipment used to connect Data Terminal Equipment (DTE) to a communications facility. Example: modem.

Data communications. The transmission of data from one network workstation to another.

Data packet. A logically assembled group of data.

Data Terminal Equipment (DTE). Device at which data transmission originates or terminates.

DCE. *See* Data Circuit-Terminating Equipment.

Decibel. Numerical indication of the relative intensity of sound.

Dedicated line. Lease of private communication line.

De facto. Commonly accepted standard.

De jure. Specified by law (or a standards organization).

Demodulator. The conversion of analog to digital signal.

Digital data. Data specified by either on or off states, ones or zeros.

Digital Network Architecture (DNA). Digital Equipment Corporation network architecture.

Digital signal. Signal symbolized by being either on or off.

Disk server. A mass storage device capable of sharing its resources.

Distributed processing. The capability of a system to hand off data processing to individual workstations to process the data and allow that central system to only handle the sharing of the data.

DNA. *See* Digital Network Architecture.

DTE. *See* Data Terminal Equipment.

Duplex. *See* Full-duplex transmission.

E

EBCDIC. Extended Binary Coded Decimal Interchange Code. Eight-bit character set developed by IBM.

Echoplexing. Error checking by means of echoing back all signals sent by the sender.

EIA. Electronic Industries Association. A set of standards that includes data communications interface standards. Best known for EIA-232-D or RS-232.

Electronic Industries Association. *See* EIA.

Emulation. One device mimicking another device.

Encryption. Changing data so that it appears differently for security purposes.

Enterprise network. A network that brings all sites together through a communications medium.

F

FCS (frame check sequence). SDLC and HDLC term corresponding to CRC, used for error checking.

FDM (frequency division multiplexing). Use of a single channel to allow multiple users to all have access to that single channel.

Fiber optics. Glass fibers used to transmit data through the glass by use of light signals.

File server. A computer system allowing for sharing of files from one source to many.

Flag. A bit commonly used for specifying a true or false condition.

Format. Structuring for messaging and data, allowing it to be understood.

Frame. Term for message block.

Frame check sequence. *See* FCS.

Frequency. Number of cycles of a signal per second.

Frequency division multiplexing. *See* FDM.

Frequency modulation. The communication is measured in the change in frequency while amplitude stays constant.

Full-duplex transmission. A two-way transmission scheme in which information can be carried in both directions simultaneously.

G

Gateway. Network node that operates as an interface between different network types, such as a NetWare LAN to an SNA network.

Global network. A network extending between countries or even continents.

H

Half-duplex transmission. A two-way transmission scheme in which information can be carried only one direction at a time.

Handshaking. Synchronization between machines through messaging.

HDLC. High-Level Data-Link Control, a standard bit-oriented communication line protocol developed by ISO.

Hertz. A unit of frequency, abbreviated Hz.

High-Level Data-Link Control. *See* HDLC.

Host. A computer that shares processing resources with other devices on a network. Generally, hosts supply the processing capability for terminals in a terminal/host environment.

Hub. A centralized point on a network through which all traffic flows.

Hz. *See* Hertz.

I

IEEE. *See* Institute of Electronic and Electrical Engineers.

Institute of Electronic and Electrical Engineers (IEEE). A committee creating standards for interfaces and local area network protocols.

Integrated Services Digital Network (ISDN). A digital communications network in which data, voice, facsimile, graphics, and video can be carried over a common circuit.

Interface. A device that allows for communications between multiple devices.

International Organization for Standardization (ISO). One of the two primary international bodies developing data communications and networking standards.

L

LAN. *See* Local area network.

Line. Communications circuits.

Line protocols. Provide handshaking and line-control over network connections.

Local area network (LAN). Computers connected together through various types of media sharing files and peripherals.

M

MAN. *See* Metropolitan area network.

Mark. For an interchange circuit, a condition representing a value of one.

Message. An ordered collection of data in a form that can be processed by a receiver.

Message switching. Descriptive of a process in which messages are stored at one or more intermediate points between sender and receiver. Sometimes called store and forward.

Metropolitan area network (MAN). A network that services an urban area.

Microwaves. Radio waves used in unbounded media transmissions. Microwave operates at radio waves above 890 MHz.

Mobile net. A network partially made up of portable devices using unbounded media for their transmission.

Modem (Modulator/Demodulator). A DCE used to connect a DTE to an analog communications circuit. Converts the DTE's digital signal to analog form for transmission and converts the received analog signals from analog circuit to digital.

Modulator. The portion of the modem that does the conversion of digital to analog signal.

Multiplexer (MUX). A device that allows multiple independent data streams to share a data link.

Multipoint. One circuit is interconnecting multiple stations.

MUX. *See* Multiplexer.

N

NetWare. Network operating system software created by Novell.

Network. A set of devices interconnected to enable them to communicate.

Network interface card (NIC). A computer board that allows computers to be connected to media for communications between stations.

NIC. *See* Network interface card.

Node. A device connected to a network.

Noise. Bad or undesired signals on a channel.

Non-dedicated. Terminology used with file servers stating that the machine will be shared as a workstation along with being a file server.

Nonproprietary. Created under the impression that it can be shared and not used for only one specific purpose, with specific equipment.

O

Open System Interconnection (OSI). A reference to a model used for creating standards for today's computer communications.

OSI. *See* Open System Interconnection.

P

Packet. *See* Data packet.

Packet switching. The routing and transmission of packets of data across a network, based on origin/destination address pairs contained within packets.

Parity bit. A bit added to the total number of bits, used in error checking at a character level.

Peer-to-peer communication. Sharing of resources on all computers contained within a network.

Peripheral device. An attached device on a computer system for mass storage or for data output, such as printing.

Phase modulation. Changing the phase of a signal for the purpose of transmitting digital data.

Point-to-point. Data-link supporting direct communication between two devices.

Polling. Process of querying stations on a multipoint line, one at a time, for pending messages or operational status.

Port. A point at which a device can be connected to a computer.

POTS (plain old telephone service). Describes traditional voice-only, dial-up telephone service.

Proprietary. Created under the impression that it will be used for only one specific purpose, with specific equipment.

Protocol. An agreement between parties on a format and sequence of control messages to be exchanged between the parties.

PSTN (Public Switched Telephone Network). Probably the largest network using circuit switching and has a total of 300 million telephone connections.

R

RAM (Random Access Memory). Data storage area that holds data only while the power is on.

Remote workstation. A computer used to dial into a LAN, but is not connected to that LAN on a full-time basis.

Repeater. A device that improves the signal as that signal moves through the device when traveling long distances on a network.

ROM (Read-Only Memory). Memory that has data stored in it before it was placed in the computer. In most circumstances, the data contents of ROM cannot be changed.

Router. A network node that ensures the delivery of a message from a station on one network to a station on another network based on the network on which the receiving device resides. The sending station includes the address of the receiving station. A router on the local network determines the best route to the receiving station. Routers are capable of interconnecting networks that utilize different topologies and protocols.

RS-232. Interface developed by EIA for communications between computers, printers, and modems.

S

Satellite microwave radio. Radio waves used in unbounded media transmission over very long distances via satellite.

SDLC (Synchronous Data-Link Control). IBM-defined link-control protocol that has the characteristics of being code-independent, transparent to the bit pattern being handled, and using a single format for the combination of data and control information.

Session. A temporary logical connection between two network addressable units.

Shielded twisted pair. Twisted pair cable surrounded by a special shielding, usually metallic or foil.

Signal splitting device. A device on the network that takes a signal and splits it to be sent to multiple destinations.

Simplex transmission. A channel that only allows for one direction transmission.

SNA (Systems Network Architecture). IBM network architecture.

Start bit. The bit added in async transmission that indicates the beginning character.

Station. A device connected to the network, typically a personal computer.

Stop bit. The bit added in async transmission that indicates the ending character.

Store-and-forward. Description of data communications applications in which messages are stored at an intermediate point until the receiver is ready to retrieve them or until a communication link to the receiver is available.

Synchronous transmission. A data transmission mode in which synchronization is established for an entire block of data.

Systems Network Architecture. *See* SNA.

T

T-connector. A piece of hardware used to connect coaxial cable to a network interface card on a linear bus topology.

Tariff. A set of regulations and rates set up for services provided by a common communications carrier.

TCP/IP (Transmission Control Protocol/Internet Protocol). A protocol introduced in the early 1970s by the U.S. Department of Defense for interconnection of DOD networks.

Terminator. A hardware device used for termination on both ends of a linear bus cable system.

Throughput. Productivity measurement for a network, computers, and their devices.

Time-sharing. The capability of multiple users to share computer resources from one common source.

Topology. The actual network configuration of all the network nodes and connectivity.

Transmission Control Protocol/Internet Protocol. *See* TCP/IP.

Transmit. The capability to send data or messages electronically.

Trunk. Multi-line circuit used to connect switching or distribution centers.

Twisted pair. Cable consisting of one or more parallel sets of two insulated wires twisted together.

U

Unbounded media. A communication path in which the signal is unconfined by a physical medium such as an electrical cable or an optical fiber.

V

Virtual machine. Having one computer work as if it were several computers.

Voice-grade. Switched or leased telephone circuit, capable of carrying analog signals, speech, and analog data.

Volt. A standard unit of electrical measurement.

W

WAN (Wide area network). A large network typically connecting multiple LANs and MANs together.

Watt. Standard unit measurement of power.

Wide area network. *See* WAN.

Workstation. A personal computer that has a network interface card and is connected to a network.

X

X.25. Standardized by CCITT, an interface between data terminal equipment (DTE) and data circuit-terminating equipment (DCE) for terminals that operate in the packet mode and are connected to public data networks by dedicated circuits.

Networking Acronyms Directory

A

AARP AppleTalk Address Resolution Protocol

ABM Asynchronous Balanced Mode

ACK Acknowledgment

ACSE Association Control Service Element

ADCCP Advanced Data Communication Control Procedures

ADMD Administration Management Domain

ADSP AppleTalk Datastream Protocol

AFI AppleTalk Filing Interface

AFP AppleTalk Filing Protocol

AM amplitude modulation

AMD Advanced Micro Devices

AMI alternate mark inversion

AMT address mapping table

ANSI American National Standards Institute

ANTC Advanced Networking Test Center

APPC Advanced Program-to-Program Communications

APPN Advanced Peer-to-Peer Networking

ARM Asynchronous Response Mode

ARP Address Resolution Protocol

ARPANET Advanced Research Projects Agency Network

ASCII American Standard Code for Information Interchange

ASE application service element

ASK amplitude shift keying

ASN.1 Abstract Syntax Notation One

ASP AppleTalk Session Protocol

ATA ARCnet Trade Association

ATM asynchronous transfer mode

ATP AppleTalk Transaction Protocol

AT&T American Telephone and Telegraph

AUI attachment universal interface

B

BB&N Bolt, Beranek & Newman

BER basic encoding rules

BOC Bell operating company

BSC bisync communication

BSD Berkeley Software Distribution

C

CA collision avoidance

CAM channel access method

CATV Community Access Television

CCITT Consultative Committee on International Telegraphy and Telephony

CD carrier detection

CD-ROM Compact Disc-Read-Only Memory

CICS Customer Information Control System

CLNP Connectionless Network Protocol

CLNS Connectionless Network Services

CMIP Common Management Information Protocol

CMIS Common Management Information Service

CMOS complementary metal oxide semiconductor

CMOT CMIP Over TCP/IP

CMS conversational monitor system

CO central office

CONS Connection Oriented Network Services

COS Corporation for Open Systems

CPU central processing unit

CR carriage return

CRC cyclic redundancy check

CRT cathode ray tube

CSMA/CA Carrier Sense Multiple Access/Collision Avoidance

CSMA/CD Carrier Sense Multiple Access/Collision Detection

CTS clear to send

D

DAP Data Access Protocol

DAS dynamically assigned sockets

dB decibel

DCE data circuit terminating equipment

DDCMP Digital Data Communication Message Protocol

DDN Defense Department Network

DDP Datagram Delivery Protocol

DEC Digital Equipment Corporation

DHA destination hardware address

DIB directory information base

DID destination identification

DIS Draft International Standards

DNA Digital Network Architecture

DoD Department of Defense

DOS disk operating system

DP draft proposal

DQDB distributed queue dual bus

DS directory services

DSA directory system alert

DSA destination software address

DSAP destination service access point

DSR data set ready

DTE data terminal equipment

DTR data transmit ready

DUA Directory User Agent

E

EBCDIC Extended Binary Coded Decimal Interchange Code

ED end delimiter

EIA Electronic Industries Association

ELAP EtherTalk Link Access Protocol

EMA Enterprise Management Architecture

EMI electromagnetic interference

ENQ enquiry

EOT end of transmission

ES end system

F

FBE free buffer enquiry

FCC Federal Communications Commission

FCS frame check sequence

FDDI Fiber Distribution Data Interface

FDM frequency division multiplexing

FEP front-end processor

FIN finish flag

FM frequency modulation

FRMR frame reject

FS frame status

FTAM File Transfer, Access, and Management

FTP File Transfer Protocol

G

GDS general data stream

Ghz gigahertz

GOSIP Government Open Systems Interconnection Profile

H

HDLC High-level Data-Link Control

HP Hewlett-Packard

Hz Hertz

I

I/O input/output

IAB Internet Activities Board

IBM International Business Machines

IC integrated circuit

ICMP Internet Control Message Protocol

IDG interdialog gap

IDP Internetwork Datagram Protocol

IEEE Institute of Electrical and Electronics Engineers

IFG interframe gap

IHL internet header length

ILD injection laser diode

IMS Information Management System

INTAP Interoperability Technology Association for Information Processing

IP Internet Protocol

IPL initial program load

IPX Internet Packet Exchange

IS intermediate system

ISDN Integrated Services Digital Network

ISN initial sequence number

ISO International Organization for Standardization

ISODE ISO Development Environment

ITI Industrial Technology Institute

ITT invitation to transmit

IWU intermediate working unit

K

kHz kilohertz

L

LAN local area network

LAP Link Access Protocol

LAPB Link Access Protocol—Balanced

LAPD Link Access Protocol—Digital

LAT Local Area Terminal

LATA Local Access and Transport Areas

LED light emitting diode

LLAP LocalTalk Link Access Protocol

LLC logical link control

LSL Link Support Layer

LU logical unit

M

MAC medium access control

MAN metropolitan area network

MAP Manufacturing Automation Protocol

MAU medium attachment unit (or multi-station access unit)

MBps megabits per second

Mbps megabytes per second

MF more fragments

MHS Message Handling Service

Mhz megahertz

MIB management information base

MOP Maintenance Operation Protocol

MOTIS Message-Oriented Text Interchange Systems

MS-DOS Microsoft disk operating system

MSAU multi-station access unit

MSG message

MTA Message Transfer Agent

MTS Message Transfer System

MUX multiplexer

MVS multiple virtual storage

N

NAK negative acknowledgment

NAUN nearest active upstream neighbor

NBP Name Binding Protocol

NBS National Bureau of Standards

NCP Network Control Program

NCP NetWare Core Protocol

NCR National Cash Register

NetBIOS Network Basic Input/Output System

NFS Network File System

NIC network interface card

NID next identifier

NIST National Institute of Standards and Technology

NLM NetWare Loadable Module

NRM normal response mode

NRZ non-return to zero

NRZ-I non-return to zero-inverted

NRZ-L non-return to zero-level

NSF National Science Foundation

NVE network visible entry

NVTS network virtual terminal service

O

ODI Open Data-Link Interface

ONC Open Network Computing

OS/2 Operating System/2

OSI Open Systems Interconnection

P

P/F poll/final bit

PAC packet

PAD Packet Assembler/Disassembler

PAP Printer Access Protocol

PARC Palo Alto Research Center

PC personal computer

PCSA Personal Computer System Architecture (DEC)

PDN public data network

PDU protocol data unit

PEP Packet Exchange Protocol

PLP Packet Level Protocol

PLU primary logical unit

POP point of presence

POTS plain old telephone service

PRMD private management domains

PSH push flag

PSK phrase shift keying

PSTN Public Switched Telephone Network

PTT Postal Telephone and Telegraph

PU physical unit

PUC public utilities company

R

RAM Random Access Memory

RBHC Regional Bell Holding Company

RD receive data

REJ reject

RFC request for comment

RIP Routing Information Protocol

RJE remote job entry

RNR receiver not ready

ROM Read-Only Memory

ROSE remote operation service element

RPC remote procedure call

RPL remote procedure load

RR receiver ready

RS recommended standard

RST reset flag

RTMP Routing Table Maintenance Protocol

RTS request to send

RTSE reliable transfer service element

RZ return to zero

S

SAP Service Advertising Protocol

SAP service access point

SAS statistically assigned sockets

SD start delimiter

SDLC Synchronous Data-Link Control

SFD start of frame delimiter

SID source identifier

SIP service identification packet

SLU secondary logical unit

SMC Standard Microsystems Corporation

SMDS switched multimegabit data service

SMT station management

SMTP Simple Mail Transfer Protocol

SNA Systems Network Architecture

SNADS Systems Network Architecture Distributed Services

SNAP Subnetwork Access Protocol

SNMP Simple Network Management Protocol

SOH start of header

SONET synchronous optical network

SPP Sequenced Packet Protocol

SPX Sequenced Packet Exchange

SQE signal quality error

SQL structured query language

SRI Stanford Research Institute

SSAP source service access point

SSCP system services control point

STP shielded twisted pair

SYN synchronize flag

T

TCP Transmission Control Protocol

TCP/IP Transmission Control Protocol/Internet Protocol

TD transmit data

TDM time division multiplexing

TFTP Trivial File Transfer Protocol

TLAP Token Ring Link Access Protocol

TLI Transport Layer Interface

TOS type of service

TP twisted pair

TPDU transport protocol data unit

TP0 (1,2,3,4) Transport Protocol 0 (1,2,3,4)

TSO Time-Sharing Option

TTL time to live

TTS Transaction Tracking System

TTY teletype

U

UDP User Datagram Protocol

UHF ultra-high frequency

UI unnumbered information

ULP upper-layer protocol

URG urgent flag

UTP unshielded twisted pair

V

VAP Value Added Process

VAX Virtual Access Extended

VHF very high frequency

VM virtual machine

VMS virtual memory system

VSE virtual storage extended

VT virtual terminal

VTAM Virtual Telecommunications Access Method

W

WAN wide area network

WD working document

X

XDR external data representation

XNS Xerox Network System

XO exactly once

Z

ZIP Zone Information Protocol

ZIT Zone Information Table

Installing NetWare 4.01

APPENDIX C

The purpose of this workshop is to provide hands-on installation and configuration experience to students who have already become familiar with NetWare 4.0 through course 526, *NetWare 3.11 to 4.0 Update*, or course 525, *NetWare 4.0 Advanced Administration*. The course outline for the *NetWare 4.0 Installation and Configuration Workshop* is as follows:

I.   Installing the Server

II.   Installing the DOS and Windows Client

III. Using NOS Object Naming

IV.   Installing the Server Using Maintenance Options

V.   Managing Directory Services Objects

VI.   Managing NOS Security

VII. Managing Print Services

VIII. Backing Up and Restoring Data

IX.   Managing the NetWare 4.0 Server

X.   Migrating to NetWare 4.0

XI.   Case Study: Installing, Partitioning, and Replicating

The background required for *NetWare 4.0 Installation and Configuration Workshop* is too extensive to be included in this book. The courses mentioned here are covered in the following books in NRP's *NetWare Training Guide* series:

NetWare 4 Update, ISBN 1-56205-285-3

NetWare 4 Administration, ISBN 1-56205-240-3

This appendix will supplement those two books with information about installing NetWare 4. To successfully prepare for the test you will need to complete either the Update or the Advanced Administration course and obtain hands-on experience at installing and administering NetWare 4.

Due to the requirement for hands-on experience, you will probably want to attend a workshop at an NAEC unless you have access to sufficient hardware and software to complete all of the tasks. The partitioning and replicating tasks require access to two NetWare 4 servers and two NetWare 4 software licenses.

Background

NetWare 4.*x* shares the NLM architecture with NetWare 3.*x* and can be considered the next step in the evolution of the NetWare 3.*x* product. NetWare 4.*x* and 3.*x* servers are installed and managed in much the same way. However, NetWare 4 is a vastly more advanced operating system than NetWare 3.*x*, largely due to the NetWare Directory Service (NDS) that is the key tool for managing multiserver networks with NetWare 4.

A complete description of NetWare Directory Services is beyond the scope of this book. If you are interested in managing NetWare 4, you will want to consult a companion to this volume, *NetWare 4 Administration*, also a volume in NRP's NetWare Training Guide series.

Although a complete discussion of NDS cannot appear here, you need to understand some definitions and concepts that relate to information you must specify during the NetWare 4 installation process. After examining those definitions and concepts, you will be taken through a typical NetWare 4 installation procedure.

NDS Basic Concepts

NetWare Directory Services are based on the concept of a directory tree that organizes the information about all of the resources in a NetWare 4 network. NDS Directories can grow to be quite extensive, and only a simple example will be presented here.

Figure C.1 shows a simple NDS tree as it is typically presented. Each tree branch and each intersection contains information about an item on the network, which may be a physical item such as a server, a user, or a logical item such as an organization. Each of these items is called an object.

In figure C.1, you can see the symbols for several object types:

- The *Root object* identifies the topmost object in the tree.

- *Organization objects* (abbreviated as O) represent the second tier of objects. One O object named Widgets appears in this tree.

- *Organization Unit objects* (abbreviated as OU) represent subdivisions of Organization objects. Two OU objects appear in this tree: Engineering and Marketing.

- *Server objects* are examples of leaf objects, which are identified by their common names, or the abbreviation CN. One server object represents each NetWare 4 server in the directory tree.

- *User objects* are also leaf objects and are labeled with the abbreviation CN. There is one user object for each user that is registered in NDS. One user object appears in this tree, named Admin.

Figure C.1

Objects in a simple
NetWare Directory
Services tree.

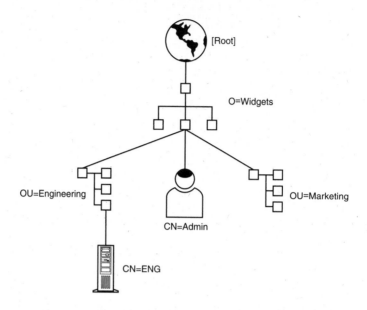

There are two distinct categories of objects. Container objects can contain other objects and appear at the intersections of branches. The Root object, Organization objects, and Organization Unit objects are the three types of container objects you are most likely to use. (You may also encounter a Country object, but it is not essential and is used infrequently.) Container objects resemble the directories and subdirectories in a file system; they contain files or other directories but don't contain data themselves.

All other objects are classified as leaf objects, which appear at the ends of the tree branches. There are many types of leaf objects. Some common examples are Server, User, Group, and Printer. All leaf objects have a common name often tagged with the label CN. The common name for the server in the diagram is ENG.

Each object in the NDS tree has a name that defines its position in the tree. These names work much like a complete file specification in DOS, which names the file and the complete list of directories that are found between the file and the root directory. There are shortcuts for names, but this chapter examines only the complete name, called the distinguished name. In figure C.1, the distinguished name for the MFG server is CN=MFG.OU=Manufacturing.O= Widgets. The Root object is implied but not stated.

The distinguished name of Admin is shorter:
CN=Admin.O= Widgets.

A distinguished name will contain exactly one CN and one O. Any number of OUs can appear, however. NDS trees can grow to contain quite a few layers by nesting OUs within OUs.

Assuming that the rightmost object in an object's distinguished name is an O object, it is possible to leave out the CN, OU, and O designations. The server's name can be expressed as MFG.Manufacturing.Widgets, for example.

Each object in an NDS tree has a context that defines its position in the tree. The context for the server MFG is Manufacturing.Widgets. The context for Admin is Widgets.

Object names are subject to the same rules:

- Each object within a given container at a given level must be uniquely named. This is similar to the requirement that each file in a DOS directory must have a unique name within the directory.

- They are case-insensitive. Widgets is treated as the same object name as WIDGETS, widgets, or wiDgETs.

- Only leaf objects can be renamed.

- Object names can be up to 64 characters in length, although they should be kept much shorter for practical purposes. Remember, you will be typing these names often and they should be easy to remember and enter.

- Object names can contain alphanumeric characters, spaces, dashes, underscores, and parentheses.

- Object names can contain spaces. However, this may not be a good idea because many commands will require you to place quotes around object names containing spaces. Under-scores are safer.

- Object names cannot contain brackets, percent signs, or periods (unless the periods are preceded by a \ character).

When you install a NetWare 4 server, you will need to specify several bits of information that define the NDS tree that will be used to manage the server. You need to specify the following:

♦ The name of the directory tree. Several directory trees can be present on the same internetwork, and each tree must be identified by a unique name. The directory tree in this installation example is named Widgets.

♦ The name of the first Organization object that will be added to the tree. This first O object becomes the context for the Admin user object that is created during installation. The Organization object used in this example is named Widgets.

♦ The names of any Organization Unit objects that define the context in which the server will be installed. In this installation example, the server will be installed in an Organization Unit object named Engineering.

♦ The name of the server you will install. This will become the common name of the server's Server object in the NDS tree. As with all object names, server names can be 42 characters long, but eight characters should be the upper limit and five is a good idea. You will be typing the server name quite often as an administrator.

♦ An internal network number for the server, which can have up to eight hexadecimal digits. This number must be different from every other internal server number or network number on the internetwork. Ideally, your network planning should establish conventions for assigning internal server numbers and network numbers on your network.

Proper initial design of the NDS tree is essential. When additional NetWare 4 servers are created for the organization, they will be installed in some context within the NDS tree that was created when the first NetWare 4 server was installed on the network.

NDS tree design is complex and trees can be difficult or impossible to modify once created. It is entirely possible to design an NDS tree hastily that will not meet the future needs of your organization. Before you install the first NetWare server, plan the future of your NDS trees as thoroughly as possible. See the Introduction for a listing of New Riders Publishing books that address the details of NDS tree design.

As mentioned, it is not the place of this chapter to tell you everything you need to know about designing NDS trees. However, this information should be sufficient to enable you to install NetWare 4 once the NDS tree has been designed for your organization.

Preparing Server Hardware

NetWare 4.01 installs on the same server hardware as NetWare 3.1x, and the server hardware discussion in Chapter 15 applies to NetWare 4.01 as well. The first NetWare 4.01 server you install will be known as the root server and will bear the greatest burden in managing the NDS directory. Therefore, this server should be at least a 25-MHz Intel 80486 computer.

NetWare 4.01 requires substantial disk space. Plan on allocating at least 55MB to the NetWare system files and the DOS boot directory. Another 30MB will be required to install the ElectroText online documents.

Like NetWare 3.12, NetWare 4.01 includes large numbers of drivers for network cards and disk drives, far more than were provided with NetWare 3.11. Chances are excellent that your hardware will be supported by driver files that shipped with your copy of NetWare 4.01. However, if your hardware is not supported, most vendors provide appropriate drivers.

Memory Requirements

Calculating memory requirements for NetWare 4.01 is more involved than for NetWare 3.*x* because NetWare 4.01 incorporates a feature called block suballocation and also supports file compression.

If the block suballocation feature is enabled for a volume, NetWare allocates file storage in 512-byte units, regardless of the block size that is defined for the volume. Block suballocation utilizes hard drive space more efficiently but requires more server RAM. File compression reduces the size of less frequently used files and requires 250KB of RAM per volume being compressed.

The following items must be added to determine the total memory requirements for a NetWare 4.01 server:

1. The base memory requirement for NetWare 4.01 is 5MB.

2. The memory required to support cache memory can be estimated using this formula:

   1MB + (total megabytes of disk space × 5KB)

3. The Media Manager requires memory that can be determined from this formula:

   150KB + (total megabytes of disk space × 0.2KB)

4. Each active user connection requires 2KB.

5. Each packet receive buffer requires 2.3KB.

6. Each directory cache buffer requires 4.3KB.

7. Each service process requires 9KB.

8. Each volume for which file compression is enabled requires 250KB.

9. 8.2 bytes per volume block is required to support the file allocation tables (FATs). Calculate the number of blocks by dividing the volume size by the block size for each volume.

10. Directory Entry tables require 10 bytes per file. Estimate the number of files that will be stored on the server by dividing the volume size by the average file size.

11. Calculate the memory in bytes for block suballocation using the following formula:

$$\frac{((\text{blocksize in } K \times 2)\text{-}1) \times 4096}{5 \times \text{number of files}}$$

12. Sum up the memory requirements for any particularly large NLMs you will be using. The following are some example memory requirements:

    BTRIEVE.NLM   700KB

    CLIB.NLM   500KB

    PSERVER.NLM   200KB

    INSTALL.NLM   600KB

As an exercise, determine the minimum memory required for a server with the following specifications:

◆ 100 users

◆ 1GB (gigabyte) disk space

◆ Average file size of 25KB

◆ 200MB SYS: volume has block suballocation enabled but does not use file compression and has a 16KB block size

◆ 800M DATA1: volume has block suballocation and file compression enabled and has a 32KB block size

◆ 50 packet receive buffers

◆ 50 directory cache buffers

◆ 10 service processes

◆ CLIB and INSTALL NLMs will be used

Try the calculations yourself first. Then check your answer against the following:

Operating System	5.0MB	
Cache memory	6.0MB	= 1MB + (1,000 × 5K)
		= 1MB + 5MB

Media Manager	.35MB	$= 150KB + (1,000 \times 0.2KB)$
		$= 150KB + 200KB$
Connections	.2MB	$= 2KB \times 100$
Packet receive buffers	.115MB	$= 2.3KB \times 50$
Directory cache buffers	.215MB	$= 4.3KB \times 50$
Server processes	.090MB	$= 9KB \times 10$
File compression on DATA1	.250MB	
FAT table for SYS:	.1MB	$= 8.2 \text{ bytes} \times (200MB, 16KB)$
FAT table for DATA1:	.2MB	$= 8.2 \text{ bytes} \times (800MB, 32KB)$
Block suballocation store 8,000 25KB files for SYS:	.17MB	$= (((16 \times 2)\text{-}1) \times 4096) + (5 \times 8000)$ 200KB can
Block suballocation for DATA1:	.42MB	$= ((32 \times 2)\text{-}1) \times 4096) + (5 \times 32,000)$
Directory Entry tables	.4MB	$= 10 \times 40,000$
NLMs	1.1MB	$= 500KB + 600KB$

The sum of these calculations is 14.61, indicating that at least 16MB of memory should be installed in the server. Always round up to at least the next 4MB interval, although adding memory in 16MB or even 32MB increments may make better financial sense. A server motherboard has a limited number of SIMM sockets.

Configuring a CD-ROM Drive for Installation

The next example demonstrates the installation of NetWare 4.01 from a CD-ROM. In addition to the basic hardware setup discussed earlier, you need to configure a SCSI controller card and a CD-ROM drive in your server.

If you are using a SCSI disk subsystem, you need to have a separate SCSI controller for your CD-ROM drive. NetWare installation accesses the CD-ROM drive by way of DOS and the CD-ROM drivers that are installed by DOS. However, NetWare uses its own SCSI drivers to support a SCSI disk subsystem. If you try a CD-ROM installation using a single SCSI controller, your system will hang when you load the NetWare SCSI card drivers.

This happens because both the DOS SCSI/CD-ROM drivers and the NetWare server SCSI drivers are attempting to control the same SCSI card. If you will be leaving the CD-ROM reader attached to the server, you will want to retain the second SCSI card in the server so that use of the CD-ROM does not reduce performance of your hard drive subsystem. If the CD-ROM reader will be removed after installation, the second SCSI card can be removed as well.

As just mentioned, the installation program reads programs from the CD-ROM by using the SCSI and CD-ROM drivers installed for DOS. You need to add the required driver files to your boot drive, and you need to modify CONFIG.SYS and AUTOEXEC.BAT to run the drivers. Most SCSI cards include setup programs that install the drivers and configure the CONFIG.SYS and AUTOEXEC.BAT FILES.

The CONFIG.SYS file usually will run two drivers: one for the SCSI card and one for the CD-ROM. These drivers are specific for each brand of SCSI controller. The following are the lines that are required for an Adaptec 1542 SCSI adapter (the parameters will vary depending on the installation):

```
DEVICE=C:\ADAPTEC\ASPI4DOS.SYS /D
DEVICE=C:\ADAPTEC\ASPICD.SYS /D:ASPICD0
```

A DOS CD-ROM routine also is required. Usually, this means using the MSCDEX program that is licensed by Microsoft. Here is the AUTOEXEC.BAT command that runs MSCDEX:

```
C:\DOS\MSCDEX.EXE /D:ASPICD0 /M:12 /S
```

Before you can proceed with a CD-ROM installation, configure the CD-ROM hardware and install the required drivers and commands in your server's DOS partition. Consult the documentation for your SCSI card and CD-ROM drive for the proper commands and syntax to use. If your equipment includes an automatic setup program, it usually simplifies driver installation.

After the drivers are configured, boot the server and see if you can access your CD-ROM drive. If you can, you are ready to continue with installation.

Creating the DOS Boot Partition

Although you can obtain a full DOS license for your server, the DOS partition can be created using only the LICENSE disk that is included with NetWare 4.01. LICENSE is a bootable DR DOS disk and contains the FORMAT and FDISK utilities in a \DOSTOOLS directory. An EDITOR program is also provided to enable you to configure CONFIG.SYS and AUTOEXEC.BAT files.

Whichever version of DOS you select, use FDISK to create a primary DOS partition on the first physical hard drive. The partition should be at least 5MB in size. A larger partition can accommodate tools such as CHECKIT PRO for diagnosing server hardware problems. After creating the DOS partition, make the partition active.

Reboot the server with a DOS disk or the LICENSE disk. Then use the FORMAT /S command to format the DOS partition and install the DOS boot system files on the drive.

Do not install any high-memory or extended-memory managers in the DOS partition. The NetWare server must control all upper memory in the server and will conflict with DOS memory managers.

The example installation in this chapter will install NetWare 4.01 from a CD-ROM. This is the most efficient way to install NetWare and the only way if you want to install the ElectroText on-line documentation.

Beginning Server Installation

If you have configured your system properly, your CD-ROM drive will be available as a DOS drive, often as drive D:. Insert the NetWare 4.01 CD-ROM in the drive and change to the drive letter that accesses your CD-ROM drive.

1. Run the INSTALL program.

The directory you install from depends on the language you want NetWare to use in displays. NetWare 4.01 includes language support for English, French, German, Spanish, and Italian.

For English, CD to the \NETWARE.40\ENGLISH directory. For other languages substitute FRANCAIS, DEUTSCH, ESPANOL, or ITALIANO for ENGLISH.

In the appropriate language directory, enter the command **INSTALL**. Soon, the installation utility screen in figure C.2 will be displayed.

As with all screens seen in the installation process, this screen shows a list of active keys at the bottom of the screen. You will find that several keys are used to move from one screen to the next, and these key lists will be extremely helpful. Also note that F1 will display help for this screen. A help option is available for each installation screen.

From the Installation option screen select the option Install new NetWare 4.*x* to proceed with the installation.

2. Verify the DOS partition.

The screen in figure C.3 displays the existing disk partitions on C:. This screen can be used to reconfigure the DOS partition. However, you have already created a bootable DOS partition, and you should choose the option Retain current disk partitions.

Figure C.2

Selecting an Installation option.

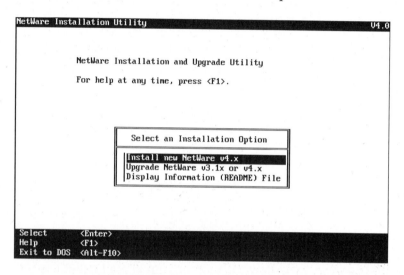

Figure C.3

Configuring disk partitions in INSTALL.

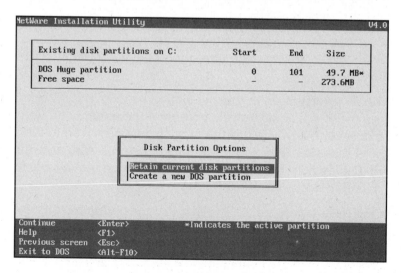

Practical TIP

Most screens in INSTALL enable you to back up to previous steps by pressing the Esc key. If you make a mistake, you can usually cancel the mistake by escaping to the previous step.

3. Name the server.

With your DOS position created, you are ready to proceed with the actual installation of server files. The screen in figure C.4 instructs you to enter a server name. This name should have been determined beforehand as part of your planning process.

```
NetWare Installation Utility                                      V4.0

   Name the new server

              Enter a unique name for this NetWare server. For guidelines, press
              <F1>.

              (Example: MY_SERVER)

              Press <Enter> to continue.




                        ┌───────────────────────────────────────────┐
                        │           Enter Server Name:              │
                        ├───────────────────────────────────────────┤
                        │Server name: ENG                           │
                        └───────────────────────────────────────────┘


 Continue          <Enter>
 Help              <F1>
 Previous screen   <Esc>
 Exit to DOS       <Alt-F10>
```

Figure C.4

Entering the server name.

With NetWare 3.*x*, you can change server names fairly freely. When you install a server in NetWare 4.01, however, its name will appear in several places in the NDS tree, and changing the name can be quite involved. For example, each volume on the server will be represented by a Volume object that incorporates the server name in its object name. Just as it was important to plan your Directory tree carefully, it is important to plan your server names carefully.

Type the server's name in the Server name field and press Enter to continue.

1145

4. Specify an internal network number.

The next screen, shown in figure C.5, requests an internal network number. The figure displays the randomly generated number that was provided by INSTALL. Ideally, you should be selecting a number based on a network management plan, and this number should have been determined as part of your network planning process. You can delete the number provided by INSTALL and enter one of your own. For this example installation, an internal network number of 2BAD was selected. This number will appear later when the AUTOEXEC.NCF file is created. Press Enter to accept the internal network number that is displayed.

Figure C.5

Entering the server internal network number.

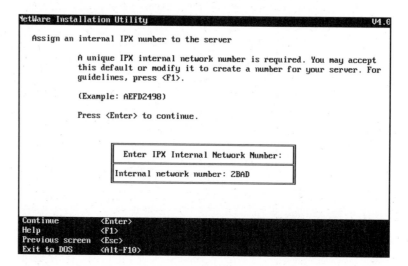

5. Specify the installation directory.

Next you must specify the directory from which the server boot files are to be installed. As shown in figure C.6, INSTALL will select a default Source path that is directed at your CD-ROM drive. A directory named _____ has been selected in the subdirectory level below the language directory you chose to begin installation. There should be no need to change the Source path.

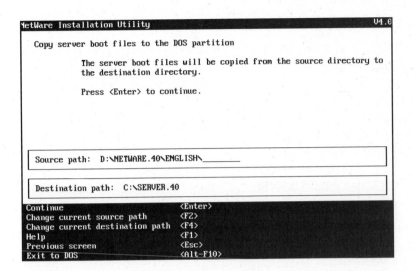

Figure C.6

Selecting the boot file source and destination.

In most cases, you will want to copy the boot files into a directory on C:. The default subdirectory is named \NETWARE.40. Usually, you will want to verify both defaults by pressing Enter. INSTALL will proceed to copy the boot files, monitoring the progress with the screen shown in figure C.7.

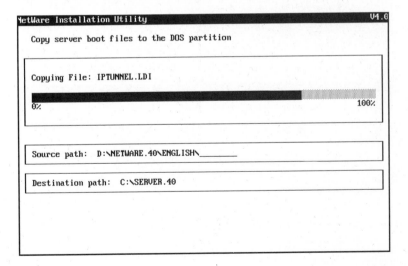

Figure C.7

Monitoring installation of the server boot files.

6. Customize the locale settings.

The screen in figure C.8 enables you to customize three locale settings of your NetWare 4.0 installation. These values are derived from your current DOS configuration. The Country Code is a three-digit number that can be determined from your DOS manual. If you select this field and press Enter, the submenu in figure C.9 will be displayed, from which you can select one of the alternative country codes.

Figure C.8

Options for customizing locale settings.

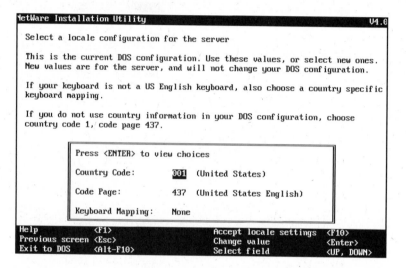

Figure C.9

The menu of available country codes.

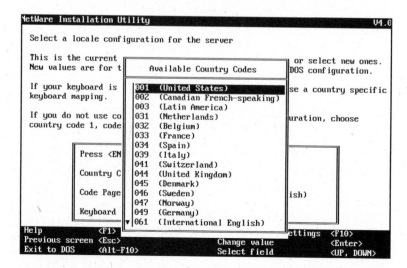

Code pages determine the character sets that can be displayed. Code page 437 is used for United States English. (Code page 437 is also known as the hardware code page because it corresponds to the display and keyboard defaults of IBM-compatible PCs.) NetWare 4.01 also supports the Multilingual code page 850, which displays international characters. You can display a menu of code pages, shown in figure C.10, by highlighting the Code Page field and pressing Enter.

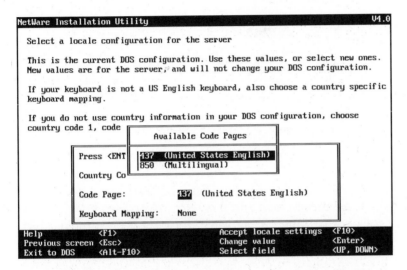

Figure C.10
The menu of available code pages.

Alternative keyboard mappings enable you to customize the console keyboard for conventions of different countries. A menu of keyboard maps, shown in figure C.11, can be displayed by highlighting the field and pressing Enter. After selecting the desired locale settings, press F10 to continue.

 Note When using INSTALL, Enter is used to continue making a menu selection; F10 continues after filling in forms.

Figure C.11

The menu of available keyboard mappings.

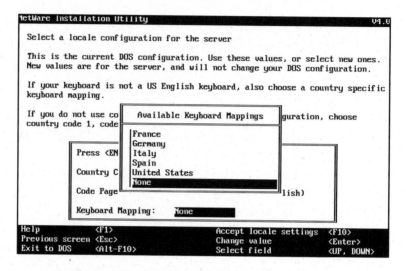

7. Select the file format.

NetWare 4.01 can support two file name formats, and you must select one from the screen in figure C.12. The recommended format obeys DOS file name restrictions. The DOS file name format is case-insensitive and converts lowercase characters to uppercase for storage. DOS format does not permit the use of many characters from the extended character set.

Figure C.12

Selecting the file server file name format.

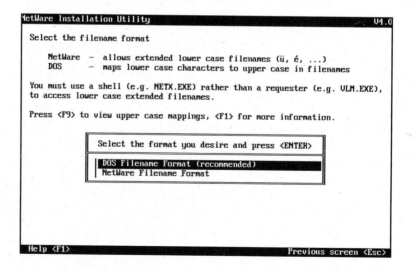

The NetWare file name format permits file names to contain upper- and lowercase characters as well as graphic and other extended characters. The NETX shell program supports the NetWare file name format. However, the NETX shell cannot be used to access the NetWare Directory Services of NetWare 4.01.

The VLM Requester that is required for NDS is restricted to using file names that obey DOS file name restrictions. If files are created that use the extended characters permitted by the NetWare file name format, you will not be able to access these files from clients that use the VLM Requester. Therefore, you will want to select DOS file name format from this screen.

8. Specify commands to be added to STARTUP.NCF.

Two files contain configuration information that is used when a NetWare server is started. A file named STARTUP.NCF is stored on the server boot drive and contains commands that are executed as the server is started. A file named AUTOEXEC.NCF is stored in the \SYSTEM directory and contains commands that are executed after the server is running, much as AUTOEXEC.BAT contains commands that are run after DOS is started.

INSTALL now displays the screen in figure C.13, giving you an option of entering commands that are to be added to the STARTUP.NCF file. You can easily add these commands in the future, and descriptions of the commands you might enter are beyond the scope of an installation tutorial. For this example, therefore, select the No response.

Figure C.13

Choosing whether to enter startup commands.

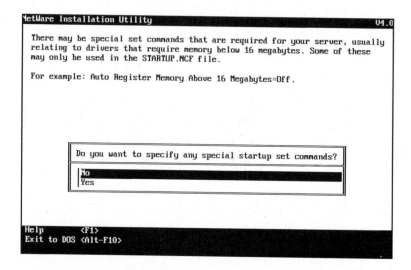

Figure C.13

Choosing whether to enter startup commands.

9. Specify whether AUTOEXEC.BAT should start the server.

Ordinarily, you will want your server to start NetWare automatically when the server is rebooted. The screen in figure C.14 gives you the option of having AUTOEXEC.BAT customized with the commands that will start SERVER.EXE whenever DOS is booted. Usually, you select Yes on this screen.

Figure C.14

Choosing whether AUTOEXEC.BAT should be customized.

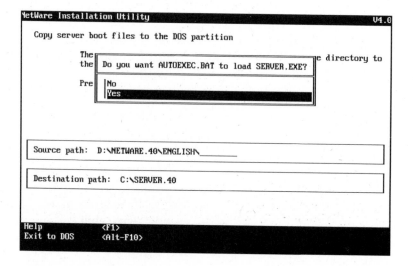

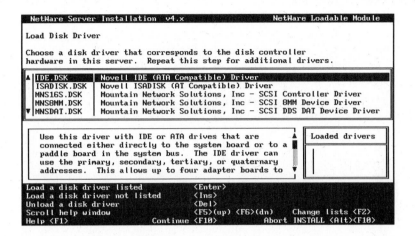

Figure C.16
Loading disk drivers.

INSTALL will attempt to load the disk driver with the parameters you specified. If successful, the screen shown in figure C.18 will confirm that the driver has been loaded. From this screen you may choose to load additional drivers or to continue to the next installation step.

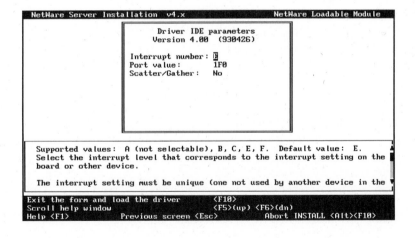

Figure C.17

Entering disk driver parameters.

Figure C.18

Loaded drivers are
displayed with a
continuation option.

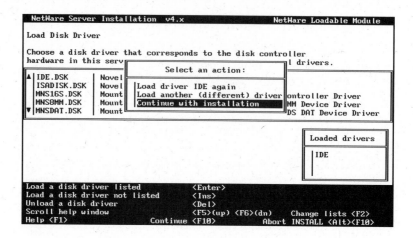

12. Create automatic or manual installation.

Now that a disk driver has been loaded, INSTALL can access the
hard drives and create NetWare partitions and volumes. The
screen in figure C.19 permits you to choose between automatic
and manual disk partitioning.

Figure C.19

Selecting automatic
or manual disk
partitioning.

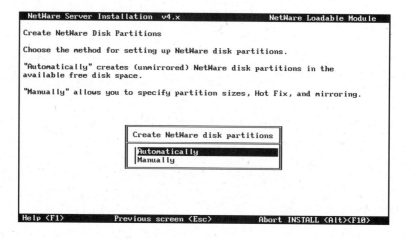

Automatic disk partitioning creates an unmirrored disk partition
on the first drive that occupies all disk space not taken up by the
DOS partition. It then proceeds to create a SYS: volume that fills
that partition.

Manual disk partitioning gives you control over each step of the process. The following steps will illustrate manual partitioning and volume creation. Select Manually to continue with the example.

13. Create partitions.

After you select manual partitioning, the screen in figure C.20 displays the partitions that are currently installed on the first hard drive. You will see specifications for the DOS partition that was created earlier. To create a NetWare partition, choose the option Create NetWare disk partition and press Enter.

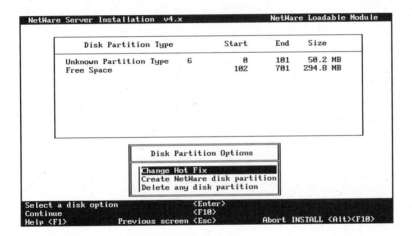

Figure C.20
Disk partition options.

The Disk Partition Information form shown in figure C.21 enables you to set the specifications for the partition you will create. The default values in this form assume that all remaining space on the disk will be set up as a NetWare partition. Only one NetWare partition can occupy a given hard drive, so you will usually want to select the defaults.

The Redirection Area value specifies the number of blocks that are to be set aside for Hot Fix redirection. The default is generally an appropriate choice, but you may choose to adjust this amount. Press Escape to accept the values that are displayed on this form. A confirmation menu will ask you, Create NetWare partition? Select Yes to create the partition or No to cancel.

Figure C.21

Setting NetWare disk partition information.

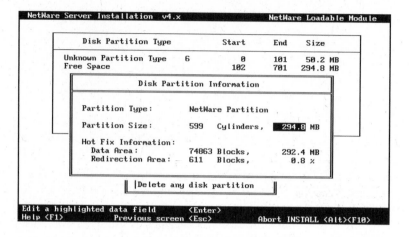

When you return to the Disk Partition Options screen, the new NetWare partition will be displayed along with the original DOS partition, as shown in figure C.22. Press F10 when all required partitions have been created.

Figure C.22

Confirmation of a NetWare partition creation.

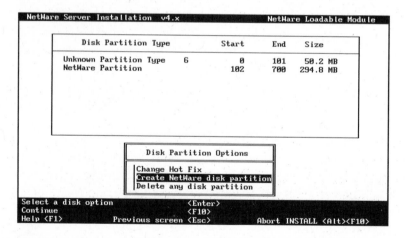

Note Some of the subforms in INSTALL do not provide a list of function keys. With these forms, you will enter the required information and press Esc to accept your entries.

14. Create volumes.

Before the partition can be used, it must be configured with one or more NetWare volumes. The first volume created on the first server hard drive will always be named SYS:. The names of additional volumes can be determined by the installation.

After F10 is pressed on the Disk Partitions Options screen, a message similar to figure C.23 confirms that INSTALL has automatically created a SYS: volume on the first disk drive (designated as Disk device 0). The SYS: volume has been assigned all of the free space in the partition on the disk. Press Enter after reading this message.

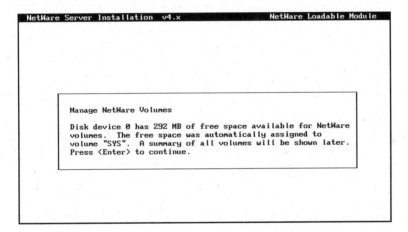

Figure C.23

INSTALL automatically creates the SYS: volume.

The screen of figure C.24 displays all of the currently created volumes. For a new installation, the only volume will be SYS:. In this exercise, the SYS: volume will be deleted and the partition space will be divided between two volumes named SYS: and DATA1:. Take a moment to examine the key options at the bottom of this screen.

Figure C.24

Volume information about the newly created SYS: volume.

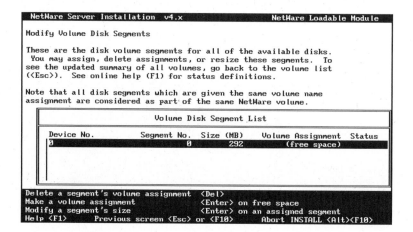

```
NetWare Server Installation  v4.x              NetWare Loadable Module

Manage NetWare Volumes

This is a summary of all proposed new volumes on this
server.  Rename or modify them as necessary.  The total
disk space occupied by the NetWare volumes is 292 MB.


        ┌──────────────────────────────────────────────────────┐
        │  Volume Name            Size (MB)                      │
        │ ┌──────────────────────────────────────────────────┐ │
        │ │ SYS                       292   (new system volume)│ │
        │ │                                                    │ │
        │ │                                                    │ │
        │ └──────────────────────────────────────────────────┘ │
        └──────────────────────────────────────────────────────┘

Save volume changes and continue      <F10>
View/Modify/Add volume segments        <F3> or <Ins>
Delete a volume                        <Del>
Modify volume parameters               <Enter>
Help <F1>            Previous screen <Esc>      Abort INSTALL <Alt><F10>
```

Highlight a volume and press Del to delete the volume. After deleting SYS:, press Ins to create a new volume.

The Modify Volume Disk Segments screen is used to create volumes and assign partition space to them (see fig. C.25). To create a volume, select one of the available segments that are displayed in the Volume Disk Segment List. Remember, SYS: must be the first volume on the first available drive, which is designated as Device No. 0.

Figure C.25

Selecting an available disk segment.

```
NetWare Server Installation  v4.x              NetWare Loadable Module

Modify Volume Disk Segments

These are the disk volume segments for all of the available disks.
 You may assign, delete assignments, or resize these segments.  To
see the updated summary of all volumes, go back to the volume list
(<Esc>).  See online help (F1) for status definitions.

Note that all disk segments which are given the same volume name
assignment are considered as part of the same NetWare volume.

 ┌────────────────────────────────────────────────────────────────┐
 │                Volume Disk Segment List                         │
 │ ┌────────────────────────────────────────────────────────────┐ │
 │ │ Device No.     Segment No.  Size (MB)  Volume Assignment  Status│
 │ │ 0                  0          292         (free space)     │ │
 │ │                                                            │ │
 │ └────────────────────────────────────────────────────────────┘ │
 └────────────────────────────────────────────────────────────────┘

Delete a segment's volume assignment <Del>
Make a volume assignment                <Enter> on free space
Modify a segment's size                 <Enter> on an assigned segment
Help <F1>        Previous screen <Esc> or <F10>    Abort INSTALL <Alt><F10>
```

Note NetWare hard drive partitions can be divided into segments that are assigned to volumes. The entire partition can be assigned to a single segment and a single volume, or a partition can be divided into a maximum of eight segments that can be assigned to one or more volumes.

A volume can consist of up to 32 segments from one or more hard drives. New segments can be added to volumes even when the volumes are mounted, enabling administrators to increase volume size "on the fly." Once a segment is assigned to a volume, it cannot be unassigned.

Creating volumes with segments on more than one hard drive significantly increases performance because both drives can be reading data simultaneously. The process of assigning segments from multiple drives to a volume is called "spanning."

When volumes are spanned, the risk of data loss due to disk failure increases. The failure of any disk supporting the volume will destroy all data in the volume. For this reason, Novell recommends that all spanned volumes be duplexed.

The disk segment parameters form enables you to specify a name and size for the volume to be created (see fig.C.26). Because this is the first volume, it must be named SYS:, and this entry cannot be changed. The disk segment size field contains a value that would allocate the entire segment to the SYS: volume. To allocate a smaller segment to SYS:, change the entry for this field to specify a segment size in megabytes. In this case, the size of SYS: will be set to 100MB. Press Esc to accept the values in the form.

1161

Figure C.26

Entering disk segment parameters.

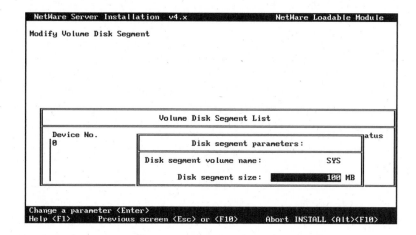

>
> **Note**
>
> For NetWare 4.01, the size of the SYS: volume must be at least 50MB. An additional 30MB are required if the ElectroText documentation will be installed.

As shown in figure C.27, the Volume Disk Segment List now indicates that SYS: occupies one segment and has a size of 150MB. The remaining free space will be assigned to a new volume. Highlight the line identified as free space and press Enter.

Figure C.27

The Volume Disk Segment List after SYS: has been created.

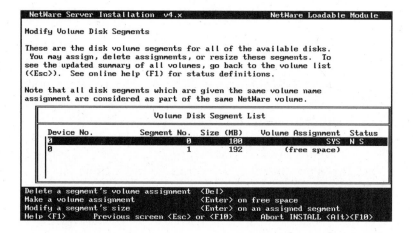

A menu now gives you two choices of what to do with the free space segment you have selected. You can Make this segment a new volume or Make this segment part of another volume. The second choice enables you to add new segments to an existing volume. However, the first choice will be chosen here to create a second volume. Highlight the choice Make this segment part of another volume and press Enter.

You can now enter the disk segment parameters for the new volume as shown in figure C.28. Because this is no longer the first volume, you can specify a different volume name. The default Disk segment size allocates the remaining space in the partition to the new volume. Enter a volume name and change the segment size if you want to allocate less than the entire segment. Then press Esc to accept the entries.

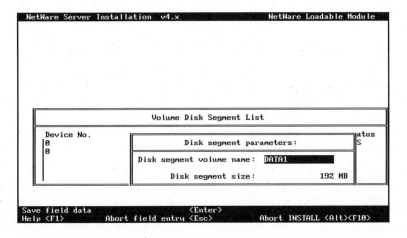

Figure C.28

Creating a second volume.

All NetWare volumes are configured with a block size, which can range from 2KB to 64KB. With older versions of NetWare, the block size was chosen as a compromise. If a server would store many small files, a small block size would be chosen to enhance efficient use of the hard drive space. If files would be large, a large block size memory met requirements for cache buffers.

NetWare 4.01 has a block suballocation feature that allocates disk storage in 512-byte units regardless of the block size that was defined for the volume. With NetWare 4.01, the choice of an appropriate block size for a volume is made primarily to reduce RAM requirements.

Novell recommends the following as default block sizes for various volume sizes:

Volume Size	Block Size
0 through 31MB	4KB
32 through 149MB	8KB
150 through 499MB	16KB
500 through 1999MB	32KB
2000+MB	64KB

All volumes created by the INSTALL program are configured with the following characteristics:

- Block size is set to the default recommended for the volume size
- Volume is MOUNTED
- Block suballocation is ON
- File compression is ON
- Data migration is OFF

Once a volume has been created, its block size cannot be altered. Once file compression is turned on for a volume, it cannot be turned off. If you want to create volumes that do not have these default characteristics, you need to leave the INSTALL program and use the INSTALL. NLM.

File compression greatly reduces the space required to store files, but it can degrade performance in some circumstances. If you have a large database file that is heavily used, however, it should not be compressed due to the time delay incurred when the file must be decompressed for use. You may want to use the IN- STALL. NLM to create a volume for such files with the file com- pression feature turned off.

The newly created volume will now appear in the Volume Disk Segment List, as shown in figure C.29. In this example, no free space remains in the segment list. The letters in the right columns describe the status of the volume. The status letters have the following meanings:

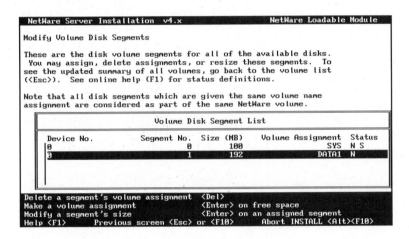

Figure C.29

The new volume in the Volume Disk Segment List.

E   Existing volume (previously created)

S   System volume (SYS)

M   Mirrored volume segment

N   Newly created volume

Newly created volumes are defined in memory but have not been created on disk. That will be accomplished in the next step. Press Esc or F10 to leave the Modify Volume Disk Segments screen.

The Manage NetWare Volumes screen summarizes the volumes that you have defined (see fig. C.30). They are still identified as "new," indicating that they have yet to be physically created on disk. These volume definitions could still be modified without having to delete them from disk. To create the volumes on disk, verify the volume names and sizes and press F10. You will be presented with the confirmation request Save volume changes?. Answer Yes to continue.

Figure C.30

The Manage NetWare Volumes screen with new volume definitions.

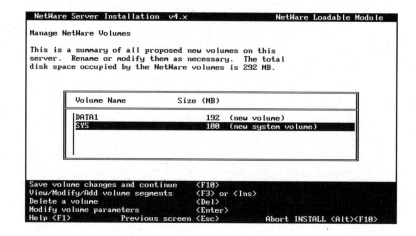

```
NetWare Server Installation  v4.x              NetWare Loadable Module

Manage NetWare Volumes

This is a summary of all proposed new volumes on this
server.  Rename or modify them as necessary.  The total
disk space occupied by the NetWare volumes is 292 MB.


     ┌──────────────────────────────────────────────────────┐
     │ Volume Name           Size (MB)                       │
     ├──────────────────────────────────────────────────────┤
     │ DATA1                   192   (new volume)            │
     │ SYS                     100   (new system volume)     │
     │                                                       │
     │                                                       │
     │                                                       │
     └──────────────────────────────────────────────────────┘

Save volume changes and continue    <F10>
View/Modify/Add volume segments      <F3> or <Ins>
Delete a volume                      <Del>
Modify volume parameters             <Enter>
Help <F1>            Previous screen <Esc>        Abort INSTALL <Alt><F10>
```

 Practical TIP

Here are some suggestions for creating volumes:

♦ Mirror or duplex disks that contain valuable data.

♦ Volume SYS: should be reserved for the system and public files. Create additional volumes for application and data files. (NetWare 3.*x* places all print queue files in subdirectories under the SYSTEM directory, requiring you to leave extra space on the SYS: volume to store queues. NetWare 4.01 can place print queue files on any volume. SYS: can, therefore, be held to a much smaller size than is possible with NetWare 3.*x*.)

♦ Span volumes when performance is most important. However, be aware that the risk of drive failure is doubled. Disk duplexing of spanned volumes is recommended.

♦ If your network will support files, such as Macintosh, that require long file names, create separate volumes for those files. The long file names require extra disk space that is not required for DOS.

◆ NetWare 4.01 supports an Auditor
function that enables an independent
auditor to monitor server operations.
Auditor accounts are set up by volume. If
you intend to have multiple auditors on
your network, create a separate volume
for each auditor.

15. Copy the license.

Now that volumes are created and on-line, INSTALL is prepared
to copy system and public files to the appropriate directories.
First, INSTALL copies the license information. If you have not
already inserted the license disk in the A: drive, INSTALL displays the message in figure C.31. Insert the license disk and press
Enter. After the license information has been successfully copied,
you will see a confirming message, `The Main Server License was
successfully installed`. Press Enter to continue.

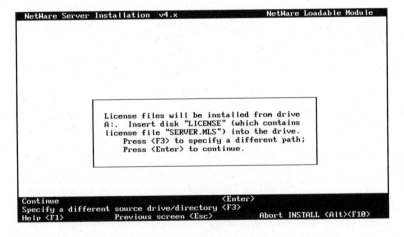

Figure C.31

INSTALL requests the
license disk.

16. Copy the system and public files.

INSTALL now displays the screen in figure C.32, which enables
you to specify a source directory for the files. If you are installing
files from another NetWare server, you can enter the drive letter
that is mapped to the file directory by pressing F3. In this example, files are being installed from CD-ROM, and INSTALL has
specified the correct path. Press Enter to confirm the path.

Figure C.32

Specifying the source directory for SYSTEM and PUBLIC files.

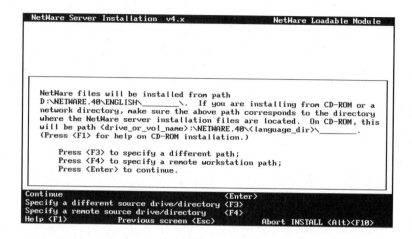

```
NetWare Server Installation  v4.x              NetWare Loadable Module


     NetWare files will be installed from path
     D:\NETWARE.40\ENGLISH_____\.  If you are installing from CD-ROM or a
     network directory, make sure the above path corresponds to the directory
     where the NetWare server installation files are located.  On CD-ROM, this
     will be path <drive_or_vol_name>:\NETWARE.40\<language_dir>_____.
     (Press <F1> for help on CD-ROM installation.)

        Press <F3> to specify a different path;
        Press <F4> to specify a remote workstation path;
        Press <Enter> to continue.

Continue                                        <Enter>
Specify a different source drive/directory <F3>
Specify a remote source drive/directory    <F4>
Help <F1>                   Previous screen <Esc>        Abort INSTALL <Alt><F10>
```

Figure C.33

Specifying NetWare files to be copied.

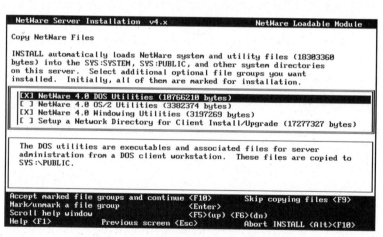

```
NetWare Server Installation  v4.x              NetWare Loadable Module
Copy NetWare Files

INSTALL automatically loads NetWare system and utility files (18303360
bytes) into the SYS:SYSTEM, SYS:PUBLIC, and other system directories
on this server.  Select additional optional file groups you want
installed.  Initially, all of them are marked for installation.

[X] NetWare 4.0 DOS Utilities (10766210 bytes)
[ ] NetWare 4.0 OS/2 Utilities (3382374 bytes)
[X] NetWare 4.0 Windowing Utilities (3197269 bytes)
[ ] Setup a Network Directory for Client Install/Upgrade (17277327 bytes)

The DOS utilities are executables and associated files for server
administration from a DOS client workstation.  These files are copied to
SYS:\PUBLIC.

Accept marked file groups and continue <F10>      Skip copying files <F9>
Mark/unmark a file group                <Enter>
Scroll help window                      <F5>(up) <F6>(dn)
Help <F1>                   Previous screen <Esc>        Abort INSTALL <Alt><F10>
```

The next screen enables you to specify which files will be copied (see fig. C.33). The SYSTEM files will always be copied, but all others are optional because the utilities may be available on another server in the network. You have a choice of the following:

◆ DOS utilities, the text-based command-line and menu utilities for use with DOS

◆ OS/2 utilities, including all utilites that are used under OS/2

◆ NetWare 4.0 Windows utilities, which you will certainly want to use if you will be administering the network from a DOS Windows workstation

◆ Client Installation and Upgrade files enabling you to upgrade client workstations with the NetWare 4 client server
by copying files from the server, a less tiresome process than
upgrading each client from disks

Press Enter to select (X) or deselect (no X) the options you want.
(DOS and Windows utilities are selected for copying in figure
C.33.) Then press F10 to continue.

INSTALL proceeds to copy files to the SYSTEM and PUBLIC
directories, displaying its progress as files are transferred (see fig.
C.34). When done, INSTALL displays the message File copying
was completed. Press the Enter key to continue.

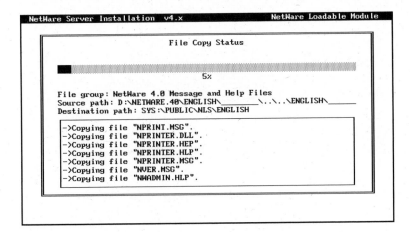

Figure C.34

Monitoring the
progress of server file
installation.

17. Install the LAN drivers.

For a few seconds, INSTALL displays the message Scanning for
available drivers. During this time, INSTALL is examining your
installation media for NIC drivers, which have the file name
extension of .LAN. When all drivers have been found, a menu will
be displayed, as shown in figure C.35.

Figure C.35

Menu for loading LAN
drivers.

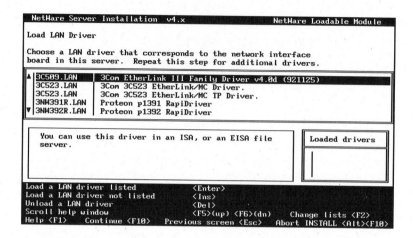

You can scroll through the list of drivers with the Up and Down
arrow keys. Find the driver for your NIC and press Enter. In this
case, a 3Com 3C509 driver was selected.

Every NIC will have certain configuration parameters, and a
driver parameters screen similar to figure C.36 will be presented
so that you may enter the settings of your board. In the example,
the server has an EISA bus and the 3C509 has been configured to
work in EISA mode. Therefore, the slot number is the only required parameter.

Figure C.36

Entering LAN driver
parameters.

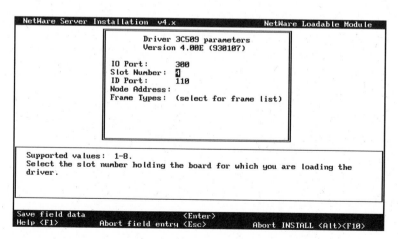

If your board type supports multiple frame types, you will want to review the frame types that can be configured for the board. Move the cursor to that field and press Enter. The board used is an Ethernet board, and figure C.37 shows that two frame types will be loaded for this board. Ethernet_802.2 is the standard Ethernet frame type for both NetWare 4.01 and 3.12, and Ethernet_802.3 is configured for backward compatibility with clients that are configured for older types of NetWare. Highlight an entry and press Enter to select (X) or deselect the entry (no X).

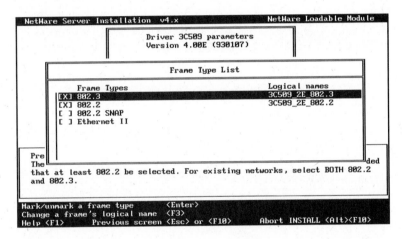

Figure C.37

Selecting Ethernet frame types.

INSTALL displays a message confirming that it is loading your LAN driver, followed by the message in figure C.38 that fully describes the drivers and protocols that were configured. Press Enter to leave this screen and to return to the Load LAN Driver screen. This time, as shown in figure C.39, the screen lists the driver you configured in the Loaded drivers list. You are presented with the choice of loading the same driver for a different network board, loading a different driver, or continuing with installation.

1171

Figure C.38

Binding IPX to LAN drivers.

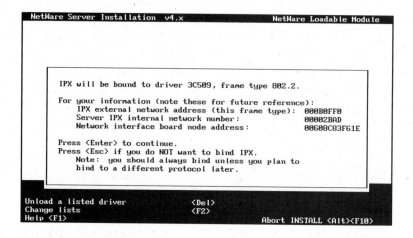

```
NetWare Server Installation  v4.x            NetWare Loadable Module

       IPX will be bound to driver 3C509, frame type 802.2.

       For your information (note these for future reference):
           IPX external network address (this frame type):  000B0FF0
           Server IPX internal network number:              00002BAD
           Network interface board node address:            00608C83F61E

       Press <Enter> to continue.
       Press <Esc> if you do NOT want to bind IPX.
           Note:  you should always bind unless you plan to
           bind to a different protocol later.



Unload a listed driver             <Del>
Change lists                       <F2>
Help <F1>                                        Abort INSTALL <Alt><F10>
```

Figure C.39

Loading additional LAN drivers.

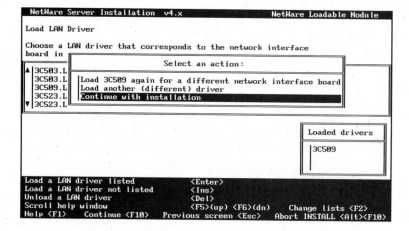

```
NetWare Server Installation  v4.x            NetWare Loadable Module
Load LAN Driver

Choose a LAN driver that corresponds to the network interface
board in
                        Select an action:
  ▲ 3C503.L
    3C503.L  Load 3C509 again for a different network interface board
    3C509.L  Load another (different) driver
    3C523.L  Continue with installation
  ▼ 3C523.L


                                           Loaded drivers

                                            3C509


Load a LAN driver listed           <Enter>
Load a LAN driver not listed       <Ins>
Unload a LAN driver                <Del>
Scroll help window                 <F5>(up) <F6>(dn)   Change lists <F2>
Help <F1>    Continue <F10>   Previous screen <Esc>  Abort INSTALL <Alt><F10>
```

Note If all of your network cards use the same driver file, NetWare is able to reuse the network driver program without loading a separate copy of the driver for each card. NetWare disk and LAN driver programs are "reentrant" programs, meaning that the program can be reused (reentered) several times. When you issue a command to load a driver that is already running, the driver is using *re-entrantly* to save memory.

18. Install the NetWare directory services.

NDS is a global database that contains information about all of the
NetWare 4.01 servers on the network. It is important, therefore,
that a new server be smoothly integrated into the network NDS
database if one already exists. After you have loaded LAN drivers
and the server can connect to the network, INSTALL displays the
message Examining network for Directory Service trees. If any NDS
trees are already installed, INSTALL will attempt to find them.

Assuming that this is the first NetWare 4.01 server on the network, INSTALL will display the screen in figure C.40. If other
NetWare 4.01 servers are installed on the network, do not proceed
with installation. You must determine why the server you are
installing is not communicating with the other servers. Either the
other servers are down, this server is improperly configured, or
there is a network failure. You must restore communication before
you proceed with installation. Because this is the first server on
the network, however, you can select the YES option.

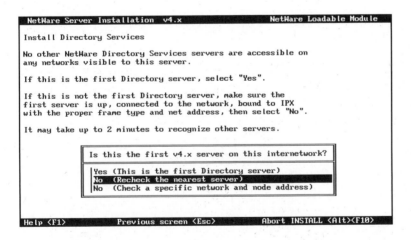

Figure C.40

Starting NDS
installation.

You will be creating a new NDS Directory tree, which must be
assigned a name using the screen in figure C.41.

Figure C.41

Entering a network directory tree name.

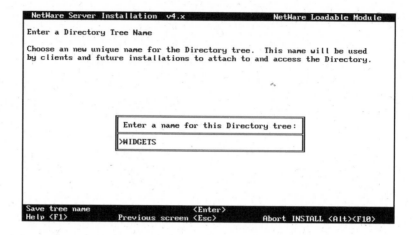

NDS uses an elaborate system of time servers to synchronize all of the copies of the NDS database that are on the network. To make this work, NDS must know the time zone for each server. From the screen of figure C.42, you will select a time zone, in this case, United States of America, Eastern Time.

Figure C.42

Selecting a time zone.

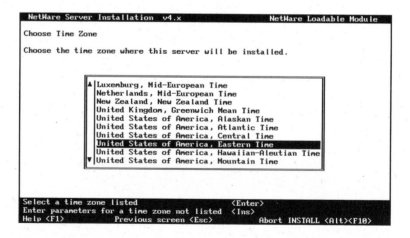

Then, in the form shown in figure C.43, you can customize the time information depending on whether and how your area observes daylight savings time. Press F10 to accept the information on this screen. INSTALL displays the prompt Save time configuration information?. Enter Yes to continue.

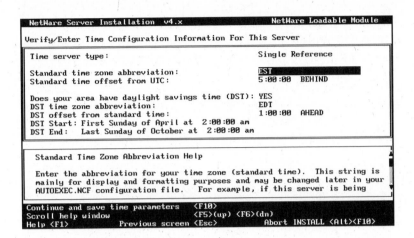

Figure C.43

Customizing time zone information.

Now you will use the screen in figure C.44 to enter the server context information for the Directory. You must enter at least one Company or Organization. You can specify three suborganizational units. Notice as you enter information that the Server Context and the Administrator Name fields are updated. You will also want to enter an Administrator password (which you will be asked to reenter to confirm your typing). Press Esc when you have entered all of the required information. INSTALL will display a message that it is Installing Directory Services. Another message will inform you that The number of volumes installed in the Directory is 2 (or another number determined by the volumes you have defined).

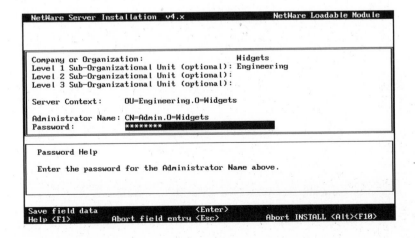

Figure C.44

Entering NDS Directory information.

After NDS has been installed, a message similar to figure C.45 will be shown. Copy this information down for future reference. You will need the complete name for the Admin user object when you log in as an administrator.

Figure C.45

NDS configuration information.

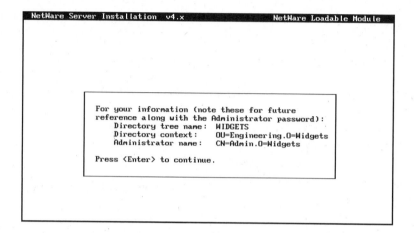

```
NetWare Server Installation  v4.x                    NetWare Loadable Module




                    For your information (note these for future
                    reference along with the Administrator password):
                         Directory tree name:  WIDGETS
                         Directory context:     OU=Engineering.O=Widgets
                         Administrator name:    CN=Admin.O=Widgets

                    Press <Enter> to continue.
```

19. Confirm the startup files.

Next, a display will present the STARTUP.NCF file that has been created by INSTALL (see fig.C.46). You can edit this file if required. Notice that this file contains the information required to load the disk driver that you configured during installation.

Figure C.46

Confirming the STARTUP.NCF file contents.

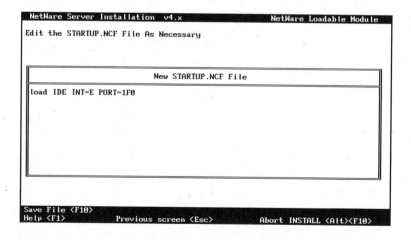

```
NetWare Server Installation  v4.x                    NetWare Loadable Module
Edit the STARTUP.NCF File As Necessary


                          New STARTUP.NCF File

load IDE INT=E PORT=1F0








Save File <F10>
Help <F1>           Previous screen <Esc>         Abort INSTALL <Alt><F10>
```

1176

As shown in figure C.47, you will also have the opportunity to confirm and modify the contents of the AUTOEXEC.NCF file. This file contains your time zone configuration, LAN driver startup commands, your server name, and various statements that configure the protocols on your network. You can edit AUTOEXEC.NCF to add other statements that you want to have executed after SERVER.EXE has started.

20. Install options.

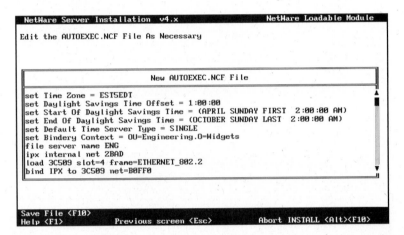

After you save the AUTOEXEC.NCF file, a menu gives you the option of installing several options (see fig. C.48). You will probably want to install the on-line documentation, so select this option and press Enter. The menu in figure C.49 enables you to select the language version or versions that will be installed. Press Enter to select (X) or deselect (no X) an option. A File Copy Status screen enables you to specify the destination for the files, which should probably be left to the default value of SYS:DOC unless there is insufficient space on the SYS volume. After you press Enter, the files will be copied.

Figure C.48

Selecting options to be installed.

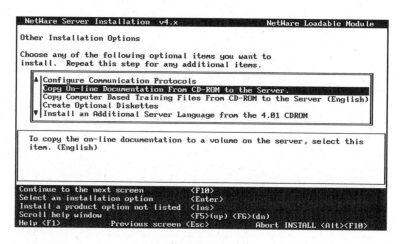

Figure C.49

Selecting on-line help language versions.

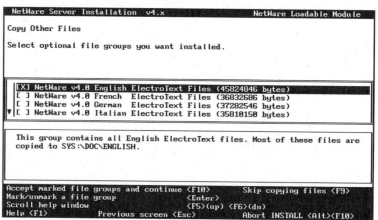

Another option you should be aware of in figure C.48 is Create Optional Diskettes. This option enables you to create the disks that are required to install the NetWare Requester on DOS and OS/2 clients. Scroll through the options in this screen to become familiar with them.

This completes installation of the first NetWare 4.01 server on the network.

21. Install a second server.

Installation of a second server is very much the same as installation of the first except that the second server will be installed into the NDS tree that was created by the first server installation. Some minor differences in the procedure should be examined.

Consider the NDS tree shown in figure C.50. This tree adds a server named MKT to the Directory tree that was presented in figure C.1. Although additional Administrators could be created, this example will be kept simple, and both servers will be managed by the same Admin user.

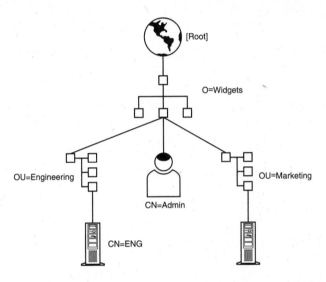

Figure C.50

The example NDS tree after adding the MKT server.

Installation proceeds as in the previous examples until the LAN drivers have been installed. Then, assuming that network communication is working properly, the search for existing NDS trees succeeds in finding the tree name Widgets, which has already been created. This is illustrated in figure C.51.

You have the option of adding the server to the existing tree or of pressing Ins and specifying a new tree. If you install the new server into a second tree, the servers will be isolated from each other and will not be able to communicate directly. Ordinarily, therefore, you will install all of the servers in your organization into the same NDS tree. Press Enter to accept the name of the existing tree.

Figure C.51

Installation identifies
an existing NDS tree
named Widgets.

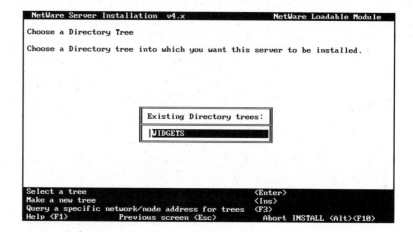

As mentioned, the same administrator will manage both the ENG
and MKT servers. In the form of figure C.52, enter the Administrator name and password. After the password has been verified
("authenticated" in NetWare 4 terminology), you will be asked to
define the context for the new server, using the form in figure
C.53.

Figure C.52

Defining the
administrator for the
new server.

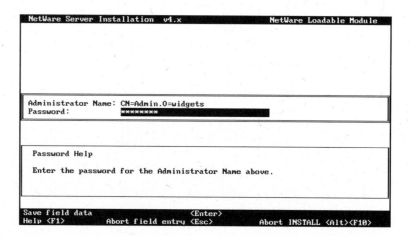

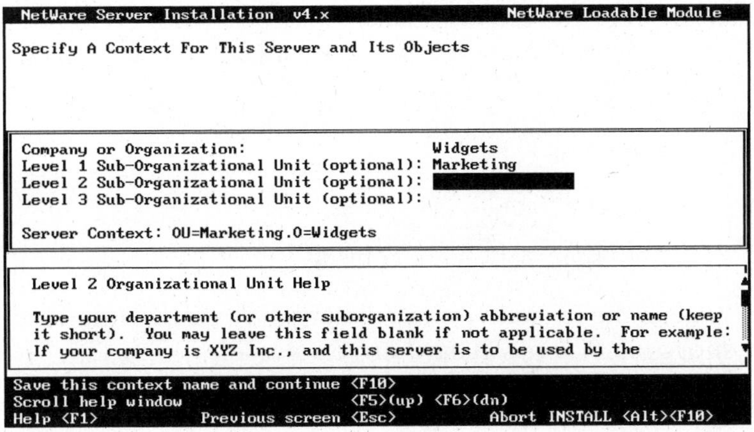

Figure C.53

Selecting on-line help
language versions.

The MKT server will be installed in the context of
OU=Marketing.O=Widgets, and Marketing should be entered as
the first level Organizational Unit in the form. Notice that the
Server Context is updated to reflect the changes.

Review Questions

1. Which of the following is *not* a factor in determining server
   memory requirements?

   ○   a.   Average file size

   ○   b.   Volume size

   ○   c.   Macintosh support

   ○   d.   Block size

2. What is the file name extension of a disk driver NetWare
   Loadable Module?

   ○   a.   NLM

   ○   b.   DRV

   ○   c.   DSK

   ○   d.   DIS

3. Which type of NetWare Directory Services object cannot be located immediately below an Organization object?

○ a. Another Organization object

○ b. A Root object

○ c. A User object

○ d. An Organization Unit object

4. What is the formula for calculating the memory required to support a Macintosh hard drive volume?

○ a. (Volume Size in MB × .023) divided by block size

○ b. (Volume Size in MB × .032) divided by block size

○ c. (Volume Size in MB × .23) divided by block size

○ d. (Volume Size in MB × .32) divided by block size

5. Which of the following statements about NDS is not true?

○ a. Server objects can be renamed.

○ b. Servers in different NDS trees can communicate directly.

○ c. Organization objects cannot be renamed.

○ d. More than one Admin user object can be created.

6. Which of the statements about NDS object names is not true?

○ a. Two User objects can have the same common name.

○ b. A Server object and a User object can have the same distinguished name.

○ c. Object names can contain percent signs, underscores, and dashes.

○ d. Object names can contain numbers, spaces, upper- and lowercase letters.

7. Which of the following is *not* required to install NetWare 4.01 and configure NDS on a server?

   ○ a. A CD-ROM drive

   ○ b. A LICENSE disk

   ○ c. A network interface card

   ○ d. Communication with any other NDS servers in the network

8. What is the context of the first Admin user to be created during server installation?

   ○ a. The server context

   ○ b. The Root context

   ○ c. The Organization object specified during installation

   ○ d. An Organization Unit object specified during installation

9. If you select Automatic volume configuration during installation, which of the following will occur?

   ○ a. Every disk drive will be automatically partitioned.

   ○ b. Disk device 0 will be partitioned and the entire partition will be assigned to SYS:.

   ○ c. A SYS: volume will be created that is the minimum size required for NetWare.

   ○ d. Volumes will be created on any partitions that have been created.

10. Which of the following is *not* true of volumes?

   ○ a. Volumes can consist of segments on more than one hard drive.

   ○ b. Spanning volumes increases performance when reading files.

    ○   c. A hard drive partition can contain as many as 12 volumes.

    ○   d. Spanned volumes should be duplexed for reliability.

11. The maximum number of segments that can be assigned to a volume is

    ○   a. 8

    ○   b. 16

    ○   c. 32

    ○   d. 48

12. Which of the following statements is true?

    ○   a. Segments can span up to eight disk drive partitions.

    ○   b. A disk drive can contain three NetWare partitions.

    ○   c. When block suballocation is used, the unit of storage allocation is 25 percent of the block size.

    ○   d. The block size of a volume can be changed after the volume is created.

Answers

1. A

2. C

3. B

4. B

5. B

6. B

7. A

8. C

9. B

10. C
11. C
12. D

Using NetWare Troubleshooting Tools

Your CNE test requires that you know how to use the MicroHouse Technical Library (MTL) and the NetWare Support Encyclopedia (NSEPro) to help you solve problems. Practicing using each tool before testing will help you to pass this test. Because your test is in the Windows environment, you can save significant time using the ALT+TAB key combination to toggle between applications. Once you open both the MTL and the NSEPro, do not close them, but instead toggle them to the background. Opening the programs is the biggest waste of time you may experience while taking the test.

The following two sections describe what you can find in MTL and NSEPro and are organized to help you determine which tool to use for the information you need. After a brief description, you are presented with several scenarios that you need to resolve. Use the appropriate tool to discover the answer. In the back of this section you will find a Hints section that will help get you going in the right direction. After the Hints section is an Answers section to see if you came up with the right answers. There may be other ways to get to the same point. If you find them, you're ready for the test!

Using MTL

To use the MicroHouse Technical Library (MTL), you will need to have a CD-ROM drive and Windows 3.1x installed on your PC. The CD-ROM included with this book includes a demonstration that illustrates many of the features of the MTL. To create a Windows program icon for the MTL demo, insert your book CD-ROM in your CD-ROM drive. Then do the following:

1. Run Windows 3.1

2. Choose File | New

3. Select Program Item and click OK

4. Enter the following information:

    Description: `MicroHouse Technical Library`

    Command Line: `D:\DEMOS\CDDEMO.EXE`

    Working Directory: `D:DEMOS`

    (If your CD-ROM drive uses a drive letter other than D: enter the appropriate drive letter in the Command Line and Working Directory entries.)

5. Click on the Change Icon and Choose an Icon from the ones that are presented.

6. Click on OK in the Program Item Properties window.

A program icon will be added to your Windows environment.

Use the MTL (MicroHouse Technical Library) to find information on:

◆ Computer main boards

◆ Hard drives

◆ Network interface boards (NIBs)

Each section gives you technical information and diagrams to help you determine hardware settings. Check into each heading to determine what type of information you can find.

Use MTL to find the answers to the following scenarios: (You do not need to know the answers to these scenarios to feel confident for testing. Concentrate on how to find the information, i.e.: *What section and what keywords would help find the answer?*).

Scenario 1:

You have a Fujitsu hard drive that you do not believe is set properly for Drive 0. The only information you have on the drive is that it is larger than 2 GB (gigabytes) and it uses an RLL interface. Find the position of the jumper block so that you can set the drive to Drive 0.

Scenario 2:

You need to figure out the possible DRAM configuration to get 32 MB using 2 SIMM/SIPP modules per bank.

Scenario 3:

Find the location of the banks in Scenario 2.

Scenario 4:

Find the cable segment length for 10BASE-T.

Scenario 5:

You want to find an FDDI network board that supports both fiber and shielded-twisted pair for a 32-bit EISA computer.

Scenario 6:

You want an Adaptec hard drive controller that supports SCSI and a 1.44 floppy on a 16 bit ISA computer. Which model should you order?

Scenario 7:

Find the number of megabytes in a terabyte.

Using NSEPro

Several versions of NSEPro have been published. The most recent versions include user interfaces for Windows, DOS, and Macintosh. Use the instructions that came with your copy of NESPro to install the software on your system.

1189

Use the NSEPro to find the following types of information:

♦ Search the NetWare product manuals

♦ Look for the "hot start" notes for installation walk-throughs

♦ Find and download patches and fixes

♦ Research Novell Application Notes on topics such as security or optimizing printing

♦ Find information on NetWare education and support centers

♦ Learn about certification programs and organizations like the NPA (Network Professional Association)

♦ Find FYI information to help solve problems

The main area to concentrate on is Service and Support, which includes the following information areas you may need to answer test questions:

> Technical Information Documents
>
> Files, Patches, Fixes
>
> Application Notes
>
> Novell Professional Developer Bullets
>
> Novell Lab Bulletins
>
> Software Testing Reports
>
> Top Issues
>
> Printing Decision Trees

Sample Scenarios:

Use NSEPro to find the answers to the following scenarios: (You do not need to know the answers to these scenarios to feel confident for testing. Concentrate on how to find the information, i.e.: *What section and what keywords would help find the answer?*).

Scenario 1:

Your file server keeps ABENDing (crashing and displaying an ABortEND message) with the message `AllocatePermanentMemory discovered invalid memory block segment`. You are running SAA 1.3 and NFS 1.2. What is the problem?

Scenario 2:

An FYI document found in the Technical Information Document area suggested that you find the latest patch for NFS. What is the most current version of this patch?

Scenario 3:

Where can you find suggestions to help you solve printing problems?

Scenario 4:

A colleague just approached you to ask your opinion on NLSP. Where could you look for more information, since she seemed so hot on the topic?

Summary

Practice as much as you can with these utilities before you test. This test is designed to test your ability to figure out problems as well as to know concepts and tools taught throughout this book.

Hints

MTL Scenario 1:

Choose the Encyclopedia of Hard Drives, then choose Drive Jumper Settings.

Enter the Make of Fujitsu, Interface of RLL and Size > 2000.

MTL Scenario 2:

Choose Encyclopedia of Main Boards, then choose Chapter 6, "System and Cache Memory." Page down through the text until you find the chart. Once you find the chart, can you think of any search words in that area that might have gotten you there quickly?

MTL Scenario 3:

Choose Encyclopedia of Main Boards, then click on the picture of a computer board. Enter Hewlett Packard as the Manufacturer and the Model as the HP Vectra 486ST PC Series.

MTL Scenario 4:

Choose The Network Interface Technical Guide, then Appendix D: Common Cable Pin Assignments. Search on 10BASE-T.

MTL Scenario 5:

Choose The Network Interface Technical Guide, then click on the picture of the computer board. Mark Fiber and STP under Wire Type, Other under Protocol and 32-bit EISA under Bus Type.

MTL Scenario 6:

Choose Encyclopedia of Hard Drives and click on the picture of a computer board. Fill in Manufacturer of Adaptec, SCSI for Hard Drive Support, 1.2/1.44 for Floppy Support and 16-bit ISA for Bus Type.

MTL Scenario 7:

Choose Encyclopedia of Main Boards, then Appendix G: Conversion Tables.

NSEPro Scenario 1:

Search Service and Support, Technical Information Documents for the exact error message.

NSEPro Scenario 2:

Search Service and Support, then Files, Patches and Fixes. Use the Query to find NFS Patch.

NSEPro Scenario 3:

Search Service and Support, then Decision Trees.

NSEPro Scenario 4:

Search Service and Support, then Novell Application Notes. Query for NLSP.

Answers

MTL Scenario 1:

Model # M2654SA

Jumper Block CN3

Lower Right Hand Corner

MTL Scenario 2:

2 4mx9 chips in Bank 0 and Bank 1

MTL Scenario 3:

Bank 3 is at the top of the board, so Bank 0 is the last row and Bank 1 is above Bank 0.

MTL Scenario 4:

328 ft., 100 Meters.

MTL Scenario 5:

3COM 3C771

MTL Scenario 6:

1522 or the 1542B

MTL Scenario 7:

1048576

NSEPro Scenario 1:

SAA 1.3 shipped with a CLIB that conflicted with NFS. Change to another revision.

NSEPro Scenario 2:

As of this printing, the file is NFS193.EXE.

NSEPro Scenario 3:

Although the FYI documents can be a help in specific issues, the decision trees are the most effective tool for helping narrow down general problems.

NSEPro Scenario 4:

The best article on NSEPro as of this printing is a May 1994 App Note article. It's really good reading, definitely a must for the CNE!

INDEX

G

I

U

NetWare Training Guide: Networking Technologies, 3/E

REGISTRATION CARD

Fill out this card to receive information about future NetWare books and other New Riders titles!

Name _____ Title _____

Company _____

Address _____

City/State/ZIP _____

I bought this book because: _____

_____

I purchased this book from:
- ☐ A bookstore (Name _____)
- ☐ A software or electronics store (Name _____)
- ☐ A mail order (Name of Catalog _____)

I purchase this many computer books each year:
- ☐ 1–5   ☐ 6 or more

I currently use these applications: _____

_____

_____

_____

I found these chapters to be the most informative: _____

_____

I found these chapters to be the least informative: _____

_____

Additional comments: _____

_____

☐ I would like to see my name in print! You may use my name and quote me in future New Riders products and promotions. My daytime phone number is: _____

New Riders Publishing 201 West 103rd Street • Indianapolis, Indiana 46290 USA

Fold Here

PLACE
STAMP
HERE

New Riders Publishing
201 West 103rd Street
Indianapolis, Indiana 46290
USA

WANT MORE INFORMATION?

CHECK OUT THESE RELATED TITLES:

Fold Here

- -

New Riders Publishing
201 West 103rd Street
Indianapolis, Indiana 46290
USA

Become a CNE
with Help from a Pro!

The NetWare Training Guides are specifically designed and authored to help you prepare for the **Certified NetWare Engineer** exam.

NetWare Training Guide: Managing NetWare Systems

This book clarifies the CNE testing process and provides hints on the best ways to prepare for the CNE examinations. *NetWare Training Guide: Managing NetWare Systems* covers the following sections of the CNE exams:

- NetWare 2.2 System Manager

- NetWare 2.2 Advanced System Manager

- NetWare 3.*x* System Manager

- NetWare 3.*x* Advanced System Manager

ISBN: 1-56205-069-9, **$69.95 USA**

NetWare Training Guide: Networking Technologies

This book covers more advanced topics and prepares you for the tough hardware and service/support exams. The following course materials are covered:

- MS-DOS

- Microcomputer Concepts

- Service and Support

- Networking Technologies

ISBN: 1-56205-145-8, **$69.95 USA**

GO AHEAD. PLUG YOURSELF INTO
MACMILLAN COMPUTER PUBLISHING.

Introducing the Macmillan Computer Publishing Forum on CompuServe®

Yes, it's true. Now, you can have CompuServe access to the same professional, friendly folks who have made computers easier for years. On the Macmillan Computer Publishing Forum, you'll find additional information on the topics covered by every Macmillan Computer Publishing imprint—including Que, Sams Publishing, New Riders Publishing, Alpha Books, Brady Books, Hayden Books, and Adobe Press. In addition, you'll be able to receive technical support and disk updates for the software produced by Que Software and Paramount Interactive, a division of the Paramount Technology Group. It's a great way to supplement the best information in the business.

WHAT CAN YOU DO ON THE MACMILLAN COMPUTER PUBLISHING FORUM?

Play an important role in the publishing process—and make our books better while you make your work easier:

- Leave messages and ask questions about Macmillan Computer Publishing books and software—you're guaranteed a response within 24 hours

- Download helpful tips and software to help you get the most out of your computer

- Contact authors of your favorite Macmillan Computer Publishing books through electronic mail

- Present your own book ideas

- Keep up to date on all the latest books available from each of Macmillan Computer Publishing's exciting imprints

JOIN NOW AND GET A FREE COMPUSERVE STARTER KIT!

To receive your free CompuServe Introductory Membership, call toll-free, **1-800-848-8199** and ask for representative **#597**. The Starter Kit Includes:

- Personal ID number and password

- $15 credit on the system

- Subscription to CompuServe Magazine

HERE'S HOW TO PLUG INTO MACMILLAN COMPUTER PUBLISHING:

Once on the CompuServe System, type any of these phrases to access the Macmillan Computer Publishing Forum:

GO MACMILLAN   **GO BRADY**
GO QUEBOOKS   **GO HAYDEN**
GO SAMS   **GO QUESOFT**
GO NEWRIDERS   **GO ALPHA**

Once you're on the CompuServe Information Service, be sure to take advantage of all of CompuServe's resources. CompuServe is home to more than 1,700 products and services—plus it has over 1.5 million members worldwide. You'll find valuable online reference materials, travel and investor services, electronic mail, weather updates, leisure-time games and hassle-free shopping (no jam-packed parking lots or crowded stores).

Seek out the hundreds of other forums that populate CompuServe. Covering diverse topics such as pet care, rock music, cooking, and political issues, you're sure to find others with the same concerns as you—and expand your knowledge at the same time.

Using the New Riders Electronic TestPrep ™

The New Riders Electronic TestPrep testing program is designed to help you become a CNE (Certified NetWare Engineer) or a CNA (Certified NetWare Administrator) by simulating the types of questions you're likely to face on the CNE or CNA exams. If you're already a CNE or a CNA, Electronic TestPrep will help you keep your skills sharpened by presenting you with up-to-date topics and information presented in an easy-to-use graphical format.

Installing the New Riders Electronic TestPrep™ Disc

The Electronic TestPrep is a Windows-based application that has the following system requirements:

Any IBM PC-compatible computer running Microsoft Windows version 3.0 or above (standard or enhanced mode). DOS version 3.1 or above. 2MB or more of RAM. A Microsoft Windows-compatible mouse. An EGA, VGA, or compatible monitor (color is recommended). A hard disk drive with at least 3MB of free space. A CD-ROM drive. A Microsoft Windows-compatible printer is recommended.

Steps to follow:

1. Place the CD-ROM in your CD-ROM drive.

2. From the Windows Program Manager, choose File, then Run.

3. In the Command Line box, type **D:\TESTPREP\SETUP.EXE** and press Enter. (If your CD-ROM drive is installed to a drive other than the default letter D, type in the letter of that particular drive.)

4. Follow the instructions on the screen. When the license agreement screen displays, read it and click on the "agree" button if you agree. Also, be sure to enter your name correctly in the Enter Your Name field.

5. Specify the start-up directory where you want the TestPrep to be stored. The default is NRP4. Click on Continue.

TestPrep will now install on your hard disk. After TestPrep installs, a program group named New Riders is created in your Program Manager. From here, you can start the TestPrep program by double-clicking on its icon. Or, if you want to review additional books published by New Riders Publishing, double-click on the NRP Books icon.

NOTE: When you take each test, it's important to use the HINT button before answering each question. This button indicates whether there is one, or more than one, correct answer.